AN ACCOUNT OF THE
BELL ROCK LIGHT-HOUSE

LECTOR HOUSE PUBLIC DOMAIN WORKS

AN ACCOUNT OF THE BELL ROCK LIGHT-HOUSE

ROBERT STEVENSON

ISBN: 978-93-5342-271-4

First Published: 1824

LECTOR HOUSE LLP
E-MAIL: lectorpublishing@gmail.com

BELL ROCK LIGHT HOUSE
DURING A STORM FROM THE NORTH EAST.

Drawn by J. M. W. Turner R. A.
Engraved by J. Horsburgh.

AN
ACCOUNT OF THE
BELL ROCK LIGHT-HOUSE,

INCLUDING THE
DETAILS OF THE ERECTION AND PECULIAR STRUCTURE OF THAT EDIFICE.

TO WHICH IS PREFIXED A
HISTORICAL VIEW OF THE INSTITUTION AND PROGRESS

OF THE
NORTHERN LIGHT-HOUSES.

ILLUSTRATED WITH TWENTY-THREE ENGRAVINGS.

DRAWN UP BY DESIRE OF
THE COMMISSIONERS OF THE NORTHERN LIGHT HOUSES,

BY

ROBERT STEVENSON,

CIVIL ENGINEER;
FELLOW OF THE ROYAL SOCIETY OF EDINBURGH;
MEMBER OF THE SOCIETY OF SCOTISH ANTIQUARIES, OF THE
WERNERIAN NATURAL HISTORY SOCIETY,
AND OF THE GEOLOGICAL SOCIETY OF LONDON;
ENGINEER TO THE NORTHERN LIGHT-HOUSE BOARD, AND TO
THE CONVENTION
OF ROYAL BOROUGHS OF SCOTLAND.

1824.

TO
THE KING.

SIRE,

It is with much diffidence that the author now lays before Your Majesty, an Account of the arduous national undertaking of erecting a Light-house on the Bell Rock,—a sunk reef, lying about eleven miles from the shore, and so situated as to have long proved an object of dread to mariners on the eastern coast of Scotland, especially when making for the Friths of Forth and Tay.

This edifice being of the utmost consequence to the safety of Your Majesty's Ships of War upon the North Sea station, and of the commercial shipping of this part of the empire, he presumes to hope for Your Majesty's favourable acceptance of his work. From the known partiality, also, of Your Majesty for naval excursions, which so recently led the Royal Squadron within a comparatively short distance of the Bell Rock Light-house, in the course of Your Majesty's most gracious Visit to your ancient Kingdom of Scotland, he flatters himself that Your Majesty may feel an additional interest in the subject of this volume.

The Introduction to this work brings generally under Your Majesty's notice, the important labours of the Scottish Light-house Board, appointed by an act of the 26th Parliament of Your Majesty's illustrious *FATHER*. Since that period, Light-house stations have been partially extended over the whole northern shores of Your Majesty's British dominions, from Inchkeith in the Firth of Forth, to the Isle of Man in the Irish Sea, including in this circuit the Hebrides, and Orkney and Shetland Islands. Much, however, still remains to be done; and the Board is gradually proceeding, as the state of its funds will permit, in placing additional Sea-Lights on certain intermediate points of the coast.

It cannot fail to be gratifying to Your Majesty to learn, as the result of the exertions of this Board, that the mariner may now navigate those regions with a degree of security and confidence quite unknown to Your Majesty's Royal Ancestor *JAMES THE FIFTH*, when he sailed around this coast in the 16th century, or even, at a recent period, to Your Majesty's Royal Brother *WILLIAM HENRY* Duke of Clarence, when in early life he traversed those seas.

With unfeigned sentiments of loyalty and attachment, the author subscribes himself,

Your MAJESTY'S
Most devoted Subject and Servant,
ROBERT STEVENSON.

CONTENTS

CHAPTER V.

CHAPTER VI.

CHAPTER VII.

APPENDIX.

NO. I.

NO. II.

NO. III.

NO. IV.

NO. V.

NO. VI.

NO. VII.

CONTENTS ix

DESCRIPTION OF PLATES

INTRODUCTION

Island of May Light-house. Patent ratified 1641; the Duty for that Light complained of after the Union. Family of Scotstarvet become Proprietors. Chamber of Commerce get that Light improved. Portland Family become Proprietors. Loss of the Nymphen and Pallas Frigates. Lord Melville, First Lord of the Admiralty, applies to the Light-house Board, by whom the Duties and Island of May are purchased. Additional apartments provided at the Isle of May. Notice of the alteration of this Light and that of Inchkeith. Pilot's guard-room.

1815.   Corsewall Light-house. Foundation-stone laid. Light exhibited.

1818.   Isle of Man Light-houses. Writer's Report in the year 1802, relative to the erection of Light-houses on the Isle of Man. Trade of Liverpool applies to the Commissioners to erect them. Act of 1815, obtained by Sir W. Rae, with regard to these Lights. Difficulty of fixing their Sites. Lights exhibited 1st February 1818. Sum expended by the Light-house Board, on the East Coast, in the course of 10 years.

1821.   Sumburgh-head Light exhibited. This House built with double walls,

Carr Rock Beacon. List of 16 vessels wrecked there in the course of nine years. Floating-Buoy moored off this dangerous Reef. Beacon of Masonry designed, with Tide-machine and Bell-apparatus. Dimensions of Carr Rock. Difficulties of this work. It is frequently damaged in Storms. The upper part ultimately completed with cast-iron, without the Alarm-Bell.

Duties exigible. Expence of Management. Accounts of the Light-house Board made public. Application of the Funds, and disposal of the Surplus. Practical Management.

ACCOUNT OF THE INSTITUTION OF THE BOARD OF COMMISSIONERS AND OF THE PROGRESS MADE IN THE ERECTION OF THE NORTHERN LIGHT-HOUSES.

Institution of Board of Northern Light-houses.

Among the Nations of Europe, the Scots have always been allowed to possess a considerable share of maritime enterprise. The local situation and circumstances of Scotland necessarily directed the genius of its people to the pursuit of nautical affairs. Their voyages to the Hanseatic Towns, and to all the commercial countries of Europe, were naturally longer than those of their more southern neighbours of England, who were separated from the Continent only by a narrow channel, which must have rendered their communication in the rude periods of maritime discovery comparatively easy. The voyages of the Scots even to the most contiguous parts of France and the Low Countries were upwards of 140 leagues, along a coast intersected by innumerable shoals; and, in the time of war, lay so open to the attacks of English ships, that, in prosecuting them, the navigators were obliged to abandon the usual track, and hold a course far from the shelter of the land, exposed to all the dangers of the seas and the vicissitudes of the weather.

In those early periods of our national history, when Britain was divided into two separate and independent states, jealous of each other, it became necessary for Scotland to form alliances with foreign powers, when distant voyages, and much intercourse by sea was indispensable. The frequent struggles with the marauding powers of the North, obliged her to keep a more considerable navy than would otherwise have been required for the protection of her commerce. The connection likewise, with Denmark and Norway, through the marriage of James III. with Margaret daughter of Christian I., in 1469, was attended with the final annexation of the Orkney and Shetland Islands to the Crown of Scotland;—circumstances which naturally extended her foreign traffic, and completely united the dominion and the navigation of the whole line of her coast.

It was reserved, however, for the influence and happy effects of the Union of the Crowns and Kingdoms of England, Scotland and Ireland, to draw forth the full energies of these countries. During the long and glorious reign of his late Majesty, the name and character of the United Kingdom have been highly advanced in arms, while her works of industry, have not only flourished at home, but been extended to the remotest parts of the world.

Improvement of the Highlands.

About the middle of the last or eighteenth century, the true value of the Highlands of Scotland, and the best interests of these extensive districts, may be said for the first time to have been understood. Since that period, the object of the Government has been more especially directed to the industry of the inhabitants, in giving every encouragement and facility to the establishment of fisheries, towns and harbours, along the shores of the north and west of Scotland; and in opening interior communications, by the introduction of a system of roads, the formation of an extensive inland navigation, and the execution of other national works.

Extension of Trade.

Soon after the internal disturbances which marked the year 1745, the trade on the coast of Scotland with sloops or vessels of small tonnage, became considerable, in consequence of the bounties and encouragement given to the extension of the British fisheries. About this time also, the important manufacture of kelp or marine alkali, from certain species of fuci abundant on the northern and western shores of Scotland, was introduced. Besides carrying the kelp to market, a considerable number of small vessels was employed in conveying salt and other articles required for the fisheries, — in the Irish coasting trade, — in carrying slates from Argyleshire, — and in transporting the rich iron-ore of Cumberland to the foundries on the eastern shores of the kingdom. A trade was likewise carried on from the Firth of Clyde, Liverpool, and the west of England in general, and north of Ireland, with Norway, the Baltic, and the other States in the north of Europe, in timber, iron, tar and other commodities; and in exchange for these were received coal, salt, and the various exports of Britain. These all became sources of commerce, which created a demand for shipping, and promoted numerous voyages along the northern and western coasts of Scotland, which now became more known and frequented. But such was the length and peril of a voyage round the coast of Scotland, by the Orkneys and Western Islands, without the aid of light-houses, or even of correct charts, that the traffic along these shores was still comparatively small.

Inland Navigation.

It was to remove these difficulties in some measure, that the formation of a navigable canal between the Friths of Forth and Clyde, had long been in agitation; and in the year 1767, the measure was brought forward in the House of Commons. This canal, upon a voyage from the Forth to the Clyde, is calculated to save no less than about 628 miles; the distance, by the inland navigation being reduced to about 35 miles. This work having been carried into execution, was opened from sea to sea in 1790, forming an important step in the progressive intercourse by water-carriage, a system which has since been so remarkably extended to all parts of the united kingdom. But the usefulness of the Forth and Clyde Canal was greatly marred by an unfortunate error in its construction, its depth having been limited to 9 feet, and its consequent incapacity for carrying sea-borne ships of large burden; so that the inconveniences of a circuitous voyage round Scotland still remains for all the larger classes of shipping. In the formation of the Caledonian Canal, the error of the Forth and Clyde navigation has been avoided; this noble work being capable of receiving ships which draw 21 feet of water.

Voyage of James V. in 1540.

Notwithstanding these great improvements, it was still found necessary, from the increasing state of trade, to give further facilities to the navigation of the northern shores, by the Orkney and Western Islands. The first step taken towards this object, was to procure accurate surveys of the coast; for it is a curious fact, deserving of notice, that the little journal and chart of the enterprising voyage of James V., with many of the Scottish Nobles, from the Firth of Forth to the Solway Firth , by the Orkneys, was long consulted as the only guide for these seas. This voyage, so honourable to the naval annals of Scotland, was undertaken by James with twelve ships in the year 1540, under the direction of Alexander Lindsay, the most skilful pilot of his time.

Original Charts.

At the request of the Philosophical Society (now the Royal Society) of Edinburgh, the Rev. Alex. Bryce of Kirknewton, about the year 1740, made a geometrical survey of the North-west coast of Scotland, including the shores of Caithness and Sutherland. This paved the way for the more extensive labours of Mr Murdoch Mackenzie, who, after finishing his excellent charts of the Orkney Islands in the year 1750, was employed by Government in a survey of the whole of the Western Highlands and Islands, from Cape Wrath in Sutherlandshire to the Mull of Kintyre. But long after the publication of these valuable charts, the navigation of the sounds and sheltered seas of this district was seldom ventured upon by the larger class of shipping employed in foreign trade. The danger of falling in prematurely with the land during the night, and the rapidity of the tides on these shores, induced the mariner to keep along the extreme points and headlands of the coast, holding his course even to the northward of Orkney and Shetland, and to the westward of the Lewis Isles by St Kilda, exposed to the heavy seas of the Atlantic Ocean. In this way, much hazard to shipping, and loss of time, were incurred; and when overtaken with gales of wind, such vessels were unable to avail themselves of the numerous bays and anchorages of the Highlands;—considerations of much importance to heavy laden ships, but especially to the smaller classes of coasting and fishing vessels. It therefore appeared, that nothing but the erection of Lighthouses, by which the mariner might identify the land under night, would render this navigation at all a safe one.

Proposition of a Light-house Board.

Representations had often been made by shipmasters to their owners, of the difficulties and dangers encountered in sailing along the coast of Scotland. The establishment of a Light-house Board, and the erection of Light-houses on our Northern Shores, became the topic of conversation among mercantile men; and the subject was at length brought forward at the meeting of the Convention of the Royal Boroughs of Scotland, in the year 1784, by the late Mr Dempster of Dunnichen, then Provost of Forfar, and Member of Parliament, as worthy of the notice of the Legislature.

Passing of the Original Act, 1786.

A bill was accordingly framed by the late Mr John Gray, writer to the Signet, agent for the Royal Boroughs, which was brought into Parliament by Mr Dempster, in the session of 1786. By this act, the 26th Geo. III. chap. 101., a Board was appointed, for the erection of Light-houses on the coast of Scotland; the preamble stating that "it would conduce greatly to the security of navigation and the fisheries, if four lighthouses were erected in the northern parts of Great Britain," viz. one on Kinnaird Head, in Aberdeenshire; one on the Orkney Islands; one on the Harris Isles, and one at the Mull of Kintyre, in Argyleshire; for which a duty of one penny per register ton, for British, and twopence per ton upon foreign ships, should be paid by every ship or decked vessel which should pass one or all of these lights.

Commissioners ex Officio.

The Commissioners appointed for putting this act in execution, are, "His Majesty's Advocate and Solicitor-General for Scotland; the Lord Provost and First Bailie of Edinburgh; the Lord Provost and First Bailie of Glasgow; the Provosts of Aberdeen, Inverness and Campbeltown; the Sheriffs of the Counties of Edinburgh, Lanark, Renfrew, Bute, Argyle, Inverness, Ross, Orkney, Caithness, and Aberdeen;" and to these have since been added, the Sheriffs of the Counties of Ayr, Fife, Forfar, and Wigton, agreeably to a clause which authorises the Commissioners to add to their number.

First Meeting of the Board.

The first meeting of the Commissioners was held at Edinburgh on the 1st day of August 1786; and consisted of the following members:

> His Majesty's Solicitor-General, Robert Dundas of Arniston.
> The Lord Provost of Edinburgh, Sir James Hunter-Blair, Bart.
> The First Bailie of Edinburgh, James Dickson, Esq.
> The Sheriff of the County of Bute, Bannatyne Macleod, Esq.
> The Sheriff of the County of Aberdeen, Alexander Elphinston, Esq.
> The Sheriff of the County of Lanark, Sir William Honyman, Bart.

Mode of raising Funds.

The meeting having elected Sir James Hunter-Blair to be their Preses, and appointed Mr Gray to be their Secretary, deliberated upon the measures to be taken for giving effect to the statute. The first object of the Board was to borrow the sum of L. 1200, which they were authorised to raise. As all the Commissioners were acting ex officio, it was suggested, that the most convenient method of arranging the security for the funds to be borrowed, would be for the Magistrates of the five boroughs mentioned in the act to become security, upon assignment of the duties leviable for the lights, — a mode which was accordingly adopted.

Progress of Northern Light-houses.

Information about Light-houses.

The preses informed the meeting, that he had corresponded with persons the most likely to afford information relative to the best construction of Light-houses, and had received answers from Liverpool to a variety of queries regarding Light-houses, where the use of coal-fires had been laid aside, and where oil lights, with reflectors, had been introduced: That he had also got various plans and estimates for Light-houses lighted with oil: That the Chamber of Commerce of Edinburgh had furnished a plan of the Light-house on the Island of May, in the Firth of

Forth, and also a description of the light on the Island of Cumbraes, in the Firth of Clyde, both of which were then open coal-fires: In particular, that he had received from the late Mr Thomas Smith of Edinburgh, plans and observations on the construction of Light-houses with Lamps and Reflectors; which having been ultimately approved of, Mr Smith was nominated Engineer to the Board. After appointing a Committee for preparing matters for a general meeting, they adjourned till the 23d of January 1787.

Transactions of 1787.

In pursuance of the act of Parliament, the Commissioners gave directions that a correspondence should be opened with the several proprietors of the land where the four original Light-houses were specified to be erected. An answer was immediately received from Mr Traill of Westness in Orkney, requesting the Board's free acceptance of the ground necessary for erecting the Light-house proposed for the Northern Isles of Orkney, on any part of his property. Application was made to the Duke of Argyle, as to the ground for the erection of a Light-house on the Mull of Kintyre; to Lord Saltoun, relative to the station of Kinnaird-Head, in Aberdeenshire; and to Mr Macleod of Harris, as to the site of a Light-house on Island Glass. Measures were also taken for obtaining fit persons to contract for erecting the necessary buildings, and for conducting the operations at the different stations.

KINNAIRD HEAD.

Kinnaird-Head Light-house.

The result of the correspondence with Lord Saltoun, was the purchase of the old building of Kinnaird Castle from his Lordship, on which a lantern or light-room was erected. After encountering considerable difficulties in the outset of this establishment, the house was got ready for the exhibition of the light by the month of December 1787, and the following notice to mariners was officially given by the Secretary in the London Gazette, and in the Edinburgh, Glasgow, and Aberdeen newspapers.

"By order of the Commissioners appointed by Act of Parliament for erecting four Light-houses in the northern parts of Great Britain, a Light-house is now erected on Kinnaird Castle, at Kinnaird-Head, near Fraserburgh, in the county of Aberdeen, Lat. 57° 42′, and Long. 2° 19′ West of London, Cairnbulg from the Light-house bearing, by compass, S.E., distant 2 miles; and Trauphead W.NW., distant 9 miles. The lantern is 120 feet above the level of the sea at high-water, and will be seen from SE. to W.NW. and intermediate points of the compass on the north of these points. The lantern will be lighted on the night of the first day of December 1787, and every night thereafter, from the going away of day-light in the evening till the return of day-light in the morning."

MULL OF KINTYRE.

Mull of Kintyre Light-house.

At the Mull of Kintyre, one of the most inaccessible and difficult of the Northern Light-house stations, the buildings were nearly prepared for the light-room by the month of November; but the season being too far advanced, and it appearing from Mr Smith's report, that there would be some risk in conveying the apparatus to the light-house at this inclement season, the Commissioners resolved to delay the further progress of the work at Kintyre till the following spring.

1788.

The operations at the Mull of Kintyre were recommenced in the month of April, but, owing chiefly to the inaccessible great difficulty that was experienced in transporting the building materials connected with the lantern or light-room, over the mountainous district of Kintyre, it was the month of October before the light could be announced for exhibition, when public advertisement was made of the lighting of the house to the following effect.

"The Mull of Kintyre Light-house is situated immediately above the rocks known to mariners by the name of The Merchants, in North Lat. 55° 17′, and Long. 5° 42′ west of London; the eastern entrance of the Sound of Isla, bearing from the Light-house by compass, N. by E., distant 33 miles; the Mull of Kinho in the Island of Isla N. NW., distant 25 miles; and the northern extremity of Rathlin Island, on the coast of Ireland, NW. ½ W. distant 13 miles; the Maiden Rocks S. by W. ½ W., distant 21 miles; and Copland Light-house S. by W. ½ W., distant 40 miles. The light-room is elevated 240 feet above the medium level of the sea, and will be seen from N. NE. to S. by W., and all intermediate points of the compass north of these points. The light will be exhibited on the 1st day of December 1788, and every night thereafter, from the going away of day-light in the evening till the return of day-light in the morning."

Light-house duty too small.

In the progress of the works of the Northern Light-houses, it soon became evident, from the diminished state of the funds, that the light-house duty of 1d. per ton upon British vessels, and 2d. upon foreign bottoms, was too small. By the original act, also, this duty was only to be levied after the whole of the lights at the four stations had been exhibited to mariners; but the Board having found that it would be expedient to commence the collection of the duties so soon as two were lighted, resolved on applying to Parliament for a new act.

Act of 1788.

A bill was accordingly brought into the House of Commons by Sir Ilay Campbell, M. P., when Lord Advocate for Scotland, and ex officio one of the Commissioners of the Northern Light-houses, which passed in the session of 1788, empowering the Commissioners to levy a duty of 1½d., or one halfpenny more per ton upon British ships, and 3d., or one penny per ton additional upon foreigners; and, in the mean time, to commence collecting half duties till the whole of the four light-houses mentioned in the former act were lighted, when the full duties were to become exigible. Already about L. 4000 had been expended on the light-houses of Kinnaird-Head and Kintyre. By this new act, however, the Commissioners being empowered to borrow a further sum of L. 3000, were not only enabled to forward the operations already commenced, but, with this additional duty, it was expected that they would soon be in a condition to answer the calls of the shipping interest for additional erections on the coast.

ISLAND GLASS.

1789.

Considerable progress had been made in the course of the former season with the erection of the Light-house at Island Glass in Harris, which was finished and lighted on the 10th day of October 1789, the following being its specification:— The Point of Island Glass, one of the Harris Isles, is situated in North Lat. 57° 50′, and Long. 6° 33′ west of London. Ru-Ushiness bears from the light-house, per compass, E. NE. ½ E., distant 8 miles; northern extremity of Shiant Isles E., ½ S., southern extremity of ditto E. by S. ½ S., distant 11 miles; Skerne Rock SE., ½ E., distant 3 miles; Skergraidish Rock S. SE. ¼ E., distant 9 miles; Point of Trotternish in Sky S. SE. ¼ E., distant 16 miles; Point of Vaternish S. SW. ¼ W., distant 15 miles; Dunvegan-Head SW. ½ S., distant 20 miles; Point of Roudil, at the entrance of the Sound of Harris, W. by S., distant 14 miles. The light-room is elevated 70 feet above the medium level of the sea, and will be seen from E. NE. ½ E., from W. by S., and intermediate points of the compass south of these points.

North Ronaldsay Light-house.

While the works of Island Glass were proceeding, a light-house was also erected, and lighted 10th October 1789, on the island of North Ronaldsay, in Orkney; but, as the light at this station was afterwards removed to the neighbouring island of Sanday, it will fall more properly to be noticed in the form of a Tower or Beacon, into which the building was converted, after a Light-house had been established at the Start Point of Sanday.

PLADDA.

Application for Pladda Light-house.

The erection of the four light-houses of Kinnaird Head, North Ronaldsay, Island Glass, and the Mull of Kintyre, completed the operations of the Northern Light-house Board, referred to in the original act of 1786; and at the time of passing that act, it was not foreseen that a greater number would be required on the coast of Scotland for a series of years. But the benefit of the lights which had already been erected, in affording much greater safety and facility to the mariner in those dangerous seas, became so apparent, that they were no sooner exhibited than applications from different quarters for new erections followed. Among these, a memorial was presented to the Commissioners by the Merchants' House of Greenock, accompanied by a letter from the Chamber of Commerce of Glasgow, setting forth the advantages which the shipping of the Clyde would derive from the erection of a light-house upon the small island of Pladda, situated at the southern extremity of the island of Arran, and entrance of the Firth of Clyde. This memorial concluded by requesting, that the Commissioners would "take such measures as should to them seem most proper, for procuring an act of Parliament, in order to carry the erection of a light-house on the island of Pladda into execution as soon as possible."

Act of 1789.

An act was accordingly obtained, in the session of 1789, not only for the erection of Pladda Light-house, but for extending the powers of the Commissioners to the erection of such other light-houses on the coast of Scotland as to them should seem necessary, whenever the free produce of the duties of 1½d. and 3d. per ton respectively on British and foreign ships should enable the Board to do so.

Collectors appointed.

In consequence of the act of 1788, authorising the collection of half duties so soon as two of the four light-houses mentioned in the original act should be lighted, collectors at the different customhouses of all the ports of Great Britain were appointed to receive the Northern Light-house duty, and for their trouble they were to be paid at the rate of 10 per cent. upon the sums they should respectively receive: But the business being scarcely organized in 1789, and only half duties being exigible, the whole money collected in that year amounted but to L. 290:14:6, and even this small sum formed part of two years' collection. From the smallness of the duties, and the extent of the operations which the Commissioners had now on hand, they were much pressed for the necessary funds, and but for the liberality of their bankers Sir William Forbes and Company, the operations of the Board must have been greatly hampered. Indeed, Sir James Hunter Blair, one of the partners of that house, when Lord Provost of Edinburgh, and ex officio a member of the Board, had been highly instrumental in forwarding the establishment of the Northern Light-houses; and it was, perhaps, from such adventitious circumstances, together with the economy of the measures originally pursued, that the progress of the Light-house works proceeded, without experiencing any interruption from want of funds.

1790.

The light-house of Pladda was finished in the course of the year 1790, and lighted on the 1st day of October. As before noticed, it is situated in the Firth of Clyde, on the small island of Pladda, near the south-west point of the island of Arran, in North Lat. 55° 30′ and Long. 5° 4′ west of London; the entrance of Campbeltown Loch bearing, by compass, W.NW. ¼ N., distant 18 miles; Island of Sana W., distant 20 miles; Craig of Ailsa SW. by S., distant 15 miles; entrance to Loch Ryan S.SW., distant 25 miles; and the Heads of Ayr E.SE., distant 16 miles. The light-room is elevated above the medium level of the sea 70 feet; and the light is seen from NE. by E. to NW. by W. and intermediate points of the compass south of these points.

1791.

Distinguishing light at Pladda.

In order to distinguish Pladda Light-house from the light upon the Promontory of Kintyre on the one hand, and that upon the island of Cumbrae, further up the Firth of Clyde, and also from the Copeland light on the Irish coast, it was found necessary, in the course of the year 1791, to erect a small Light-room, immediately under the principal light, that, by shewing two distinct lights at this station, the one 20 feet higher than the other, it might be distinguishable from those above alluded to. This small light-room being rather of a temporary construction, the Board have it in view to erect one upon a more efficient plan, when certain repairs which are in contemplation at Pladda shall be made.

Annual supply and inspection of the Lights.

The Northern Light-houses being situated in parts of the country remote and inaccessible, it became necessary to arrange some systematic and proper plan for managing the ordinary business of the Board, which, at this time, had only one stated meeting, held by act of Parliament in the month of July annually. A special meeting was accordingly convened by the Secretary, in the month of March 1791; at which there were present, the Lord Advocate of Scotland; the Lord Provost of Edinburgh; the Sheriff of Aberdeen; the Sheriff of Renfrew; and the Sheriff of Orkney, Mr Charles Hope, now Lord President of the Court of Session. This meeting having taken into consideration the proper mode of supplying the light-houses, and of attending to the conduct of the light-keepers, it was resolved, That the engineer should charter a vessel annually, to carry a full complement of stores and other necessaries for the use of the lights, and such artificers, implements and materials as might, from time to time, be found necessary for making repairs at the light-houses; and also, that the engineer should annually visit each light-house, and report upon the state and condition of the buildings, and upon the conduct of the respective light-keepers in keeping the lights, and in the management of the stores and appurtenances committed to their charge; with power to dismiss them for neglect of duty.

Light-keepers' Salary.

The light-keepers already engaged in the service, had been verbally informed by the engineer, that they would be paid L. 30 of yearly salary; and this meeting having before it a range of salaries paid to light-keepers both in England and Scotland, varying from L. 20 to upwards of L. 70, it was resolved, That in ordinary situations, the salary of the light-keepers in the service of the Northern Light-houses should be L. 30 per annum, with a piece of garden-ground and pasture for a cow, and a sufficient quantity of fuel for the use of their families.

First voyage of the Engineer.

In consequence of this arrangement, a vessel of about 100 tons burden was chartered and fitted out with stores and other necessaries for the use of the Northern Light-houses; and in the course of the summer of 1791, Mr Smith made his first annual visit by sea to the light-houses—the journeys of the engineer having hitherto been performed chiefly by land. On this voyage, every thing was reported to be in good order at the several stations, excepting at the Light-house of North Ronaldsay, which he found to be very improperly kept: it appeared also that the light-keeper at this station had been embezzling the stores committed to his charge. This person was formerly a ship-master, who, finding it difficult to get employment in the line of his profession, had been very improperly recommended to the attention of the Light-house Board.

Light-house keeper dismissed the service.

Under circumstances of such misconduct, the engineer immediately dismissed him from the service, and his conduct was further taken cognizance of by the Sheriff of the county.

Economical plan of the early Light-houses.

The business of the Light-houses was now so arranged, that matters went on in a very prosperous and successful manner. So well, indeed, had the plans and buildings of their engineer been considered, and made to meet the slender funds of the Board, that, with an expenditure of little more than L. 10,000, five lights had been exhibited upon the coast. Though these buildings were unavoidably very much circumscribed in their accommodations, and even temporary in their construction, yet the speedy exhibition of the lights was of great benefit to navigation, while the improving state of the light-house duties enabled the Commissioners to extend their influence along a greater range of coast; and the different buildings have since been enlarged and completed in a much more substantial manner, by applying the surplus funds to these purposes.

1793.

Application for additional light-houses.

In the year 1793, the prosperous state of funds induced and enabled the Commissioners to attend to the applications of mariners for additional light-houses on the coast. In particular a letter, to be afterwards more fully noticed, was addressed to the Light-house Board by Admiral Sir Alexander Cochrane, then commanding his Majesty's ship Hind upon the Leith station, setting forth the great benefit that would accrue to shipping, from the erection of a light-house upon the Bell Rock. Representations were likewise made at this time by the merchants of Liverpool, regarding the propriety of erecting a light-house upon the Skerries, situated in the middle of the Pentland Firth , which separates the Orkney Islands from the Mainland of Caithness. The object of a light here, was to open this Firth as a passage to shipping in general, and to enable the mariner to avoid a circuitous and dangerous voyage to the northward of the Orkney Islands.

State of the Light-house funds.

At this period, however, the Commissioners could not venture to undertake a work of such magnitude and difficulty, as the erection of a light-house upon the Bell Rock. The amount of the light-house duties at first was extremely limited; and though in a progressive state, yet, for 1789, as before stated, they only amounted to L. 249:14:6. For 1790, the sum was L. 1477:5:1; for 1791, it was L. 2736:9:2; for 1792, it rose to L. 3160:18:1. But in the year 1793, of which we are now treating, the duties rather declined, and they only netted L. 2868, 3s. 5d. The Commissioners were nevertheless enabled to pay off L. 4200, which, by the acts of 1786 and 1788, they had been empowered to borrow, and likewise to discharge the advances made by Sir William Forbes and Company; still leaving a balance of about L. 2000 of surplus duties in the hands of their treasurer. The funds being, therefore, still very limited, and only in a condition to enable the Board to erect a light-house of the ordinary construction, the erection of the light-house on the Pentland Skerries was resolved on; and the further consideration of the Bell Rock light-house reserved, until the funds should be in a more advanced state.

PENTLAND SKERRIES.

Regarding the site of the Pentland Firth Light-house.

Some difference of opinion arising among the gentlemen and merchants of Orkney, whether the light-house proposed for the Pentland Skerries should not rather be erected upon the island of Copinsha, situate about fifteen miles northward of the Portland Firth , the matter was referred to the opinion of the Association of Ship-owners of Liverpool, and to the Chambers of Commerce of Glasgow and Greenock, when these public bodies unanimously and strongly recommended the erection of the light-house on the Pentland Skerries, as the site best calculated for a direction to the Pentland Firth ; which was accordingly fixed upon by the Board. To mark this Light-house from the other lights upon the coast, it was necessary to make it a Distinguishing-light, which was effected by the erection of a higher and lower light-house tower, respectively 80 and 100 feet above the medium level of the sea, built at the distance of 60 feet asunder, and each having a light-room with reflectors, so as to show two distinct stationary lights, for as yet the Revolving-light had not been introduced upon this coast.

1794.

The author's first voyage to the north.

The works at the Pentland Skerries were begun early in the spring of 1794. The masonry was executed by builders of Orkney; and the materials having been prepared, were partly landed on these small islands in the course of the preceding summer. The Skerries consist of two uninhabited islands, with some contiguous sunken rocks. They lie exposed to the uninterrupted force of the waves of the North Sea, and to the rapid tides and currents of the Pentland Firth , and present many convincing proofs of the wasting state of the land, by the action of the sea. The works here had been so laid out, that the towers should be in readiness for the erection of the light-rooms by the month of August; and it was expected that the lights would be ready for exhibition in the month of October. The author, to whose superintendance the completing of these light-houses was to be entrusted, as his first work for the Board, sailed from Leith on this service on the 2d July 1794; and after touching at Kinnaird Head Light-house, he landed at the Pentland Skerries on the 11th of that month, and found the masonry of the two light-house towers in such a state of forwardness, as to be then nearly ready for the light-rooms. In the month of September, these works were completed, and the lights were exhibited on the 1st day of October 1794.

These lights are from oil, with reflectors, and may be described as erected on the largest of the Pentland Skerries, in Lat. 58° 43′ and Long. 3° 3′ west of London; the northmost or highest light-room being elevated 100 feet, and the lower light-room 80 feet above the medium level of the sea. The two light-rooms, relatively to each other, bear S. SW. and N. NE., distant 60 feet. The bearings, as taken from the highest light-room, by compass, are the western extremity of the Little Pentland Skerry S. by W., distant 1¼ mile; extremity of the foul ground off that Skerry SE., distant 1½ mile; Duncan's Bay Head in Caithness; W. SW. distant 4½ miles; Noss Head SW. by W., distant 14 miles; northmost point of the Island of Stroma NW. by W., distant 6½ miles; south-western extremity of the Loather Rock on the Orkney shore N. by W., distant 3½ miles; Island of Copinsha NE. by E. ¼ E., distant 17 miles.

Loss of the sloop Elizabeth.

The author, having remained to complete the works at the Pentland Skerries, and to see the house lighted, sailed from Orkney on the 9th of October, in the sloop Elizabeth of Stromness. On the following day, the vessel got within three miles of Kinnaird Head Light-house, in Aberdeenshire; but the wind having suddenly shifted to the south-east, Mr Sinclair, the master, with much attention and kindness, landed the author, who continued his journey to Edinburgh by land. A very different fate, however, awaited his shipmates; for the Elizabeth having put back to Cromarty Roads, was afterwards driven to Orkney, and ultimately lost, when all on board perished.

Mr Balfour and Mr Riddoch presented with pieces of Plate.

In the affairs connected with the erection of light-houses in Orkney, Mr Balfour of Elwick, and Mr Riddoch, collector of the customs at Kirkwall, having respectively taken much friendly interest and trouble in the advancement of the Light-house works in the Orkney islands, the Commissioners of the Light-houses presented a small piece of plate to each of these gentlemen, with a suitable inscription, in testimony of the services they had thus rendered to the public.

Act for Incorporating the Commissioners.

Some inconveniency having been experienced in conducting the business of the Light-house Board, in consequence of its not being an incorporated body, and not having a common seal, particularly in the holding of stock and other property, in laying out and investing the surplus funds arising from the light-house duties, application was made to Parliament, and an act passed in 1798, 38th Geo. III. c. 57. erecting the Commissioners into a Board or Body-politic, by the name of "The Commissioners of the Northern Light-houses;" and under that title to have perpetual succession, and hold a common seal.

Additional Works at the first erected Light-houses.

After the completion of these two light-houses on the Pentland Skerries in 1794, a period of ten years elapsed before the erection of any additional light-house was undertaken on the coast of Scotland. This delay was rendered necessary, chiefly on account of the necessity of extending the accommodation of the light-keepers at the different stations,—in making landing places and roads,—enclosing grounds,—and, in short, putting the whole establishment of the light-houses into a more complete and finished state.

Light-House proposed as a direction for Cromarty Firth .

In the mean time, several propositions for new light-houses were brought under the notice of the Commissioners. In the year 1797, for example, the late Mr Dempster of Dunnichen proposed the erection of a light-house as a direction for the entrance of Cromarty Firth , one of the principal inlets for shipping on the eastern coast of Great Britain. Mr Dempster also suggested, in connection with this, that a Beacon should be erected, and a floating buoy moored, to point out the dangerous channel of Dornoch Firth , which is too often fatally mistaken for the entrance to Cromarty Firth . The proposition of a beacon and buoy for Dornoch, was considered by the Commissioners as not strictly in the high seas, and therefore not properly belonging to the concerns of the Board, and, together with the light-house, were delayed for the present, that attention might be paid to more urgent demands on other parts of the coast.

Proposition for altering the site of Kinnaird Head Light-House.

Notwithstanding the benefit derived from the erection of Kinnaird Head lighthouse, shipwrecks were still occurring on a dangerous reef of rocks called Rattray Brigs, situate about 12 miles southward of Kinnaird Head, and 6 miles north of Peterhead. In the year 1798, petitions were presented to the Commissioners from certain merchants and traders, setting forth, that the light-house upon Kinnaird Head would be much more beneficial to shipping, were it removed to Rattray Head. This matter was remitted to the author to report upon, who accordingly made a survey of this part of the coast. After maturely considering the subject, it was deemed advisable to decline the removal of the light-house from Kinnaird Head, which was found to be extremely useful for directing ships into the Moray and Cromarty Friths, and also to vessels making the land from the northward. Although it might not, perhaps, be so useful to coasters bound from the south, yet the Commissioners found, that it would be better, under all circumstances, to preserve Kinnaird Head as a light-house station, and, at some future period, to erect an additional light upon this important part of the coast, at or near Peterhead, in a position calculated to be useful as a guide for the sunken reef of Rattray Brigs, and also for the south-eastern shores of Aberdeenshire.

START POINT BEACON.

1801.

Numerous Wrecks on the Island of Sanday.

Among the several applications brought before the Board for additional light-houses, something still appeared to be necessary for averting the misfortunes which were annually happening on the low shores of the Northern Isles of Orkney. It had now been found, by the experience of about twelve years, that the light-house of North Ronaldsay was not calculated to prevent the numerous wrecks on the islands of Sanday and Stronsay. In the year 1796, when the author was on his annual visit to the Northern Light-houses, he was struck at seeing the wreck of three homeward-bound ships upon the island of Sanday, though situate only about eight miles southward of the light-house of North Ronaldsay. Again, in 1797, he found one wrecked ship on Sanday; but in 1798 he saw the remains of no fewer than five vessels upon that fatal island; and, in the month of December 1799, two of the numerous vessels which were driven from Yarmouth Roads in a dreadful gale of wind at south-east, were also wrecked there. The author having laid this continued and alarming state of things before the Light-house Board, in his annual report of 1801, it was resolved, that a beacon or tower of masonry should be erected upon the Start Point or eastern extremity of the low shores of the island of Sanday; the building to be constructed in such a manner that it might, if found necessary, be converted into a light-house.

1802.

Proofs of a severe winter in Orkney.

In the year 1802, the author sailed on his annual voyage to the Northern Light-houses so early as the 14th of April, in the Pharos of Leith, carrying with him a foreman and sixteen artificers, to commence the works of the Start Point Tower. After rather a boisterous passage, the vessel reached Orkney in six days, and, at this advanced period of the season, these Islands were found covered to the depth of six inches with snow. This, at any time, is rather uncommon in Orkney; but such had been the severity of the season in the northern regions, that a flock of wild swans which, in severe winters, visit this country, were still seen in considerable numbers upon the fresh-water lakes of Sanday. These large birds are supposed to migrate from Iceland, but are rarely seen here later than the month of March, so that their appearance in the latter end of the month of April, was considered by the Orcadians as a mark of a very severe and long-continued winter in the higher latitudes.

Quarries at Sanday and Eda.

It having been ascertained that there was no workable sandstone on the island of Sanday, where the Beacon was to be erected, permission was granted by Mr Laing, the proprietor of the contiguous island of Eda, to open a quarry at Calf Sound, where sandstone of a pretty good quality was obtained. With a view to render this building substantially water-tight, it had been originally intended to make it wholly of hewn stone, built in regular courses, technically called ashlar or aisler-work, a term derived from the aisle of a church, where this sort of masonry predominates; but the quarry of Eda being about fourteen miles distant from the work, the stones had to be brought by sea through rapid tides; and there being but indifferent creeks or havens both at the quarry and at the Start Point, it was found necessary to make only the principal stones of hewn-work, while the body of the work was executed in ruble-building, for which excellent materials were got at the Start Point, the property of the Right Honourable Lord Dundas, consisting of sandstone-slate, of a greyish-smoke colour, intermixed with shining particles of mica. The rock here is disposed in strata, from 1 to 8 inches in thickness, and could easily be raised in pieces containing from 15 to 20 square feet.

Encroachments of the Sea upon the Land.

Indeed, the encroachments of the sea had heaped up immense quantities of these schistose stones at high-water mark, all round the Start Point, the shores of which appeared like the ruins of the wall of some large city.

Of Ruble Building.

These stones, however, were more applicable for the purposes of dike-building, or interior walls, than for external work; for, after having been exposed on the beach for ages to the alternate changes of moisture and dryness, heat and cold, they were found to have many small fissures, or were split horizontally; and although the pieces still seemed to adhere closely, yet they were sufficiently open to admit moisture into the heart of the walls, which, in these stormy and exposed situations, is forced through the building: hence it is, that houses built with drift-stones of this description, are said by the cottagers of these islands to keep out moisture much better when built with puddle or clay, than with the best lime-mortar, which, under certain circumstances, is known to attract moisture, while the clay resists it. But after all the care that can be taken in building with these slaty stones, even when taken fresh from the quarry, they still have a tendency to split into lamellæ, after they are built in the walls. Experienced builders, therefore, generally lay the outward stones of such walls with a slight inclination downwards, or dip, as the workmen term it, the more readily to prevent the admission of wetness.

Houses built with Double walls.

I have been thus particular, because it is hardly possible to prevent walls built of these materials from drawing moisture, until they have been rough cast,—an operation which is so very troublesome, from requiring to be occasionally renewed, that I have found it necessary, in these exposed situations, to build the outward walls double, as the only effectual method of obtaining a comfortable house free of dampness.

Laying the foundation stone of Beacon.

The weather continued to be so extremely boisterous here, that it was the middle of the month of May before a sufficient stock of materials was laid down for commencing the building at the Start Point. A wish having been expressed by the workmen, to have the foundation-stone of the Beacon laid with masonic ceremony; and considering the dreary prospect which the artificers had before them, the author was the more willing to embrace so fair an opportunity of affording them the enjoyment of a little convivial happiness. The influx of so many strangers to the island of Sanday for this work, and the novelty of the intended ceremony, made the news soon find its way to every house. Preparations were accordingly made;—the year of our Lord 1802, was cut upon the foundation-stone, in which a hole was perforated for depositing a glass phial, containing a small parchment scroll, setting forth the intention of the building; the official constitution of the Commissioners of the Northern Light-houses; and the name of their Engineer. It also contained several of the current coins of George III. in gold, silver, and copper. The day fixed for the ceremony was the 15th of May. The weather was dry and tolerably agreeable, though cold, with snow upon the ground; the thermometer by Fahrenheit's scale indicating 35° in the shade at noon. A number of the principal inhabitants, and a crowd of cottagers assembled. Things being arranged for the ceremony, the author, assisted by Mr James Cleghorn, foreman for the works, applied the square and plummet-level to the foundation-stone, in compliance with the ancient custom of the craft. The phial was then deposited in the cavity prepared for it in the stone, and carefully covered up with sand, when the masonic ceremony concluded in the usual manner. The Reverend Walter Traill, minister of the parish, who obligingly attended on this occasion, now stood forward, and, after a most impressive prayer, imploring the blessing of heaven upon the intended purposes of the building, delivered an address, which, from the singularity of the subject, and the excellency of the matter, shall here be inserted.

Rev. Walter Trail's Address.

"This moment is auspicious. The foundation-stone is laid of a building of incalculable value;—a work of use, not of luxury. Pyramids were erected by the pride of kings, to perpetuate the memory of men, whose ambition enslaved and desolated the world. But it is the benevolent intention of our Government, on this spot to erect a tower, not to exhaust, but to increase the wealth, and protect the commerce of this happy kingdom.—To the goodness of God, in the first place, we are indebted for a degree of prosperity unknown to other nations. In the next place, we owe our happiness to our insular situation, and attention to maritime affairs. Faction and civil war have, at this period, laid waste the fairest countries of Europe; while peace has flourished within our walls. Agriculture, commerce, and their kindred arts, have prospered in our land. British oak hath triumphed; victory hath been attached to the British flag; and British fleets have ridden triumphant on the wings of the wind.—Consider the great national objects for which this building will be erected. To protect commerce, and to guard the lives of those intrepid men who for us cheerfully brave the fury of the waves, and the rage of battle. The mariner, when he returns to the embraces of his wife and children, after ascribing praise to the Great Giver of safety, shall bless the friendly light which guided him over the deep, and recommend to the protection of heaven, those who urged, who planned, and who executed the work.—This day shall be remembered with gratitude. It shall be recorded, that at the beginning of a new century, the pious care of Government was extended to this remote island. Those rocks, so fatal to the most brave and honourable part of the community, shall lose their terror, and safety and life shall spring from danger and death.—Even you, my friends, who are employed in the execution of this work, are objects of regard and gratitude. You have, for a season, left the society of your families and friends, to perform a work of high interest to your country and to mankind. I am confident, that you will act, in all respects, so as to deserve and obtain the esteem of the people who now surround you. I hope that they will discharge to you every duty of Christian hospitality, and that you will have no occasion to feel that you are strangers in a strange land.—It becomes us to remember, that all the affairs of men are dependent on Providence. We may exert talents and industry, but God only can bless our exertions with success. Let our trust be in him. Let us humbly hope that he will bless this day and this undertaking. Through his aid, may there arise from this spot, a tower of safety and protection to the mariner of every tongue and nation."

The whole of this scene was very impressive; and the plain, decent, and respectable appearance of the people collected on the occasion, was none of the least interesting parts of it.

Beacon Completed.

Having now got the works at the Start Point of Sanday fairly commenced, and some progress made in opening the quarries, the author left the Orkney Islands, and continued his voyage westward to the other Light-houses on the coast. Every thing having succeeded well at the Start Point, the Beacon was finished in the month of September. It was terminated at the height of 100 feet above the medium level of the sea, with a circular ball of masonry measuring fifteen feet in circumference.—But this tower having been afterwards converted into a light-house, it seems to be unnecessary here to enter into a more particular specification of the building.

INCHKEITH LIGHT-HOUSE.

1803.

Much inconveniency had been experienced, and many fatal accidents had occurred, in the Firth of Forth, from the want of a light to direct ships past the island of Inchkeith into the Roads of Leith. In the course of the winter of 1801, from this cause, a very severe misfortune happened at the rocks lying off Kinghornness, on the Fifeshire coast, by the loss of the smack Aberdeen, Freeman, master, one of the traders bound from Aberdeen to London. This vessel had been put up the Firth in a storm, loaded with a general cargo, which was valued at upwards of L. 10,000, and had on board 13 passengers, besides the ship's crew, all of whom perished, excepting the master, the mate, and a lady. So very distressing an accident, with other instances of a similar nature, produced a strong sensation with the public. It was also found, that vessels which, by the direction of the light of May, had entered the Firth of Forth in the course of a long winter night, could not yet venture to hold on their course, up the Firth , owing to the difficulty of passing the island of Inchkeith, and the foul and rocky ground in its neighbourhood. The mariner was thus obliged to lie off and on in this narrow sea, without being able to run for the anchorage of Leith Roads till day-light: but, before morning, the wind perhaps had shifted; and, instead of being in a safe anchorage, he was too often driven to sea. The author has, indeed, known of a ship in this situation, which drifted before the wind even to the coast of Norway.

Inchkeith Light-house resolved on.

It was from considerations of this kind that an application was brought forward by the Corporation of the Trinity House of Leith, for the erection of a light-house upon Inchkeith; and the Commissioners of the Northern Light-houses, also viewing Leith Roads as a naval station and rendezvous for his Majesty's ships on the North Sea station, resolved upon the propriety and expediency of this measure in the year 1802. Various difficulties occurred about procuring the ground necessary for this establishment, not indeed with the noble proprietor of the island, the Duke of Buccleuch, who forthwith ordered every facility to be given to the work; but time was lost in arranging matters with his Grace's agent. It was not, therefore, till the summer of the year 1803, that the building on Inchkeith commenced, and the masonry of the light-house was not ready for the light-room till the following year, when the light was exhibited on the 1st day of September 1804. Its position is described as follows:

Description of Inchkeith Light-house.

"The Light-house erected on the island of Inchkeith, situate in the Firth of Forth and county of Mid-Lothian, in North Lat. 56° 2′, and Long. 3° 8′. west of London, is elevated 220 feet above the medium level of the sea, of which height the building forms 45 feet. The light is from oil with reflectors, and will be seen from every point of the compass as a Stationary light" (since altered to a Revolving light, as shall be afterwards noticed). "From the light-house Ely-ness bears, by compass, E. NE., distant 16 miles; Light of May E. ½ N., distant 23 miles; Fidra Island E. by S., distant 14 miles; Craig Waugh Rock SE. by S. ½ S., distant 4¾ miles; Leith-Harbour Light SW. ¼ S., distant 3½ miles; Gunnet Rock W., distant 1½ mile; Ox-Scares W. by N. ½ N., distant 4½ miles; Inchcolm W. NW. ¼ N., distant 6½ miles; Pettycur Light N. NW. ¼ N., distant 2½ miles; Kinghorn-ness N. NW. ¾ N. distant 2¼ miles."

Originally proposed to be a Leading light.

This light-house was originally proposed to have been made a double or leading light, to guide ships up the Firth , and especially past the dangerous rock called the Ox-Scares, to the anchorage above Queensferry; but it was thought advisable to erect a light, in the first instance, upon the top of the island, and to defer the erection of a lower or western light till the effect of a single light should be tried. Such, however, appears to have been the benefit of the light on the top of the island, together with a cast-iron Beacon, which, at this time, was erected on the Ox-Scares, that the want of a second light-house on Inchkeith does not seem to have been much felt.

Light duty for Inchkeith modified.

By the existing acts of Parliament, the light-house Board is entitled to take the full duties of three halfpence per ton, from the local trade of the Firth of Forth, for the light of Inchkeith, instead of which, only one halfpenny per ton is exacted from such vessels as are not liable to the duty, in consequence of passing some other of the Northern Light-houses. The great utility of this light-house, and the equitable and liberal manner in which these duties are exacted, gave much satisfaction to the maritime and commercial interests of the country.

Accommodation of Light-keepers' houses extended.

It may here be proper to observe, that the erection of Inchkeith Light-house, forms a new era in the works of the Commissioners of the Northern Light-houses; which, as formerly observed, had been necessarily executed on the smallest, plainest and most simple plan that could be devised, and with such materials as could be easily transported, and most speedily erected, so as to meet the urgent calls of shipping, and answer the very limited state of the funds. But from the thriving condition of the trade of the country, the yearly duties which, in 1790, amounted only to L. 1477:5:1; in the year 1802 encreased to L. 4386:7:5. It was, therefore, considered advisable, from its being ultimately more economical, to erect and finish the several works of the light-house Board in the most substantial manner, and more like the buildings of a permanent National Establishment.

Houses covered with leaden roofs.

From the vicinity of Inchkeith to sandstone quarries, the buildings there were executed of aislar masonry. A platform roof covered with lead, and defended by a parapet wall, was adopted for the light-keepers' house, instead of a slated roof, with garrets of the common construction; a slated roof being not only more liable to be injured by high winds, but when the attic apartments of such houses are occupied, the premises became more exposed to accident from fire.

Disadvantage of slated roofs.

The slated roof, with iron nails, is also subject to decay, owing to the saline particles with which the air is impregnated, and the sprays of the sea, which, even in such situations as Inchkeith, are often blown over the island, though the site of the light-house is about 175 feet in height. Indeed, at all the original light-house stations in the north, the nails were soon rusted, and the slates getting loose, were often blown off in great numbers, so that in the very depth of Winter, the light-keepers have been obliged to make such a requisition as the following: "A slater is much wanted here, to repair the roof of the house, as upwards of 50 slates have been blown away during the late gales." Instead, also, of a dwelling-house consisting of only two small apartments as formerly, the house at Inchkeith has four rooms, with other conveniencies, laid out for the accommodation of the families of a principal light-keeper and an assistant, who are now appointed to the charge of each of the Northern Light-houses.

Construction of Light rooms improved.

An entire change also took place at this period upon the construction of the Light-rooms and the reflecting apparatus, as well as in the extension and enlargement of the accommodation for the light-keepers. The early light-rooms were constructed wholly of timber, excepting the window-sash frames, which were made of cast-iron. The outside of the wooden cupola, covered with sheet copper, and the ceiling and floor with fire-proof plates of tinned iron. But it soon appeared that this construction was liable to great objections, particularly to the risk of accidental fire. The timber roof being also unavoidably shut up from the air, and exposed to a degree of heat sufficient to dry it to the state of tinder, its strength and fibrous qualities were soon lost, and the buildings in danger of being destroyed by the storms of winter.

Rendered Fire-proof.

At Inchkeith, on the contrary, the roof is framed of iron, and covered with copper, and the floor is laid with flag-stones; while the window-frames, and all the materials exposed to the immediate action of the weather, are made of copper; the windows are glazed with plates of polished glass, measuring 29 inches by 18 inches, and ¼ of an inch in thickness, instead of sash panes of crown-glass, measuring only 12 inches by 8 inches, by which so many astragals were unavoidably introduced into the windows, that much of the light was obstructed and lost.

Reflectors of Silvered Mirror-glass.

The reflectors of the first of the Northern Light-houses were formed to the parabolic curve, upon principles susceptible of considerable accuracy; their powers were, however, small from their reflecting surfaces being composed of facets of silvered mirror-glass, and one point only of each facet coinciding with the curve of the parabola. As many of the rays are thus lost or weakened by transmission through the glass of the reflector, the light is much less brilliant than when reflected from a metallic speculum of a uniform parabolic figure, of a more white and dense body, such as silver. Another objection to mirror-glass reflectors, is the great number of interstices or subdivisions between the pieces of glass, which unavoidably induces a want of cleanliness and uniformity in the reflecting surface as a whole.

Reflectors of Copper, plated with Silver.

The improvement upon this part of the reflecting apparatus, as more recently fitted up, consists in employing sheets of copper, plated or coated with silver, which, with much labour and great nicety of workmanship, are formed as nearly as may be into the parabolic curve,—a subject to which we shall again recur, in treating of the reflectors for the Bell Rock Light-house.

The use of Argand lamps and Spermaceti Oil introduced.

Instead, also, of whale oil, and the use of the Common lamp, spermaceti oil, and the Argand lamp, were introduced at Inchkeith. Upon these principles, all the new erections of the Northern Light-houses are constructed; and such of the original light-houses, as require considerable repairs, are directed by the Board to be altered to the improved construction. But the erection of such a light-house as that of Inchkeith, in place of requiring an expenditure of only about L. 1000 like the original establishments, cost upwards of L. 5000.

Inscription on Inchkeith Light-house.

The light-house of Inchkeith having been erected before the late Mr Smith, the author's predecessor, had retired from the situation of Engineer for the Northern Light-houses, and being the first of the light-houses erected upon the coast of Scotland on the recently improved principles, it is thought proper to give a plan and elevation of the house and offices, in one of the plates of this work, as a specimen of what is considered a very complete light-house establishment. It may also be noticed here, that the elevation of the light-house tower bears a tablet with the following inscription:—"For the direction of Mariners, and for the benefit of Commerce, this Light-house was erected by order of the Commissioners of the Northern Light-houses. It was founded on the 18th day of May, in the year 1803, and lighted on the 1st of September 1804. Thomas Smith, Engineer."

Pilots and Shipwrecked Seamen receive shelter.

As part of the establishment at Inchkeith, a guard-room is provided for pilots. In the event also of shipwreck upon the coast, in the neighbourhood of any of the light-house stations, from the more extended state of the buildings, the unfortunate seamen are not only directed to be lodged in the best manner that the circumstances of the case will admit, but, in necessitous cases, ship-wrecked mariners have even been allowed a sum of money by the Light-house Board, to clothe and carry them to their respective homes. In this way, it has not unfrequently fallen to the lot of the keepers of the Northern Light-houses, to save the lives of perishing seamen, to succour many poor fishermen and pilots, as well as the half starved and unlucky individuals of water parties, when driven by stress of weather to these lone places of abode, for safety and shelter. In these varied forms, it will not be too much to suppose, that the practice of protecting the navigator in distress, which is said to have formed a chief part of the design of the Fire Towers and Nautical Colleges of the ancients, is thus in some measure restored.

START POINT LIGHT-HOUSE.

1806.

Shipwrecks still take place on Sanday.

Notwithstanding the precautions which had been taken to prevent the frequent occurrence of shipwreck upon the island of Sanday, by the erection of a Beacon or Tower of masonry on the Start Point, the loss of ships did not appear to be diminished. It had even become proverbial with some of the inhabitants to observe, "that if wrecks were to happen, they might as well be sent to the poor island of Sanday as any where else." On this and the neighbouring islands, the inhabitants have certainly had their share of wrecked goods; for here the eye is presented with these melancholy remains in almost every form.

Striking examples of this.

For example, although quarries are to be met with generally in these islands, and the stones are very suitable for building dikes, yet instances occur of the land being inclosed, even to a considerable extent, with ship timbers. The author has actually seen a park paled round, chiefly with cedar wood and mahogany from the wreck of a Honduras built ship; and in one island, after the wreck of a ship laden with wine, the inhabitants have been known to take claret to their barley meal porridge, instead of their usual beverage. On complaining to one of the pilots of the badness of his boat's sails, he replied to the author with some degree of pleasantry, "Had it been His (God's) will that you came na here wi' these lights, we might a' had better sails to our boats and more o' other things." It may further be noticed, that when some of Lord Dundas's farms are to be let in these islands, a competition takes place for the lease, and it is bona fide understood, that a much higher rent is paid than the lands would otherwise give, were it not for the chance of making considerably by the agency and advantages attending shipwrecks on the shores of the respective farms. The author was so struck with some of these circumstances, that he collected, and shall here insert a list of shipwrecks for the twelve years immediately following the erection of North Ronaldsay light-house, in procuring which he was obligingly assisted by the Rev. William Grant, minister of Cross-kirk parish, including the island of North Ronaldsay, and part of Sanday.

List of Shipwrecks for Twelve Years.

LIST OF WRECKS on the contiguous islands of North Ronaldsay, Sanday and Stronsay, during a period of Twelve Years, immediately after the erection of North Ronaldsay Light-house, in 1789.

Year.	Voyage.	Cargo.	Tonnage.	Supposed Value of Ship and Cargo.
1789.	Norway to America,	Spirits, &c.	150	L. 3500 0 0
1790.	Hamburgh to do.	Cordage, &c.	100	2800 0 0
1792.	Norway to Wales,	Wood and Iron,	90	1100 0 0
— —	Sweden to Liverpool,	Grain,	120	3100 0 0
— —	Do. to Greenock,	Timber,	400	3400 0 0
1793.	Norway to Spain,	Fish and Oil,	100	2000 0 0
— —	Copenhagen to Santa Cruz,	Silks, &c.	250	35,000 0 0
1794.	Copenhagen to Surinam,	Muslins, &c.	250	20,000 0 0
— —	Do. to Dundee,	Flax, &c.	90	2000 0 0
1795.	Do. to America,	Cloth, &c.	300	12,200 0 0
1796.	Do. to Liverpool,	Timber,	250	2500 0 0
— —	Do. to Whitehaven,	Timber,	150	1300 0 0
— —	Liverpool to Ostend,	Wine and Rum,	400	15,300 0 0
1797.	Baltic to Liverpool,	Grain,	120	3000 0 0
1798.	Sweden to Hull,	Timber and Iron,	200	2500 0 0
— —	Norway to Liverpool.	Timber,	200	1800 0 0
— —	Do. to America,	Cloth, &c.	200	5000 0 0
— —	Altona to Do.	Spirits and Cloth,	450	18,000 0 0
— —	London to Gibraltar,	Stores,	300	5000 0 0
1799.	Do. to Dublin,	Staves,	150	2200 0 0
1800.	Hamburgh to America,	Cambric and Linen,	200	45,000 0 0
— —	Dantzic to Liverpool,	Timber,	900	10,000 0 0
22 vessels wrecked in 12 years, supposed value				L. 196,400 0 0

. Start Point Tower proposed to be converted into a Light-house.

This list of shipwrecks strongly points out the dangerous nature of the navigation of the seas and friths of the northern islands of Orkney. From a consideration of these numerous accidents, being almost at the rate of two wrecks in the year, and seeing the mangled remains of some fine ships which still appeared upon the island of Sanday, the author was induced to bring this matter again under the notice of the Commissioners of the Northern Light-houses, in his report to the Board in the year 1805, when he proposed that the Start Point Beacon should be converted into a light-house, and that North Ronaldsay light should be discontinued, and its tower converted into a beacon, as wrecks were found to happen comparatively seldom upon that island, while hardly a year passed without instances of this kind on the island of Sanday; for, owing to the projecting points of this strangely formed island, the lowness and whiteness of its eastern shores, and the wonderful manner in which the scanty patches of land are intersected with lakes and pools of water, it becomes even in day-light a deception, and has often been fatally mistaken for an open sea.

North Ronaldsay Light-house to be converted into a Beacon.

The removal of the light from North Ronaldsay to Sanday, was also calculated to be equally, if not more, useful to the navigation of North Ronaldsay Firth ; the Start Point being only four miles from the sunken rock called the Reef-dyke, as will be seen from the general chart of the coast which accompanies this work. It therefore appeared that if only a single light were allowed for the protection of this coast, it would be much better upon Sanday than on North Ronaldsay.

Opinion of persons conversant with the Navigation of these Seas.

On this subject, however, the author was instructed to take the opinion of persons acquainted with the navigation of these seas. Accordingly, when on his annual voyage to the Northern Light-houses, he submitted the subject to the consideration of Mr William Ellis, Commander of the Ross Revenue Cutter, who had then been cruising for several months off these islands, by order of Government, for intelligence relative to the motions of the Dutch fleet, which then threatened to attempt a landing on the Western Coast of Ireland. It was also submitted to Mr Riddoch, Collector, and Mr Manson, Comptroller of the Customs, at Kirkwall; to Mr John Traill, Mr Fotheringham, and Mr Strang of Sanday; and to the ship-masters of Kirkwall and Stromness. These gentlemen all united in opinion as to the superior usefulness of a light upon the island of Sanday.

Light-house resolved on.

This measure having been resolved on by the Board, the plans were remitted, with powers to proceed, to Mr William Rae, (now Sir William Rae, Bart. Lord Advocate of Scotland,) who was then Sheriff of the county of Orkney. The works at the Start Point were accordingly commenced early in the summer of 1805; by the month of November the light-room was finished, and the light exhibited on the 1st day of January 1806. Intimation was at the same time given to the public, that the beacon or tower of masonry erected in the year 1803, upon the island of Sanday, having been found insufficient for preventing the numerous shipwrecks upon the low shores of that island, had been converted into a light-house.

Description of Start Point Light.

The Start Point of Sanday is situate in the county of Orkney, in North Lat. 59° 20′, and Long. 2° 34′ west of London, from which North Ronaldsay light-house Tower bears by compass, N. NE. ½ E., distant 8 miles, and the Lamb Head of Stronsay SW., distant 15 miles. The light at the Start Point is from oil with reflectors, elevated 100 feet above the medium level of the sea, and is visible from all points of the compass, at the distance of 15 miles, in a favourable state of the atmosphere. To distinguish this light from the other lights on this coast, it is known to mariners as a Revolving light, without colour, exhibiting a brilliant light once in every minute, and becoming gradually less luminous; to a distant observer it totally disappears. In this manner, each periodic revolution of the reflector-frame, alternately shows a brilliant light, and a light becoming fainter and more obscure, until it be totally eclipsed.

The Foreman and Artificers sail for Leith in the Traveller.

The alteration of the Start Point beacon into a light-house, and the erection of houses for the light-keepers, were placed under the management of Mr George Peebles, an experienced mason, and executed with every possible attention. When the works were completed, he, and such of the artificers as had been retained, proceeded to Stromness on the mainland of Orkney, from whence they were most likely to get a passage to the southward. The party consisted of six in number; and Charles Peebles, the foreman's brother, wishing to go directly to his native place, took his passage in a vessel bound from Stromness to Anstruther, while Mr George Peebles, and the remaining four men, embarked on board of a schooner, called the Traveller, Cruickshanks master, bound for Leith.

The Traveller is wrecked.

This vessel sailed with a fair wind early on the 24th of December 1806. On the following morning they got sight of Kinnaird Head light-house, in Aberdeenshire, and had the prospect of speedily reaching the Firth of Forth; but the wind having suddenly shifted to the south-east, increased to a tremendous gale, which did much damage on the coast. The Traveller immediately put about, and steered in quest of some safe harbour in Orkney. At two o'clock in the afternoon, she passed through the Pentland Firth , and got into the bay of Long Hope; but could not reach the proper anchorage; and, at three o'clock, both anchors were let go in an outer roadstead. The storm still continuing with unabated force, the cables parted or broke, and the vessel drifted on the island of Flotta.

Captain Manby's Apparatus much wanted.

The utmost efforts of those on board to pass a rope to the shore, with the assistance of the inhabitants of the island, proved ineffectual, (for want of some apparatus like Captain Manby's); the vessel struck upon a shelving rock, and, night coming on, sunk in three fathoms water.

The Foreman and four of the Artificers are drowned.

Some of the unfortunate crew and passengers attempted to swim ashore, but in the darkness of the night, they either lost their way, or were dashed upon the rocks by the surge of the sea; while those who retained hold of the rigging of the ship, being worn out with fatigue and the piercing coldness of the weather during a long winter night, died before morning,—when the shore presented the dreadful spectacle of the wreck of no fewer than five vessels, with many lifeless bodies, the mournful subjects of the care and pity of the islanders. In one of these wrecks, all on board were lost; and, in the Traveller, only the cabin-boy escaped. This poor boy, from whom these particulars were learned, had, for a time, been sheltered from the severity of the blast, by one of the crew, but being at length left alone, he clung to the top-mast, from which he was with great difficulty removed in the morning, when the storm had somewhat abated.

A very trifling circumstance prevented the vessel bound for Anstruther, from leaving Stromness along with the Traveller, so that Charles Peebles escaped this gale, and arrived with the sad tidings of the fate of his brother and companions. In Mr George Peebles, the light-house service lost a most active and faithful servant, whose next charge would have been at the operations of the Bell Rock light-house. From the peculiar circumstances of this case, the Commissioners were pleased to grant small annuities to the mother of the foreman, and also to the family of another of the sufferers.

BELL ROCK LIGHT-HOUSE.

1807.

In the prosecution of the plan of this introductory account of the Northern Light-houses, we may observe that the attention of the Commissioners was occupied with the erection of the Bell Rock Light-house, during the years 1807, 8, 9, and 10. But as the detail of the operations of these four years forms the chief object of this work, it is not necessary that they should be further noticed here. We therefore proceed to the next operations of the Board, in the order of time.

NORTH RONALDSAY BEACON.

1809.

North Ronaldsay Light extinguished, and its Tower converted into a Beacon.

It having been considered superfluous to have two light-houses on this part of the coast, within 8 miles of each other, the Light-house Board resolved to extinguish North Ronaldsay light, and convert its tower into a sea-mark, or beacon without a light. It was accordingly intimated in the newspapers of the principal ports of the United kingdom that the light on the Island of North Ronaldsay, in Orkney, situated in North Lat. 59° 40′, Long. 2° 15′ west of London, would be discontinued, and cease to be lighted from and after the 1st day of June 1809; but that the Light-house Tower would be preserved as a Beacon on the coast, by the erection of a Circular Ball of masonry, measuring 8 feet in diameter, instead of a Light-room. This beacon bears from the revolving light on the Start Point of Sanday, N.NE., ½ E. by compass, distant 8 miles, which continues to be lighted as heretofore, the Start Point having been found the most centrical position for a light-house to warn the mariner of his approach to the low shores of the North Isles of Orkney.

ISLE OF MAY.

1814.

Light of May first Lighted 1635.

The island of May holds a prominent position at the entrance of the Firth of Forth, as will be seen by referring to the charts of the coast which accompany this work. From its connection also with the estuary leading to the Capital of Scotland, and the principal ports of her commerce, the light of May seems to have been the earliest public light on our shores. Over the entrance door of the old light-house tower, a stone, neatly cut into the figure by which the sun is usually represented, bears the date 1635. It appears, also, from the printed acts of the Scottish Parliament, Vol. v. p. 585., that power was granted, in the reign of Charles I., to James Maxwell of Innerwick, and John Cunninghame of Barnes, to erect a light-house upon the Isle of May, and collect certain duties from shipping for its maintenance:

Patent ratified 1641.

The patent for this purpose, was ratified by the Scots Parliament in 1641.

Much complained of after the Union.

The duties leviable for the light of May produced much dissatisfaction after the Union, English and Irish vessels having been charged with double rates, as foreigners. There was, besides, a general dislike to any thing that was payable in the form of a tax being held as private property. This light being also a coal-fire, exposed in an open choffer to the vicissitudes of the weather, was found to be very insufficient. After the appointment of a Light-house Board in Scotland, in the year 1786, the shipping interest often expressed a desire that the light of May should be included as one of the Northern Lights; that it might undergo the most recent improvements; that, according to the spirit and conditions of the Northern Light-house acts, the invidious distinction between the shipping of the same kingdom, with regard to the light-house duties, might be done away; and also that there might be some prospect of the duties being modified, and ultimately ceasing. In the year 1809, the author foreseeing, that notwithstanding the erection of the Bell Rock light-house, the navigation of this part of the coast would still be very incomplete, unless the light of May were improved, took an opportunity of bringing this subject under the notice of the Commissioners of the Northern Light-houses; but it did not then appear that this could be taken up by the Board, unless it were at the instance of the proprietor.

Family of Scotstarvit become Proprietors of the Island.

The family of Scotstarvit, into whose hands the property of the island and light of May came by purchase, in 1714, along with the estate of Westbarnes, in East Lothian, had long been solicited by the trade of the Firth of Forth, to have the light made better, either by enlarging the choffer for containing the coals, or by altering it to an oil light with reflectors.

Chamber of Commerce get the Light Improved.

Statements to this effect having been laid before the proprietor, by the Chamber of Commerce of Edinburgh, a Committee of that body visited the island in the year 1786, and reported on the state of the light. In consequence of the representation of this Committee, the choffer was enlarged to the capacity of a square of three feet; and, instead of about 200 tons of coal per annum, formerly consumed, the quantity of fuel was now doubled.

Wemyss Coal preferred for the Lights.

The Chamber further recommended, that the stock of coals, hitherto exposed to the open air on the island, should in future be kept under cover, and that the supply should be invariably got from the collieries of Wemyss, which were preferred as fittest for maintaining a steady light, Wemyss coal being then used at Heligoland, and other coal-lights upon the Continent.

Light of May considered the best Coal-Light in the kingdom.

These conditions were most readily complied with by the tutors of Miss Scott, the proprietor; and the light of May, from that period, was found to be very considerably improved, the choffer for containing the fuel being about double the capacity of any other light-house choffer on the coast of Great Britain. The light of May, from this period, may therefore be described as the most powerful coal-light in the kingdom, although, from its exposure, it was still found to be very unsteady, in bad weather, when most required by the mariner. Lime-kilns and other accidental open fires upon the neighbouring shores, were also apt to be mistaken for the Isle of May choffer. To obviate such dangerous mistakes, there was no other method but the introduction of a light from oil, with reflectors, inclosed in a glazed light-room.

Portland Family get possession of the Island.

The Trinity-house of Leith, in the year 1790, presented a memorial to this effect, to the Duke of Portland, into whose possession the light and Isle of May had come by his Grace's marriage with Miss Scott of Scotstarvit. But after many fruitless applications urged from time to time by the Merchants of Leith, to have the light altered, the measure was at length given up by them as hopeless.

Loss of the Nymphen and Pallas Frigates.

Early in the morning of the 19th day of December 1810, however, two of his Majesty's ships, the frigates Nymphen and Pallas, had the misfortune to be wrecked near Dunbar, in consequence, it is believed, of the light of a lime-kiln on the coast of Haddingtonshire having been mistaken for the coal light of the island of May. These frigates having come along the northern coast of Scotland, their situation, as may be seen from the annexed maps, was very different from that of ships approaching the land from a distant voyage, who are much more liable to mistakes of this kind.

Their prize-ship arrives in safety.

But what renders the error in this instance more unaccountable is, that one of the ships had even sent a boat ashore at Johnshaven, on the opposite coast of Kincardineshire, in the afternoon of the day preceding their loss; and the other, about the same time and place, dispatched a small prize for Leith Roads, under the command of a Midshipman,—who, in his course up the Firth of Forth, saw the Bell Rock floating light, (for at this time the light-house was not completed),—then the lights on the islands of May and Inchkeith in succession, and before day-light in the morning of the 19th he anchored his little vessel in the Roads. In reporting the prize to the Admiral at Leith, this young gentleman expressed his surprise that the frigates had not reached their station before him. In the course of the forenoon of the same day, however, an express arrived, stating the circumstance of the loss of the Pallas, which had happened in the course of the night, about two miles to the eastward of Dunbar. Soon afterwards, another notice arrived announcing to the Admiral the loss of the Nymphen Frigate in the same manner, and from the same mistake. It is not a little surprising, that although these ships had sailed in company, and were wrecked within a few miles of each other, their similar fate was perfectly unknown by the respective crews, till late in the day on which the accidents happened.

Nine men drowned.

It was, however, so far fortunate, that although the ships became total wrecks, only nine men were lost of their joint crews, amounting to about 600 men; all of whom might probably have perished, from the rocky and exposed shore on which they were stranded, had not the weather been very moderate.

Lord Melville applies to the Light-house Board about the Isle of May Light.

Immediately after the loss of these two fine frigates, valued at not less than L. 100,000, Lord Viscount Melville, first Lord of the Admiralty, applied to the Commissioners of the Northern Light-houses, proposing that the light of May should be assumed as one of the northern lights, and forthwith put under proper regulations.

Duke of Portland proposes to alter the Light;

It may here be proper to notice, that, prior to this accident, the Duke of Portland entertained serious intentions of altering this light; and the author had been employed to report to his Grace on its alteration, from the use of pit-coal to oil, with reflectors, the expence of which he had estimated at the annual sum of L. 600.

And proposes that the Commissioners should become Lessees, which is rejected.

The communication from the Admiralty gave rise to a correspondence between the Light-house Commissioners and the Duke of Portland, who proposed to give the Light-house Board an allowance of L. 600 per annum, for taking burden of the light of May, while his Grace was to continue to levy the duties. This proposal was rejected on the part of the Commissioners, who declined becoming lessees, under the existing acts or constitution of their Board; and it was ultimately concluded, that they could only take up this measure as purchasers for the public, in order to abolish the charge on English and Irish vessels paying as foreigners, and to lessen the duty for that light to the trade in general. In the present state of the light-house funds, this purchase could only be made by a special act of Parliament, and with pecuniary aid from Government:

The Duke demands L. 63,000 for the Light duties and Island.

as the sum demanded by the Duke for the island, and the right to the light-duties, was unavoidably great, amounting to no less than Sixty Thousand Guineas.

Memorial presented to the Admiralty.

In the mean time, Mr Cuningham, Secretary to the Light-house Board, was directed to acquaint Mr Walker, the Duke of Portland's agent, that the Commissioners could not treat for upholding the light of May for payment of an annual sum. A memorial was then drawn up for the Admiralty, of the whole proceedings in this measure, which was presented by Sir William Rae, Bart., on the part of the Light-house Board; when their Lordships were pleased to give their countenance and support to a bill for the purchase of the light duties and island of May.

Isle of May and Duties purchased at L. 60,000.

This bill was accordingly brought into Parliament, and passed in the Session of 1814, authorising a loan of L. 30,000 to be made from the Treasury to the Commissioners of Northern Light-houses, and empowering them to make the purchase from the Duke of Portland, for the sum of L. 60,000.

Duty of the Light of May reduced by the Act of 1814.

This important transaction having been closed, the Light-house Board, in terms of this act (46th George III. chap. cxxxvi.) were empowered to reduce the light-duty of the Isle of May, to all British vessels, from one penny half-penny, as collected heretofore, to one penny per ton, when English and Irish ships were no longer treated as foreigners, by paying double dues. Immediate measures were also taken for altering and improving the light. It was, however, too late at the end of the session of 1814, to commence operations on the island; but, in the following summer, the new light-house was erected, and a light from oil with reflectors was exhibited, on the 1st day of February 1816, after a coal-light had been continued here for 181 years, or from 1635.

Additional Apartments at the Isle of May.

As the island of May lies about half way between the light-houses of Inch Keith and the Bell Rock, it was thought proper to have two or three apartments in the May Light-house for the reception of such members of the Light-house Board, as might happen to be detained by contrary winds in occasional visits to the Bell Rock, upon which landing is often very difficult and precarious, depending both on the state of the weather and the tides. The dwelling-house at the Isle of May, therefore, is larger than would otherwise have been required for the accommodation of the two light-keepers and their families.

Notice given of the alterations at Isle of May and Inchkeith.

In consequence of this change upon the light of May, notice was given to the public, that it had been assumed one of the Northern Light-houses, and that the Commissioners had directed a new light-house, upon improved principles, to be erected, which would not only alter its former appearance, but also occasion a change on the light of Inchkeith, situate about twenty-two miles farther up the Firth of Forth. The following description of the Isle of May light was published.

Description of the Light of May.

"The light-house on the Island of May, is situate at the entrance of the Firth of Forth, in North Lat. 56° 12′, and Long. 2° 36′ west of London. From the light-house, Fifeness bears, by compass, N. by E. ½ E., distant five miles, and the Staple Rocks lying off Dunbar, S. by W. ½ W., distant ten miles. The light being formerly from coal, exposed to the weather in an open grate or choffer, was discontinued on the night of the 1st day of February 1816, when a light from oil, with reflectors, known to mariners as a Stationary Light, was exhibited. The new light-house tower, upon the Island of May, is contiguous to the site of the old one, and is elevated 240 feet above the medium level of the sea, of which the masonry forms 57 feet, and is therefore similar to the old tower in point of height. The new light is defended from the weather in a glazed light-room, and has a uniformly steady appearance, resembling a star of the first magnitude, and is seen from all points of the compass, at the distance of about seven leagues, and intermediately according to the state of the atmosphere." —

Old Light-house converted into a Pilot's Guard-room.

The old light-house tower on the Island of May, has been reduced in height to about 20 feet, and by directions of the Light-house Board, it has been converted into a guard-room like that upon Inchkeith, for the use and conveniency of pilots and fishermen.

INCHKEITH REVOLVING LIGHT.

Description of Inchkeith Revolving Light.

The above description, in so far as regards the appearance of the light of May being exactly applicable to that of Inchkeith, described at page 25. of this Introduction, it was found expedient to alter it from a stationary to a revolving light, that it might be distinguished from the light of May, where a revolving light would have been liable to be mistaken for the Bell Rock light, owing to the more contiguous position of the May island to the Bell Rock.

The light upon Inchkeith, hitherto a stationary light from oil, with reflectors, was therefore altered and converted into that description of light known to mariners as a Revolving light without colour, on the same night that the change took place upon the Isle of May. The light of Inchkeith is seen from all points of the compass, at the distance of five leagues in favourable weather, exhibiting a bright light once in every minute, and gradually becoming less luminous, it totally disappears to a distant observer. In this manner, each periodic revolution of the reflector-frame, alternately shows a brilliant light, which becomes fainter, and more obscure, until it is totally eclipsed. By this alteration, the same description and appearance of the other lights upon the coast is preserved, and the possibility of mistaking Inchkeith light for the numerous lights on the land, with which it is surrounded, is now also effectually prevented.

CORSEWALL.

1815.

Additional Light proposed for the western coast on Corsewall Point.

It had long been the wish of the mercantile interest of the Firth of Clyde and St George's Channel, to have a light on the coast of Galloway, to direct ships, on the Scotch side, into the Irish Channel. From the great amount of light-house duties collected upon the western coast, and the extent of light-house works which had of late years been erected upon the eastern shores, including the Bell Rock and Isle of May light-houses, the Commissioners were desirous of accommodating the trade of the western coast, as far as the demands of shipping required, or the state of the light-house funds would permit. It was accordingly resolved, that a report upon this subject, made to the Light-house Board by the author, should be submitted to the trade of Liverpool, Glasgow and Greenock, for their observations. Having in this manner procured the necessary information, it was resolved that a light-house should be erected for the benefit of this coast, upon the northern extremity of the Mull of Galloway in Wigtonshire, on the point of Corsewall; because, in addition to the advantages of this situation, as an excellent direction both for the entrance of the Irish Channel and Firth of Clyde, it would answer as a guide to the Roadstead or anchorage of Loch Ryan.

Light-houses necessary for the navigation of the Irish Channel.

In the course of the correspondence on this subject, it had been stated by Mr Quintin Leitch, Chief Magistrate of Greenock, a gentleman well acquainted with the navigation of these seas, that if light-houses were erected upon the Isle of Man, these, with the lights of Copeland and Kilwarlin, on the Irish side of the channel, together with the proposed light on Corsewall Point, and another on the Hulin or Maiden rocks, off the coast of Antrim, would fully protect this important part of the coast.

Foundation-stone of Corsewall Light-house laid.

After considering the subject in its various bearings, the Board resolved, as before noticed, on the erection of a light-house on Corsewall Point, in the month of January 1815, and on the 17th day of June following, the foundation-stone was laid, by Mr Quintin Leitch, as master mason, when Mr James Spreull, Chamberlain of the city of Glasgow, Mr Lachlan Kennedy, under whose charge the works were placed, and the Engineer, assisted at the ceremony. In the course of the Summer and Autumn, the tower of this light-house was got to the height of 35 feet, and some progress was also made with the walls of the house for the light-keepers.

1816.

Light-house finished.

The works at Corsewall being suspended during winter, were again resumed in the ensuing spring. The light-room was completed in the autumn, and the light was exhibited to the public on the night of the 15th day of November 1816, agreeably to the following description.

Description of Corsewall Light.

"Corsewall light-house is situate in the county of Wigton, in North Lat. 55° 1′, and West Long. 5° 5′. It bears by compass, from Millour Point, on the western side of the channel leading into Loch Ryan, W. by S., distant about two miles; from Turnberry Point, SW. 21 miles; from the Craig of Ailsa SS. W. 15 miles; from the Mull of Kintyre S. E. S. 31 miles; from the Hulin or Maiden rocks on the coast of Antrim, E. by S. 20 miles; from Copeland Light-house, near the entrance of Belfast loch, NE. ½ E. 22 miles, and from Laggan point in Galloway, NE., distant 3½ miles. To distinguish this light, which is from oil, with a reflecting and revolving apparatus, from the other lights upon the coast, it is known to mariners as a Revolving light with colour, and exhibits from the same light-room a light of the natural appearance, alternating with a light tinged with a red colour. These lights, respectively, attain their greatest strength, or most luminous effect, at the end of every two minutes. But, in the course of each periodic revolution of the reflector-frame, the lights become alternately fainter and more obscure, and, to a distant observer, are totally eclipsed for a short period. The light-room at Corsewall is glazed all round, but the light is hid from the mariner by the high land near Laggan Point, towards the south, and by Turnberry Point towards the north. This light is elevated 112 feet above the medium level of the sea, and its most luminous side may be seen like a star of the first magnitude, at the distance of five or six leagues, but the side tinged red being more obscured by the colouring shades, is not seen at so great a distance."

ISLE OF MAN.

Rate of Light-house duties for the Isle of Man.

The subject of the erection of the light-houses on the Isle of Man, having again been agitated by the merchants of Liverpool, the rates of duty which would probably be demanded for the erection of a light-house upon the Calf of Man, was procured from one of the agents of the Trinity-House of London upon that coast. This schedule of duties appearing to be high, a correspondence took place between Mr William Laird of Liverpool, and Mr Quintin Leitch of Greenock, respecting the rate of Scotch light-house duties, which was ultimately brought under the notice of the Commissioners of the Northern Light-Houses, by Sir William Rae, Bart.

1802.

Author's Report on this subject.

Reference having been made to the author relative to the expence of erecting a light-house upon the Calf of Man, he stated to the Board, that, in the course of a tour which he had made in the year 1802, round the coast of Great Britain, he visited the Isle of Man, with a view to ascertain the most eligible places for light-houses on that island, where he considered two light-house stations to be indispensably necessary, viz. one on the Calf of Man, to the south, and another on the Point of Ayre, towards the north of the island. From the numerous shipping of that district, he only calculated upon the duty of one farthing per ton upon shipping for the light-houses of both stations. The Commissioners took this matter under consideration at the time, as appears from their minutes of the 14th January 1803, which state, that "Mr Stevenson had reported very strongly of the great utility which would attend the erection of light-houses on the Isle of Man; but that island not being within the jurisdiction either of the Commissioners of the Northern Light-houses or Trinity Board of London, both boards seem thereby to be prevented from accomplishing an object so much wished for by mariners, as such an improvement upon the coast would prove a great additional security to the navigation of those seas, and especially to the trade of a great number of the ports of England and Ireland. In order, therefore, that this circumstance might not be overlooked, the Commissioners direct this notice to be taken of it in their minutes, that if an application to Parliament should, at a future period, be deemed necessary, they may judge how far it may not be proper in them to apply for power to erect lights upon the Isle of Man."

Scotch Light-house Board applied to for lights on the Isle of Man.

When these circumstances were intimated to the merchants of Liverpool, and especially that the rate of one farthing per ton was considered a sufficient rate of duty, the business was brought under the notice of the Association of Shipowners and other public bodies of Liverpool, by Mr John Gladstone, when a representation and petition from them was presented to the Commissioners of the Northern Light-houses, praying, that they would bring a bill into Parliament, to enable them to erect the necessary light-houses on the Isle of Man.

Act of 1815.

This application having been complied with, Sir William Rae was requested to attend to the progress of the bill, and to take the assistance of any of the other members of the light-house board who might happen to be in London at the time. The Isle of Man Light-house Bill was accordingly brought forward by Mr Huskisson, in absence of Mr Canning, member of Parliament for Liverpool, as a measure in which that port was specially interested. But when the subject was communicated to the late Mr Rose, M. P., one of the elder brethren of the Trinity House of London, he requested that nothing might be done in this measure, until he should have an opportunity of consulting with the gentlemen of the Trinity-House, as he considered the Isle of Man to be within the district of that board. After repeated meetings, at which Mr Rose attended, he ultimately stated, that the Trinity Board did not consider the Isle of Man as coming under their line of coast; and that the Commissioners of the Northern Light-houses might, therefore, go on with their bill. It was accordingly brought forward in the House of Commons, and the author attended to prove the preamble of the bill in the House of Lords; and in June 1815 it received the Royal assent.

Difficulty in fixing the position of the Isle of Man lights.

In returning towards Scotland, I embarked in the Light-house Yacht at Liverpool, and visited the Isle of Man. It appeared, on examining the site for the erection of a light-house on the Point of Ayre, or northern extremity of the island, that there would be no difficulty in fixing its place. But the case was different at the Calf Island, as there seemed an evident advantage in having the house on a low situation, to keep it more free from fog, and where it might also be more in the line of direction with a dangerous reef called the Chickens, lying about a mile into the offing. On this low position, called Kaager Point, the high land of the Calf would have shut in the light very much from the northward. Another situation, however, presented itself; but, as this last station was considerably higher, it might perhaps be found more uncertain with regard to fog resting upon it in thick and hazy weather; and it was therefore thought prudent to place a trusty person on the island, with directions for observing and communicating the state of the weather for about six months, previously to determining the site of the light-house on the Calf of Man. This mode of inquiring into the subject, was strengthened by the report of some intelligent persons relative to the prevailing state of the weather at the Isle of Man, who represented that the Calf Island was less liable to be enveloped in fog than the higher parts of the Main Island.

A person stationed on the Island to observe the state of the weather.

In the month of August 1815, when Sir William Rae, Bart. then Sheriff of the shire of Edinburgh, Mr Robert Hamilton, Sheriff of Lanarkshire, and Mr Adam Duff, Sheriff of Forfarshire, Commissioners of the Northern Light-houses, visited this island, they concurred in judging it highly proper to make special observations on the state of the weather at the Calf Island. In the beginning of November following, the author accordingly sent Mr Macurich, a shipmaster in the light-house service, to that island, with directions to reside there, and make monthly returns of the state of the weather, agreeably to a printed form. During his stay of seven months, it appears, upon the whole, that the fog rested only twice upon the highest land of the Calf, while it cleared partially below. On one of these occasions, I was on board of the Light-house yacht, then at anchor off the island, when the fog was for a time general; and as the weather became clear, I observed that it first disappeared upon the lower parts of the island; and that in half an hour the whole of the Calf was seen. In the journal of the weather alluded to, the Calf Island is represented as often perfectly free of fog, while the higher parts of the opposite mainland of Man, was hid in mist. To account for this, it may be noticed, that the mass of matter in the Calf island is much less, and the land is also much lower, than in the main island. Part of this effect may also be ascribed to the rapidity of the tides, which create a current of wind, particularly in the narrow channel between the Main and Calf islands; which have a direct tendency to clear away the fog; as I have observed at the Skerries in the Pentland Firth , and in similar situations on different parts of the coast, where rapid currents prevail.

1816.

Distinguishing Light for the Calf of Man.

From these observations, the author was led to report to the Commissioners, that the light-house on the Calf of Man should hold an intermediate position between the highest part of the island, called Bushel's Hill, and the lower site called Kaager Point; and, further, that by erecting two light-house towers in a certain relative position to each other, they would point out the line of direction of the dangerous sunken rocks called the Chickens, and by adopting that description of light known to mariners as a Revolving light without Colour, this station would be sufficiently distinguished from the lights which surround the Isle of Man on the Scotch, Irish, and English shores.

1817.

Lights of the Isle of Man completed.

A difficulty occurred in proceeding with the Isle of Man light-houses, from the want of funds to enable the Commissioners to proceed with the works. The Board had already become liable for a large sum to liquidate the payment of the purchase-money of the private right of the Portland Family to the duties of the light of May. On this measure, and in the erection of the Bell Rock light-house, as before noticed, there had been expended upwards of L. 160,000 in the course of the last ten years; so that it became necessary to borrow L. 10,000, agreeably to the act, for the Isle of Man. In this state of things, the works at the Isle of Man were delayed for a time; but, in the month of August 1816, they were commenced. The light-rooms were completed in the month of December 1817; and, on the night of the 1st of February 1818, the lights, both at the stations of the Point of Ayre, and Calf Island, were exhibited to the public, agreeably to the following descriptions.

POINT OF AYRE.

1818.

Description of the Point of Ayre Light-house.

The only consideration to be taken into view in fixing the site of the Point of Ayre Light-house, was the wasting appearance of the shores by the effects of the sea at this part of the coast. Although, therefore, it would have answered fully better, for the purposes of the light, to have erected the tower close upon high-water-mark, yet the beach being composed of a loose shifting gravel, it became a matter of prudence rather to keep the buildings at some distance from it.

"The Point of Ayre light-house is situate about 650 feet from the sea, at high-water of spring tides, upon an extensive plain in the Main Island of Man, in north latitude 54° 27′, and longitude 4° 20′ west of London. The light-house bears, by compass, from the Mull of Galloway, S. S. E. and is distant 22 miles; from Burrowhead, S. S. W. ½ W. distant 16 miles; from St Bees, in Cumberland, W. by N. ¾ N. distant 29 miles; and from Rue Point, E. by S. distant 4 miles.

"The light is from oil, with a reflecting and revolving apparatus, and is known to mariners as a "Revolving-coloured-light," exhibiting from the same Reflector-frame a light of the natural appearance, alternating with one tinged red. These lights respectively attain their most luminous effect, at the end of every two minutes. But, in the course of each periodic revolution of the reflector-frame, both lights become alternately fainter and more obscure, and, to a distant observer, are totally eclipsed for a short time.

"The Light-room at the Point of Ayre is glazed all round, but the light is hid from the mariner by the high land of Maughold Head towards the south, and by Rue Point towards the west. Being elevated 106 feet above the medium level of the sea, its most luminous side may be seen, like a star of the first magnitude, at the distance of five leagues; but the side tinged red, being somewhat obscured by the coloured shades, cannot be seen at so great a distance."

CALF OF MAN.

Description of Calf of Man Light.

"There are two leading lights on the Calf of Man, situate on the western side of the small island called the Calf, in north Lat. 54° 5′, and Long. 4° 46′ west of London. These two light-houses are distant from each other 560 feet. The higher light bears by compass from the Mull of Galloway, S. SW. distant 37 miles; Peelhead, in the Isle of Man, SW. distant 11 miles; Langness Point, W. by N. ½ N. distant 6 miles; and from the sunken rocks, called the Chickens, NE. ⅓ E. distant about 1¼ mile.

"These lights are from oil, each light-room being furnished with a distinct reflecting and revolving apparatus, by which they are distinguished from the other lights on the coast, and rendered useful as leading lights for passing the dangerous rocks called the Chickens. The light-house towers, as before noticed, are built at the distance of 560 feet apart, bearing from each other NE. ⅓ E. and SW. ¼ W. Consequently, to an observer, in the direction of the Chickens, both lights will appear in one, or be seen in the same line of direction, and be known to mariners as "Double-revolving and Leading-lights without colour." These lights will respectively attain their most luminous effect at the end of every two minutes; but, in the course of each periodic revolution of the reflector frames, they alternately become fainter and more obscure, and, to a distant observer, are totally eclipsed for a short time. The two light-rooms at the Calf of Man are glazed all round, but are hid from the mariner by the high land of Peel Head towards the NE. and by Spanish Head in an eastern direction; both lights, however, will be visible at about ¼ of a mile from Langness Point. The lower light is elevated 305 feet above the medium level of the sea, and the high light 396 feet, and they will be seen like two stars of the first magnitude, at the distance of six or seven leagues, in a favourable state of the atmosphere."

Extension of the Northern Lights to the Irish Sea.

By the extension of the works of the Scotch Light-house Board to the Isle of Man, the system of the Northern Light-houses may now be said, in a general way, to extend over the whole of the coast of Scotland, while the lights of Man are of immediate importance to the extensive shipping of the coasts of England and Ireland, which bound the Irish Sea. The trade of Dublin and Newry, &c. on the one side, and of Liverpool, Lancaster, Whitehaven, and Workington, &c. on the other, find the traffic with those ports much more safe since the erection of these lights. Instead of shunning the Isle of Man, as formerly, owing to the projecting points, sunken rocks, and sand-banks connected with it, the mariner now steers boldly for this island, and takes shelter under it in stormy weather.

SUMBURGH HEAD.

Shetland Islands.

According to the existing acts of Parliament relative to the Northern Lights, no additional duty is exigible for any new erections of the Board, as the only part of the coast not liable, prior to the extension of the Scots Light-house Acts to the Isle of Man, was that of the Solway Firth , now also subject to the duty. These acts, however, empower the Commissioners to erect additional light-houses; and when a sufficient number shall have been exhibited on the coast, and a surplus fund provided for their maintenance, the duty on shipping is ultimately to cease, and be no longer payable. Presuming, therefore, upon the prosperity of the commerce of the country, for an increase of funds, the Commissioners, though there were large sums to pay, both in the form of interest for Government loans, and instalments for borrowed money, taking into consideration the unprotected state of the Shetland Islands, a part of their district still without the immediate benefit of light-houses, had in view to erect an additional Light-house, as soon as their funds would admit, on some of the most prominent points of that group of Islands. The winters of 1817 and 1818 having been very unfortunate to the shipping of the North Seas, and some very distressing shipwrecks having occurred at Shetland, Mr William Erskine, now Lord Kineddar, then Sheriff of the County of Orkney and Shetland, and ex officio one of the Commissioners, brought the subject again under the notice of the Board; and, in the month of January 1819, it was finally resolved that a Light-house should be erected on Sumburgh Head in Shetland, the position of which will be seen by inspecting Plate III. This work having been accordingly contracted for by Mr John Reid, builder, of Peterhead, the first stone of the building was laid on the 10th day of May 1820, and the light exhibited on the night of the 15th day of January 1821, agreeably to the following specification of the position of the house, and appearance of the light:

Description of Sumburgh Head Light-house.

"Sumburgh Head Lighthouse is situate on the southern promontory of the Mainland of the Shetland Islands, in north latitude 59° 52′, and longitude 1° 15′ west of London. The Lighthouse, by compass, bears from Hangcliff-head in Noss Island SW. by W. ¼ West, distant 21 miles. From Fair Island NE. by E. ½ East, 26 miles. And from the Island of Foula, SE. by S. ¼ South, distant 28 miles. In reference to these bearings, the light is visible to the mariner from the southward, between Noss and Foula Islands. This light is known to mariners as a "Stationary light from oil with reflectors;" and being elevated 300 feet above the medium level of the sea, it is seen, like a star of the first magnitude, at the distance of seven or eight leagues, and at intermediate distances, according to the state of the atmosphere."

Built with double walls.

From the very exposed situation of the promontory of Sumburgh Head, and the great difficulty experienced in preserving the walls of light-houses in a water-tight state, the writer followed a new plan with the buildings at this station, in having made the whole of the external walls double; the masonry of the outward wall being lined with brick instead of lath-work, with a space of three inches left between the double walls. This method was of course, more expensive in the first instance, but will ultimately be much more economical, as repairs, in these remote situations, are unavoidably very expensive.This house is free of dampness, and has not admitted a single drop of water through any part of the walls during the storms of two successive winters, although the force of the wind is such, that the light-keepers, when out of doors, are frequently obliged to move upon their hands and knees, to prevent their being blown off the high land. In such states of the weather, accompanied by rain, it is hardly possible to prevent a single wall from admitting water.

CARR ROCK.

The Carr forms the seaward termination of a reef of sunken rocks which appear at low-water, extending about a mile and three quarters from the shore of Fifeness, on the northern side of the entrance of the Firth of Forth. The very dangerous position of this rock, as a turning point, in the navigation of the northern-bound shipping of the Firth , will be seen from the chart of the coast, Plate IV. It seemed necessary, therefore, for the safety of navigation, that the Carr Rock, in connection with the several light-houses of the Bell Rock, Isle of May, and Inchkeith, should be made as easily distinguishable to the mariner as possible.

Shipwrecks at the Carr Rock.

The author, while occupied with the works at the Bell Rock, having been often struck with the frequent and distressing occurrence of shipwreck at the Carr Rock, was induced to collect information as to the probable numbers of these wrecks; and he accordingly obtained, from persons who had good access to know, the following list of wrecked vessels, for a period of nine years prior to the commencement of the works at the Carr Rock.

List of Shipwrecks off Fifeness, between the Years 1800 and 1809.

VESSELS' NAMES.	MASTERS' NAMES.	DESCRIPTIONS.	PORT BELONGING TO.
Unknown.	Simpson.	Sloop.	South Ferry.
Martha.	Clark.	Do.	Crail.
Leven.	Phillip.	Do.	Leven.
Neptune.	Finlay.	Do.	Dundee.
Unknown.	Brown.	Do.	Kincardine.
Aurora.	Leslie.	Brig.	Arbroath.
Lady Charlotte.	Duncan.	Sloop.	Aberdeen.
Two Brothers.	Carfrae.	Brig.	Dundee.
Expedition.	Nicol.	Sloop.	Kincardine.
Isabella.	Rintoul.	Do.	Perth.
Unknown.	Johnston.	Do.	Do.
Do.	Unknown.	Do.	John's Haven.

New Deer.	Banks.	Do.	Kirkaldy.
Unknown.	Hamson.	Galliot.	Christiansand.
Countess of Elgin.	Gowans.	Sloop.	John's Haven.
Unknown.	Small.	Do.	South Ferry.

Floating-buoy moored off the Carr.

By this melancholy list we find, that no fewer than sixteen vessels have, in the course of nine years, been either lost or stranded on the Carr Rocks, being almost at the rate of two wrecks in the year. From this alarming state of things, it was thought advisable to bring the subject under the notice of the Commissioners of the Northern Light-houses, when the Board immediately ordered a Floating-buoy, of a large size, to be moored off the Carr. The moorings for this buoy were laid down, upon the 18th of September 1809, in 10 fathoms water, at the distance of about 200 fathoms, in a north-eastern direction, from the rock. But, owing to the heavy swell of sea, and the rocky sandstone bottom on this part of the coast, it was found hardly possible to prevent the buoy from occasionally drifting, even although it had been attached to part of the great chain, made from bar-iron, measuring 1½ inch square, with which the Bell Rock floating light had been moored for upwards of four years, without injury. The moorings of the Carr Rock-buoy, from the continual rubbing upon the sandstone bottom, were worn through with the friction in the course of ten months; and during the four years which it rode here, though regularly examined and replaced, in the proper season of the year, it was no less than five times adrift, to the great inconveniency and hazard of shipping.

A Beacon of masonry is resolved on.

Under these circumstances, the Light-house Board was induced to erect a Beacon of masonry upon the Carr Rock itself, instead of the Floating-buoy. This work was commenced in the month of June, in the year 1813, under the direction of the writer. The stone for this building was taken from an excellent sandstone quarry on the property of Lord Kellie, near the mouth of Pitmilly Burn: But, owing to the smallness of the rock, the depth of water upon it, and the exposed nature of the situation, the work was afterwards attended with very great difficulty.

Dimensions of the Carr Rock.

The length of the Carr Rock, from south to north, measures 75 feet; but its greatest breadth, as seen at low-water of spring-tides, being only 23 feet, it was found to be impracticable to obtain a base for a building of greater diameter than 18 feet. Such also was the fractured and rugged state of the surface of this rock, that it became necessary to excavate part of the foundation-pit of the building to the depth of seven feet. The difficulties of this part of the work were also greatly increased, owing to the foundation, on the eastern side, being under the level of the lowest tides: so that it became necessary to construct a coffer-dam. Part of this coffer-dam it was necessary to remove, and carry ashore, after each tide's work; and on the return of the workmen at ebb-tide, a considerable time was unavoidably occupied in fixing the moveable part of the coffer-dam, and in pumping the water out of the foundation-pit.

Difficulties of this work compared with those of the Bell Rock.

But, to enable the reader to form a comparative estimate of the difficulties attending the early stages of the Carr Rock Beacon, with those of the Bell Rock Light-house, it may be noticed, that the period which the artificers were actually at work upon the Carr Rock, as ascertained by the foreman during the first season, or the summer of 1813, was 41 hours; and in 1814, after the experience of one year's work, these were only extended to 53 hours. Now, if we compare 1807 and 1808, the two first years' work at the Bell Rock, we find the artificers were respectively about 180 and 265 hours upon that rock. The first two years at the Carr Rock were entirely occupied in excavating and preparing the foundation, and in laying 10 stones, or the half-course of masonry, which brings the foundation to a uniform level, for the first entire course of the building, as shewn in Plate II.; while, at the Bell Rock, in the two first seasons three courses were erected, as represented in Plate IX., of a building situate 12 miles from the shore, and measuring 42 feet in diameter at the base, besides the erection of a Beacon-house or Barrack for the workmen. The establishment for the works at the Bell Rock was of course on a much larger scale than that of the Carr Rock; but still the latter was equally effective, and the same apparatus, artificers and seamen, were employed at both.

Third year's work at the Carr Rock.

During the third year's work, or 1815, the second course of the masonry was completed upon the Carr, and nine stones of the third course had been got laid by the 3d of October, when a heavy ground-swell obliged the artificers precipitately to leave the rock and take to their boats. This swell was immediately accompanied by a gale of easterly wind, and before the cement had taken bond or firmness, the surge of the sea washed it out; when the oaken trenails, used as a temporary fixture during the progress of the work, were wrenched off, and the stone-joggles broken asunder. The whole of the nine blocks of stone were thus swept off the rock and lost in deep water, though they had been completely dove-tailed, and fitted on the same principles as the masonry of the Bell Rock Light-house, where not a single stone was lost during the whole progress of the work.

Fourth year's work.

In the year 1816, or fourth season, the work was continued till the month of November, when the building had attained the height of about 20 feet, or the 16th course, and still wanting 18 courses to complete the masonry. In this state, it was left till the following season, having been previously loaded with about four tons of lead, cast in suitable pieces, and suspended within the void or central hollow of the building. The operations of the fourth season had been also much retarded by several untoward accidents. In particular, a heavy gale overtook the workmen while they were laying the 7th course, which obliged them to leave the rock before the precautionary measures could be taken, for closing and completing the work immediately in hand; in consequence of which, the stones on the eastern, or weather-side of this course, were lifted off their bases, the oaken trenails broken, and five of the blocks of stone swept away. At another period, the Pozzolano mortar of the beds of two of the stones was washed out, and so much injured, that the stones required to be lifted and relaid. The works were this season intended to have been closed early in the month of October, when another unlucky gale sprung up, just as the sixteenth course had been laid, which lifted seven of the stones off their beds; but they were fortunately held by the oaken trenails, and in this state they remained for about three weeks, before a landing could possibly be effected, to replace them.

Fifth year's work.

In the month of June 1817, the fifth year's work was begun, and the remaining courses of the masonry were built; but in the month of November, the coast was visited with a gale of wind at south-east, accompanied with a heavy swell of sea, which, unfortunately, washed down the upper part of the building, and reduced it to the height of the fifth course, which formed part of the fourth year's work.

Beacon finished with cast-iron pillars and ball.

Instead, therefore, of completing this Beacon with masonry, as had been originally intended, and providing the Machine and large Bell, which was to have measured 5 feet across the mouth, to be tolled by the alternate rise and fall of the tide, it now became a matter of consideration in what form the upper part of this design should be finished. The Board ultimately determined on the erection of six columns of cast-iron upon the remaining courses of masonry. These columns are put together with spigot and facet joints, strongly connected with collars and horizontal bars of malleable iron; the whole terminating with a cast-iron ball, formed in ribs, elevated about 25 feet above the medium level of the sea. In this manner the Carr Rock Beacon was at length completed, in the month of September 1821, after six years work. The following is the notice and description of it given to the public:

Bearings and Description of the Carr Rock Beacon.

"The Carr Rock forms the seaward ledge of a range of sunken rocks, extending about two miles from Fifeness, on the eastern coast of Scotland, in North Latitude 56° 17′, and Longitude 2° 35′ west of London. By compass the Carr Rock Beacon bears SW. by W. from the Bell Rock, distant 11 miles; and from the Isle of May Light-house N.N.E. ¼ E., distant 6 miles.

"The lower part of the beacon is a circular building of masonry, 18 feet in diameter, forming a basement for six pillars of cast-iron, terminating in a hollow ball of that metal, which measures 3 feet across, and is elevated about 25 feet above the medium level of the sea.

"The erection of this beacon has been attended with much difficulty, having occupied six years in building; in the course of which the works sustained occasional damage. Mariners are therefore warned, when they run for the Carr Rock Beacon, to do so with caution, both on account of its exposure to the breach of the sea, and its liability to receive damage from vessels under sail."

Application of the tide-machine described.

The form and construction of the Carr Rock Beacon, both as originally intended, and ultimately executed, will be better understood by referring to Plate II., and to the annexed Description of the Plates. The motion to be given to the bell-apparatus, or tide-machine, was to be effected by admitting the sea water through a small aperture, of three inches in diameter, perforated in the solid masonry, communicating with a cylindrical chamber, in the centre of the building, measuring two feet in diameter, in which a float or metallic air-tank, was to rise and fall with the tide. The train of machinery for this apparatus was calculated for a perpendicular rise of only six feet, being equal to the lowest neap-tides on this coast. During the period of flood-tide, the air-vessel, in its elevation, by the pressure of the water, was to give motion to machinery for tolling the bell, and winding up a weight; which last, in its descent, during ebb-tide, was to continue the motion of the machine, until the flood-tide again returned to perform the joint operation of tolling the bell and raising the weight. A working model of a machine upon this principle having been constructed, it was kept in motion for a period equal to several months: this was effected by water run through a succession of tanks, raised by a pump from the lower one to the higher, thus producing the effect of flood and ebb tides. The time during which this apparatus was in action, having been ascertained by an index, a constant attendance upon the machine, during this protracted experiment, became unnecessary.

General application of tide-machinery.

The upper termination of the Beacon, in its present form, does not admit of the application of the tide-machine with the bell-apparatus. Experiments as applicable to this have, however, been tried with a wind-instrument, to be sounded by the pressure of the sea water; but it has not succeeded to the extent that seems necessary for a purpose of this kind. We have indeed thought, that the application of pressure as a power, communicated by the waters of the ocean, in mechanical operations, might be carried to almost any extent, by simply providing a chamber or dock, large enough for the reception of a float or vessel, of dimensions equivalent to the force required. This description of machinery is more particularly applicable in situations where the tides have a great rise, as in the Solway Firth , Bristol Channel, and other parts of the British seas; and at St Malo, on the coast of France.

Leading Lights suggested.

A Beacon of any form, unprovided with a light, must always be considered an imperfect land-mark, and therefore various modes have been contemplated, for more completely pointing out the position of the Carr Rock. It has been proposed that phosphoric lights should be exhibited from the top of the Building. This object, however, would be more certainly accomplished, by the erection of leading lights, upon the Island of May and Mainland of Fife. But these, with other plans which have been under the writer's consideration, would necessarily be attended with a great additional expence, which, in the present instance, it is not thought advisable to incur.

Expence of the Carr Rock works.

Owing to the necessarily slow progress of the operations at the Carr Rock, the works were carried on partly in connection with the new Light-house on the Isle of May, and with the assistance of the ordinary shipping of the Light-house establishment. This renders it difficult to give a distinct estimate of the expence of the Beacon; but in so far as it can be collected, it may be stated, including all charges, at about L. 5000.

STATIONS ON THE COAST OF SCOTLAND, WHERE LIGHT-HOUSES HAVE BEEN SUGGESTED AS STILL NECESSARY.

Having now taken notice of the works of the Light-house Board, so far as they have been completed, up to and including part of the year 1823. We may farther advert to the Light-house on the Rhins of Ilay, founded on the 23d of August last. The Northern Light-houses accordingly amount to seventeen, erected at fourteen stations; and besides these, there are the Beacons of North Ronaldsay and the Carr Rock. The position of these establishments has not been chosen in regard to their respective distances from each other, but agreeably to the commercial importance and dangers connected with particular parts of the coast. Six of them, for instance, are on the Friths of Forth and Clyde, at not more than from 20 to 25 miles apart; while Kinnaird-Head, on the east coast, is about 72 miles from the Bell Rock, and 70 miles from the Pentland Skerries. The Light-house upon Island Glass, is about 130 miles south-west from the Pentland Skerries, and 120 miles northward from the Rhins of Ilay, being a stretch of 250 miles of coast, with only one Light-house intervening. It must therefore be obvious, that fourteen Light-house stations, which include two on the Isle of Man, are too few for the Scottish coast, rendered formidable and dangerous, by a vast number of islands and sunken rocks. The Commissioners have still, accordingly, a wide field of operations before them, which they are gradually occupying, as their funds will admit, and as the demands of navigation and commercial intercourse seem to require. In the Appendix, No. I. notice is taken of the most prominent points of land on the coast, which have been brought under consideration as fit Stations for additional Light-houses; and of these, one at Buchan-Ness, on the east coast, has already been fixed on by the Board.

CONSTITUTION OF THE BOARD, AND SYSTEM OF MANAGEMENT.

Constitution of the Board.

The affairs of the Northern Light-houses are managed by the Commissioners named in the different acts already noticed; but the direction of the whole concerns of the establishment almost entirely devolves upon the Commissioners resident in Edinburgh, viz. The Lord Advocate and Solicitor-General, the Lord Provost, and Senior Magistrate of that City, and the different Sheriffs, Commissioners ex officio, who attend the Courts of Law. They hold frequent meetings, and bestow their time and labour without any salary or remuneration whatever. At their Meetings, all matters falling under the economy, and connected with the arrangement of the Light-houses, are regulated; full powers being conferred upon them as a Board to erect and maintain such additional Light-houses as they shall deem necessary; so that the system in this respect will at no very distant period be rendered complete.

Rate of Duties.

By the Statutes, the general rate of duty upon British ships is 2d. per register ton for passing one of, or all the Scottish Lights; together with certain local duties of ½d. per ton, connected with the Lights of May and Inchkeith; and for vessels which only pass the Lights on the Isle of Man, one farthing per ton is the sole duty. Foreign ships in all cases pay double rates. These duties are exigible at all the Ports in the United Kingdom, and are remitted to the General Collector at Edinburgh, at the end of three or six months, according to the extent of the respective collections.

The application of the Funds, and disposal of the Surplus, are fixed by the Acts; which also require, that an account of the moneys received and expended by the Board, be annually presented to the Lords of the Treasury, the Convention of Royal Burghs of Scotland, and that two copies be sent to the Board of Customs at Edinburgh, to be laid before both Houses of Parliament.

Expence of Management, &c.

The only permanent expence of management in the way of remuneration to the Officers of the Board, are a salary of L. 500 to the Engineer; L. 380 to the Clerk, who is also Cashier, and a fee of 50 guineas to the Auditor or Accountant. The revenue of the Board may be stated at about L. 24,000 yearly; and as the department of the Engineer is unconnected with the financial arrangements, this fund is, in fact, managed for about L. 432, 10s. per annum.

As to the practical arrangement, the Engineer visits all the Light-houses annually, and Reports to the Board upon the various works and operations connected with the different Light-houses,—the conduct of the light-keepers,—and also upon the stores and supplies required for the ensuing year,—and these, when approven of, are authorised and ordered by the Commissioners. All accounts for supplies are laid before the Board, and paid twice in the year.

At each ordinary Light-house, a Principal and an Assistant Light-keeper are appointed, whose salaries are respectively L. 45, and L. 35 per annum, besides a piece of ground, not less than 10 acres, with fuel, a suit of uniform clothes every three years, and some other small perquisites. At the Bell Rock, there are four light-keepers, three of whom are always at the Light-house, while one is, by rotation, on shore at the establishment at Arbroath for the families of the light-keepers. Their salaries are respectively L. 63, and L. 57, 15s., and for each of the two ordinary Assistants L. 52, 10s. with provisions for themselves while at the Rock, and apartments for their families ashore. The light-keepers act under certain Instructions, and make Monthly Returns to the Engineer's office, copies of which will be found under Appendix, No. I.

Shipping of the Establishment.

The shipping belonging to the Light-house service, besides attending boats, for visiting Light-houses on insulated situations, consists of a vessel of about 50 tons register, which is chiefly employed in attending the Bell Rock, to supply the house with necessaries, and relieve the light-keepers in their turn. For general service, another vessel of 140 tons is kept, which carries oil and other stores for the lights, together with fuel and necessaries, for the use of the light-keepers, and artificers, with their implements and apparatus, for making repairs at the different stations. The Engineer makes his annual voyage of inspection in this vessel, which is provided with cabins suitable for the reception of such of the Commissioners as may occasionally visit the Light-houses.

Voyages of Inspection.

This duty has been undertaken by various members of the Board. In the Summer of 1814 a Committee, consisting of Mr Hamilton, Sheriff of Lanarkshire, Mr Erskine, Sheriff of Orkney, and Mr Duff, Sheriff of Forfarshire, with the Engineer, made a voyage to inspect the different Light-houses already erected, as also the most prominent of the stations on the coast, suggested for the erection of Additional Lights. They sailed from Leith in the Yacht, having for their companion Mr Walter Scott, and having visited the Light-houses on the Isle of May and Bell Rock, with the establishment at Arbroath, and that upon Kinnaird-Head in Aberdeenshire, they next landed at Sumburgh-head in Shetland, on which a Light-house has since been erected. Returning southward, they visited the Light-houses on the Start Point of Sanday, and the Pentland Skerries in Orkney. Then steering westward, they landed at Cape Wrath, one of the projected Stations for a Light-house. They next touched at the Light-house on Island-Glass, one of the Harris Isles. From thence they proceeded and landed upon the Rock called Skerryvore, lying off the Island of Tiree, and were satisfied of the practicability of erecting a Light-house there. Having visited the Light-house on Ennistrahul, on the coast of Donegal, one of the Irish Lights, and inspected their own establishments on the Mull of Kantire and Isle of Pladda, the Commissioners landed at Greenock, after a voyage of nearly seven weeks.

In July 1815, Mr Hamilton and Mr Duff, accompanied by the writer, sailed in the Yacht from the Troon for Liverpool, where they were joined by Sir William Rae; and after having had a meeting with Mr Gladstone on the subject of the Lights on Man, they sailed thither, and fixed on the Stations for the Lights on that Island, and on the Calf. They then proceeded to Dublin, and communicated with the Irish Board for the affairs of Light-houses, regarding certain arrangements for the advancement of the public service committed respectively to their charge. Mr Crossthwaite, and other Members of the Irish Board, accompanied them to the Light-house upon Houth: and having visited the Tuskar Light-house, situate on an insulated rock off the coast of Wexford, they bent their course to Holyhead, landed at the Light-house on the South Stack; and on their return surveyed the operations at the Light-house at Corsewall in Galloway then building, and having visited Pladda, landed at Greenock.

In the Summer of 1818, Messrs Hamilton and Duff, with the writer, sailed from Clyde, and inspected the Light-houses of Corsewall and on the Isle and Calf of Man. The Yacht being then bound through the British Channel, they availed themselves of the opportunity to visit some of the English Light-houses, particularly the Smalls, off St David's Head, the Longships, off the Land's End, the Edystone, the Caskets off Alderney, Hurst Castle, Dungeness, and the North Foreland. By these voyages, the Commissioners greatly enlarged their knowledge of the important concerns entrusted to their charge. Some of them had thus seen and examined all the Light-houses already established on the coast of Scotland, and most of the Sites in contemplation for new erections on the northern parts of the Island.

ACCOUNT OF THE
BELL ROCK LIGHT HOUSE

Drawn by Miss Stevenson.
Engraved by J. Horsburgh.

Pharos loquitur
Far in the bosom of the deep
O'er these wild shelves my watch I keep
A ruddy gem of changeful light
Bound on the dusky brow of Night
The Seaman bids my lustre hail
And scorns to strike his timorous sail

See page 500.

BELL ROCK LIGHT-HOUSE.

CHAPTER I.

NAME OF THE ROCK,—SITUATION AND DIMENSIONS,— NATURAL HISTORY,—DEPTH OF WATER, AND CURRENT OF TIDES.

In the Introduction, I have given an account of the institution of the Board of Commissioners of the Northern Light-houses; of the progress made in the erection of Light-houses on the coast of Scotland; the probable future operations of the Board, and the general economy or management of its affairs. I now come to treat in detail of the Bell Rock Light-house, as the chief object of this work; and, in the present chapter, I propose to give the general history, and a description of this dangerous Rock.

NAME OF THE ROCK.

Name.

Origin of the Name.

There is perhaps nothing in history more arbitrary, or difficult to account for, than the origin of proper names, nor, in general, any research more unsatisfactory, than a prolix inquiry into their etymology. The charts of the nautical surveyor are the proper records for the names of places upon the sea-coast; but such maps are comparatively of late invention. The first sea-chart which we hear of in England, was that brought from Spain in 1489, by Bartholomew Columbus, to illustrate his brother's theory of the discovery of America; and the earliest, applicable to the coast of Scotland, is the chart of the voyage of James V., from the Firth of Forth, by the Orkney and Western Islands, to the Firth of Clyde and coast of Galloway, in the year 1540. This map was published at Paris by Nicolay D'Arfiville, Seigneur Du d'Aulphinois, &c. chief Cosmographer to the King of France, in 1583; and afterwards in Edinburgh, in the year 1688, by John Adair, F. R. S., Geographer for Scotland.

Inch Cape.

The French writer gives a hydrographical description of the coast of Scotland, in relation to the Royal voyage, from Leith to the Solway Firth , noticing the distances of places, the tides, and the rocks and sand-banks, or "dangers," as they are more generally termed, which it was necessary to avoid. In adverting to the course from Leith by the east coast to Duncansby-Head, in Caithness, he observes, "Entre Finismes [Fifeness] et la pointe nommé Redde, xii mille à l'est sud-est du costé de la dicte pointe Redde, gist un danger appelé Inchkope." This is unquestionably the

Bell Rock, the inch or island of the Cape, and with a reference to the Redhead, to the north of Aberbrothock, the highest and most remarkable point on that coast. In Adair's collection of nautical charts, and descriptive account of the eastern coast of Scotland, published in 1703, the Bell Rock is indifferently termed Scape and Cape; and the fishermen on the shores of Angus uniformly call it the Cape Rock. In some old charts, particularly by the Dutch, whose name for a headland is kappe, it is also called skape and scaup. It does not, however, seem that any inference can be drawn from these various appellations; and, although it were to be conjectured, that the Inch Cape was, at a very remote period, permanently above water, and in all respects an island, the most rational hypothesis would still remain, and be indeed confirmed, that this name was given it on account of the relation it bore, especially in situation, to the cape of Redhead.

Bell Rock.

It is perhaps more difficult to assign the true origin for the modern term of Bell Rock, by which this dangerous reef is now universally known. There is a tradition, that an Abbot of Aberbrothock directed a bell to be erected on the Rock, so connected with a floating apparatus, that the winds and sea acted upon it, and tolled the bell, thus giving warning to the mariner of his approaching danger. Upon similar authority, the bell, it is said, was afterwards carried off by pirates, and the humane intentions of the Abbot thus frustrated. This story has, by a modern poet, been made the subject of the ballad of "Sir Ralf the Rover," which, for the reader's amusement, is inserted in the Appendix, No. II.

Erection of a Bell.

Of the erection of the Bell, and of the machinery by which it was rung, if such ever existed, it would have been interesting to have had some authentic evidence. But, though a search has been made in the chartularies of the Abbey of Aberbrothock, preserved in the Advocates' Library, and containing a variety of grants and other deeds, from the middle of the 13th to the end of the 15th century, no trace is to be found of the Bell Rock, or any thing connected with it. The erection of the bell is not, however, an improbable conjecture; and we can more readily suppose that an attempt of that kind was made, than that it had been intentionally removed, which in no measure accords with the respect and veneration entertained by seamen of all classes for land-marks; more especially, as there seems to be no difficulty in accounting for the disappearance of such an apparatus unprotected, as it must have been, from the raging element of the sea. It is not therefore unlikely, that the popular appellation by which this Rock has more recently been known, may owe its origin to the tradition of the Abbot's humanity and public spirit; and when we consider that the churchmen of those days were well acquainted with the history of the celebrated Pharos of Alexandria, and may have heard of the fire-towers and sea-marks, which Mr Bryant, in his Mythology, conjectures existed in very remote times, it is natural to suppose, that these learned persons had, at a pretty early period, turned their attention to the subject, and had attempted, in the mode which has been figured, to point out and guard against the danger.

Amidst these speculations, it must not, however, be overlooked, that this Rock may have acquired its present name from its shape or figure; for at the commencement of the author's operations, he remarked, that the site of the light-house, at some distance, had much the appearance of a large bell; and although this part was not more than four feet above the general level of the Rock, yet by supposing it to have been the nucleus of a larger mass, in the central part of the Rock, gradually wasted away by the washing of the sea, it may at a former period, from that resemblance, have obtained the appellation it now retains.

SITUATION AND DIMENSIONS.

Situation.

The Bell Rock may be described as a most dangerous sunken reef, situate on the northern side of the entrance of the great estuary or arm of the sea called the Firth of Forth; and as such directly affecting the safety of all vessels entering the Firth of Tay. Its position, as will be seen from the Charts, Nos. 3. and 4., which accompany this work, is in west longitude from Greenwich 2° 22′, and in north latitude 56° 29′. From St Abb's Head in Berwickshire, it bears north by east per compass, (variation 27° 20′ west in the year 1819), and is distant about 30 miles; from the Island of May north-east 17 miles; and from the promontory or cape called the Redhead, in Forfarshire, it bears south-west, and is distant 14 miles. But in easterly directions no land intervenes between the Bell Rock and the coasts of Norway, Denmark, Germany and Holland.

Dimensions.

The dimensions of the north-eastern or higher compartment of the Rock where the light-house is built, are about 427 feet in length, and 230 feet in breadth. Besides these dimensions, the south-western reef extends about 1000 feet from the main rock. The greatest length, therefore, of the Bell Rock, which may be said to be dangerous to shipping, is about 1427 feet, and its greatest breadth is about 300 feet; but the outline or margin of the Rock is quite irregular, as will be seen from the Plates marked Nos. 5. and 6.

NATURAL HISTORY.

Mineralogy.

The Bell Rock consists of sandstone of a reddish colour, which in some places contains whitish and greenish spots of circular and oval forms, irregularly interspersed through the rock. It is of a fine granular texture, containing minute specks of mica. It is very hard, and, in the language of the artificer, is tough, and rather difficult to work; and in some parts it is found to rise in masses having a conchoidal fracture. Its angle of inclination with the horizon is about 15 degrees, dipping towards the south-east. The strata are thick and unequal, strongly cemented together, and running in the direction of north-east and south-west. The surface of the Rock is rugged, and full of cavities, so that walking upon it becomes rather difficult. A longitudinal section of the Bell Rock, taken in a north-easterly and south-westerly direction, may be described as consisting of a higher and a lower level. The cross section, taken in a south-easterly and north-westerly direction, exhibits the abrupt and pointed terminations of the strata, though it appears level when seen from a distance.

Wasting effects of the Sea.

Natural History.

It would be a speculation highly interesting to the geologist, to inquire into the probable early history of the Bell Rock, and the changes produced on it by the wasting effects of the waters of the ocean. When we consider the similarity of the red sandstone of this rock with the Redhead of Forfarshire, and opposite shores of Berwick in the neighbourhood of Dunglass, and take into view that there is a ridge or shallower part of the bottom, which extends a considerable way from the Bell Rock in the direction of these shores, we may infer, that the Rock itself had extended at one time much further. We are also enabled to trace the same formation, penetrating to the northward through Ross-shire, and quite across the kingdom, in a southern direction, to Cumberland. At a period indefinitely remote in the history of the globe, we may therefore imagine that one continuous bed of red sandstone had stretched across the Firth , forming a barrier by which the great collection of waters of the Forth and Tay have been pent up.

Proofs of the Sea having occupied a higher level.

In support of this opinion, we have the most unequivocal proofs of the waters of those friths having formerly occupied a much higher level. Of these we may notice the general appearance of their water-worn shores, and a bed of oyster-shells near Borrowstounness, which has been traced to the extent of three miles in length, and about two fathoms in thickness, lying in their natural state, but now upwards of 35 feet above the present level of the sea. Under these circumstances, and many others which might be adduced, it is not improbable that the Bell Rock has at one time been connected with the opposite coasts; and when we consider the general waste of the land, which is apparent in all directions from the impulse of the sea, it may at least be concluded, that at no very remote period, the Rock has been of much greater superficial extent, and above the level of the highest tides. Nor need we be surprised that such changes upon this remote and insulated spot should have been lost sight of, owing to their gradual and almost imperceptible effects, compared with the short period of the life of man, and in absence of all testimony excepting that which is oral.

Plants.

With regard to the marine Plants which grow upon the Bell Rock, we may observe that the lower parts of it are covered with the stronger or larger sorts, as the great tangle, Fucus digitatus, the roots of which rarely appear above the water, while it is seen at the depth of several fathoms, growing with the greatest luxuriance, and has often been observed by the author from a boat in fine weather, as a means for ascertaining, by the direction of the leaf, the changes of the currents of the tide at the bottom. The Badderlock, or Henware, Fucus esculentus, is found only on the north-eastern and south-eastern extremities of the Rock, growing at low water-mark of spring-tides, and seems to prefer the most rapid currents of the sea, and places where the heaviest breach takes place. In such situations it grows in great abundance at the Bell Rock, where it has been measured of the length of eighteen feet, and of proportionally increased breadth. Perhaps some of these plants are of considerable age; but at the works of the Carr Rock Beacon, off Fifeness, it was found that the growth of the badderlock was so very rapid, that the plant attained to the length of seven feet upon the new building, in the course of the winter and spring months. The higher parts of the Bell Rock abound with the smaller fuci, as Fucus mamillosus, and F. palmatus, or common dulse. F. lycopodiodes, alatus, and coccineus, are found on the older stalks of the great tangle, and F. subfuscus and confervoides occupy the smaller pools. In some places, the rocks are rendered slippery with Ulva compressa and umbilicalis; and the higher parts of the Rock, and the basement or lower courses of the light-house, are so covered with Conferva rupestris, as to produce the appearance of a sward of grass.

Animals.

Of the feathered tribe of animals at the Bell Rock, we notice the shag, cormorant, and herring-gull, which sometimes rest upon the Rock when in search of codlings and other small fishes. It also formed the resting-place of numerous seals at the commencement of the operations of the Light-house, but these amphibious animals, as well as the birds, have now almost entirely left it. The common crab and lobster are sometimes found here in the crevices of the rock. The Lepas balanoides, or acorn-shell, the common limpet, mussels of a small size, and the white buckey or Buccinum lapillus, abound on the rock. The Actinia crassicornis, Asterias glacialis and oculata, are common. A minute crustaceous insect, called, by Dr Leach, Limnoria terebrans (Lin. Trans, vol. XI. p. 371.), appeared in great numbers in the submersed wood work of the temporary erections on the Rock.

Insect destructive to Timber.

So destructive to timber is this small insect, that the Norway logs, laid down to support the temporary railways in 1807, when lifted in 1811, were found to have been reduced by its ravages from 10 inches square to 7 inches, or at the rate of about an inch in the year. The author having had occasion afterwards to examine the timber-bridge of Montrose, found the attacks of this insect upon the wooden piers to be so alarming as to endanger that fabric; and after many trials for the preservation of timber in such situations, the Trustees were ultimately induced to cover the upright beams with sheet-copper. Upon another occasion, when the author was called to inspect the Crinan Canal, he found the gates of the sea-locks so destroyed, chiefly by this little animal, that the locks lost seven feet of their depth of water in the course of the night. It is further remarked, that the deserted cavities, formed by the perforations of the Limnoria, frequently become the residence of larger marine insects, belonging to the Linnæan genus Oniscus.

Experiments with pieces of timber trenailed to the Rock.

In the year 1814, with a view to experiment on the effects of these destructive vermes, I fixed down specimens of teak-wood, oak, black birch, Memel and Norway fir timber, on the Bell Rock. The only specimen which remained imperforate till 1820, was the teak-wood. The rest were almost entirely destroyed in the course of two or three years. This may be regarded as a matter of some importance, in a national point of view, in directing the employment of teak-wood for the sea-lock gates of canals and for ship-timbers. From the excellency of the situation of the Bell Rock for such experiments, I have caused another set of timbers to be trenailed to the rock, in a situation where, like the former, they are occasionally uncovered by the water. These last pieces of timber were laid down in the month of October 1821. They are eighteen in number, each measuring 5 inches square, and 30 inches in length; and are of the following kinds, viz. British and American oaks and firs, Memel fir, Scotch elm, beech, sycamore, larch, teak-wood, mahogany, bullet-tree, locust-wood, and blue gum-wood from Van Dieman's Land.

Attempt to plant Muscles on the Rock.

When the workmen first landed upon the Bell Rock, limpets of a very large size were common, but were soon picked up for bait. As the limpets disappeared, we endeavoured to plant a colony of muscles, from beds at the mouth of the river Eden, of a larger kind than those which seem to be natural to the rock. These larger muscles were likely to have been useful to the workmen, and might have been especially so to the light-keepers, the future inhabitants of the rock, to whom that delicate fish would have afforded a fresh meal, as well as a better bait than the limpet; but the muscles were soon observed to open and die in great numbers. For some time this was ascribed to the effects of the violent surge of the sea, but the Buccinum lapillus having greatly increased, it was ascertained that it had proved a successful enemy to the muscle. The buccinum being furnished with a proboscis capable of boring, was observed to perforate a small hole in the shell, and thus to suck out the finer parts of the body of the muscle; the valves of course opened, and the remainder of the fish was washed away by the sea. The perforated hole is generally upon the thinnest part of the shell, and is perfectly circular, of a champhered form, being wider towards the outward side, and so perfectly smooth and regular, as to have all the appearance of the most beautiful work of an expert artist. It became a matter extremely desirable to preserve the muscle, and it seemed practicable to extirpate the buccinum. But after we had picked up and destroyed many barrels of them, their extirpation was at length given up as a hopeless task. The muscles were thus abandoned as their prey: and in the course of the third year's operations, so successful had the ravages of the buccinum been, that not a single muscle of a large size was to be found upon the rock; and even the small kind which breed there, are now chiefly confined to the extreme points of the rock, where it would seem their enemy cannot so easily follow them.

Habits of Fishes.

In speaking of the habits of fishes, it deserves notice that they have their particular grounds and shores which they frequent; for while the vessels attending the works at the Bell Rock were stationed there, different kinds of fish were caught as the depth and bottom varied. About high-water, and especially during ebb-tide, when the sea is smooth on the rock, the Podley (chiefly the fry of the coal-fish, but including also the young of the Gadus virens) is so numerous, as almost entirely to cover it from view. Near the rock, the small red cod is often found in abundance: at some distance, as the bottom, which is covered with marine plants near the rock, alters to coral, gravel, shell sand, fine sand and mud, all of which occur in a range of depths from 4 to 23 fathoms towards the north, different kinds of fish are found; first, the codling, which ceases to be wholly red, but becomes only speckled with reddish spots; then, upon the finer or mud grounds in the track of the tides of the Firth of Tay, whiting, haddock, flounder, and occasionally the sole. On the southern side of the rock, where the water deepens to 35 fathoms, the large white cod, in company with ling, conger-eel, halibut, skate, thornback, plaise, turbot, wolf-fish and large coal-fish are found. The dog-fish appears to be very general, and seems to prey chiefly upon the haddock and cod. The mackerel and gurnard are found together near the surface, and do not seem to be confined to particular grounds, but occur wherever the water is of a considerable depth. Herrings are found in the bays of the opposite shores in great abundance at the fishing season, when they are understood to be migrating towards the south. It has often been observed, in the course of the Bell Rock operations, that, during the cold weather of spring and autumn, and even at all seasons, in stormy weather, when the sea is much agitated by wind, the fishes disappear entirely from the vicinity of the rock, probably retreating into much deeper water, from which they do not seem to return, until a change of weather has taken place; so much was this attended to by the seamen employed on this service, that they frequently prognosticated and judged of the weather from this habit of the fishes, as well as from the appearances of the sky.

DEPTH OF WATER.

Depth of Water.

Depth of Water upon the Bell Rock.

At the time of high-water of spring-tides, the south-western reef is about 16 feet, or nearly the whole rise of the tide, under the surface of the water; while the part of the rock on which the light-house is built, is about 12 feet below high water-mark of spring-tides: At low-water of neap-tides, hardly any part of the rock is visible: But at low-water of spring-tides, the general level of the north-eastern end where the light-house is built, is about four feet perpendicular above the level of the sea, though particular points measure six or even seven feet in height above the low-water mark of spring-tides.

Depth at the distance of 100 yards, and upwards from it.

At the distance of about 100 yards from the rock in all directions, excepting on the south-western reef, there is a depth of water varying from two to three fathoms at low water of spring tides. On the north-west side, or in the direction of the shores of Forfar and Fife, the greatest depth is 23 fathoms; but on the south-eastern or seaward side, in the direction of the dip or inclination of the strata, the water deepens more suddenly to 35 fathoms; in the same direction from the rock, however, the soundings again become less, being only 22 fathoms upon Mars Bank, distant about 33 miles; this bank appears to be a deposition formed by the joint operation of the waters of the Friths of Forth and Tay, influenced by the great tidal wave of the German Ocean. It may here be noticed as a fact connected with the depth of the German Ocean, that at Queensferry passage, in the Firth of Forth, the depth of the water is about 35 fathoms, while the greatest depth of the sea across to Denmark, does not exceed 45 fathoms. The depths of the German Ocean will be seen, by inspecting Chart No. 3., where sectional lines are delineated between various points of Great Britain and the opposite Continent, on which the reader will see the relative depths marked by shaded lines, in a new and it is hoped a perspicuous manner.

CURRENT OF THE TIDES.

Currents of the Tide.

Tides at the Bell Rock.

The tides at the Bell Rock, are observed to follow the same laws as on the opposite shores of the Firth of Forth. The currents along the coast take their direction from the figure of the land, and, in their course, they are therefore occasionally deflected from, and inclined towards it. At the Bell Rock the flood-tide sets south-west, and the ebb-tide north-east, being nearly in the direction of the shores of Forfar and Kincardine. The velocity of the water in spring-tides, or when the sun and moon are in conjunction, and in opposition, is about three miles per hour, but in neap-tides, or at the quadratures of the moon, the current is only at the rate of about one mile per hour. On the days of new and full moon it is high-water upon the Bell Rock at half past one o'clock, being about the same periodic time as at the harbour of Arbroath, or nearest point of the mainland. In the ordinary state of the weather, the perpendicular rise and fall of the sea at the Bell Rock, in spring-tides, is 15 feet, and in neap-tides, 8 feet; but so much depends upon the direction of a prevailing tract of winds, that the tides are often found to vary from 1 to 3 feet above and below these numbers. This irregularity in the tides of the German Ocean and its subsidiary friths or inland seas will be easily accounted for, by considering the effect of westerly winds passing for a length of time over the Atlantic, which must naturally force an undue quantity of water from thence into the entrance of the North Sea, between the coasts of Scotland and Norway; while the Strait of Dover, to the southward, from the same cause, is gorged by the surplus waters of the British Channel flowing in an opposite direction, and checking the tide of the German Ocean. When the winds blow from southerly and easterly directions, the reverse of this happens, and the waters are then proportionally low.

In and Off shore Currents.

A curious anomaly connected with the flowing and ebbing of the sea, in the early part of each tide, is observable in the contrary currents which take place along the shore, and at a distance from it. For example, the flood-tide begins to flow in many situations two or even three hours sooner on the shore than at the distance of from one mile to four miles in the offing. The same thing also happens with regard to the ebb-tide, which begins to fall and run in a contrary direction to the flood-tide, two or three hours sooner on the shore than at a distance. These effects are very different from the state of things three or four leagues from the land, or in the open sea, where the lateral motion of the tide-waters is scarcely sensible. That an extensive tract of coast should produce changes on the current of the tides, is perhaps what we should expect; but it is somewhat curious to find the same appearances connected with small islets, and, as in the case of the Bell Rock, even with an insulated reef, situate at the distance of 12 miles from the land, and sunk to the depth of from 2 to 3 fathoms under the surface of high-water. So strikingly observable is this, that the tide begins to ebb about two hours sooner on the Bell Rock than at the short distance of one mile from it. In the course of the light-house operations this was rendered sufficiently obvious, by the swinging round of the several vessels at their moorings according to the flood and ebb tides. For example, the Floating Light-ship was moored about three miles in a north-west direction from the Bell Rock, and the moorings of the Tender and two Stone Lighters, were respectively laid down at the distance of ¾ and ½ mile from it, as will be seen from Plate V. Now, these vessels were all found to swing to the tide at periods proportional to their distance from the rock. Although it may, therefore, seem strange, that this comparatively small object should affect the tides in its vicinity in a manner similar to the shores of an extensive coast; yet, as the rock shelves outwards, with an extensive base, especially on the northern side, it must impede the under current of the tide, and indeed forcibly proves the existence of such under currents.

Not accounted for by Writers on the subject.

To account for these in and off shore tides, or central and marginal streams, would be interesting. But to what cause shall we ascribe them? Sir Isaac Newton, and the other eminent philosophers who have followed that great man in considering the theory of the tides, confine their attention chiefly to an explanation of the influences of the sun and moon, and the laws of gravitation, in affecting the waters of the ocean, leaving it to the result of experience and observation to account for such anomalies as those to which we now allude. It is noticed by Adair, Mackenzie, and other nautical surveyors, that the tides run longer upon the shore than in the offing, and the advantage of working a ship with in and off shore tides, is familiar to every mariner. The existence of these opposite currents was also known to the author, prior to the commencement of the Bell Rock works, but they had not struck him so forcibly till that period. For here, even after the flood-tide had overflowed the rock, and put a stop to the operations, the boats in carrying the artificers on board of the Tender, had still to row against the current of a strong ebb-tide.

Currents along Shore considered as Eddy-tides.

It would be foreign to this work to enter into the theory of the tides generally; all, therefore, that is here proposed, is to endeavour to account for these in and off shore currents. In doing this, however, it will be necessary to observe, that the great wave or "theoretical tide," as it has been termed by the late eminent Professor Robison, is produced by the united attraction of the sun and moon, which, between the Tropics, has been calculated by philosophers to raise the water from 8 to 14 feet perpendicularly. It is observable, that the attractions of these heavenly bodies elevate the parts of the ocean to which they are vertical, without having any direct tendency to progressive or lateral motion. The currents along our coasts, may therefore be considered merely as Eddy-tides, occasioned by the interposition of the land, which obstructs the undulating motion incident to the rise or fall of a fluid. In this manner the land may be said to displace a portion of the tidal waters which have been elevated above the medium level of the sea; and were it not for such obstruction, the great waves of the tide might be supposed to undulate indefinitely over the expanse of the ocean. To compare small things with great, these effects may be conceived as in some degree exemplified, by the disturbing effect of a vessel passing along a navigable canal, or the undulations which are observable in the wake of a ship or wheels of a steam-boat in motion on a smooth sea.

Progress of the Great Waves of the Tides.

The great wave which supplies the British tides, appears to be propagated between the coast of Labrador and Greenland, on the one hand, and the European shores on the other; and this great wave seems to be divided into two lesser waves. One of these flows between Ireland and the coast of France, into the British and St George's Channels; while the other enters by the North Sea into the German Ocean; and in its course from north to south, supplies all the friths, rivers, and bays connected with it, invariably in the form of In and Off shore tides, which are every where observable along the margin of this great basin. This northern wave is found to occupy about 12 hours in flowing southward from the 58th to the 52d degree of latitude, or from the Orkney Islands to the numerous Sand-banks which pervade and encumber the apex of the German Ocean, where the currents become extremely desultory and irregular. The coast of the British Isles, accordingly, may be said to, displace a portion of this northern wave, and thus to produce the irregularities which we are endeavouring to account for.

Progressive periods of High-Water in the Firth of Forth.

At present, we shall confine our attention to the tides of the Firth of Forth. Here, as on other parts of the coast, the tidal waters have a tendency to flow towards the shores and higher parts of the Forth, till the instant of high-water upon the shore, when the tide begins to ebb, and run in a contrary direction. A central stream, however, continues to run with unabated force, as flood-tide, during two or even three hours longer, as before noticed, according to the situation and local circumstances of the coast. It appears, from a comparison of the several periods of high-water on the shores of the Firth of Forth, as nearly as some of them could be ascertained, that the precise time of high-water becomes later and later in the same tide, as we proceed westward; at the Bell Rock, for example, it is high-water on the days of new and full moon, as before noticed, at ½ past 1 o'clock; at the Carr Rock, at ¾ past 1; at Elie, still further up the Firth , at 2; Kinghornness, at ¼ past 2; Queensferry, at ¾ past 2; and at Alloa, at ¾ past 3 o'clock. The off-shore stream of the tide continues to flow proportionally longer till it has supplied the higher parts of this estuary with its portion of tidal waters; and in like manner, the central stream of ebb-tide continues its course till these waters are again run off.

Currents at the Mouth of the Dee and other Rivers.

In many points, it is found, that the operation of the tidal waters of extensive arms of the sea, bears a close resemblance to what is observable upon the small scale in the currents of rivers, especially at their junction with the ocean. An interesting example of this occurs on the river Dee, which falls rapidly into the harbour of Aberdeen. Here the author having occasion to make some observations on the tides in the summer of 1812, stationed several assistants at low-water mark, between the entrance of the harbour and the bridge, about two miles up the river. The waters of the Dee, even at the entrance of the harbour, have almost a constant current seaward, notwithstanding the opposite direction of the flood-tide of the Ocean. On the occasion alluded to, one of his assistants, a very intelligent ship-master, continued at his post while the water flowed up to his middle; and, when accosted about his situation, he significantly observed, "That it was rather extraordinary, as the stream had never ceased to indicate the continuance of an ebb-tide, while the water was still rising upon his body."

Water salt at bottom and fresh at top.

In connection with these observations on the tides, some experiments were also made with an instrument adapted for lifting water from considerable depths, without the possibility of its intermingling with the surface water. By means of this instrument, the water at the bottom of the Dee, at Aberdeen, was found to be salt, while that at the surface was quite fresh. These streams of fresh and salt water run in distinct currents, and in contrary directions, the salt water, from its greater specific gravity, flowing at the bottom of the river, and fluctuating with the level of the ocean, while the fresh water is actually lifted upwards, and continues all the while to flow seaward on the surface of the salt water. Towards the point of high-water, however, the flood-tide gains strength on the margin of the basin of the harbour, where the water becomes salt, and forms an eddy-tide in a contrary direction to the central stream, which is observed still to run toward the sea. Having made similar observations on the waters of the Thames, the Garonne, and other rivers, with nearly the same results, after making allowance for the more level state of the country, in the track of these great streams,—it is concluded, that the currents at the embouchure of rivers bear a strong resemblance to the operation of the in and off shore tides of the ocean.

Phenomena of in and off shore Tides accounted for.

We further observe, that the great wave of the German Ocean produces its tides in regular succession, and at stated periods, as it moves from north to south; but the tides of the more inland seas are subject to many irregularities, both in their periodic times, and in the direction of their currents. Let us suppose, then, that we have arrived at the instant of high-water on the shores at the entrance of the Firth of Forth, and that the tidal waters are then moving in a body, and with a certain pressure, towards the higher parts of the Firth , and even affecting the river above the bridge of Stirling. We find, that at the entrance of this estuary, on the days of new and full moon, it is high-water at a quarter past one o'clock; but at Alloa, situate 70 miles above the Bell Rock, it is not high-water till about two hours and a half later. The in-shore tidal waters having to encounter the shelving shores, islands, sunken rocks, and projecting points of land, which lie in their course up the Firth , acquire lateral as well as perpendicular motion, and being thus checked in their progress, are brought sooner to a maximum state than the off-shore stream, which flows in deeper water, and comparatively free of obstruction, till it reaches its ultimate limits; though it gradually diminishes in breadth, till the stream of the new tide gaining strength becomes general; and the central current, formerly running in a contrary direction, at length disappears, and takes the course of the new tide.

We would, therefore, be understood to ascribe this anomaly in the flowing and ebbing of the sea, to the obstruction which the current of its waters meets not only at the surface or margin, but at the bottom, which, from the variety of the soundings of the depths, appears to be as various as the face of the land. A striking proof of this is afforded at the Bell Rock: on the northern side of which there are 11 fathoms, at the distance of about three quarters of a mile; while, on the southern side, and at a similar distance, the water deepens to 35 fathoms; so that a perpendicular section of this rock under water forms a precipitous declivity, such as we are quite accustomed to see on the land. Now, if we apply this irregular conformation of the bottom of the sea, to the production of the in and off shore tides, and conceive that the tidal currents extend their motion to the bottom, it must be evident, that this obstruction presented to the stream will bring the tides to a maximum state sooner on the northern side of the rock, where the water is so much shallower, than on the southern side. This is also agreeable to observation; for, the tides upon the Bell Rock begin to flow and ebb one hour sooner than at the distance of about three quarters of a mile from it on the northern side, and about two hours and a half sooner than at the same distance on the southern side. The marginal current is thus checked by the shallowness of the water, and the projecting points of land; while the central stream, flowing comparatively without obstruction, continues to run till the most inland creeks are supplied with tidal water; and vice versâ, it continues its stream outwards, till these waters are again run off.

Progressive times of high-water.

The progressive times of high-water, at intermediate points between the Bell Rock and the port of Alloa in the Firth of Forth, appear to follow the same general law, as the great wave of the German Ocean in its progress from the Orkneys southward. These observations on the tides of the Forth apply equally to the Firth and River of Tay, and indeed to all the tributary streams and arms of the sea which communicate with the German Ocean, according to their local situations and magnitudes.

Tides of the Mediterranean and Baltic Seas.

If due allowance be made for the peculiar situation and circumstances of the Mediterranean and Baltic seas, it is apprehended, from all that we have been able to learn of the operation of the currents at the Strait of Gibraltar, and Sound of the Cattigate, that these seas are supplied and discharged by in and off shore tides or currents, under certain modifications, and making due allowance for local circumstances, in the same manner as on all other parts of the coast.

I have been thus particular relative to the in-shore and off-shore tides, because they appear in a very puzzling form to the mariner, while writers on the theory of the tides are almost silent on this subject.

CHAPTER II.

DANGEROUS POSITION OF THE BELL ROCK.—SIR ALEX-
ANDER COCHRANE'S LETTER TO THE LIGHT-HOUSE
BOARD.—DESIGNS FOR THE BELL ROCK LIGHT-
HOUSE.—BILL BY LORD ADVOCATE HOPE IN 1803.—
REPORT OF TRADERS OF LEITH.—RESOLUTION
OF THE LIGHT-HOUSE BOARD TO APPLY AGAIN
TO PARLIAMENT.—MEMORIAL TO THE BOARD OF
TRADE.—BILL BY LORD ADVOCATE ERSKINE.—RE-
PORT OF THE COMMITTEE OF THE HOUSE OF COM-
MONS.—THE BILL PASSED.

DANGEROUS POSITION OF THE BELL ROCK.

Dangerous Position of the Bell Rock.

Whatever may have been the early state of the Inch Cape or Bell Rock, as an Island, its present character is strictly that of a sunken rock; and, as such, its relative situation on the eastern shores of Great Britain has long rendered it one of the chief impediments to the free navigation of that coast. It is almost unnecessary to remark, that there are only three great inlets or estuaries upon this coast, to which the mariner steers, when overtaken by easterly storms in the North Sea or German Ocean. These are the Humber, and the Friths of Forth and Moray; of which the Firth of Forth is the principal rendezvous. The mouth of the River Thames, excepting in certain narrow and intricate channels, has not a sufficient depth of water, and is so much encumbered with sand-banks, that no vessel can enter it under night, or approach it in bad weather. On the coast and shores in the neighbourhood of the Humber, the land is flat, and defective in those bold and characteristic features which are essential to the situation of an anchorage for ships in bad weather when they cannot keep at sea. The entrance of the Humber is also considerably obstructed with sand-banks, of which the mariner is, if possible, more afraid than of rocks, because more liable to uncertainty, by the shifting of their position, and thereby changing the direction of the accustomed channels. The great places of resort for ships, therefore, in the North Sea, are the Roads of Leith and Cromarty, lying in the Friths of Forth and Moray, as will be seen from Plate III., in both of which we find the natural advantages of an ample entrance, and a coast so strongly marked as to be easily recognised by the mariner. But from the dangerous position of the Bell Rock, his approach to the shores of this coast, prior to the erection of the Light-house there, was liable to the greatest peril and uncertainty.

Great storm in December 1799.

A memorable example of this occurred during a storm from the south-east, in the month of December 1799. This storm having continued with little intermission for three days; a number of vessels were driven from their moorings in the Downs and Yarmouth Roads; and these, together with all vessels navigating the German Ocean at this time, were drifted upon the coast of Scotland. Many found shelter, both in Leith and Cromarty Roads, which, from the state of the winds, lay quite open for their reception. But still, from the dread of the Bell Rock, in the one case, and the danger of mistaking the entrance to the Firth of Dornoch for that of Moray, by taking the northern instead of the southern side of Tarbetness, in the other, a great number of vessels were lost, or much hardship was sustained by the mariner in seeking safety in higher latitudes. It has even been reckoned, that seventy sail of ships were either stranded or lost upon the eastern coast of Scotland during that gale, when many of their crews perished.

At the Bullers of Buchan, near Peterhead, alone, on the first night of this storm, the wrecks of seven vessels were found in a small cove, without one survivor of the crews, to give an account of their disaster. As a remarkable instance of escape on this occasion, it may be mentioned, that a coal-ship, in ballast, returning from London to Newcastle, was carried completely round the coast of Great Britain and Ireland, the first land made by this vessel, after leaving Flamborough Head in Yorkshire, being the Land's End of Cornwall. Having put into Falmouth to refit the ship and refresh the exhausted crew, she continued her voyage up the British Channel to the Straits of Dover, and so to Newcastle, thus making a complete circuit of the British shores. In the summer of 1800, the writer saw the wrecks of two fine vessels on the Orkney Islands; one of which, on her way to Gibraltar, had been as far as Ushant on the coast of France, when, by contrary winds, she had been driven back to the Downs, and, in the month of December 1799, she was ultimately stranded on the Island of Sanday, along with the other vessel, which in that gale had been driven from Yarmouth Roads.

From the situation and circumstances attending the Bell Rock, it may well be supposed, that this dangerous sunken reef was found to be either the direct or ultimate cause, in many cases of shipwreck upon the eastern coast of Great Britain, and as such, every scheme which had for its object the fixing of some distinguishing mark upon it, was regarded as a matter of public interest, claiming a degree of attention proportionate to its apparent practicability and usefulness. The traditionary story of the Bell said to have been erected by the Abbots of Aberbrothock upon this rock may, perhaps, have given rise to many plans of this nature. But, on account of the limited advantages which must have attended any erection merely in the form of a beacon, without a light, upon a sunken rock, at so great a distance from land,—none of the many proposals of this kind which were from time to time suggested, ever met with the serious attention of the public. It was evident, that nothing but a light-house could not be essentially useful, and that all temporary erections in a situation of this kind were to be avoided.

Sir Alex. Cochrane's Letter.

The following letter from Sir Alexander Cochrane, while stationed on the eastern coast in the year 1793, is particularly deserving of a place in this work, as well from being the first official application made to the Commissioners on the subject of the Bell Rock, as on account of that officer's great experience in nautical affairs, and the clear and decided manner in which the advantages which would result from the erection of a light-house there, are pointed out.

"On board his Majesty's ship Hind, Leith Roads, January 7. 1793. Gentlemen, I think it a duty I owe to the public, to call your attention, as Trustees for the Northern Lights, to the great hazard and peril that the trade of the east of Scotland is subject to, from the want of a light-house being erected on the Bell or Cape Rock, the only dangerous one upon this coast, from the Staples to Duncansbay-head, except the Carr, which lies so close to Fifeness and the Isle of May as to render it comparatively of less consequence.

"The situation of the Cape being about 12 miles from the nearest shore, bearing off the Redhead, by compass, S. ¾ W. — Taybar, SE. by E. ¼ E. — Fifeness, NE. by E. — Isle of May Light, NE. 17 miles, (consequently, too distant to be useful to shipping during the night); this rock is therefore placed in the most dangerous situation possible, for the trade of the Friths of Forth and Tay; the more so, from the prevailing winds on the coast, being from the W.NW. to SW., which occasion vessels bound inwards, to stretch across from shore to shore, that is, from the south to the north, or the opposite, according to their situations. This they can do in the day time; but at night, the danger of falling in with the Cape Rock, prevents them from standing to the northward of the Firth of Forth, and they are thereby prevented from taking the advantage of working up under the land in St Andrew's Bay, by which they would get into smooth water, and avoid the heavy swell and gusts of wind that are always met with in the opening of this Firth .

"Ships from the Baltic, which have not made the land, are often driven off the coast, from the caution they are obliged to take, in consequence of their not knowing what their situation is respecting this rock; which, from being covered early in the tide, and having little or no sea or breakers on it in moderate weather, the wind being off the shore, the soundings are no guide whatever; for, within one mile of the south-east side, the depth of water is 32 fathoms, (the general soundings on the coast); from all which circumstances, a ship standing in for the shore, perhaps without having had an observation of the sun for some days, runs the utmost danger of being wrecked. From the experience I have, in consequence of cruizing on this coast, I give it as my most decided opinion, that the greatest good consequence would arise to the trade of Scotland, were a light-house erected on it; but, in the event of its being so, a distinction must be made between it and the light of May, such as is adopted at Scilly and the Caskets, the light on which revolves, I believe, once in a minute, so as to be obscured and visible alternately."

Expence of a Light-house on the Bell Rock, as estimated by the Public.

Although the subject of this letter had occasionally occupied the attention of the Commissioners of the Northern Light-houses, yet the Bell Rock, as the site of a light-house, was then for the first time brought formally under the notice of the

Board; and some erection there, was considered a primary object, whenever the funds should be in a state to meet the expence of such a work. But, the estimates for such an undertaking admitted of an almost unlimited range of amount, both from the nature of the buildings which were proposed, and on account of works of this kind being subject to unavoidable risk in all their stages, from the commencement till the completion. In conversation, it was common to compare the situation of the Bell Rock with the rocks of the Eddystone off Plymouth Sound, and Corduan at the mouth of the Garonne.

Designs for the Bell Rock Light-house.

The expence of erecting a light-house on the Eddystone, though understood to have been about L. 20,000, has never been communicated to the public by the lessees of the light-house duties, from the consideration, perhaps, of their being obliged, by their agreement with the Trinity Board of London, to erect and uphold the building, and also from claims which they afterwards made, for having the value of the light-house reimbursed to them at the end of their lease; but it was well known that the present building is no less than the third erection which the lessees had made upon the Eddystone, between 1696 and 1759, or in the space of 63 years. It was therefore natural to conclude that a building on the Bell Rock, situate under a greater depth of water, being nearly on a level with low-water mark, would be a work of greater difficulty and expence, than the Eddystone light-house, where the top of the rock is on a level with high-water mark. We are also left in the dark in forming any opinion on the important point of expence with regard to the French work at Corduan, but we know that it met with repeated misfortunes while in progress, and that it occupied from 1584 till 1610, or 26 years in building. The main rock here is about a mile in length, and half a mile in breadth, and, in its position as a sunken reef, it resembles the Bell Rock more than the Eddystone. From the difficulties which attended the erection of these two celebrated light-houses,—both of which the writer has visited,—the erection of a light-house upon the Bell Rock, in comparison with these, was estimated by the public at so wide a range as from L. 20,000 even to L. 100,000.

Funds for the Light-house Board inadequate.

In the year 1793, when Admiral Cochrane addressed his letter to the Light-house Board, its surplus funds amounted only to a few hundred pounds; a sum so inadequate to meet the necessary expenditure of such a work, that the Commissioners judged it better for the interests of navigation, to go forward with the less expensive improvements on other parts of the coast, aware that nothing essential could be undertaken at the Bell Rock without the effectual aid of Government.

In this state, matters were allowed to rest till the great storm in December 1799, already noticed, which roused the public mind to fresh speculations about the necessity of some erection being made upon the Bell Rock; not merely as a local improvement, but as one essentially calculated to benefit the ships navigating the German Ocean, by opening the Firth of Forth more effectually as a place of safety in easterly storms, so that the Bell Rock, in place of being the dread of mariners, might in future become a point from which they would take their departure, and for which they might steer in sailing for the coast. Nautical and commercial men, especially, were interested, and felt this state of things in its fullest extent. Remarks were accordingly made in several of the periodical publications of the day, calling the attention of the public to the erection of a light-house there, as a subject of national importance.

In order to advance this object, the Corporation of the Trinity-House of Leith, made public advertisements, calling on persons likely to produce some practical plan that might lead to the means of making the erection in question. This, of course, produced various propositions on the subject.

DESIGNS FOR THE BELL ROCK LIGHT-HOUSE.

Designs by Captain Brodie and Mr Couper.

The late Captain Joseph Brodie of the Royal Navy, prepared and brought forward a model of a cast-iron light-house, supported upon four pillars, to be built and connected together in a very strong manner. This model was made by Mr Joseph Couper, Iron-Founder in Leith, who, in conjunction with Captain Brodie, proposed to erect a light-house on this plan on the Bell Rock, on being authorised to draw certain duties from shipping for their mutual remuneration. With this view, they sent their model, and made certain propositions to the different commercial towns on the coast, as Newcastle, Dundee, and Aberdeen. After having been at considerable trouble and expence with this scheme, as a private adventure, these gentlemen applied to the Commissioners of the Northern Light-houses, requesting their inspection of this model. The design, however, was not altogether approved of by the Light-house Board, in the form in which it had been modelled; yet such was the confidence of its projectors, that at different times, in pursuance of their plan, they erected two temporary beacons, constructed with spars of fir-timber; these unfortunately were almost immediately washed down. The Merchants of Leith, applauding the great perseverance of these gentlemen, aided their exertions by a subscription of about L. 150, when they erected a third beacon on the Bell Rock on a more extended scale. It consisted of four spars of fir-timber, each about 40 feet in length, strengthened by flat bars of iron, laid the lengthway of the spars, which were kept in their places by rings or hoops of iron, firmly wedged over them. These spars, when erected upon the rock, formed a common diameter of about 20 feet at the base, and crossed each other about 6 feet from the top. They were let into holes made in the rock, of about ten inches in depth, and were fixed by straps of iron, forming bats of about two inches square, and about six inches in length, which were also let into the rock, and run up with melted lead. At the place of junction, near the top, the spars were bolted together with iron, and above this, they were connected with small pieces of timber, nailed to the principal spars. After much labour and difficulty, with the assistance of a number of workmen, this temporary erection was fixed on the Bell Rock, in the month of July 1803. In the month of August the writer landed on the rock and examined it; but when the gales of winter set in, this erection also disappeared, having never been seen after the 20th of December. Nothing further was attempted to be done upon the Bell Rock till the author commenced the Light-house operations in the year 1807, by direction of the Commissioners of the Northern Light-houses.

Make further proposals to the Light-house Board.

Not discouraged, however, by the failure of these trifling works, Captain Brodie and Mr Couper addressed a letter to the Light-house Board, in which an offer was made to erect a cast-iron light-house, in the space of two years, agreeably to the model already alluded to, and on the following terms, viz. L. 6000 to be paid over to them during the first year of the work, together with the produce of a certain Duty for the erection, to be exacted from shipping, as a Northern Light, until the original cost of the work should be paid off. But this description of building having been considered objectionable, Captain Brodie proposed to construct a new model, upon an improved plan, by which the base of the building, instead of being raised on pillars, was to be continuous, with small interstices or holes in its circumference, or outer casing, to admit the water into the interior void, with a view to lessen the weight and expence of metal, and check the force of the sea. But this also appeared to the Commissioners to be defective, when compared with an erection of stone, like the Eddystone and Tour de Corduan Light-houses.

Captain Brodie's remuneration.

Captain Brodie having, however, shewn a most laudable zeal in this work, and considering that he must have expended a sum of money beyond what had been subscribed for the erection of the Spar Beacon, the Commissioners proposed to make him a liberal allowance for the last model, to the preparation of which they had given their countenance. He was according ly requested to state the expence of this model, with a view to his reimbursement. But, under an erroneous impression, he brought forward an account, containing an enumeration of charges connected with the Bell Rock, from the year 1792; and by applying these items to the imaginary profits of trade, the sum amounted to several thousand pounds. This appeared so contrary to the views of the Commissioners, that the account was returned, with an offer of L. 400 in full of all claims. This sum, however, was refused, and another proposition made, that the Board should apply to Government to have his services publicly rewarded. But it was finally intimated, that L. 400 were at his disposal; and here the matter rested till after Captain Brodie's decease, when that sum, with interest, was, in 1816, paid to his widow.

The Author's early designs for the Bell Rock Light-house.

In noticing the progress of the designs of the Bell Rock Light-house, it will here be necessary to give some detail of the writer's own exertions in the preliminary stages of this measure, in his capacity of Engineer for the Light-house Board. In the summer of 1794, when on a voyage to the Northern Light-houses, in passing the Bell Rock, he directed the vessel to be brought near it, when he had an opportunity of observing the sea breaking heavily upon it. From this period, the difficulties which must attend the erection of a habitation on this rock, appeared in a stronger point of view than they had hitherto done. He, nevertheless, was resolved to embrace every opportunity of forwarding this great object. In the year 1796, he visited the operations of the Kilwarlin light-house, then erecting on the South Rock, a sunken reef, situate three miles off the coast of Downshire in Ireland, as a work resembling that which was in contemplation for the Bell Rock.

His pillar-formed Light-house.

The disastrous shipwrecks which occasionally happened at the entrance of the Friths of Forth and Tay, deeply impressed every one conversant in nautical affairs, with the most convincing proofs of the necessity for some distinguishing mark being erected upon the Bell Rock. As yet, the writer had not landed upon the rock; though he had begun to prepare a model of a pillar-formed light-house, to be supported upon six columns of cast-iron, under the impression that this description of building was alone suitable to its situation. The general features of this model may be understood, by examining Plate VII., which represents the author's original designs for the Bell Rock Light-house.

In the summer of the year 1800, this model was presented to the Light-house Board, when an official application was made to the Commissioners of his Majesty's Customs, for the use of the Osnaburgh cutter, then lying in the harbour of Elie, on the coast of Fife, to carry the writer to the Bell Rock, that, by landing there, he might be enabled to judge of the applicability of his pillar-formed design to the situation of the rock. Upon reaching Elie, the Osnaburgh was found to be under repair, and could not possibly go to sea for several days, by which time the spring-tides would be over. On consulting with the commander, as to the most advisable course to be followed, in order to avoid losing these tides, it was resolved to go to St Andrew's in quest of a boat; but being there also disappointed, the journey was continued along the coast to West Haven, on the northern side of the Firth of Tay, where a large boat was procured, and manned with fishermen who were in the habit of visiting the rock to search for articles of shipwreck.

His first visit to the Bell Rock, with Mr Haldane, architect.

On this first visit to the Bell Rock, the writer was accompanied by his friend Mr James Haldane, architect, formerly principal assistant to the late eminent Mr John Baxter. The crew being unwilling to risk their boat into any of the creeks in the rock, very properly observing that the lives of all depended upon her safety, and as we could only remain upon the rock for two or three hours at most, we landed upon a shelving part on the south side of the rock, at the spot marked "First Landing" on Plate VI. Having been extremely fortunate both as to the state of the weather and tides, an opportunity was afforded of making a sketch of the rock at low water: meantime, the boatmen were busily employed in searching all the holes and crevices in quest of articles of shipwreck, and by the time that the tide overflowed the rock, they had collected upwards of 2 cwt. of old metal, consisting of such things as are used on shipboard. A few of these were kept by the writer, such as a hinge and lock of a door, a ship's marking-iron, a piece of a ship's coboose (or kambuis, cover of the cooking-place), a soldier's bayonet, a canon ball, several pieces of money, a shoe-buckle, &c.; while the heavier and more bulky articles, as a piece of a kedge-anchor, cabin-stove, crowbars, &c. were left with the crew, who were, however, disposed to make very light of their booty, when it was urged in extenuation of an extravagant demand which they made for the boat's freight, being at the rate of one guinea per man, and one guinea for the use of the boat, besides expences, amounting altogether to about eleven guineas.

He concludes that a building of stone is most suitable for the Bell Rock.

The immediate result of this visit on the mind of the writer and of Mr Haldane, was a firm conviction of the practicability of erecting a building of stone upon the Bell Rock; and from that moment the idea of a pillar-formed light-house was rejected, as unsuitable to the situation. This opinion was chiefly founded upon the area or extent of the part which dried, or was exposed to view in the spring-tides, being found to measure about 280 by 300 feet, and consequently affording a sufficient space for a foundation, and even a degree of shelter from the force of the waves, for the lower courses of a building.

Pillar-formed building compared with one of stone.

The depth at high-water upon the Bell Rock was much against the design of a building with pillars, as a vessel drawing 12 feet water, and loaded with 100 or even 200 tons, may come with full sail against any erection made there. Were such a circumstance to happen to a pillar-formed building, and a ship to get thus entangled among the openings of the under part of the light-house, there is little doubt that the event would prove fatal to a building of that construction, however strongly framed. On the contrary, supposing a vessel to strike a building of stone, under these circumstances, it is not at all likely, that she could have any effect upon a mass of matter extending to 2000 or 3000 tons, so as to injure such a fabric.

Author's designs and models of a stone-building.

Under these impressions, the writer, after his first visit to the Bell Rock, in the year 1800, made a variety of drawings, and constructed new models for a building of stone, shewing various methods of connecting the stones, by dove-tailing them laterally, like those of the Eddystone light-house, and also course to course into one another perpendicularly. Other methods were likewise modelled, for connecting the whole building in a more simple manner, by means of joggles, or square blocks of stone, and also by dove-tailed bats of iron cased in lead, as delineated in the various designs of Plate VII. These plans and models were duly submitted to the Light-house Board, accompanied with estimates of the expence, amounting to the maximum sum of L. 42,685, 8s.

Mr Telford requested to visit the Bell Rock.

Sir William Pulteney having taken an interest in forwarding a bill for this measure in Parliament in the year 1803, gave Mr Thomas Telford, engineer, instructions to inquire into the circumstances of the Bell Rock, in the course of his journey to the Works of the Caledonian Canal. Mr Telford had accordingly taken some preparatory steps for making a Design; and, with this view, he had engaged Mr Murdoch Downie, author of several Marine Surveys, to accompany him to the Bell Rock. But the weather proved unfavourable at the time for effecting a landing upon the rock; and, the bill then in progress having been withdrawn before another opportunity occurred, Mr Telford's visit was not resumed.

Mr Downie's pillar-formed Light-house of Stone.

Mr Downie, however, who had previously been upon the rock, when making his Nautical Survey of the Eastern Coast of Scotland, prepared a drawing and an estimate of the expence of erecting a light-house upon it, which he stated at about L. 29,000. His light-house was to have consisted of eight columns of stone, of an elliptical or egg form, as he expressed it, ranged round a common centre, having the longer axis and smaller end towards a circular column in the centre of the plan. These columns were to support a circular building of stone for the habitation of the light-keepers and the site of the light room. By this plan it was meant to give less resistance to the waves. But it did not seem to be well adapted for the situation, as it wanted that solidity and unity of parts which are so essential to the stability of a building upon a sunken rock. Such a work would have been of difficult execution. It would have required similar apparatus with the solid masonry for its construction, and while in progress, it would have been in greater danger of being destroyed than a solid fabric. There seemed, therefore, upon the whole, to be but two opinions as to the proper description of a light-house for this situation, viz. either that it should be constructed of iron, as was maintained by Captain Brodie, or of solid masonry, as proposed by the writer.

BILL BY LORD ADVOCATE HOPE.

Bell Rock Light-house proposed at a Meeting of the Royal Burghs.

The erection of a light-house upon the Bell Rock had been occasionally alluded to at the Convention of the Royal Burghs of Scotland, which meets annually at Edinburgh; and, in consequence of recent losses on that reef, the Convention of 1802 was moved, by Provost Duncan of Arbroath, to take this subject under its serious consideration. It was accordingly resolved, That the Lord Advocate Hope, one of the Commissioners of the Northern Light-houses, and Member of Parliament for the City of Edinburgh, should be requested to use his influence in forwarding this desirable object. His Lordship being present, readily engaged to undertake the measure, and declared that he would not allow it to rest until something satisfactory should be done.

The Commissioners of the Light-houses having afterwards furnished the particulars, the heads of a bill were arranged, which, in the session of 1803, was brought forward by his Lordship and the late Sir William Pulteney, who took a great interest in the Scotch business before the House of Commons. This bill had for its object to empower the Commissioners to borrow L. 30,000, and to exact the Northern Light-duty of 1½d. per ton upon British shipping, and 3d. per ton upon Foreigners, from all vessels bound to or from any port on the eastern coast of Great Britain, that should cross the latitude of the Bell Rock.

Bill lost in the House of Lords.

This bill passed the House of Commons in the session of 1803; but having met with opposition from the corporation of the City of London, as including too great a range of coast in the collection of the duties, such amendments and alterations were proposed in the House of Lords, as rendered it necessary for the Lord Advocate to withdraw the bill.

Works proposed of less expence than a stone building.

The expectations of nautical and commercial men were severely disappointed by the loss of this bill, which occasioned a delay of several years in the prosecution of the object. It was obvious, that, without considerable funds at command, it was impossible to undertake a work of such magnitude. The annual funds of the Light-house Board at this period amounted only to about L. 4000, and the maintenance of the light-houses already erected was equal to one-half of this sum, which would leave a surplus fund of about L. 2000 per annum. But, as the Commissioners found it to be their duty to go on with their improvements on the other parts of the coast, without confining their attention to one object, however important, it was impossible that this great work could be undertaken for a series of years, without the direct aid of the Government, or an extension of the Light-house duties, on the security of which money might be borrowed. In consequence of the loss of this bill, the dangers of the Bell Rock now became very generally the topic of conversation; and various schemes were again suggested for constructing economical and temporary buildings to remedy the evil.

Difficulty of determining among these proposals.

In a work of so much apparent difficulty, it was not easy for the Light-house Board to determine what was the most advisable design. The pillar-formed building was supported by many arguments. It would have been executed in a very short period, and would not, perhaps, have cost one-sixth part of the expence of a building of stone. A light-house, supported upon wooden pillars, had also stood for many years, and still remains, upon the Smalls Rocks, off St David's-Head, in Pembrokeshire, although the sea, in high tides, and stormy weather, occasionally breaks over the building. But a fabric of stone, for such a situation as the Bell Rock, was evidently preferable, and the examples of the Tour de Corduan, the Eddystone, and the Kilwarlin light-houses, already noticed, were all in favour of it.

Mr Rennie consulted and agrees with the Author in recommending a building of stone.

Amidst a diversity of opinion as to the practicability of the undertaking, and especially as to the description of the building, whether it should be of cast-iron or stone, and in the form of pillars or solid, the Commissioners ultimately determined upon submitting the several views of the subject to Mr John Rennie, engineer. In the year 1804, Mr Rennie and the writer accompanied Mr Hamilton, Sheriff of Lanarkshire, one of the Commissioners, and who had turned much of his attention to the subject, on a visit to the Bell Rock. They made a favourable landing; and Mr Rennie had only been a short time upon the rock, when he gave his decided opinion upon the practicability of the proposed erection of stone. He had examined the author's designs and models, and afterwards made a Report, in which he coincided with him in recommending to the Board the adoption of a building of stone, on the principles of the Eddystone Light-house. Sanctioned with such authority, the Commissioners were finally confirmed in the resolution, that the Bell Rock Light-house should be a tower of masonry similar to that of the Eddystone.

The Light-house Board takes the sense of the Mercantile Interest in this measure.

Hitherto the general opinion throughout the country, and especially at all the sea-ports, had been anxiously expressed for the erection of a light-house of some kind on the Bell Rock. But before going a second time to Parliament with this measure, the Commissioners thought it advisable to take the sense of the mercantile interest at the ports more immediately connected with the navigation of the Firth of Forth, such as Leith, Aberdeen, Dundee, Montrose, Arbroath, and Berwick-upon-Tweed, as to the utility of the light-house, and the propriety of obtaining an act of Parliament, to empower them to levy duties for the erection and maintenance of the proposed building. A number of Reports were accordingly received, all approving of the measure; but one of these only need be inserted, from the Corporation of Traders in Leith, as it may be considered as conveying the sentiments of all the others.

Report of the Traders of Leith.

Report of the Committee appointed by the Incorporation of the Traders in Leith, relative to the expediency of erecting a Light-house on the Cape or Bell Rock.

"The Committee, justly sensible of the great importance of the object referred to their consideration, have endeavoured to inform themselves, more especially on those points to which their attention is particularly called by the letter of the Commissioners.

"The result of these inquiries, as far as regards the number of vessels known, from the safety of the crews, to have been wrecked upon the Bell Rock, within these last ten years, amount to four, viz. two smacks trading between London and Banff, one brig from Holland, and a sloop from Hamburgh.

"These losses, although the vessels were all valuable, may at first view appear comparatively small, but to your Committee, they serve as a powerful evidence, in support of the opinion given by all maritime people, of the fatal position and nature of this rock, where, from the tremendous sea which even a moderate gale occasions, total destruction is almost the inevitable consequence of any vessel striking upon it.

"Situate off the openings of the two Friths of Tay and Forth, the Bell Rock stands a frightful bar, to deter vessels making the land from attempting it in the night-time, when they require most to seek its shelter; and, if unhappily overtaken with a gale at SE., when near the latitude of this rock, the alternative, dangerous as it must appear, of stretching to the northward, along a scarce less frightful coast, to gain the Murray Firth , is frequently, in such perilous cases, had recourse to.

"In the beginning of 1800, fifty or sixty vessels were cast away; and, from the circumstances of most of them being bound south of the Forth, but driven towards it by the violence of the storm, there can be no reason to doubt, that, had it been possible for these vessels to have attempted with safety the shelter of the Firth of Forth, many lives and much property would by this means have been preserved.

"The dread, however, of the Bell Rock, induced them on that occasion to prefer hauling to the northward, and encountering a sea and tide surpassed in few places of the globe. This fatal apprehension was followed by the disastrous consequences already mentioned.

"The Committee have, indeed, no hesitation in giving it as their opinion, that the greater part of the losses which occur, even from the Coquet Island, as far as the Murray Firth , arise from vessels either actually striking upon, or from an over-solicitude to keep at a distance from, this fatal rock. To the latter cause, there is great reason to believe, from many concurrent circumstances attending her loss, and from parts of her wreck being washed ashore near Buchanness, his Majesty's ship York, of 64 guns, fell a sacrifice, with all her crew. Indeed, if the number of vessels is calculated, which, within these last ten years, have been cast away within the above-mentioned extent of coast, they will be found to amount to more than one hundred.

"That the erection of a light-house upon the Bell Rock would obviate many of these dangers is sufficiently evident, and merchants, as well as seafaring men, trading to the east coast of Scotland, as well as to the north of England, are alike interested in the accomplishment of this desirable object.

"In a national point of view, the advantages that would result from it are incalculable; but none more forcible need be adduced, than that of its serving as the direct means of preservation to the invaluable lives of numerous British seamen.

"All these considerations induce your Committee to give this measure their full approbation; and that such a necessary object has not been sooner attained, must rather have proceeded from the supposed difficulty of the execution, than any hesitation as to the expediency of it.

"Your Committee, in reply to that part of the letter of the Commissioners, in which the Traffickers of Leith are required to signify, in the event of their concurrence in the measure, whether they will support the application of the Commissioners by petition to Parliament, have again to state, that giving, as they do, their full approbation to the expediency of erecting a light-house on the Bell Rock, they can have no hesitation in joining in any petition to Parliament to that effect. But the funds of this Incorporation being appropriated to specific purposes, no pecuniary aid can be afforded by them as a Society.

"To so great a national benefit as this will certainly prove, they will contribute, by willingly submitting to a tax on all shipping passing the Bell Rock, provided the duty so imposed does not exceed that laid on for any light in England, whose situation may bear resemblance to that to be erected upon the Bell Rock.

"The Trinity-House of Leith, to whom, the Committee is informed, the Commissioners have likewise applied, must be supposed better qualified to give detailed information upon the whole of this subject than your Committee; and the more especially, as one among their number has, for a period exceeding twenty years, made the dangers of the Bell Rock, and the means to be applied to avoid or lessen them, his peculiar study. Captain Joseph Brodie has, at great risk, and certainly at no little expence, and without any expectation of recompence, beyond that of having served his country, frequently visited the Bell Rock, and at one time succeeded in erecting a Beacon upon it, which withstood the fury of the sea for several months.

"The Committee, therefore, consider him well qualified to give the Commissioners information on the subject; and the various models of light-houses applicable to this rock, which, with much labour and ingenuity, he has invented, will be found highly valuable, whenever the execution of the business shall come to be taken into final consideration. — (Signed) James Searth, Master; Wm. Mowbray, Assist.; Wm. Dougal, Assist.; Arch. Geddes, James Pillans junior."

Report of the Merchants of Berwick.

The dangerous situation of the Bell Rock, and the losses which have either occurred upon, or in consequence of it, were also strongly expressed in all the other documents communicated to the Light-house Board; and we may further form a judgment of the extent of the serious consequences of this rock to the shipping on the coast, by what was stated in the communication from Berwick-upon-Tweed. It was therein mentioned, that two vessels had struck upon this rock in one night; and that other two, which had been built at Berwick, and sold to a Shipping Company at Banff, were afterwards lost upon the same reef. It also deserves notice, that Captain Allardice, who commanded one of those vessels, had the misfortune, in the course of his profession, to have been twice wrecked upon the Bell Rock.

Resolution of the Light-house Board to apply again to Parliament.

These statements, furnished upon unquestionable authority, of the losses occasioned by the Bell Rock, satisfied the Commissioners of the propriety of persisting in their original plan of obtaining an act of Parliament and a loan for this special purpose. After various meetings of the Board, for adjusting the heads of a bill, the measure was finally resolved upon at a meeting, held on the 19th February 1806, at which the following members were present: Mr James Clerk, Sheriff-Depute of Edinburghshire, Mr Robert Hamilton, Sheriff-Depute of Lanarkshire, Mr William Rae, Sheriff-Depute of Orkney and Shetland, Mr James Trail, Sheriff-depute of Caithness, Mr John Connell, Sheriff-Depute of Renfrewshire, Mr Edward M'Cormick, Sheriff-Depute of Ayrshire, and Mr David Monypenny, Sheriff-Depute of Fife.

This meeting having also taken into consideration a memorial, prepared by Mr Hamilton, pointing out the importance and urgency of the measure, ordered it to be printed; and requested him to proceed to London, to submit the memorial, and the documents on which it was founded, to the consideration of His Majesty's Ministers, and other Members of Parliament.

Mr Hamilton and the Author go to London.

Mr Hamilton went to London in the month of April 1806, when the author also attended, with his plans and estimates, to prove the preamble of the bill. Mr Hamilton having transmitted the memorial to the heads of the departments of the Treasury, the Admiralty, and the Board of Trade, requested an audience from them on the subject. He had a meeting with the Board of Trade, and urged the proposition for a loan, or advance from Government, of L. 25,000, on the security of the duties which the proposed light-house would produce. It was, however, recommended that application should also be made to the other two Boards. Some time thereafter, a conference on the matter was held with Lord Howick, then at the head of the Admiralty, and Admiral Markham,—when the plans of the projected building were shewn to them,—it was stated that all that was wanting to enable the work to be proceeded with, was the advance from Government,—and the importance of the proposed light-house was at this interview pointed out, not only as to trade, but as a guide and protection for the Navy while cruising in the German Ocean. But their Lordships still considered the undertaking chiefly as of a local nature, and comparatively of little benefit to the Navy. Not discouraged, however, by this unsuccessful application, Mr Hamilton soon after obtained an audience of Lord Grenville, First Commissioner of the Treasury, who examined the charts, plans, elevations and sections of the projected building with much attention,—declared himself fully convinced of the importance and expediency of the measure,—and promised that the loan by Government, and every other expedient for the advancement of the design, should have his support. The patronage of the First Minister of State having been thus obtained, Mr Hamilton returned to his public duties in Scotland, leaving the farther proceedings in the application to the charge of the writer, with the assistance of Mr Longlands, solicitor for the Light-house Board in London.

BILL BY LORD ADVOCATE ERSKINE.

The Loan from Government becomes doubtful.

The Hon. Henry Erskine, Lord Advocate of Scotland, took charge of the Bill in Parliament. But, notwithstanding his Lordship's attention to the business, so much time was lost in furnishing various statements, relative to the probable amount of the new duties to be levied, and the security to be given for repayment of the loan, that little progress was made with the bill, till the middle of the month of June. By this time, the prospect of the loan became so doubtful, that it was thought advisable by some friends to the measure to take the bill without it. But the Commissioners, after considering the tendency of such a bill, in tying up their funds for an indefinite period for one object, and thus preventing the extension of the benefit of additional light-houses to other parts of the coast, were of opinion, that, unless the loan was granted, they must withdraw their petition for the bill, and allow the business to lie over till the duties were in such a condition as to enable the work to be undertaken. The author was therefore directed to consider himself as at liberty to leave London, if it should appear that the loan could not be obtained.

Board of Trade favourable to the Loan.

Lord Auckland, President of the Board of Trade, was favourable to the proposal of the loan; and Sir Joseph Banks, the Vice-President, having entered warmly into the measure, and at a meeting of the 7th June, urged its necessity so strongly, that the Board desired a Memorial to be presented on the following points:—Of the coast to be subjected to the Duty of the Northern Lights, by the erection of the Bell Rock light-house;—of the trade and mercantile interest to pay this additional duty;—of the security to be given to Government for the repayment of the loan of L. 25,000;—and of the assurance to be given, that this sum, together with the surplus funds in the possession of the Commissioners, would accomplish a building of so much hazard.

The following Memorial was accordingly presented.

"To the Right Hon. the Lords of the Committee of Council, relating to Trade,— The Humble Memorial of the Commissioners, for erecting Light-Houses on the Northern parts of Great Britain;

Sheweth,

Memorial to the Board of Trade.

"That the memorialists have taken the liberty of stating, in a former Memorial hereunto annexed, the reasons that have induced them to apply to the Lords Commissioners of his Majesty's Treasury, for their support to an application to Parliament, for the loan of so much money as will enable them to build a light-house upon the Cape or Bell Rock,—an object of much consequence to the navigation of the North Sea, from the many fatal shipwrecks it has occasioned. The Memorialists have been much pressed and solicited by the commercial interest of the country, to get this accomplished; and by opening the Firth of Forth as a place of safety, by the erection of this light-house, the navigation of the northern coasts of the kingdom will be greatly facilitated.

"It now appears, by the accompanying Custom-House returns, on an average of three years, that the duties which would be received for a light-house on the Bell Rock would amount to L. 2617:3:9½; and by the accounts of the Commissioners of Northern Lights, annually laid before Parliament, it will be seen, that the memorialists have of annual surplus duties L. 1350, amounting together to L. 3967, which, it is thought, will be considered a sufficient security for the interest of the sum that may be advanced by the public.

"On erecting a light-house on the Bell Rock, the Commissioners, by the existing acts, would be empowered to levy the above duties of L. 2617, 3s. 9½d.; and it appears by the representations from the ports more immediately interested, that they highly approve of the measure.

"The memorialists have received several estimates of the expence of erecting a light-house upon the Bell Rock. They have more particularly had recourse to the professional abilities and advice of Mr Rennie and Mr Stevenson, Civil Engineers, from whose reports they have reason to believe that the sum will not exceed L. 48,000. The memorialists have already in the 3 per cent. consols L. 28,000 of surplus duties, (about L. 16,800). If the public, therefore, are induced to advance L. 25,000 by instalments in the course of three years, making together about L. 41,800, the memorialists presume, that, with the application of the whole surplus duties for a time, this sum will be perfectly sufficient to enable them to complete a work so long recommended, and so anxiously desired." (For the statements above referred to, see Appendix, No. III.)

Sir Joseph Banks makes further exertions for the Loan.

Observations by the several members of the Board of Trade having been made upon this memorial, it was more especially referred to Sir Joseph Banks, to give an opinion, as having himself sailed along that coast. Sir Joseph, knowing from experience the horrors of sunken rocks, supported the proposition of the loan, not only as one of expediency, but of necessity and humanity to the seafaring people of a great portion of the kingdom, and gave his most decided and hearty concurrence to the recommendation to the Treasury. After describing the extensive advantages to be derived by shipping from the establishment of a light-house upon the Bell Rock, he pointedly alluded to the probable loss of the York Man-of-war upon it; and observed, that the security and facility to be derived to the extensive shipping of this coast, should not be overlooked for the advance of so small a sum as L. 25,000. After the matter had been deliberated on for some time at the Board, Lord Auckland intimated to Mr Longlands, and the author, that a report would be made to the Treasury.

Bill Read a first time in the House of Commons.

This was communicated to the Lord Advocate, who, at an early day, moved for leave to bring in a bill, "To enable the Commissioners of the Northern Light-houses to levy certain duties upon the shipping, and also to enable the Lords of His Majesty's Treasury to grant a loan of L. 25,000 from the 3 per cent. consolidated fund for the erection of a light-house upon a certain dangerous sunken reef, called the Bell Rock, lying at the distance of twelve miles from the nearest land, at the entrance of the Friths of Forth and Tay, upon the eastern coast of Scotland." His Lordship had no sooner made the motion, than Lord Henry Petty, then Chancellor of the Exchequer, stated, that he could not answer for the support which this bill might ultimately meet with from his Majesty's Ministers;—that he spoke not from his own knowledge of the subject, but merely from the views of the First Lord of the Admiralty, who had expressed his doubts as to the propriety of the loan in the then low state of his Majesty's Exchequer, and the great demands which were made upon the country; but that he did not mean to oppose the present motion, only, under these circumstances, he thought it proper to state this much, in absence of the noble Lord alluded to. Leave having been given to bring in the bill, it was accordingly read a first time.

Second Reading of the Bill.

On the second reading of the bill, the Lord Advocate introduced the business with his usual display of eloquence, pointing out, in forcible language, the horrors of a sunken rock so situate as the Bell Rock; and concluded, by observing, that, as there could be but one opinion as to the important object of this bill, he hoped, through the exertions of the Light-house Board, to which he had the honour to belong, and of other public functionaries, appointed for similar purposes, on other parts of the coast, the day would come, when every sunken rock and dangerous shoal, of similar importance to navigation, would be distinctly pointed out to the mariner. The only reply made was by Mr Spencer Perceval, who remarked, that he had no intention to oppose the present measure, the importance of which he would not call in question, but he must agree with those who thought that this was not a favourable time for granting loans of public money. The bill was then read a second time. In its progress through the House of Commons, it was detained, from various causes, beyond the regular time. The Lord Advocate had also unfortunately been taken ill; but in his absence, Sir John Sinclair attended to the bill in the Committee, of which he was chairman, and brought up the following Report:

REPORT OF THE COMMITTEE OF THE HOUSE OF COMMONS.

Report of the Committee.

Report brought up by Sir John Sinclair.

"The Committee, to whom was referred the Petition of the Commissioners of the Northern Light-houses, and to report the matter to the House, as it shall appear to them,

"Proceeded to examine Mr Robert Stevenson, Civil Engineer, who, in his capacity of engineer for the Northern Light-houses, has erected six light-houses in the northern parts of the kingdom; and has made the erection of a light-house on the Cape or Bell Rock, more particularly his study,—especially, since the loss of about 70 sail of vessels, in a storm which happened upon the coast in the month of December 1799, by which numerous ships were driven from their course along the shore, and from their moorings in Yarmouth Roads, and other places of anchorage, southward of the Firth of Forth, and wrecked upon the eastern coast of Scotland, as referred to in the report made to this House, in the month of July 1803; the particulars of which he also confirms: That the Bell Rock is most dangerously situate, lying in a track which is annually navigated by no less than about 700,000 tons of shipping, besides his Majesty's ships of war, and revenue cutters: That its place is not easily ascertained, even by persons well acquainted with the coast, being covered by the sea about half flood, and the land-marks, by which its position is ascertained, being from 12 to 20 miles distant from the site of danger.

"That from the inquiries he made at the time the York Man-of-war was lost, and pieces of her wreck having drifted ashore upon the opposite and neighbouring coast; and from an attentive consideration of the circumstances which attend the wreck of ships of such dimensions, he thinks it probable that the York must have struck upon the Bell Rock, drifted off, and afterwards sunk in deep water: That he is well acquainted with the situation of the Bell Rock, the yacht belonging to the light-house service, having, on one occasion, been anchored near it for five days, when he had an opportunity of landing upon it every tide: That he has visited most of the light-houses on the coast of England, Wales and Ireland, particularly those of the Eddystone, the Smalls, and the Kilwarlin or South Rock, which are built in situations somewhat similar to the Bell Rock: That at high-water, there is a greater depth on the Bell Rock than on any of these, by several feet: and he is therefore fully of opinion, that a building of stone, upon the principles of the Eddystone light-house, is alone suitable to the peculiar circumstances which attend this rock, and has reported his opinion accordingly to the Commissioners of the Northern Light-houses as far back as the year 1800; and having given the subject all the attention in his power, he has estimated the expence of erecting a building of stone upon it at the sum of L. 42,685, 8s.

"Your Committee likewise examined Mr John Rennie, civil-engineer, who, since the report made to this House in 1803, has visited the Bell Rock, who confirms the particulars in said report, and entertains no doubt of the practicability of erecting a light-house on that rock, is decidedly of opinion that a stone light-house will be the most durable and effectual, and indeed the only kind of building that is suited to this situation: That he has computed the expence of such a building, and, after making every allowance for contingencies, from his own experience of works in the sea, it appears to him that the estimate or expence will amount to L. 41,843, 15s.

"It appears further to your Committee, from the accounts presented to this House by the Commissioners of the Northern Light-houses, in the years 1803, 1804, and 1805, that, on an average of these years, the surplus duties arising from the light-houses already erected by that Board, is L. 512:18:8. But your Committee find, that the average of general expenditure for these years has been higher than usual, owing to the erection of additional light-houses, viz. one on the Island of Inchkeith, in the Firth of Forth, and a revolving light upon the Start-Point of Sanday, one of the Orkney Islands, on which there was expended, during these years, about L. 4800, causing an annual extra charge of L. 1600 upon the duties collected in that period.

"That, agreeably to the act of the 26th of the King, the said Commissioners of the Northern Light-houses have invested in the public Funds L. 28,000, affording dividends to the annual amount of L. 840.

"That the duties that would be collected for the Bell Rock light, as appears by the returns from the customs presented to this House, and the resolution they have come to, would amount to about L. 2617: 3: 9 annually.

"That if the sum of L. 25,000 was to be advanced, by way of loan, from the consolidated fund, this, with the L. 28,000 now invested in the 3 per cent. Consolidated Annuities, would enable the Commissioners to erect the proposed light-house, and that there would remain a sufficient fund for the payment of interest of the loan from the surplus duties, as well as for the repayment of the principal, in a reasonable time."

Bill meets with some opposition at the third reading.

The bill passed through the Committee of the Commons without any impediment, but, on the third reading, it met with some opposition in the House, upon new and unexpected grounds. One of the members for Liverpool opposed the loan, on the ground that that Port maintained its own sea-lights, and that the trade of the Firth of Forth ought also to support its lights. But this objection was withdrawn, upon explaining the position of the Bell Rock relatively to the Firth of Forth, and the difficulty and expence of the proposed building, and shewing that the collection of its Light-duties were proportionally as much confined to the Firth of Forth, though extending between Berwick to the south, and Peterhead to the north, as the more limited sphere of the Liverpool lights were to the ports and havens in the Mersey. This difficulty was no sooner got over, than the bill was likely to have met with another check, from a clause which had been introduced, exempting this work from the duty on stone carried coastwise, which, it was calculated, would have amounted to between L. 2000 and L. 3000. This clause was withdrawn, by the advice of Mr Vansittart, Secretary to the Treasury, as being improper to appear in the shape of an enactment.

Is Passed, and receives the Royal Assent.

The bill then went through the third reading, and passed the House Commons on the 16th of July. It was afterwards brought up to the House of Lords, where it went through the Committee, and the several readings; and having received the Royal Assent, became an act of the Legislature.

The writer immediately returned to Scotland, with feelings of the greatest satisfaction, on the accomplishment of a measure which, in its tendency, was so eminently calculated to meet the wishes of the mercantile interest of the country. But, along with these sensations, there was also a degree of responsibility, and a crowd of difficulties, which still presented themselves, in the execution of a work of so peculiar a nature. Hitherto this undertaking had been viewed only at a distance, clogged with many previous obstacles, which, by the passing of the bill, were removed; and the whole measure now pressed fully upon his mind.

CHAPTER III.

PHAROS FLOATING LIGHT-SHIP.—COMMENCEMENT
OF THE OPERATIONS ON THE BELL-ROCK.—EREC-
TION OF THE BEACON-HOUSE, AND FURTHER PRO-
GRESS OF THE LIGHT-HOUSE WORKS IN 1807.

Floating-Light.

The Act of Parliament, by which the Commissioners of the Northern Light-hous-es were empowered to undertake the works at the Bell Rock, having only received the Royal Assent late in the month of July 1806, there was not sufficient time for making the necessary preparations for their commencement that season. But the writer, on his return from London, received instructions from the Board to have such preliminary steps in view, as would enable him to begin the operations early in the summer of 1807. This being arranged, he sailed in the month of August, on his annual voyage, for the inspection of the Northern Light-houses.

Act provides for a Floating-Light and Beacon.

The bill for the Bell Rock Light-house was drawn up, under a strong impres-sion of the uncertainty which must attend the whole of the works at the rock, and doubts were accordingly entertained as to the estimated expence being adequate to the accomplishment of the undertaking. A clause had, therefore, been intro-duced, authorising the collection of the light-house duties of one penny halfpenny per register ton from British vessels, and threepence per ton from foreigners, "im-mediately upon mooring or anchoring a ship or vessel, and exhibiting a floating or other light, at or near the Bell Rock," and "half the amount of the said duties respectively," on the erection of "a proper beacon or distinguishing mark or object on the said Bell Rock." The measures first in order were, consequently, to fit out and moor a floating-light and to erect a beacon on the Bell Rock, that shipping might derive immediate advantage from them, while the light-house was in prog-ress; and also that the funds of the Board might, as early as possible, have the benefit of the additional duties. We therefore proceed to give an account of the outfit and mooring of this vessel, and of the erection of the beacon-house, without attending strictly to the chronological order of the works.

The writer had frequent communications with the late Captain Huddart, of the Trinity-House of London, and other nautical men, both as to the form of a vessel, and the moorings proper for a situation like the Bell Rock: here the depth of water could not be less than from seventeen to nineteen fathoms at the lowest tide, whereas, on the English coast, the depth where floating lights are, in general, moored, does not exceed seven or eight fathoms, and their moorings, consequently, much more easily managed. The writer had also visited the floating light of the Nore, at the entrance of the river Thames; and he was induced, upon the whole, to conclude, that a vessel built after the manner and construction of the Dutch fishing-doggers, would be the most suitable for riding at anchor in the open sea, and that her moorings should consist partly of an iron chain, and partly of a hempen cable.

PHAROS FLOATING LIGHT-SHIP.

Fishing Dogger purchased, and named The Pharos.

In the year 1806, a great number of vessels were taken by our cruizers, upon the coasts of Holland, Denmark, and Norway, many of which were carried into Leith to be sold. One of these, a Prussian, which happened to be captured while fishing on the Dogger Bank, was purchased for the Bell Rock service. This vessel was of a flat construction, rounded off both at the stem and stern, agreeably to the ordinary make of these doggers. She was called the Tonge Gerrit, but was afterwards named the Pharos, in allusion to the celebrated Pharos of Alexandria. She measured 67 feet in length, and 16 feet in breadth, upon deck, 8 feet depth of hold, and was 82 tons register. It was, however, only the form of her hull that fitted her for our purpose; her rigging and whole equipment having to undergo a complete alteration, for the light-house service.

Fitted out under the direction of the Trinity-House, Leith.

The establishing of a floating-light being quite new upon the coast of Scotland, and that every thing connected with this vessel might be done upon the best principles, the writer procured the assistance of Mr Joseph Webb, an experienced pilot of Yarmouth, who had attended the fitting up of one of the floating lights stationed off that coast, and who had been recommended by the Trinity Board of London as a person of skill, for instructing the master of the vessel in all the details of the service. Several of the Captains of the Trinity-House of Leith also obligingly formed themselves into a committee, and from time to time assisted in giving directions as to the necessary repairs and outfit of the vessel.

Agreeably to this arrangement, the Prussian dogger was put into one of the graving docks of Leith, in the month of March 1807, and underwent a complete examination, when it was found that she required a few new timbers in her bottom; and that to strengthen her upper works, several new beams and additional knees were necessary. Her bottom had to be new trenailed and caulked, and then sheathed with fir plank. Her ceiling, or interior lining, was also caulked, and made water-tight, in case of accident to the outer plank, in the event of her breaking adrift, and getting upon the Bell Rock. Her deck-plank and upper works were also entirely renewed; and from stem to stern, under deck, her accommodations were laid out anew. She was furnished with three masts, of a length calculated to enable her to ride with as little incumbrance as possible in a storm; the main-mast being only thirty-five feet above the deck, while the fore and mizen masts were each twenty-five feet. The rigging was also made of light cordage, and she was provided with storm-sails, to be used in the event of her breaking adrift in bad weather.

By the time, therefore, that this vessel came from the hands of the carpenters, very little of the old work remained, as nothing had been omitted, which could, in any manner, add to her strength and durability. She was fitted up with births for about thirty artificers, besides her ordinary crew and officers, amounting to thirteen in number, independently of her hold for oil and stores of various descriptions. In the distribution of these, the fore-peak of the ship was allotted for the sailors; the waist for the artificers; and galley appropriated to the cooking of the victuals. Next to this, a large cabin was set off for the master, mate, and principal light-keeper, and for the foremen of the works; while the after or stern part of the ship formed a cabin for the use of the engineer.

Peculiar construction of Lanterns.

The Pharos was furnished with a large copper lantern for each mast, containing ten lamps, with small silver-plated reflectors, ranged upon a chandelier, moveable at pleasure, in a horizontal direction, for the conveniency of turning the lamps to trim them and clean the reflectors. To make the vessel ride as easily as possible, in a situation so exposed, the lanterns were made of a peculiar construction, so as to screw together upon the masts, in two pieces, longitudinally, as represented in Plate X., Figs. 1, 2, and 3. By these means, the light could be seen in every direction, without the necessity of suspending them in the usual manner from yards, or other weighty apparatus, which tend not only to obscure the light, but also to make the ship ride heavily in bad weather.

Construction of Moorings.

The moorings of the floating light consisted of a large mushroom anchor, of cast-iron, weighing about a ton and a half, and made with a shank and head, resembling in form, as nearly as may be, the vegetable from which it takes its name. This anchor was made with a malleable iron shank, but latterly these mushroom anchors were made wholly of cast-iron, as represented in Plate X., Fig. 4. A chain of fifty fathoms in length, was attached to the anchor, made of inch and half bars of iron, to which a hempen cable, of 14 inches in circumference, and 120 fathoms in length, was connected, to be veered out according to the state of the weather.

Pharos is towed to the Roads.

The Pharos being ready for sea, was, on the 9th of July, towed out of the harbour of Leith to the Roads, by the Light-house Yacht, a cutter-rigged vessel attached to the general service of the Northern Light-houses. The Yacht had the Pharos' moorings on board, and was appointed to conduct her to the Bell Rock, and lay them down. A curious enough circumstance took place, when the crew of the floating-light was mustered, before leaving the harbour: two of the seamen having taken alarm, at the destination of the ship, and the nature of the service in which they were about to embark, suddenly turned about, and, to the great surprise of their comrades, ran with the utmost precipitation from the ship; to which they never again returned. Their places, however, were supplied with others, without much inconvenience.

COMMITTEE OF THE TRINITY-HOUSE GO TO THE BELL ROCK.

As the gentlemen of the Trinity-house of Leith, had all along taken a particular interest in the fitting out of the floating-light, the Commissioners requested their assistance in fixing upon the precise spot in which she should be moored, for the direction of ships passing the Bell Rock. This they readily complied with, suggesting, at the same time, that some of the shipmasters of Arbroath, who were locally acquainted with the coast, should also be invited to give their opinion and advice upon this point. A few of the most experienced ship-masters and merchants of Arbroath were accordingly invited to come off, when the floating light should make her appearance in their neighbourhood. Matters being thus arranged, the writer went on board of the Light-house Yacht, on the 10th, accompanied by Mr Thomas Grindlay, master of the Trinity-house of Leith, with Mr John Hay, and Mr Thomas Ritchie, Assistant-Masters.

Pharos sails for the Bell Rock.

At 8 A. M. the Pharos got under way in Leith Roads, and sailed for her station at the Bell Rock, under the command of Mr George Sinclair, with a crew of twelve in number. But as she sailed very heavily, the Yacht, with her party, did not follow till noon, and about 2 P. M. came up with her, and took her in tow, when it came to blow fresh breezes from SW. At 6, both vessels anchored for the night on the eastern side of the Isle of May, as, by continuing our course, we should have reached the Bell Rock under night, which was then an object of terror to every seaman, and must have been attended with danger, from its then undistinguished state.

Committee from Arbroath join the party.

While the Yacht and Pharos lay at anchor at the Isle of May, Mr David Balfour, Mr Andrew Duncan, Mr David Cargill, Mr John Fleming, and Mr William Kidd, as a Committee from Arbroath, having hired a vessel, left that place in the morning, and hailed the Yacht, soon after she came to an anchor, when some of their party joined us on board. As the accommodations of the floating light were very ample, having only the ship's company on board, it was proposed that the whole party should meet in her, and pass the night; but she rolled from side to side, in so extraordinary a manner, that even the most sea-hardy of our number were content to remain in a state of separation, rather than accept of the best birth in the floating light. It was humorously observed of this vessel, "that she was in some danger of making a round turn, and appearing with her keel uppermost." Another said, "she would roll out her masts;" and a third that she would "even turn a halfpenny, if laid upon deck." These, and such like remarks, afforded much pleasantry on board of the Light-house Yacht, and were suggested by the manner in which the Pharos rolled and yawed about, when compared with the more easy motion of the other vessels. Being then in light ballast trim to fit her for riding in bad weather, and very flat in the bottom, the smallest wave set her in motion, when at anchor; and when under way, she was little better, for she answered the helm with so much difficulty, that a large decked Praam-boat, which she had in tow, was upset in the passage from Leith. The writer is the more particular on this subject, as the rolling motion of the floating-light became proverbial in the Light-house service, and continued a source of much trouble and uneasiness to all concerned, especially while she was used as a tender or store-ship for the works.

Pharos anchors in a temporary birth.

Early in the morning of the 11th, the vessels left their anchorage at the Isle of May, and sailed for the Bell Rock; but on reaching it, in the course of the forenoon, the wind came to the eastward, accompanied with thick hazy weather, and drizzling showers of rain, which so completely hid the distant landmarks from view, that there was a necessity for ordering the Pharos to come to an anchor with her best bower, on the smoothest spot of ground that could be found, until a change of weather should admit of her being moored in a proper manner. The weather afterwards became so foggy that every object was lost sight of. The vessel which had brought our friends from Arbroath, put into that harbour in the course of the evening, but the Light-house Yacht kept at sea till the morning of the 12th, when it came to blow so fresh, that she also went into that harbour, to wait a change of weather. On the 14th, it improved, and the Yacht again sailed for the Bell Rock. On returning to the floating light, we were happy to find that all was well on board, though Mr Sinclair and Mr Webb, the pilot, complained that their anchorage was not very good, as the bottom was hard, and the soundings or particles brought up with the lead exhibited sharp coral and coarse gravel. After plying about for some time with the Yacht, and sounding in every direction, a place was at length fixed upon, about a mile and a half in a north-westerly direction from the Bell Rock. The Yacht, as before noticed, having on board the floating-light's moorings, anchored on the spot most approved of for laying them down.

In laying down her Moorings, the whole chain goes overboard.

Some arrangements having been made among the nautical gentlemen, as to the precise mode of going about this operation, it was resolved to suspend the mushroom anchor over the gunwale of the Yacht, and before letting it into the water, to bring the greater part of the chain upon deck, taking the precaution to make the further end of it fast to the lower part of the mast, in the vessel's hold, with a very strong and perfectly new stopper, or piece of rope, measuring 7 inches in circumference. It was not doubted but that this strong rope would have held the chain against any strain that might have been brought upon it, in the process of letting down the moorings. But the mushroom-anchor was no sooner let go from the ship's tackle, than the part of the chain which had been coiled upon deck went overboard with such velocity, that it communicated a similar impetus to the remainder of the chain in the hold, and the strain coming ultimately upon the stopper, snapped through the several parts which fixed the end of the chain to the mast, and, consequently, the whole went to the bottom with the mushroom-anchor.

Moorings recovered with great difficulty.

This untoward circumstance greatly disconcerted and embarrassed the operations of mooring the floating-light, as the chain had now to be fished or hooked at the bottom, and raised from the depth of seventeen fathoms. After many trials, we at length succeeded in hooking it with a grappling-iron, but as it happened to lay hold only a few fathoms from the anchor, it required all the purchase-blocks and tackle of the Yacht and Pharos to raise it: for the weight, including the anchor, and so large a portion of the chain, could not be less than about three tons. This operation was begun at mid-day, and, although the united force of the crews of both ships was fully mustered, it was not till two o'clock on the following morning,—being a period of fourteen hours,—that the moorings were got up, and the Pharos brought alongside of the Yacht, to receive the hempen cable, which was made fast to the clinch, or great ring, connected with the chain moorings. The weather was fortunately the most favourable that could have been desired for this operation; and it is impossible for the writer to describe the anxiety and exertions of all on board in getting this matter adjusted. Were he to judge by his own feelings, he has no doubt that all on board would join in saying, that it was one of the most painfully laborious days they had spent in the course of their existence. For the space of about twenty hours, the crews of both ships had never been off deck, and during twelve of these the hand-spike, or the tackle, had not been five minutes together out of their hands, as the refreshments which they got were served up at the windlass. The same observations are literally applicable to the gentlemen of the quarter-deck, who divided their attention severally to the different tackles and purchases employed in raising the moorings.

The perplexing and tedious business of mooring the floating-light having been happily got over, it was judged necessary to see how she would ride at anchor for a time, before advertising the light to the public. The writer accordingly returned on board in the course of three weeks, and examined the moorings, which were found in good order. The anchorage ground was also considered of a very proper description, in so far as observations, made during a tract of favourable weather, had afforded the means of judging. The vessel lay in an excellent position for the direction of shipping; and being at this time only about a mile from the Bell Rock, her situation as a hulk or store-ship for the light-house operations, was as favourable as the relative position of the rock would admit. In this state of things, notice to the following effect was given in the newspapers, for the direction of mariners, and along with a copy of the notice, a chart or sketch of the opposite coast was sent to the different Custom-houses.

Description of the Floating-Light.

"In virtue of an Act of Parliament of the 46th year of Geo. III. chap. 132. authorising the Commissioners of the Northern Light-houses to erect a Light-house on the Bell Rock, to place a floating light there, and to collect duties thereupon,—notice is hereby given, that a vessel, fitted out for a floating-light, is now moored off the Cape or Bell Rock, situate at the entrance of the Friths of Forth and Tay, in North Lat. 56° 27', and West Long. 2° 27'.

"The moorings of the floating-light consist of a mushroom anchor, and chain, laid down in 17 fathoms water, the Bell Rock bearing, by compass, E. S. E. distant one mile; the Red Head, N. by E. ¼ E. distant thirteen miles; Fifeness, S. W. ¾ W. distant twelve miles; and the island of May S. W. ¾ S. distant seventeen miles.

"A light from oil, with reflectors, will be exhibited upon the night of the 15th day of September 1807, and thereafter every night, from the going away of day-light in the evening, till the return of day-light in the morning. To distinguish this light from the double lights at the entrance of the Firth of Tay, and on the Scares off the coast of Northumberland, and also from the single light on the Island of May, three distinct lights will be shown from the Bell Rock Floating-light, by a lantern hoisted to the top of each mast, which will be visible from every point of the compass, at the distance of from two to three leagues; the lanterns on the fore and mizen masts being elevated 23 feet, and that on the main mast 31 feet, above the vessel's deck; the lights, when seen from either side of the ship, have the appearance of a triangle, but if seen end-on, they appear as two lights, the one above the other.

"This vessel is called the Pharos; she was formerly a fishing dogger, and appears like a ship under jury masts; during the day-time, a blue flag, with a light-house in the field, will be displayed from the main-mast; and, in thick and foggy weather, a bell will be tolled, night and day, on board, with an interval of about one minute.

"Although this vessel has been fitted out in the completest manner, and every attention paid to mooring her properly, yet, as all floating-lights are liable to break adrift in tempestuous weather, mariners are requested not to neglect their land-marks, and to run with caution for the floating-light.

"The Pharos being also intended to answer the purpose of a store-ship, while the light-house is building on the Bell Rock, it may be found necessary, in the course of the works, to alter her present station, of which due notice will be given."

Commencement of the Operations on the Bell Rock.

1807, August.

As the commencement of works of masonry, requiring stones of large dimensions, is unavoidably tedious, especially in the collecting of materials, we shall at present only notice, that the Light-house Board having resolved on the use partly of granite and partly of sandstone, for the erection at the Bell Rock, measures were duly taken for procuring a supply of the former from the quarry of Rubeslaw near Aberdeen, and of the latter from Mylnefield near Dundee. But, instead of following out this part of our subject in its order, we shall first proceed to a detail of the operations afloat, as they may be termed, or of the works upon the rock itself, during the season of 1807,—particularly of the erection of the principal beams of the beacon-house, or temporary residence for the artificers on the rock, and of the progress made in the preparation of the foundation or site of the main building.

Sloop Smeaton.

We therefore observe, that a vessel had been built at Leith, in the course of the spring, expressly for the Bell Rock service, to be employed as a tender for the floating-light, and as a stone-lighter for the use of the work. This vessel was launched in the month of June; she measured 40 tons register, was rigged as a sloop, and fitted in all respects in the strongest manner, to adapt her as much as possible for the perilous service in which she was to be employed. She was called The Smeaton,—a name which the writer had great pleasure in suggesting, as a mark of respect for the memory of the celebrated engineer of the Eddystone Light-house, whose narrative was to become a kind of text-book for the Bell Rock operations. The Smeaton was ready for sea in the beginning of August, and reached Arbroath upon the 5th day of that month. Arbroath being the most contiguous harbour to the Bell Rock, naturally pointed out itself as the proper place for establishing the works, and preparing the materials, before shipping them for the rock. The writer had, accordingly, been here for some time, making the necessary preparations; and when the Smeaton arrived, he found himself in a condition for commencing the operations, in a systematic manner, upon the rock itself.

The Positions of the Light-House and Beacon fixed on.

The floating-light rode in safety at her moorings, and had hitherto been supplied with necessaries by the Yacht belonging to the general service of the Light-house Board. In this vessel, occasional trips had also been made to the rock; but on the arrival of the Smeaton, the Yacht sailed on a voyage, with stores for the use of the Northern Light-houses. In these preliminary trips, the writer had fixed, in his own mind, upon the parts of the rock most favourable for the position of the light-house, and on the south-west of it, he chose the site of the beacon-house, that it might be sheltered, in some measure, from the breach of the north-east sea; and by placing them contiguous, or about twenty-five feet apart, they admitted of a ready communication with each other in the more advanced stages of the work.

1807, 7th August.

First trip of the Artificers to the Bell Rock.

The Smeaton having got on board necessaries for the floating-light, and three sets of chain-moorings with mushroom-anchors, and large floating buoys, the writer sailed on another preliminary visit to the Bell Rock on the 7th day of August, carrying with him Mr Peter Logan, foreman builder, and five artificers, selected, on this occasion, from their having been somewhat accustomed to the sea; the writer being aware of the distressing trial which the floating-light would necessarily inflict upon landsmen, from her rolling motion. Here he remained till the 10th, and as the weather was favourable, a landing was effected daily, when the workmen were employed in cutting the large sea-weed from the sites of the light-house and beacon, which were respectively traced with pick-axes upon the rock. In the mean time, the crew of the Smeaton was employed in laying down the several sets of moorings within about half a mile of the rock, for the conveniency of vessels riding at the buoys by a hawser, instead of letting go an anchor, which, in that situation, could seldom have been purchased or lifted again, as it would constantly have hooked the rocky bottom, a disadvantage to which the mushroom anchor, from its figure and construction, is not liable, as will be understood by examining the diagram representing it in Plate X. Fig. 4. The artificers having fortunately experienced moderate weather, returned to the work-yard at Arbroath, with a good report of their treatment afloat; when their comrades ashore began to feel some anxiety to see a place of which they had heard so much, and to change the constant operation with the iron and mallet in the process of hewing, for an occasional tide's work on the rock, which they figured to themselves as a state of comparative ease and comfort.

Rate of Artificers' wages fixed on.

In answer to some advances which had been made on this subject by the artificers, the foreman was instructed to select fourteen of the stone-cutters, who had been accustomed to the use of the pick-axe, and to boring or drilling holes with a jumper, after the manner of quarriers, to go off to the rock in the course of a few days. When these men, however, came to be spoken to more closely, some of them were disposed to hold their services rather at a high rate, demanding two guineas per week if they were to find their own provisions, and L. 1, 10s. if provisions were found to them. But they were informed, that the nominal rate of wages was to be L. 1 per week, being the same for those employed at the rock, as for those in the work-yard at Arbroath. The artificers at the rock were, in addition, to have their provisions, with certain premiums, to be arranged in the further progress of the work, particularly for each tide's work on Sunday, which was to be accounted and paid for as a day's work. After a good deal of trouble, two or three of the men acceded to the foreman's proposals, others refused to engage themselves, excepting at the highest rate; while a third party objected only to working on Sunday. In any agreement to be entered into, it was held as an express condition, "That every man who embarked for the work at the Bell Rock, should remain for the space of four weeks, without returning ashore." Those chiefly wanted at this time were masons from Aberdeen, who were accustomed to the use of the boring-iron and pick, in working granite. Being engaged only from week to week in the work-yard, they were desirous of knowing the reason for remaining a month at the rock; when they were informed that it was not unlikely some of them might suffer from sea sickness, and wearying of confinement on board of ship, might wish to return ashore, which would be attended with much inconveniency to the work, by too frequent a change of hands. They were further told, that, by continuing for one month afloat, they would, in the course of that time, become so sea-hardy as probably to feel no desire to return till the end of the working-season, which, at this advanced period, could not last for many weeks. This condition was considered of importance in the commencement of the work, and it was the more readily agreed to, as the writer assured them that he should himself remain with them during that period. As one condition, however, had been made to the Aberdeen masons, they felt no hesitation in proposing another on their own part, and they accordingly handed the following offer of service, addressed to the foreman, dated 12th August 1807, which, from the tenor of the document, we shall here insert.

Letter from the Aberdeen Masons.

"In consequence of our communing with one another concerning the Bell Rock, we hereby agree to stay with you from the above date, till August 1808, being twelve months certain, and to take our turn at whatever work may start up concerning the Bell Rock business,—only, it is to be understood, that the rest of the masons must take turn and turn about with us: the terms of our agreement to be 20s. per week, summer and winter, wet and dry, with free quarters ashore, and likewise our victuals when we are at the rock.—As for the Sunday's work and premiums, we leave that to the honour of our employers. (Signed) William Bonyman, John Bruce, John Cruickshanks, Alexander Sherif, John Bonyman, Alexander

Davidson, James Macdonald, Robert Ferres, John Mason, William Chalmers."

Every thing being arranged for sailing to the rock on Saturday the 15th, the vessel might have proceeded on the Sunday; but understanding that this would not be so agreeable to the artificers it was deferred until Monday. Here we cannot help observing, that the men allotted for the operations at the rock seemed to enter upon the undertaking with a degree of consideration, which fully marked their opinion as to the hazardous nature of the undertaking on which they were about to enter. They went in a body to church on Sunday, and whether it was in the ordinary course, or designed for the occasion, the writer is not certain, but the service was, in many respects, suitable to their circumstances. Indeed, the Reverend Mr Gleg, the minister of the parish, was in the constant habit of enquiring after the success and safety of the works. Throughout this day the weather was remarkably serene, and the best hopes were entertained of a favourable tract of weather, which the inhabitants of Arbroath were disposed to consider as an omen of good fortune.

Monday, 17th.

Twenty-four Artificers embark for the Rock.

The tide happening to fall late in the evening of Monday the 17th, the party, counting twenty-four in number, embarked on board of the Smeaton about 10 o'clock P. M., and sailed from Arbroath with a gentle breeze at west. Our ship's colours having been flying all day in compliment to the commencement of the work, the other vessels in the harbour also saluted, which made a very gay appearance. A number of the friends and acquaintances of those on board having been thus collected, the piers, though at a late hour, were perfectly crowded, and just as the Smeaton cleared the harbour, all on board united in giving three hearty cheers, which were returned by those on shore in such good earnest, that, in the still of the evening, the sound must have been heard in all parts of the town, re-echoing from the walls and lofty turrets of the venerable Abbey of Aberbrothwick. The writer felt much satisfaction at the manner of this parting scene; though he must own, that the present rejoicing was, on his part, mingled with occasional reflections upon the responsibility of his situation, which extended to the safety of all who should be engaged in this perilous work. With such sensations he retired to his cabin; but as the artificers were rather inclined to move about the deck than to remain in their confined births below, his repose was transient, and the vessel being small, every motion was necessarily heard. Some who were musically inclined occasionally sung; but he listened with peculiar pleasure to the sailor at the helm, who hummed over Dibdin's characteristic air,

> "They say there's a Providence sits up aloft,
> To keep watch for the life of Poor Jack."

ERECTION OF THE BEACON-HOUSE.

The weather had been very gentle all night, and, about four in the morning of the 18th, the Smeaton anchored on the spot where it was intended to lay down an additional set of chain-moorings which she had on board. Agreeably to an arranged plan of operations, all hands were called at 5 o'clock, A. M., just as the highest part of the Bell Rock began to shew its sable head among the light breakers, which occasionally whitened with the foaming sea. The two boats belonging to the floating-light attended the Smeaton, to carry the artificers to the rock, as her boat could only accommodate about six or eight sitters. Every one was more eager than his neighbour to leap into the boats, and it required a good deal of management on the part of the coxswains, to get men unaccustomed to a boat, to take their places for rowing and at the same time trimming her properly. The landing-master and foreman went into one boat, while the writer took charge of another, and steered it to and from the rock. This became the more necessary in the early stages of the work, as places could not be spared for more than two, or at most three seamen to each boat, who were always stationed, one at the bow, to use the boat-hook in fending or pushing off, and the other at the aftermost oar, to give the proper time in rowing, while the middle oars were double banked, and rowed by the artificers.

Tuesday, 18th.

Commence work at 6 A. M.

As the weather was extremely fine, with light airs of wind from the east, we landed without difficulty upon the central part of the rock at half-past 5, but the water had not yet sufficiently left it for commencing the work. This interval, however, did not pass unoccupied; the first and last of all the principal operations at the Bell Rock were accompanied by three hearty cheers from all hands, and, on occasions like the present, the steward of the ship attended, when each man was regaled with a glass of rum. As the water left the rock about 6, some began to bore the holes for the great bats or holdfasts, for fixing the beams of the Beacon-house, while the smith was fully attended in laying out the site of his forge, upon a somewhat sheltered spot of the rock, which also recommended itself from the vicinity of a pool of water for tempering his irons. These preliminary steps occupied about an hour, and as nothing further could be done during this tide towards fixing the forge, the workmen gratified their curiosity, by roaming about the rock, which they investigated with great eagerness till the tide overflowed it. Those who had been sick picked dulse (Fucus palmatus), which they ate with much seeming appetite; others were more intent upon collecting limpets for bait, to enjoy the amusement of fishing when they returned on board of the vessel. Indeed none came away empty handed, as every thing found upon the Bell Rock was considered valuable, being connected with some interesting association. Several coins, and numerous bits of shipwrecked iron were picked up, of almost every description; and, in particular, a marking-iron lettered James, — a circumstance of which it was thought proper to give notice to the public, as it might lead to the knowledge of some unfortunate shipwreck, perhaps unheard of till this simple occurrence led to the discovery. When the rock began to be overflowed, the landing-master arranged the crews of the respective boats, appointing twelve persons to each. According to a rule, which the writer had laid down to himself, he was always the last person who left the rock. Another maxim was, to allow the landing-master's boat to proceed about twice or three times her own length a-head of the other boats, that in case of accident he might be ready to assist; and when he had thus cleared the rock, he waited till the others got out of the respective creeks; after which they proceeded in company. Upon the present occasion, the boats reached the tender about half-past 8, after having been two hours upon the rock, and three hours absent from the ship.

In a short time, the Bell Rock was laid completely under water, and the weather being extremely fine, the sea was so smooth, that its place could not be pointed out from the appearance of the surface,—a circumstance which sufficiently demonstrates the dangerous nature of this rock, even during the day, and in the smoothest and calmest state of the sea. During the interval between the morning and the evening tides, the artificers were variously employed in fishing and reading, others were busy in drying and adjusting their wet clothes, and one or two amused their companions with the violin and German-flute.

Method of fixing iron-bats into the Rock.

About 7 in the evening the signal bell for landing on the rock was again rung, when every man was at his quarters. In this service it was thought more appropriate to use the bell than to pipe to quarters, as the use of this instrument is less known to the mechanic than the sound of the bell. The landing, as in the morning, was at the eastern harbour. During this tide, the sea-weed was pretty well cleared from the site of the operations, and also from the tracks leading to the different landing-places; for walking upon the rugged surface of the Bell Rock, when covered with sea-weed, was found to be extremely difficult, and even dangerous. Every hand that could possibly be occupied, was now employed in assisting the smith to fit up the apparatus for his forge. The frame-work of iron, forming the hearth, was now got into its place; and the four legs which supported it were let into holes, bored from six to twelve inches into the rock, according to the inequalities of the site: and then firmly wedged, first with wood, and then with iron, a method followed in all the operations of batting at the Bell Rock, and found greatly preferable to running in melted lead. The block of timber for supporting the anvil was fixed in the same manner, on which the anvil was simply laid, without any other fixture than the small stud, fitted as usual into its seat, depending upon the gravity of the mass for preserving its place against the effects of the sea. In this state things were left on the rock at 9 P. M., when the boats returned to the tender, after other two hours work, in the same order as formerly, perhaps as much gratified with the success that attended the work of this day, as with any other in the whole course of the operations. Although it could not be said that the fatigues of this day had been great, yet all on board retired early to rest. The sea being calm, and no movement on deck, it was pretty generally remarked in the morning, that the bell awakened the greater number on board from their first sleep; and, though this observation was not altogether applicable to the writer himself, yet he was not a little pleased to find, that thirty people could all at once become so reconciled to a night's quarters within a few hundred paces of the Bell Rock.

Wednesday, 19th.

Landing-master's duty.

It was a rule laid down and adhered to by the writer, throughout the whole of the Bell Rock works, that, as far as possible, the charge should be arranged into departments. It therefore fell to the officer termed the Landing-master, who was also master of the Floating-light, to take the responsibility of the safe and proper landing of the artificers and materials upon the rock. With him, the writer generally arranged the business of the following day; his crew watched the ebbing of the water, and the appearance of the rock, and from the state of the weather, he judged of the proper time for causing the signal bell to be rung, when the boats were to leave the ship for the rock. It was also a special injunction laid upon him to say, from the state of the weather, when it was necessary for the boats to leave the rock and return to the tender.

Indications of the weather.

Being extremely anxious at this time to get forward with fixing the smith's forge, on which the progress of the work at present depended, the writer requested that he might be called at day-break to learn the landing-master's opinion of the weather, from the appearance of the rising sun, a criterion by which experienced seamen can generally judge pretty accurately of the state of the weather for the following day. About 5 o'clock, on coming upon deck, the sun's upper limb or disk had just begun to appear, as if rising from the ocean; and in less than a minute he was seen in the fullest splendour; but after a short interval he was enveloped in a soft cloudy sky, which was considered emblematical of fine weather. His rays had not yet sufficiently dispelled the clouds which hid the land from view, and the Bell Rock being still overflowed, the whole was one expanse of water. This scene in itself was highly gratifying; and when the morning bell was tolled, we were gratified with the happy forebodings of good weather, and the expectation of having both a morning and an evening tide's work on the rock.

Wednesday, 19th.

The boats left the ship at a quarter before 7 this morning, and landed upon the rock at 7. The water had gone off the rock sooner than was expected, for, as yet, the seamen were but imperfectly acquainted with its periodic appearance, and the landing-master being rather late with his signal this morning, the artificers were enabled to proceed to work without a moment's delay. The boat which the writer steered happened to be the last which approached the rock at this tide; and, in standing up in the stern, while at some distance, to see how the leading boat entered the creek, he was astonished to observe something in the form of a human figure, in a reclining posture, upon one of the ledges of the rock: he immediately steered the boat through a narrow entrance to the eastern harbour, with a thousand unpleasant sensations in his mind. He thought a vessel or boat must have been wrecked upon the rock during the night; and it seemed probable that the rock might be strewed with dead bodies, a spectacle which could not fail to deter the artificers from returning so freely to their work. Even one individual found in this situation, would naturally cast a damp upon their minds, and, at all events, make them much more timid in their future operations. In the midst of these reveries, the boat took the ground at an improper landing place; but, without waiting to push her off, he leapt upon the rock, and making his way hastily to the spot which had privately given him alarm, he had the satisfaction to ascertain, that he had only been deceived by the peculiar situation and aspect of the smith's anvil and block, which very completely represented the appearance of a lifeless body upon the rock. The writer carefully suppressed his feelings, the simple mention of which might have had a bad effect upon the artificers, and his haste passed for an anxiety to examine the apparatus of the smith's forge, left in an unfinished state at the evening tide.

Dangerous situation in foggy weather.

After an excellent tide's work of three hours at the forge, and boring the bat-holes for fixing the Beacon-house, we again took to our boats, and left the rock at 10 o'clock, the one boat preceding and waiting for the other till it cleared the rock, as formerly. In the course of this morning's work, two or three apparently distant peals of thunder were heard, and the atmosphere suddenly became thick and foggy. But as the Smeaton, our present tender, was moored at no great distance from the rock, the crew on board continued blowing with a horn, and occasionally fired a musket, so that the boats got to the ship without difficulty. The occurrence of thick weather, however, became a serious consideration, in looking forward to the necessary change of quarters to the Pharos, distant about one mile from the rock, instead of a few hundred yards, as in the case of the Smeaton.

Artificers amuse themselves with fishing.

The continuation of the thick and foggy weather was transient, being what seamen term an easterly hoar, arising from the heat of the weather, which disappeared soon after mid-day. The weather being clear in the evening, the boats landed again at half-past 6 o'clock, when the artificers were employed for two hours, as in the morning, and returned again to the ship about a quarter past 8. The remainder of the day-light was eagerly spent in catching fish, which were got, at this time, in great abundance, both alongside of the vessel and in the boats at a distance; and in the course of an hour about five dozen of codlings were caught, which not only afforded an agreeable relaxation, but afforded a plentiful dish of fish for the different messes on board.

Thursday, 20th.

Complete the fixing of the smith's forge.

The wind this morning inclined from the north-east, and the sky had a heavy and cloudy appearance, but the sea was smooth, though there was an undulating motion on the surface, which indicated easterly winds, and occasioned a slight surf upon the rock. But the boats found no difficulty in landing at the western creek at half-past 7, and, after a good tide's work, left it again about a quarter from 11. In the evening the artificers landed at half-past 7, and continued till half-past 8, having completed the fixing of the smith's forge, his vice, and a wooden board or bench, which were also batted to a ledge of the rock, to the great joy of all, under a salute of three hearty cheers. From an oversight on the part of the smith, who had neglected to bring his tinder-box and matches from the vessel, the work was prevented from being continued for at least an hour longer.

Valuable services of the smith at the Bell Rock.

It may here be proper to notice, that although a considerable quantity of jumpers or boring-irons, picks, and other quarry-tools, had been brought, in good order, for the use of the work; yet, from the extent of work in preparing the foundations, together with the hard and compact nature of the sandstone, of which the Bell Rock is composed, the tools soon became blunt, and the work must have often been completely at a stand, had it not been for the conveniency of having a smith and his forge so near at hand. The writer doubts not that his readers may be at a loss to account for the operation of the bellows and other apparatus upon a sunken rock, and it may therefore be necessary, in the accompanying description of the plates of this work, to give some explanation of this arcanum of Vulcan, on which the work had so great a dependence. The smith's shop, represented in Plate XI. was of course in open space: the large bellows were carried to and from the rock every tide, for the serviceable condition of which, together with the tinder-box, fuel and embers of the former fire, the smith was held responsible. Those who have been placed in situations to feel the inconveniency and want of this useful artizan, will be able to appreciate his value in a case like the present.

Much wanted at the Eddystone.

Mr Smeaton often felt the want of a forge permanently upon the rock, and had the foundation of the Eddystone Light-house required more extensive preparations, this useful implement could hardly have been dispensed with; but the Eddystone rock was so small as hardly to have room for it, in addition to other no less necessary apparatus. Could the operations of the blacksmith, at the Bell Rock, have been continued, from the commencement of the operations, even for half an hour longer every tide than the pickmen or quarriers, it would have added much to the facilities and progress of the work. But a stage or platform, in that case, must have been erected, to which there were a number of intervening obstacles, that more than counter-balanced the temporary inconveniency felt from the want of this additional time. It often happened, to our annoyance and disappointment, in the early state of the work, when the smith was in the middle of a favourite heat, in making some useful article, or in sharpening the tools, after the flood-tide had obliged the pickmen to strike work, a sea would come rolling over the rocks, dash out the fire, and endanger his indispensable implement the bellows; or if the sea was smooth, while the smith often stood at work knee-deep in water, the tide rose by imperceptible degrees, first cooling the exterior of the fire-place, or hearth, and then quietly blackening and extinguishing the fire from below. The writer has frequently been amused at the perplexing anxiety of the blacksmith, when coaxing his fire, and endeavouring to avert the effects of the rising tide. In this state of things, the erection of the Beacon was looked forward to as a happy period, when the smith should be removed above the reach of the highest tides.

Friday, 21st.

Seals desert the Bell Rock.

The weather still continued to be very fine; though the winds were variable, they rather prevailed from the eastward, and were occasionally accompanied with a hazy atmosphere, inclining to fog. The boats landed to-day upon the rock at half-past 7 o'clock A. M., and left it at a quarter past 11, the artificers having had an excellent tide's work of three hours and three-quarters. Every thing connected with the forge being now completed, the artificers found no want of sharp tools, and the work went forward with great alacrity and spirit. It was also alleged that the rock had a more habitable appearance, from the volumes of smoke which ascended from the smith's shop; and the busy noise of his anvil; the operations of the masons; the movements of the boats, and shipping at a distance, all contributed to give life and activity to the scene. This noise and traffic had, however, the effect of almost completely banishing the herd of seals which had hitherto frequented the rock as a resting place, during the period of low water. Though these animals were thus prevented from reposing upon the higher parts of the rock, yet they ventured, for a time, to lie upon the more detached outlayers which dry partially: here they seemed to look with that sort of curiosity which is observable in these animals when following a boat. But after the smith established himself, it was rare to see more than one or two of these amphibious animals about the rock, which seemed to be peculiarly adapted to their habits; for, excepting two or three days at neap tides, a part of it always dries at low water, at least during the summer season; and as there was good fishing ground in the neighbourhood, without a human being to disturb or molest them, it had become a very favourite residence of the seal, if we may judge from their numbers, the writer having occasionally counted from fifty to sixty of these animals playing about the rock at a time. But when they came to be disturbed every tide, and their seclusion was broke in upon by the kindling of great fires, together, with the beating of hammers and picks during low water, after hovering about for a time, they changed their place, and seldom more than one or two were to be seen about the rock. The writer felt a desire to protect these animals, with a view to observe their habits, and in hopes of taming them, at least so far as he had observed was done at the Small's Light-house, off the coast of Pembrokeshire, another favourite resort of seals, where, by gentle treatment, they have become so tame and familiar as to eat bread out of the hands of the light-keepers. But here, indeed, they constantly find a resting place, as some of the Small's rocks are always above water.

Progress of the work.

We had now been six days out from Arbroath, and, in that time, had the good fortune to have seven successive tides' work upon the rock, during which, the smith's forge had been fixed, and twelve holes of 2 inches in diameter and 18 inches in depth, had been bored or drilled into the rock, in the process of excavating the bat or stanchion-holes for fixing the principal beams of the Beacon-house. Hitherto the artificers had remained on board of the Smeaton, which was made fast to one of the mooring buoys, at the distance only of about a quarter of a mile from the rock, and of course a very great conveniency to the work. Being so near, the seamen could never be mistaken as to the progress of the tide, or state of the sea upon the rock, nor could the boats be much at a loss to pull on board of the vessel during fog, or even in very rough weather; as she could be cast loose from her moorings at pleasure, and brought to the lee side of the rock. But the Smeaton being only about forty register tons, her accommodations were extremely limited.

Hampered state of the artificers.

It may, therefore, be easily imagined, that an addition of twenty-four persons to her own crew, must have rendered the situation of those on board rather uncomfortable. This vessel served as a tender only in fine weather, with the assistance of the boats of the floating-light, for she could not stow boats sufficiently large for attending the rock with such a complement of artificers. The only place for the men's hammocks on board being in the hold, they were unavoidably much crowded; and if the weather had required the hatches to be fastened down, so great a number of men could not possibly have been accommodated. To add to this evil, the co-boose or cooking place being upon deck, it would not have been possible to have cooked for so large a company in the event of bad weather.

The stock of water was now getting short, and some necessaries being also wanted for the floating-light, the Smeaton was dispatched for Arbroath; and the writer with the artificers, at the same time, shifted their quarters from her to the floating-light.

Saturday, 22d.

Inconveniencies of the Pharos as a tender.

The operations still continued to be favoured with pleasant weather; to-day there were light airs of wind from south-east, and the morning bell was rung at 6. Although the rock barely made its appearance at this period of the tides till 8 o'clock, yet, having now a full mile to row from the floating-light to the rock, instead of about a quarter of a mile from the moorings of the Smeaton, it was necessary to be earlier astir, and to form different arrangements; breakfast was accordingly served up at 7 o'clock this morning. From the excessive motion of the floating-light, the writer had looked forward rather with anxiety to the removal of the workmen to this ship. Some among them, who had been congratulating themselves upon having become sea-hardy while on board of the Smeaton, had a complete relapse on returning to the floating-light. This was also the case with the writer. From the spacious and convenient birthage of the floating-light, the exchange to the artificers was, in this respect, much for the better. The boats were also commodious, measuring sixteen feet in length on the keel, so that, in fine weather, their complement of sitters was sixteen persons for each, with which, however, they were rather crowded, but she could not stow two boats of larger dimensions. When there was what is called a breeze of wind, and a swell in the sea, the proper number for each boat could not, with propriety, be rated at more than twelve persons.

The act of getting into or out of a boat, when alongside of the floating-light, was at all times attended with more or less difficulty; her rolling motion was so great, that the gunwale, though about five feet above the surface of the water, she dipped nearly into it, upon the one side, while her keel could not be far from the surface on the other. This was her state, even in moderate weather, in certain directions of the wind, especially for the period of about an hour, when she was thwarting to the tide, or rode in what sailors call the trough of the sea. The act of getting on board was then attended with great difficulty, even to seamen, and was particularly so to landmen, requiring all the attention which the landing-master could bestow, in getting the artificers safely transferred from the boats to the ship, and vice versa.

Difficulty of getting on board and leaving the Pharos.

When the tide-bell rung, the boats were hoisted out, and two active seamen were employed to keep them from receiving damage alongside. The floating-light being very buoyant, was so quick in her motions, that when those who were about to step from her gunwale into a boat, placed themselves upon a cleat or step on the ship's side, with the man or rail ropes in their hands, they had often to wait for some time, till a favourable opportunity occurred for stepping into the boat. While in this situation, with the vessel rolling from side to side, watching the proper time for letting go the man-ropes, it required the greatest dexterity and presence of mind to leap into the boat. One who was rather awkward, would often wait a considerable period in this position: at one time his side of the ship would be so depressed, that he would touch the boat to which he belonged, while the next sea would elevate him so much, that he would see his comrades in the boat on the opposite side of the ship, his friends in the one boat calling to him to "Jump," while those in the boat on the other side, as he came again and again into their view, would jocosely say, "Are you there yet? You seem to enjoy a swing." In this situation it was common to see a person, upon each side of the ship, for a length of time, waiting to quit his hold. A stranger to this sort of motion was both alarmed for the safety, and delighted with the agility of persons leaping into the boat, under those perilous circumstances. No sooner had one quitted his station on the gunwale, than another occupied his place, until the whole were safely shipped.

Difficulty of keeping boats alongside.

It also formed a critical operation with the sailors to keep the boats at a convenient distance from the vessel, to guard against being too far off; as, in that case, the man, in the act of stepping off the ship's side, might have been in danger of falling into the sea. If, on the other hand, the boat was allowed to come in contact with the vessel, she would have been in danger of being staved or damaged. This state of things was fortunately not what we had to commence with, as the weather happened to be, as before noticed, serene, and the Smeaton's sides were comparatively low in the water. The excessive rolling of the Pharos did not therefore come upon the artificers all at once, otherwise some unpleasant accidents must have happened, for in these rolling operations, if a stranger had, in a moment of alarm, let go his hold, at an improper time, he must have been pitched with violence into the sea.

The party being seated in their respective boats, they were pulled to the Bell Rock in about twenty minutes, from the moorings of the Pharos, when the water was smooth and the wind moderate. This morning the boats reached the rock at 8 o'clock; the work commenced exactly at a quarter past 8, and at half-past 11, the water again began to overflow the parts on which the artificers were at work. Every tide now gave the writer more pleasant prospects of the progress of the work than another, especially since the erection of the smith's forge.

Artificers become expert rowers.

On leaving the rock to-day, a trial of seamanship was proposed amongst the rowers, for by this time the artificers had become tolerably expert in this exercise. By inadvertency, some of the oars provided had been made of fir instead of ash, and although a considerable stock had been laid in, the workmen, being at first awkward in the art, were constantly breaking their oars; indeed, it was no uncommon thing to see the broken blades of a pair of oars floating astern, in the course of a passage from the rock to the vessel. The men, upon the whole, had but little work to perform in the course of a day; for though they exerted themselves extremely hard while on the rock, yet, in the early state of the operations, this could not be continued for more than three or four hours at a time,

Rations of artificers.

and as their rations were large, consisting of one pound and a half of beef,—one pound of ship-biscuit,—eight ounces oatmeal,—two ounces barley,—two ounces butter,—three quarts of beer,—with vegetables and salt, they got into excellent spirits, when free of sea-sickness. The rowing of the boats against each other became a favourite amusement; which was rather a fortunate circumstance, as it must have been attended with much inconvenience, had it been found necessary to employ a sufficient number of sailors for this purpose. The writer, therefore, encouraged this spirit of emulation, and the speed of their respective boats became a favourite topic. Premiums for boat races were also instituted, which were contended for with great eagerness, and the respective crews kept their stations in the boats, with as much precision as they kept their beds on board of the ship. With these, and other pastimes, when the weather was favourable, the time passed away, among the inmates of the fore-castle and waist of the ship. The writer looks back with interest upon the hours of solitude which he spent in this lonely ship, with his small library.

"Saturday night at Sea."

This being the first Saturday that the artificers were afloat, all hands were served with a glass of rum and water at night, to drink the sailors favourite toast of "Wives and Sweethearts." It was customary, upon these occasions, for the seamen and artificers to collect in the galley, when the musical instruments were put in requisition; for, according to invariable practice, every man must play a tune, sing a song, or tell a story. In this manner Saturday night, in particular, passed away in a very happy manner, when much boisterous mirth and loud peals of laughter occasionally broke forth. It is true, that this could not proceed from a single glass, but every man sat down with a determination to be pleased. They had, besides, a pretty liberal allowance of good small beer, which the rations of the sick increased; and they contrived to make the glass go round, and seemed to feel no want whatever, while the ship kept from her excessive rolling motion.

Sunday, 23d.

The operations at the Bell Rock were still fortunate with regard to the weather. The morning of Sunday set in with light airs from the south-west, which, towards mid-day, came to what sailors term fresh breezes, but towards evening it fell calm, and the weather became foggy.

Reasons for continuing the work on Sunday.

To some, it may require an apology, or, at least, call for an explanation, why the writer took upon himself to step aside from the established rules of society, by carrying on the works of this undertaking during Sundays. Such practices are not uncommon in the dock-yards and arsenals, when it is conceived that the public service requires extraordinary exertions. Surely, if, under any circumstances, it is allowable to go about the ordinary labours of mankind on Sundays, that of the erection of a light-house upon the Bell Rock, seems to be one of the most pressing calls which could in any case occur, and carries along with it the imperious language of necessity. When we take into consideration, that, in its effects, this work was to operate in a direct manner for the safety of many valuable lives and much property, the beautiful and simple parables of the Holy Scriptures, inculcating works of necessity and mercy, must present themselves to every mind unbiassed by the trammels of form or the influence of a distorted imagination. In this perilous work, to give up every seventh day, would just have been to protract the time a seventh part. Now, as it was generally supposed, after taking all advantages into view, that the work would probably require seven years for its execution, such an arrangement must have extended the operation to at least eight years, and have exposed it to additional risk and danger, in all its stages. The writer, therefore, felt little scruple in continuing the Bell Rock works in all favourable states of the weather.

Preparations for reading prayers on deck.

Having, on the previous evening, arranged matters with the landing-master as to the business of the day, the signal was rung for all hands at half past 7 this morning. In the early state of the spring-tides, the artificers went to the rock before breakfast, but as the tides fell later in the day, it became necessary to take this meal before leaving the ship. At 8 o'clock all hands were assembled on the quarter-deck for prayers, a solemnity which was gone through in as orderly a manner as circumstances would admit. Round the quarter-deck, when the weather permitted, the flags of the ship were hung up as an awning or screen, forming the quarter-deck into a distinct compartment with colours; the pendant was also hoisted at the main-mast, and a large ensign flag was displayed over the stern; and, lastly, the ship's companion, or top of the staircase, was covered with the flag proper of the Light-house Service, on which the Bible was laid. A particular toll of the bell called all hands to the quarter-deck, when the writer read a chapter of the Bible, and, the whole ship's company being uncovered, he also read the following impressive prayer, composed by the Reverend Dr Brunton, one of the ministers of Edinburgh.

A PRAYER FOR THE USE OF THOSE EMPLOYED AT THE ERECTION OF THE BELL ROCK LIGHT-HOUSE.

"Almighty and ever blessed God! Thou art not confined to temples made with man's hands: The temple most acceptable to thee is the heart of thy worshipper: Thou hast promised, that wherever thy servants are assembled, thou wilt be with them, to bless them and to do them good. Unto us, O our Father! may the promise be fulfilled. Even here, where no temple invites, and where no ordinances cheer us, be with us, we beseech thee, while we meet in thy presence; and strengthen us to discharge the duties of thy holy day.

"The Sabbath was appointed to celebrate thy creating power: And here, where the magnificence of thy works surrounds us,—where we see thy wonders in the deep,—where we behold every morning thy Sun arise from the world of waters, to spread, as at the first, light and beauty over Nature,—shall not our souls pour forth abundantly the tribute of adoration to thee, whose word alone spake the Universe into being!

"The Sabbath commemorates that Providence which watcheth continually over the works of thy hand: And shall not we, whom dangers so often threaten, and whom difficulties so often alarm; shall not we, conscious of our frailty, and removed far from human aid; shall not we raise the voice of thanksgiving to God, who alone protecteth us, and who, even in the midst of danger, causeth us to dwell in safety!

"The Sabbath was appointed to commemorate the triumphs of redeeming love: And shall not we hail it with delight, whose earliest infancy was hallowed in the name of Jesus; on whose opening minds the doctrines of his faith were poured; who, even in this remote abode, are permitted to call upon thy holy name in prayer,—to read the Oracles of everlasting truth,—to speak one to another of the God who hath loved and blessed us!

"Our souls do magnify the Lord, our spirits rejoice in God our Saviour; for he that is mighty hath done great things for his people, and his mercy is on them that fear him. We bless thee for the doctrines which our Master taught,—for the example which he set before us,—for the atonement by which he relieves us from the load of guilt,—for the hope which he hath restored of grace and glory. We bless thee for the institutions which thou hast appointed for enlightening thy people in religious knowledge, and for training them to lives of usefulness and purity. With shame we remember how often we have abused our Christian privileges,—how often we have neglected the exercises of private devotion,—how often we have failed to study thy holy word,—how often, while yet it was in our power to go up to the house of God, we have forsaken the assembling of ourselves together,—how often we have worshipped thee with our lips, while our hearts were far from thee. Visit us not, O God! in anger, for our transgression; but do thou enable us to lament and forsake it. Let not the circumstances in which we now are placed, be permitted to wean our affections from thy worship. But, while the service of humanity calls us to labour even on this day of rest, save us,—O thou, who wilt have mercy and not sacrifice!—save us from the temptation which might lead us to forget our God, and the duties which we owe to him. Rather, while we are deprived of thine ordinances for a season, do thou give us grace, through prayer and holy meditation, to compensate the loss; that we may, with delight, look forward to the time when the courts of thy sanctuary shall be opened to us again; when we, and those whom we love and value, shall again take sweet counsel together, and walk in company to the house of God. Give to us, even now, O God of our salvation! those pious and holy dispositions which will prepare us for the nobler worship, offered to thee by the Angels of Heaven, and by the Spirits of just men made perfect.

"We pray to our common Father in behalf of all mankind. May the day-spring from on high arise on those who now sit in darkness; and, where the light of the Gospel already shines, may its influences be felt reviving and purifying.

"We pray especially for our native land;—for her peace,—her prosperity,—her liberties,—and her honour. We pray for our king, and for all who are in authority over us. We pray particularly for those by whose command we are engaged in this arduous work. Bless them in their persons, in their families, and in the discharge of their official duty. Prosper, we beseech thee, the work itself in which we are engaged. May it remain long after our eyes have ceased to behold it. Long after our ashes are cold in the dust, may he that was ready to perish have cause to bless the memory of those by whom it was reared.

"We pray for the people of our land. Purify them unto thyself a peculiar people, zealous of good works: Bless them in their commerce, and in their harvests: Bless them in the pursuits of honest industry: Bless them in the relations of domestic life: Bless them, above all, with spiritual blessings in Christ Jesus.

"May the sons and daughters of affliction be enabled to profit by the bitter lesson with which thou hast seen it meet to visit them. Restore the sick to usefulness, or prepare the dying for judgment and eternity. May the living lay it to heart that they must die, and act as it becometh those who know not how soon they shall be called hence.

"Our friends and families, from whom we are separated for a time, we commit to thy protection, O God of love! Unspeakably precious is the thought, that thou carest for them,—that thine eye is upon them continually,—and thine everlasting arms around them. Grant that, in thy good time, we may meet them in peace;—Grant that we may be united hereafter in that land where separation and pain are unknown for ever.

"Our enemies we beseech thee to forgive and bless. Bless us, even us also, O our Father! Give us thy grace in every season of trial;—give us thy protection in every hour of danger. Prepare us for the dispensations of thy Providence;—prepare us for the discharge of duty;—prepare us for the inheritance of the just.

"And may grace, and mercy, and peace, from the Father, the Son, and the Holy Ghost, be with us for ever."

Some of the artificers decline working on Sunday.

Upon concluding this service, which was attended with becoming reverence and attention, all on board retired to their respective births to breakfast, and, at half-past 9, the bell again rung for the artificers to take their stations in their respective boats. Some demur having been evinced on board, about the propriety of working on Sunday, which had hitherto been touched upon as delicately as possible, all hands being called aft, the writer, from the quarter deck, stated generally the nature of the service, expressing his hopes that every man would feel himself called upon to consider the erection of a light-house on the Bell Rock, in every point of view, as a work of necessity and mercy. He knew that scruples had existed with some, and these had, indeed, been fairly and candidly urged before leaving the shore; but it was expected, that, after having seen the critical nature of the rock, and the necessity of the measure, every man would now be satisfied of the propriety of embracing all opportunities of landing on the rock, when the state of the weather would permit; and, in short, of exerting every effort in this as a common cause, at least until the Beacon should be erected, being an undertaking, on which the lives and safety of all connected with these works had a constant dependence. The writer, farther, took them to witness, that it did not proceed from want of respect for the appointments and established forms of religion that he had himself adopted the resolution of attending the Bell Rock works on the Sunday; but, as he hoped, from a conviction that it was his bounden duty, on the strictest principles of morality. At the same time it was intimated, that if any were of a different opinion, they should be perfectly at liberty to hold their sentiments, without the imputation of contumacy or disobedience; the only difference would be in regard to the pay.

Upon stating this much, he stepped into his boat, requesting all who were so disposed to follow him. The sailors, from their habits, found no scruple on this subject, and all of the artificers, though a little tardy, also embarked, excepting four of the masons, who, from the beginning, mentioned that they would decline working on Sundays. The boats reached the rock at a quarter past 10 o'clock A. M., and after a very active tide's work of two hours and a half, the water again overflowed the rock. It may here be noticed, that throughout the whole of the operations, it was observable that the men wrought, if possible, with more keenness upon the Sundays than at other times, from an impression that they were engaged in a work of imperious necessity, which required every possible exertion. On returning to the floating-light, after finishing the tide's work, the boats were received by the part of the ship's crew left on board, with the usual attention of handing ropes to the boats, and helping the artificers on board; but the four masons who had absented themselves from the work did not appear upon deck.

Additional pay on Sunday.

As the season advanced, the period of low water occurred later, and the writer did not consider it advisable, in the present state of the works, to land on the rock under night, there being nothing to mark its place prior to the erection of the Beacon. Under more favourable circumstances, he would willingly have landed this evening, to entitle the artificers who accompanied him in the morning, to additional wages, as every tide's work on Sunday counted a day, according to the rate of pay and premiums which he had laid down.

Monday, 24th.

Neap-tides. Artificers working knee-deep in water.

The weather, upon the whole, was very fine to-day, and the winds, though variable, were gentle; but from the mildness of the season, it got rather foggy towards the evening. The boats left the floating-light at a quarter past 9 o'clock this morning, and the work began at three-quarters past 9; but as the neap tides were approaching, the working-time at the rock became gradually shorter, and it was now with difficulty that two and a half hours work could be got. But, so keenly had the workmen entered into the spirit of the Beacon-house operations, that they continued to bore the holes in the rock till some of them were knee deep in water. In this work the sailors were also engaged, taking their turns at the boring and other works.

Operations entirely confined to the Beacon.

The operations at this time, were entirely directed to the erection of the beacon, in which every man felt an equal interest, as at this critical period the slightest casualty to any of the boats at the rock might have been fatal to himself individually, while it was perhaps peculiar to the writer more immediately to feel for the safety of the whole. Each log or upright beam of the beacon, was to be fixed to the rock by two strong and massive bats or stanchions of iron, of a construction which will be better understood by inspecting the diagrams on Plate VIII., and the accompanying description. These bats, for the fixture of the principal and diagonal beams and bracing-chains, required fifty-four holes, each measuring two inches in diameter, and eighteen inches in depth.

Description of the operation of boring the rock.

The operation of boring or drilling these deep holes in the rock, was conducted with great dexterity in the following manner: Three men were attached to each jumper or chisel; one placed himself in a sitting posture, to guide the instrument and give it a turn at each blow of the hammer; he also sponged or cleaned out the hole, and supplied it occasionally with a little water; while the other two, with hammers of sixteen pounds weight, struck the jumper alternately, generally bringing the hammer with a swing round the shoulder, after the manner of blacksmiths' work. The three men relieved each other in the operation of guiding the jumper and striking with the hammers. The forms of the jumper, hammer, and sponging-rod, are represented in Plate X., Figs. 7, 8, and 9. After many observations, as to the time occupied in boring these holes, the writer found that, when the tools were of a very good temper, they could be sunk at the rate of one inch per minute, including stoppages. The holes for the stanchions, when completed, measured seven inches in length, two inches in breadth, and eighteen inches in depth. After a jumper had been sunk to the necessary depth at each end of these holes, the most tedious part of the operation was to cut out the piece of rock which remained between the two jumper-holes, so as to clear it fully for the reception of the great iron stanchions, which were of a dove-tail form.

Progress of the work.

There had already been so considerable a progress made in boring and excavating these holes, that the writer's hopes of getting the beacon erected this year, began to be more and more confirmed, although it was now advancing towards what was considered the latter end of the proper working season at the Bell Rock. The foreman joiner, Mr Francis Watt, was accordingly appointed to attend at the rock to-day, when the necessary levels were taken for the step or seat of each particular beam of the beacon, that they might be cut to their respective lengths, to suit the inequalities of the rock; several of the stanchions were also tried into their places, and other necessary observations made, to prevent mistakes on the application of the apparatus, and to facilitate the operations, when the beams came to be set up, which would require to be done in the course of a single tide.

Tuesday 25th.

We had now experienced an almost unvaried tract of light airs of easterly wind, with clear weather in the fore-part of the day, and fog in the evenings. To-day, however, it sensibly changed; when the wind came to the south-west, and blew a fresh breeze. At 9 A. M. the bell rung, and the boats were hoisted out, and though the artificers were now pretty well accustomed to tripping up and down the sides of the floating-light, yet it required more seamanship this morning than usual. It therefore afforded some merriment to those who had got fairly seated in their respective boats, to see the difficulties which attended their companions, from the hesitating manner in which they quitted hold of the man-ropes in leaving the ship. As it blew pretty fresh, the passage to the rock was tedious, and the boats did not reach it till half-past 10. By working upon the higher parts of the site of the beacon 1¼ hours work was got, though not without difficulty, and the men left off at a quarter past 12 noon, completely drenched in water.

Difficult situation of the Smith.

The masons and pickmen were employed in boring the bat-holes, and in dressing and preparing the rock between the holes, at the places on which the beams of the beacon-house were to rest. It being now the period of neap-tides, the water only partially left the rock, and some of the men, who were boring on the lower ledges of the site of the beacon, stood knee-deep in water. The situation of the smith to-day was particularly disagreeable, but his services were at all times indispensable. As the tide did not leave the site of the forge, he stood in the water, and as there was some roughness on the surface, it was with considerable difficulty that, with the assistance of the sailors, he was enabled to preserve alive his fire; and, while his feet were immersed in water, his face was not only scorched, but continually exposed to volumes of smoke, accompanied with sparks from the fire, which were occasionally set up, owing to the strength and direction of the wind.

Wednesday, 26th.

Wind-gauge, and nomenclature for the winds much wanted.

The wind had shifted this morning to N. NW. with rain, and was blowing what sailors call a fresh breeze, — for as yet a correct and efficient wind-gauge remains a desideratum with the mechanical philosopher; and we have unfortunately no proper or satisfactory nomenclature for expressing the force of the wind. To speak, perhaps, somewhat intelligibly to the general reader, the wind was such, that a fishing-boat could just carry full sail. The weather did not look very favourable in the morning; but as it was of importance, especially in the outset of the business, to keep up the spirit of enterprise for landing on all practicable occasions, the writer, after consulting with the landing-master, ordered the bell to be rung for embarking, and at half-past 11 the boats reached the rock, and left it again at a quarter past 12, without, however, being able to do much work, as the smith could not be set to work from the smallness of the ebb and the strong breach of sea, which lashed with great force among the bars of the forge.

Difficult passage from the Rock to the Floating-Light.

Just as we were about to leave the rock, the wind shifted to the SW., and, from a fresh gale, it became what seamen term a hard gale, or such as would have required the fisherman to take in two or three reefs in his sail. The boats being rather in a crowded state for this sort of weather, they were pulled with great difficulty towards the floating-light. Though the boats were handsomely built, and presented little obstruction to the wind, as those who were not pulling sat low, yet having the ebb-tide to contend with, the passage was so very tedious, that it required two hours of hard work before we reached the vessel.

It is a curious fact, before noticed, that the respective tides of ebb and flood are apparent upon the shore about an hour and a half sooner than at the distance of three or four miles in the offing. But what seems chiefly interesting here is, that the tides around this small sunken rock should follow exactly the same laws as on the extensive shores of the mainland. When the boats left the Bell Rock to-day, it was overflowed by the flood-tide, but the floating-light did not swing round to the flood-tide for more than an hour afterwards. Under this disadvantage the boats had to struggle with the ebb-tide and a hard gale of wind, so that it was with the greatest difficulty they reached the floating-light. Had this gale happened in spring-tides when the current was strong, we must have been driven to sea in a very helpless condition.

Life-buoy streamed.

The boat which the writer steered, was considerably behind the other, one of the masons having unluckily broken his oar. Our prospect of getting on board, of course, became doubtful, and our situation was rather perilous, as the boat shipped so much sea that it occupied two of the artificers to bale and clear her of water. When the oar gave way, we were about half a mile from the ship, but being fortunately to windward, we got into the wake of the floating-light, at about 250 fathoms astern, just as the Landing-master's boat reached the vessel. He immediately streamed or floated a life-buoy astern, with a line which was always in readiness, and by means of this useful implement, the boat was towed alongside of the floating-light, where, from her rolling motion, it required no small management to get safely on board, as the men were much worn out with their exertions in pulling from the rock. On the present occasion, the crews of both boats were completely drenched with spray, and those who sat upon the bottom of the boats to bale them, were sometimes pretty deep in the water, before it could be cleared out. After getting on board, all hands were allowed an extra dram, and having shifted, and got a warm and comfortable dinner, the affair, it is believed, was little more thought of.

Tender ordered exclusively for the service of the Rock.

This was the first difficult or tedious passage which had been experienced in landing at the Bell Rock; it was also the first time that the writer had really felt the inconveniency of not having a vessel entirely set apart for the purposes of a tender. The floating-light, from the construction of her moorings, and the service for which she was specially employed, could not be cast loose or brought to the lea side of the rock in any case of emergency. Neither could she be risked to ride at moorings near enough to the rock, to place her in a more eligible situation for the purposes of the work. When these circumstances were brought under the notice of the Commissioners, it was ordered that a vessel should be provided, exclusively as a tender for the operations of the rock; and this was accordingly done before the commencement of the works of another season.

Thursday, 27th.

Depth of water in the site of the building in Neap-tides.

The tides were now in that state which sailors term the dead of the neap, and it was not expected that any part of the rock would be seen above water to-day; at any rate, it was obvious, from the experience of yesterday, that no work could be done upon it, and therefore the artificers were not required to land. The wind was at west, with light breezes, and fine clear weather; and as it was an object with the writer to know the actual state of the Bell Rock at neap-tides, he got one of the boats manned, and, being accompanied by the landing-master, went to it at a quarter past 12. The parts of the rock that appeared above water being very trifling, were covered by every wave, so that no landing was made. Upon trying the depth of water with a boat-hook, particularly on the sites of the Light-house and Beacon, on the former, at low water, the depth was found to be three feet, and on the central parts of the latter it was ascertained to be two feet eight inches. Having made these remarks, the boat returned to the ship at 2 P. M., and the weather being good, the artificers were found amusing themselves with fishing. The Smeaton came from Arbroath this afternoon, and made fast to her moorings, having brought letters and newspapers, with parcels of clean linen, &c. for the workmen; who were also made happy by the arrival of three of their comrades from the work-yard, ashore. From these men they not only received all the news of the work-yard, but seemed themselves to enjoy great pleasure in communicating whatever they considered to be interesting with regard to the rock. Some also got letters from their friends at a distance, the postage of which, for the men afloat, was always free, so that they corresponded the more readily.

Friday, 28th.

To-day the weather was not quite so agreeable as it had been yesterday, the wind being south-east, and blowing what sailors term a fresh breeze, by which we understand a force of wind that would be sufficient to cause the sails of a fishing-boat to be reefed. At ½ past 1 P. M., the writer again went to the rock, accompanied by the landing-master, when a depth of about four feet of water was found upon the site of the Light-house, which may be considered a medium depth, as nearly as this could be ascertained in its present unworked state, but there was some surf upon the rock.

Saturday, 29th.

Some of the Artificers wish to go ashore.

In the course of the night, the wind had shifted from SE. to SW., and it blew very hard, being technically termed a stiff gale, or rather too much wind for a fishing-boat. It was therefore considered unsafe for the Smeaton to continue at her moorings, and the signal was made for her to sail for Arbroath; she therefore got under way, but although there was a packet of letters for the shore, and the artificers had their memorandums in readiness, yet the floating-light rolled so unmercifully, that it would have been at the imminent hazard of staving or dashing a boat to pieces, had it been attempted to put one out. This was a disappointment in one way, though it answered a good purpose in another, as two of the three men, who had come last from the work-yard, earnestly entreated that they might be allowed to return, as they could no longer endure the rolling of the floating-light, a request in which they were anxiously accompanied by one of the masons, who had all along been much afflicted with sea-sickness. These applications were necessarily refused; they then applied to have an interview with the writer, when they urged the misery they were likely to suffer on board, without their being able to do any work at the rock. To the two strangers the difficulty and danger of putting out a boat was stated, as rendering it impossible for them to leave the ship; while the third person was reminded of his engagement to remain afloat for one month. In this manner these two men were put off, with the prospect of better weather in the course of a day or two. With regard to the other, he had suffered so severely, that the writer would have been happy to have had him ashore, and he was informed that if his comrades would ask leave for him, it would be granted. This being readily complied with, he was left at full liberty to return to the work-yard. But, for the present, the Smeaton was obliged to pass at a considerable distance, without being able to communicate with the floating-light.

Sunday, 30th.

Land upon the Rock after five days absence.

The wind was N.NE. this morning, in light airs, and the weather was clear. This being Sunday, the usual ceremony was observed at 12 noon, when the writer read prayers on the quarter-deck. The ensuing set of spring-tides were now coming to hand, and, at 3 P. M., all the artificers embarked for the rock, excepting the four men who had declined it last Sunday. Their places, however, were willingly taken by the three men who came last from the shore, who were happy to get relief from the disagreeable motion of the floating-light upon any terms. The boats reached the rock at half-past 3; but being rather early in the tide, the men rested on their oars till 4 o'clock, and then landed on the different spots as they dried, where they remained till the tide ebbed sufficiently to allow them to commence work. This was the first time the artificers had landed on the rock for five days, owing to the state of the weather and tides, and it was not a little flattering, on this occasion, to see with what eagerness the workmen leaped upon it. Those who were not troubled with sea-sickness, felt a degree of languor on board from which their working hours formed rather a relaxation, while the sickly (by far the greater number) felt immediate relief upon setting their foot upon terra firma, even in its most circumscribed boundary. While the water was going off the rock, the workmen were all busily employed in picking dulse, the Fucus palmatus of botanists, and indeed any other of the marine plants which happened to lie within their reach. Those who were the greatest sufferers from sea-sickness always ate the most greedily upon these occasions. Such incidental circumstances tended greatly to keep up the desire for landing at the rock, and seemed, in some measure, to compensate for the labour of rowing to and from it.

Method of fixing the stanchions in the rock.

The operation of boring the bat-holes being in great forwardness, the men were now chiefly employed in chiselling or cutting out the piece of rock which remained between each pair of jumper-holes, forming a ridge of about two inches in thickness. When this was cleared away, the bat-hole was of the proper form, and, as before noticed, it measured about seven inches in length, two inches in breadth, and eighteen inches in depth, an excavation which, from its dimensions, must readily appear to have been attended with much difficulty. The holes, though bored with the same size of chisels, as nearly as might be, were not precisely of the same size; but this was not essential, as the stanchion, when wedged in its place, completely filled the aperture. This operation of chiselling out the middle piece, and widening the hole in the form of a dove-tail, was a much more intricate and tedious operation than boring perpendicularly with the jumper. At that process three men worked with great celerity, whereas two only could be employed in cutting out the divisions and widening the holes.

The site of the building having already been carefully traced out with the pick-axe, the artificers, this day, commenced the excavation of the rock, for the foundation or first course of the light-house. Four men only were employed at this work, while twelve continued at the site of the Beacon-house, at which every possible opportunity was embraced, till this essential part of the operations should be completed. After having been two hours upon the rock this tide, the water began to rise upon the smith's forge and the site of the Beacon-house, and at ¼ past 6 o'clock P. M. the artificers left the rock.

Monday, 31st.

Longest day's work hitherto had on the Bell Rock.

The winds varied to-day from N.NE. to S. Though it blew pretty fresh, it was not accompanied with any swell in the sea, and the weather upon the whole was very pleasant. At half-past 3 in the morning, the writer was called by the landing-master, to consult about the state of the weather, and the practicability of landing upon the rock. After some hesitation, the result was to proceed: the signal bell for getting the boats ready was rung at 4 A. M., when all hands took to their respective boats, and at half-past 4 the work commenced at the rock: it continued till half-past 7, allowing an excellent tide's work of three hours, when the artificers again returned to the floating-light, and remained till the evening tide. At 4 P. M. they landed, but did not begin to work till a quarter from 5 o'clock, when the water had sufficiently left the rock. At a quarter past 7 it was overflowed, when the boats returned to the ship, and the writer was not a little elated, as the morning and evening tide had afforded no less than five and a half hours work, being the greatest day's work hitherto obtained on the Bell Rock.

September, Tuesday, 1st.

The weather was extremely pleasant throughout these twenty-four hours, though the wind veered and shifted about from N.W. to W.SW. At 4 o'clock this morning the bell made rather an unwelcome call, but all hands readily turned out. As before mentioned, when the work commenced at these early hours, a dram and a biscuit were served out to the artificers; and the writer, upon these occasions, found a cup of coffee very salutary. Having landed at a quarter from 5, the work was continued for three and a half hours, four men, as before noticed, being employed on the site of the Light-house, and twelve at the Beacon-house. The water overflowed the rock at a quarter past 7, when the boats returned to the floating-light.

Smeaton brings off the experimental cargo of stone.

The Smeaton had arrived from Arbroath in the course of the last night, and made fast to her moorings at the eastern buoy, which was nearest to the rock, as will be seen from Plate V. Agreeably to appointment, she had brought off six blocks of granite, for the purpose of making an experiment regarding the landing of the stones on the rock. She also had in tow the praam, or decked boat, brought from Leith astern of the Pharos, of which mention has already been made. This boat, in smooth water, could carry about six or seven tons upon deck.

Various suggestions about landing the stones.

The writer had looked forward to the trial of landing weighty materials upon the rock, as a matter which was to determine an important point in the operations of the Bell Rock light-house, and which could hardly be resolved by any other means than actual trial. This part of the operation had always been a matter of the greatest uncertainty with those conversant in such matters, and it became essential to determine the point at this period, by actual trial, before proceeding to the preparation of the craft and apparatus requisite for the works of next season, which it would not have been safe or prudent to rest upon doubtful hypothesis. In speculating upon this point, some had suggested that each particular stone should be floated to the rock, with a cork-buoy attached to it, while others would convert the float into an air-tank for this purpose; a third proposed to sail over the rock at high water, in a vessel of a flat construction, and drop the stones one after another, while under way, or at anchor on the rock. Others took up a still more extraordinary view of the case, and proposed to build so much of the Light-house ashore, in a kind of coffer-dam or vessel, as would raise the building to the level of the highest tide, and having previously prepared the rock for its reception, they would scuttle the vessel, and settle this ponderous mass, weighing perhaps 1000 tons, at once upon the rock. But it were endless to follow the various conceptions, even of men of experience, upon subjects of this kind. Though some of these propositions were ingeniously conceived, yet they could not be carried into effect in such a situation as the Bell Rock. Taking into view the uncertain state of the weather, the brittle nature of stone, when worked to a delicate edge and formed into angular points,—and, above all, considering the disadvantages that would attend the loss, even of a single stone, by the unavoidable delay it would occasion to the work, which might even in some instances hazard a great part of the building,—the writer judged it safest to keep the vessels that were to bring the stones from the work-yard at moorings, laid down at a convenient distance from the rock, so as to enable them to clear it, in case of drifting. He also determined, as the safest method, that their cargoes should be unloaded at these moorings, laid on decked praam-boats, and towed to the rock by the landing-master's crew, at low water, when the artificers were at work, and ready to lay and secure the stones in their places on the building. To put this to the test of actual experiment, the trial praam-boat had been built, and the six rough blocks of stone were brought to the rock.

Experiment of landing six blocks of Granite.

The middle part of this day was occupied by the writer on board of the Smeaton, at her moorings, where he carefully attended to the process of bringing the praam alongside, fixing her head and stern-ropes, and stationing the seamen at their respective posts, for the purpose of landing this small, but, in his view, important cargo. The mode by which the stones were taken out of the Smeaton's hold, and lowered on the praam's deck, will be understood from Plate XI. This was done by means of a gaff-boom, which traversed upon the Smeaton's mast, with the necessary tackles for guying it. An essential part of this tackle was a travelling-crance, or ring of iron, by which the stone might be lifted either at the extremities or at the central parts of the boom, as best suited its position in the ship's hold, or its intended place on the praam's deck. The length of this gaff-boom was thirteen feet, being sufficient for lowering the stone upon the praam. Another part of this apparatus, for lifting the stone, was a winch, fixed before the Smeaton's mast, consisting of a wheel two feet in diameter, worked by a pinion. The stone being raised from the vessel's hold, was laid on her deck, in order to shift the crance tackle to the extremity of the gaff-boom. The chief charge of the stone was then taken by the landing-master, till it was laid on the praam's deck, landed on the rock, and ultimately delivered over to the foreman builder. In the act of working this apparatus, one man was placed at each of the guy-tackles, who also assisted at the purchase-tackle for raising the stone; and one of the ablest and most active of the crew was appointed to hold on the end of the tackle-fall or purchase, which often required all his strength, and his utmost agility in letting go, for the purpose of lowering the stone at the instant when the word "Lower" was heard. Much depended upon the promptitude with which this part of the operation was performed, in a rolling sea, as our nautical readers will readily understand. For this purpose, the man who held the end of the tackle placed himself before the mast in a sitting, but more frequently in a lying posture, with his feet stretched under the winch, and abutting against the mast, as, by this means, he was enabled to exert his greatest strength. The signal being given by the men in the hold, that the Lewis-bat was fixed into the stone, and the tackle hooked, every man took his post. If the stone was very weighty, the two men who were to receive it on board of the praam, assisted in working the purchase, till the stone was got out of the hold, to be laid upon deck, when the word "Lower" was given, in an audible and stern tone of voice. After the traveller was shifted upon the gaff boom, the praam-men returned to their post, and the stone was again lifted to a sufficient height, to clear the vessel's gunwale, when great attention became necessary in working the guy-tackles, till the stone was brought over the praam's deck, and the watchword

"Lower" given, if possible, with greater force than before. The tackles were then unhooked, and in this manner the operation proceeded until the stones were got on board of the praam-boat.

This description may seem particular; but the reason will appear obvious, when it is recollected, that the landing of the materials has been considered one of the most nice and difficult parts of seamanship, and on which the best informed seamen were unable to say how it might answer, without great risk to the crew, and damage to the stones, and even occasionally losing them between the ship and the praam-boat. Both vessels being afloat, and riding in the open sea, at the distance of about a quarter of a mile from the Bell Rock, their motion was instantly communicated to the landing-gaff, and so to the stone in the tackle. The six blocks of granite having been placed upon the praam's deck, she was towed to a floating-buoy, where she was made fast, until the proper time of tide, for taking her into one of the creeks of the rock.

Stones first landed on the Rock.

At a quarter past 4 P. M., the boats, with the artificers, left the floating-light, and the work of the evening tide commenced at a quarter before 5. The sailors having previously decorated the ships and the praam-boat with flags, she was towed to the rock by two boats. The writer having resolved personally to attend the whole progress of this experiment went on board of the praam-boat, when she entered the eastern creek, where the foreman builder, at the head of the artificers, gave three hearty cheers. As the praam had not water to float her so far up the creek as the site of the building, her cargo was delivered upon Smith's Ledge, on the north side of this creek, as marked on Plate VI. In the present unprepared state of the machinery and implements upon the rock, the stones, in the present case, were raised with pinches, and pushed ashore upon planks. The whole of this experiment succeeded to the writer's utmost expectation, who was thus led to conclude, that the materials might be landed with much more expedition and certainty than he had previously supposed. All hands spontaneously collected to witness the landing of the first stone, which had no sooner touched the rock, than other three cheers were given, and, on this occasion, a glass of rum was served out by the steward. Having continued two hours upon the rock this evening, the artificers left it at 7, and returned to the floating-light, while the landing-master's crew towed the praam-boat off to the Smeaton, that she might be taken to Arbroath, having completed all that was intended with her, this season.

1807, September.

Wednesday, 2d.

First mode of attaching the vessels to their moorings.

The floating-light's bell rung this morning at half-past 4 o'clock, as a signal for the boats to be got ready, and the landing took place at half-past 5. In passing the Smeaton, at her moorings near the rock, her boat followed with eight additional artificers who had come from Arbroath with her at last trip, but there being no room for them in the floating-light's boats, they had continued on board. The weather did not look very promising in the morning, the wind blowing pretty fresh from W.SW.; and had it not been that the writer calculated upon having a vessel so much at command, in all probability he would not have ventured to land. The Smeaton rode at what sailors call a salvagee, with a cross-head made fast to the floating-buoy. This kind of attachment was found to be more convenient, than the mode of passing the hawser through the ring of the buoy, when the vessel was to be made fast. She had then only to be steered very close to the buoy, when the salvagee was laid hold of with a boat-hook, and the bite of the hawser thrown over the cross-head, instead of being obliged to put out the boat, in order to pass the rope through the ring of the buoy. But the salvagee, by this method, was always left at the buoy, and was, of course, more liable to chaff and wear than a hawser passed through the ring, which could be wattled with canvas, and shifted at pleasure. The salvagee and cross method is, however, much practised; but the experience of this morning showed it to be very unsuitable for vessels riding in an exposed situation, for any length of time.

Smeaton breaks adrift from her moorings.

Soon after the artificers landed, they commenced work; but the wind coming to blow hard, the Smeaton's boat and crew, who had brought their complement of eight men to the rock, went off to examine her riding ropes, and see that they were in proper order. The boat had no sooner reached the vessel than she went adrift, carrying the boat along with her, and both had even got to a considerable distance before this situation of things was observed, every one being so intent upon his own particular duty, that the boat had not been seen leaving the rock. As it blew hard, the crew with much difficulty set the mainsail upon the Smeaton, with a view to work her up to the buoy, and again lay hold of the moorings. By the time that she was got round to make a tack towards the rock, she had drifted at least three miles to leeward, with the praam-boat astern; and having both the wind and a tide against her, the writer perceived, with no little anxiety, that she could not possibly return to the rock till long after its being overflowed; for, owing to the anomaly of the tides formerly noticed, the Bell Rock is completely under water before the ebb abates to the offing.

Perilous situation of those left on the Rock.

In this perilous predicament, indeed, he found himself placed between hope and despair,—but certainly the latter was by much the most predominant feeling of his mind,—situate upon a sunken rock in the middle of the ocean, which, in the progress of the flood-tide, was to be laid under water to the depth of at least twelve feet in a stormy sea. There were this morning thirty-two persons in all upon the rock, with only two boats, whose complement, even in good weather, did not exceed twenty-four sitters; but, to row to the floating-light with so much wind, and in so heavy a sea, a complement of eight men for each boat, was as much as could, with propriety, be attempted, so that, in this way, about one-half of our number was unprovided for. Under these circumstances, had the writer ventured to dispatch one of the boats in expectation of either working the Smeaton sooner up towards the rock, or in hopes of getting her boat brought to our assistance, this must have given an immediate alarm to the artificers, each of whom would have insisted upon taking to his own boat, and leaving the eight artificers belonging to the Smeaton to their chance. Of course, a scuffle might have ensued, and it is hard to say, in the ardour of men contending for life, where it might have ended. It has even been hinted to the writer, that a party of the pickmen were determined to keep exclusively to their own boat against all hazards.

The unfortunate circumstance of the Smeaton and her boat having drifted, was, for a considerable time, only known to the writer, and to the landing-master, who removed to the farther point of the rock, where he kept his eye steadily upon the progress of the vessel. While the artificers were at work, chiefly in sitting or kneeling postures, excavating the rock, or boring with the jumpers, and while their numerous hammers, and the sound of the smith's anvil continued, the situation of things did not appear so awful. In this state of suspense, with almost certain destruction at hand, the water began to rise upon those who were at work on the lower parts of the sites of the Beacon and Light-house. From the run of sea upon the rock, the forge fire was also sooner extinguished this morning than usual, and the volumes of smoke having ceased, objects in every direction became visible from all parts of the rock. After having had about three hours work, the men began, pretty generally, to make towards their respective boats for their jackets and stockings, when, to their astonishment, instead of three, they found only two boats, the third being adrift with the Smeaton. Not a word was uttered by any one, but all appeared to be silently calculating their numbers, and looking to each other with evident marks of perplexity depicted in their countenances. The landing-master, conceiving that blame might be attached to him for allowing the boat to leave the rock, still kept at a distance. At this critical moment, the author was standing upon an elevated part of Smith's Ledge, where he endeavoured to mark the progress of the Smeaton, not a little surprised that her crew did not cut the praam adrift, which greatly retarded her way, and amazed that some effort was not making to bring at least the boat, and attempt our relief. The workmen looked steadfastly upon the writer, and turned occasionally towards the vessel, still far to leeward. All this passed in the most perfect silence, and the melancholy solemnity of the group made an impression never to be effaced from his mind.

Pilot boat accidentally comes to our relief.

The writer had all along been considering of various schemes,—providing the men could be kept under command,—which might be put in practice for the general safety, in hopes that the Smeaton might be able to pick up the boats to leeward, when they were obliged to leave the rock. He was, accordingly, about to address the artificers on the perilous nature of their circumstances, and to propose, That all hands should unstrip their upper clothing, when the higher parts of the rock were laid under water; that the seamen should remove every unnecessary weight and encumbrance from the boats; that a specified number of men should go into each boat, and that the remainder should hang by the gunwales, while the boats were to be rowed gently towards the Smeaton, as the course to the Pharos or floating-light lay rather to windward of the rock. But when he attempted to speak, his mouth was so parched, that his tongue refused utterance, and he now learned by experience that the saliva is as necessary as the tongue itself for speech. He then turned to one of the pools on the rock and lapped a little water, which produced immediate relief. But what was his happiness, when, on rising from this unpleasant beverage, some one called out "A boat, a boat!" and, on looking around, at no great distance, a large boat was seen through the haze making towards the rock. This at once enlivened and rejoiced every heart. The timeous visitor proved to be James Spink, the Bell Rock pilot, who had come express from Arbroath with letters. Spink had, for some time, seen the Smeaton, and had even supposed, from the state of the weather, that all hands were on board of her, till he approached more nearly, and observed people upon the rock; but not supposing that the assistance of his boat was necessary to carry the artificers off the rock, he anchored on the lee-side and began to fish, waiting, as usual, till the letters were sent for, as the pilot-boat was too large and unwieldy for approaching the rock, when there was any roughness or run of the sea at the entrance of the landing creeks.

The boats have a rough passage from the rock.

Upon this fortunate change of circumstances, sixteen of the artificers were sent, at two trips, in one of the boats, with instructions for Spink to proceed with them to the floating-light. This being accomplished, the remaining sixteen followed in the two boats belonging to the service of the rock. Every one felt the most perfect happiness at leaving the Bell Rock this morning, though a very hard and even dangerous passage to the floating-light still awaited us, as the wind, by this time, had encreased to a pretty hard gale, accompanied with a considerable swell of sea. The boats left the rock about 9, but did not reach the vessel till 12 o'clock noon, after a most disagreeable and fatiguing passage of three hours. Every one was as completely drenched in water as if he had been dragged astern of the boats. The writer in particular, being at the helm, found, on getting on board, that his face and ears were completely coated with a thin film of salt from the sea spray, which broke constantly over the bows of the boat. After much baling of water and severe work at the oars, the three boats reached the floating-light, where some new difficulties occurred in getting on board in safety, owing partly to the exhausted state of the men, and partly to the violent rolling of the vessel.

Smeaton bears away for Arbroath.

As the tide flowed, it was expected that the Smeaton would have got to windward, but, seeing that all was safe, after tacking for several hours, and making little progress, she bore away for Arbroath, with the praam boat. As there was now too much wind for the pilot-boat to return to Arbroath, she was made fast astern of the floating-light, and the crew remained on board till next day, when the weather moderated. There can be very little doubt, that the appearance of James Spink with his boat, on this critical occasion, was the means of preventing the loss of lives at the rock this morning. When these circumstances, some years afterwards, came to the knowledge of the Board, a small pension was ordered to our faithful pilot, then in his seventieth year; and he still continues to wear the uniform clothes and badge of the Light-house service.

Indispensable utility of the Beacon-house.

The experience of this day's hard passage to the floating-light strongly impressed the writer with the inconveniency and danger arising from the want of a proper tender, which could be cast loose at pleasure, and brought to the lee-side of the rock, and could, at all times, be moored nearer than it would have been safe or proper to have risked a vessel of the description of the floating-light. Another circumstance, no less deeply interesting to the safety of those on the rock, was the erection of the beacon-house, as a place of refuge in cases like the present. Here the writer could not help congratulating himself not only upon the near prospect of completing this work, but also on the perseverance with which he had maintained the indispensable necessity of the erection of the beacon. He was aware of the well grounded fears for the safety of all concerned, in the event of its being washed away by the sea; but, without such an erection on the Bell Rock, it is impossible to describe the continual hazard which must have attended the undertaking, or to determine the period when works so peculiarly situate, and especially so low in the water, might have been brought to a conclusion.

Thursday, 3d.

Eighteen of the artificers decline embarking for the rock.

The bell rung this morning at 5 o'clock, but the writer must acknowledge, from the circumstances of yesterday, that its sound was extremely unwelcome. This appears also to have been the feelings of the artificers, for when they came to be mustered, out of twenty-six, only eight, besides the foreman and seamen, appeared upon deck, to accompany the writer to the rock. Such are the baneful effects of any thing like misfortune or accident connected with a work of this description. The use of argument to persuade the men to embark, in cases of this kind, would have been out of place, as it is not only discomfort, or even the risk of the loss of a limb, but life itself, that becomes the question.

The boats proceed with eight.

The boats, notwithstanding the thinness of our ranks, left the vessel at half-past 5. The rough weather of yesterday having proved but a summer's gale, the wind came to-day in gentle breezes, yet the atmosphere being cloudy, it had not a very favourable appearance. The boats reached the rock at 6 A. M., and the eight artificers who landed, were employed in clearing out the bat-holes for the beacon-house, and had a very prosperous tide of four hours work, being the longest yet experienced by half an hour.

The boats left the rock again at 10 o'clock, and the weather having cleared up as we drew near the vessel, the eighteen artificers who had remained on board were observed upon deck; but as the boats approached, they sought their way below, being quite ashamed of their conduct. This was the only instance of refusal to go to the rock which occurred during the whole progress of the work, excepting that of the four men who declined working upon Sunday, a case which the writer did not conceive to be at all analogous to the present. It may here be mentioned, much to the credit of these four men, that they stood foremost in embarking for the rock this morning. Indeed, it seemed quite evident, that the backwardness of the artificers to-day arose from certain doubting expressions about the state of the weather, made through the inadvertency of some of the nautical people on board, in allusion to the state of the weather of yesterday.

A second landing was made in the evening tide, at a quarter past 6, with twenty of the artificers, six having been left on board for want of sitting-room in the boats; but as the work was not carried on with torch-light, till after the erection of the beacon-house, the boats left the rock again at a quarter past 7, the men having been employed chiefly at the bat-holes of the beacon-house.

Friday, 4th.

All hands, twenty-six in number, landed this morning, having been assisted by the Smeaton's boat, as she had again returned from Arbroath to her moorings at the rock. After three hours' work, the boats returned to the Pharos at a quarter past 10, leaving eight hands on board the Smeaton, as formerly, which preserved a convenient complement of sitters in the other two boats.

Captain Pool's account of the drifting of the Smeaton.

From the late accident of the Smeaton's drifting, precautionary measures were taken to impress upon Captain Pool, and his mate Mr Macurich, that their ship was not once to be put in competition with the safety of the people on the rock. Orders were also more strictly enforced upon the landing-master, that on no occasion whatever should the boats attending the rock be permitted to leave it, without carrying along with them the complement of men which they respectively brought to the rock. Upon examining the master of the Smeaton as to the circumstances of his vessel breaking adrift, it appeared that the salvagee had been chaffed, and that it had given way by the excessive motion of the vessel. Being also examined as to his intentions with regard to the people left on the rock on the 2d instant, he stated, that, when tacking the ship, he had seen the Pilot-boat a considerable time before it was likely that she could be seen at the rock; and that he was just about to cut the praam adrift, when he got sight of the boat. After setting sail on the Smeaton, his intentions were to try a tack or two, to see if she gained to windward, but if, on trial, she appeared to lose way, his intentions were to lash the helm to leeward, and leaving the boy on board of the vessel, he was to man the boat and make towards our relief. Captain Pool, in concluding his account of this matter, added, that "both ship and praam should have gone to the d— —l, rather than that the people upon the rock should have been left to perish." But he stated, that he was in much confusion for a time;—indeed, until he got sight of the pilot boat, that he was almost in a state of distraction, he and his ship's company being in a continual wrangle about what was best to be done in so critical a situation. This accident put an end to the mode of riding at the Bell Rock floating buoys by a salvagee and cross-head, the hawser being in future passed through the ring of the buoy, and the end of it taken on board of the vessel; which was found to be much more safe, though not quite so expeditious as the other.

Saturday, 5th.

The wind having shifted to N.NW., the weather had a favourable appearance this morning. But on landing at the rock at 7 A. M., there was a considerable swell from the eastward, so that the boats had some difficulty in approaching the eastern creek. The artificers, however, had a most excellent tide's work, having continued four hours at work, or till 11 o'clock. The boring and preparations for the Beacon-house being nearly completed, only twelve of the artificers were employed at this work, while fourteen were excavating and preparing the site of the Light-house.

Ascertain the comparative level of the site of the building.

This being the third day after new moon, it was estimated the lowest ebb of the present spring-tides. The writer therefore caused a part of the site of the building to be reduced to what he considered a medium level of the whole. This he compared with low water-mark, as noted by the landing-master, at the moment when the tide ceased to ebb and began to flow. An assistant with a rod having been stationed at low water-mark previously determined, another was placed at the spot ascertained to be the medium level of the site of the building; a spirit-level was then set at a convenient position between these upright rods, when the writer found that the medium height of the site of the building, in the present rough and irregular state of its surface, was about three feet three inches above low water-mark of spring tides. By further observation, it was also found, that the highest part of the foundation of the building, in its present unprepared state, was six feet above low water-mark. This highest part consisted of a large rounded mass, which declined gradually on all sides, excepting on the north-east, where it was more abrupt. The writer had originally some thought of taking advantage of this part of the rock, by connecting it, after Mr Smeaton's plan, with the lower courses of the building. But after working for some time, with this object in view, it was found to contain several large fissures, which rendered it more advisable to clear away the whole, and reduce the site of the building to a uniform level.

Full complement of Floating Buoys moored.

Finding it impossible, with any degree of safety, to carry to the floating-light, in the two boats belonging to this ship, more than eighteen artificers, and four seamen, together with the landing-master, the foreman and the writer, eight of the present complement of men were lodged on board of the Smeaton, and when she went to Arbroath for water and fuel, they necessarily accompanied her. Before sailing, she laid down a fourth mushroom-anchor, and mooring-chain, with a floating buoy, for the use of the praam-boat. It was not at all likely that there would be much use for so many sets of moorings for the operations of this season; but it was desirable to have the probable number laid down that might ultimately be required for the works, in order that the fitness of their respective situations might be ascertained, before they came to be wanted for the purposes of the building. This last buoy was laid down in four fathoms water, with twelve fathoms of chain, at the distance of about ninety fathoms, in a N.E. direction from the rock. The other three buoys were respectively moored at greater distances from the rock, in depths varying from seven to eleven fathoms, the mushroom anchors lying on a hard rocky bottom.

Floating-Light rides out a heavy gale of wind.

As before noticed, the work could not be carried on by torch-light with any degree of safety, till the Beacon was erected, and the tide fell rather late for landing this evening. Although the weather would have admitted of this, yet the swell of the sea, observable in the morning, still continued to increase. It was so far fortunate that a landing was not attempted, for at 8 o'clock the wind shifted to E. SE. and at 10 it had become a hard gale, when fifty fathoms of the floating-light's hempen cable were veered out. The gale still increasing, the ship rolled and laboured excessively, and at midnight eighty fathoms of cable were veered out; while the sea continued to strike the vessel with a degree of force which had not before been experienced.

Sunday, 6th.

During the last night there was little rest on board of the Pharos, and daylight, though anxiously wished for, brought no relief, as the gale continued with unabated violence. The sea struck so hard upon the vessel's bows, that it rose in great quantities, or in "green seas," as the sailors termed it, which were carried by the wind as far aft as the quarter-deck, and not unfrequently over the stern of the ship altogether. It fell occasionally so heavily on the skylight of the writer's cabin, though so far aft as to be within five feet of the helm, that the glass was broken to pieces before the dead-light could be got into its place, so that the water poured down in great quantities. In shutting out the water, the admission of light was prevented, and in the morning all continued in the most comfortless state of darkness. About 10 o'clock A. M., the wind shifted to NE., and blew, if possible, harder than before, and it was accompanied by a much heavier swell of sea; when it was judged advisable to give the ship more cable. In the course of the gale, the part of the cable in the hause-hole had been so often shifted, that nearly the whole length of one of her hempen cables, of 120 fathoms, had been veered out, besides the chain-moorings. The cable for its preservation, was also carefully served or wattled with pieces of canvass round the windlass, and with leather well greased in the hause-hole. In this state things remained during the whole day. Every sea which struck the vessel,—and the seas followed each other in close succession,—causing her to shake, and all on board occasionally to tremble. At each of these strokes of the sea, the rolling and pitching of the vessel ceased for a time, and her motion was felt as if she had either broke adrift before the wind, or were in the act of sinking; but when another sea came, she ranged up against it with great force, and this became the regular intimation of our being still riding at anchor.

State of the vessel during the gale.

About 11 o'clock, the writer, with some difficulty, got out of bed, but in attempting to dress, he was thrown twice upon the floor, at the opposite side of the cabin. In an undressed state, he made shift to get about half way up the companion-stairs, with an intention to observe the state of the sea and of the ship upon deck, but he no sooner looked over the companion, than a heavy sea struck the vessel, which fell on the quarter-deck, and rushed down stairs into the officers' cabin, in so considerable a quantity, that it was found necessary to lift one of the scuttles in the floor, to let the water into the limbers of the ship, as it dashed from side to side in such a manner, as to run into the lower tier of beds. Having been foiled in this attempt, and being completely wetted, he again, got below and went to bed. In this state of the weather the seamen had to move about the necessary or indispensable duties of the ship, with the most cautious use both of hands and feet, while it required all the art of the landsman to keep within the precincts of his bed. The writer even found himself so much tossed about, that it became necessary, in some measure, to shut himself in bed, in order to avoid being thrown into the floor. Indeed, such was the motion of the ship, that it seemed wholly impracticable to remain in any other than a lying posture. On deck the most stormy aspect presented itself; while below all was wet and comfortless.

About 2 o'clock P. M., a great alarm was given throughout the ship, from the effects of a very heavy sea which struck her, and almost filled the waist, pouring down into the births below, through every chink and crevice of the hatches and sky-lights. From the motion of the vessel being thus suddenly deadened or checked, and from the flowing in of the water above, it is believed there was not an individual on board who did not think, at the moment, that the vessel had foundered, and was in the act of sinking. The writer could withstand this no longer, and as soon as she again began to range to the sea, he determined to make another effort to get upon deck. In the first instance, however, he groped his way in darkness from his own cabin through the births of the officers, where all was quietness. He next entered the galley and other compartments occupied by the artificers: here also all was shut up in darkness, the fire having been drowned out in the early part of the gale: several of the artificers were employed in prayer, repeating psalms, and other devotional exercises in a full tone of voice: others protesting, that if they should fortunately get once more on shore, no one should ever see them afloat again. With the assistance of the landing-master, the writer made his way holding on step by step, among the numerous impediments which lay in the way. Such was the creaking noise of the bulk-heads or partitions, the dashing of the water, and the whistling noise of the winds, that it was hardly possible to break in upon such a confusion of sounds. In one or two instances, anxious and repeated inquiries were made by the artificers, as to the state of things upon deck, to which the Captain made the usual answer, that it could not blow long in this way, and that we must soon have better weather. The next birth in succession, moving forward in the ship, was that allotted for the seamen. Here the scene was considerably different. Having reached the middle of this darksome birth, without its inmates being aware of any intrusion, the writer had the consolation of remarking, that although they talked of bad weather, and the cross accidents of the sea, yet the conversation was carried on in that sort of tone and manner which bespoke an ease and composure of mind, highly creditable to them, and pleasing to him. The writer immediately accosted the seamen about the state of the ship. To these inquiries they replied, that the vessel being light, and having but little hold of the water, no top rigging, with excellent ground-tackle, and every thing being fresh and new, they felt perfect confidence in their situation.

It being impossible to open any of the hatches in the fore part of the ship, in communicating with the deck, the watch was changed by passing through the several births to the companion-stair leading to the quarter-deck. The writer, therefore, made the best of his way aft, and on a second attempt to look out, he succeeded, and saw indeed an astonishing sight. The seas, or waves, appeared to be ten or fifteen feet in height of unbroken water, and every approaching billow seemed as if it would overwhelm our vessel, but she continued to rise upon the waves, and to fall between the seas in a very wonderful manner. It seemed to be only those seas which caught her in the act of rising, which struck her with so much violence, and threw such quantities of water aft. On deck there was only one solitary individual looking out, to give the alarm, in the event of the ship breaking from her moorings. The seaman on watch continued only two hours; he who kept watch at this time, was a tall slender man of a black complexion; he had no great coat nor over-all of any kind, but was simply dressed in his ordinary jacket and trowsers: his hat was tied under his chin with a napkin, and he stood aft the foremast, to which he had lashed himself with a gasket or small rope round his waist, to prevent his falling upon deck, or being washed overboard. When the writer looked up, he appeared to smile, which afforded a farther symptom of the confidence of the crew in their ship. This person on the watch was as completely wetted as if he had been drawn through the sea, which was given as a reason for his not putting on a great coat, that he might wet as few of his clothes as possible, and have a dry shift when he went below. Upon deck, every thing that was moveable was out of sight, having either been stowed below, previous to the gale, or been washed overboard. Some trifling parts of the quarter boards were damaged by the breach of the sea; and one of the boats upon deck was about one-third full of water, the oyle-hole or drain having been accidentally stopped up, — and part of her gunwale had received considerable injury. These observations were hastily made, and not without occasionally shutting the companion, or covering up the stair-case, to avoid being wetted by the successive seas which broke over the bows, and fell upon different parts of the deck, according to the impetus with which the waves struck the vessel. By this time it was about 3 o'clock in the afternoon, and the gale, which had now continued with unabated force for 27 hours, had not the least appearance of going off.

Consultation about the probable event of her breaking adrift.

In the dismal prospect of undergoing another night like the last, and being in imminent hazard of parting from our cable, the writer thought it necessary to advise with the master and officers of the ship as to the probable event of the vessel's drifting from her moorings. They severally gave it as their opinion, that we had now every chance of riding out the gale, which, in all probability, could not continue with the same fury many hours longer; and that even if she should part from her anchor, the storm-sails had been laid to hand, and could be bent in a very short time. They further stated, that from the direction of the wind being NE., she would sail up the Firth of Forth to Leith Roads. But if this should appear doubtful, after passing the Island and Light of May, it might be advisable at once to steer for Tyningham Sands, on the western side of Dunbar, and there run the vessel ashore. If this should happen at the time of high-water, or during the ebbing of the tide, they were of opinion, from the flatness and strength of the floating-light, that no danger would attend her taking the ground, even with a very heavy sea. The writer seeing the confidence which these gentlemen possessed with regard to the situation of things, and their knowledge and ability, should the ship break adrift, found himself as much relieved with this conversation, as he had previously been with the seeming indifference of the forecastle-men, and the smile of the watch upon deck, though literally lashed to the foremast. From this time he felt himself almost perfectly at ease; at any rate he was entirely resigned to the ultimate result.

The gale takes off.

About 6 o'clock in the evening, the ship's company was heard moving upon deck, which, on the present occasion, was rather the cause of alarm. The writer accordingly rung his bell to know what was the matter, when he was informed by the steward, that the weather looked considerably better, and that the men upon deck were endeavouring to ship the smoke-funnel of the galley, that the people might get some meat. This was a more favourable account than had been anticipated. During the last twenty-one hours he himself had not only had nothing to eat, but he had almost never passed a thought on the subject. Upon the mention of a change of weather, he sent the steward to learn how the artificers felt, and on his return he stated that they now seemed to be all very happy, since the cook had begun to light the galley-fire, and make preparations for the suet-pudding of Sunday, which was the only dish to be attempted for the mess, from the ease with which it could both be cooked and served up.

The principal change felt upon the ship, as the wind abated, was her increased rolling motion, but the pitching was much diminished, and now hardly any sea came farther aft than the foremast; but she rolled so extremely hard, as frequently to dip and take in water over the gunwales and rails in the waist, though, as before noticed, she was in light ballast trim. By 9 o'clock, all hands had been refreshed by the exertions of the cook and steward, and were happy in the prospect of the worst of the gale being over. The usual complement of men was also now set on watch, and more quietness was experienced throughout the ship. Although the previous night had been a very restless one, it had not the effect of inducing repose in the writer's birth on the succeeding night, for having been so much tossed about in bed, during the last thirty hours, he found no easy spot to turn to, and his body was all sore to the touch, which ill accorded with the unyielding materials with which his bed-place was surrounded.

Monday, 7th.

Appearance of the sea upon the Bell Rock.

This morning about 8 o'clock, the writer was agreeably surprised to see the scuttle of his cabin sky-light removed, and the bright rays of the sun admitted. Although the ship continued to roll excessively, and the sea was still running very high, yet the ordinary business on board seemed to be going forward on deck. It was impossible to steady a telescope, so as to look minutely at the progress of the waves, and trace their breach upon the Bell Rock, but the height to which the cross-running waves rose in sprays, when they met each other, was truly grand, and the continued roar and noise of the sea was very perceptible to the ear. To estimate the height of the sprays at forty or fifty feet, would surely be within the mark. Those of the workmen who were not much afflicted with sea-sickness, came upon deck, and the wetness below being dried up, the cabins were again brought into a habitable state. Every one seemed to meet as if after a long absence, congratulating his neighbour upon the return of good weather. Little could be said as to the comfort of the vessel, but after riding out such a gale, no one felt the least doubt or hesitation as to the safety and good condition of her moorings. The master and mate were extremely anxious, however, to heave in the hempen cable, and see the state of the clinch or iron ring of the chain-cable. But the vessel rolled at such a rate, that the seamen could not possibly keep their feet at the windlass, nor work the hand-spokes, though it had been several times attempted since the gale took off.

Floating-Light breaks adrift.

About 12 noon, however, the vessel's motion was observed to be considerably less, and the sailors were enabled to walk upon deck with some degree of freedom. But, to the astonishment of every one, it was soon discovered that the floating-light was adrift! The windlass was instantly manned, and the men soon gave out that there was no strain upon the cable. The mizzen sail, which was bent for the occasional purpose of making the vessel ride more easily to the tide, was immediately set, and the other sails were also hoisted in a short time, when, in no small consternation, we bore away, about one mile to the south-westward of the former station, and there let go the best bower anchor and cable in twenty fathoms water, to ride until the swell of the sea should fall, when it might be practicable to grapple for the moorings, and find a better anchorage for the ship.

Cable supposed to have been cut by a piece of wreck.

As soon as the deck could be cleared, the cable-end was hove up, which had parted at the distance of about fifty fathoms from the chain-moorings. On examining the cable, it was found to be considerably chafed, but where the separation took place, it appeared to be worn through, or cut shortly off. How to account for this would be difficult, as the ground, though rough and gravelly, did not, after much sounding, appear to contain any irregular parts. It was therefore conjectured, that the cable must have hooked some piece of wreck, as it did not appear, from the state of the wind and tide, that the vessel could have fouled her anchor, when she veered round with the wind, which had shifted, in the course of the night, from NE. to N.NW. Be this as it may, it was a circumstance quite out of the power of man to prevent, as, until the ship drifted, it was found impossible to heave up the cable. But what ought to have been the feeling of thankfulness to that Providence which regulates and appoints the lot of man, when it is considered, that if this accident had happened during the storm, or in the night after the wind had shifted, the floating-light must inevitably have gone ashore upon the Bell Rock. In short, it is hardly possible to conceive any case more awfully distressing than our situation would have been, or one more disastrous to the important undertaking in which we were engaged.

In the present untoward state of things, the writer had chiefly to regret the necessity of making a permanent change in the position of the moorings of the floating-light, after her station had been publicly advertised, and within a week of the time of exhibiting the light. It had also become more evident that this vessel could not be continued as a tender or store-ship for the work. The object of consideration, therefore, was to place her in a situation where she would be most useful to shipping. It was evident that she must now be stationed at about double her former distance from the rock, or, instead of one mile, that she must be moored upwards of two miles from it, on ground formerly ascertained to have been good, but considered too distant from the operations.

Difficulty of manning the Floating-light.

In the evening the Smeaton came off from Arbroath, with provisions and necessaries for the work. There being little wind, and a heavy swell in the sea, it was not safe that the vessels should come in contact with each other. Mr Macurich, the mate, who came within hail, in the Smeaton's boat, informed us, that two seamen had come off to make up the complement of the crew of the floating-light, and that they would be brought on board the first opportunity. From the manner in which this address was made, and the enquiry as to how we rode out the gale, it was evident that the crew of the Smeaton were not aware that the floating-light had shifted her place; nor, indeed, was this at all obvious, unless by a particular observation made by the mariner's compass, in reference to the position of the rock.

The peculiarity of this service rendered it difficult to procure good seamen to embark in it, and the original crew dropped off one after another as the winter season began to advance; for as yet our naval heroes had not shewn the possibility of remaining for months together, even off an enemy's coast. It was therefore found to be an extremely difficult matter to get the crew of the floating-light recruited from time to time; and, under the perplexity of our present situation, it was some alleviation to be told that there were men voluntarily offering their services.

In the course of this day the wind had veered from N.NW. to NE., but the weather was mild, and the sea had fallen considerably, so that the boat came alongside with the two seamen, and a supply of necessaries. The Smeaton was then dispatched to Arbroath for another set of moorings for the floating-light, in case of our not finding those from which she had drifted. Letters were also dispatched to the Light-house Board, intimating the particulars of the floating-light's new ground, that additional notice might be given to shipping.

Wednesday, 9th.

Floating-light anchored in her new station.

The weather continued to be extremely agreeable, though the wind kept shifting about. Having got every thing in readiness for moving to the new station, which had again been carefully sounded, the floating-light was got under way,—which the author had fondly hoped never to have seen, till after her purpose as a temporary light had been supplied by a permanent building upon the Bell Rock. At 9 o'clock A. M. the best bower anchor was let go upon the new ground, in twenty fathoms water, on clean sand mixed with fine silt or mud, appearing to be the deposited matters borne along by the currents from the river Tay; the Bell Rock bearing SE. ½ S. distant about 2½ miles.

Monday, 14th.

It is found impracticable to land to-day.

The Smeaton returned to Arbroath, after landing her dispatches; but the wind and the swell of the sea having again increased, she was obliged to remain in port till the 14th. As the floating-light still rode at single anchor, it was often an anxious wish to have her once more properly fixed with chain moorings; but, as yet, no opportunity had occurred for recovering the old chain, and it took some time to prepare a new one. The Smeaton having returned from Arbroath this morning, the writer went on board of her, carrying with him all the artificers. At 6 an attempt was made to land, but the sea ran so heavily, and the breakers rushed with such fury in every direction, that after rowing all around the rock, the boats were obliged to return without success. It deserves remark, however, that this was the first attempt to land this season, in which it had been found impracticable, after actually embarking in the boats.

Tuesday, 15th.

State of matters at the rock, after a lapse of ten days.

This morning at 5 A. M., the bell rung as a signal for landing upon the rock, a sound which, after a lapse of ten days, it is believed was welcomed by every one on board. There being a heavy breach of sea at the eastern creek, we landed, though not without difficulty, on the western side, every one seeming more eager than another to get upon the rock, and never did hungry men sit down to a hearty meal with more appetite than the artificers began to pick the dulse from the rocks. This marine plant had the effect of reviving the sickly, and seemed to be no less relished by those who were more hardy.

While the water was ebbing, and the men were roaming in quest of their favourite morsel, the writer was examining the effects of the storm upon the forge, and loose apparatus left upon the rock. The six large blocks of granite which had been landed, by way of experiment, on the 1st instant, were now removed from their places, and, by the force of the sea, thrown over a rising ledge into a hole at the distance of twelve or fifteen paces from the place on which they had been landed. This was a pretty good evidence, both of the violence of the storm and the agitation of the sea upon the rock. The safety of the smith's forge was always an object of essential regard. The ash-pan of the hearth or fire-place, with its weighty cast-iron back, had been washed from their places of supposed security: the chains of attachment had been broken, and these ponderous articles were found at a very considerable distance, in a hole on the western side of the rock; while the tools and picks of the Aberdeen masons were scattered about in every direction. It is, however, remarkable, that not a single article was ultimately lost. A mushroom-anchor, weighing about 22 cwt., had been driven from its station at some distance, and thrown upon the rock, being found in one of the landing creeks. The floating-buoy being still attached to it, had received no material damage, though it had been chafed and was water-logged. This buoy, with its moorings, consisting of 24 fathoms of chain, and the anchor, had been given up as lost, ever since the gale; but just as the boats were about to leave the rock, they were fortunately observed between two ledges of rock, by one of the seamen.

Work, this tide, continues only for one hour.

After having been two hours and a half upon the rock this morning, boats left it at a quarter past 8. At half-past 6 P. M., they again returned; but the smith having fallen into the water in landing, got the tinder so wetted, that he could not strike fire, and the work was left off at 7, after one hour's work, for want of sharp tools. — The site of the beacon being now prepared, and the stanchion-holes excavated, the mode of employing the artificers was reversed, only four being occupied at the beacon works, and twelve in preparing the foundation of the light-house.

Floating-light first exhibited.

This being the night on which the floating-light was advertised to be lighted, it was accordingly exhibited, to the great joy of every one. For, besides the benefit to be derived by shipping in general, from this temporary light, it was also to be of great service to the operations at the Bell Rock, as it became a point of reference for the conveniency and safety of the light-house vessels, either in riding at the buoys, or in cruising about the rock. The event of lighting up this ship, was, therefore, ushered in with three hearty cheers, and a dram was served out to all hands.

Wednesday, 16th.

The weather continuing to be moderate, with gentle breezes from NW. to N.NE., this morning the work commenced at the rock at half-past 6, and the boats left it again at a quarter from 9, after the artificers had been at work two hours and a half.

Light-house Yacht becomes a Tender to the works.

The writer was made happy to-day, by the return of the Light-house Yacht, from a voyage to the Northern Light-houses. She had sailed from the Bell Rock on the 5th of last month for the Orkneys, and had passed the Western Islands to the Clyde, returning to the eastern coast by the Forth and Clyde Canal, after having discharged stores at the several Light-houses in her track. The arrival of this vessel was a great relief, as she brought a set of moorings with her for the floating-light, which still rode at single anchor. Having immediately removed on board of this fine vessel of eighty-one tons register, the artificers gladly followed, for, though they found themselves more pinched for accommodation on board of the Yacht, and still more so in the Smeaton; yet they greatly preferred either of these to the Pharos or floating-light, on account of her rolling motion, though in all respects fitted up for their conveniency.

Artificers agree to remain at the rock after their engagement had expired.

The writer called them to the quarter-deck, and informed them that having been one month afloat, in terms of their agreement, they were now at liberty to return to the work-yard at Arbroath, if they preferred this to continuing at the Bell Rock. But they replied, that, in the prospect of soon getting the beacon erected upon the rock, and having made a change from the floating-light, they were now perfectly reconciled to their situation, and would remain afloat till the end of the working season. This was considered a matter of the greatest importance to the success of the work; for, from the circumstances of the bad weather, and the drifting of the floating-light, it seemed extremely doubtful but the whole of the workmen might have been induced to go on shore, which would have deterred others from embarking in this perilous service, at so advanced a period of the season. At all events, it must have required no small trouble to have brought a new set of men to expertness in the minutiæ of the traffic in boats, and getting in and out of the vessels. Of those who had originally come off to the work on the 17th of August, only one man, already alluded to, who was a great martyr to sea-sickness, had returned to the work-yard.

Thursday, 17th.

Accident happens to one of the boats.

The wind was at NE. this morning, and though there were only light airs, yet there was a pretty heavy swell coming ashore upon the rock. The boats landed at half-past 7 o'clock A. M., at the creek on the southern side of the rock, marked Port Hamilton in Plate VI., which to-day was found to be the most accessible landing-place. But as one of the boats was in the act of entering this creek, the seaman at the bow oar, who had just entered the service, having inadvertently expressed some fear, from a heavy sea which came rolling towards the boat, and one of the artificers having at the same time looked round and missed a stroke with his oar, such a preponderance was thus given to the rowers upon the opposite side, that when the wave struck the boat, it threw her upon a ledge of shelving rocks, where the water left her, and she having kanted to seaward, the next wave completely filled her with water. After making considerable efforts, the boat was again got afloat in the proper track of the creek, so that we landed without any other accident than a complete ducking. This accident caused us to lose some time; but, as the boats could not conveniently leave the rock till flood-tide, and there being no possibility of getting a shift of clothes, the artificers began with all speed to work, so as to bring themselves into heat, while the writer, and his assistants, kept as much as possible in motion. Having remained more than an hour upon the rock, the boats left it at half-past 9; and after getting on board, the writer recommended to the artificers, as the best mode of getting into a state of comfort, to strip off their wet clothes, and go to bed for an hour or two. No farther inconveniency was felt, and no one seemed to complain of the affection called "catching cold."

It was a standing order in the landing department, that every man should use his greatest exertions, in giving the boats sufficient force or velocity to preserve their steerage-way in entering the respective creeks at the rock, that the contending seas might not have the command of the boat at places where the free use of the oars could not be had, on account of the surrounding rocks. The late accident, accordingly, put all hands more upon their guard, as such an occurrence might have proved fatal to all on board, under a very slight change of circumstances.

Friday, 18th.

Floating-light moored in her new station.

The first object to be accomplished, with the assistance of the Light-house Yacht, was to get the floating-light secured at her new station, an operation which required the finest of weather. To-day, the wind was at NE., and although moderate, it was, of all others, most dreaded at the Bell Rock, the heavy gale of the 6th instant having been from this direction. The writer, however, judged it advisable to proceed with the laying down of the new moorings, and in case of any accident by the slipping of the chain, as formerly, the artificers, instead of going to the rock this tide, were kept on board, that the seamen and all hands might be on the spot to render assistance. These new moorings consisted of 40 fathoms of chain, made from iron-bars of one inch square, with a cast-iron mushroom-anchor, weighing 1 ton 1 cwt. 2 qrs. 4 lb. This anchor and chain, were let down in a depth of twenty-one fathoms, the Bell Rock being from the new station SE. ½ S., distant two and a half miles; Redhead N. by E., distant ten miles; Arbroath N.NW., distant about ten miles; Fifeness SW. by W., distant about eleven miles, and Isle of May SW. by S., distant sixteen miles. The moorings having been laid down on this spot, a buoy was placed upon them. The Yacht then took the floating-light in tow to her new station, where she was made fast to the chain, with a new cable measuring sixteen inches in circumference. This business was successfully accomplished at about 2 o'clock P. M., after six hours of very hard work.

The first cables of the floating-light were of patent cordage, made of the very best materials, and most beautifully laid by machinery. But the sailors complained that these ropes were so stiff and unpliable, that they could neither be got stowed in the hold, nor run freely out of the hause-holes. These difficulties were also more felt with the patent laid cables, after the weather became somewhat cold. It was, therefore, found necessary to get a new cable, laid in the ordinary way, for the winter months.

Smeaton arrives with the beams of the Beacon in tow.

Another important occurrence, connected with the operations of this season, was the arrival of the Smeaton at 4 P. M., having in tow the six principal beams of the Beacon-house, together with all the stanchions and other work on board for fixing it on the rock. The mooring of the floating-light was a great point gained, but, in the erection of the beacon at this late period of the season, new difficulties presented themselves. The success of such an undertaking, at any season, was precarious; because a single day of bad weather occurring, before the necessary fixtures could be made, might sweep the whole apparatus from the rock. Notwithstanding these difficulties, the writer had determined to make the trial, although he could almost have wished, upon looking at the state of the clouds, and the direction of the wind, that the apparatus for the beacon had been still in the work-yard.

Saturday, 19th.

Preparations for erecting them.

The weather to-day did not prognosticate any thing very favourable; the wind, though in light breezes, continued at NE., and it was occasionally almost calm. The main beams of the Beacon were made up in two separate rafts, fixed with bars and bolts of iron. One of these rafts, not being immediately wanted, was left astern of the floating-light, and the other was kept in tow by the Smeaton, at the buoy nearest to the rock. The Light-house Yacht rode at another buoy, with all hands on board that could possibly be spared out of the floating-light; including also ten additional men, as carpenters, smiths and sailors, brought off for this operation. The party of artificers and seamen which landed this morning on the Bell Rock, counted altogether forty in number. At half-past 8 o'clock, a Derrick or mast of thirty feet in height, was erected and properly supported with guy-ropes, for suspending the block for raising the first principal beam of the beacon; and a winch-machine was also bolted down to the rock for working the purchase-tackle. The necessary blocks and tackle were likewise laid to hand and properly arranged. The artificers and seamen were severally allotted in squads to different stations; some were to bring the principal beams to hand, others were to work the tackles, while a third set had the charge of the iron-stanchions, bolts, and wedges, so that the whole operation of raising the beams, and fixing them to the rock, might go forward in such a manner that some provision might be made, in every stage of the work, for securing what had been accomplished, in case of a change of weather.

Upon raising the derrick, all hands on the rock spontaneously gave three hearty cheers, as a favourable omen of our future exertions in pointing out more permanently the position of the rock. Even to this single spar of timber, could it be preserved, a drowning man might lay hold. When the Smeaton drifted on the 2d of this month, such a spar would have been sufficient to save us, till she could have come to our relief. These preparations for the erection of the Beacon having been previously made, the writer collected the heads of the several departments on board of the Light-house Yacht, particularly the foremen of the builders and joiners, and the masters and mates of the vessels. Here the operation of raising and fixing the first four beams was again talked over and arranged, as, from the very limited period of working on the rock, every thing required to be performed in the most prompt and systematic manner, as previously settled.

Sunday, 20th.

Four of the principal beams erected.

The wind this morning was variable, but the weather continued extremely favourable for the operations throughout the whole day. At 6 A. M. the boats were in motion, and the raft, consisting of four of the six principal beams of the Beacon-house, each measuring about sixteen inches square, and fifty feet in length, was towed to the rock, where it was anchored, that it might ground upon it as the water ebbed. At 7 A. M. the boats of the Floating-light, the Yacht, and the Smeaton, arrived at the rock, when the work immediately commenced. The sailors and artificers, including all hands to-day, counted no fewer than fifty-two, being perhaps the greatest number of persons ever collected upon the Bell Rock. It was early in the tide when the boats reached the rock, and the men worked a considerable time up to their middle in water, every one being more eager than his neighbour to be useful. Even the four artificers, who had hitherto declined working on Sunday, were to-day most zealous in their exertions; they had indeed become so convinced of the precarious nature and necessity of the work, that they never afterwards absented themselves from the rock on Sunday, when a landing was practicable.

Method of raising the principal beams of the Beacon-house.

Having made fast a piece of very good new line, at about two thirds from the lower end of one of the beams, the purchase-tackle of the derrick was hooked into the turns of the line, and it was speedily raised, by the number of men on the rock, and the power of the winch tackle. When this log was lifted to a sufficient height, its foot, or lower end, was stepped into the spot which had been previously prepared for it. Two of the great iron stanchions were then set into their respective holes, on each side of the beam, when a rope was passed round them and the beam, to prevent it from slipping, till it could be more permanently fixed. The derrick or upright spar used for carrying the tackle to raise the first beam, was placed in such a position as to become useful for supporting the upper end of it, which now became, in its turn, the prop of the tackle for raising the second beam, which was laid in such a position, that when hoisted up, its foot slipped into its place, when it was, in like manner, lashed to its great iron stanchions on each side. The first and second beams being lashed to one another at the top, served as a pair of sheers, from which the purchase tackle was now suspended, for raising the other two beams, which were also speedily got into their places. The whole difficulty of this operation was in the raising and propping of the first beam, which became a convenient derrick for raising the second, these again a pair of sheers for lifting the third, and the sheers a triangle for raising the fourth. Having thus got four of the six principal beams set on end, it required a considerable degree of trouble to get their upper ends to fit. Here they formed the apex of a cone, and were all together mortised into a large piece of beechwood, and secured, for the present, with ropes, in a temporary manner. During the short period of one tide, all that could further be done for their security, was to put a single screw-bolt through the great kneed bats or stanchions on each side of the beams, and screw the nut home. In this manner each beam, with its respective pair of bats, was fixed, besides being strongly bound together with ropes.

Method of fixing the great iron stanchions into the rock.

While one set of the artificers were employed in this operation, another fixed the great iron-stanchions into the rock, into which they were sunk to the depth of about twenty inches. They were of a dove-tail or wedge form, at the lower end, where they measured an inch and a half in thickness; were about four inches in their medium breadth; and were let perpendicularly into the rock, but kneed or bent to suit the angle which the beams formed with it. These great bats or stanchions had much the figure and appearance of a soldier's musket; they were five feet in length, and weighed about 140 lb. each. Instead of running the bat-holes full of melted lead, as is common in operations of this kind, but which, in case of friction or movement, is apt to be squeezed out of the holes, all the bats made use of at the Bell Rock, as before noticed, were fixed by means of wedges. Several of the artificers were therefore employed in wedging these stanchions first with fir-timber, then with oak, and lastly with iron, driven into spaces left for this purpose, between the bats and the rock. These wedges were driven so firmly, that although the stanchions were the only fixture for this wooden house, it had not been found necessary to drive any of the wedges a second time.

Have seven hours work upon the rock.

In this manner these four principal beams were erected, and left in a pretty secure state. It, however, required the whole tide to get this much accomplished. Indeed, the men had commenced during ebb-tide, while there was about two or three feet water upon the site of the Beacon, and as the sea was smooth, they continued the work equally long during flood-tide. Two of the boats being left at the rock to take off the joiners, who were busily employed on the upper parts till 2 o'clock P. M., this tide's work may be said to have continued for about seven hours, which was the longest that had hitherto been got upon the rock by at least three hours.

When the first boats left the rock with the artificers employed on the lower part of the work during the flood-tide, the Beacon had quite a novel appearance. The beams erected, formed a common base of about thirty-three feet, meeting at the top, which, independently of ulterior works, was about forty-five feet above the rock, and here half a dozen of the artificers were still at work. After clearing the rock, the boats made a stop, when three hearty cheers were given, which were returned with equal good will by those upon the Beacon, from the personal interest which every one felt in the prosperity of this work, so intimately connected with his safety.

All hands assemble to prayers.

All hands having returned to their respective ships, they got a shift of dry clothes, and some refreshment. Being Sunday, they were afterwards convened by signal on board of the Light-house Yacht, when prayers were read; for every heart, upon this occasion, felt gladness, and every mind was disposed to be thankful for the happy and successful termination of the operations of this day. The crews then returned to their respective ships, and as nothing further could be done to the Beacon during the night tide, there was no landing made in the evening.

Monday 21st.

The weather most fortunately continued favourable for the operations, the wind being westerly, with fresh breezes. The boats landed at half-past 7 A. M., the number of persons on the rock being, as formerly, fifty-two; the work was carried on till half-past 12, making four hours and a half upon the rock. The remaining two principal beams were erected in the course of this tide, which, with the assistance of those set up yesterday, was found to be a very simple operation. In hoisting up the sixth and last log, however, and just when it was about to be kanted into its place, the iron-hook of the principal purchase-block gave way, and this great beam, measuring fifty feet in length, fell upon the rock with a terrible crash; but what is not a little wonderful, although there were fifty-two people engaged round the beacon, yet not one was hurt in the slightest degree by its fall. The beam itself was only a little shaken near the upper end, but was not materially damaged. Another block was immediately hooked, in the place of that which had failed, and the beam was got into its place without much delay. Every possible exertion was now made to fix the lower ends of the beams to the rock, by connecting them with their respective stanchions, while three strong hoops of malleable iron were employed, for securing the whole in one mass at the top.

The six principal beams of the beacon were thus secured, at least in a temporary manner, in the course of two tides, or in the short space of about eleven hours and a half. The only inconveniency attending this operation, arose from the derrick for raising the first beam being rather too short. It was only thirty feet in height, whereas it was found that it would have answered better had it been about forty-five feet. We were also a good deal troubled and perplexed with the logs afloat, from having the six principal beams in two rafts: it would have been more convenient had they been lashed together in pairs, and then rafted in one lot. The writer concludes, upon the whole, that about eight hours only were actually employed in raising the beams of the beacon, and fixing them in a temporary manner. Such is the progress that may be made, when active hands and willing minds set properly to work in operations of this kind.

Tuesday, 22d.

Four of the supporting beams set up.

Having now got the weighty part of this work over, and being thereby relieved of the difficulty both of landing and victualling such a number of men, the Smeaton could now be spared, and she was accordingly dispatched to Arbroath, for a supply of water and provisions, and carried with her six of the artificers who could best be spared. The wind to-day was due west, and blowing so fresh, that the boats had some difficulty in landing the remaining thirty-six persons at 8 A. M. who continued on the rock till half-past 12, having had four and a half hours work. During this tide four of the struts, or supporting beams, were set up, butting against the inside of four of the principal beams. These supports were each about twenty feet in length, varying somewhat according to the inequalities of the rock. At the foot they were fixed to the rock with stanchions, similar to those of the principal beams, and at the top they were connected with pieces of oak, strongly strapped with iron, collapsing around the principal beams to which they were bolted.

Wednesday, 23d.

The boats have some difficulty in leaving the rock to-day.

Landed at half-past 9 this morning, and succeeded in getting up the two remaining supports, and in fixing several of the bracing chains. But, instead of entering at present into any farther details about the several parts of the beacon, it will be better to refer these to the letter-press description of Plate VIII. After having been four and a half hours at work on the rock to-day, the boats left it, though not without considerable difficulty, as the wind had been blowing fresh all the last night, and to-day it was shifting and veering about from N.W. to N.N.E., which had already set up a pretty heavy sea. In going out of the eastern harbour, the boat which the writer steered shipped a sea, that filled her about one-third with water. She had also been hid for a short time, by the waves breaking upon the rock, from the sight of the crew of the preceding boat, who were much alarmed for our safety, imagining for a time that she had gone down.

Shipping separated by a gale.

The Smeaton returned from Arbroath this afternoon, but there was so much sea that she could not be made fast to her moorings; she therefore let go her small bower anchor, in order to get a supply of provisions put on board of the Light-house yacht, and receive other six of the artificers to carry ashore. But the anchor was no sooner let go than it broke among the rocks, and the vessel was obliged to return to Arbroath, without being able either to deliver the provisions, or take the artificers on board. The Light-house yacht was also soon obliged to follow her example, as the sea was breaking heavily over her bows. After getting two reefs in the mainsail, and the third or storm-jib set, the wind being SW., she beat to windward, though blowing a hard gale, and got into St Andrew's Bay, where we passed the night under the lee of Fifeness. In these circumstances, it was impossible for the writer to divest himself of much anxiety for the fate of the newly erected beacon, which was still but imperfectly fixed to the rock.

Thursday, 24th.

At 2 o'clock this morning we were in St Andrew's Bay, standing off and on shore, with strong gales of wind at SW.; at 7 we were off the entrance of the Tay; at 8 stood towards the rock, and at 10 passed to leeward of it, but could not attempt a landing. The beacon, however, appeared to remain in good order, and by 6 P. M. the vessel had again beaten up to St Andrew's Bay, and got into somewhat smoother water for the night.

Friday, 25th.

The wind still continues at SW., blowing very hard; at 7 o'clock bore away for the Bell Rock, but finding a heavy sea running on it, were unable to land. The writer, however, had the satisfaction to observe, with his telescope, that every thing about the beacon appeared entire, and although the sea had a most frightful appearance, yet it was the opinion of every one, that, since the erection of the beacon, the Bell Rock was divested of many of its terrors, and, had it been possible to have got the boats hoisted out and manned, it might have even been found practicable to land: the vessel was, therefore, kept in the track of the rock, till it could be determined if a landing might be effected with the afternoon's tide. The Yacht, in the mean time, stood towards the Redhead on the opposite shore, and at 5 P. M. returned; but both the wind and sea had rather increased. At 6 it blew so hard, that it was found necessary to strike the topmast and take in a third reef of the mainsail, and under this low canvas we soon reached St Andrew's Bay, and got again under the lee of the land for the night. The artificers being sea-hardy, were quite reconciled to their quarters on board of the Light-house Yacht; but it is believed that hardly any consideration would have induced them again to take up their abode in the floating-light.

Saturday, 26th.

Land on the rock after an absence of four days.

In the course of the last night, the wind had shifted from SW. to W. NW., with moderate weather. At day-light, the Yacht steered towards the Bell Rock, and at 8 A. M., made fast to her moorings; at 10, all hands, to the amount of thirty, landed, when the writer had the happiness to find that the beacon had withstood the violence of the gale and the heavy breach of sea, every thing being found in the same state in which it had been left on the 21st. The artificers were now enabled to work upon the rock throughout the whole day, both at low and high water, but it required the strictest attention to the state of the weather, in case of their being overtaken with a gale, which might prevent the possibility of getting them off the rock. To-day, one half of the artificers remained on the beacon till half-past 6 P. M., having been eight hours and a half at work upon it.

Smith's forge removed from the rock to the Beacon.

Two somewhat memorable circumstances in the annals of the Bell Rock attended the operations of this day; one was the removal of Mr James Dove, the foreman smith, with his apparatus, from the rock to the upper part of the beacon, where the forge was now erected on a temporary platform, laid on the cross beams or upper framing. The other was, the artificers having dined for the first time upon the rock, their dinner being cooked on board of the Yacht, and sent to them by one of the boats. But what afforded the greatest happiness and relief, was the removal of the large bellows, which had all along been a source of much trouble and perplexity, by their hampering and incommoding the boat which carried the smiths and their apparatus. The men belonging to that boat were so delighted with this occurrence, that while the bellows were in the act of being hoisted up to their new station, they gave three such hearty cheers, from below, as astonished and surprised those who were working the tackle on the beacon, to such a degree, that, for a moment, they let the rope slip through their hands, and had they not speedily caught hold again, this useful implement might have been dashed to pieces,— which would have been a misfortune of no small import, considering the state of the works at the present crisis.

Sunday 27th.

It being now the period of neap-tides, other ten of the artificers were sent ashore to the work-yard at Arbroath, which reduced our complement at the rock to twenty. The boats landed the people this morning at 11, but the masons had only about an hour's work on the highest part of the foundation of the light-house, which was only partially left by the water, the joiners and two blacksmiths being busily employed in completing and securing the several parts of the beacon, particularly in screwing the bolts of the stanchions and bracing-chains, and in staying the lower part of the beams. They continued at these operations till 6 o'clock P. M., having been nine hours upon the rock.

Monday, 28th.

The writer sails for Arbroath after having been four weeks afloat.

The joiners and smiths were landed on the beacon at 7 A. M., where they continued all day, and were brought off again at 5 P. M. The Smeaton had just returned from Leith, where she had been sent for sundry materials connected with the work. The joiners and smiths were ten hours upon the rock to-day, which was the longest period they had hitherto been upon it at any one time. They now had their dinner regularly sent to the beacon, and could continue at work throughout the whole day, while the weather was sufficiently moderate to admit of the boats plying to and from the rock. To-day the water did not leave it, and it was now the seventh day since the lowest part of the foundation or site of the light-house had been seen. The Beacon being now in a comparative state of security, the Smeaton was left at the rock as a tender, and the writer sailed in the Light-house yacht, this afternoon, to inquire into the operations of the work-yard at Arbroath. After setting sail, and looking back upon the Bell Rock, it was quite astonishing to observe the change in the appearance of things, which the erection of these beams had produced. To shipping they became an excellent beacon; while they induced the greatest confidence of safety in all who were actively engaged in this work. The vessel anchored in the bay of Arbroath, at a late hour, when the writer landed, for the first time since the commencement of the working season, on the 17th of August; after having been between four and five weeks afloat.

Tuesday, 29th.

This morning was occupied in going over the work-yard with Mr David Logan, clerk of works, who had charge of the hewing department. The first entire course of the building was now partly laid upon the platform: a few stones of the second course, and several of the higher courses, were also in progress. But from the backward state of the quarries in the production of stones of large dimensions, it was found necessary to make some additional exertions for procuring a more regular supply, and a person was therefore dispatched to the quarries of Aberdeen and Mylnefield for this purpose.

Sails again for the Bell Rock.

Having made some further arrangements in the work-yard, the writer again embarked in the Yacht, and sailed for the Bell Rock this forenoon, carrying with him Mr Peter Logan, the foreman builder, and the artificers who had formerly been at the rock; but who had expressly stipulated that they were not to be obliged to continue longer afloat than the approaching spring-tides, when it was expected the Beacon works would be completely secured for the winter. In the early part of this day, there was little or no wind, but in the afternoon it came to blow very hard from south by west, and in the evening it had increased to a hard gale. Having stood off to the Bell Rock, and put the vessel under low canvas, we hailed the floating-light, and found her labouring very hard with sixty fathoms of cable out. We then stretched to the southern side of the Bell Rock, when the vessel was laid to; but the Smeaton, which was also in company, being a small vessel, and much hampered with boats, was not in a condition to keep at sea, and as soon as the gale got up she stood in for Arbroath, and landed Mr Francis Watt, the foreman-joiner, and the artificers under his charge, to wait a favourable change of weather.

Wednesday, 30th.

The vessels again separated by a gale.

This morning it was calculated, by Mr Gloag, the commander of the Light-house Yacht, that she had drifted about thirty miles, in a SE. direction from the Redhead. About mid-day, the wind shifted to NW., and we steered for St Abb's Head, which was seen about twilight in the evening, and our course was directed across the Firth of Forth. When in the act of putting about the ship, the stem boat was very nearly lost, having been struck by a heavy sea which unhooked the fore-tackle. At midnight we got within a few miles of the light of May, and soon afterwards found smooth water in St Andrew's Bay, where we tacked, or "stood to and again," as the sailors term it, all night.

1807, October.

October, Thursday 1st.

This morning the wind shifted to NE. with moderate breezes. In the course of the forenoon we beat towards the Bell Rock, and sailed round it, when every thing appeared to be in good order about the beacon. Having no shelter in St Andrew's Bay with this wind, the Yacht stood alternately towards Arbroath and the Bell Rock for the night. The floating-light being a most excellent guide for putting about, before the vessel got too near to the rock. The older sailors on board of the Yacht, on this occasion, made frequent observations as to the utility of this temporary light, expressing their admiration at the change of circumstances which had led to their cruising with so much confidence, both by day and night, in the immediate vicinity of this dangerous rock.

Friday 2d.

Effect a landing at the rock.

The wind having come round to NW. with fresh breezes, it soon run down the north-easterly swell of the sea, and at half-past 1 P. M., all hands, to the amount of twenty, landed on the rock, though not without difficulty. Twelve of the masons were engaged during three hours, or till 4 o'clock, in excavating the foundation of the light-house, while the eight joiners and smiths, who also had arrived with the Smeaton, were employed at the works of the beacon for nine hours and a half; and having continued at work by torchlight, they left the rock at half-past 10 o'clock P. M.

State of the Beacon after the late gale.

On carefully examining into the state of things at the Bell Rock, after the late gale, the writer had the satisfaction to find, that the principal beams of the beacon, with their diagonal supports, cross-beams and stanchions connecting them to the rock, had not the smallest appearance of working or shifting, as mechanics express it. One of the tie chains had indeed given way, and hung loosely from the beacon, and one of the bracing screws had wrought off its nut. This was an evidence that the principal beams from the elasticity of the timber, had been acted upon by the sea, and that they still required some additional stay in the middle. Such, however, were the fixtures of the beacon to the rock with the iron stanchions, and its connection at the top, where it was strongly girt with circular hoops of iron, that it was perfectly firm at both extremities. The central support was intended to be effected by means of strong bars of iron, stretching between the principal beams; but the season was now too far advanced for such an undertaking, and therefore, the bracing-chains, represented in Plate VIII., were attached for the present.

It was not a little remarkable, that notwithstanding the impression which the sea had produced during the late gale, in shaking the beacon, so as to break one of the tie-chains, unscrew one of the bracing-bolts, and in shaking several of the smith's tools from his hearth on the platform at the top, yet these tools, and other small articles of iron, were all found lying on the rock. The nut of the bolt, for example, was got immediately under the chain from which it had dropped. Several other striking examples of this kind were observable, shewing how little will shelter articles somewhat ponderous in themselves, when they lie at a considerable depth in water.

Saturday 3d.

Working hours greatly extended.

The wind being west to-day, the weather was very favourable for the operations at the rock, and during the morning and evening tides, with the aid of torch-light, the masons had seven hours' work upon the site of the building. The smiths and joiners, who landed at half-past 6 A. M., did not leave the rock till a quarter past 11 P. M., having been at work, with little intermission, for sixteen hours and three quarters. When the water left the rock, they were employed at the lower parts of the beacon, and as the tide rose or fell, they shifted the place of their operations. From these exertions, the fixing and securing of the beacon made rapid advancement, as the men were now landed in the morning, and remained throughout the day. But, as a sudden change of weather might have prevented their being taken off at the proper time of tide, a quantity of bread and water was always kept on the Beacon.

Sunday 4th.

The wind was southerly during the fore part of the day, and towards evening it became quite calm. The boats landed the artificers this morning at a quarter before 7 o'clock; when the masons had three and a half hours ' work at the foundation of the building, but the spring-tides were now taking off; the best of them having unfortunately been lost during the late gale. The smiths and joiners, however, continued their operations throughout the whole of the day, and did not leave the rock till half-past 12 at night.

During this period of working at the Beacon all the day, and often a great part of the night, the writer was much on board of the Tender; but, while the masons could work on the rock, and frequently also while it was covered by the tide, he remained on the Beacon; especially during the night, as he made a point of being on the rock to the latest hour, and was generally the last person who stepped into the boat. He had laid this down as part of his plan of procedure; and in this way had acquired, in the course of the first season, a pretty complete knowledge and experience of what could actually be done at the Bell Rock, under all circumstances of the weather. By this means also his assistants, and the artificers and mariners, got into a systematic habit of proceeding at the commencement of the work, which, it is believed, continued throughout the whole of the operations.

Beacon works finished for the season.

The external part of the beacon was now finished, with its supports and bracing-chains, and whatever else was considered necessary for its stability, in so far as the season would permit; and although much was still wanting to complete this fabric, yet it was in such a state that it could be left without much fear of the consequences of a storm. The painting of the upper part was nearly finished this afternoon; and the Smeaton had brought off a quantity of brush-wood and other articles, for the purpose of heating or charring the lower part of the principal beams, before being laid over with successive coats of boiling pitch, to the height of from eight to twelve feet, or as high as the rise of spring-tides. A small flag-staff having also been erected to-day, a flag was displayed for the first time from the Beacon, by which its perspective effect was greatly improved. On this, as on all like occasions at the Bell Rock, three hearty cheers were given; and the steward served out a dram of rum to all hands, while the Light-house Yacht, Smeaton, and Floating-light, hoisted their colours in compliment to the Erection.

Monday 5th.

To-day the wind was westerly, and the weather was very wet; but this was thought nothing of at the Bell Rock, so long as the wind kept moderate. At a quarter past 8 A. M. the boats landed the artificers. The masons had only 2½ hours' work at the site of the building, owing to the smallness of the ebb-tide; but the joiners and smiths continued their operations till half-past 11 P. M., and were consequently 15 hours and a quarter upon the Rock.

Mr Rennie and one of his sons visit the Rock.

In the afternoon, and just as the tide's work was over, Mr John Rennie, engineer, accompanied by his son Mr George, on their way to the harbour-works of Fraserburgh, in Aberdeenshire, paid a visit to the Bell Rock, in a boat from Arbroath. It being then too late in the tide for landing, they remained on board of the Light-house Yacht all night, when the writer, who had now been secluded from society for several weeks, enjoyed much of Mr Rennie's interesting conversation; both on general topics, and professionally upon the progress of the Bell-Rock works, on which he was consulted as chief engineer. The weather continued very moderate all night; but although there was little swell in the sea, yet our quarters on board of the Yacht were not the most agreeable, especially to strangers. The vessel, being perfectly new, was so completely water-tight, that it was hardly possible to keep her free of bilge-water, and so strong was the hydrogenous gas or offensive effluvia arising from it, that it had affected the colour of the paint of the cabin floor-cloth, and even, to a certain degree, blackened the silver plate, coins and watch-cases on board, notwithstanding the frequent pumping of the ship, and other means which were taken to sweeten her.

Tuesday 6th.

Works given up for the season.

The artificers landed this morning at 9, after which one of the boats returned to the ship for the writer and Messrs Rennie, who, upon landing, were saluted with a display of the colours from the Beacon, and by three cheers from the workmen. Both the weather and the tide were pretty favourable for the operations, and the masons continued about three hours at work. Every thing was now in a prepared state for leaving the rock, and giving up the works afloat for this season, excepting some small articles, which would still occupy the smiths and joiners for a few days longer. They, accordingly, shifted on board of the Smeaton, while the Yacht left the rock for Arbroath, with Messrs Rennie, the writer, and the remainder of the artificers. But, before taking leave, the steward served out a farewell-glass, when three hearty cheers were given, and an earnest wish expressed, that every thing, in the spring of 1808, might be found in the same state of good order as it was now about to be left.

In concluding the account of the first season's work, the writer may observe, that he had not at any time previously to his engaging in the Bell Rock works, been more than five or six days at sea on a stretch, even in the course of his voyages to the Northern Light-houses. But on the present occasion he had now been afloat upwards of seven weeks, with the exception of a single day spent in the Work Yard. Upon his return to the shore, therefore, after having successfully closed these critical operations, he felt a mixed emotion of happiness and gratitude, for so prosperous a termination; and, participating in those feelings which are known to actuate the mariner, after a dangerous voyage, he looked with thankfulness to that Providence which had preserved those engaged in the work under so many perilous circumstances.

Number of days the artificers were actually at work.

The period during which the works had been continued, appeared of much longer duration to every one than it really was, for, upon calculating the actual time spent upon the rock, it amounted to about 180 hours, of which only 133 or about 13½ days, of 10 hours each, could be said to have been actively employed. Upon looking back on this result, the writer is astonished at what had been accomplished in so short a period; for besides the erection of the principal beams of the Beacon-house, something considerable had also been done towards the preparation of the site of the Light-house. He cannot, therefore, help thinking, that the experience of this season's work at the Bell Rock, affords a good example of what may be executed under similar circumstances, when every heart and every hand is anxiously and zealously engaged; for the artificers wrought at the erection of the Beacon as for life; or somewhat like men stopping a breach in a wall to keep out an overwhelming flood.

PROGRESS OF THE WORK.

In stating the progress of the Bell Rock works at the close of the first season, it is hardly necessary to say, that, for success, and ultimate utility, they far exceeded the writer's most sanguine expectations. By the erection of the frame-work of the Beacon-house, the rock had in a great measure been robbed of its terrors to those employed in building the Light-house. At all times when a boat could be put to sea, or approach this sunken reef, there was not now that actual danger in landing which formerly presented itself. Should the Tender in future go a-drift, or a boat happen to be wrecked on the rock, the Beacon could now be looked to as a place of shelter, till more efficient means could be resorted to. This work had always been a great desideratum with the writer, who had now chiefly to consider how the future steps were to be attained, having much less to occupy his attention in regard to the safety of the people employed.

The whole of the artificers being collected at the work-yard of Arbroath, in the latter end of the month of October, their number amounted to forty-four. It, therefore, became indispensably necessary to get forward with the quarries, otherwise a number of experienced workmen must have been paid off, which would have been attended with much disadvantage to the operations at the rock next year. There was now every prospect that by mid-summer, the foundation or site of the Light-house would be completely excavated and ready for commencing the building; while as yet the hewing of one entire course had not been completed, for want of materials, although the stones of three or four successive courses were in progress. For example, 10 blocks of granite were still wanting of the first course, 30 blocks of the second, which measured 18 inches in thickness, and 20 blocks of the third, and so of other courses. The procuring of a sufficient stock of materials, and getting the quarries into a more regular system of supply, became an object which we shall more particularly notice under the article Building Materials, in the following chapter.

Work-Yard.

The Work-Yard at Arbroath, where the stones were collected and hewn, consisted of an inclosed piece of ground, extending to about three quarters of an acre, conveniently situate on the northern side of the Lady Lane, or street, leading from the western side of the Harbour, being only about 200 yards distant from the Light-House shipping birth, as will be seen from Plate XII. Upon this plot of ground there was built a suite or range of barrack-rooms for the artificers, and the several apartments connected with the engineer's office, mould-makers' drawing-room, stores, work-shops for smiths and joiners, stable, &c. extending 150 feet along the north side of the work-yard, which were now fully occupied. Shades of timber were also constructed for the workmen in wet weather, and a kiln for burning lime. In a centrical position of this ground, a circular platform of masonry was built, on which the stones were laid when dressed, and each course tried and marked, before being shipped for the rock. This platform measured 44 feet in diameter; it was founded with large broad stones, at the depth of about 2 feet 6 inches, and built to within 10 inches of the surface with ruble work; on which a course of neatly dressed and well jointed masonry was laid, of the red sandstone from the quarries to the eastward of Arbroath, which brought the platform on a level with the surface of the ground. Here the dressed part of the first entire course of the Light-House was now lying, and the platform was so substantially built as to be capable of supporting any number of courses which it might be found convenient to lay upon it, in the further progress of the work.

1807, November.

Mr Gloag, who commanded the Light-house Yacht, had been successful in grappling and finding the old moorings of the Pharos floating-light, from which that vessel had drifted after the dreadful gale of the 6th of September. These he had weighed, and removed to within about 400 fathoms of the new ground taken up by that vessel, and had placed a buoy upon them, that, in case of her again drifting, any vessel carrying the floating-light could immediately be brought to ride at these spare moorings. The Yacht had also lifted three of the four floating buoys, with their chains and mushroom anchors, from the neighbourhood of the

Bell Rock, leaving one set for the use of the vessel occasionally attending for the purpose of inspecting the Beacon. In the course of the month of November several very severe gales of wind occurred, and Mr Watt, the foreman joiner, who had been appointed to examine the rock at spring-tides, when the weather would permit, with three or four artificers, found some small repairs necessary, in consequence of damage which the Beacon had sustained.

Sunday 22d.

The Writer visits the Rock.

On the morning of the 22d of this month, the writer landed at the Bell Rock, when the greater part of the bracing-chains of the Beacon were in a loosened state, and hanging from their eye-bolts, like so much shipwreck. Two of the chain-bats were also drawn, which had lifted considerable masses of the rock along with them. But after a most careful and minute examination of the six principal beams of the beacon, and their respective supports, it was satisfactory to find that the great iron-stanchions had not the smallest appearance of working or shifting; the wedges of timber and iron having exactly the same appearance as when they were at first driven home by the hammer; the coating of pitch and tar was also as entire upon the seams and joints as when first applied. Every thing connected with the fixing of the beams at the top was likewise in good order. Nor was it less surprising, after so much stormy weather, to find that the ruble building, with Pozzolano's mortar, used in filling several holes in the site of the Beacon, remained in its place, having now become fully as hard as the adjoining parts of the rock.

Although it was found that the bracing-chains could not withstand the shaking and tremulous motion of the Beacon, yet they were again set up and tightened, with the exception of the two that had lifted their bats, with a mass of the rock; which were knocked off altogether. It is here worthy of remark, that the bolts of the bracing screws had always a tendency to unlock, and one of the nuts, as before noticed, had even unscrewed no less than three inches. To prevent this in future, a piece of small wire was turned round the threads of each screw, which had a tendency to preserve them; but still the chains stretched, became loose, and broke their eye-bolts, or lifted part of the rock with the strain. The bracing-chains may, however, be conceived to have had some effect in checking the force of the waves, as was observable in the operation of the sea upon the extensive beds of marine plants. It often happened, when heavy seas were rolling along the Bell Rock, which at a distance threatened to overrun the whole, that, upon reaching these beds of fuci, with which the flat and level parts of the rock were thickly coated, the velocity and force of the waves were immediately checked, and in a great measure destroyed.

Professor Playfair's observations about the unlocking of screws.

The unlocking of screws, where washers had been introduced as a security, was rather unexpected, and the writer took an opportunity of conversing with his much respected friend Professor Playfair of Edinburgh, regarding this circumstance. The Professor observed, that he had experienced some inconveniency of this kind from the unlocking of almost all the screws of a telescope, which had been sent to him from London by the mail-coach. Indeed from the spiral form of the screw, which is, in fact, an inclined plane, Mr Playfair readily accounted for such an occurrence; and when reflected upon, it seems to be an effect rather to be looked for, and is a reason why rivetting the point of a bolt, in preference to screwing it, should generally be resorted to, where much friction or motion is to be apprehended.

1807, December.

State of the Floating-light.

At this visit to the Bell Rock, the writer went also on board of the Floating-light, where every thing was found in good order. On some occasions Mr Sinclair, the commander, stated, that the vessel had rolled excessively hard; that she had shipped two or three very heavy seas over the waste-boards, and that he had found it occasionally necessary to veer out 80 fathoms of cable. He also stated, that the floating-light had been run foul of by a large smack-rigged vessel, with all her canvas set, though the lights were burning perfectly clear. This vessel had struck upon the larboard quarter, damaged the taff-rail, and started three of the floating-lights' trenails. That they immediately hailed the vessel, but she sheered-off, and her crew made no reply. The smack was beating to the northward, and was much lumbered on the quarter-deck with packages of earthen-ware, which were distinctly seen upon her deck from the brilliancy of the lights.

The sailors on board of the floating-light were all in good health, and appeared to be satisfied with their situation. The master, however, mentioned, that his crew, particularly the young men, calculated very sharply about their turns for leave on shore, which came round in the course of about six weeks. Indeed, the probability is, that had the seamen not been rather compelled to this duty, as a protection against the Impress-service, it might have been found extremely difficult to get able seamen to undertake so dreary a life as the continual round of riding at anchor in the open sea, without the company of other shipping, or the pleasure of intercourse with the shore, as is the case in the ordinary road or anchorage for shipping.

The several departments of the Bell Rock works being arranged for the winter months, the sloop Smeaton was appointed to make several trips to the quarries for stones, while the Light-house Yacht, being stationed at Arbroath, was to attend the Floating-light, and carry off the artificers to examine the state of the Beacon at spring-tides. The writer having adjusted these matters, returned to Edinburgh on the 4th of December. Here he was employed in preparing the necessary implements, procuring materials, and in other objects connected with the work, which will fall more properly to be noticed in the transactions of the year 1808.

CHAPTER IV.

SHIPPING.—IMPLEMENTS.—BUILDING MATERIALS,— AND PROGRESS OF THE BELL ROCK WORKS IN THE YEAR 1808.

1808, January.

After taking some notice of the preparations made during the winter months, or early part of the year 1808, it is proposed, in describing the progress of the works of this season, to adopt the form of a journal or diary, as in the preceding chapter. The last year's operations being more of a preliminary nature, the implements and apparatus employed were few in number, and simple in their construction. But the facilities to be afforded by the erection of the Beacon were such, that not only the site of the building was expected to be prepared, but it was hoped that some of the courses of masonry would also be laid during the ensuing summer. It therefore became necessary to be provided with shipping, and every article, both of implements and building materials, however small the actual progress of the work might ultimately be.

SHIPPING.

The New Tender.

It has already been noticed, in the course of last year's operations, that much inconveniency, and no small degree of hazard, were experienced in making the numerous passages between the Bell Rock and the Floating-light, especially when the boats were crowded with artificers. Not having previously been so fully aware of these circumstances, and with a view to save expence, the Floating-light was likewise applied to the purpose of a tender. She was consequently moored at a more considerable distance from the rock, as will be understood from Plate V.; but as, from the nature of her tackling, she could not be cast loose upon any emergency, she was found to be but ill adapted to the uses of a tender.

Is named The Sir Joseph Banks.

The writer having represented this to the Light-house Board, was immediately authorised to provide a vessel, to be exclusively employed for the service of the rock. He accordingly purchased one upon the stocks at Arbroath, in such forwardness, that she was launched upon the 18th of January 1808. This vessel was built by a Mr Thomas Fernie, and was considered so complete in the mould or figure of her hull, that some of the best judges of shipping have described her as one of the handsomest vessels which perhaps had hitherto been built in Scotland. On account of the exertions of the late Sir Joseph Banks, in his capacity of one of the Lords of Trade, in procuring the loan from Government, for the use of the Bell Rock Light-house, already alluded to in the Introduction to this work, the writer suggested, as a mark of respect, that the new tender should be named "The Sir Joseph Banks," to which the Light-house Board most readily acceded.

Is rigged as a schooner.

She was no sooner launched, than her rigging and equipment, in the best manner, were undertaken by professional people; but the inspection of the interior fitting and accommodations was kindly undertaken by the late Provost Balfour of Arbroath, a gentleman who took great delight in architectural pursuits, and who, upon all occasions, felt the most lively interest in the operations of the Bell Rock. In order that this vessel might stow two large boats upon deck, and be got as quickly as possible under sail, in the event of her breaking adrift, she was rigged as a schooner; and that, by the application of a tackle from each mast, the boats might be conveniently managed, in getting them in and out of the vessel. The Sir Joseph Banks being only 81 tons register, it was necessary to lay out the births, for the several departments of the service, with all possible attention to the economising of room. The forepeak was accordingly fitted up with a coboose for cooking; immediately aft of this birth, a compartment was set off for the ship's company and the landing-master's crew, with births for fifteen sailors. But Jack is by no means ill to satisfy with his sleeping-place, and it was often found necessary to encroach upon the allotted number for this birth, according to the exigencies of the service. The waist or middle of the ship was set apart for the artificers, and was capable of containing forty men. Still proceeding aft, a small birth was set off for the mate and steward, which communicated both with the artificers' birth, and also with the cabin for the engineer's assistants, the landing-master, and the captain of the tender. In the sternmost part of the ship, a cabin was fitted up for the use of the writer; the whole being found extremely commodious and suitable. From the great proportion of the ship required for the birthage of seamen and artificers, the hold of this small vessel was much curtailed, there being hardly more room left than was sufficient for containing a stock of provisions, water and fuel, for any length of time, besides stowing two or three tiers of casks of lime, cement, and other necessaries for the use of the work.

Praam-boats, or Stone-lighters.

Continuing the description of the marine part of the establishment, we next notice three new praam-boats, or stone-lighters, built for conveying the building materials to the Bell Rock, from the vessels employed in bringing them from the work-yard at Arbroath. The term Praam-boat is applied to a certain description of Norwegian boats, having their stem and stem rounded after a peculiar fashion. The introduction of this phrase, in the Bell Rock service, was purely accidental, having been applied, by Captain Grindlay, Master of the Trinity-House of Leith, to the first or experimental stone-lighter, from its resemblance to the praams of Norway. Those now alluded to, however, were built of a more rounded form, after the Dutch manner. They measured over all, on deck, about 28 feet by 8 feet 6 inches, and their depth of hold may be stated at 2 feet, for, being built by different carpenters, they were not exactly of the same dimensions. They had a considerable spring or sheer, and were constructed for carrying their cargoes entirely upon deck, which formed a kind of cockpit in the waist, having a high gunwale on each side, and a break, both fore and aft, as will be seen in Plate XI., the first tier of stones seldom reaching above the level of the gunwale. They had, consequently, little or no hold, having only what was sufficient for stowing some pig or cast iron ballast, a few empty casks, with the necessary warps, kedge-anchors, and grappling-irons.

Precautions taken for rendering them water-tight and buoyant.

These lighters were built of uncommonly strong materials, both in their timbers, outward planks, and ceiling or lining, which last was caulked and secured in a manner similar to that described for the Floating-light, so that although the outward skin were damaged, by striking or rubbing on the rock, there would still be an additional defence against sinking. Such, however, was the presentiment of danger attached to the landing-department, that besides the precaution of a water-tight lining, each praam was provided with twelve strong empty casks, which were stowed in the hold, and were sufficient to float and render her buoyant, in case of accident. The praams, therefore, became so many life-boats moored in the neighbourhood of the rock.

Method of mooring the Praam-boats.

These praams had but one hawse-hole, and that they might ride more easily at their moorings in the open sea, it was placed amid-ships, and as low or near the water-line as possible. The chain-hawsers with which they were connected to their respective floating-buoys and mushroom-anchors, were made of rod-iron, one-half inch in diameter, turned into as short links as possible. This piece of chain was about five fathoms in length, and was attached to the praam by a strong hook, connected with her bits, the farther end being made permanently fast to the mooring-chain of the mushroom-anchor. From the lowness of the hawse-hole, and its central position in the praam, and from having only a short piece of chain to carry, which connected the boat to the mooring-buoy, may be attributed the astonishing ease and safety with which these boats rode at anchor. So remarkable was this, that while the tender, and the other vessels in the service, were tossed about, and shipping a great deal of sea, and even at times obliged to slip their moorings, the praams floated with an easy undulating motion, and were generally as dry upon deck during a gale, though loaded with ten tons of stone, as if, to use a sailor's phrase, they had been riding in a mill-pond. The facility, also, with which the praams were attached and disengaged from their moorings, was another very great conveniency to the work. In unmooring them, all that became necessary was to unhook the hawser-chain from the bits, and throw it overboard, with a small floating-buoy attached to it, for the purpose of suspending the hawser-chain for the time. In the same manner, in making the praams fast to their moorings, this chain was simply to be laid hold of, by taking the small floating-buoy on board. The chain was then slipped into the hawse-hole, by a corresponding slit in the stem of the praam, and then attached to the bits, when the process was complete. By inspecting the diagrams in Plate XI., this process will be better understood.

Attending Boats.

The two cutters or boats employed last year for transporting the artificers from the Floating-light to the Bell Rock, were found to be rather too small in rough weather. They measured 16 feet in length of keel, 5 feet 3 inches in breadth, on the mid-ship thwart or seat, and 2 feet 6 inches in depth. These boats were of as large dimensions as the floating-light could stow, after making the necessary allowance for ranging her cables on deck. They had square sterns, were rowed with four oars, and accommodated twelve sitters, including sailors. But the Sir Joseph Banks being entirely fitted as a tender for the works, the stowing of large landing-boats became a principal object. Her boats were therefore made as large as possible, due regard being had to their convenient management and fitness for the small creeks or landing-places at the rock. After a careful consideration of these circumstances, it was resolved that the two new attending-boats should measure 20 feet in length of keel, 5 feet 8 inches in breadth, and 2 feet 10 inches in depth. They were rowed with eight oars, double banked, or two upon each thwart, and could accommodate eighteen sitters each. They were round in the stern, fitted with a backboard and a convenient seat for the cockswain, who steered with a yoke and lines, instead of a tiller.

Life-Boat.

One of these boats was called The Mason, the other The Seaman. The latter was fitted up as a Life-boat, somewhat after Greathead's method, being lined and girded with cork, to the depth of three streaks below the gunwale. In case of accident, therefore, by the bilging of either boat upon the rock, she was rendered more buoyant by the cork lining and sheathing. They were built in Leith, and before being sent to the rock, the buoyancy of the Life-boat was tried, when it was found that she would float with thirty people on board.

IMPLEMENTS.

Railways.

From the wasting effects of the sea, the Bell Rock is formed into numerous benches and gullies, and its surface is consequently extremely rough and irregular. The site of the Light-house being in a central position on the rock, it became necessary to make some provision for conveying the large blocks of stone speedily from the respective landing-places to the site of the building; or at least within the range of the cranes or machinery to be employed in laying them. In ordinary situations, the most obvious method would have been to clear away the inequalities of the rock; but here, from the lowness of its position in the water, such an operation would have been extremely tedious and difficult. Besides, every portion of the Bell Rock was held sacred, excepting in so far as it was absolutely necessary to excavate or remove part of it, in fixing the Beacon-house, and in preparing the foundation of the Light-house. Instead, therefore, of quarrying the rock, the writer found that the most advisable process would be, to lay cast-iron railways round the site of the Light-house, projecting to the several landing-places, on which waggons could easily be wheeled in all directions, as will be seen by tracing the dotted lines on

Plate VI.

For this purpose, patterns were prepared in the course of the winter, from which castings of the several compartments of the railways were made by Mr John Baird, of the Shotts Iron Works. These rails were cast in lengths of four feet, and supported upon props and frames of cast-iron, varying in height from six inches to five feet, according to the inequalities of the rock, that the whole might be laid upon one level. Besides the tracks for the wheels of the waggons, it was necessary also to provide a tracking-path of the same metal, which was formed of ribbed work, rested upon the supports of the rails, as will be understood from the diagrams in Plate X. The waggon-tracks were of the form technically termed Plate-rails, which were found convenient for making the necessary fixtures. The edge-rail is less liable to friction, and is certainly greatly preferable to the plate-rail, where the track is liable to be impeded with dust, and other adventitious matters; objections which do not apply at the Bell Rock, where the rails were every tide considerably under water.

Waggons.

It was necessary that every thing intended to be left on the Bell Rock during the working season, should have as little buoyancy as possible, and as it would have been extremely inconvenient to have removed the waggons from the rock, which were to be employed in conveying the blocks of stone from the landing-places to the Light-house, they were constructed entirely of iron, excepting two pieces of oak timber, which were bolted upon the top, to form a seat for the stones. These waggons, represented in Plate X., moved upon four trucks or wheels of cast-iron, measuring one foot two inches in diameter, placed two feet six inches asunder, being the length of the axle, and breadth of the railway. Each waggon was provided with a handle, which shifted at pleasure to either end, for the conveniency of reversing the motion, without the necessity of turning the vehicle. But what was more peculiar to these waggons, was a joint in the middle of the perch or double frame, connecting the wheels, by means of which they were made applicable to the circular tracks of the railway round the site of the building.

Triangular Crane.

Connected with the cast-iron railways, preparations were also made at the eastern landing place, for lifting the stones by means of cranes or other machinery from the Praam-boats, and laying them upon the waggons to be conveyed to the building. After a good deal of consideration, patterns were prepared for an apparatus consisting chiefly of six pieces of cast-iron, four of which measured 12 feet in length, and of a corresponding strength. As will be seen in Plate XI., these bars met at the top in the form of two sets of sheers, but their lower ends were placed about 9 feet asunder. Connected with these, a pair of sheers were set up, which were moveable upon a bolt, and worked with a crab or winch machine, the whole being strongly batted to the rock. When the moveable pair of sheers, with their attached chain and hook, were suspended outwards over the stone to be lifted from the praam, the chain was hooked to the Lewis-bat, previously inserted into the block. The sheers were then raised till they were brought to a perpendicular position, when the motion of the winch was reversed, and the sheers were lowered inwards upon the wharf, and the stone thus laid upon the waggon. The chain was then unhooked, and the sheers were ready for lifting another stone, as will be better understood by referring to Plate XI., with its letter-press description.

Crane with moveable Beam.

Having, in the foregoing article, described the implement employed in landing the stones on the Bell Rock during the year 1808, we are now to notice the crane employed in laying or building them. It appears from Mr Smeaton's Narrative, that the implements chiefly used for building at the Edystone, were a pair of moveable sheer-poles and a set of triangles, most ingeniously applied to their respective purposes. But such implements must have come far short of the expedition which the writer had conceived to be necessary at the Bell Rock, both on account of the much greater extent of the building, and also from its foundation being so much lower in the water. After considering the subject, and making minute inquiries into the practice at various public works, he found no implement of the description, which he considered applicable to his purpose. The common sheer-poles, still chiefly in use, were recommended as having upon the whole been successfully employed at the Edystone. In some instances, the common crane, with the beam fixed at the top, at right angles to the shaft, was applied for laying heavy materials. The writer, however, laid it down as a proposition to himself, That a more effective mode of building must be adopted at the Bell Rock than had hitherto been in use, by which all the stones at any time likely to be landed in the course of a tide, might be built and secured before the artificers left the rock.

The chief difficulties attending the application of the common crane in such a situation, consisted in the laying the stones perpendicularly into their respective places, as they were all of a dove-tail or angular form, as will be seen from Plate XIII. The fixed beam of the common crane was further objectionable, from its being more liable to interfere with the guy ropes. It would also have been difficult to have lifted it either laterally or perpendicularly upon the building, from one course to another. To these may also be added the great obstruction which the beam would have presented to the waves of the sea at high water. All these objections, however, were in a great measure got over, by substituting a moveable beam to work upon a bolt at the foot or lower end of the upright shaft, instead of a fixed beam at the top in the usual manner. But as we shall have occasion again to notice this machine in the operation of building, we shall here refer to Plate XIV. with its letter-press description. Three of these cranes, with moveable beams, were prepared for the work, in the course of the winter, one with an upright shaft of 28 feet in length, for laying the prepared stones upon the platform in the work-yard at Arbroath, and other two, with shafts of 21 feet, for building at the rock.

Sling Cart.

Though none of the stones of the Bell Rock Light-house were likely to exceed two tons in weight, in their finished state; yet, in their undressed state, they were much more ponderous. From the waste attending their dove-tailed form, and the working them square on all their sides, the blocks from the quarry were greatly reduced; in many instances, to one-half of the cubical contents of their quarry dimensions, before they were brought to the size of the moulds. The stones had not only to be conveyed from the harbour of Arbroath to the work-yard, a distance of from two to three hundred yards, but also required to be frequently lifted from place to place; as, for example, when in a hewn or dressed state, they were removed to the circular platform, in the middle of the work-yard, to be tried and marked;—they were again shifted from this position, and ultimately carried to the harbour to be shipped for the rock. From the various movements which each stone had thus to undergo, it became an object of importance to the facility and economy of the work, to consider how this could be most conveniently accomplished. Had a cart or carriage, with four wheels of the ordinary construction for great loads, been employed, it would have been extremely troublesome, in all the operations of loading, turning and moving from place to place. To have attempted to avoid this by the use of waggons with low wheels, and the introduction of railways along the quays and public streets of Arbroath, would also have been objectionable, especially as the object could be much more conveniently obtained by the use of what is called the Woolwich Sling-cart, represented in Plate X. By this machine, the weight is simply raised off the ground with a wheel and pinion apparatus fixed upon the frame of the cart, and in this manner, the stone, instead of being lifted upon the body of the carriage, had only to be suspended at the necessary height for overcoming the inequalities of the road. This vehicle had long been used with great advantage by military engineers, in moving ordnance; but was probably first employed at Mylnefield Quarry, and the Bell Rock works, in transporting blocks of stone.

Carpenter's Jack.

Another implement prepared, in the course of the winter, for the Bell Rock work-yard, was the Carpenter's jack, used for raising ships upon the blocks or props for the purposes of repair. This machine, which is simple in its construction, and direct in its application, consists of a rack and pinion, enclosed in a frame of oak timber, strongly bound with iron, as represented in Plate X. By working the handle of the jack, the stone-cutter is enabled, without the assistance of his fellow workmen, to turn and lay the heaviest stone to his hand. This apparatus the writer first saw used to much advantage, by the quarriers at Portland Island, in the year 1801; and though it had not perhaps at that time been put into the hands of the stone-cutter, it was obvious that it might also be applied to his purpose with equal effect.

It may further be noticed, regarding this useful implement, as strongly marking the prejudices of habit, that Mr Mylne, the proprietor of Mylnefield Quarry, who, with enlightened views, furnished his works with machinery of the very best description, among other articles, provided a number of these jack-machines for his quarriers, but, for a long time, they could not be induced to make use of them. One of the men, however, happening, of his own accord, to apply the jack in turning a heavy block, its utility soon became apparent; and Mr Allan the manager, who had previously taken considerable pains to get the jack introduced, was at length not a little pleased to find it, after having been laid up in store as useless, in much request throughout that extensive quarry.

Lewis Bat.

A Lewis Bat, of some form, for lifting large stones, is believed to have been known to the ancients. But that now in common use is generally understood to have been at least improved by the French engineers, who, in honour of their Sovereign, gave it the name of Lewis. This useful implement is so universally known in practice, for its great utility in building with heavy materials, that it is hardly necessary to do more than simply allude to it. It consists of five pieces of iron, three of which, forming a dovetail, like an inverted wedge or the keystone of an arch, are inserted into a corresponding hole cut in the stone. The fourth is the bolt connecting the shackle-piece, by which the weight is suspended, as will be better understood by referring to the sketch or diagram illustrative of it in Plate XI. Of this implement, it became necessary to furnish several dozens, as well from the variety in the weight, as from the figure of the stones, many of them requiring two Lewises to produce a proper balance. But the number was more particularly encreased, from the different sets required for the workyard, the stone-lighters, and for the Bell Rock, where it was necessary to provide against loss, to which this service was so peculiarly liable.

Moulds.

As the whole of the stones of each course or tier of this building were connected or let into one another, by a system of dovetails, diverging from the centre to the circumference, after the manner of the Edystone Light-house, as will be seen from Plate XIII., each particular stone required to be cut with accuracy, to fit its precise place in the building; and as even the form into which the blocks of granite were made, often depended upon the adventitious produce of the quarries, it became a very considerable operation to prepare the necessary moulds or patterns for the respective courses. When, therefore, the thickness was ascertained that a lot of these stones would admit being dressed, a plan of the particular course was first drawn upon paper by the Clerk of Works; a certain compartment of the course was then protracted of the full size, upon a platform of polished pavement, measuring 70 feet in length, and 25 feet in breadth, and occupying part of the ground floor of the workmen's barrack. From this enlarged draught, Mr James Slight, the principal mould-maker, took his dimensions in making the moulds of the full size of the ground-plan of each stone, on which were marked the necessary directions for the stone-cutter, both as to the thickness of the course, and the position of the connecting joggle-holes, trenails and wedges.

These moulds being made with great precision, were carefully marked and numbered with oil paint, according to the positions which the respective stones were to occupy. They were made of well seasoned fir timber, and dressed clean in the form of open frame-work, measuring from three to four inches in breadth, and from one-half to three-fourths of an inch in thickness. At the angles and joints, thin plates of iron were screwed upon these frames, to strengthen and preserve them, while the workmen were making their draught-lines, and in their numerous applications of them in the process of hewing the stones. Each course of the solid part of the building required from three to five moulds, of the form delineated in Plate X., which were carefully laid aside in sets, till the particular course to which they belonged should be landed upon the rock, and secured in the building. In a work of this kind, such a precaution was indispensably necessary; for, in case of loss or accident to any of the stones, in landing them at the Rock, it would then only have been necessary to send to the work-yard, referring to the particular number of the mould, from which another stone could speedily have been prepared.

Cofferdam.

In the first designs for the Bell Rock Light-house, the writer had modelled a cofferdam, five feet in height, intended to have been erected of cast-iron, round the site of the building, that the work in its early stages might be continued for a longer period, both during the ebb and flood tides. The experience of last season's work, however, shewed that the erection of the proposed cofferdam would have been attended with considerable difficulty; and, to have rendered such an apparatus equally useful during ebb-tide as flood-tide, would have required the pumping of water by machinery more complicated and powerful than the situation of the Bell Rock would have admitted.

Pumps.

This idea was therefore laid aside, and two Pumps, of a simple construction, were prepared, for clearing the foundation-pit of water. They measured about twelve feet in length, and were of a square form, both externally and internally, having each a void of ten inches. They were made of fir timber, three inches in thickness, strongly jointed, and put together with white-lead paint, having also a number of cross bars and bolts of iron, to strengthen them for withstanding the atmospheric pressure upon so considerable a surface. These pumps were furnished with a wooden spear or rod, having a cross head or handle at one end, and a leathern valve attached to the other. This valve was of a very simple construction; it collapsed when plunged into the water, and was inflated by the return draught delivering a quantity of water equal to the cubical contents of the void or chamber of the pump.

Winch-machines.

There were four Crabs or Winch-machines prepared for working the different purchases required in the various departments of the work, as, for example, in lifting the stones from the praam-boats, as represented in Plate XI. Another of these machines was fixed on the temporary wooden bridge of communication, erected between the Beacon-house and Light-house, as will be seen in Plate IX. Other two of these machines are likewise represented for raising the stones from stage to stage upon the building, as will be more particularly described in the letter-press description of this Plate. These machines were made wholly of iron, excepting the bushes for the gudgeons working in, which were of bell-metal. They were calculated to work with what is called double and single purchases, according to the weight of the stones to be lifted. They were very powerful in their operation: the winch or barrel being twelve inches in diameter, gave the single purchase a power of about fifteen to one, and the double purchase about sixty to one. These machines were calculated to work with five tons. The weight of the largest size was altogether about 10 cwt., so that they were not easily shifted by the impulse of the sea, when batted to the rock, as represented in Plate XI.

BUILDING MATERIALS.

Stone.

The Commissioners of the Northern Light-houses, as before noticed, having finally resolved that the erection upon the Bell Rock should be of stone, constructed upon principles similar to the Edystone Light-house, it became a question of importance in the economy of the work, to fix the quality and description of stone to be used. Considering this subject in reference to the Edystone Light-house, it appears that the hearting or interior of the solid part is of sandstone from Portland Island, and that the exterior of that building is of Cornish granite, both of which were highly suitable in quality, and were fortunately procurable from quarries the most contiguous to Plymouth, where these works were situate.

Mineralogy of the southern and eastern shores of Britain.

It may farther be noticed, that granite is perhaps the only stone upon the coast of England, which possesses durability for withstanding the effects of the weather in a situation so exposed, or strength sufficient for undergoing the process of landing the stones when in their prepared state. In Scotland, however, the case is widely different, for here, the country abounds with excellent building materials of almost every description; and excepting in those districts which produce granite, that stone is rarely had recourse to for buildings of any description. It is curious to observe, and it may here not be out of place to remark, in looking into the mineralogy of the British coast, on the great scale, that we find the shores of the whole southern parts of the kingdom, or from Portland Island in Dorsetshire, to Flamborough Head in Yorkshire, consist chiefly of chalk, limestone, clay, and beds of gravel. But if we continue our course from thence northward, to Stonehaven in Kincardineshire, including the Firth of Forth, the strata, with little exception, are sandstone, greenstone, limestone and coal. The Aberdeenshire coast is chiefly of granite, syenite, and gneiss, while a part of Banffshire consists of serpentine and porphyry: but here the sandstone again makes its appearance, and stretches along the northern shores of the Moray Firth , Caithness and Sutherland, nearly as far to the westward as Cape Wrath. To this great extent of sandstone country, may also be added the islands of Orkney and Shetland, with some considerable exceptions, however, in so far as regards Shetland; but, in Orkney, these are confined to comparatively small portions of gneiss with granite veins, which occur in Pomona or the Mainland, and in the Island of Græmsay.

From this state of the mineral strata, it naturally follows, that those who inhabit the sandstone districts employ that beautiful, easily worked, and, in many instances, highly durable stone, in architecture; and so of the other districts, according to the predominating species of their stone. For a building, therefore, in a country situate like that of the Bell Rock, abounding with sandstone of the first quality, this description of stone obviously presented itself, both as the most accessible and economical. But when the importance of this work came to be fully considered in all its relations, a little additional expence was not to be allowed to regulate a point so essential, without a due regard to what might ultimately prove the most durable and permanent fabric.

The use of granite and sandstone is resolved upon.

The attention of the Commissioners was consequently directed to the use of granite, as combining the greatest number of properties for such a building. Some doubts, however, having existed, as to the certainty of procuring blocks of that stone of sufficient dimensions, it became a matter of importance to determine this point, and also to ascertain the quality of the sandstone, of which it had been proposed to form at least the hearting of the solid part. The Commissioners, therefore, in the month of November 1806, required a special opinion from Mr Rennie and the writer upon this subject; who accordingly visited the sandstone quarry of Mylnefield near Dundee, and the granite quarries in the neighbourhood of Aberdeen, and made a report to the Board, which is given in the Appendix, No. IV.

Report of Mr Rennie and Mr Stevenson.

This report sets forth, that many granite quarries were found in activity at Aberdeen, some of which were capable of producing larger blocks of stone than are usually met with, but that still it was doubtful, whether any single quarry would be found to produce a sufficient number of large blocks for this work in any reasonable time. Upon the quality of the stones respectively; the report states, that "the granite of Aberdeen is very strong and durable in its nature, and having been used in works where the sea has acted upon it for time immemorial, no doubt can possibly be entertained as to its adaptation to a work of this kind. There is also every reason to believe that the Mylnefield stone resists the sea and weather equally well, but we have not been able to collect such positive proof of this as of the other; for, although a great number of Mylnefield stones have been used in the piers of the harbour of Dundee, yet, as these works consist of stones from other quarries, having the same appearance, and nearly the same composition, there is no possibility of our saying whether some of the stones that appear in a wasting state, may not have been from that quarry, although we have great reason to believe they have not. However, where facts cannot be positively ascertained doubts exist, and we think that a Light-house upon the Bell Rock is too important a work to permit the leaving of the slightest doubt about the durability of the materials. We have, therefore, no hesitation in recommending that the outer part of the building, at least as high as the first apartment, should be of granite; and as this is the great bulk of the work, it may be as well to complete the outer course of granite."

The Reporters then go on to state, from a review of the several quarry prices, that, for the outer casing, the sum of about L. 2,500 would be saved by the use of sandstone from Mylnefield, instead of granite from Aberdeen; and that, for the hearting of the solid part, an additional saving of about L. 1000 would further be made, if the sandstone of the Redhead quarries, in the immediate neighbourhood of Arbroath, instead of the Mylnefield stone, was used. On considering this subject, however, in all its bearings, the Commissioners resolved that measures should be taken for procuring granite for the whole outward casing of the Light-house, and that the Mylnefield sandstone should be used for the interior work. To the other properties of these stones, one of some consideration for a work of this description was their ponderosity, there being only about 13½ cubic feet of Rubislaw granite to the ton, and 15 feet of Mylnefield stone, while the more common kinds of sandstone contain about 15½ feet to the ton.

These, and other matters of minor importance alluded to in this report, having been adjusted by the Light-house Board, the writer took the necessary measures for entering into contracts and agreements for the supply of stones from these quarries. The difficulties which subsequently attended the procuring of a regular supply of stones for the work have already been alluded to; and to this subject we shall again have occasion to recur, as it was ultimately found necessary to restrict the use of granite to the outward casing of the first thirty feet or solid part of the building.

Mortar of the ancients.

The best composition for building-mortar appears to have been a problem from the earliest history of the arts. Vitruvius, who lived about 130 years before the Christian æra, seems to have been practically, as well as scientifically, acquainted with the whole subject of architecture. But, although he, and other eminent authors who followed him, have minutely treated of the composition of mortar, stating, no doubt, all that was known of the practice of the ancients; yet, it has always been a favourite maxim to maintain, that the secret of compounding mortar has at some period of its history been irrecoverably lost. It is certainly true, that many of the works of ancient times exhibit wonderful specimens of the excellency of their building materials. It may, however, be drawn no less conclusively from the writings of intelligent travellers, that many of their finest edifices have been subject to premature decay, which affords a proof that at least no systematic rule was universally observed in the preparation of their calcareous cements; but that, like the artists of the present day, the quality of their materials depended much upon those adventitious circumstances which too often regulate the views of their successors, by an over-anxious desire for economy, without keeping duly in view the permanency of their works.

Attention of the moderns to this subject.

In Great Britain, the composition of mortar does not seem to have occupied much of the attention of the learned, prior to the beginning of the 18th century, or the time of Sir Christopher Wren. And, indeed, the subject was not pursued with much intelligence and effect, till after the great discoveries of Dr Black, about the year 1754, which unfolded the principles of latent caloric, and the expulsion of fixed air, by which limestone loses about one-half of its weight in the process of calcination. These discoveries were succeeded by the excellent treatise of Dr Higgins on Water Cements, published in 1780; and in 1793, Mr Smeaton's Narrative of the Edystone Light-house appeared, containing, not only an account of the preparation of the mortar for that celebrated building, but also of his experience for thirty-six years, as an engineer of the most extensive practice of his day. The composition of mortar has also occupied the attention of several French authors, as Belidor, Loriot, Viccat and others, but without perhaps adding much to our stock of practical knowledge.

Experience of the writer.

Were the writer permitted to state the result of his professional observations for the last twenty years, he might notice, that no error is more commonly met with in water buildings, than that of employing house or common mortar in the erection of sea-walls. It may also be stated, generally, in compounding mortar, that the cheapest article is too apt to be made use of in the greatest proportion. We accordingly find, that lime is not unfrequently made too rich, as it is technically termed when a small proportion of sand is applied to the mixture; an error, which is attended even with worse consequences than when the lime is made poor, or when too great a proportion of sand is used. But, perhaps, the worst of all mortar is that wherein very fine pit-sand, containing a portion of earthy matters, is used, and when the whole is mixed up with impure water. So little attention is often paid to the quality of mortar, in common buildings, that one would imagine it were applied, as if intended more to prevent the sifting winds from penetrating the walls, than as the medium by which they were ultimately to be bound or formed into a compact fabric.

It is not possible to give any formula for the composition of mortar which will apply generally; so much depends upon the quality of the limestone, the mode of its treatment in burning, the use of clean sharp sand and pure water. When these ingredients are judiciously selected, duly apportioned, and well beaten together, they will immediately form a paste of some tenacity, which will ultimately take bond and give a consistency to the work. From all the experiments that have been made, it seems to be essential to the composition of the best water-cements, that the limestone should contain about one-seventh of alumine or clayey matter. But as this description of limestone admits of a less proportion of sand in the mortar compounded of it, than that which is more purely calcareous, it is not so much in request for the common operations of building, as being less economical. It may, however, be stated, as a pretty general maxim, that where comparatively pure calcareous matter is met with, at least three measures of clean sharp sand, free of earthy particles, mixed with one of burned lime, in the state of powder, and a due portion of pure water, well beaten together, will form good mortar for common use.

Mortar of the Edystone.

From the similarity of the situations and the buildings upon the Edystone and Bell Rocks, and from Mr Smeaton's celebrity as an engineer, his Narrative of the former work became a text-book to the writer in the erection of the latter. In considering the importance of this subject, with a view to the erection of the Bell Rock Light-house, the judicious remarks, and numerous experiments, of Dr Higgins on water cement, were carefully examined, and they will always be consulted with interest by the professional reader. The composition of the Edystone mortar consisted of equal portions, by measure, of Aberthaw lime and Pozzolano earth, both in the state of powder, mixed up with sea-water. When the writer first visited Plymouth in the year 1801, the Edystone Light-house had been erected about 42 years; and he was informed by Mr Tolsher, agent for the establishment, that the original pointing of the joints of that building had never required repair.

Bell Rock Mortar.

Of the ingredients of the Bell Rock mortar, as the pozzolano was not only the most expensive, but, from the distracted state of Europe, during the progress of the works, could hardly be procured at any price, it became an object to be as independent of that article as possible. A train of experiments was therefore undertaken by the writer, when it was ultimately found, that pozzolano and lime, in the state of a dry impalpable powder, and clean sharp sand, in equal proportions by measure, mixed with sea-water, formed a mortar equally good in all respects as when no sand was added. Under favourable circumstances, this mixture did not seem to be more tardy in fixing, than when the sand was excluded, while nothing could exceed the compact and indurated state of the composition. The writer accordingly built some small rubble-walls with it within sea-mark, which were allowed to stand for a few months, and when pulled down, they appeared like so many pieces of conglomerated rock, the mortar being as hard and compact as the sandstone of good quality with which these little walls were built. From the excellency of the Bell Rock mortar, it may not be amiss to go a little farther into detail, by noticing each of the ingredients of which it was composed.

Lime.

In the course of investigating this subject, specimens of lime, from the counties of Edinburgh, Haddington, Fife and Forfar, were subjected to various trials with mixtures of pozzolano and sand. The results were not a little curious, as the experimental balls, made with different proportions of these limes, did not set or harden; but, on the contrary, the particles seemed to repel each other as the mixture became heated, and ultimately crumbled into its constituent ingredients. From these experiments, it was found advisable to bring a cargo of limestone from Aberthaw in Wales, being the same as that used for the Edystone Light-house. This lime is found imbedded in a clayey matrix, in the state of water-worn nodules, varying in size from a cubic inch to that of a cubic foot. This limestone is of a bluish or beautiful French grey colour, of the specific gravity of 2.70. It is easily calcined, and in that state is reducible to the finest powder. It is the mountain or first flœtz limestone of geologists; and, when broken, it pretty generally displays the Cornua ammonis, and many other curious animal remains. This limestone is found in great abundance on the sea-shore at Aberthaw, where the softer matters being washed away from the lower stratum of certain high cliffs, containing these rounded masses, the upper parts fall in great quantities, from which the succeeding tides wash away the earthy matters, leaving the limestone upon the beach in the state of debris. When a vessel is to load limestone here, she is grounded on the shore at about half-tide, and loaded when the water recedes. The price paid to the proprietor for a cargo is at the rate of one shilling per ton, as a lordship.

Pozzolano.

Pozzolano, the second mentioned ingredient of the Bell Rock mortar, is a kind of earthy lava, of a brownish red or greyish colour. It contains in the hundred parts, silica 55, alumina 20, lime 5, and oxide of iron 20. It was not so easily procured as the limestone from Aberthaw. It is very abundant on the coast of Italy and shores of Sicily, where it is found in considerable masses, and is usually imported in a crude earthy state, requiring to be pounded, or beat in a mill, to fit it for the finer purposes of mortar. It is generally brought to this country as ballast; and, in time of peace, when the ports are open, is sold for about L. 5 per ton. During the progress of the Bell Rock works, however, from the long continued and almost universal restrictions upon British trade with foreign ports, as much as L. 15 per ton has been paid for pozzolano for the use of these works. The writer having had great difficulty in procuring a supply of it for commencing the works, got a quantity of Tarras from Holland, the Dutch ports being, at this time, open to British vessels. Tarras or Trass is found near Andernach, and is brought down the Rhine to Holland. It is very similar in its nature and properties to pozzolano, and, like it, is of a reddish or greyish colour. It contains 37 parts silica, 28 alumina, 6.5 lime and 8.5 iron. Its property of setting in water is very remarkable, and, when good, it admits even a greater proportion of lime in the composition of mortar than pozzolano. The Dutch are very attentive in ascertaining the quality of the trass before using it in building their dikes. The following simple experiment is always employed. A small vessel, made of a mixture of lime and trass, is filled with water, and if at the end of three days the water does not filter through the vessel, the trass is considered good; if, on the contrary, water passes through, the trass is rejected as bad.

Sand.

According to Dr Higgins, the sand used for mortar should be free of earthy particles, and have as many sharp angular points as possible. The writer having accordingly examined the shores in the neighbourhood of Arbroath, for sand answerable to this description, he found it of excellent quality about a mile and a half westward from that place. Upon examining this sand with a magnifying-glass, its appearance was like so many small shining crystals shooting into numerous points.—It is often a difficult question with mineralogists, to account for the production of sand in many situations upon the coast; but here the question involves no perplexity, as St Andrew's Bay, which is generally understood to extend from Fifeness to the Redhead, a distance of about 25 miles, is not only bounded by sandstone, but forms the embouchure of the river Tay, and of several other considerable streams, which fall into the sea upon its shores.

Water.

It usually forms a condition in the Specification of mortar for house-building, that it shall be mixed with pure water, free of earthy or saline particles. In situations where water is scarce, many impurities are apt to be mixed with it, which injure and even destroy the adhesive quality of the mortar. The use of sea or salt water is guarded against in these cases, from its liability to produce an efflorescence on the walls; when the saline particles deliquesce with the changes of the weather, and produce the appearance of dampness.

To have attempted to avoid the use of salt-water in the preparation of the mortar for the Bell Rock Light-house,—which was all prepared on the spot,—independently of the risk of deteriorating the mortar, would have been attended with much additional trouble and expence. Besides the practice at the Edystone, the writer had previously ascertained, that the use of sea-water produced no bad effect upon the tenacity or adhesive quality of the mortar into which it was introduced, and the object of avoiding the appearance of dampness in this building was extremely trifling. The stones were to be very correctly jointed, and the whole of the interior walls to consist of polished masonry, so that the fine lines of the joints exposed to the action of the air were so inconsiderable, as hardly to be taken into account. Salt-water was, therefore, uniformly used in the preparation of the Bell Rock mortar.

Cement.

The recent discovery of a very excellent water-cement, for which Mr Parker of London obtained a patent, under the title of "Roman Cement," became another matter of importance to the Bell Rock works. This substance is produced from calcined nodules of argillaceous limestone, found upon the southern shores of England. It is of a brownish colour, and from its excellent property of setting in water, when good and fresh, its application as a mortar, for the lower courses of the Light-house, demanded attention. But, for general use as a mortar, it would not only have been expensive, but often highly inconvenient in building, from the speedy manner in which it hardens. It is also of too brittle a nature to be suitable for the general purposes of common mortar; though it forms a paste of great value for lipping or pointing the outward joints of water buildings, not only by preserving the mortar till it gets into a fixed state, but also as forming a durable joint. A considerable supply of this cement was accordingly used throughout the building, for pointing the exterior joints. This cement is sold at the rate of five shillings per Winchester bushel, in the state of powder, packed into casks, lined with paper, to prevent it, in some measure, from imbibing humidity from the atmosphere, by which its adhesive properties are destroyed.

Oaken Trenails and Wedges.

Following out the principle of the Edystone Light-house in most of its details, the oaken trenail and wedge were used for fixing the stones, till the mortar took band, and a superincumbent weight was got upon them to prevent the sea from sweeping them away. These being also introduced into all the lower courses of the Bell Rock Light-house, a sufficient quantity was procured for the probable number of courses that might be built during the ensuing season. The precise lengths of the trenails and wedges could not be fixed, from the uncertainty of the granite quarries, which regulated the thickness of the courses of the building; but, for the present, the trenails were provided of the length of 2 feet, and 1¼th inch in diameter. The wedges were of the length of 18 inches, measuring 3 inches in breadth, 1 inch in thickness at the top, and tapering to ¼th of an inch in thickness at the point, as will be seen in Plate X. Figs. 10. and 11. But when we come to speak of the process of building, their respective uses will be described.

1808, March.

The writer visits the Bell Rock.

On the writer's visit to Arbroath, in the end of March, he was anxious to land upon the Bell Rock, to ascertain the precise state of the Beacon, after the storms of the winter, that he might be enabled to judge of the propriety of converting it into a habitable place for the artificers during the working season. He accordingly sailed from Arbroath on the 30th current, at 1 A. M. in the Light-house Yacht. The wind was from E.NE., but the weather, though cold, was upon the whole favourable for the trip. At 7 the Floating-light was hailed, and all on board found to be well. It was now unfortunately too late in the tide for landing upon the rock this morning; and it became necessary to cruise about till the following day, there being at this season only one tide with daylight. In the mean time, in sailing round the rock, just as it was beginning to be covered with the tide, the base of the Beacon was distinctly seen between the rolling seas, which broke upon it; while at the top, the flag-staff proudly continued to surmount the whole.

Floating-Light.

In the course of the day the writer examined the Floating-light, where every thing connected with the security of the vessel, and her moorings, was in good order. What seemed chiefly to please Mr Wilson the commander, was a late improvement in the application of a winch, with wheel and pinion fixed at the break of the quarter-deck, which was now employed to great advantage in working the cable with stoppers as on board of war-ships, the hempen cable, forming part of her moorings, being too thick and unwieldy for holding-on by hand. The vessel's manner of riding during some late gales was described as having been very difficult, and even alarming at times; but it was nevertheless, added, that nothing had been felt so severely as the gale of the 6th and 7th of September last, when the writer was on board.

The crew spend their time happily.

The crew were observed to have a very healthy-like appearance, and looked better than at the close of the works upon the rock. They seemed only to regret one thing, which was the secession of their cook, Thomas Elliot,—not on account of his professional skill, but for his facetious and curious manner. Elliot had something peculiar in his history, and was reported by his comrades to have seen better days. He was, however, happy with his situation on board of the Floating-light, and, having a taste for music, dancing, and acting plays, he contributed much to the amusement of the ship's company, in their dreary abode during the winter months. He had also recommended himself to their notice as a good shipkeeper, for as it did not answer Elliot to go often ashore, he had always given up his turn of leave to his neighbours. At his own desire, he was at length paid off, when he had a considerable balance of wages to receive, which he said would be sufficient to carry him to the West Indies, and he accordingly took leave of the light-house service.

The Light is comparatively feeble.

Mr John Reid, the principal light-keeper, stated, that every thing specially connected with his department on board, answered its purpose to his entire satisfaction. In stormy weather, however, when the ship rolled much, great difficulty was experienced in trimming the lights, which often required the assistance of all hands. In the course of this night's cruise, the writer had a good opportunity of observing the lights at different distances from the vessel. Even at the distance of two or three leagues, it appeared feeble, compared with a regular reflecting-light. It was also upon the whole so unsteady, from the rolling motion of the ship, that, in running for it, mariners could never venture to make very free with their course.

Landing at the rock found difficult.

At day-break, on the following morning, the Light-house Yacht, attended by a boat from the Floating-light, again stood towards the Bell Rock. On coming within a proper distance of it, the usual tools carried by the artificers on such occasions were put into this boat, and every thing was got into a state of readiness for making an attempt to land. The weather felt extremely cold this morning, the thermometer being at 34 degrees, with the wind at east, accompanied by occasional showers of snow, and the marine barometer indicated 29.80. At half-past 7, the sea ran with such force upon the rock, that it seemed doubtful if a landing could be effected. At half-past 8, when it was fairly above water, the writer took his place in the Floating-light's boat with the artificers, while the Yacht's boat followed, according to the general rule of having two boats afloat in landing expeditions of this kind, that in case of accident to one boat, the other might assist. After several unsuccessful attempts, the boats for a time were beat back by the breach of the sea upon the rock. On the eastern side, it separated into two distinct waves, which came with a sweep round to the western side where they met; and at the instant of their confluence, the water rose in spray to a considerable height. Watching what the sailors term a smooth, we caught a favourable opportunity, and in a very dexterous manner the boats were rowed between the two seas, and made a favourable landing at the western creek.

State of the Beacon.

At the latter end of last season, as was formerly noticed, the Beacon was painted white, and from the bleaching of the weather and the sprays of the sea, the upper parts were kept clean; but within the range of the tide, the principal beams were observed to be thickly coated with a green stuff, the conferva of botanists. Notwithstanding the intrusion of these works, which had formerly banished the numerous seals that played about the rock, they were now seen in great numbers, having been in an almost undisturbed state for six months. It had now also, for the first time, got some inhabitants of the feathered tribe: in particular the Scarth or Cormorant, and the large Herring-gull, had made the Beacon a resting-place, from its vicinity to their fishing grounds. About a dozen of these birds had rested upon the cross beams, which, in some places, were coated with their dung; and their flight, as the boats approached, was a very unlooked for indication of life and habitation on the Bell Rock, conveying the momentary idea of the conversion of this fatal rock, from being a terror to the mariner, into a residence of man, and a safe-guard to shipping.

Propriety of converting it into a Barrack.

Upon narrowly examining all the parts of the Beacon, then in the state represented in Plate VIII., and especially the great iron stanchions with which the beams were fixed to the rock, the writer had the satisfaction of finding that there was not the least appearance of working or shifting at any of the joints or places of connection; and excepting the loosening of the bracing-chains, every thing was found in the same entire state in which it had been left in the month of October. This, in the estimation of the writer, was a matter of no small importance to the future success of the work. He, from that moment, saw the practicability and propriety of fitting up the beacon, not only as a place of refuge in case of accident to the boats in landing, but as a residence for the artificers during the working months. With a view to this, he determined on the entire removal of the bracing-chains, which, in general, were either so relaxed or loosened by the unlocking of the screws, the stretching of the links, or the drawing of the chain-bats, from the tremulous motion of the beacon, as to be comparatively of little use. Measures were therefore taken for procuring great iron-bars to fix in a horizontal position between each pair of the principal beams, at the height of about 8 feet from the rock, as the best means of strengthening them.

Bread and water chest.

Having made these remarks upon the lower parts of the beacon, and its connection with the rock, the writer ascended to the higher parts, where he had also the satisfaction to find that the fixtures of the cross beams were in the same good condition. Upon looking into the bread and water-chest fixed on the top, in case of accident to the boats, or in the event of shipwreck upon the Bell Rock, the sea-biscuits which had been carefully put into a tin cannister, were in good order; but, in the compartment of the chest allotted for water, the fragments of several of the quart bottles in which it was contained were found, which had probably burst with the freezing of the water, for it can hardly be supposed to have arisen from the shaking or tremulous motion of the beacon; be this as it may, only twelve of the eighteen bottles remained entire.

Advantages of the Beacon in its present state.

While upon the top of the beacon, the writer was reminded by the Landing-master, that the sea was running high, and that it would be necessary to set off while the rock afforded any thing like shelter to the boats, which, by this time, had been made fast by a long line to the Beacon, and rode with much agitation, each requiring two men with boat-hooks to keep them from striking each other, or from ranging up against the beacon. But even under these circumstances, the greatest confidence was felt by every one, from the security afforded by this temporary erection. For, supposing that the wind had suddenly encreased to a gale, and that it had been found unadvisable to go into the boats; or, supposing they had drifted or sprung a leak from striking upon the rocks; in any of these possible and not at all improbable cases, those who might thus have been left upon the rock had now something to lay hold of, and, though occupying this dreary habitation of the sea-gull and cormorant, affording only bread and water, yet life would be preserved, and, under all such circumstances, the mind would still be supported, by the hope of being ultimately relieved. After, with some difficulty, getting off the Beacon, a proper time was again watched, and, by active rowing, the boats soon cleared the Rock in safety, though not without shipping two or three pretty heavy seas. About

12 noon the Light-house Yacht bore away, and at 7 in the evening she reached the Bay of Arbroath, where the writer landed about 8 P. M., and on the following day returned to Edinburgh.

Impress Service, how it affected the Bell Rock operations.

The Impress Service—that much-to-be-regretted system—being in great activity, not only at the larger ports, but, owing to the pressure of the war with France and the Northern Powers, orders having likewise been issued for the establishment of an Impress at Dundee, Arbroath and Aberdeen, it became necessary to be doubly careful in obtaining protections for all our seamen. There being now five vessels employed in the service of the Commissioners of the Northern Light-houses, including the Bell Rock craft, a requisition was accordingly made to the Admiralty for a protection for 35 seamen, which was readily granted. In so far as the liberty of the subject is infringed by the impress service, its existence is much to be regretted; but, in regard to the works in question, it had the effect of rendering them popular, instead of their being shunned by seamen, which might otherwise have been the case.

Protection Medal.

As the impress officers were extremely rigid in the execution of their duty, it became necessary to have the seamen carefully identified; and, therefore, besides being described in the usual manner in the Protection-bills, which, agreeably to the Admiralty regulations, must always remain on board of the respective ships for which they are granted, it was found advisable to give each man a ticket, descriptive of his person, to which was attached a silver medal emblematical of the Light-house service, as represented in Plate XII. On the one side of this medal was the figure of the Bell Rock Light-house, and on the other, the word 'Medal,' referring to the Admiralty Protection, and a description of the person by the Engineer. The following is a copy of the ticket of one of our best seamen.

1808, April.

Protection Ticket.

"Bell Rock Work-yard, Arbroath, 31st March 1808.

"John Pratt, seaman in the service of the Honourable the Commissioners of the Northern Light-houses, aged 35 years, 5 feet 8 inches high, black complexion, and slightly marked with the small-pox.

"Robert Stevenson,
"Engineer for Northern Light-houses."

Obverse.

"The bearer John Pratt, is serving on board of the Sir Joseph Banks Tender and Craft, employed at the erection of the Bell Rock Light-house.

The signature of the Master of the Tender, "David Taylor.
The signature of the bearer, "John Pratt."

These tickets were found to be indispensably necessary in the Light-house service, as it was impossible that every man, or even each boat's crew, could carry the ship's protection about with them. But the check afforded by the several signatures as noted above, was generally respected by the Impress officers.

Light-house Yacht again visits the Rock.

Directions having been given in the month of March for tightening the bracing-chains, and fixing certain ring-bolts, both at the eastern and western landing places of the rock, for the conveniency of the boats, the Light-house Yacht again sailed on the 12th of April, carrying off artificers and all necessaries for the service. After accomplishing this duty she returned to Arbroath on the 14th, and in this state things remained till the commencement of the works in the month of May.

Preparatory state of the Works.

The several implements already alluded to and described, were in a state of great forwardness about the close of the winter, having been prepared in Edinburgh, under the immediate directions of the writer. At Aberdeen, Mr Alexander Gildowie, stone-agent, used every exertion to procure an additional supply of granite from Rubislaw and other quarries. But the severity of the winter was such as to prevent much progress from being made. At Mylnefield Quarry, owing to the liability of that stone to board or split in frosty weather, from its lying in regular strata, by which moisture is more readily absorbed and acted upon in the laminæ, the operations had been entirely suspended for several months.

Use of Granite restricted to the lower courses.

In the month of April, the writer visited the works at Arbroath, which he found still in a much retarded state, for want of a regular supply of granite. Owing to this, it had not as yet been possible to complete even one entire course of the building, although the figure and dimensions of the moulds had been repeatedly altered to accommodate the quarries. It had already become apparent, that the works would unavoidably be stopped, if the whole of the outward casing were to consist of granite. In order, therefore, to avoid a circumstance which might prove hazardous to the whole operations, the Light-house Board resolved to restrict the use of this material to the lower courses of the building.

Use of Sandstone extended.

It having thus been found necessary to lessen the quantity of granite at the Bell Rock, and proportionally to encrease the quantity of sandstone, a new engagement was entered into with the proprietor of Mylnefield, for an additional supply, at the rate of one shilling and sixpence per cubic foot, put free on board. On visiting this quarry in the month of April, the writer had assurance of being largely supplied with stone, if a greater range or variety in the thickness of the courses were allowed. This, however desirable, was altogether impossible, in so far as regarded the lower courses; the thickness of which could only be regulated piecemeal, as the dimensions of the granite stones could be determined.

Mr Skene's contract to supply Granite.

Every exertion had already been made on the part of Mr Skene of Rubislaw, who had entered into a contract with the Light-house Board to supply granite, at the rate of one shilling and threepence per cubic foot, for the use of the Bell Rock,—having been chiefly induced to enter into this contract, on account of the celebrity of the work;—but after furnishing a few of the lower courses, he found that he could not implement his agreement without incurring considerable loss, and running the risk of retarding the building: he therefore applied to be relieved of his contract. From the commencement of the work, Mr Skene had, with much liberality, stated, that in case the quarries upon his estate should be found defective in producing the necessary size and quantity of materials, his contract should never be allowed to form any bar or stoppage to the Commissioners in applying to others. This had accordingly been acted upon by the Stone-agent; but after making every exertion for the space of about 12 months, he had been able to procure only a few additional blocks of the requisite dimensions, even with the range of all the quarries of Aberdeen, besides those of Rubislaw. The price of suitable blocks had, in the mean time, advanced to three shillings and threepence, and even to five shillings per cubic foot. At the commencement of the Bell Rock works, the quarries of Aberdeen were chiefly worked for paving-stones, and for common house purposes, and were consequently unprovided with implements or tools suitable either for working or transporting stones of large dimensions, for which they had hitherto had no regular demand.

He is remunerated for loss.

Mr Skene having sustained considerable pecuniary loss, in opening additional quarries for the Light-house, he had certain claims upon the Board, which were remitted to Mr Kennedy, advocate, of Aberdeen, upon whose opinion and report remuneration was made to the extent of about L. 370.

The Sir Joseph Banks takes the station of the Light-house Yacht.

The Light-house Yacht being employed in the general service of the Northern Light-houses, she left the Bell Rock on the 16th of April, to load stores at Leith. But the Sir Joseph Banks Tender being now completely equipped, she sailed to supply her station, for the first time, on the 20th of May, having on board several sets of moorings for the use of the vessels in attendance at the Rock. The mushroom-anchors of these moorings weighed about one ton each, and had about thirty-two fathoms of chain attached to them, which was made from iron, measuring seven-eighths of an inch in thickness. These moorings were laid down in fourteen fathoms water, at about 200 fathoms apart, on a rocky bottom, and at the distance of about a quarter of a mile on the north-western side of the Rock, as will be seen from Plate V. After completing this operation, and supplying the Floating-light with necessaries, the Tender returned to Arbroath previously to the commencement of the operations at the Rock for the season.

1808, May.

Wednesday 25th.

The writer begins the operations of the season.

In the month of May, the number of artificers in the work-yard, consisting of masons, smiths, mill-wrights, joiners and labourers, amounted to sixty. On the

25th, the writer embarked at Arbroath, on board of the Sir Joseph Banks, for the Bell Rock, accompanied by Mr Logan senior, foreman-builder, with twelve masons, and two smiths, together with thirteen seamen, including the master, mate and steward. The vessel sailed at 3 o'clock P. M., under a salute of three hearty cheers from a great assemblage of people on the quays; but before getting to the Rock, it was too late for making fast to the moorings that night; and she kept cruising about, with the Floating-light in view, which proved a great comfort to the seamen, in directing them to tack the ship, before she got too near the Rock.

On this occasion, the prospects of the writer were very different from the state of things upon his sailing to commence the last year's operations, when much doubt and uncertainty attended every step. The experience of last season, together with the facility and confidence afforded by the erection of the Beacon, which had withstood the storms of a winter, together with the use of a new Tender, which could now be moored so near to the Rock as to be perfectly convenient for the boats, and was at the same time capable of being cast loose from her moorings, to take the people on board on any emergency;—these circumstances gave a degree of security and promptitude to the work, which relieved all concerned of much anxiety.

Thursday 26th.

The wind to-day was at south-east, and though the weather was not very pleasant, yet it was moderate. Mr James Wilson, now Commander of the Pharos Floating-light, and Landing-master, in the room of Mr Sinclair, who had left the service, came into the writer's cabin this morning at 6 o'clock, and intimated that there was a good appearance of landing on the rock. The bell being accordingly rung, the boats were hoisted out, and at half-past 7 the artificers were seated and arranged by the landing-master in their respective boats, who, with the foreman-builder, went into the boat on the off-side, while the writer steered the one on the side of the ship next to the Rock. Every thing being arranged, both boats proceeded in company, and at 8 A. M. they reached the Rock. The light-house colours were immediately hoisted upon the flag-staff of the Beacon, a compliment which was duly returned by the tender and floating-light, when three hearty cheers were given, and a glass of rum was served out to all hands, to drink success to the operations of 1808.

State of the Bell Rock after the storms of winter.

When the writer made a landing here, in the month of March, he was so entirely occupied in examining all the parts of the Beacon, that little attention was paid to the general appearance of the Rock. Its surface was now found to be covered with a new crop of Fuci, where it had been destroyed and rubbed off in the course of the last season. Even the iron work, and lower parts of the Beacon, and the site of the foundation of the Light-house, where it had been dressed and worked with the pick, was now also thickly coated with a species of Conferva, of a deep green colour, resembling very fine grass where the water had left it, while in the pools it had the most beautiful arborescent appearance. The limpets and white bucky were, as formerly, in considerable numbers, and the barnacle had coated all the higher parts of the rock, giving it a whitish appearance. On the extreme points, a few detached clusters of mussels were seen, of a very diminutive size, varying from a quarter to half an inch in length. The six blocks of granite, which had been landed as an experiment on the 1st of September 1807, were now scattered about in different directions, covered with the delicate looking plant above described. The general aspect of the rock remained otherwise unaltered.

State of the Foundation-pit.

The north-western half of the site of the building being higher than the other, it had, in the course of last season, been wrought down to a regular surface; but the other half contained depressions or holes, varying in depth from six inches to no less than three feet. By 8 o'clock the tide had left the higher parts of the foundation dry, when it appeared from observation, that the water ebbed at the rate of one inch in two minutes and thirty seconds, and that the difference of the perpendicular height, between the lowest and highest parts of the foundation-pit, at the commencement of the works this season, was still about four feet. After having been an hour and three quarters at work, the water began to overflow the site of the building, when the boats left the rock, the landing-master taking the lead; but after getting clear, he waited, agreeably to usual practice, till the other boat got out of the creek, when both proceeded for the Tender.

Landing attended with considerable difficulty.

In the evening tide the artificers landed at a quarter past 7, though the sea ran pretty high, and the boats shipped a good deal of water. Being rather early in the tide for working at the site of the building, the time was occupied in getting the smith's forge put in order upon the cross-beams of the Beacon, a step of great importance to the future progress and advancement of the work. At half-past 7, the higher parts of the foundation being left dry, a few of the artificers set to work, the others beginning as the water went off. At half-past 9 the tide again overflowed the rock, when the boats left it, after the artificers had been two hours at work. In coming out at the eastern creek this evening, the landing-master's boat was struck by a heavy sea, and thrown to one side of the creek; but, by his dextrous management, the boat's head was fortunately kept seaward, and she got out in safety, though not without having shipped a good deal of water.

Friday, 27th.

This morning the wind was at east, blowing a fresh gale, the weather being hazy, with a considerable breach of sea setting in upon the rock. The morning-bell was therefore rung, in some doubt as to the practicability of making a landing. After allowing the Rock to get fully up, or to be sufficiently left by the tide, that the boats might have some shelter from the range of the sea, they proceeded at 8 A. M., and upon the whole made a pretty good landing; and after two hours and three quarters' work returned to the ship in safety.

Found necessary still to excavate to the depth of fourteen inches.

In the afternoon the wind considerably increased, and as a pretty heavy sea was still running, the Tender rode very hard, when Mr Taylor, the commander, found it necessary to take in the bowsprit, and strike the fore and main top-masts, that she might ride more easily. After consulting about the state of the weather, it was resolved to leave the artificers on board this evening, and carry only the smiths to the Rock, as the sharpening of the irons was rather behind, from their being so much broken and blunted, by the hard and tough nature of the rock, which became much more compact and hard as the depth of excavation was increased. Besides avoiding the risk of encumbering the boats with a number of men, who had not yet got the full command of the oar in a breach of sea, the writer had another motive for leaving them behind. He wanted to examine the site of the building without interruption, and to take the comparative levels of the different inequalities of its area; and as it would have been painful to have seen men standing idle upon the Bell Rock, where all moved with activity, it was judged better to leave them on board. The boats landed at half-past 7 P. M., and the landing-master, with the seamen, was employed during this tide, in cutting the sea-weeds from the several paths leading to the landing-places, to render walking more safe, for, from the slippery state of the surface of the rock, many severe tumbles had taken place. In the mean time the writer took the necessary levels; and having carefully examined the site of the building, and considered all its parts, it still appeared to be necessary to excavate to the average depth of fourteen inches, over the whole area of the foundation. Having made these remarks, we again left the rock, at half-past 9, after having been two hours upon it. At the entrance of the eastern creek, the sea ran high, and all on board got a thorough wetting; but so long as the boats were kept from striking upon the rock, the sprays which came on board were but little regarded.

Saturday 28th.

Artificers much afflicted with sea-sickness.

The wind still continued from the eastward, with a heavy swell; and to-day it was accompanied with foggy weather, and occasional showers of rain. Notwithstanding this, such was the confidence which the erection of the Beacon had inspired, that the boats landed the artificers on the Rock, under very unpromising circumstances, at half-past 8, and they continued at work till half-past 11, being a period of three hours, which was considered a great tide's work, in the present low state of the foundation. Three of the masons on board were so afflicted with sea-sickness, that they had not been able to take any food for almost three days, and they were literally assisted into the boats this morning by their companions. It was, however, not a little surprising, to see how speedily these men revived upon landing on the Rock and eating a little dulse. Two of them afterwards assisted the sailors in collecting the chips of stone, and carrying them out of the way of the pickmen; but the third complained of a pain in his head, and was still unable to do any thing. Instead of returning to the tender with the boats, these three men remained on the Beacon all day, and had their victuals sent to them along with the smiths. From Mr Dove, the foreman-smith, they had much sympathy, for he preferred remaining on the Beacon at all hazards, to be himself relieved from the malady of sea-sickness. The wind continuing high, with a heavy sea, and the tide falling late, it was not judged proper to land the artificers this evening, but in the twilight the boats were sent to fetch the people on board who had been left on the Rock.

Sunday 29th.

Misunderstanding among the Artificers about their wages.

The wind was from the S. W. to-day, and the signal-bell rung, as usual, about an hour before the period for landing on the Rock. The writer was rather surprised, however, to hear the landing-master repeatedly call, "All hands for the Rock;" and, coming on deck, he was disappointed to find the seamen only in the boats. Upon inquiry, it appeared, that some misunderstanding had taken place about the wages of the artificers for Sundays. They had preferred wages for seven days stately, to the former mode of allowing a day for each tide's work on Sunday; as they did not like the appearance of working for double or even treble wages on Sunday, and would rather have it understood that their work on that day arose more from the urgency of the case, than with a view to emolument. This having been judged creditable to their religious feelings, and readily adjusted to their wish, the boats proceeded to the Rock, and the work commenced at 9 A. M. The artificers were chiefly employed in removing the iron-stanchions, or frame-work of the forge, which had last year been fixed on the rock, and which was now set on a temporary scaffold erected for it on the Beacon. Having now got two smiths' hearths above the reach of the tide, the work of this department made great progress, both in the sharping of the numerous picks and irons, and in making bats for fixing the different railway tracks upon the Rock. After getting three and a half hours' work, the boats returned to the ship at 12 noon, when the excellent prayer, composed by the Rev. Dr Brunton, given in a former part of this work, was read upon the ship's quarter-deck, in the same manner as had been done last year.

The sloop Smeaton arrived this afternoon with a quantity of cast-iron rails, to be laid upon the Rock, for transporting the blocks of stone from the different landing-places to the site of the building. She had also on board some Norway logs, intended to be batted on the Rock, for supporting the railways across the gullies, or inequalities of the surface. The boats of the Sir Joseph Banks and Floating-light, being employed during the evening tide in delivering the Smeaton, by landing the cast-iron on the Rock, and bringing the timber on board of the Tender, the artificers could not be landed this evening.

Monday 30th.

Fish very abundant at the rock.

The weather to-day was moderate, and there was much less breach in the sea than there had been since the commencement of the work this season. The wind kept steadily in the south-west, and the barometer had changed its range from 29.40 to 29.90, and the thermometer from about 40° to 45°. The abundance of fish caught near the Rock was another proof of the more favourable state of the weather; for the fish never failed to come upon the anchorage-ground during good weather, while they as regularly disappeared on a change for the worse.

The Tender's bell rung this morning, as the signal for going to the Rock, at

9 o'clock; and at half-past 9, the water having partially left the foundation-pit, the work commenced, and continued two and three-fourth hours, or till a quarter from 1 o'clock P. M., when the tide again overflowed the whole site of the building. The masons and seamen returned with the boats on board the Tender, but the mill-wrights and joiners, who had come off with the Smeaton to fit up the railways, and such of the masons as were apt to be sick, remained with the smiths on the Beacon throughout the day.

General usefulness of Sailors as men of all works.

The number of workmen at the Rock was now increased to twenty-eight, including six sailors from the landing-master's crew, who were constantly employed in baling water, and keeping the foundation clear of the chips, struck off by the pick. They also conveyed the irons to the forge, by hoisting them up to the Beacon by a whip-tackle. The seamen were of the greatest service in many of the operations, for Jack is a man of all trades; but as they had their boats to attend, and were always at the landing-master's call, they were not taken into account in the enumeration of artificers.

Mortar Gallery fitted up.

Mr Francis Watt commenced, at this tide, with five joiners, to fit up a temporary platform upon the Beacon, about twenty-five feet above the highest part of the Rock. This platform was to be used as the site of the smith's forge, after the Beacon should be fitted up as a barrack; and here also the mortar was to be mixed and prepared for the building, and it was accordingly termed the Mortar Gallery. This platform was supported with joisting, well framed, and properly fixed to the principal beams; but the flooring or boarding, though two inches in thickness, was only slightly nailed to the joisting, so that when the sea rose, and struck it in bad weather, it might lift, without endangering the general frame of the fabric. At the end of the working season this floor was lifted, and the joisting only left during the winter months.

Smeaton is ballasted at the Bell Rock.

The landing-master's crew completed the discharging from the Smeaton of the remainder of her cargo of the cast-iron rails and timber. It must not here be omitted to notice, that the Smeaton took in ballast from the Bell Rock, consisting of the shivers or chips of stone, produced by the workmen in preparing the site of the building, which were now accumulated in great quantities on the Rock. These the boats loaded, after discharging the iron. The object in carrying off these chips, besides ballasting the vessel, was to get them permanently out of the way, as they were apt to shift about from place to place, with every gale of wind; and it often required a considerable time to clear the foundation a second time of this rubbish. The circumstance of ballasting a ship at the Bell Rock afforded great entertainment, especially to the sailors; and it was perhaps with truth remarked, that the Smeaton was the first vessel that had ever taken on board ballast at the Bell Rock.

Tuesday, 31st.

The winds were variable to-day, but chiefly from the north, accompanied with fine weather. On landing at a quarter from 11 A. M., the higher parts of the site of the building were dry, and the work continued two and a quarter hours, when it was again stopped by the return of the flood-tide. The joiners and smiths, together with those who were apt to be sick on board of the Tender, remained on the Beacon throughout the day, and at a quarter past 1 P. M. the boats left the Rock with the masons.

There were eighteen seamen from the Smeaton, Sir Joseph Banks, and Floating-light, employed to-day under the direction of Mr Wilson, the landing-master, in laying the cast-iron work of the railways in a compact manner, into the various crevices and holes in the Rock, to prevent its being tossed about by the sea, until it should be wanted in the course of fixing the tracks to the Rock.

Chips of the rock in great request at Leith.

The Smeaton being finally discharged, and partly loaded with stone shivers from the Bell Rock, she sailed for Leith, in order to fetch the remainder of the cast-iron, and some additional logs of timber. Mr Pool, the commander of this vessel, afterwards acquainted the writer, that when the ballast was landed upon the quay at Leith, many persons carried away specimens of it, as part of a cargo from the Bell Rock; when he added, that such was the interest excited, from the number of specimens carried away, that some of his friends suggested, that he should have sent the whole to the Cross of Edinburgh, where each piece might have sold for a penny.

Fish caught at the Bell Rock.

In the evening the boats went to the Rock, and brought the joiners and smiths, and their sickly companions, on board of the Tender. They also brought with them two baskets full of fish, which they had caught at high water, from the Beacon, reporting, at the same time, to their comrades, that the fish were swimming in such numbers over the rock at high water, that it was completely hid from their sight, and nothing seen but the movement of thousands of fish. They were almost exclusively of the species called the Podlie, or young Coal-fish. This discovery, made for the first time to-day by the workmen, was considered fortunate, as an additional circumstance likely to produce an inclination among the artificers to take up their residence in the Beacon, when it came to be fitted up as a barrack.

1808, June.

Wednesday, 1st.

The boats landed to-day at 11 A. M., but the tides being neap, the water went off very slowly, and it was 12 noon before it left the site of the building. After continuing at work one hour and three quarters, the artificers left the rock with all hands, when the tender immediately got under weigh, or rather cast off from her moorings, by simply letting go one end of the mooring hawser, and sailed for Arbroath. But the wind being N.N.W., it was 8 o'clock P. M. before she got into the harbour.

Saturday, 4th.

First course finished to-day. Its cubical contents, &c.

This being the birth-day of King George III., who now entered into the 70th year of his age, and 50th of his reign, a considerable effort was made to get the first entire course of the building laid upon the platform at Arbroath, where it was to be marked and numbered, and made ready for shipping for the Rock. It may seem strange, that after continuing the operations of the work-yard for about twelve months, there should only have been but one course ready to ship for the Rock. Such also was the difficulty of procuring granite of a large size, that this course was obliged to be hewn of the thickness of only one foot. The chief advantage of thick courses in water buildings, besides a saving of hewing, is that of getting sooner out of the reach of the tide, there being nearly as much time necessary for laying a thin course as a thick one. The stones for the first entire course were not quarried particularly for it, but were taken from the whole materials in the yard. The enumeration of the various kinds and quantity of work in this single course of the Light-house, may perhaps surprise the reader. Though only one foot in thickness, it contained 508 feet cubic of granite in outward casing; 876 feet cubic of Mylnefield stone in the hearting; 104 tons of solid contents; 132 feet superficial of hewing in the face work; 4519 feet superficial of hewing in the beds, joints and joggles; 420 feet lineal boring of trenail holes; 378 feet lineal cutting for wedges; 246 oaken trenails; 378 oaken wedges in pairs.

Certainty of commencing building this season.

In the work-yard, about sixty stone cutters were employed in hewing and preparing the various courses of the solid part of the building. Stones were now got pretty readily from Mylnefield quarry; and besides the quarries at Aberdeen, others had been opened near Peterhead, belonging to Mr John Hutchison, which produced a great many fine blocks. As much of the Aberthaw limestone had been broken and prepared for burning as would charge the kiln. A number of casks of the capacity of about 32 gallons, had also been provided and were ready to be filled, in equal numbers, of clean sharp sand, lime and pozzolano earth, in the state of fine powder. After much trouble and correspondence with timber-merchants in Leith, London, and other parts, a considerable quantity of trenails and wedges of British oak were procured, which were to be used in connecting the courses of the solid part of the building, while the works were low, and in danger of being washed away or injured by the sea. These oaken trenails and wedges were made up in bundles, containing about 20. In short, every thing was in a state of readiness in the work-yard, for building the first three courses of the Light-house. The preparations for its foundation at the Rock were now also in considerable forwardness, and the works, upon the whole, put on an appearance which left no doubt as to the commencement of the building this season.

Artificers sail for the Rock.

The writer sailed from Arbroath in the evening of the 6th of June in the Tender, with a fine breeze of northerly wind, having on board 34 artificers, consisting of masons, smiths, mill-wrights and joiners, besides the landing master's crew, consisting of twelve seamen, who worked the ship. There were also on board Mr Peter Logan, foreman builder; Mr Francis Watt, foreman mill-wright; Mr James Dove, foreman smith; Mr James Wilson, landing master; Mr David Taylor, master;

Mr William Reid, mate, and Mr John Peters, steward, counting in all fifty-four persons. The weather was clear, and the vessel had no sooner got out of the harbour, than the lights of the float were distinctly seen; and before day-break, the Tender was made fast to her moorings off the Bell Rock.

Tuesday, 7th.

Arrangements at landing at an early hour on the Rock.

At 3 o'clock in the morning, the ship's bell was rung as the signal for landing at the Rock. These artificers, to which this had been the first trip, found their quarters rather confined in the ship, and some of them being sickly, were glad of an opportunity of landing, and came almost immediately upon deck, notwithstanding the earliness of the hour at which the tide happened. But those who were more accustomed to the business, calculated their time, knowing that sufficient warning was always given, especially at hours so early. When the landing was to be made before breakfast, it was customary to give each of the artificers and seamen a dram and a biscuit, and coffee was prepared by the steward for the cabins. Exactly at 4 o'clock, the whole party landed from three boats, including one of those belonging to the Floating-light, with a part of that ship's crew, which always attended the works in moderate weather. The landing-master's boat called the Seaman, but more commonly the Life-boat, took the lead. The next boat called the Mason, was generally, steered by the writer; while the Floating-light's boat Pharos, was under the management of the boatswain of that ship.

How the Artificers are employed.

Having now so considerable a party of workmen and sailors on the Rock, it may be proper here to notice how their labours were directed. Preparations having been made last month for the erection of a second forge upon the beacon, the smiths commenced their operations, both upon the lower and higher platforms, where forges had been erected. They were employed in sharpening the picks and irons for the masons, and in making bats and other apparatus of various descriptions, connected with the fitting of the railways. The landing-master's crew were occupied in assisting the mill-wrights in laying the railways to hand. Sailors, of all other descriptions of men, are the most accommodating in the use of their hands. They worked freely with the boring irons, and assisted in all the operations of the railways, acting by turns as boatmen, seamen, and artificers. We had no such character on the Bell Rock as the common labourer. All the operations of this department were cheerfully undertaken by the seamen, who, both on the rock and on ship-board, were the inseparable companions of every work connected with the erection of the Bell Rock Light-house. It will naturally be supposed, that about twenty-five masons, occupied with their picks in executing and preparing the foundation of the light-house, in the course of a tide of about three hours, would make a considerable impression upon an area even of forty-two feet in diameter. But in proportion as the foundation was deepened, the rock was found to be much more hard and difficult to work, while the baling and pumping of water became much more troublesome. A joiner was kept almost constantly employed in fitting the picks to their handles, which, as well as the points of the irons, were very frequently broken. At 8 o'clock, the water overflowed the site of the building, and the boats left the rock with all hands for breakfast. Several of the artificers would willingly have remained upon the beacon to avoid the rolling motion and sickness incident to the ship; yet, being all wetted, and those especially who were employed in excavating the site of the light-house and railways, being completely bespattered with the chips and particles elicited from the Rock, the whole party embarked in the boats; but such as chose were at liberty to return to the beacon with the smiths after breakfast.

Interesting appearance of the Rock.

Excepting at the erection of the principal beams of the beacon, the Bell Rock this morning presented by far the most busy and active appearance it had exhibited since the erection of the Beacon. The surface of the Rock was crowded with men, the two forges flaming, the one above the other, upon the Beacon, while the anvils thundered with the rebounding noise of their wooden supports, and formed a curious contrast with the occasional clamour of the surges. The wind was westerly to-day, and the weather being extremely agreeable, as soon after breakfast as the tide had sufficiently overflowed the rock to float the boats over it, the smiths, with a number of the artificers, returned to the Beacon, carrying their fishing-tackle along with them, which had all been put in a state of requisition before they left the shore. In the course of the forenoon, the Beacon exhibited a still more extraordinary appearance than the Rock had done in the morning. The sea being smooth, it seemed to be afloat upon the water, with a number of men supporting themselves in all the variety of attitude and position; while, from the upper part of this wooden house, the volumes of smoke which ascended from the forges, gave the whole a very curious and fanciful appearance.

Artificers remain on the rock all day.

The length of the day now afforded two tides with day-light. The boats, therefore, landed the artificers at 5 o'clock P. M., and after three hours' work, as in the morning, all hands again left it at 8 o'clock, and returned on board of the Tender. Those who had been left upon the beacon, complained of being very tired, with supporting themselves so long in one position without motion, or even a sufficient space to rest their feet upon.

From the excellence of the weather, and for the greater conveniency of the work, the Tender had been made fast to one of the Stone-lighter's floating buoys, to be nearer to the Rock than her own moorings, which were placed at such a distance as might enable her, in casting off, to clear the Rock on any tack. But, in the course of this tide, it was observed that a heavy swell was setting in from the eastward; and the appearance of the sky indicated a change of weather, while the wind was shifting about. The barometer also had fallen from 30 to 29.60. It was therefore judged prudent to shift the vessel to the SW. or more distant buoy. Her bowsprit was also soon afterwards taken in, the top-masts struck, and every thing made snug, as seamen term it, for a gale. During the course of the night, the wind increased and shifted to the eastward, when the vessel rolled very hard, and the sea often broke over her bows with great force.

Wednesday, 8th.

Tender bears away for Leith Roads.

Although the motion of the Tender was much less than that of the Float-ing-light, at least in regard to the rolling motion; yet, she sended or pitched much. Being also of a very handsome build, and what seamen term very clean aft, the sea often struck her counter with such force, that the writer, who possessed the aftermost cabin, being unaccustomed to this new vessel, could not divest himself of uneasiness; for, when her stern fell into the sea, it struck with so much violence, as to be more like the resistance of a rock than the sea. The water, at the same time, often rushed with great force up the rudder-case; and forcing up the valve of the water-closet, the floor of his cabin was at times laid under water. The gale contin-ued to increase, and the vessel rolled and pitched in such a manner, that the haw-ser by which the Tender was made fast to the buoy snapped, and she went adrift. In the act of swinging round to the wind, she shipped a very heavy sea, which greatly alarmed the artificers, who imagined that we had got upon the Rock. But this, from the direction of the wind, was impossible. The writer, however, sprung upon deck, where he found the sailors busily employed in rigging out the bow-sprit, and in setting sail. From the easterly direction of the wind, it was considered most advisable to steer for the Firth of Forth, and there wait a change of weather. At 2 P. M. we accordingly passed the Isle of May; at 6 anchored in Leith Roads, and at 8 the writer landed, when he came in upon his friends, who were not a little surprised at his unexpected appearance, which gave an instantaneous alarm for the safety of things at the Bell Rock.

Wednesday, 9th.

The wind still continued to blow very hard at E. by N., and the Sir Joseph Banks rode heavily, and even drifted with both anchors ahead, in Leith Roads. The artificers did not attempt to leave the ship last night; but there being upwards of fifty-people on board, and the decks greatly lumbered with the two large boats, they were in a very crowded and impatient state on board. But to-day they got ashore, and amused themselves by walking about the streets of Edinburgh, some in very humble apparel, from having only the worst of their jackets with them, which, though quite suitable for their work, were hardly fit for public inspection, being not only tattered, but greatly stained with the red colour of the rock.

Friday, 10th.

To-day the wind was at S. E., with light breezes and foggy weather. At 6 A. M. the writer again embarked for the Bell Rock, when the vessel immediately sailed. At 11 P. M., there being no wind, the kedge-anchor was let go off Anstruther, one of the numerous towns on the coast of Fife, where we waited the return of the tide.

Saturday, 11th.

Before leaving Leith Roads, the muster-roll was called, to see that all hands were on board; and we also shipped an additional seaman. The vessel, therefore, required a great stock of provisions and water, and, from her very hampered sit-uation, with the stores and apparatus of various kinds which she had on board, it became necessary to embrace every opportunity of filling up the stock of water, as landsmen use a much greater quantity of that indispensable article for every purpose than seamen. Mr Taylor, who commanded the Tender, and whose attention in this respect was quite indefatigable, sent the boat ashore at Anstruther, at a very early hour this morning, for an additional supply.

Work continued on the Rock till midnight.

Throughout these twenty-four hours, the winds were variable and the weather was hazy. At 6 A. M. the Sir Joseph got under weigh, and at 11 was again made fast to the southern buoy at the Bell Rock. Though it was now late in the tide, the writer being anxious to ascertain the state of things after the gale, landed with the artificers, to the number of forty-four. Every thing was found in an entire state; but, as the tide was nearly gone, only half an hour's work had been got when the site of the building was overflowed. During the period of high-water, the boats were employed in bringing stores and provisions from on board the Smeaton, which had also returned from Arbroath, whither she had run for shelter. In the evening the boats again landed at 9, and, after a good tide's-work of three hours, with torch-light, the work was left off at midnight.

Appearance of the Rock at night.

To the distant shipping, the appearance of things under night on the Bell Rock, when the work was going forward, must have been very remarkable, especially to those who were strangers to the operations. Mr John Reid, principal light-keeper, who also acted as master of the Floating-light during the working months at the rock, described the appearance of the numerous lights situate so low in the water, when seen at the distance of two or three miles, as putting him in mind of Milton's description of the fiends in the lower regions; adding, "for it seems greatly to surpass Will-o'-the-Wisp, or any of those earthly spectres of which we have so often heard."

Sunday, 12th.

The weather was somewhat blowy to-day, and the wind veered from E. to S.W. The boats landed at a quarter past 9 this morning, but not without considerable difficulty, owing to a heavy swell of sea which accompanied the change of wind. After continuing at work for three hours and a half at the site of the building, and the fixtures for the railways, the water came in upon the artificers, and the boats left the rock with all hands, after having experienced some difficulty at the entrance of the eastern landing creek, by the breach of the sea. In this respect, the larger boats of the new Tender were not found to be so well adapted for pulling through a swell of sea in these narrow creeks, as the smaller boats of the Floating-light. The breadth of the former being greater, the oars were more apt to get entangled with the sea-weed and jutting points of the rock, so that it was with difficulty they could be equally pulled on each side; and if they did not exactly stem the sea, but got a preponderance to one side, the waves were apt to throw them upon the shelving rocks. Smaller boats, under these particular circumstances, would have been more handy, but of two evils we are often left to choose the least, and the larger boats were found to be more generally useful. For the conveniency of accommodating a greater number of artificers, it was necessary to have the boats of as large dimensions as the Tender could stow; it being hardly possible in this service to have more than two upon deck, and one over the stern.

Sixty persons on the quarter-deck at prayers to-day.

About 1 P.M. the boats returned to the Tender in safety; and prayers were soon afterwards read upon deck, when all hands, including the boats crews from the Floating-light and Smeaton, being present, they counted sixty individuals. Owing to the difficulty experienced in getting clear of the rock this morning, and the swell of the sea still continuing, a landing was not attempted in the evening.

Monday, 13th.

The wind blew fresh from the S.W. this morning, and the tides were again getting into the state of neap; yet the ebb was very considerable yesterday, and some parts of the rock were even dry about half an hour before the calculated time. The boats landed to-day at 11, and left the Rock again at half-past 2 o'clock P. M. The artificers were again landed in the evening, but the tide did not leave the foundation-pit. All hands, however, were employed on the higher parts of the rock, in the tracks of the railways, where bat-holes were to bore and seats for the cast-iron props or supports of the railways to level. After being employed in this manner for an hour and a half, the boats returned to the Tender.

Artificers appear backward in landing on the Rock to-day.

From the difficulties attending the landing on the rock, owing to the breach of sea which had for days past been around it, the artificers showed some backwardness at getting into the boats this morning; but after a little explanation this was got over. It was always observable, that for some time after any thing like danger had occurred at the Rock, the workmen became much more cautious, and on some occasions their timidity was rather troublesome. It fortunately happened, however, that, along with the writer's assistants and the sailors, there were also some of the artificers themselves who felt no such scruples, and in this way these difficulties were the more easily surmounted. In matters where life is in danger, it becomes necessary to treat even unfounded prejudices with tenderness, as an accident, under certain circumstances, would not only have been particularly painful to those giving directions, but have proved highly detrimental to the work, especially in the early stages of its advancement.

Tuesday, 14th.

Tender sails for Arbroath.

The wind was at south this morning, accompanied with very heavy showers of rain; and though the boats effected a landing at 12 noon; yet, during the whole tide, there was not less depth than 15 inches of water on the highest part of the site of the building, while the sea was continually ranging into it. The artificers were, therefore, employed on the higher parts of the eastern railway-track. After an hour and three-quarters work, the boats returned to the Tender, which had already cast off from her moorings, and kept plying about till they left the rock with the artificers, when she immediately sailed for Arbroath, and got into the harbour at 6 P. M.

Here the artificers were employed in the work-yard for six days, until the return of spring-tides. During this interval ashore, the smiths were busily employed in giving the picks and other tools a thorough repair. Every measure was also adopted that could possibly facilitate the fitting up of the railways, without the aid of which the blocks of stone could not possibly be conveyed along the rugged surface of the rock after they were landed.

First entire course removed from the platform.

The operations at the rock, both in the preparation of the foundation of the building, and in the fitting up of the railways for landing the materials, became more and more urgent as the work advanced ashore. The first course had now been removed from the platform, and the greater part of the second was laid in its place; and, in the course of three weeks, it was also expected to be in readiness to ship for the rock, while a number of the higher courses were in a considerable state of forwardness. Some of the Aberthaw limestone having been burnt, and reduced to a state of powder, it was put into casks, while equal quantities of pozzolano and clean sharp sand were also made up in the same manner, to be used in building up the inequalities on the south east or lowest part of the margin of the foundation-pit, that by this means the water might be more speedily pumped out, and a longer period of the tide obtained for carrying on the work.

Trial of the landing apparatus.

It being apparent, from the present state of things, that we should be ready for building in the course of the next spring-tides, if the weather proved favourable, it was necessary to have all the apparatus for landing the stones at the rock in a working state. While at Arbroath, the writer had a trial made of one of the new praams or stone-lighters, by towing her into the bay of Arbroath, with a large stone upon deck, where the sloop Smeaton had been previously anchored with her gaff-boom and tackle rigged. This experiment was made in pretty rough weather, when the block of stone was lifted with the tackle in and out of the Smeaton's hold, and again placed on the praam's deck, as was to be done in the operation of landing at the rock. The apparatus is represented in Plate XI., and the trial was highly satisfactory, the tackle requiring only some trifling alterations. The Smeaton was then brought into the harbour and trimmed with ballast, consisting of pieces of granite, neatly fitted into her hold, over which a platform was laid, which completed her for the service of taking the stones from Arbroath to the Bell Rock.

Monday, 20th.

Tender sails for the Rock.

Things on shore having been thus arranged, the writer again embarked on the 20th in the Sir Joseph Banks Tender, and sailed for the Bell Rock at 1 P. M., accompanied by the sloop Smeaton, and having on board of both vessels sixty-two artificers and seamen. At 8 the Floating-light was hailed, and at 9 the Tender and Smeaton were made fast to their respective buoys.

Tuesday, 21st.

Fifty-eight artificers land.

At 3 o'clock this morning, the bell was rung, as a signal for landing at the rock. From the number of artificers, it required considerable management and exertion on the part of the landing-master to get them properly seated in the four boats belonging to the Tender, the Smeaton, and Floating-light, which last attended the rock during the morning tides, and assisted in all the operations of the landing-master's department. At 4 o'clock fifty-eight persons landed; but the tides being extremely languid, the water only left the higher parts of the rock, and no work could be done at the site of the building. A third forge was, however, put in operation, during a short time, for the greater conveniency of sharpening the picks and irons, and for purposes connected with the preparations for fixing the railways on the rock.

Advantage of a Bell as a signal at the Rock.

The weather towards the evening became thick and foggy, and there was hardly a breath of wind to ruffle the surface of the water; had it not therefore been the noise from the anvils of the smiths who had been left on the Beacon throughout the day, which afforded a guide for the boats, a landing could not have been attempted this evening, especially with such a company of artificers. This circumstance confirmed the writer's opinion with regard to the propriety of connecting large bells to be rung with machinery in the light-house, to be tolled day and night during the continuance of foggy weather, by which the mariner may be forewarned of too near an approach to the Rock, while every distant object is obscured in the mist.

The tides went so little back at the Rock to-day, that no work was done excepting to the railways; it being impossible to pump the water out of the foundation-pit, as the tide never left the south-eastern margin of it. After remaining two hours, all hands returned towards the Tender, where guns were occasionally fired, horns sounded, and the ship's bell tolled, as signals for the boats to find their way from the Rock to the vessels; and, in this manner, the whole party got safely on board about 8 o'clock P. M.

Wednesday, 22d.

At 6 A. M. the artificers landed, but the foundation could only be partially cleared of water, so as to enable a few hands, standing ankle-deep in water, to work round the edges where the site of the Light-house was highest. After two and a half hours' work, the boats, with the artificers, returned to their respective ships.

Building materials landed for the first time this season.

This morning several casks of pozzolano, lime and sand were landed, to make mortar, in order to build round the lower edges of the foundation-pit. This being something like an approximation to the long wished-for commencement of building the Light-house, the artificers thought the opportunity too good to pass over in silence, and the casks were accordingly landed under a salute of three hearty cheers. At half past 6 P. M. the boats again landed upon the rock, but, even when the tide was at the lowest, the water stood to the depth of 18 inches upon the site of the building, and no work was done. This was rather a relief to the smiths, who having no irons to sharp, got rapidly forward with the necessary fixtures for the railways.

Thursday, 23d.

Small ruble walls built instead of cofferdam.

The weather continued to be extremely mild, and the winds were generally from the eastward and southward, accompanied with thick and hazy weather, which, in communicating with the rock, was not only irksome but even dangerous. At 7 o'clock this morning, the tide proving more favourable, the artificers began to work. At 9 the rock was again overflowed, and the boats returned to the Tender after two hours' work. Part of the operations of this morning's tide consisted in building up the crevices and inequalities of the rock round the margin of the foundation, with pozzolano mortar, and the chips produced from the excavation, with a view to dam out the water. These little walls varied from six inches to eighteen inches in height; a small sluice or aperture being formed in one of them by which the water, during ebb-tide, was allowed to drain off.

It formed part of the writer's original design, as formerly noticed, to erect a cast-iron coffer-dam of about five feet in height, round the site of the building; but the surface of the rock was so irregular, that the difficulty of tightening it, and also of emptying the contained water, so as to get the benefit of it during ebb-tide, would have been so great, that, taking these circumstances into account, together, with the loss of time which would attend the erection of such a preparatory work, the idea of a coffer-dam was laid aside, soon after entering upon the actual execution of the work.

Inconveniencies of foggy weather.

The boats landed this evening, when the artificers had again two hours' work. The weather still continuing very thick and foggy, more difficulty was experienced in getting on board of the vessels to-night, than had occurred on any previous occasion, owing to a light breeze of wind which carried the sound of the bell, and the other signals, made on board of the vessels, away from the Rock. Having, fortunately, made out the position of the sloop Smeaton, at the N.E. buoy,—to which we were much assisted by the barking of the ship's dog, we parted with the Smeaton's boat, when the boats of the Tender took a fresh departure for that vessel, which lay about half a mile to the south-westward. Yet such is the very deceiving state of the tides, that although there was a small binnacle and compass in the landing-master's boat, we had, nevertheless, passed the Sir Joseph a good way, when, fortunately, one of the sailors catched the sound of a blowing-horn. The only fire-arms on board, were a pair of swivels of one inch caliber; but it is quite surprising how much the sound is lost in foggy weather, as the report was heard but at a very short distance. The sound, from the explosion of gunpowder, is so instantaneous, that the effect of the small guns was not so good as either the blowing of a horn, or the tolling of a bell, which afforded a more constant and steady direction for the pilot. It may here be noticed, that larger guns would have answered better, but these must have induced the keeping of a greater stock of gunpowder, which, in a service of this kind, might have been attended with risk. A better signal would have been a bugle-horn, the tremulous sound of which produces a more powerful effect in fog, than the less sonorous and more sudden report of ordnance.

Friday, 24th.

The artificers landed to-day, both with the morning and evening tides. During the first, they had two hours and three-quarters, and in the latter, two hours and a quarter, making together five hours work; the weather still continuing thick and foggy, with the wind at south-east.

Saturday, 25th.

The boats landed this morning at a quarter from 8 o'clock, and the artificers left off work at half-past 10. During the evening's tide, the operations were again continued with torch-light, from half-past 7 till 11 o'clock P. M., having to-day had four hours and three-quarters work upon the rock.

Force of the sea upon the Rock.

A remarkable fact may here be mentioned as an evidence of the force of the sea upon the Bell Rock. The reader may remember, that the mushroom anchor, with its chain and buoy, which had drifted during the very hard gale of the 6th September 1807, were found upon the Rock after the gale: at that time the buoy and chain were taken up, but the anchor having got into a pretty large hole or cavity of the rock, no convenient opportunity occurred for lifting it last season. No doubt, however, was entertained that a mass of iron, weighing about a ton, without any timber or buoyant matter attached to it, would remain in this position undisturbed, till a convenient time should occur for recovering it. But, at the commencement of the works this season, to the surprise of every one, the anchor in question could not be seen. To-day, however, it was discovered at the opposite side of the Rock, by one of the smiths who was at work upon the highest platform of the beacon; and the weather being extremely fine, it was weighed or lifted by the landing-master's crew. For this purpose, spars were laid across two boats, between which the anchor was made fast: as the tide rose the boats floated, and the anchor thus suspended, was conveyed to one of the vessels in the offing; when a chain and buoy being attached to it, it was again laid down in a proper birth, as the moorings of one of the praam-boats.

Sunday, 26th.

The weather kept still very favourable for the operations at the rock, though, from the prevailing fogs, it was not only inconvenient, but hazardous, to ply even in the short distance between the rock and the vessels in the offing. The boats landed this morning at half-past 8, and again returned to the Tender at 12. In the evening, they landed at half-past 8 and continued with torch-light till half-past 11 P. M., having had five hours work during the two tides.

Monday, 27th.

The weather was still thick and hazy, but the sea kept smooth, and the tides were very favourable, so that in the morning, the artificers were at work from half-past 8 till half-past 11 o'clock; and in the evening, from a quarter past 9 till midnight; or had altogether five hours and three-quarters work to-day.

The writer wishing, in such favourable weather, to try the practicability of bringing the Stone-lighters directly into the landing creeks of the Rock, with the stones and building materials, by which great facility might occasionally be given to the work, in landing the stones directly from the vessels, instead of doing it on all occasions by loading and discharging the praam-boats; an experiment was accordingly made this evening, and the sloop Smeaton was towed into the eastern creek, when it was ascertained that her cargo, in such weather, might have been very speedily landed. But when the tide left the rock, the vessel heeled to the one side, her sails hung loose, and she had so much the appearance of a wreck, that the sight cast an immediate gloom particularly upon the countenances of the sea-men, to whom a vessel, in this state, could not be viewed without some degree of horror. Whether it was partly from this circumstance, or that the tide and weather would so seldom answer this nice operation, or that the landing-master's crew had become so expert in transporting the praam-boats, the idea of laying the stone-vessels upon the rock, was, from this night's experiment, completely abandoned.

Tuesday 28th.

Land in the morning at 9, and continue at work till 1 P. M., and again in the evening, when the work is continued by torch-light, from half-past 10 till half-past 12, having had five hours' work to-day.

Wednesday, 29th.

The wind was at south-east this morning, with gentle breezes and clear weath-er. The boats landed at 11 A. M., and the foundation pit having been speedily cleared of water, the work was continued till half-past 1. P. M., being three hours. The evening tides now falling late, and becoming neap, no landing was made this night.

Monday, 30th.

Artificers leave the Rock. Progress of the works.

The boats landed the artificers on the rock at half-past 11 this morning, but the tides being extremely languid, there was only about an hour's work got upon the site of the building, and about 2½ hours' at the Railways. Finding that little more could be got done during the present set of spring-tides, on returning to the vessel at 3 P. M., she was got under way, and sailed for Arbroath, which she reached at 7 P. M.; but, being too early in the tide for getting into the harbour, the author landed with the boat, and felt not a little satisfied with the progress and success of the work. The site of the building had been excavated as low in some parts as it was necessary or proper to carry it, and there was now a good prospect of having it completely prepared in the course of the next spring-tides. About 100 feet of the eastern branch of the Railway had also been laid, while the best of the season was still to come. The business of the work-yard was going on with no less vigour ashore. The greater quantity of the stones wanted from Aberdeen for the courses in hand, had been brought to Arbroath, and the supply was becoming both more regular and abundant from the quarry of Mylnefield. The second course, which contained very weighty stones, being 18 inches in thickness, was now nearly all laid down upon the platform in the middle of the work-yard, where each stone was carefully fitted and marked as it was to lie in the building, in the same manner as had been done with the first course.

The Artificers' pay and premiums this month.

It so happened that the artificers employed afloat, or, at the Bell Rock, were upon this occasion ashore on the regular pay-day, which took place on the first of every month. The seamen's wages were paid once a quarter, and their premiums at the end of the working season. Such of the artificers as had been off at the Rock this month, had each a considerable sum to receive for wages and premiums, say L. 6, the stated wages being L. 1 for six days; and having no disbursement to make for victuals, the situation of those afloat became enviable, and the workmen who had not been at the Rock, now began to make application for what they called their turn afloat. This change was not a little gratifying, considering the hesitation and backwardness shewn last season to this part of the service.

1808, July.

Tuesday, 5th.

Artificers embark for the Rock.

At 11 o'clock P. M., the Sir Joseph Banks Tender set sail from Arbroath for the Bell Rock, to commence the operations for the ensuing spring tides, having on board 38 masons, 6 joiners, 3 smiths, and the landing-master's crew, consisting of 12 seamen, in all 59. The winds being variable, the vessel only got a short way off the shore in the course of the night, and did not reach her moorings till the next day at noon.

Wednesday, 6th.

Commence operations for the ensuing Spring-tides.

Landed on the Rock, with the three boats belonging to the Tender, at 5 P. M., and began immediately to bale the water out of the foundation-pit, with a number of buckets, while the pumps were also kept in action with relays of artificers and seamen. The work commenced upon the higher parts of the foundation, as the water left them, but it was now pretty generally reduced to a level. The pumps were laid in a diagonal position as represented in Plate XI.; four men wrought at the cross handle and guided the pump-spear, to which a rope was attached, and in this manner, about 20 men could be conveniently employed at each pump, and it is quite astonishing in how short a time so great a body of water could be drawn off. The water in the foundation-pit at this time, measured about two feet in depth, on an area of 42 feet in diameter; and yet it was drawn off in the course of about half an hour. After this, the artificers commenced with their picks, and continued at work for two hours and a half, some of the sailors being at the same time busily employed in clearing the foundation of chips, and in conveying the irons to and from the smiths on the beacon where they were sharped. At 8 o'clock, the sea broke in upon us, and overflowed the foundation pit, when the boats returned to the Tender.

Thursday, 7th.

How employed.

The landing-master's bell rung this morning about 4 o'clock, and at 5 the boats landed the artificers, when the pumps and buckets were set to work to clear the foundation-pit of water. The pumps, as formerly noticed, were left upon the Rock, being fixed between four bars of iron, batted or wedged into it, upon which plates were fitted with forelocks, which kept them from shifting. It was common also to drive a few wedges of iron between the pumps and these fixtures, for greater security against their being lifted by the pressure of the water, which, in spring tides, was from 12 to 14 feet in depth. At half-past 5, the foundation being cleared, the work commenced on the site of the building. But from the moment of landing, the squad of joiners and mill-wrights was at work upon the higher parts of the Rock, in laying the railways, while the anvils of the smiths resounded on the Beacon, and such columns of smoke ascended from the forges, that they were often mistaken by strangers at a distance, for a ship on fire. After continuing three hours at work, the foundation of the building was again overflowed, and the boats returned to the ship at half-past 8 o'clock. The masons and pickmen had, at this period, a pretty long day on board of the Tender, but the smiths and joiners were kept constantly at work upon the Beacon; the stability and great conveniency of which had now been so fully shewn, that no doubt remained as to the propriety of fitting it up as a barrack. The workmen were accordingly employed, during the period of high-water, in making preparations for this purpose.

Foundation stone prepared.

The foundation-pit now assumed the appearance of a great platform, and the late tides had been so favourable, that it became apparent that the first course, consisting of a few irregular and detached stones for making up certain inequalities in the interior parts of the site of the building, might be laid in the course of the present spring-tides. Having been enabled to-day to get the dimensions of the foundation or first stone accurately taken, a mould was made of its figure, when the writer left the Rock, after the tide's work of this morning, in a fast rowing boat, for Arbroath; and upon landing, two men were immediately set to work upon one of the blocks from Mylnefield quarry, which was prepared in the course of the following day, as the stone-cutters relieved each other, and worked both night and day, so that it was sent off in one of the Stone-lighters without delay.

On returning to the Rock, the writer found that the artificers had been able to land regularly, both at the morning and evening tides, and that they had added eight hours to the working period. He was, however, extremely sorry to find that he had missed the visit of his excellent friend Mr Patrick Neill, who, in the zeal of his pursuits in botany and natural history, had expressed a strong desire to examine the fuci and animals upon the Bell Rock, and had taken the opportunity of a passage with the Smeaton from Leith. But his engagements did not admit of his remaining till the writer's return; and he had left the rock in a boat going to the Redhead, about seven miles east from Arbroath, where he expected to overtake the writer, but instead of which, they unluckily passed each other under night.

Saturday, 9th.

The weather still continued to be very agreeable, the wind being moderate and chiefly from the S.W. At 6 A. M. the signal bell was rung for embarking for the Rock. At 7 the artificers landed, and began to clear the foundation-pit of water, and the work continued from a quarter past 7 till half-past 11, having had three hours' and a quarter's work, when the Rock was again overflowed, and the boats returned to the Tender.

Foundation stone landed at high-water.

The site of the foundation-stone was very difficult to work, from its depth in the Rock, but being now nearly prepared, it formed a very agreeable kind of pastime, at high-water, for all hands to land it upon the Rock. The landing-master's crew and artificers accordingly entered with great spirit into this operation. The stone was placed upon the deck of the Hedderwick Praam-boat, which had just been brought from Leith, and was decorated with colours for the occasion. Flags were also displayed from the shipping in the offing, and upon the Beacon. Here the writer took his station with the greater part of the artificers, who supported themselves in every possible position while the boats towed the praam from her moorings, and brought her immediately over the site of the building where her grappling anchors were let go. The stone was then lifted off the deck by a tackle hooked into a Lewis-bat, inserted into it; when it was gently lowered into the water, and grounded on the site of the building, amidst the cheering acclamations of about sixty persons. The landing of this stone at high-water became necessary, from there being still a want of a sufficient length of railway for conveying it along the Rock at low-water to the site of the building. But this method was rarely resorted to, as it was apt to skirt or break the edges of the stones; and as a continuation of good weather was not to be calculated upon, it was observed as a rule never to land more stones in any one tide than could be built, because the force of the sea was more than sufficient to remove the heaviest stones, as we have seen in the case of the first six blocks of granite which were landed by way of experiment, and also of the cast-iron mushroom anchor, which was drifted about the Rock, although it weighed upwards of a ton.

The boats landed at half-past 7 this evening, and the artificers immediately began to bale and pump the water from the foundation-pit, and the work was afterwards continued by torch-light till a quarter-past 11, having had three hours' and a quarter's work this tide.

Sunday, 10th.

Foundation-stone laid with masonic ceremony.

The wind to-day was variable, with gentle breezes varying from S.E. to N.E.; and every thing being in a state of preparation for laying the foundation-stone, which had yesterday been landed with so much eclat, the sailors again displayed their flags at all points, and a cheerful happiness was discernible in every countenance. At half-past 8 the boats landed the artificers, and the weather being remarkably fine, as many of the crews of the Floating-light, the Tender and the Smeaton, as could be spared from their respective ships, landed this morning, to witness the long-wished-for ceremony of laying the first stone of the Light-house. We had, besides, an acquisition to our numbers, in a party consisting of about sixteen persons from Dundee, who came to the Rock, just as preparations were making for laying the stone.

Whether we consider this building as an erection of great difficulty, or, in a nautical point of view, as adding much to the comfort and protection of the mariner, and safety of property, upon a range of coast extending almost to the whole eastern shores of Great Britain, its importance is evident. If it be proper, therefore, on any occasion, to attach importance to the act of laying the first stone of a public building, that of the Bell Rock Light-house cannot be said to yield to any in point of celebrity, either for the peculiarity of its situation, or the importance of its object. Under these considerations it is obvious, that but for the perilous and uncertain nature of any arrangement which could have been made for this ceremony, instead of its having been performed only in the presence of those immediately connected with the work, and of a few accidental spectators from the neighbouring shore, counting in all about eighty persons, many thousands would have attended upon an occasion which must have called forth the first dignitaries of the country, in conferring the highest honours of masonry. The writer may, however, confidently affirm, that, situate as the work was, nothing could add to the satisfaction felt by all present, in having now got matters in so advanced a state, as to be able to commence the building operations.

At 11 o'clock, the foundation stone was laid to hand. It was of a square form, containing about 20 cubic feet, and had the figures or date of 1808 simply cut upon it with a chisel, a derrick or spar of timber having been erected at the edge of the hole and guyed with ropes. The stone was then hooked to the tackle and lowered into its place, when the writer, attended by his assistants Mr Peter Logan, Mr Francis Watt, and Mr James Wilson, applied the square, the level, and the mallet, and pronounced the following benediction: "May the Great Architect of the Universe complete and bless this building," on which three hearty cheers were given, and success to the future operations was drunk with the greatest enthusiasm.

Prayers read after the tide's work.

By 12 o'clock noon, the tide had overflowed the site of the building, and the boats left the Rock after a tide's work of three hours and a half. On returning to the ship, prayers were read, when every heart perhaps felt more than ordinary thankfulness. The artificers were again landed in the evening at half-past 8, and continued at work, with torch-light, till a quarter past 12, having been three hours and three quarters' at work, or seven hours in all to-day.

Monday, 11th.

The boats landed at 9 o'clock this morning, and after three hours' and a quarter's work, they left the Rock at a quarter past 1 P. M. The artificers landed again in the evening, and work with torch-light from 10 to a quarter past 12, having had two hours' and a quarter's work.

Tuesday, 12th.

After clearing the foundation-pit of water, by means of the two pumps and a number of buckets, the work commenced at a quarter past 10, and left off at half-past 12 noon, having had two hours' and a quarter's work. In the evening, the artificers again landed at 9, but it was not till a quarter past 11 that the water was cleared out, and it began to overflow the site of the building again at midnight, so that only three quarters of an hour's work was got upon the Rock with the evening tide.

Wednesday, 13th.

Land at a quarter before 10 A. M., and begin to work at half-past 10, and left off at a quarter from 1 P. M., having had two hours' and a half. In the evening at 12 o'clock, the foundation-pit was cleared of water; but at a quarter past 12, the sea broke into it again, so that no work was done, owing to the state of the tide.

Thursday, 14th.

Tender leaves the Rock.

Land to-day at half-past 12 noon, and had one hour's work. But the tides being now in the state of neap, the Tender sailed with the artificers and landing-master's crew to Arbroath, to wait the return of spring-tides. The work now put on a very promising appearance. The first stone had been laid, and the levelling of the site of the building was in such a state, as to afford every prospect of being able to commence the building of the first entire course, after a few good tides. The reach of the Railways from the site of the building, to the eastern landing-place, was also in a state of great forwardness, and the other parts of the apparatus being now in readiness, there was every prospect of making rapid progress after the foundation course was laid, and building operations were fairly begun.

Price of granite advanced.

In the work-yard, however, things had not so prosperous an appearance, as a number of blocks of granite were still wanting to complete the first four courses of the building; and such was the urgency of the demand, lest the work should be stopped in its progress, that the writer authorised Mr Gildowie of Aberdeen to advance the price of stone, according to circumstances, as an additional stimulus to the exertions of the quarriers. From this state of matters, it was now pretty obvious, that not more than two or three courses of the light-house could be built this season.

Friday, 22d.

Artificers sail for the Rock.

To-day, at 1 o'clock P. M., the Tender left Arbroath for the Bell Rock, having on board 16 masons, 5 mill-wrights and joiners, 2 black-smiths, and 13 seamen, in all 35 persons, including the officers of the ship. The wind was at E. N. E., with light breezes and fine weather; but as it fell calm, the boats left the Tender at 5 P. M. with the artificers, while yet about 5 or 6 miles from the rock: but owing to the strength of the ebb-tide, it was found impossible to reach it in time for the tide, and they returned to the vessel at 9 P. M. without having effected a landing.

Saturday, 23d.

At half-past 5 A. M., the Tender was made fast to the south-west buoy, when the artificers landed. The two pumps were immediately set to work, and at half-past 7 the work commenced, and continued till a quarter past 9, when the site of the building was again overflowed, and the boats left the Rock after an hour and three-quarters' work. In the evening the work commenced at 7, and left off at half-past 9, after two hours' and a half's work.

Sunday, 24th.

A raft of timber goes adrift.

The wind was at S.S.E., with strong gales, accompanied with a heavy breach of sea, so that the boats could not land, and there was consequently no work done to-day. The ship had also such a rolling motion, that the people could not be collected on deck, as usual, for reading prayers. The wind was at east, accompanied with a pretty heavy swell of sea to-day, so that it was not without considerable difficulty that the boats landed, when two hours' and a quarter's work were got, having been on the Rock from three quarters past 7 till 10 A. M. But in this state of the weather a landing was not attempted in the evening. In the course of this night, a raft of six Norway logs, intended for laying the railways over certain gullies or inequalities of the rock, drifted from one of the floating buoys to which it had been made fast. It was afterwards picked up by some fishermen in the Firth of Forth, near Anstruther, who were paid L. 2 for their trouble, in name of salvage and expences.

Tuesday, 25th.

The weather was more settled to-day, and the sea had become much smoother. At a quarter past 8 A. M. the work commenced, and left off again at half-past 11, after an excellent tide's work of three hours and a quarter. The masons were chiefly employed at the foundation of the building,—the millwrights and joiners at the railways,—the blacksmiths were kept busy at both operations,—while the landing-master's crew took part in the whole.

The boats landed again in the evening at 8 P. M., and the foundation having been cleared, the artificers began to the low-water works at a quarter past 9, and continued till 11. After an hour and three-quarters' work they left the rock, but the joiners and blacksmiths had been employed on the beacon since morning.

State of things, at night, upon extinguishing the torches.

The wind being at S.E. this evening, we had a pretty heavy swell of sea upon the rock, and some difficulty attended our getting off in safety, as the boats got a-ground in the creek, and were in danger of being upset. Upon extinguishing the torch-lights, about twelve in number, the darkness of the night seemed quite horrible; the water being also much charged with the phosphorescent appearance which is familiar to every one on ship-board, the waves, as they dashed upon the rock, were in some degree like so much liquid flame. The scene, upon the whole, was truly awful.

Wednesday, 26th.

The first, or foundation course is finished to-day.

The work on the rock began this morning at 9 o'clock, and left off at a quarter past 12 noon, when the tide overflowed the site of the building. The masons then went on board of the Tender, but the smiths and joiners, as usual, continued their operations on the beacon. The weather being moderate, the boats landed again in the evening, at a quarter past 10, and left off at midnight, having had altogether four hours' and three quarters' of low-water work to-day, when the last of the eighteen detached pieces of stone, forming the Foundation-course, were laid. The several holes or cavities in it, varying in depth from six to eighteen inches, had now been built up with stones, exactly cut and fitted to their respective places, as represented in Plate XV.; and which brought the whole surface to a uniform level.

The force of habit exemplified in landing at night on the Bell Rock.

In leaving the Rock this evening, every thing, after the torches were extinguished, had the same dismal appearance as last night, but so perfectly acquainted were the landing-master and his crew with the position of things at the Rock, that comparatively little inconveniency was experienced on these occasions, when the weather was moderate: such is the effect of habit, even in the most unpleasant situations. If, for example, it had been proposed to a person accustomed to a city life, at once to take up his quarters off a sunken reef, and land upon it in boats at all hours of the night, the proposition must have appeared quite impracticable and extravagant; but this practice coming progressively upon the artificers, it was ultimately undertaken with the greatest alacrity. Notwithstanding this, however, it must be acknowledged, that it was not till after much labour and peril, and many an anxious hour, that the writer is enabled to state, that the site of the Bell Rock Light-house is fully prepared for the First entire course of the building.

Thursday, 28th.

First cargo of an entire course landed.

The sloop Smeaton had accordingly loaded the first cargo of cut stone at Arbroath for the Light-house, consisting of twenty blocks of the First entire course, and had last night come to her moorings; and this morning the praam-boats were employed in landing her cargo upon the Rock. From the want of a complete line of Railway from any of the landing-places to the site of the building, this operation could only be effected at high-water, when the stones were let down, one after another, upon the unincumbered area of the foundation of the Light-house, by means of a slip-rope passed through the Lewis-bat of each stone. This, as before noticed, was by no means a very desirable mode of landing the materials, and was indeed, one that could rarely be resorted to, except in the finest weather. The artificers having landed at 9 A. M., the foundation was cleared of water by 10, when the masons made preparations for commencing the building operations. Having had two hours' and three quarters' work, they left the Rock, after laying the blocks of stone which had been landed, in a compact and regular manner upon the site of the building.

Friday, 29th.

The wind was at east to-day, with a gentle breeze. At 10 A. M. the workmen landed, but the tides becoming neap, it was two hours and a half before the foundation could be cleared of water, and at a quarter from 2 P. M. it was again overflowed, having only had an hour and a quarter's work with the morning tide, when the twelve remaining blocks of the Smeaton's cargo were laid to hand, and ready for being built with mortar. In the present state of the tides, it was not judged necessary to land this evening.

The Smeaton makes a second trip for a cargo in 20 hours.

The Smeaton having been unloaded yesterday forenoon, she was again dispatched to Arbroath for another cargo of the First course, which she got on board that same night by 12 o'clock, and had returned to her moorings at the Bell Rock this morning; Captain Pool, with his usual activity, having only been absent from the Rock about twenty hours. In the mean time, the writer visited the operations of the work-yard, to ascertain more fully what prospect there was of having a supply of prepared stones for continuing the works of this season, to the extent of three or four courses of the Light-house. Some arrangement also was necessary for the removal of Cranes and other articles of machinery for the use of the building operations.

Saturday, 30th.

Tender sails for Arbroath.

The Tender left her moorings at the Rock this morning for Arbroath, with such of the artificers as could be spared. Those left shifted on board of the Smeaton, and were to be employed at the Beacon, and in laying the Railways, now much wanted, for transporting the stones along the Rock. They also attended to the arrangement of the materials landed upon the site of the building, where, from the lowness of its situation, they lay in safety. In the work-yard considerable progress had now been made with the Second entire course of the building, and after much trouble, the necessary blocks of granite had at length come to hand, for completing it, but still many stones were wanting for the higher ones.

1808, August.

August, Wednesday, 3d.

Returns to the Rock.

The Tender sailed this afternoon from Arbroath, having on board two of the cranes already alluded to, as in preparation for the work, upon a new construction, as will be seen in Plate XIV. These were intended to be erected on the site of the building, for laying the stones in a more perfect and expeditious manner than had hitherto been followed in operations of this kind. She carried also forty-seven persons, including artificers and seamen; but as the winds were light, little progress was made during the afternoon, for, as yet, the utility of the Steam-boat, in cases of this kind, had not been developed.

Thursday, 4th.

Four stones laid.

At 4 o'clock this morning the Tender reached her moorings, and was made fast to the south-west buoy, as laid down upon Plate V. At 5 o'clock, 32 artificers and

11 seamen landed upon the Rock, from three boats. The landing-master's crew transported one of the cranes from on board of the Tender, on one of the praams, and landed it at high-water upon the Rock. Having again landed in the evening, the foundation-pit was cleared of water by 6 o'clock, when the Crane was set up and properly guyed with ropes. The center-stone and three others were then laid with mortar, and trenailed to the Rock. After two hours' work, the site of the building was again overflowed, and at 8 o'clock the artificers returned on board of the Tender.

Advantages of the new cranes over sheer-poles.

As the stones were all dove-tailed into one another, they required to be laid perpendicularly into their respective places, which was also essential to preserving a proper bed of mortar under them. This could only be effected in a speedy and dextrous manner by means of a crane; but it will further be seen, from the angular figure of the stones, that this could not be effected by one of these machines of the ordinary construction, as has formerly been noticed. It had been recommended to the writer to use the common sheer-poles, with which the Edystone Light-house was built, which, notwithstanding all the improvements in machinery, were still chiefly in use for laying heavy stones; but sheer-poles, besides being difficult to preserve on a sunken rock, could neither have laid the materials so well, nor with a tenth part of the expedition, as the crane with the moveable beam delineated in Plate XIV.

Mr Smeaton's plan of Trenails and Wedges followed.

Stones laid at the depth of about 14 feet under high-water mark, required more than merely laying them on their respective beds, and trusting to their own gravity. For this purpose nothing seemed to be so well adapted as the oaken trenails which Mr Smeaton used in the erection of the Edystone Light-house. Two jumper-holes, of an inch and a half in diameter, had accordingly been drilled through each stone, which were continued or perforated to the depth of six inches into the rock or course immediately below, which became the most tedious part of the building operation. When the oaken trenail was inserted into the hole, it had a saw-draught across the lower end, into which a small wedge was inserted: and when driven home, it became quite firm. The trenail was then cut flush with the upper bed of the stone, and split with a chisel, when another wooden wedge was inserted and driven into the upper end of the trenail, as represented in diagram 10. of Plate X. Nor was this all, for, in following up Mr Smeaton's principle, two pairs of oaken wedges, as represented in Plate X., Fig. 11. were also driven gently into the perpendicular joints, prior to grouting them with mortar. The whole stones of a course had thus to be laid with great nicety, corresponding to a number of checks and marks, previously arranged in the work-yard, that the wedges might fit without trouble at the Rock, and preserve the respective positions of the superincumbent courses, and make band throughout the whole fabric.

Friday, 5th.

16 Stones laid.

The boats landed the artificers this morning at half-past 5 o'clock, and the foundation-pit being cleared of water, seven stones were laid and secured with trenails by 8 o'clock. The artificers are again landed at 6 P. M. and in the course of two hours nine additional stones were laid.

Saturday, 6th, till Wednesday, 10th.

92 Stones laid.

From Saturday the 6th till Wednesday the 10th inclusive, the weather and tides were favourable, which afforded an opportunity of landing both with the morning and evening tides, and in the course of these five days twenty-six hours' work were obtained, and ninety-two stones were laid. The landing-master's crew also continued their operations in delivering the Smeaton, and laying her cargoes on the Rock.

Thursday, 11th.

11 Stones laid.

The boats landed the artificers to-day at 9 A. M., and in about three quarters of an hour the site of the building was cleared of water, when eleven stones were laid in the course of an hour and three quarters. There being a considerable swell in the sea to-day from south-east, the praams could not land any materials upon the Rock at high-water, and nothing could be done in this way at low-water, as the Railways were not yet in a working condition.

A party of Gentlemen narrowly escape being drowned.

During the morning-tide, while the work was in progress, a very serious accident was like to have happened to a party of gentlemen from Leith, who came to see the operations at the Rock. They attempted to land in a very small boat belonging to their yacht; but, as a considerable swell of sea set round it in all directions, after several attempts, they found this to be impracticable. The writer then hailed the gentlemen, and advised them to return, and remain on board of their vessel, until the state of the tide would enable him to send a proper boat for them. In the mean time, however, a boat from the Floating-light, pretty deeply laden, with lime, cement and sand, approached, when the strangers, with a view to avoid giving trouble, took their passage in her to the Rock. The accession of three passengers to a boat, already in a lumbered state, put her completely out of trim, and, as it unluckily happened, the man who steered her was not in the habit of attending the Rock, and was not sufficiently aware of the run of the sea at the entrance of the eastern creek. Instead, therefore, of keeping close to the small rock called "John Gray," the situation of which will be seen in Plate VI., he gave it a wide birth, as the sailors term it; a heavy sea having struck the boat, drove her to leeward, and the oars getting entangled among the rocks and sea-weed, she became unmanageable, and was thrown on a ledge by another heavy swell, which instantly leaving her, she kanted seaward upon her gunwale, when the people, and part of the cargo, were thrown into the sea. Before she righted, or any assistance could be rendered by those on the Rock, another sea came which filled her and scattered the passengers, eight in number, in all directions. Some clung to the boat, others to the sea-weed, and two or three having got hold of oars and loose thwarts, which floated about, were carried out of the creek, to a considerable distance from the spot where the accident happened. By the very prompt and active assistance of Mr James Wilson, the landing-master, and his crew, the whole were, however, speedily got out of the water, excepting a Mr Strachan, one of the strangers, who had clung to the sea-weed upon a small insulated rock, bearing his name, in Plate VI., to which it was impossible at this time of tide to approach, without the assistance of a boat. Mr Wilson, with a dexterity peculiar to himself, made towards this spot, where Mr Strachan, with great resolution and perseverance, still kept his hold, although every returning sea laid him completely under water, and even hid him from the view of the spectators on the Rock. In this situation he must have remained for ten or twelve minutes. When the boat reached the insulated rock, the most difficult part was still to perform, as it required the greatest nicety of management to guide her in a rolling sea, so as to prevent her from being carried forcibly against Mr Strachan, who was in danger of being struck with the stem of the boat, to which he lay completely exposed. Notwithstanding the breach of the sea, however, and the narrowness of the passage, the boat was conducted at the proper moment close to Mr Strachan, without either touching him or the insulated rock to which he clung, till he was lifted into the boat. Mr Strachan was of course much exhausted, from having been so completely overrun by the sea, and having had but a very short space for breathing between the returning waves.

The gentlemen thus extricated in safety from the most imminent peril, were immediately removed on board of their own vessel, no doubt very thankful for the narrow escape they had made, and with grateful recollections of the exertions made by Captain Wilson and his crew. With regard to the people belonging to the Light-house service, none of them were materially injured beyond the disagreeable ducking which they experienced; but the boat was almost completely wrecked: her cargo was also injured, and partly lost.

Friday, 12th.

First entire course completed.

The artificers landed this morning at half-past 10, and after an hour and a half's work, eight stones were laid, which completed the First entire course of the building, consisting of 123 blocks, the last of which was laid with three hearty cheers. Immediately after this tide the Tender left the Rock for Arbroath, with all hands on board; and having a fine breeze at south, she got into the harbour at half-past 6 P. M., to wait the return of the spring-tides.

Artificers are welcomed into Arbroath Harbour.

Those on board felt not a little happy, when the ship, which, on her passage, had been decorated with colours, intimating that the First entire course was laid, was received with cheering from the workmen ashore, and the inhabitants of Arbroath. The service of the Bell Rock now became every trip more desirable with the artificers, who, having been enabled to work both during the morning and evening tides, with the exception of the evening of the 11th, the premiums over and above their stated wages became more and more an object, while the experience acquired in landing 123 blocks of stone, had fully established the practicability of the whole operation.

One of the Artificers disabled. He receives an annuity.

On the writer's arrival at the work-yard this evening, he learned, with much regret, that an unfortunate accident had happened to one of the masons, of the name of Hugh Rose, while employed in raising a block of stone, of between two and three tons weight, with the carpenter's jack, represented in Plate X. The jack had not been set with sufficient care, and slipped from under the stone, which instantly fell upon his knees. For a considerable time Rose was thus kept in a sitting posture, with a great part of the weight of this large stone resting upon his legs, till relieved by the other workmen who came to his assistance, and again applied the jack to raise the stone. His legs were, however, sprained in a very painful and distressing manner, which kept him from work for upwards of a twelvemonth. He was one of the best workmen in the Yard, and a man of great bodily strength; but became so much disabled by this accident, that the Light-house Board was afterwards pleased to settle an annuity of L. 20 per annum upon him.

Friday, 19th.

Granite Stones much wanted.

The work at this moment had much the appearance as if it would be retarded, as several blocks of stone were still wanted from the quarries at Aberdeen, to complete the Third entire course, the Second being now ready to be removed from the work-yard to the Rock. This course was 18 inches in thickness, the granite stones of which measured from 4 to 7 feet in length, varying in breadth from 3 feet to 4 feet 6 inches. Stones of these dimensions could not be landed with safety at high-water, but the railways on the Rock were nearly completed from the eastern landing-place to the site of the building, so that every thing was now in readiness for commencing the landing of the materials with low-water.

Wednesday, 24th.

10 Stones laid.

Having made all the necessary arrangements for making dispatch with the Third course, the writer sailed at mid-day on the 24th, with the Tender, for the Bell Rock, having on board forty-three persons in all, and the wind being favourable, the vessel was made fast to her buoy at the Rock at 7 P. M. The Smeaton also came to her moorings with a cargo of the Second course, when the landing-master's crew brought the praam-boat along-side, and was loaded with 10 stones, which were landed, and laid this evening after three hours' work.

Saturday, 27th.

136 Stones laid in 7 tides.

The weather having been extremely favourable, regular tides' work were got both morning and evening, so that the Second entire course, containing 136 stones in number, and 152 tons weight, was laid in the course of seven tides; the sloop Smeaton having been kept constantly plying between the Bell Rock and Arbroath, where, on her arrival, she was immediately loaded, whether by night or day.

From the favourable state of the weather, the complete and effective condition of the landing apparatus, and the dexterity of the landing-master's crew, a cargo of stones was discharged from the vessel, and landed on the Rock in as short a time as the stones could be built, and the holes bored into the course below, and trenails fixed into them. To facilitate the lifting of the stones off the waggons, after they were brought on the railways to the site of the building, and for laying them at once on every part of its area, though measuring 42 feet in diameter, a second crane was erected on the First entire course, as represented in Plate IX., which thus admitted of the Second course being built with great facility, without once requiring to shift the cranes horizontally; as the beams, when extended in opposite directions, reached from the centre to the extremity of the course.

1808, September.

Second course completed.

On completing the laying of the Second entire course, the Light-house began to assume the appearance and form of a building; for, although still under a part of the excavated rock, it was, nevertheless, 4 feet above the level of the lower bed of the foundation-stone,—a consideration which was highly gratifying to those immediately connected with the work. Having successfully completed this course, the writer sailed with the Smeaton for Arbroath, accompanied by such of the artificers as had been employed in building, and leaving the Tender at the Rock, with the mill-wrights, joiners, smiths, and masons, who worked at the Railways, and in preparing the upper part of the Beacon as a barrack. After landing at Arbroath, the Smeaton was immediately dispatched for Aberdeen, in quest of a few blocks of granite, still much wanted for the courses in hand.

Friday, 9th.

Artificers go off to the Rock. 10 Stones laid.

Having now got the Third entire course nearly ready for shipping, the Tender returned to Arbroath for the artificers, and a supply of water and provisions; and sailed again this morning at two o'clock for the Bell Rock, having forty persons on board. At 9 she was made fast to the S.W. buoy, when the boats were hoisted out and landed the artificers, who remained till 12 noon. These two hours were occupied in adjusting the cranes, and making preparations for commencing the building operations. A landing is again made in the evening at 9, and at midnight the artificers returned on board of the Tender, having been three hours on the Rock, when ten stones of the Third course were laid and trenailed to the course below.

Saturday, 10th.

Pumping of Water discontinued.

Land at 9 A. M., and by a quarter past 12 noon, 23 stones had been laid. The works being now somewhat elevated by the lower courses, we got quit of the very serious inconvenience of pumping water to clear the foundation-pit. This gave much facility to the operations, and was noticed with expressions of as much happiness by the artificers as the seamen had shewn when relieved of the continual trouble of carrying the smiths' bellows off the Rock, prior to the erection of the

Beacon.

One of the Artificers loses a finger.

While the workmen were laying the closing or last stone of the former course, John Bonnyman, one of the most active and expert of the masons, met with an unlucky accident in the following manner. The moveable beam of the building-crane having been lowered to a horizontal position, for the purpose of laying the stone at the circumference of the course, Bonnyman, who was directing it into its birth with a small pince in his right hand, had inadvertently rested his left hand on the beam, near the sheave or pulley, at its extremity, when one of the links unfortunately caught his hand, and before the crane could be stopped, the chain had passed over the middle joint of the fore-finger, and cut it so nearly off, that he applied to the writer, who was standing by, to relieve him of the almost detached part. But having no great inclination for the performance of operations of this kind, the severed parts were set together and bandaged in as careful a manner as circumstances would admit, when the patient was sent in a fast-rowing boat to Arbroath for medical aid. It was nevertheless soon afterwards found necessary to amputate the finger, and Bonnyman became a successful candidate for a light-keeper's birth.

Sunday, 11th.

Progress of the works stopped for want of granite.

Having landed this morning at 10, the work was continued during four hours, when 14 stones were laid; but its regular progress had now to be stopped for a time, owing to the want of stones from the work-yard, where some blocks of granite were waited for from the quarries. In the afternoon the Smeaton arrived with a few hearting or interior stones of the course in hand; but the wind having been for some days past in the N.E., accompanied with a considerable swell of sea, it was not found practicable to make a landing, and the praam-boat, after having been loaded, was made fast to her moorings: consequently no landing was made on the Rock with the night tide.

Monday, 12th.

Building level with the higher parts of the Rock.

The wind being still at N.E., the swell was so great that the boats landed with much difficulty on the Rock this morning at half-past 11 o'clock, but could only remain for an hour and a half, owing to the heavy sea which ran upon it. This tide was employed in completing the boring of the trenail-holes, and in securing the stones which had been laid. The cranes were also raised from the second to the third course, which being 18 inches in thickness, the artificers who worked them now stood nearly on a level with the highest parts of the Rock.

Tuesday, 13th.

Experience great difficulty in landing.

The wind being still at N.E., accompanied with a heavy breach on the Rock, no attempt would have been made to land to-day, had not the writer felt a more than ordinary desire to examine the state of the work, from the manner in which the sea broke upon the building. In accomplishing this about noon, the boats were frequently put back, but were at length successful, when it was found that the force of the sea had raised two of the stones exposed to its immediate wash, which, in the unfinished state of the course, formed an abrupt face to the waves. These two stones were lifted perpendicularly off their beds, the one to the height of 6, the other of 10 inches; but they were fortunately still held by the trenails, and supported as if on stilts. Had this not been timeously observed, the probability is, that the operation of another tide might have swept them into deep water, which would have been attended with much additional hazard, by delaying the work in its present state, at so advanced a period of the season.

Two Stones loosened but are again secured. The vessels slip their moorings.

The trenails of these stones having been drawn or bored out, the stones were laid a second time, when every precaution was taken to secure the mortar, by stuffing bagging-cloth round the joints, and loading them with bars of iron. The guy-ropes of the cranes were also tightened, and every thing put in as complete a state of security as circumstances would admit. At 1 P. M. the boats again returned to the Tender, which now rode so heavily at her moorings that it was found necessary to get her under way, when she sailed for Arbroath with the artificers. The Smeaton also slipped her moorings; but instructions were previously given to Mr Pool, to keep as close as possible to the loaded praam-boat, still riding at her moorings, that, in the event of her breaking adrift, he might be at hand to take her in tow. In the evening, however, the weather moderated considerably, and, after landing the masons at Arbroath, to remain till the return of spring-tides, the Tender returned to her station at the Rock, with the workmen employed at the Beacon-house and Railways.

Saturday, 17th.

10 Stones are laid. The praam-boats ride out the gale.

The Light-house Yacht having to-day returned from the Northern Light-houses, she transported the builders from Arbroath to the Rock, and supplied the Floating-light and Tender with provisions and necessaries. By this means, the latter vessel was enabled to remain at her moorings during the present neap-tides, by which the operations on the higher parts of the Beacon made great progress. The writer also embarked this morning in the Light-house Yacht, and having hailed the Floating-light at noon, found that she had rode out the late gales with great ease. At 3 o'clock P. M. the Yacht was made fast to a set of moorings which had been laid down for her early in the season; and at 5, thirty artificers landed, when 10 stones were laid in two hours and a quarter. Notwithstanding the heavy seas which had run upon the Rock since the completion of the Second course, every thing was found in good order. The stones of the course in hand were all in their respective places, and the joints were full of mortar. The cranes also stood quite firm, with their guys and tackling. It was no less satisfactory to find that the loaded praam rode at her moorings in perfect safety, without having apparently shipped any sea during the gale.

Sunday, 18th.

31 Stones laid in 6¼ hours.

The artificers landed this morning at 5 o'clock, and continued at work till a quarter past 8. The railways being now in a pretty complete state, and a further supply of stones having been brought to the Rock, the landing-master got 21 blocks conveyed from the eastern wharf to the building. In the same manner, with the evening tide, 10 stones were landed, and the work continued from half-past 5 to half-past 8, having had six hours' and a quarter's work to-day, during which no fewer than 31 stones were laid.

Monday, 19th.

12 Stones are laid. The western track of Railway much wanted.

The artificers landed this morning, and continued at work for three hours, when 7 stones were laid. The wind being at S.E. there was a very heavy swell of sea in the eastern creek; and not having as yet been able to lay the Railway-track to the western creek, the stones were obliged to be landed on the eastern side of the Rock, which was often attended with great disadvantage to the work. For it was only in the very finest weather that materials could be dropped or lowered upon the Rock at high-water; an operation which was further attended with great inconveniency, from the sparse manner in which it was found necessary to drop them from the praam, to prevent their being injured. The fear also of a storm overtaking the work while the stones were in this situation, was none of the least sources of uneasiness which attended this practice: for, though the sea might not carry them entirely off the Rock, they might nevertheless be so damaged, as to render them unfit for the work, and the loss of a single stone could not be replaced without returning to the work-yard, and having recourse to the mould from which it was cut.

One of the beams cannot be got out of the eastern creek.

As the landing-master's crew were in the act of towing one of the praam-boats into the eastern creek this morning, an unlucky sea struck her, and carried her upon the same ledge of the Rock, which, on the 11th of last month, had almost proved fatal to the Floating-light's boat. By the active exertions of the crew, however, the praam on the present occasion was got off without sustaining much damage, her bottom being only slightly rubbed; and the cargo, consisting of 7 blocks of stone, with cement, &c. was landed in safety. The boats returned to the Rock at 6 P. M., and left it again at 9, after having had three hours' work, and laid 5 stones, being all the materials that could be got this tide, owing to the rough state of the weather; for it was not till after three successive attempts had been made, that Mr Wilson succeeded in getting the praam into the creek this evening, the wind being at S.E., and still continuing to blow fresh with a heavy swell of sea, insomuch, that it was found impracticable to get her out again after unloading; and she, therefore, remained till the tide had flowed sufficiently to float her over the lower parts of the Rock to the westward.

Tuesday, 20th.

15 Stones are laid. The weather continues to be very boisterous.

The artificers landed this morning at 6 o'clock, and left the Rock again at a quarter past 10, having had four hours' and a quarter's work, when seven stones were laid. In the evening, the artificers landed at 6, and continued at work till 10, having had a tide of four hours, in which time eight stones were laid. Owing to the surf of sea upon the Rock to-day, it was with the utmost difficulty that the heavy blocks could either be got out of the Smeaton into the praams, or conveyed in safety to the Rock. It was only by the experience now acquired, and the activity of the landing-master's crew, that any thing was done to the building during the whole of these spring-tides. Indeed the Smeaton was forced to leave her moorings, and return to Arbroath, before the whole of her last cargo could be delivered. In this state of the weather, the workmen could not be regularly employed in building; but there was so much to do with each course, in boring trenail holes, and laying railways during the time of low-water, that the artificers were always fully employed, when it was possible to land. During the period of high-water, the mill-wrights and joiners were occupied in framing the upper part of the Beacon-house.

Wednesday, 21st.

Engineer's clerk most active in dispatching the shipping.

To-day the wind was at S.W., blowing a fresh gale, and it was not expected that the Smeaton could have possibly returned from Arbroath, with the remaining stones of the course in hand, consisting of 17 blocks, with which, from the advanced period of the season, and the boisterous state of the weather, it was proposed to terminate the building for this year. The Smeaton, however, got to Arbroath last night, at a late hour; and Mr Lachlan Kennedy, Engineer's clerk,—whose department it was to attend to the dispatch of the vessels,—with that promptitude and zeal in the service which uniformly marked all his transactions, called the artificers in the work-yard barrack at midnight, when they commenced, with torch-light, to cart the stones to the quay, and had loaded the Smeaton, by half-past 2 A. M., so that she saved tide out of the harbour, and at half-past 6 got to her moorings at the Rock.

The unfortunate loss of James Scott, one of the seamen.

Mr Thomas Macurich, mate of the Smeaton, and James Scott, one of the crew, a young man about 18 years of age, immediately went into their boat to make fast a hawser to the ring in the top of the floating-buoy of the moorings, and were forthwith to proceed to land their cargo, so much wanted at the Rock. The tides at this period were very strong, and the mooring-chain, when sweeping the ground, had caught hold of a rock or piece of wreck, by which the chain was so shortened that when the tide flowed, the buoy got almost under water, and little more than the ring appeared at the surface. When Macurich and Scott were in the act of making the hawser fast to the ring, the chain got suddenly disentangled at the bottom, and this large buoy, measuring about 7 feet in height, and 3 feet in diameter at the middle, tapering to both ends, being what seamen term a Nun-buoy, vaulted or sprung up with such force, that it upset the boat, which instantly filled with water. Mr Macurich, with much exertion, succeeded in getting hold of the boat's gunwale, still above the surface of the water, and by this means was saved; but the young man Scott was unfortunately drowned. He had, in all probability, been struck about the head by the ring of the buoy, for although surrounded with the oars and the thwarts of the boat which floated near him; yet he seemed entirely to want the power of availing himself of such assistance, and appeared to be quite insensible, while Pool, the master of the Smeaton, called loudly to him: and, before assistance could be got from the Tender, he was carried away by the strength of the current, and disappeared! A signal of distress was immediately hoisted, when one of the boats of the landing-master's crew instantly attended to Macurich's safety, and picked him up in a very exhausted state, but he happily soon recovered.

His mother gets a small annuity.

The young man Scott was a great favourite in the service, having had something uncommonly mild and complaisant in his manner; and his loss was therefore universally regretted. The circumstances of his case were also peculiarly distressing to his mother, as her husband, who was a seaman, had, for three years past, been confined to a French prison, and the deceased was the chief support of the family. In order, in some measure, to make up the loss to the poor woman for the monthly aliment regularly allowed her by her late son, it was suggested, that a younger boy, a brother of the deceased, might be taken into the service. This appeared to be rather a delicate proposition, but it was left to the landing-master to arrange according to circumstances: such was the resignation, and at the same time the spirit of the poor woman, that she readily accepted the proposal, and in a few days the younger Scott was actually afloat in the place of his brother. On representing this distressing case to the Board, the Commissioners were pleased to grant an annuity of L. 5 to Scott's mother.

17 stones are laid. The Building operations completed for the season.

The Smeaton not having been made fast to the buoy, had, with the ebb-tide, drifted to leeward, a considerable way eastward of the Rock, and could not, till the return of the flood-tide, be worked up to her moorings, so that the present tide was lost, notwithstanding all exertions which had been made both ashore and afloat with this cargo. The artificers landed at 6 A. M., but as no materials could be got upon the Rock this morning, they were employed in boring trenail holes, and in various other operations, and after four hours' work they returned on board the Tender. When the Smeaton got up to her moorings, the landing-master's crew immediately began to unload her. There being too much wind for towing the praams in the usual way, they were warped to the Rock, in the most laborious manner, by their windlasses, with successive grapplings and hawsers laid out for this purpose. At 6 P. M., the artificers landed, and continued at work till half-past 10, when the remaining seventeen stones were laid, which completed the Third entire course, or Fourth of the Light-house, with which the building operations were closed for this season.

Summary of the Building operations at the Rock.

The building, being now on a level with the highest part of the margin of the foundation-pit, or about 5 feet 6 inches above the lower bed of the foundation-stone, is computed to contain about 388 tons of stone; consisting of 400 blocks, connected with 738 oaken trenails, and 1215 pairs of oaken wedges. The number of hours of low-water work upon the Rock this season, amounted to about 265, of which number only 80 were employed in building. It was further highly satisfactory to find, that the apparatus, both in the work-yard at Arbroath, and also the craft and building apparatus at the Rock, were found to answer every purpose much beyond expectation. The operations of this season, therefore, afforded the most flattering prospects of the practicability of completing the solid part, or first 30 feet of the building, in the course of another year.

Sunday, 25th.

Shipping obliged to run for Arbroath.

Owing to very heavy gales of wind from a north-eastern direction, the Sir Joseph Banks Tender, the Sloop Smeaton, and Light-house Yacht, were, on the 22d, obliged to slip their moorings, and proceed with all hands for Arbroath. The Tender and the Smeaton again returned to their stations at the Bell Rock on the 25th; the former to attend the mill-wrights, joiners, and smiths, while they completed certain operations connected with the Railways, and Beacon-house, that everything might be left in as secure a state as possible for the winter months; the crew of the Smeaton being at the same time occupied in lifting the several sets of moorings, building-cranes, and other apparatus connected with the works, which she carried to Arbroath.

Appearance of things at the Rock after the late gale.

Writer sails for the Northern Light-houses.

The writer having also sailed on the 25th in the Light-house Yacht, on his annual inspection of the Northern Light-houses, wished, in passing the Bell Rock, to have landed, but this he found impossible, owing to the heavy sea which still ran upon it. The vessel, however, sailed as near the Rock as possible, that he might, in some measure, learn the state of matters after the late gales of the 22d and 23d. He could discern that the Beacon was in good order, but found that the strong Triangular-sheers of cast-iron, represented in Plate XI., at the Eastern wharf, were thrown down and broken to pieces; and that the North-west buoy had drifted from its moorings. The circumstance of the breaking of these sheers greatly surprised the writer, as they consisted of bars of iron, whose cross section was about 10 inches; having each four longitudinal ribs, of about an inch and a half in depth, and thus forming a common circumference of 16 inches.

1808, October.

Monday 31st.

Visits the Rock on his return.

After sailing by the Orkney Islands, and visiting all the Light-houses on the coast of Scotland, the writer landed at Greenock on the 19th of October, and soon afterwards returned to the works at Arbroath. At half-past 11 A. M. on the 31st, he landed on the Bell Rock, and remained till half-past 3 P. M., examining every thing minutely, when he had the satisfaction of finding the stones and joints of the building quite entire. The Railways and Beacon were also in good order; while the moorings, and all the moveable apparatus, had been conveyed to Arbroath.

December.

Arrangements for the Writer.

During the months of November and December, the affairs of the work-yard went forward in the usual busy manner. A small squad of artificers went off to the Bell Rock at each period of spring-tides, when the weather permitted, with tools and implements to repair and refit any temporary damage which the Beacon or Railways might sustain, and likewise to examine the state of the several courses of masonry. In the work-yard the masons were employed in hewing or cutting stones for the next year's operations; the joiners, in preparing the upper framing of the accommodation part of the Beacon-house. The Tender was occupied in carrying off the workmen who landed at the Rock; in relieving the crew of the Floating-light in their turns ashore, and supplying that ship with provisions and necessaries; while the sloop Smeaton made several trips to the granite quarries of Aberdeen and Peterhead, and the Light-house Yacht was laid up in ordinary at Leith.

In this state of arrangement, the business of the Bell Rock was left during the winter months; and the writer is now to continue the narrative, by giving the account of the operations of the year 1809.

CHAPTER V.

PROGRESS OF THE WORKS IN THE YEAR 1809.

1809, January.

In the month of January 1809, the winds prevailed much from the east and north-east, which never fail to produce a heavy sea on the eastern shores of Great Britain, and particularly at the Bell Rock, from its exposed position to these points. This state of the weather, therefore, rendered it extremely difficult to communicate with the Floating-light, for the purpose of relieving the seamen in their turns ashore, and supplying the ship with provisions and necessaries.

Railways injured, and Bracing chain-bolts unlocked.

It was also found impracticable to land upon the Rock itself sooner in this month than the 20th, when, after several attempts, Mr Francis Watt and Captain Wilson, two of the engineer's assistants, landed with four seamen, and four artificers with their tools, at 12 noon, and remained till a quarter past 1 P. M. By this time several of the supports of the iron-railways on the Rock had got loose, and two of the castings forming the waggon-track and footpath had broken adrift. One of these was found at a considerable distance from its place, but the other had entirely disappeared, and must have been washed off the Rock, although it weighed upwards of 100 lb. In these gales, no fewer than ten of the bracing-chains of the Beacon were shaken entirely loose, seven of which had unscrewed the tightening-bolts, and the remaining three lifted the pieces of rock into which the chain-bats had been fixed. The tightening-bolts were again screwed up, and pieces of small wire twisted round the points of the screws, to prevent the nuts from unlocking. The three bolts, with their chains, which had lifted the parts of the rock, were disengaged from the Beacon altogether, to prevent injury to the wooden beams, by their motion with the force of the sea; and things were otherwise left in as serviceable a state as the circumstances of a limited stay upon the Rock at this season of the year would admit. It was, upon the whole, highly satisfactory to learn, that the Beacon, this important auxiliary to the operations, had received no material injury, after such a continued tract of stormy weather; the great iron stanchions sunk into the Rock, which kept the main beams in their places, and all the joints and fixtures of the higher parts of the framed work, being quite entire, and without the smallest appearance of having shifted.

Proofs of strong currents in the Sea.

On this trip to the Rock, the Light-house Yacht picked up a floating-buoy belonging to the navigation of the river Weser. It was marked "Bremen 1808, W. R.

No. 2.," and measured six feet in length, and three feet in diameter over the head, being of the form known to mariners as a Cann buoy. It appeared to have drifted, in the course of this winter, from the shores of Germany, which, in a direct line, is a distance of at least 340 miles. This circumstance, as the buoy presented, while afloat, but a small surface for the wind to act upon, being heavily bound with iron, and having about two fathoms of mooring chain appended to it, affords an extraordinary proof of the effects of the tides and currents in the ocean. We may likewise here notice, among other instances corroborative of this curious anomaly of the tides, the drifting, within the same period, of part of the apparatus belonging to the works of the Bell Rock; particularly the two buoys, formerly mentioned, that parted from their moorings, and came ashore, the one, along with a raft of timber, at Fifeness, and the other at the Island of May, after having been upwards of two months at sea. But, perhaps, the most remarkable occurrence of this kind, was that of the Praam-boat, also formerly mentioned, which broke loose from the Floating-light, and was found at the Redhead about 13 miles distant, having been at sea for the space of three months and eight days.

Three large drift-stones found upon the Rock.

The artificers again landed at the Rock on the morning of the 31st at 7 o'clock, being rather before day-break, and left it again at 10, after having been on it about three hours. Several of the bracing-chains were found loosened, notwithstanding the precautions hitherto used for preventing the bolts from unlocking. But the writer had resolved, when the weather would admit, to remove these chains altogether, and introduce strong bars of malleable iron, about eight feet above the Rock, as represented in Plate VIII., to connect the several beams in a horizontal direction. At this landing, three large masses of rock were found close to the Beacon, which had been drifted upon the Rock by the force of the sea. They were of various dimensions, the largest containing no less than about 20 cubic feet, equal perhaps to a ton and a quarter in weight. After a careful examination, in every direction, of the low-water surface of the rock, it was ascertained that these stones had formed no part of it, though of the same description of rock; and it was therefore concluded, they must have been thrown up from deep water. The refitting of the chains of the Beacon and the cast-iron Railways, so occupied the time of the artificers, that they could not get the stones so broken as to be removed, and thereby prevent their being perhaps thrown, by the force of the sea, against the Beacon and Railways, like so many battering rams.

February.

During the month of February, the weather continued to be extremely boisterous, and it was not without considerable difficulty that the Floating-light could be visited at the stated periods; while two unsuccessful attempts were made, on the 1st and 20th, to land at the Bell Rock.

Progress of the Works at Arbroath, and exertions made at the Quarries.

In the work-yard, the preparation of the several courses of the building was going progressively forward. The Ninth course was now finished, and part of the Tenth laid upon the platform. At Mylnefield Quarry, the operations were at a stand; for in winter, as formerly mentioned, no work is done here, owing to the liability of the stones to split in frosty weather, especially when newly taken from the quarry, the laminæ of the strata being then charged with moisture. But, as granite imbibes water very slowly, and is not liable to those changes, every exertion continued to be made at the quarries of Aberdeenshire, that, if possible, the outside casing of granite might be carried to the height of 30 feet, or to the top of the solid part of the building, instead of 16 feet, or to high-water mark, as had been latterly intended. The stone-agent at Aberdeen, accordingly, had a person traversing the numerous quarries in that neighbourhood, while one of the foremen from the work-yard at Arbroath, was similarly employed, during the winter months, at Peterhead; and whenever a stone was found answerable to the Light-house moulds, it was immediately purchased, and laid aside for the use of the Bell Rock.

1809, February.

Employment of Shipping.

The sloops Smeaton and Alexander made several trips to the North, and also to Mylnefield, near Dundee, for stones which had been quarried in the course of the summer months, and were in no danger from the frost; but owing to the difficult nature of the navigation of the Tay in winter, these voyages were frequently attended with considerable danger. On the last trip which the Smeaton made to this quarry, she had a very narrow escape, and lost both her boat and an anchor; but the hazardous state of the vessel and all on board, will be better understood by the following very distinct and explicit letter or journal from Mr Thomas Calder, commander of the Light-house Yacht, who, on this occasion, was acting master on board of the Smeaton.

Captain Calder's account of a trip to the Tay.

"Arbroath, 25th February 1809.

"Mr Stevenson.

"Sir,—At 3 o'clock P. M., on the 21st inst., I got under way from the South Ferry Roads for Mylnefield quarry, wind at West. At 7 were about a mile from the quarry pierhead. Light airs of wind. Got beset amongst ice, and brought up with the small bower-anchor. At midnight, all hands employed hanging fenders over the bows and sides, to save the vessel from getting cut with the ice.

"At day-light, on the 22d., being high-water, got under way; ice all round, and had frequently to let go an anchor, to allow it to drift past us. Could not get up to the quarry, and at 10 put into Dundee. During the remainder of this day had light breezes, with hard frost.

"On the 23d, at 7 A. M. got again under way, with a westerly wind, but still could not make up to the quarry. At 10, had drifted down as far as the Lights of Tay, having little wind, but a heavy sea from E.SE. At 11, the boat filled, and was turned bottom up; nothing could be done for her safety; cut her adrift. At noon, had a very heavy sea on our broadside, breaking over all, with little or no wind. Got into three fathoms water, the sea sweeping every thing off the deck that was moveable. All hands in the rigging for safety, except the man at the helm. Endeavour if possible to get back, but all in vain. Let go our anchor in two fathoms water, the sea breaking over all. At 9 o'clock P. M., being then high-water, let go the best bower-anchor. At midnight calm weather, with heavy breaking seas.

"At 9 A. M. of the 24th, got under way again, and took our fate, being in much peril to ride longer. Could not purchase our anchor, and were therefore obliged to cut the cable. Had light airs of wind, but still a heavy sea. Went over the bank in going out of the Tay, and, at 9 in the evening, had the good fortune to get into Arbroath. In the course of this trip we saw one sloop sink with all hands in the rigging, while close by us, but we could render them no assistance, and we were still drifting towards the shore. Another sloop, named the Lady Kinnaird, I believe bound for Leith, God only knows what her fate was; being thick with snow I lost sight of her frequently. It was often impossible for a man to stand on deck; and we took to the rigging for safety. The Smeaton and these two vessels being a long way a-head of six of the Dundee London smacks, were certainly the means of saving them. The ship's company is now employed in rigging the Light-house Yacht, and fitting her for sea. I am, Sir, your humble servant,

Thos. Calder."

1809, March.

Large Stones removed. Joisting of platform lifted by the sea.

The month of March set in with some pretty good weather, and eight artificers landed upon the Rock on the 5th, at half-past 11 A. M., and remained till half-past 1, when they got the three large stones, formerly mentioned as lying near the Beacon, broken, and reduced to such a size as to admit of their removal. Several of the fixtures of the Railways had got loose, and were again secured; and two lengths of the waggon-tracks were broken to pieces by the movement of the above mentioned stones, which, in their progress across the rock, had made indelible ruts upon it. The bracing-chains of the Beacon still required to be screwed up; but the essential parts of this fabric were in the most entire and perfect state; although all the joisting of the lower platform, excepting three pieces, had been carried away. The deals of this floor had been lifted at the end of the working season, being only about 30 feet above the Rock, but the joisting presented so little resistance to the waves, that it had been allowed to remain, being only fixed in a slender manner, that both the floor and the joisting might lift with the force of the sea, without endangering the safety of the Beacon.

A vessel in danger of being wrecked on the Bell Rock.

On this occasion, the people of the Floating-light informed the landing party, that they had just been spoken to by the crew of a large brig from Gottenburgh, bound for Liverpool. This vessel having got out of her reckoning, had been lying-to in the entrance of the Firth for three days, not knowing the land. But having been directed as to their situation, the strangers now shaped their course for the Orkneys. Had it not been for these instructions, this vessel, in all probability, might have been wrecked on the Bell Rock; and, therefore, looking prospectively to the completion of this work, we may see its extensive and important advantages to shipping.

Fourteenth course laid on the platform, and further progress of the Work.

During the remainder of this month, no opportunity occurred for landing on the Rock, but the other departments of the service went forward with all possible dispatch. The Thirteenth course was nearly completed, and a part of the Fourteenth had been laid on the platform. The last of the moulds for the granite stones, to the height of 30 feet, had now been sent to the quarries of Aberdeen and Peterhead, where the Smeaton, and the hired sloop Alexander, were each loading a cargo. Mr Peter Logan had now left the quarries at Peterhead, where he had been for some months; and Alexander Davidson, one of the principal granite masons, appointed to attend the quarries at Aberdeen, was also soon to be removed from that station, to perform the same duty at the sandstone quarry of Mylnefield. Measures had likewise been taken for providing the necessary castings for the extension of the Railways to the western landing place at the Rock, which altogether were to include a range of about 800 feet.

Cast-iron Mushroom Anchors. Difficulty in procuring Trenails.

The uncertainty attending the fixing of the malleable iron shank into the large cast-iron head of the mushroom anchor, represented in Plate X. Fig. 4., from its liability to shake loose, had induced the writer to make trial of a mushroom anchor, made wholly of cast-iron, which was finished in a very complete manner by the Shotts Iron Company. At the same works, castings were also made for a set of new sheers for those broken in the month of September at the eastern landing creek, which answered all the purposes of a crane, as represented in Plate XI. The two new praam-boats building at Arbroath, had advanced considerably in the course of this month, and were now ready for the laying of the decks. Of all the materials connected with those which may be termed of a trifling nature, none was more difficult to be procured than the oaken trenails, for fixing the stones of the lower or solid part of the building while the work was in progress. After much correspondence with London and other ports, a considerable quantity was procured from trenail merchants of Wapping. But such was the demand for oak timber at this period, owing to the great supply wanted for the Navy, that it was not only at a considerable expence, from about L. 3 to L. 5 per hundred, but with great difficulty, that trenails of the dimensions wanted could be collected. It was found by a calculation, at this time, that 2544 trenails, from 20 to 26 inches in length, and 1¼ inches in diameter, and 3720 pairs of wedges, from 15 to 19 inches in length, 3 inches in breadth, and 1 inch in thickness at the top, would still be wanted. Fortunately, however, a great quantity of oak timber, suitable for trenails, was brought about this time from the Highland districts to Perth, for making the spokes of carriage-wheels. A supply of these was accordingly got, at a much cheaper rate than the ordinary trenails of the carpenter, and which were also considered better for the purposes of the work.

Purchase of the Sloop Patriot.

In order that the building operations at the Rock might suffer as little delay as possible, from the difficulty attending the regular transportation of the stones from Arbroath, and also to provide against the numerous accidents to which the vessels in this service were incident, it was judged proper to have another vessel besides the Smeaton for this department of the service. The writer consequently corresponded with various ports, with a view to procure a vessel of about 40 tons burden, or nearly the size of the Smeaton. Two vessels of this description were offered for sale, at the same price of L. 470; but one of them, the sloop Patriot of Kirkaldy, was stated to be a new vessel, which had hardly been at sea, while the other was several years old; the Kirkaldy vessel was therefore preferred.

1809, April.

On the 5th and 6th April, the boats of the Floating-light landed the artificers on the Bell Rock at 11 o'clock A. M., and they remained till 1, having had two hours' work each tide in refitting the railways, and setting up the bracing-chains of the Beacon, which were still found in a loose state. Notwithstanding all the precautions used, one of them had unscrewed its nut to the extent of 3 inches, by the friction arising from the agitation of the sea, but every thing else was found to be in good order.

Floating-light encounters some heavy seas.

From the 6th to the 20th, the weather was particularly boisterous, the winds being chiefly from the eastward, with occasional showers of snow. On the 16th it was found necessary to veer out the cable of the Floating-light from the 30th to the 90th fathom service; and, on the 17th, at 2 o'clock A. M., she had shipped so heavy a sea, that it filled both of the boats amid-ships, and ran down the companion and hatches in such quantities as to give great alarm to all on board, who, for a time, concluded that the vessel was sinking.

Twelfth course completed by the Stone-cutters.

About the beginning of this month, the stone-cutters in the workyard had just completed the hewing of the sandstone or hearting of the Fourteenth course of the building: but those employed at the granite blocks of the course were at a stand, both with that and the Thirteenth course, for want of materials: a supply, however, having timeously arrived from Aberdeen and Peterhead, these courses were proceeded with, though, as yet, none higher than the Twelfth was in a finished state. As the sandstone masons were considerably ahead of those who wrought the granite, the former were chiefly employed in laying the courses on the platform, and boring the trenail holes. The necessary implements were also prepared, and in readiness for shipping for the Rock, with 62 barrels of lime, 78 barrels of pozzolano, and 60 barrels of sand.

Employment of Shipping.

The Light-house Yacht was now fitted out for her voyage with stores for the Northern Light-houses, and the other general business connected with her department. The Sir Joseph Banks Tender was ready for sea by the 17th of April; and the Smeaton and Alexander were still making trips to the quarries, and occasionally supplying the Floating-light with provisions.

Sloop Patriot condemned.

Opinion of Mr Solicitor-General Boyle.

The sloop Patriot, of 45 register tons, formerly mentioned as having been purchased for the work, had her hatches enlarged, for the conveniency of loading and delivering stones; and was otherwise fitted up for the service at the Rock. On the 20th, she took on board five cast-iron mushroom anchors, with chains and floating-buoys, together with a quantity of cast-iron work for extending the Railways. With this cargo she sailed from Leith on the 21st of April, reached the Bell Rock on the morning of the 22d, and was discharged with the assistance of the boats of the Tender and Floating-light. In the course of this trip, the Patriot was observed to make a considerable quantity of water; and instead, therefore, of proceeding for the quarries for a cargo of stone, it was found necessary to send her to Arbroath for examination, when James Macdonald, the master, reported that he could not proceed to sea until the vessel underwent repair. A warrant was accordingly obtained from the Judge-Admiral for a survey of carpenters, who declared her "not sea-worthy." On farther opening the bottom planks, it appeared, that, upon the starboard-bow, both planks and trenails were in a state of decay, and the expence of the necessary repairs was estimated at L. 80. Upon this report of the carpenters being produced, a correspondence was entered into with the late owner of the vessel, who resisted the charge; and the matter being submitted by the Light-house Board to Mr Solicitor-General Boyle, then ex officio one of the Commissioners, (now Lord Justice-Clerk,) he was of opinion, from the circumstance of the Patriot's having been sold as an almost new vessel, that the late owner was liable for the estimated repairs. Upon this opinion being made known, the sum of L. 80 was immediately paid, and the vessel was put under repair.

Two Praams launched.

Two of the praam-boats built at Arbroath had been launched, by the names of "Fernie," and "Dickie," after the respective builders, and were fitted out with complete sets of warps and grapplings for landing the stones at the Bell Rock. Every thing being in readiness for commencing the operations, it was fully expected that the solid part would be completed in the course of the ensuing season, and the Light-house thus carried to the height of 30 feet.

Thursday, 20th.

Tender sails. Floating light put under charge of Mr Reid.

The Sir Joseph Banks Tender, having been fitted out for sea, sailed on the 20th of April, with the Hedderwick praam-boat in tow, to attend the works at the Bell Rock. She had also on board 15 artificers, consisting of mill-wrights, joiners, smiths and masons, to be employed in extending the Railways, and fitting up the Beacon-house as a place of residence for the workmen. Having left the harbour of Arbroath at 5 A. M., the Floating-light was hailed at 8, when her boat came alongside with Captain Wilson, the landing-master, who was now to leave his charge on board of the Floating-light for a time, and attend as landing-master at the Bell Rock, while Mr John Reid, mariner, and principal light-keeper, took charge as master of the Floating-light, acting in these capacities with much credit to himself and advantage to the service.

Two sets of Moorings laid down.

The first attention of the landing-master was to lay down a mushroom-anchor, weighing 18 cwt. 1 qr. with 32 fathoms of ⅞th inch chain, in 13 fathoms water, as the future moorings of the Tender; the Beacon on the Bell Rock bearing E. by S. distant ¼ mile. A set of moorings were also laid down about 300 fathoms to the eastward of this for the praam-boat, with a mushroom-anchor, weighing 15 cwt. 24 lb., with 25 fathoms of chain, in 11 fathoms water. The artificers, having left the Tender in two boats, landed on the Rock at 9 A.M. and returned on board again at half-past 12 noon. But, in the afternoon, the weather becoming more coarse, with the wind from the NE., accompanied with showers of snow, a landing was not attempted in the evening.

Friday, 21st.

Tender slips her moorings.

The wind to-day being still from the NE., a heavy sea set upon the Rock. The artificers, notwithstanding, left the Tender in two boats, at 10 A. M., but, after various attempts to land at the western creek, it was found impracticable, and the boats returned to the vessel at half past 11; when the Tender was found to ride so heavily at her moorings, that it was judged advisable to slip her hawser; when she set sail, and at 5 P. M. anchored in the bay of Arbroath; but, in the course of the night, she again returned to her moorings off the Bell Rock.

Saturday, 22d.

Other three sets of Moorings laid down.

The wind having come round to the south to-day, the weather had moderated; and at 10 A. M. the artificers landed, their number having been augmented by nine additional men from Leith, so that they now counted twenty-five. The latter part of this day was employed in laying down three sets of moorings with mushroom-anchors, weighing from 15 to 23 cwt., for the use of the Stone-Lighters, and other craft employed at the work. The positions of these, as nearly as may be, will be seen in Plate V.

Sunday, 23d.

Artificers cannot land.

At 6 A. M. the artificers left the vessel, with an intention to land on the Beacon at high-water, but there being too much sea, they returned without effecting their purpose. At one P. M., being low-water, fifteen of them made a landing, and remained till 4 o'clock, making preparations for commencing the operations at the Railways and Beacon-house. This afternoon the Smeaton supplied the Floating-light and Tender with necessaries, and returned to Arbroath, carrying with her twelve of the artificers for the work-yard.

Monday, 24th.

At 7 A. M. the artificers left the Tender, and landed on the Beacon, where they remained all the day. The masons, who could only be employed on the Rock during low-water, in boring holes for the bats, and in dressing the Rock for the supports of the Railways, landed at 1 P. M., and left off work at 3, having been two hours at work, when the tide overflowed the Rock; but the joiners and smiths continued on the Beacon till 7 P. M.

Tuesday, 25th.

During these twenty-four hours the wind was from the westward, with moderate breezes and showers of rain. At half-past 6 A. M., the smiths and joiners landed on the Beacon, and continued the whole day. At half-past 3 P. M., the low-water artificers landed, and the whole returned again on board of the Tender at half-past 8.

Wednesday, 26th.

Sailors account for the unsettled state of the weather.

The weather continued to be very unsettled, and there being still great quantities of snow lying on the hills of Angus, it was an observation made by the sailors, "That the wind never continued twenty-four hours in one direction, while there was any whiteness on the Braes of Angus." To-day, it was at E.NE., with strong breezes and hazy weather. At half-past 8 the joiners and smiths left the vessel for the Rock, but could not make a landing, and returned again at half-past 9, when she immediately slipped her moorings and sailed for Arbroath, to wait the return of the spring-tides.

Progress of the work.

At Arbroath, the several departments of the work went forward with alacrity, and the courses of the building, as high as the 19th, were now ready for shipment. The Patriot having undergone a complete repair, was equipped for sea. The Smeaton was employed chiefly in attending the quarries at Mylnefield, and the Alexander those of Aberdeenshire. The Tender took on board provisions, water, and other necessaries for the supply of the Floating-light and artificers, and also some of the dressed timber for fitting up the cabins of the higher parts of the Beacon-house.

Sunday, 30th.

Tender sails for the Rock.

The Tender accordingly left the harbour of Arbroath this morning, under the command of Mr David Taylor, and sailed for the Bell Rock with Mr Francis Watt and eighteen artificers. At 6 A. M. they spoke the Floating-light, and got Mr James Wilson, the landing-master, on board. The wind being from the westward with moderate breezes, the artificers were landed at 7 A. M., and remained on the Rock till 11 P. M. While the water was low they were employed at refitting and extending the Railways; and when the Rock was overflowed, they ascended to the Beacon, and continued their operations. The wind came to blow so fresh from the N.W., or in the direction of the Tender's moorings from the Rock, that it was not judged safe to make her fast; and as soon as the artificers got on board, she beat to windward and got into St Andrew's bay for the night.

1809, May.

Monday, 1st.

In the morning the Tender stood again towards the Bell Rock. In the course of the day the wind shifted from W.NW. to N.E. The writer reached the Rock this morning, in the Smeaton, at half-past 7, when he landed with nineteen artificers, and remained till noon, and then went on board of the Tender, now at her moorings.

Writer visits the Rock.

The several tides' work which had been got upon the Rock this season, had enabled the artificers to refit the damage which the railways had sustained during the winter months, and to make further progress with the great circular track round the building, which measured fifty-five feet in diameter; but, as yet, the western reach had made but little advancement. The fitting up of the temporary residence on the higher part of the Beacon, began to make some more habitable-like appearance; the joistings for the respective floors were laid, and a few of the upright spars of the framing had also been set up. This work continued to create much interest with every one connected with the operations, as its completion was to relieve those affected with the sea-sickness, and the whole troop from the continual plague of boating to and from the Rock by day and night. Having examined the works here, the writer left the Rock at 11 P. M. with the artificers, who went on board of the Tender, while he embarked in the Smeaton and sailed for Arbroath.

Tuesday, 2d.

It blew so fresh, from West to N.W., that no landing could be made to-day, and the Tender was obliged to slip her moorings, and beat up into St Andrew's bay, to pass the night in smooth water.

Wednesday, 3d.

Some timber is landed.

The wind was still blowing fresh from the same quarter, and, of course, directly upon the Rock from the moorings of the Tender; it was therefore judged proper, in the present unsettled state of the weather, that she should keep under sail, instead of making fast. At 9 A. M. the artificers landed, and returned on board at 1 P. M. In the evening they again landed and remained till 9. Notwithstanding the state of the weather, several boat-loads of timber and iron were landed for the use of the Railways and Beacon.

Thursday, 4th.

From the state of the winds at W.NW., instead of making fast to her moorings, the Tender kept plying about the Rock all day, and passed the night reaching about in St Andrew's Bay, and returned to the Rock at the proper time of tide in the morning. At 7 A. M., eighteen artificers landed, and remained at work till 6 P. M., when they again returned on board.

Friday, 5th.

This morning, Captain Taylor embraced the opportunity of the wind having veered to the north, to make the Tender fast to her moorings, but there was too much wind and sea for landing on the Rock. The vessel was, therefore, made as snug as possible, with her top-masts struck, her yards lowered, and boltsprit run in, to enable her to ride more easily.

Saturday, 6th.

Tender in danger of drifting upon the Rock.

The wind was at North to-day, and the weather being more moderate, Mr Watt, with eight of the artificers, landed at 6 A. M., on the Beacon, and at 10, being then low-water, the remaining twelve followed. At half-past 3 P. M., the whole returned on board, as the wind blew very hard. The boltsprit was launched out, and the ship was got ready for sea, in case of the wind shifting to the N.W., which might endanger the vessel's drifting upon the Rock.

Sunday, 7th.

The wind remained in the same direction, but the weather was much more moderate, and at 7 A. M., eight artificers left the vessel for the Beacon, where they were employed at the upper works. At 10 the remaining twelve artificers landed and continued at work till 4 P. M., when the whole returned on board of the vessel. At 5, the joiners and smiths again went to the Beacon, and remained till half-past 8.

Monday, 8th.

At 6 A. M., the artificers employed at the Beacon landed, and at noon the low-water workmen followed, and returned on board again at 5 P. M. At 9, the joiners and smiths also returned to the vessel for the night. The weather was so fine to-day, that the crew of the Tender were enabled to paint her upper works; for, although this had been intended all the season, yet the present was the first favourable opportunity.

Tuesday, 9th.

Artificers return to Arbroath.

The weather still continued moderate, but as the tides became neap, little could now be done to the Railways. The operations were, therefore, confined, at this time, chiefly to the upper works of the Beacon. At 6 A. M., eight artificers went to the Beacon, and at half-past 10, the other twelve landed on the Rock, and remained till half-past 1. At 6 P. M., the whole came on board, when the vessel made sail for Arbroath, to wait the return of spring-tides.

Saturday, 13th.

Tender sails for the Rock.

The Sir Joseph Banks having been supplied with necessaries for the ensuing spring-tides, left Arbroath at 2 A. M., having in tow the Hedderwick praam-boat; and at 2 P. M., both the ship and praam were made fast to their respective moorings, when six joiners and two smiths were landed on the Beacon. At 5, the remaining eighteen artificers landed on the Rock, and continued till 9, when the whole returned on board of the Tender, after a good evening's work at the Railways and cabins of the Beacon.

Sunday, 14th.

Joiners get high premiums. One of them is hurt.

At half-past 6 A. M., twenty-seven artificers landed on the rock, and returned again at half-past 9. At half-past 10, the joiners and smiths again went to the Beacon, and at 6 P. M. the remaining eighteen artificers landed, and the whole returned to the ship at half-past 9; the masons having been six hours and a half on the rock to-day, while the joiners and smiths were about fourteen hours at work on the rock and Beacon together, so that their premiums for extra hours' work, independently of their stated pay and allowances, were considerable, averaging about L. 3 per month for the workmen, and double that sum for the foremen. Unfortunately, one of the joiners was pretty severely hurt, by the fall of a mason's pick upon one of his feet, from the smith's gallery on the Beacon, which disabled him for some time from working in the water.

Monday, 15th.

The work makes rapid progress.

The weather continuing moderate, and the tides being good, the work went on without interruption during these tides. This morning at half-past 6 o'clock, twenty-seven artificers landed on the rock, and continued till a quarter past 10. At noon, the joiners and smiths returned to the Beacon, and commenced their operations, as usual, at the higher parts of it; and at half-past 6, or at low-water, the remaining eighteen artificers landed, when the whole were employed at the railways, fixing mooring rings, and laying down small floating-buoys as guides for the landing-master, in approaching the rock from the westward with the loaded praams. In all these operations, the sailors took an active part, and the number of hands at work to-day, including them, amounted to thirty-eight. In this manner, the work was continued without any material interruption during five days. The low-water operations, including the night-tides, generally continued for six hours, and the joiners and smiths, for twelve or fourteen hours each day.

Saturday, 20th.

One of the Buoys gets water-logged. Tender leaves her station.

The wind, which had been easterly during these spring-tides, continued moderate till yesterday, when it blew what sailors term a stiff breeze, which soon set up a considerable sea upon the Rock, and the tides being now in the state of neap, no landing was attempted to-day. One of the mooring buoys having got water-logged, must soon have disappeared and sunk, had not the Tender been hauled alongside, when it was taken upon deck. An auger-hole was bored in it and the water let off, being what the sailors term "bleeding;" when the hole was closed with a plug, and the buoy was again lowered in the water, and floated as before. The spring-tides being now considered over, the Tender sailed for the bay of Arbroath, where she was made fast to a set of moorings laid down for the conveniency of the work during the summer months, and at 8 P. M. the artificers came on shore in the boats.

Sunday, 21st.

Tender again sails for the Rock.

The operations at the Rock, during the last spring-tides, had exhausted the stock of timber, of which a great quantity could not be kept either on board of the Tender, or on the Beacon, while much loss and inconveniency had frequently been experienced by attempting to keep it afloat in rafts. At 5 o'clock this morning, the boats left Arbroath with seventeen artificers, and two rafts of timber, which were taken on board of the Tender, when she immediately sailed for the Bell Rock. But there being little wind, it was 7 in the evening before she was made fast to her moorings; and, from the state of the tide, no landing was made this evening.

Monday, 22d.

Great exertions made in laying the circular track of Railway.

The weather was moderate to-day, and, at 9 A. M., Mr Watt and the artificers left the vessel for the Beacon; but the wind having been at S.E., it was with great difficulty that a landing was effected. At half-past 11, the masons and other low-water artificers landed, and proceeded with the operations of the railways; but the spring-tides being as yet very languid, little work was done, and the boats returned to the Tender in about an hour and a half. The joiners and smiths, however, continued their operations on the higher parts of the Beacon till 9 P. M. Had it not been a matter of extreme importance to get the circular track of the Railway completed, so that the waggons might be wheeled round the site of the building, and the materials brought within reach of the building-cranes in every direction, as will be understood from Plates VI. and IX., the artificers, at this period of the tides, would not have remained at the Rock, but have returned to the work-yard at Arbroath. In this stage of the work, however, the gaining of a single tide was an object of great moment to its future progress.

Tuesday, 23d.

Attempt made to erect one of the cranes.

The artificers employed at the Beacon, landed upon it at 6 o'clock A.M., being then high-water. At 12 noon, one of the building cranes was brought to the Rock in a praam, by the landing-master's crew; but, as the water did not leave the Rock sufficiently for getting hold of the ring-bats of the guy-tackles, the crane could not be set up: it was therefore laid upon the building, and made fast to Lewis-bats fixed in the upper course, and left in that state for the present. The praam-boat was towed to her moorings at 2 o'clock P. M.; but the joiners and smiths continued at work till 10 o'clock, when they came on board of the Tender.

Smeaton sails with the first stones this season.

Things being now in a state of preparation for commencing the building operations for the season, the sloop Smeaton was loaded with twenty-six blocks of stone belonging to the Fifth course. She had also on board a few casks of pozzolano, cement, lime, and sand, with trenails, wedges, and other materials connected with the building. At 5 P. M., the writer embarked with Mr Peter Logan the building-foreman, Captain Wilson the landing-master, and fifteen masons, and sailed for the Bell Rock with the first cargo of stones for this season's operations. The wind was moderate, but being easterly, it was not till 9 o'clock that the vessel reached the floating-light, when the writer, accompanied by the landing-master, went on board to examine her moorings after the gales of winter, while the Smeaton continued her course to the Bell Rock.

Wednesday, 24th.

Floating light's moorings examined.

The last night was the first that the writer had passed in his old quarters on board of the Floating-light for about twelve months, when the weather was so fine, and the sea so smooth, that even here he felt but little or no motion, excepting at the turn of the tide, when the vessel gets into what the seamen term the trough of the sea. At 5 A. M., all hands were called to man the windlass for heaving up the moorings, consisting of a cast-iron mushroom anchor, weighing 17 cwt., and forty fathoms of chain, made from bars of iron one and a half inch square, and a hempen cable of 120 fathoms, measuring 16 inches in circumference. At 6, the crew began to lay the part of this cable upon deck that had been in the hold, and afterwards to heave up that which was in the water: the whole was found in a serviceable condition, excepting where the operation of worming and rounding had been used to defend the part which was most liable to be chafed on the ground. This operation consists in warping a small rope of about two and a half inches in circumference, round between the strands or hollows in the cable, so as to give the whole a more uniform surface. This small rope, however, was found in several places, to cut yarns of the cable, and appeared to be attended with very bad consequences. The master and mate therefore concurred in opinion, that the worming should be discontinued in future, as the small rope stretched more than the cable, and chafed it. There was also a small rope wound round the cable in a circular form, which, being laid with parcelling, or strips of canvas, was a good defence to it.

Wednesday, 24th.

State of the Floating-light's Moorings.

At 8 A. M., the best bower-anchor and cable were in readiness to be let go, to hold the ship while the mushroom-anchor was lifted. The crew then began to heave up the mooring-chain, which had now been in the water upwards of two years. The first 10 fathoms of the chain were distinctly observed to have suffered by the action of the marine acid. The links had a grooved-like appearance, perhaps, from the softer parts of the iron being wasted, in the lengthway of the link, and those parts which were more hard were observed in a raised form like threads; but at the weldings or joinings of the links, where the iron was more consolidated, from having received additional beating, it had not suffered oxidation in the slightest degree. The next 10 fathoms of the chain had also a slight appearance of waste. It may be remarked, that the half of the chain next to the hempen cable, was generally suspended between the ship and the ground, in moderate weather, and was therefore more exposed to waste from the current of the tides than the half next to the anchor. On heaving up this last part, which lay chiefly on the ground, it was found to be almost as free of rust, some trifling spots excepted, as when it was first laid down: in general, the hammer marks, and even somewhat of the bluish appearance peculiar to the surface of forged iron, were perceptible. The mushroom-anchor had not sustained the slightest change, and, although the ground was rather soft, did not appear to have been imbedded in the mud; so that the ship had rode chiefly by the weight of the chain. On narrowly examining it, when laid upon deck, two of the links were observed to be insufficient, the rust having exposed the faulty parts to view. These defective links were accordingly broken out or removed, and the sound ones connected by means of shackles, kept on board for this purpose. At noon, after seven hours of hard labour, the examination of the moorings was completed, and the writer left the Floating-light, accompanied by the landing-master, to attend the work on the Rock at low-water.

State of the works at the Rock.

At 6 A. M. Mr Watt, who conducted the operations of the Railways and Beacon-house, had landed with nine artificers. At half-past 1 P. M., Mr Peter Logan had also landed with fifteen masons, and immediately proceeded to set up the crane, which still lay lashed to the building. The sheer-crane or apparatus for lifting the stones out of the praam-boats at the eastern creek had been already erected, and the Railways now formed about two-thirds of an entire circle round the building: some progress had likewise been made with the Reach towards the western landing-place. The external framing of the cabins of the Beacon was in the state described in the second year's work, and partly represented in Plate IX. The floors being also laid, the Beacon now assumed the appearance of a habitation. The Smeaton was at her moorings, with the Fernie Praam-boat astern, for which she was laying down moorings, and the Tender being also at her station, the Bell Rock had again put on its former busy aspect. At 11 A. M., the Hedderwick praam was loaded with 11 stones, which were safely landed upon the Rock: and at 2 P. M. the Fernie was loaded with 16 stones, and towed to her moorings, to wait the proper time of tide for getting to the Rock. The Smeaton being discharged, she sailed for Arbroath at 5 P. M.

Plants and Animals on the building.

The wind was from the east, with light airs, and there was hardly any ruffle or motion on the surface of the water. The masons were chiefly employed during this tide in clearing the upper course of the building from sea-weed, of which, since the month of September, it had acquired a thick coating. The weed consisted chiefly of Fucus digitatus, which, on the new wall, had attained the length of about 18 inches, with a proportional thickness of stalk and breadth of frond, during the preceding eight or nine months. The barnacle was also pretty numerous, and a good many white buckies and small mussels had attached themselves to several parts of the building. The masons left the Rock this evening at 6 o'clock, having had four hours and a half's work; but the joiners and smiths continued till 10 P. M., and had therefore been 16 hours on the Rock to-day.

Thursday, 25th.

At half-past 2 this morning, the landing-master's bell was rung on board of the Tender; and at a quarter past 3, the writer landed with fifteen masons, nine millwrights and joiners, two blacksmiths, and ten seamen, in all thirty-six, with their respective foremen. The low-water work continued two hours and a half, when those employed at the Beacon were left as usual to continue their operations. In the afternoon, at 3 o'clock, the builders were again landed, and remained on the Rock till 8, having been five hours at work, when all hands returned on board of the Tender.

Friday, 26th.

The wind had shifted to the south, with fresh breezes, which set a considerable sea upon the Rock. The boats landed the artificers at a quarter past 3 this morning, who continued on the Rock till a quarter past 6, when it was overflowed. They landed again at a quarter past 3 P. M., and remained till a quarter past 6, when all hands returned on board of the Tender for the night. The masons, for the two last days, were employed in cutting out the square joggle-holes in the upper course of last season's work, represented with deep shaded lines in Plate XIII., which were not, as usual, cut in the respective stones before they left the work-yard, that there might be the less resistance to the waves during the storms of winter. The seamen were employed this tide in landing wedges and trenails, with cement, lime, sand, and pozzolano, the necessary materials for mortar: these were stowed on the mortar gallery or the lower floor of the Beacon-house; which, in a work of this nature, was found to be of inestimable value for this purpose. The mill-wrights, joiners, and smiths continued their operations as formerly at the Railways and upper part of the Beacon.

Saturday, 27th.

Builders commence and lay 5 stones.

The landing-master's bell rung this morning at half-past 4, and at a quarter past 5, the artificers and seamen, thirty-six in number, commenced work, and continued for 2 hours and a half. The crane having been raised, and the necessary preparations made for beginning the building for the season, five stones of the Fifth course were landed and laid. In the afternoon, the artificers returned to the Rock at a quarter past 4, and remained till 9, when other five stones were laid. The seamen landed six stones with the Hedderwick praam, and sixteen stones with the Fernie, being her first cargo. The mill-wrights, joiners, and smiths, were employed at the Railways, and fitting up the cabins of the Beacon-house.

Sunday, 28th.

22 stones laid.

Landed this morning at half-past 5, and continued at work till a quarter to 9; and, in the evening tide, the work commenced at a quarter past 5, and continued till 9, when all hands left the Rock. The landing-master's crew brought two cargoes of the praam-boats to the Rock, consisting of 22 stones, which were laid or built. During the first and middle parts of these twenty-four hours, the wind was from the west, blowing fresh, but towards the evening it shifted to the N.E., with rain.

Monday, 29th.

Tender rides very hard.

The wind having blown fresh all night, and a considerable sea set up, there was no possibility of landing on the Rock to-day. In the course of the night it blew so fresh, that Captain Taylor struck the top-masts of the Tender, launched in her boltsprit, hoisted the boats on board, and had every thing in a state calculated to make her ride at her moorings as easily as possible. At 2 P. M. the vessel pitched very hard, and one of the mooring-hawsers having got foul of the cathead or timber, the ship came with such a jerk, from the run of the sea, as was sufficient to carry it away. But the Tender still kept her station, in company with the sloop Smeaton, and the praam-boats Hedderwick and Fernie.

Tuesday 30th.

Apparatus on the Rock viewed from a boat.

To-day the wind shifted from N.E. to west, but there was still too heavy a sea for landing on the Rock. The writer being on board, looked often and anxiously for the safety of the crane and the unfinished course of the building. At low-water, he accompanied the landing-master in a boat, and went round the Rock, when he had the satisfaction to find that every thing had the appearance of being in good order.

Wednesday, 31st.

13 stones laid. Landing rendered difficult from snow showers.

The landing-master's bell, often no very favourite sound, rung at 6 this morning; but on this occasion, it is believed, it was gladly received by all on board, as the welcome signal of the return of better weather. At a quarter past 7, the artificers landed, and continued at work four hours and a half. At 7 P. M. they landed again, and at 10 all hands, 36 in number, returned to the Tender. The masons laid 13 stones to-day, which the seamen had landed, together with other building materials. During these twenty-four hours the wind was from the south, blowing fresh breezes, accompanied with showers of snow. In the morning, the snow showers were so thick, that it was with difficulty the landing-master, who always steered the leading-boat, could make his way to the Rock through the drift. But at the Bell Rock, neither snow, nor rain, nor fog, nor wind, retarded the progress of the work, if unaccompanied by a heavy swell or breach of the sea.

1809, June.

Thursday, 1st.

State of the weather. Zeal of the Writer's assistants.

The weather, during the months of April and May, had been uncommonly boisterous, and so cold that the thermometer seldom exceeded 40°, while the barometer was generally about 29.50. We had not only hail and sleet, but the snow, on the last day of May, lay on the decks and rigging of the ship to the depth of about three inches; and, although now entering upon the month of June, the length of the day was the chief indication of summer. Yet such is the effect of habit, and such was the expertness of the landing-master's crew, that, even in this description of weather, seldom a tide's work was lost. Such was the ardour and zeal of the heads of the several departments at the Rock, including Mr Peter Logan, foreman builder, Mr Francis Watt, foreman mill-wright, and Captain Wilson, landing-master, that it was on no occasion necessary to address them, excepting in the way of precaution and restraint. Under these circumstances, however, the writer not unfrequently felt considerable anxiety, of which this day's experience will afford an example.

Eleven of the artificers left on the Beacon.

This morning, at a quarter past 8, the artificers were landed as usual, and, after three hours and three quarters' work, 5 stones were laid, the greater part of this tide having been taken up in completing the boring and trenailing of the stones formerly laid. At noon, the writer, with the seamen and artificers, proceeded to the Tender, leaving on the Beacon the joiners, and several of these who were troubled with sea-sickness, among whom was Mr Logan, who remained with Mr Watt, counting altogether eleven persons. During the first and middle parts of these twenty-four hours, the wind was from the east, blowing what seamen term "fresh breezes;" but, in the afternoon it shifted to E.N.E., accompanied with so heavy a swell of sea, that the Smeaton and Tender struck their topmasts, launched in their boltsprits, and "made all snug" for a gale. At 4 P. M. the Smeaton was obliged to slip her moorings, and passed the Tender, drifting before the wind, with only the foresail set. In passing, Mr Pool hailed that he must run for the Firth of Forth, to prevent the vessel from "riding under."

They encounter a severe gale.

On board of the Tender the writer's chief concern was about the eleven men left upon the Beacon. Directions were accordingly given that every thing about the vessel should be put in the best possible state, to present as little resistance to the wind as possible, that she might have the better chance of riding out the gale. Among these preparations, the best bower cable was bent, so as to have a second anchor in readiness, in case the mooring hawser should give way, that every means might be used for keeping the vessel within sight of the prisoners on the Beacon, and thereby keep them in as good spirits as possible. From the same motive the boats were kept afloat, that they might be less in fear of the vessel leaving her station. The landing-master had, however, repeatedly expressed his anxiety for the safety of the boats, and wished much to have them hoisted on board. At 7 P. M., one of the boats, as he feared, was unluckily filled with sea from a wave breaking into her, and it was with great difficulty that she could be baled out and got on board, with the loss of her oars, rudder, and loose thwarts. Such was the motion of the ship, that in taking this boat on board, her gunwale was stove in, and she otherwise received considerable damage. Night approached, but it was still found quite impossible to go near the Rock. Consulting, therefore, the safety of the second boat, she also was hoisted on board of the Tender.

The Tender is also very uncomfortable.

At this time, the cabins of the Beacon were only partially covered, and had neither been provided with bedding nor a proper fire-place, while the stock of provisions was but slender. In these uncomfortable circumstances, the people on the Beacon were left for the night, nor was the situation of those on board of the Tender much better. The rolling and pitching motion of the ship was excessive; and, excepting to those who had been accustomed to a residence in the Floating-light, it seemed quite intolerable. Nothing was heard but the hissing of the winds and the creeking of the bulk-heads or partitions of the ship: the night was therefore spent in the most unpleasant reflections upon the condition of the people on the Beacon, especially in the prospect of the Tender being driven from her moorings. But even in such a case, it afforded some consolation that the stability of the fabric was never doubted, and that the boats of the Floating-light were at no great distance, and ready to render the people on the Rock the earliest assistance which the weather would admit. The writer's cabin being in the sternmost part of the ship, which had what sailors term a good entry, or was sharp built, the sea, as before noticed, struck her counter with so much violence, that the water, with a rushing noise, continually forced its way up the rudder case, lifted the valve of the water-closet, and overran the cabin floor. In these circumstances, daylight was eagerly looked for, and hailed with delight, as well by those afloat, as by the artificers upon the Rock.

Friday, 2d.

The Artificers are relieved.

In the course of the night, the writer held repeated conversations with the officer on watch, who reported that the weather continued much in the same state, and that the barometer still indicated 29.20 inches. At 6 A. M., the landing-master considered the weather to have somewhat moderated; and from certain appearances of the sky, he was of opinion that a change for the better would soon take place. He accordingly proposed to attempt a landing at low-water, and either get the people off the Rock, or at least ascertain what state they were in. At 9 A. M., he left the vessel with a boat well manned, carrying with him a supply of cooked provisions, and a tea-kettle full of mulled port wine, for the people on the Beacon, who had not had any regular diet for about 30 hours, while they were exposed, during that period, in a great measure, both to the winds and the sprays of the sea. The boat having succeeded in landing, she returned at 11 A. M. with the artificers, who had got off with considerable difficulty; and who were heartily welcomed by all on board.

Mr Logan's account of the state of the Beacon.

Upon enquiry, it appeared that three of the stones last laid upon the building had been partially lifted from their beds by the force of the sea, and were now held only by the trenails, and that the cast-iron sheer-crane represented in Plate XI., had again been thrown down and completely broken. With regard to the Beacon, the sea, at high-water, had lifted part of the mortar gallery or lowest floor, and washed away all the lime casks and other moveable articles from it; but the principal parts of this fabric had sustained no damage. On pressing Messrs Logan and Watt, on the situation of things in the course of the night, Mr Logan emphatically said: "That the Beacon had an ill-fared twist when the sea broke upon it at high water, but that they were not very apprehensive of danger." On enquiring as to how they spent the night, it appeared that they had made shift to keep a small fire burning, and, by means of some old sails, defended themselves pretty well from the sea sprays.

James Glen's exertions.

It was particularly mentioned that, by the exertions of James Glen, one of the joiners, a number of articles were saved from being washed off the mortar gallery. Glen was also very useful in keeping up the spirits of the forlorn party. In the early part of life, he had undergone many curious adventures at sea, which he now recounted somewhat after the manner of the Tales of the Arabian Nights. When one observed that the Beacon was a most comfortless lodging, Glen would presently introduce some of his exploits and hardships, in comparison with which, the state of things at the Beacon bore an aspect of comfort and happiness. Looking to their slender stock of provisions, and their perilous and uncertain chance of speedy relief, he would launch out into an account of one of his expeditions in the North Sea, when the vessel being much disabled in a storm, was driven before the wind with the loss of almost all their provisions; and the ship being much infested with rats, the crew hunted these vermin, with great eagerness, to help their scanty allowance. By such means, Glen had the address to make his companions, in some measure, satisfied, or at least passive, with regard to their miserable prospects upon this half-tide rock in the middle of the Ocean. This incident is noticed, more particularly, to shew the effects of such a happy turn of mind, even under the most distressing and ill-fated circumstances.

State of matters after the gale.

The people from the Beacon had no sooner got safely on board of the Tender, and were provided for, than the writer went to the Rock with the landing-master, carrying along with them five artificers, and landed, though not without considerable difficulty; for, although the wind had shifted to the westward, yet there was still a very heavy swell of sea. The first object at the Rock was to relay the three stones which had been lifted about three inches off their beds. On examining the Beacon narrowly, it appeared to be all in good order, excepting the mortar gallery, which, as before noticed, had been lifted, and all the lighter articles that could not be stowed in the upper apartments, carried into the sea; and two of the four legs of the sheer-crane were broken in pieces. But the crane upon the building, fortunately still kept its erect position. After fixing the three stones and making these remarks, the boat after two hours' absence returned to the Tender.

Saturday, 3d.

Tender obliged to leave her station.

The wind was at N.W. to-day, so that the vessel rode with her stern towards the Rock; and as it came to blow excessively hard, there was some danger, in the event of any thing giving way, that she might drift upon the Rock. Accordingly, Mr Taylor, who commanded the Tender, came into the writer's cabin between 1 and 2 o'clock this morning, and, after some consultation, it was thought advisable to slip the hawser, and to stand with the ship towards the land. It then blew so fresh, that though the sails were double reefed when the vessel got under way, it was still found necessary to take in a third reef in the mainsail, and at 6 A. M. she got into the harbour of Arbroath.

Sunday, 4th.

At this time the sea was in such a state of agitation with the shifting and violence of the winds, that apprehensions were entertained about the safety of the sloop Smeaton, as she was deeply laden when she left her moorings, especially as her cargo was quite invaluable to the progress of the works of this season. At 5 o'clock this morning, however, Mr Pool made his appearance with the vessel, and got safely into the harbour of Arbroath.

Thursday 8th.

Progress of the works at Arbroath.

In the work-yard, the hewing or cutting of the several courses went on with great alacrity: the freestone masons were now at work as high as the Twentieth and Twenty-first courses, and the granite masons had completed the Sixteenth course, which was now lying on the platform, marked and ready for shipment. A great stock of lime, in a pounded state, had been prepared, and a quantity of clean sharp sand collected, which were put up in separate casks. A large supply of oaken trenails and wedges was also made up in bundles, each containing twenty-four trenails, and a like number of pairs of wedges. The hewing of the stones, and the preparation of the building materials, were placed under the charge of Mr David Logan, as clerk of works; and the writing of the books, disbursement of cash, and the dispatch of the vessels with the materials, provisions and necessaries for the Rock, formed the department of Mr Lachlan Kennedy, engineer's clerk.

Friday 9th.

4 Stones are laid.

The Tender and Smeaton having remained in port till last evening, both vessels sailed for the Rock, and reached their moorings at 5 o'clock A. M. The boats were immediately hoisted out, when the mill-wrights, joiners and smiths, ten in number, landed on the Beacon, with their foreman, and proceeded to the fitting up of the cabins. Notwithstanding the hazardous situation upon the Beacon in which these artificers had lately been placed, Mr Watt, with his principal assistant James Glen, were not to be moved with trifles, and the work, as formerly, was continued by the joiners' squad of artificers during the whole day, trusting to the eventual prospect of their being taken off by the boats at night. At low-water, or about 3 P. M., Mr Peter Logan landed, with the sixteen artificers who composed the builders' squad, and the whole left it again at 8 P. M. The three stones which had been re-laid on the 2d of this month, having had the pozzolano mortar washed out by the heavy sea, before it had time to fix, it was found necessary to lift again, and lay them a third time. In the late gales, the casks of lime and cement left on the Beacon having been washed off by the sea, an entirely new stock was required. The praams were accordingly employed in delivering the Smeaton and landing a supply of these articles, together with four blocks of stone. The operations of the building-artificers continued only three hours to-day, and no more than four additional stones were laid.

Saturday, 10th.

Patriot obliged to slip her moorings.

The Patriot having now undergone a complete repair, she was loaded with stones for the first time, and the writer took a passage in her to the Bell Rock, when he had the pleasure of finding that she wrought or sailed extremely well. She was made fast to her moorings at 6 A. M., but only one praam-load had been discharged from her to-day, when the wind came suddenly from the N.E., and it was found necessary to let slip her moorings at 6 P. M., when she made sail for the Firth of Forth.

10 Stones laid.

Artificers divided into squads.

Notwithstanding the boisterous state of the weather, the artificers were enabled to continue their visits to the Rock, and landed this morning at 5. At this time they counted twenty-six, and were, as formerly, divided into two squads; the mill-wrights, joiners, and smiths, ten in number, wrought at the fitting up the Railways while the Rock was accessible, and when it was covered with the tide, they were employed in fitting up the Beacon-house. The operations of the builders were as yet wholly confined to low-water work. Both squads were attended, and occasionally assisted, by the landing-master's crew of about twelve sailors, who were always ready for every sort of work. Including the low-water periods of morning and evening tides the whole had six hours' and a quarter's work to-day, when ten stones were laid. But those employed at the Beacon did not leave off till half-past 9 P. M., having been sixteen hours upon the Rock, when all hands returned to the Tender; and, owing to the bad state of the weather, the boats were immediately hoisted on board.

Sunday, 11th.

No landing on the Rock to-day.

The wind was still from the N.E., accompanied with so heavy a swell of sea, that it was found impossible to land this morning. At 12 noon, all hands, forty-two in number, were assembled on deck, when prayers were read as usual. At 5 P. M., the weather being somewhat more moderate, the boats left the vessel with the artificers. But on a more narrow inspection of the state of the sea upon the Rock, it was found impracticable to effect a landing, and they returned to the Tender, after having been about an hour absent. This evening, the Light-house Yacht came to the Bell Rock from her first voyage to the Northern Light-houses for the season, but there was too much sea for making her fast to any of the moorings. Captain Calder, after ascertaining that all was well, laid the Yacht to for the night, and kept the Floating-light in view.

Monday, 12th.

17 stones laid.

Ships belonging to the service.

The wind having fortunately shifted to the S.W., in the course of the night, the weather became more moderate, and at a quarter past 6 the artificers landed. Including both tides, the builders had seven hours' work to-day, and laid seventeen stones, those employed at the Beacon continuing at work throughout the day. The Smeaton having arrived from Arbroath with another cargo of stones, and the

Patriot from Largo Bay , in the Firth of Forth, where she had run for shelter, the Rock had now a very busy appearance, the following vessels belonging to the service being at their respective moorings, viz. the Light-house Yacht; the Sir Joseph Banks Tender; the Sloops Smeaton and Patriot, besides the Hedderwick and Fernie decked Praam-boats; and at the distance of about two miles and a half, the Floating-light was stationed as represented in Plate V.

Tuesday, 13th.

12 stones laid.

The artificers landed this morning at the Rock, at a quarter past 6, and had three hours' and a half's work; and in the evening, the builders again returned at 7 o'clock, and remained three hours and a quarter, when the whole left the Rock. In the course of this day twelve stones were laid, which discharged the Patriot, and she returned to Arbroath for another cargo.

Wednesday, 14th.

21 stones laid.

At 7 this morning, the whole of the artificers land, and have four hours and a quarter of low-water work, when 21 stones are laid. In the evening, they land again at half-past 6, and have three hours' and three quarter's work in completing the boring and trenailing of the stones of the course which had already been built. The landing-master's crew discharged the Smeaton's cargo to-day, consisting of twenty-six blocks, together with four casks of pozzolano, four casks of lime, four casks of sand, one cask of cement, three bundles of oaken trenails, and six bundles of wedges; and at 8 o'clock P. M. she sailed for Arbroath. The cargo of the Smeaton was partly landed upon the Rock; but, calculating upon the settled appearance of the weather, the greater part of it kept on board of the praams at their moorings.

Thursday, 15th.

18 stones laid.

At a quarter from 7 o'clock this morning the artificers landed, and having had five hours' and a quarter's work, eight stones were laid, and the remainder of the tide was occupied in boring and trenailing. In the evening, at half-past 6, they again landed and laid eighteen stones, having had five hours' and a half's work. The Patriot arrived from Arbroath with another cargo, consisting of thirty-nine blocks of stone, four casks of pozzolano, four casks of lime, four casks of sand, four bundles of wedges, and four bundles of trenails. There were thirty-six blocks of stone landed to-day on the Rock, with the above materials. The stones, when landed, were laid on the south-west side of the building till those previously built were trenailed; and the lime, &c. were carried up to the mortar-gallery on the Beacon. The three remaining stones of this cargo were left on board of one of the praams at her moorings, and the Patriot thus discharged, again sailed for Arbroath at 9 P. M. to load another cargo.

Friday, 16th.

24 stones laid.

Great exertions used in supplying materials.

This morning, at a quarter past 7, the artificers landed on the Rock, and had an excellent tide's work, which continued for five hours and a quarter, when 24 stones of the Patriot's last cargo were laid. Landing again at half-past 8 in the evening, they continued at work an hour and a quarter, when four stones were laid; and at 10 o'clock all hands left the Rock; the joiners, smiths, and such of the masons as were inclined, having been, as usual, left all day on the Beacon, had their victuals sent to them from the Tender. In the present favourable state of the weather, through the exertions of Mr Lachlan Kennedy, in dispatching the vessels, both by night and day, and also by the activity of Captains Pool of the Smeaton, and Macdonald of the Patriot, the work was largely and regularly supplied with building materials. The Smeaton having returned with a cargo from Arbroath, was made fast to her moorings at 11 this morning; but, as the wind blew strongly from the westward, it was found impracticable to land any stones to-day, without the greatest risk of injuring the materials. About mid-day, after the landing-master's crew had taken the artificers on board of the Tender, they towed the Fernie praam-boat alongside of the Smeaton, and endeavoured to load her, but it was found impracticable; and, after three stones had been laid on the praam's deck, any further attempt was given up.

Saturday, 17th.

7 stones laid.

Artificers left all night on the Beacon.

At 8 A. M., the artificers and sailors, forty-five in number, landed on the Rock, and, after four hours' work, seven stones were laid. The remainder of this tide, from the threatening appearance of the weather, was occupied in trenailing, and making all things as secure as possible. At 12 noon, the Rock and Building were again overflowed, when the masons and seamen went on board of the Tender, but Mr Watt, with his squad of ten men, remained on the Beacon throughout the day. As it blew fresh from the N.W. in the evening, it was found impracticable either to land the building-artificers, or to take the artificers off the Beacon, and they were accordingly left there all night, but in circumstances very different from those of the 1st of this month. The house being now in a more complete state, was provided with bedding, and they spent the night pretty well; though they complained of having been much disturbed at the time of high-water, by the shaking and tremulous motion of their house, and by the plashing noise of the sea upon the mortar gallery. Here James Glen's versatile powers were again at work, in cheering up those who seemed to be alarmed, and in securing every thing as far as possible. On this occasion, he had only to recall to the recollections of some of them the former night which they had spent on the Beacon, the wind and sea being then much higher, and their habitation in a far less comfortable state.

Smeaton and Patriot slip their moorings.

The Patriot came to the Rock this morning from Arbroath, loaded chiefly with timber and apparatus for the works of the Beacon. At 5 A. M., Captain Wilson, the landing-master, and his crew, made a second attempt to deliver the Smeaton of her cargo, but were only enabled to get out other five stones, with which the Fernie praam was towed to her moorings, without being able to land upon the Rock. The wind still continuing to blow fresh from the N.W., at 5 P. M., the writer caused a signal to be made from the Tender for the Smeaton and Patriot to let slip their moorings, when they ran for Lunan Bay, an anchorage on the east side of the Redhead. Those on board of the Tender spent but a very rough night, and, perhaps, slept less soundly than their companions on the Beacon, especially as the wind was at N.W., which caused the vessel to ride with her stern towards the Bell Rock; so that, in the event of any thing giving way, she could hardly have escaped being stranded upon it.

Sunday, 18th.

16 stones laid.

The weather having moderated to-day, the wind shifted to the westward. At a quarter past 9 A. M., the artificers landed from the Tender, and had the pleasure to find their friends who had been left on the Rock quite hearty, alleging that the Beacon was the preferable quarters of the two. The builders laid 16 stones in four hours and a half, when the whole returned on board of the Tender; and at 3 P. M. all hands, counting fifty-four, assembled upon deck to prayers. In the evening, at 9, the artificers again landed, and left off work at a quarter from 12 o'clock at night, having been employed in boring, trenailing, and wedging the stones which had been built in the morning.

Monday, 19th.

Remarkable breach of sea upon the Rock.

The wind was at N.E. to-day, with gentle breezes, but accompanied by the heaviest swell of sea which had yet been observed at the Bell Rock. It was what seamen term a Ground Swell, and, although the landing-master's crew were employed alongside of the Smeaton, in loading the praams, the surface of the water being comparatively smooth, yet the breach upon the Rock was truly surprising. It is when the sea is in this state,—being the result no doubt of a distant gale of wind,—that the sprays conducted by a building, rise to such a height as is represented in the Vignette of Smeaton's Narrative of the Edystone Light-house. In the forenoon, the writer, accompanied by the landing-master, in a well manned boat, went off to observe the effect of the breach of the sea upon the building and apparatus. The work had now attained the height of about 8 feet, on which one of the cranes was erected, the top of which was about 30 feet above the low-water mark. In the course of this tide, the sea, at the meeting of the waves round the building, was observed to rise in the most beautiful conical jets, of about 30 or 40 feet in diameter at the base, to the height of 10 or 15 feet above the crane. Between these seas, but more particularly at low-water, it was observed with a telescope, that some of the last laid stones had been partially lifted; but others, which had not been trenailed, it was feared had been washed off the building.

Tuesday, 20th.

3 stones in danger of being washed away.

At 11 A. M., the boats landed, with much difficulty to-day, in order to ascertain the state of the building and apparatus. On examination it was happily found, that none of the stones were lost, and that those observed yesterday to have been lifted off their beds, were the three which had not been trenailed, but which being fortunately confined by two of the jumpers or boring-irons left in the trenail holes of the lower course, were thus held in their places. After laying these stones, the remainder of this tide, which lasted for three hours and a quarter, was occupied in grouting or filling the perpendicular joints, and plastering them over with Parker's Roman cement, to preserve the pozzolano mortar. At this period, it not only happened to be rough weather, but the building being now at that height, relatively to the tides, which seamen term "Between wind and water," the upper part of the work was exposed to the wash of every wave towards high-water. It was, therefore, often found necessary to repeat the grouting of the same joints with mortar several times. As the evening tide fell wholly under night, the building artificers did not land; but the squad employed at the Beacon and Railways remained at the Rock throughout the day, and were, indeed, only restrained from taking up their quarters also for the night, in consequence of a positive injunction which the writer thought it prudent to enforce, until the Beacon should be in a more habitable state.

Wednesday, 21st.

22 stones laid.

The artificers employed at the Beacon landed upon it this morning at 7 o'clock; and, at a quarter past 11, the builders landed, and continued at work till 4 P. M., having had five hours' and a quarter's work, when 22 stones were laid. The landing-master's crew, at the same time, transported 19 blocks to the Rock with the praam-boats, which completely discharged the Smeaton of her cargo of 32 stones, four casks of pozzolano, and a similar quantity of cement, lime, and sand, with four bundles of trenails, and the like number of wedges, when she immediately left her moorings.

Thursday, 22d.

Great waste of mortar.

The artificers landed upon the Rock this morning at half-past 11, and, from the advanced state of the building, they were enabled to continue at work for six hours and a half, being the longest tide's work which had yet been got upon the Rock by the building artificers. During this tide only four stones were laid, but the time was otherwise occupied in boring, trenailing, wedging, and grouting the joints of the stones last built. From the great waste of mortar, owing to the wash of the sea, in the present stage of the building, the usual proportions of its ingredients were not found sufficient for the courses in hand; and having no conveniency for keeping more than a few casks on the Beacon, while it was an object to have the lime always fresh, it was found necessary to dispatch a boat to-day express to Arbroath, for additional supplies of pozzolano, lime and sand.

Friday, 23d.

The work commenced at 12 noon, and continued six hours and a quarter;

but, owing to the roughness of the weather, no stones were laid to-day, as, not-withstanding every precaution in pointing the joints with cement, the mortar was continually washed away. This tide was, therefore, occupied in the operation of grouting, and securing the mortar with tow, loaded with pieces of iron laid hori-zontally along such of the joints as were accessible to this, which had the effect of preserving them until the cement dried sufficiently to defend it against the wash of the sea.

Saturday, 24th.

57 Stones laid.

Cooking commenced on the Beacon.

Mr Peter Logan, the foreman builder, and his squad, twenty-one in number, landed this morning at 3 o'clock, and continued at work four hours and a quarter, and, after laying 17 stones, returned to the Tender. At 6 A. M., Mr Francis Watt, and his squad of twelve men, landed, and proceeded with their respective operations at the Beacon and Railways, and were left on the Rock during the whole day, with-out the necessity of having any communication with the Tender, the kitchen of the Beacon-house being now fitted up. It was to-day also, that Peter Fortune,—a most obliging and well known character in the Light-house service,—was removed from the Tender to the Beacon, as cook and steward, with a stock of provisions as ample as his limited store-room would admit. At 2 P. M. the building-artificers again landed, and continued at work till a quarter past 8, when 40 of the stones, formerly landed, were now laid, making no fewer than 57 blocks which had been built to-day in the course of both tides. The weather being extremely fine, with light airs of wind from the S.E., the landing-master's crew discharged the Patri-ot into the praam-boats, which were then towed to their moorings, as the stones could not at this time be received at the Rock.

Situation of the Mortar-makers and smiths.

When as many stones were built as comprised this day's work, the demand for mortar was proportionally encreased, and the task of the mortar-makers on these occasions was both laborious and severe. This operation was chiefly performed by John Watt,—a strong active quarrier by profession,—who was a perfect character in his way, and extremely zealous in his department. While the operations of the mortar-makers continued, the forge upon their gallery was not generally in use; but, as the working-hours of the builders extended with the height of the build-ing, the forge could not be so long wanted, and then a sad confusion often ensued upon the circumscribed floor of the mortar-gallery, as the operations of Watt and his assistants trenched greatly upon those of the smiths. The casks with the ingre-dients for the mortar, consisting of pozzolano, lime, and sand, were laid to hand by the sailors. These materials were lifted in spadefulls, and thrown into the cast-iron mortar tubs, represented in Plate X. Fig. 12., where they were beat with an iron-shod pestle, to a consistency suitable to the respective purposes of the work. Under these circumstances, the boundary of the smiths was much circumscribed, and they were personally annoyed, especially in blowy weather, with the dust of the lime in its powdered state. The mortar-makers, on the other hand, were often not a little distressed with the heat of the fire and the sparks elicited on the anvil, and not unaptly complained that they were placed between the "Devil and the Deep-sea."

Sunday, 25th.

27 stones laid.

Rope-ladder distended.

The work being now about 10 feet in height, admitted of a Rope-ladder being distended between the Beacon and the Building, as represented in Plate IX. By this "Jacob's-Ladder," as the seamen termed it, a communication was kept up with the Beacon, while the Rock was considerably under water. One end of it being furnished with tackle-blocks, was fixed to the beams of the Beacon, at the level of the mortar-gallery, while the further end was connected with the Upper-course of the building by means of two Lewis-bats, which were lifted from course to course as the work advanced. In the same manner, a rope furnished with a travelling-pulley, was distended, for the purpose of transporting the mortar-buckets, and other light articles, between the Beacon and the building, which also proved a great conveniency to the work. At this period the rope-ladder, and tackle for the mortar, had a descent from the Beacon to the building; by and by they were on a level; and, towards the end of the season, when the solid part had attained its full height, the ascent was from the mortar-gallery to the building; as will be understood by examining the second year's work, as shewn in the Plate above alluded to, and when viewed in connection with the progress of the work. The building-artificers were accordingly enabled to land this morning at 3 A. M., and to continue at work five hours and a quarter, when 27 stones were laid of the Seventh course. The praam-boats were brought from their moorings, where they lay loaded with 43 stones, besides a supply of pozzolano, lime, sand, cement, trenails, and wedges. The Smeaton having made a trip ashore for a supply of the castings for the western Reach of the Railway, she discharged 15 tons of cast-iron work, and returned to Arbroath for a cargo of stones. At 12 noon, all hands, fifty-seven in number, being collected upon the deck of the Tender, prayers were read as usual. At three quarters past 2 o'clock P. M., the building-artificers again landed, and had five hours' and three quarters' work, at boring, trenailing, wedging, and grouting the stones laid during the two previous tides, which completed the Seventh course of the building.

Monday, 26th.

21 stones laid.

Builders stopped by a simple mistake.

The weather still continuing to be very favourable for the operations, the building-artificers landed on the Rock at a quarter past 3 A. M., and continued at work five hours and a half, when 21 stones were laid. In the course of this tide, it was discovered that the Patriot had by mistake carried off the trainer or gauge-rule to be used for regulating the position of the stones in building the Eighth course, which, for a time, stopped the progress of building. A fast rowing boat was dispatched to Arbroath for this useful implement, a diagram of which will be seen in Plate X. In the mean time, the remainder of the landing-master's crew were employed in laying the cast-iron work in order upon the Rock, so as to be at hand in the course of fitting up the Railways. In the evening, at a quarter past 4 P. M., the artificers landed, and had five hours and a half at boring, trenailing, wedging, and grouting the last laid course of the building.

Tuesday, 27th.

33 stones laid, and 66 landed.

The Joiners' squad of artificers, with Mr Fortune, their cook and steward, landed this morning at 5 A. M. for the day, and the Builders' squad continued on the Rock till a quarter past 10. They again landed, at half-past 4, and returned on board of the Tender with all hands, at 10 P. M. The express-boat came from Arbroath with the trainer this forenoon: 33 stones were laid to-day, and the weather being extremely fine the landing-master's crew delivered no fewer than 66 blocks at the Rock.

Wednesday, 28th.

32 stones laid.

Artificers now at work while the Rock is under water.

As the work was daily getting higher, the artificers landed on the Beacon, and began this morning at a quarter before 6 o'clock, having passed along the rope-ladder, distended between it and the Building, while the Rock was yet under water, when the builders got five hours and a quarter's work. In the evening, they landed again at 6 o'clock, and remained till 11. In the course of this day 32 stones were laid, but, owing to the wind blowing fresh from N.NE., the praams could not approach the eastern creek, and the western reach of Railway being yet unfinished, no materials were landed. The Joiners' squad, as usual, remained all day on the Rock, and were enabled to make great progress with the lodging part of the Beacon or "Hurricane-house," as the seamen termed it.

Thursday, 29th.

25 stones laid, and 50 landed.

The wind was still in the N.E., but being more moderate, the work, in all its departments, proceeded with great spirit; 50 blocks of stone were accordingly landed to-day, with the necessary proportions of lime and other materials. At half-past 6, the whole of the artificers landed, and remained till half-past 11, having been five hours on the Rock. The builders again landed at 6 P. M.; and at midnight, all hands left the Rock. The builders having to-day been no less than ten hours and a half at work, had laid 25 stones. The roughness of the weather yesterday washed a great part of the mortar out of the joints, and this morning's tide was chiefly occupied in grouting and pointing the Eighth course, which being closed, the work was brought to the height of about 11 feet above the lower bed of the Foundation-stone.

Friday, 30th.

18 stones are laid.

Michael Wishart meets with a serious accident.

The artificers landed on the Rock this morning at a quarter past 6, and remained at work five hours. The cooking apparatus being now in full operation, all hands had breakfast on the Beacon at the usual hour, and remained there throughout the day. The crane upon the building had to be raised to-day from the Eighth to the Ninth course, an operation which now required all the strength that could be mustered for working the guy-tackles; for, as the top of the crane was at this time about 35 feet above the Rock, it became much more unmanageable. This will be better understood by examining the apparatus in Plate IX., and comparing the appearance of the crane-tackle of the second year's work with that of the first. In order, to give an additional purchase in tightening the tackle, one of the blocks of stone was suspended at the end of the moveable-beam of the crane, which, by adding greatly to the purchase or weight, tended to slacken the guys in the direction to which the beam with the stone was pointed, and thereby enabled the artificers more easily to brace them one after another. While the beam was thus loaded, and in the act of swinging round from one guy to another, a great strain was suddenly brought upon the opposite tackle, with the end of which the artificers had very improperly neglected to take a turn round some stationary object, which would have given them the complete command of the tackle. Owing to this simple omission, the crane, with the large stone at the end of the beam, got a preponderancy to one side, and the tackle alluded to having rended, the crane fell upon the building with a terrible crash. The surrounding artificers immediately flew in every direction to get out of its way; but Michael Wishart, the principal builder, having unluckily stumbled upon one of the uncut trenails, fell upon his back. His body fortunately got between the moveable-beam and the upright shaft of the crane, and was thus saved; but his feet got entangled with the wheels of the crane, and were severely injured. Wishart being a robust young man, endured his misfortune with wonderful firmness: he was laid upon one of the narrow framed beds of the Beacon, and dispatched in a boat to the Tender; where the writer was when this accident happened, not a little alarmed, on missing the crane from the top of the building, and at the same time seeing a boat rowing towards the vessel with great speed. When the boat came alongside with poor Wishart stretched upon a bed, covered with blankets, a moment of great anxiety followed, which was, however, much relieved, when, on stepping into the boat, he was accosted by Wishart, though in a feeble voice, and with an aspect pale as death, from excessive bleeding. Directions having been immediately given to the coxwain to apply to Mr Kennedy at the work-yard, to procure the best surgical aid, the boat was sent off without delay to Arbroath. The writer then landed at the Rock, when the crane was in a very short time got into its place, and again put in a working state. The builders commenced work with it at 7 o'clock in the evening, and continued till midnight, and in the course of this day 18 stones were laid. Robert Selkirk was appointed by Mr Logan to succeed Wishart, as principal builder.

1809, July.

Saturday, 1st.

Artificers have no less than ten hours' work, and lay 59 stones.

The artificers landed this morning at half-past 7, and as the building was gradually rising out of the reach of the tide, the work was continued no less than six hours and a half at this time, being the longest tide's work which the builders had hitherto had. They again landed at half-past 7 in the evening, and did not leave off till midnight, having, to-day, had ten hours and a half's work, when no fewer than 59 blocks of stone were built; 56 of which were landed on the Rock to-day, being the entire cargo of the Patriot, including six casks of pozzolano, and a similar quantity of lime and sand; besides twenty parcels containing 200 trenails and 200 pairs of wedges; together with six sacks of moss (hypnum), two bales of green woollen-cloth, a bale of red binding tape, with nails, &c. for lining the cabins of the Beacon-house.

Sunday, 2d.

The Writer visits the Carr Rock. Some of the vessels slip their moorings.

After a trip which he had taken in the Light-house Yacht to examine the Carr Rock, with a view to the erection of a Beacon, as described in the Introduction of this work, page 53., the writer landed on the Bell Rock this evening. He found that the artificers had commenced work at a quarter from 8 o'clock A. M., and continued for seven hours and a quarter, when seven blocks of stone were laid, with which the Ninth course of the building was completed. The remainder of this long tide's-work was occupied in boring trenail holes, driving trenails and wedges, and in filling the perpendicular joints of the course with thin mortar, mixed up into that consistency which is technically termed Grout. Having again landed in the evening, the same operation was continued from 8 till 11 o'clock P. M.; but the wind having shifted from south to E.NE., it blew so fresh that the torches could not be kept burning, being now more exposed, and without the shelter which the foundation-pit formerly afforded. The work was, therefore, obliged to be dropt, before the tide had overflowed the Rock. From the state of the weather, it was also judged necessary to give directions to the landing-master to employ his crew in removing the iron-jumpers and other implements to the Beacon; and to remove every encumbrance from the boats, so as to lighten them as much as possible, and fit them the better for carrying the artificers, thirty-two in number. At midnight, all hands left the Rock in four boats, two of which belonged to the Tender, one to the Light-house Yacht, and one to the Smeaton; and, after much difficulty, they reached their respective vessels. The Yacht and Smeaton then slipped their moorings, and proceeded for Arbroath, as they rode very hard, but the Tender kept her position.

Monday, 3d.

No landing on the Rock to-day.

The wind still continued to blow so fresh, that no landing could be made to-day on the Rock. As the Tender's stock of provisions was getting low, a considerable effort was made by the Patriot, which had come from Arbroath with supplies, to prevent the necessity of her leaving her moorings. After several vain attempts however, the Patriot was obliged to bear away for the Firth of Forth to wait a change of weather.

Michael Wishart is recovering.

The writer having come to Arbroath with the Yacht, had an opportunity of visiting Michael Wishart, the artificer who had met with so severe an accident at the Rock on the 30th ult., and had the pleasure to find him in a state of recovery. From Dr Stevenson's account, under whose charge he had been placed, hopes were entertained that amputation would not be necessary, as his patient still kept free of fever or any appearance of mortification; and Wishart expressed a hope that he might, at least, be ultimately capable of keeping the light at the Bell Rock, as it was not now likely that he would assist farther in building the house.

Progress of the Works at Arbroath.

In the work-yard, the operations were going on as usual, under the direction of Mr David Logan, and the stone-cutters were now working at the Twenty-third course. The Twentieth course being nearly finished, it was partly laid on the platform, and ready to be fitted, marked, and numbered for shipping to the Bell Rock. Dispatch was also making in the joiners' shop where Mr James Slight, was preparing the moulds for the succeeding courses, diagrams of which will be seen in Plate X.

Tuesday, 4th.

The Tender had kept her station at the Rock. Though the wind was still at N.E., it had abated a little, and the artificers landed at 11 A. M., to the number of twenty-four, and were employed for three hours in completing the trenailing of the Ninth course. At 3 P. M., the building artificers, fourteen in number, left the Rock, and went on board of the Tender, but the joiners and smiths remained upon the Beacon till half-past 9 P. M., when they also returned on board of the vessel.

Wednesday, 5th.

19 stones laid.

Joiners left on the Beacon.

The wind having shifted to the east, and the weather being moderate, the artificers landed at half-past 11 this forenoon, when 19 stones were laid after four hours work. At 8 P. M. the boats again left the vessel, and made an attempt to land on the Rock, but it was found impracticable, there being then too much sea. The joiners' squad were therefore left on the Beacon all night.

Thursday 6th.

16 stones laid.

Joiners resolve to remain on the Beacon.

The building artificers having landed at a quarter past 12 to-day, 16 stones were laid, when they again left the Rock at a quarter past 4, having been four hours at work. The weather having a very unfavourable appearance, the landing-master expressed a wish to bring all hands with him; but the Joiners' squad, with Mr Fortune their cook, had now resolved to continue their quarters on the Beacon-house, instead of having "the continual plague of boating;" and being now better provided with necessaries, they felt much more at ease. The boats were now less crowded, and this arrangement was a great relief to the landing-master's crew. The writer was at Arbroath when the Beacon was thus taken possession of; and though he felt no uneasiness as to its permanency in withstanding the effects of the sea, yet he was not without scruples about the danger of accidental fire, from the chips of wood which unavoidably encumbered the place while the joiners were at work. Considering, therefore, the awful circumstances to those inhabiting the Beacon under such a possible calamity, together with its disastrous consequences to the work, it became a matter of much solicitude to guard against such a misfortune.

Favourable to the possession of the Light-house.

This practical expression of the opinion of the mill-wrights, joiners and smiths, with regard to the safety of the Beacon, was nevertheless highly satisfactory to the writer, as it shewed a degree of confidence in this temporary erection, which left no doubt as to its utility in the future operations. It was also an excellent prelude to the inhabitation of the Light-house itself when completed, as some were even doubtful if light-keepers would be found disposed to take up their residence permanently upon a rock, which, every tide, was sunk under water to the depth of from 10 to 16 feet, of which no instance had hitherto occurred, as the First entire course of the Edystone Light-house is understood to have been on a level with high-water mark.

Friday, 7th.

15 stones laid.

The wind having shifted to the S.E. to-day, with easy weather, the Patriot returned from Largo Bay to her moorings, when the praam-boats discharged 19 stones of her cargo, and landed them on the Rock. The artificers landed at 10 A. M. and remained at work no less than nine hours and a half, when 15 stones of the Tenth course were laid. The builders then went on board of the Tender, leaving the mill-wrights, joiners and smiths, in possession of the Beacon-house.

Saturday, 8th.

11 stones laid.

The Tide, for the first time, does not overflow the Building.

The builders landed to-day at a quarter past 12 noon, and remained seven hours and three quarters, when they laid 11 blocks, while the landing-master's crew transported 46 stones to the Rock. The tide's work was now so much lengthened, that time was afforded for boring the trenail holes into the course below, fixing the trenails and wedges, and grouting up the perpendicular joints with pozzolano mortar, in a more deliberate manner than when the work was lower in the water. It was remarked to-day, with no small demonstration of joy, that the tide—being neap—did not, for the first time, overflow the building at high-water. Flags were accordingly hoisted, on the Beacon-house, and crane on the top of the Building, which were repeated from the Floating-light, Light-house Yacht, Tender, Smeaton, Patriot, and the two Praams. A salute of three guns was also fired from the Yacht at high-water, when all the artificers being collected on the top of the building, three cheers were given, in testimony of this important circumstance. A glass of rum was then served out to all hands on the Rock, and on board of the respective ships.

Number of Joiners reduced. Balance Crane begun.

Having thus got the Light-house above the sea-level in ordinary neap-tides, and the Beacon into a habitable state, while the Railway operations were confined to the western reach, it was now found expedient to diminish the number of mill-wrights and joiners at the Rock. At this period, the writer went to Edinburgh to attend a general meeting of the Commissioners of the Northern Light-houses, and to report the advanced state of the works,—news which was received with the greatest satisfaction by the Board. He also visited the Shotts Iron-works, and took measures for the immediate construction of a Crane, upon a new principle. This had occupied his attention, along with the general scheme of the work. But, since the unfortunate accident which happened to Wishart, by the fall of the Moveable-beam-crane, it had became more apparently necessary, as the increasing height of this machine rendered the guy-tackles too taunt, to use a sailor's expression for any thing that is high, or when the ropes, which support a spar or mast, form too small an angle at the top. Instead of these unmanageable tackles, the upright shaft of the new crane was to be kept in an erect position by a balance-weight acting upon the opposite end of the loaded working-beam, which was thus to be kept in a state of equilibrium. As Mr Watt, foreman of the Beacon and Railway works, could now be spared from the Rock for a time, he was sent to Shotts to get the patterns made for this machine, and other implements connected with the progress of the higher parts of the building; from whence the castings were sent to Edinburgh to be fitted up.

Sunday, 9th.

Tenth course completed.

On the writer's return to the Bell Rock to-day, it appeared from the notes of the foreman builder, and log-book of the landing-master, that the work had made very good progress, of which the building itself bore testimony, being now about 13 feet in height. The wind was at N.E. this morning, and blowed so fresh that a landing could not be made till a quarter past 4 o'clock P. M., when the closing-stone of the Tenth course was laid, after three hours and a quarter's work; but the landing-master's crew could not approach the Rock with the praam-boats.

Monday, 10th.

Twenty of the artificers landed this morning at half-past 5, and continued at work till half-past 7. Again, in the evening, the work was resumed at 6, and continued till a quarter from 9. The artificers were employed to-day in dressing off and completing the last laid course. Still the wind being from the N.E., accompanied with a heavy sea, the praams could not approach the Rock, and consequently no materials were landed.

Tuesday, 11th.

31 stones laid, and numerous articles landed.

The wind having shifted to the westward, the sea was greatly run down; and the landing-master's crew being early at work this morning, transported no fewer than 65 blocks to the Rock in the course of the day. At 6 A. M. the artificers landed, when 19 stones of the Eleventh course were laid. They again landed at 4 P. M. and laid 22, making altogether nine hours and a quarter upon the Rock to-day, when 31 stones were built. The Patriot had left Arbroath last night, and got to the Rock this morning with 43 pieces of stone, twelve bundles containing 396 wedges, five bundles containing 165 trenails, three casks of cement, six casks of pozzolano, six casks of lime, six casks of sand, besides provisions for the use of the Beacon-house and Tender, viz. five hogsheads of water, five bags of coals, three casks of beef, five bags of biscuit, one cask of oatmeal, one firkin of butter, one cask of flour, one cask of pot barley, with salt and vegetables.

Wednesday, 12th.

37 stones laid.

At a quarter past 5 this morning, the artificers, 21 in number, landed, and re-mained eight hours on the Rock, when 21 stones were laid. They landed again in the afternoon at half-past 3, and remained till 9 P. M., when 16 stones were laid. The landing-master's crew transported three stones to the Rock to-day, which completed the Eleventh course. The Smeaton arrived from Leith this forenoon, with 53 casks of pozzolano earth, 39 of which were stowed on board of the Tender to be at hand: the Smeaton then proceeded with the remainder to Arbroath, where she loaded stones for the Rock.

Thursday, 13th.

29 stones laid.

The weather still continuing favourable, the artificers landed this morning at half-past 6 and remained till half-past 11, when 15 stones were laid. They landed again at 5 and remained till 11 P. M., when 14 stones were laid. 29 stones were transported to the Rock to-day in the praam-boats.

Friday, 14th.

27 stones laid.

The artificers landed this morning at a quarter from 7, and remained six hours and a quarter on the Rock, when 18 stones were laid. They landed again in the evening and remained four hours and a quarter, when 9 stones were laid, which completed the Twelfth course; the praam-boats having landed 27 stones.

Saturday, 15th.

52 Stones landed and laid.

The wind was southerly, with occasional showers of rain to-day, but the sea was smooth. The artificers landed at a quarter past 7 this morning, and as the wa-ter did not overflow the building, they continued on the Rock till midnight, being 16 hours and a half, and laid no fewer than 52 stones, which, in the early part of the day, had also been transported to the Rock by the landing-master's crew. This was the most successful day's work which had hitherto been made. The Twelfth course was thus completed, which brought the building to the height of 15 feet above the lower bed of the foundation-stone.

Sunday, 16th.

32 Stones laid.

Hitherto no order had been given for loading the Bell Rock vessels with stones on Sundays, but Mr Kennedy, to whose department this belonged, had, with his usual unwearied attention, commenced on Sunday night, at 12 o'clock, which enabled the Patriot to sail at 5, and reach the Rock at 10 A. M., with a cargo of stones. The artificers landed at half-past 7, and laid 21 stones in the course of seven hours and a half; and having again landed in the evening at 7, they laid 11 stones in four hours, all of which had been landed on the Rock to-day from the praams. Besides laying, boring, trenailing, wedging, and grouting these stones, several other operations were proceeded with on the Rock, at low-water, when some of the artificers were employed at the Railways, and at high-water at the Beacon-house. The seamen having prepared a quantity of tarpaulin, or cloth laid over with successive coats of hot tar, the joiners had just completed the covering of the roof with it. This sort of covering was lighter and more easily managed than sheet-lead in such a situation. As a farther defence against the weather, the whole exterior of this temporary residence was painted with three coats of white-lead paint. Between the timber-framing of the habitable part of the Beacon, the interstices were to be stuffed with moss, as a light substance that would resist dampness, and check sifting winds: the whole interior was then to be lined with green baize-cloth, so that both without and within the cabins were to have a very comfortable appearance.

Monday, 17th.

9 Stones laid.

The artificers landed this morning at half-past 7, and remained at work five hours and a half, when 9 stones were laid; but the wind having shifted to the N.E., which increased to a hard gale, in the course of this afternoon, both the Smeaton and Patriot were obliged to slip their moorings, when they proceeded in company to Leith Roads for shelter. The Tender, however, being in a more light trim, and better adapted for riding, continued at her station.

One of the Artificers is accidentally killed in the work-yard.

While some of the masons were employed to-day in raising a large stone in the work-yard at Arbroath, the purchase unfortunately slipped, and the stone fell upon William Walker, one of the labourers, who was putting a prop under it, to preserve its position till a better purchase could be taken. By this accident, Walker's thigh-bone was unfortunately broken, and, though medical assistance was procured without delay, the poor man died in the course of a few hours, leaving a wife and two young children. The Commissioners of the Light-houses, in consideration of the circumstances of this case, settled an annuity of L. 5 upon his widow.

Tuesday 18th.

One of the workmen remains in the Beacon alone.

The wind still continued to blow fresh from the N.E., but the artificers were enabled to land on the Rock at a quarter from 11, where they remained two hours and three quarters, employed in shifting the crane on the building, and making other preparations for laying the Thirteenth course. Although the building-artificers generally remained on the Rock throughout the day, and the mill-wrights, joiners, and smiths, while their number was considerable, remained also during the night, yet the Tender had hitherto been considered as their night-quarters. But the wind having, in the course of the day, shifted to the N.W., and as the passage to the Tender, in the boats, was likely to be attended with difficulty, the whole of the artificers, with Mr Logan, the foreman, preferred remaining all night on the Beacon, which had, of late, become the solitary abode of George Forsyth, a jobbing-upholsterer, who had been employed in lining the Beacon-house with cloth, and in fitting up the bedding. Forsyth was a tall, thin, and rather loose-made man, who had an utter aversion at climbing upon the trap-ladders of the Beacon, but especially at the process of boating, and the motion of the ship, which he said, "was death itself." He, therefore, pertinaciously insisted with the landing-master in being left upon the Beacon, with a small black dog as his only companion. The writer, however, felt some delicacy in leaving a single individual upon the Rock, who must have been so very helpless, in case of accident. This fabric had, from the beginning, been rather intended by the writer to guard against accident from the loss or damage of a boat, and as a place for making mortar, a smith's shop, and a store for tools, during the working months, than as permanent quarters: nor was it at all meant to be possessed until the joiner-work were completely finished, and his own cabin, and that for the foremen, in readiness, when it was still to be left to the choice of the artificers to occupy the Tender or the Beacon. He, however, considered Forsyth's partiality and confidence in the latter, as rather a fortunate occurrence.

Wednesday, 19th.

Artificers remove with Peter Fortune to the Beacon.

The whole of the artificers, 23 in number, now removed, of their own accord, from the Tender, to lodge in the Beacon, together with Peter Fortune, a person singularly adapted for a residence of this kind, both from the urbanity of his manners, and the versatility of his talents. Fortune, in his person, was of small stature, and rather corpulent. Besides being a good Scotch cook, he had acted both as groom and house-servant; he had been a soldier, a suttler, a writer's clerk, and an apothecary, from which he possessed the art of writing and suggesting recipes, and had hence, also, perhaps acquired a turn for making collections in natural history; but in his practice in surgery, on the Bell Rock, for which he received an annual fee of three guineas, he is supposed to have been rather partial to the use of the lancet. In short, Peter was the fac-totum of the Beacon-house, where he ostensibly acted in the several capacities of cook, steward, surgeon, and barber, and kept a statement of the rations or expenditure of the provisions, with the strictest integrity.

Thursday, 20th.

Praam-boats cannot approach the Rock.

The wind was at the S.E. to-day, accompanied with a considerable swell of sea; and, although the Smeaton and Patriot had returned from Leith Roads, and the praams had been loaded, and were riding at their moorings, yet they could not approach the Rock. The building artificers, however, found employment in boring, trenailing, wedging, and grouting the last laid course. The smiths and mill-wrights worked at the western Railway, and the joiners at sundry jobs about the Beacon-house.

Friday, 21st.

18 Stones laid and 69 landed.

The weather having improved, the Smeaton was entirely discharged to-day of her cargo of 69 stones, which were also landed on the Rock, with a due proportion of other building materials, as pozzolano, lime, and sand, &c.; and 18 stones of the Thirteenth course were laid to-day.

Saturday, 22d.

An embargo is laid on Shipping.

In the present important state of the building, when it had just attained the height of 16 feet, and the upper courses, and especially the imperfect one, were in the wash of the heaviest seas, an express-boat arrived at the Rock, with a letter from Mr Kennedy of the work-yard, stating, that, in consequence of the intended Expedition to Walcheren, an embargo had been laid on shipping at all the ports of Great Britain; that both the Smeaton and Patriot were detained at Arbroath, and that, but for the proper view which Mr Ramsay, the port-officer, had taken of his orders, neither the express-boat, nor one which had been sent with provisions and necessaries for the Floating-light, would have been permitted to leave the harbour. The writer set off without delay for Arbroath, and, on landing, used every possible means with the official people; but their orders were deemed so peremptory, that even boats were not permitted to sail from any port upon the coast. In the mean time, the collector of the Customs at Montrose applied to the Board at Edinburgh, but could, of himself, grant no relief to the Bell Rock shipping.

Mr Sheriff Duff corresponds with the Board of Customs.

At this critical period, Mr Adam Duff, then Sheriff of Forfarshire, now of the county of Edinburgh, and ex officio one of the Commissioners of the Northern Light-houses, happened to be at Arbroath. Mr Duff took an immediate interest in representing the circumstances of the case to the Board of Customs at Edinburgh. But such were the doubts entertained on the subject, that, on having previously received the appeal from the Collector at Montrose, the case had been submitted to the consideration of the Lords of the Treasury, whose decision was now waited for.

Operations at the Rock while the vessels were under embargo.

In this state of things, the writer felt particularly desirous to get the Thirteenth course finished, that the building might be in a more secure state, in the event of bad weather. An opportunity was therefore embraced on the 25th, in sailing with provisions for the Floating-light, to carry the necessary stones to the Rock for this purpose, which were landed and built on the 26th and 27th. But so closely was the watch kept up, that a Customhouse-officer was always placed on board of the Smeaton and Patriot while they were afloat, till the embargo was specially removed from the Light-house vessels. The artificers at the Bell Rock had been reduced to fifteen, who were regularly supplied with provisions, along with the crew of the Floating-light, mainly through the port-officer's liberal interpretation of his orders. After completing the Thirteenth course, they were employed in erecting a kind of stool or prop of masonry on the western side of the building, for which the stones had fortunately been landed previous to the embargo. This prop, as will be understood by examining the second year's work of Plate IX., consisted of large blocks of stone, measuring 5 feet in length, 2 feet 6 inches in breadth, and 15 inches in thickness, and, when completed, it was 6 feet in height, and 6 feet square at the top, so that the men in working the crane had a sufficient space for standing. By this means, the foot of the lower crane was elevated 6 feet above the Rock, which, added to the length of the working-beam, made a height of about 18 feet, and, in the present state of the building, the stones were thus raised to the level of the last built course. The crane on the top of the building, with which the stones were laid, was, therefore, now only employed to take them from the lower crane, instead of lifting them at once from the waggons on the Railway. During this period, also, the Beacon-house and Railways were completely overhauled, and matters of minor importance attended to, which were obliged to be left behind when the works were going on briskly.

1809, August.

The embargo is taken off the Light-house vessels.

The Lords of the Treasury had no sooner received the appeal from the Board of Customs at Edinburgh, than an order was issued for all vessels and boats belonging to the service of the Commissioners of the Northern Light-houses, to be released and permitted to sail upon their respective voyages. But before this order could be made effective, ten days of the finest weather of the season had elapsed. Every one connected with the work had now become impatient to be again at work, when the writer had the happiness to receive a letter from Mr Charles Cuningham, Secretary to the Commissioners of the Northern Light-houses, stating that an order might be expected to reach the Collector of the Customs at Montrose on the 30th. Mr Kennedy was consequently sent to Montrose to wait the arrival of the post, which happened at midnight, when Mr Paton the Collector, with much attention, gave immediate orders for the liberation of the Bell Rock vessels; and as both the Smeaton and Patriot were loaded and ready for sea, they sailed from Arbroath on Sunday the 30th, with the wind at E.S.E., and arrived at their moorings at the Rock early on the 31st.

The necessity of stopping the Bell Rock shipping doubted, under any circumstances.

On the subject of this embargo, as applicable to the boats and vessels in the Bell Rock service, it would be difficult, and perhaps improper, to give any opinion regarding the discretion or prudence exercised by the Officers of the Customs, especially as the Board itself found it necessary to appeal to the Treasury for instructions. If, however, the Superior Officers at Montrose, aware of all the circumstances of this peculiar case, had allowed the work at the Bell Rock to proceed, till special orders could have been received on this peculiar point, there is reason to believe it would not have been called in question by the Board of Customs at Edinburgh. But when the vessels were peremptorily stopped, and the matter brought formally under its notice, an appeal to the Treasury was considered indispensable.

Tuesday, 1st.

78 stones landed, and 40 laid.

24 artificers inhabit the Beacon.

There being a considerable swell and breach of sea upon the Rock yesterday, the stones could not be got landed till the day following, when the wind shifted to the southward, and the weather improved. But to-day no less than 78 blocks of stone were landed, of which 40 were built, which completed the Fourteenth, and part of the Fifteenth courses. The number of workmen now resident in the Beacon-house were augmented to 24; including the landing-master's crew from the Tender, and the boat's crew from the Floating-light, who assisted at landing the stones. Those daily at work upon the Rock at this period amounted to 46. A cabin had been laid out for the writer on the Beacon, as will be seen from Plate VIII. but his apartment had been the last which was finished, and he had not yet taken possession of it; for though he generally spent the greater part of the day, at this time, upon the Rock, yet he always slept on board of the Tender.

Wednesday, 2d.

Mr Sheriff Duff visits the works at the Rock.

To-day the wind was from the S.E., accompanied with a pretty heavy swell of sea, which, in the early part of the season, would perhaps have been sufficient to deter the attempt of landing building materials; but such was the dexterity of the landing-master and his crew, that 23 stones were transported to the western creek, and afterwards, by great exertions, got along the Rock, though the Railways were still in an incomplete state. With these, the builders were enabled to finish the Sixteenth course, consisting of 53 stones. The work was visited to-day by Mr Sheriff Duff, who, with his accompanying friends, were much gratified in landing on the Bell Rock, and viewing the advanced state of the works.

Thursday, 3d.

23 stones laid.

The wind being from south-east, a heavy swell of sea ran upon the Rock, so that no stones were landed to-day. The building being now about 19 feet in height, it was found to produce a smoothness on the lee-side, and as the north-east wind produced the heaviest seas, the lower crane, erected on the prop, being placed on the south-west side, was somewhat sheltered from that quarter, and admitted of a considerable quantity of materials being occasionally laid around it; and, therefore, although none were landed to-day, yet 23 blocks of the Seventeenth course were built.

Friday, 4th.

2 stones laid.

The weather proved very fine, and the seamen were employed on board of the Floating-light in shifting her winter cable, and inspecting her chain-moorings, as she had just undergone such repair in her upper-works, as could be conveniently given her while afloat. The artificers on the Rock laid two stones to-day, and were otherwise employed in trenailing and grouting the Seventeenth course.

Saturday, 5th.

8 stones laid.

The weather still continued favourable, and the landing-master's crew discharged the Patriot of her cargo, of which 40 stones were landed on the Rock, and the remaining 12 were kept on board of one of the Praam-boats at her moorings. The artificers built 8 stones to-day, so that 32 of the 40 which had been landed, were either laid without mortar, upon the building, or ranged round the stool of the lower crane, in readiness for next tide.

Sunday, 6th.

In the course of the last night, however, the wind had shifted to the N.E., accompanied by a heavy swell of sea, and it was impossible for the landing-master's boats to approach the Rock. But the artificers being now stationary upon the Beacon, they could pass from it to the building at all times of tide, by means of the rope-ladder, formerly noticed, as will be understood by examining the second year's work, represented in Plate IX. They accordingly laid 25 stones to-day, and completed the Seventeenth course, consisting of 60 blocks. The Praam-boat, with the remaining 12 stones of the Patriot's cargo on board, rode at her moorings with great ease, and although the swell was very considerable, yet she had very little motion; and even when deeply loaded, these decked boats shipped no water. So easily did they ride at anchor, that the sickly artificers, while on board of the Tender, though much easier than the Floating-light, were often heard to express a wish that their births could be shifted to a Praam-boat.

Narrow escape from ship-wreck.

At day-break, this morning, a large schooner, the Fly of Bridport, Green, master, bound from London to Dundee, was observed standing right upon the Bell Rock, when she was suddenly taken aback on seeing the Beacon and works on the Rock. The crew of this vessel being entire strangers, had hoisted a signal, when the landing-master immediately went on board, and after some consultation, Pool, the master of the Smeaton, was sent to conduct the Fly into the Firth of Tay.

Monday, 7th.

The wind had shifted to the S.W. to-day, but still a heavy swell of the sea prevented the landing of materials, and the artificers were accordingly employed in shifting the crane on the building, and at low-water they were all engaged in fixing and extending the Railways towards the western creek.

Tuesday, 8th.

12 stones laid.

Mr Sheriff Hamilton visits the works.

The sea having fallen considerably, the loaded Praam-boat got to the Rock, and the artificers laid the 12 stones which had now been on board of her since the 5th. The works at the Rock were visited to-day by Mr Robert Hamilton, Sheriff of Lanark, and ex officio one of the Commissioners of the Northern Light-houses, who expressed much satisfaction at the progress of the operations.

Wednesday, 9th.

36 stones laid.

Additional supports for the Beacon landed to-day.

The number of artificers were augmented from 24 to 26, and measures were taken for leveling the necessary sites on the Rock for some additional supports for the legs or principal beams of the Beacon. These supports had been prepared in the course of the winter, but had not yet been applied, from the pressing nature of the building operations. They consisted both of iron and of timber, the former to connect the principal beams horizontally, and the latter diagonally, in order that, by every possible means, this essential part of the establishment might be preserved through the winter, and divested of the twist so expressively felt and complained of by Mr Logan, on the 30th of May. To-day 36 stones were landed and built, which finished the Nineteenth course, and brought the building to the height of about 23 feet.

Thursday, 10th.

To-day 26 stones of the Twentieth course were landed and laid.

Friday, 11th.

Sheer-crane broken by the force of the sea.

The wind was at S.E. on the 11th, and there was so very heavy a swell of sea upon the Rock, that no boat could approach it. Such indeed was the force of its breach, that one of the legs of the cast-iron Sheer-crane at the eastern creek, represented in Plate XI., was again broken. It is not a little remarkable, that these bars, which contained about 16 square inches of section, should nevertheless have been snapped, by the force of the sea, on three different occasions. It must, however, be remarked, that these sheers, in their operation, had necessarily a certain action laterally, in effecting the laying of a stone upon the waggon; in heavy seas, therefore, the apparatus was subject to a jerking motion, which proved sufficient to break it; so essential is it, that every thing within the range of the sea should be Dead-fast, as workmen emphatically express it, or as firm and steady as possible.

Saturday, 12th.

Some of the Artificers become alarmed and leave the Beacon.

The gale still continuing from the S.E., the sea broke with great violence both upon the Building and the Beacon. The former being 23 feet in height, the upper part of the crane erected on it having been lifted from course to course as the building advanced, was now about 36 feet above the Rock. From observations made on the rise of the sea by this crane, the artificers were enabled to estimate its height to be about 50 feet above the Rock, while the sprays fell with a most alarming noise upon their cabins. At low-water, in the evening, a signal was made from the Beacon, at the earnest desire of some of the artificers, for the boats to come to the Rock; and although this could not be effected without considerable hazard, it was however accomplished, when twelve of their number, being much afraid, applied to the foreman to be relieved, and went on board of the Tender. But the remaining fourteen continued on the Rock, with Mr Peter Logan, the foreman builder. Although this rule of allowing an option to every man either to remain on the Rock or return to the Tender, was strictly adhered to; yet, as it would have been extremely inconvenient to have had the men parcelled out in this manner, it became necessary to embrace the first opportunity of sending those who had left the Beacon to the workyard, with as little appearance of intention as possible, lest it should hurt their feelings, or prevent others from acting according to their wishes, either in landing on the Rock or remaining on the Beacon.

Sunday, 13th.

Effects of the late gale.

All hands were employed at low-water to-day, in refitting the sheer-crane at the eastern landing-place, and in adjusting other things about the Beacon and Rock, which had been scattered and deranged during the late gale. In particular, the guy-ropes of the cranes required to be tightened; for, although they were of patent-cordage, and had often been well tried, yet, upon this occasion, they were stretched and much relaxed with the excessive motion of the sea. The whole appurtenances of the mortar-gallery had been sent adrift; even the blacksmith's anvil was upset! and found lying at the foot of the Beacon, while his bellows, and the greater part of the deals with which the floor was laid, were forced up and carried away, with all the lime and cement casks.

Monday, 14th.

The wind still continued from the S.E., and though blowing with less force, yet the sea rolled over the Rock too heavily for approaching it with building materials. But, in the course of the day, efforts were made for getting the landing-apparatus again into a working state.

Tuesday, 15th.

5 stones laid.

The Writer takes possession of his cabin in the Beacon.

The wind had fortunately shifted to the S.W. this morning, and though a considerable breach was still upon the Rock, yet the landing-master's crew were enabled to get one Praam-boat, lightly loaded with five stones, brought in safety to the western creek: these stones were immediately laid by the artificers, who gladly embraced the return of good weather to proceed with their operations. The writer had this day taken possession of his cabin in the Beacon-house. It was small, but commodious, and was found particularly convenient in coarse and blowing weather, instead of being obliged to make a passage to the Tender in an open boat, at all times, both during the day and the night, which was often attended with much difficulty and danger.

Wednesday, 16th.

52 stones landed and 18 built.

The sea was much run down to-day, but the wind from the west, prevented the landing of stones on the western side of the Rock, and the repairs of the sheer-crane were still incomplete. Captain Wilson undertook, however, to land two Praam-boats of stones on the top of the building at high-water. He accordingly laid the Hedderwick and Fernie in succession, alongside of the building, and in this manner 30 stones were landed; the repairs of the sheer-crane were completed, and during the evening tide, other two praam-loads were landed at low-water at the eastern creek, making in all 52 stones, of which 18 of the Twentieth course were built.

Thursday, 17th.

The wind had shifted from W. to N.E. to-day, but the weather being fine, 29 stones were landed, and 25 built.

Friday, 18th.

The weather is rather boisterous to-day, accompanied with rain, and a considerable swell of sea. The two praam-boats, however, were got to the Rock, when 16 stones were landed, which, with those already at hand, finished the Twentieth and commenced the Twenty-first course.

Saturday, 19th.

Floating-light boat loses her way.

For some days past, the weather had been occasionally so thick and foggy, that no small difficulty was experienced in going even between the Rock and the Tender, though quite at hand. But the Floating-light's boat lost her way so far in returning on board that the first land she made, after rowing all night, was Fifeness, a distance of about 14 miles, as will be seen from Plate IV. The weather having cleared in the morning, the crew stood off again for the Floating-light, and got on board in a half famished and much exhausted state, having been constantly rowing for about 16 hours.

29 stones built.

The wind shifted this morning from E. to S.W. with much rain. The sloop Patriot returned from the Firth of Forth this forenoon, to which she had been driven by the late gales. The weather being more favourable to-day, 31 stones were landed on the Rock, and 29 stones were built, with which the Twenty-first course was finished, which brings the building to the height of 25 feet. The crane was also shifted, and every preparation made for commencing with the next course.

Sunday, 20th.

An entire course laid to-day. Prayers read on the Rock.

The weather being very favourable to-day, 53 stones were landed, and the builders were not a little gratified in having built the Twenty-second course, consisting of 51 stones, being the first course which had been completed in one day. This, as a matter of course, produced three hearty cheers. At 12 noon, prayers were read for the first time on the Bell Rock: those present, counting thirty, were crowded into the upper apartment of the Beacon, where the writer took a central position, while two of the artificers joining hands supported the Bible.

Monday, 21st.

Smeaton arrives with the last course of the solid.

The wind was from the S.W. this morning, blowing fresh, with rain. The Praam-boats, however, landed thirty-two stones, which were also built. At 6 P. M. the Smeaton arrived from Arbroath, having on board the last cargo of the solid part of the building. She was, of course, decorated with all her colours; and, in compliment to the advanced state of the work, there was a display of flags from the Floating-light and the other vessels on the station, and also from the Beacon-house and the Building itself.

Tuesday, 22d.

Floating-light breaks adrift.

During last night it blew excessively hard, and the operations to-day were much interrupted by the breaking loose of the Floating-light. At 5 o'clock this morning an alarm was given throughout the Beacon-house of this circumstance, when a signal was instantly made for the Tender to get under way; at the same time one of her boats came to the Rock, and the writer left the Beacon, and sailed with the Tender to the assistance of the Floating-light. It was some time before the watch on the deck had observed, by their greater distance from the buoy upon the spare moorings, that the vessel had actually got adrift. Mr John Reid, acting master, was immediately called, when the best bower anchor was let go with a sufficient scope of cable, about a mile from her original station. Here she was obliged to be left till the weather should become moderate enough to admit of her being towed to her former station.

Wednesday, 23d.

From the untoward circumstance of the Floating-light's breaking adrift, the landing-master and his crew were fully employed with the Tender in this service, so that no materials could be got landed on the Bell Rock, either yesterday or to-day.

Thursday, 24th.

The wind was still from the westward, but had now moderated considerably, when 28 stones of the Smeaton's cargo were landed on the Rock, and 14 blocks were laid, with which the Twenty-third course was completed.

Friday, 25th.

Building operations concluded for the season.

To-day, the remainder of the Smeaton's cargo was landed, and the artificers laid 45 stones, which completed the Twenty-fourth course, reckoning above the first entire one, and the twenty-sixth above the Rock. This finished the solid part of the building, and terminated the height of the outward casing of granite, which is 31 feet 6 inches above the Rock or site of the foundation-stone, and about 17 feet above high-water of spring-tides. Being a particular crisis in the progress of the Light-house, the landing and laying of the last stone for the season was observed with the usual ceremonies.

Probable height of waves in free space.

Inducements for stopping the building operations.

From observations often made by the writer, in so far as such can be ascertained, it appears that no wave in the open seas, in an unbroken state, rises more than from 7 to 9 feet above the general surface of the ocean. The Bell Rock Light-house may therefore now be considered as from 8 to 10 feet above the weight of the waves; and, although the sprays and heavy seas have often been observed, in the present state of the building, to rise to the height of 50 feet, and fall with a tremendous noise on the Beacon-house, yet such seas were not likely to make any impression on a mass of solid masonry, containing about 1400 tons: its form being at the same time circular, and diminishing in diameter from the base to the top, as represented in the second year's work, Plate IX. It had for some time been a matter of doubt with the writer, whether he might not attempt to carry the building to the top of the stone stair-case, or 13 feet above the solid, the wall being here of the medium thickness of 6 feet. Several considerations, however, induced him to stop for the season with the completion of the solid, especially as it left the work in a more entire and defensible condition than if the door and part of the void had been built. One of the chief objections to continuing the operations, was the dread of encountering the gales experienced in former years early in the month of September. Another special obstacle was the difficulty and danger attending the guying or fixing of the present crane on the top of the building, which had now got to too great a height for its stability, as the guy-ropes which supported it were of the unmanageable length of about 80 feet. Even in the month of July, as before noticed, this state of things had become so obvious, that it was then determined to make the crane upon a new construction, which was to be kept in equilibrium by means of a balance-weight, and thus do away with the guy-ropes altogether. This crane had accordingly been prepared, but, like most machines upon a new construction, it was not found to operate in so satisfactory a manner as to warrant its immediate removal to the Bell Rock. It was therefore resolved rather to perfect the Balance-crane in the course of the winter months, and begin with a better prospect of success in the spring. The building operations were therefore brought to a conclusion; and the writer now took his leave of the Bell Rock till the ensuing season, excepting in so far as an occasional visit might occur.

Tuesday, 29th.

The Floating-light had been made fast to the spare moorings to-day, but those which had given way were again fished up, when she was towed back to her former station for the winter. It appeared that one of the shackles had got loose when she went adrift.

Wednesday, 30th.

Tender to continue her station, and Beacon to be occupied for a time.

From the 25th till the 30th, the seamen and artificers were busily employed, at the proper time of tide, in removing every thing from the Rock that was not farther wanted for the season, and in securing such things as were to be left. It was still necessary, however, to keep the Tender on the station, and also to occupy the Beacon-house, and to retain the floor of the open gallery for the smiths, as an additional strut or support was to be erected on the inside of each of the six principal beams of the Beacon. There were also 36 strong tie-bars of malleable-iron to be bolted to these beams, in a horizontal direction, as represented in Plate VIII., in lieu of the bracing-chains, which were not found to answer, for connecting the whole together.

Congratulations on the Artificers returning ashore after several months' absence.

These operations being arranged with Mr Francis Watt, as foreman, the whole of the artificers left the Rock at mid-day, when the Tender made sail for Arbroath, which she reached about 6 P. M. The vessel being decorated with colours, and having fired a salute of three guns on approaching the harbour, the work-yard artificers, with a multitude of people, assembled at the harbour, when mutual cheering and congratulations took place between those afloat and those on the quays. The Tender had now, with little exception, been six months on the station at the Bell Rock, and, during the last four months, few of the squad of builders had been ashore. In particular, Mr Peter Logan, the foreman, and Mr Robert Selkirk, principal builder, had never once left the Rock. The artificers having made good wages during their stay, like seamen upon a return-voyage, were extremely happy, and spent the evening with much innocent mirth and jollity.

1809, September.

Reflections on the very proper conduct of the Artificers.

In reflecting upon the state of matters at the Bell Rock, during the working months, when the writer was much with the artificers, nothing can equal the happy manner in which these excellent workmen spent their time. They always went from Arbroath to their arduous task cheering, and they generally returned in the same hearty state. While at the Rock, between the tides, they amused themselves in reading, fishing, music, playing cards, drafts, &c. or in sporting with one another. In the work-yard at Arbroath, the young men were almost, without exception, employed in the evening at school, in writing and arithmetic, and not a few were learning architectural drawing, for which they had every convenience and facility, and were, in a very obliging manner, assisted in their studies by Mr David Logan, Clerk of Works. It therefore affords the most pleasing reflections, to look back upon the pursuits of about 60 individuals, who, for years, conducted themselves, on all occasions, in a sober and rational manner.

Tuesday, 5th.

Tender again returns to her station at the Rock.

The operations at the Bell Rock for the remainder of the season being confined to the lower parts of the Beacon and Railways, were chiefly low-water works. The Tender had again been fitted out for her station, with a supply of provisions and necessaries for ten seamen and nineteen artificers, carrying with her supplies for the Floating-light and Beacon-house. At 11 A. M. she left Arbroath on this service; but the wind being S.E., it was not till Thursday the 7th, at 8 o'clock P. M. that she was made fast to her moorings.

Friday, 8th.

Experiences very bad weather.

At 6 o'clock this morning, Mr Watt, with eighteen artificers, landed on the Rock, commenced the work, and remained on the Beacon till Thursday, the 14th, when the vessel returned to Arbroath, having had extremely boisterous weather, and been twice obliged during that period to slip and leave her moorings. The prevailing winds were S.E., and the barometer oscillated between 29.5 and 29.60.

Monday, 17th.

Writer makes a trip to Flamborough-head Light-house.

Looking forward with confidence to the completion of the Bell Rock Light-house in the course of the next year, the writer, with much expectation, began to prepare every part of the establishment. He had early anticipated the necessity of fixing upon the description of light which would be necessary for characterising and distinguishing its range or compartment of the coast. With this in view, he had already made a train of experiments with shades of different coloured glass at Inchkeith Light-house, the result of which tended to shew that light passing through Red-coloured shades, alternating with periodic intervals of Darkness, and light of the Natural appearance, were the most effectual and suitable means for answering this purpose. Notwithstanding that his opinion on this subject was quite decided, he was still desirous of seeing the effect produced by the light of Flamborough-head, on the coast of Yorkshire, which was the first erection of this description on the British coast, and had, indeed, been only lately exhibited. That his observations might therefore be the more certain and complete, he embarked in the sloop Smeaton, on the 16th of this month, reached the Yorkshire coast on the 18th, and in the course of that night had the light in view, at various distances, both in clear and foggy weather, which extended the range of his remarks.

Experiences a sudden gale of wind.

In the course of this night, the wind blew fresh from the S.W., and an immense number of large vessels, chiefly in the Coal-trade, passed our small ship, which obliged the crew to keep a sharp look-out, to avoid the imminent danger of being run down, especially after the weather became thick. As our course lay close to Flamborough-head, we had several hairbreadth escapes; for the vessel had no sooner put about to avoid the land, than she was in danger of being run foul of by the passing vessels. In this situation things remained from about 1 o'clock on the morning of the 19th till 5, when, all of a sudden, the wind shifted, in the most surprising manner, from W.SW. to N.W., when the weather immediately clearing, was succeeded by a heavy gale, which forced our ship into Burlington-Bay, where she was safely anchored.

Storm described.

Great want of a Public Harbour on this coast.

As this was one of the most extraordinary tornadoes that the writer ever witnessed, he will endeavour to give some account of it. On the morning of the 18th, the day preceding the storm, when off Scarborough, he had requested to be called early, that he might see the coast, and enjoy the sight of the rising sun. The weather was then extremely fine, but the sun had a most piercingly brilliant appearance as it came into view upon the horizon; and he was assured by Captain Pool, that the general aspect of the heavens indicated a change of weather for the worse. In the course of the 18th the sky became cloudy, and the wind shifted from point to point, but prevailed chiefly from the S.W. At midnight, the weather was foggy, and the wind blew so fresh that the second reef was taken into the Smeaton's mainsail, and her topmast was struck. During the whole of the night, a fleet of vessels passed to the northward with a fair wind: these were understood to be colliers, in ballast, on their return voyage from London to Sunderland and Newcastle. At 5 A. M., however, while the Smeaton was lying-to, and waiting for day light, the wind shifted so suddenly to N.W., that it appeared to those below as if she had been upset, or had run upon a rock. In an instant all was bustle and confusion, till the vessel was got before the wind. The writer being in bed, immediately sprung up, and, on inquiring into the matter, the answer was, "It blows mere fire." The man at the helm, at the same time, pointed out a vessel in a disabled state, having been dismasted with the sudden change of the wind. Our small bark was fortunately in the opening of Burlington Bay, where she got to an anchor about 6 o'clock A. M. In the course of the day, not fewer than 160 vessels took shelter in the same place, many of them in a mutilated and dismantled state, having, to use a sea phrase, had their sails "split in ribbons;" and two were towed into the Bay, one of which, a large brig, already alluded to, was totally dismasted. Such a scene, arising from what may be termed a "Summer's Gale," had rarely been seen on this coast. Three vessels were also driven ashore and wrecked in Robin Hood Bay, a few miles north of Flamborough-head, and several others, as the writer afterwards learned, had been stranded on various parts of the coast, between Yarmouth Roads and the Shetland Islands. The want of some place of refuge for the extensive shipping of this coast in disastrous circumstances like the present, is very apparent. Had there been a harbour at Bridlington of sufficient capacity for large ships, perhaps not fewer than 100 sail would have refitted there, which were obliged to go to sea in a very crippled condition. Probably a Northern Ramsgate could not be better set down than here or somewhere upon the Norfolk coast.

Progress of the gale along the coast.

The writer is the more particular in noticing the anomalous state of the weather on this occasion, because the progress of this gale seems to have been comparatively slow. It appeared upon inquiry, from the date of various shipwrecks, to have visited Shetland on the evening of the 17th, Peterhead on the 18th, and Yarmouth at noon of that day. Now, as the distance between Sumburgh-head in Shetland and Yarmouth is about 430 miles, and if we allow 42 hours, as nearly as could be ascertained, for the progress of the wind between these points, it thus appears that the N.W. gale had not made its way against the S.W. wind, at a greater rate than about 10 miles per hour, though, from a train of experiments made in the neighbourhood of Leith, by Mr Andrew Waddell, F. R. S. E., and obligingly communicated to the writer, he has often observed the velocity of the wind to be about 60 miles per hour. But here we cannot enough regret the want of an efficient Anemometer, or instrument for measuring the force of the wind. Indeed, we hardly know any desideratum of more universal interest, for, notwithstanding the labours of Lind and others on this subject, from the want of a proper scale, we are still groping in the dark with the use of such indefinite terms, as "Light airs, inclining to calm," — "Fresh breezes," — "Fresh gales," — "Hard gales," — and "Very hard gales;" for it rarely happens that the sailor will admit the term "Storm" into his nomenclature.

Monday, 25th.

Mr B. Mills suggests distinguishing-lights with colours.

Having landed at Bridlington on the 20th, the writer had the pleasure of meeting with Mr Benjamin Mills, Collector of the Customs there, and agent for Flamborough-head Light-house. This gentleman accompanied the writer to the Light-house, about six miles distant. He was also at pains to explain the mode in which he had originally proposed the erection of a Distinguishing-light, from oil, with reflectors, for this station; as a Coal-light, formerly here, had long since been actually extinguished, on account of its being often mistaken for other lights on the coast. Mr Mills, observing the consequent disasters to shipping on these shores, proposed to construct a Revolving-light, distinguishable by means of colours, the machinery to be kept in motion by the agency of a neighbouring rill of water. Though the apparatus described to the writer seemed, upon the whole, not very applicable in practice, yet it is believed that Mr Mills was the first who suggested the idea of a distinguishing light, by means of coloured shades of glass. Some useful remarks having been made on the effects of Flamborough-head light, the writer sailed for the Firth of Forth, and reached Edinburgh on Monday the 25th.

Voyage to the Northern Lights.

Soon afterwards, he embarked at Greenock in the Light-house Yacht, on his annual voyage for the inspection of the Northern Light-houses, proceeding down the Clyde by the Mull of Kintyre, through the sounds of the Western Islands to Cape Wrath and the Orkneys, and from thence, along the eastern coast to the Firth of Forth, which he reached in the beginning of November; when he found the Bell Rock works about to be concluded.

1809, November.

State of the works when concluded for the season.

The complement of artificers which had been employed at the Rock, and lodged in the Beacon-house, from the period of completing the building operations in the month of August, till November, was twenty-four, who, as before noticed, were chiefly employed in fixing additional supports to the Beacon, and in extending and completing the Railways leading to the western creek. The works therefore, were only continued during the period of spring-tides; and in neap-tides the artificers returned to the work-yard. The plate-iron-forge, anvil, and other weighty articles, had been removed from the Beacon, and set up in a centrical position on the top of the building, where the smiths had been for some time at work: the rope-ladder of communication, which had been found so useful this season, was taken down, and every thing arranged in the most compact and orderly manner for the winter. In the course of these latter operations, the Tender had been twice obliged to slip her moorings, and leave the artificers upon the Beacon. At one of these times, she proceeded for Leith Roads, when Mr Watt stated that very bad weather had been experienced on the Beacon, and that, on several occasions, considerable alarm was felt, more particularly when the Tender was driven off her station, the artificers conceiving themselves in a more forlorn and helpless situation while she was out of view. Having made the necessary arrangements for the Rock being visited during the winter months, the writer left the works on the 8th November.

Wednesday, 22d.

The prop of the crane is demolished.

The Tender sailed to-day at 2 P. M., and next morning at 8, Mr Watt and five artificers were landed from two boats, and remained on the Rock till 11, when they had great difficulty in returning to the vessel, as the wind blew fresh from the N.E. The boats were no sooner hoisted on board, than, instead of sailing for Arbroath, the Tender was obliged to steer for Leith Roads, where she lay till the 29th: she then again made sail for Arbroath; but, from the severity of the weather, was put past her port, and went into Montrose. When the artificers landed, at this time, they found that the prop of the lower building-crane had been demolished during the late gales, and that the stones were scattered about the Rock in every direction, having done considerable damage to the contiguous Railways.

1809, December.

Thursday, 14th.

Artificers again visit the Rock. A large buoy has drifted.

The Tender sailed early in the morning of the 14th December for the Rock, having on board six artificers and twelve seamen, with a supply of provisions for the Floating-light. The artificers landed in the evening, and though the tide did not leave the Railways, every thing appeared to be in the same state as at their former visit. Two of the large stones which had formed the prop of the crane, had been thrown forcibly against the Beacon; but it was impossible, under the present circumstances, to effect their removal. The large buoy placed upon the spare moorings of the Floating-light, had drifted between the night of the 9th and the morning of the 10th December, the wind then blowing hard at S.SW.; and the two spar-beacons, attached to small mushroom anchors, used as a direction to the western creek, had also been washed away during the same gale. But, on the whole, no material damage had been sustained either at the Rock or on board of the Floating-light.

Saturday, 8th.

Artificers visit the Rock. Floating-light has had bad weather.

At 3 o'clock this morning, the Tender sailed for the Rock, and carried off a mushroom-anchor and chain, which were laid down as spare-moorings for the Floating-light, to be in readiness in case of her accidentally drifting, as the season would not admit of the old moorings being grappled for. On landing the artificers, they found every thing much in the same state as at their former visit, excepting two additional lengths of the Railways, extending to about eight feet, which had been broken by the loose stones of the prop of the crane. The crew of the Floating-light had also experienced some very bad weather, and on several occasions the ship is represented as having laboured much. In particular, on the 15th, with the wind at S.E., when in the act of swinging round to the tide, she was boarded by a heavy sea which unshipped the boats; and found its way below, in such quantity, that it extinguished the fires, and created considerable alarm; but the vessel, being strongly built, and well found in all her materials, sustained no damage.

Having now gone through the journal of the Bell Rock operations for the year 1809, we shall proceed with a narrative of the works for the year 1810, in the course of which the Bell Rock Light-house was completed.

CHAPTER VI.

PROGRESS AND COMPLETION OF THE WORKS IN THE
YEAR 1810.

1810, January.

The shipping establishment connected with the Bell Rock service during the winter of 1809 and 1810, consisted only of the Pharos Floating-light and Sir Joseph Banks Tender; the other vessels being laid up in ordinary. The latter vessel was appointed to carry artificers to the Rock at spring-tides, for the inspection of the works, and to repair any small damage that might occur at the Beacon-house and Railways. She also supplied the Floating-light with provisions and necessaries, and changed the crew in their respective turns of leave on shore. The landing-master, Captain Wilson, was the appointed commander of this vessel; but as he and part of his crew were occupied constantly at the Rock during the building-season, they were occasionally relieved from the unpleasant duty of the Pharos, by such of the officers and seamen belonging to the other ships in the Light-house service, as were kept in pay during the winter months.

Friday 5th.

The Tender visits the Floating-light and Bell Rock.

Five artificers from the work-yard at Arbroath were allotted for visiting the Bell Rock, with Mr Francis Watt, the foreman mill-wright. They accordingly sailed on one of their trips on the 5th of January at 12 noon; but the Tender did not reach the Floating-light till next morning at 1 o'clock. The weather being moderate, a supply of fuel, water, and provisions, was immediately sent on board, when Captain Taylor, with Mr William Reid his mate, and four seamen, shifted to the Tender, and Captain Calder of the Light-house Yacht, with John Blackwood his mate, and four seamen, took their station in the Floating-light. The Tender then stood towards the Rock, when the artificers landed with the boats at 9, and remained till 12 noon, and in the afternoon, the vessel returned and got into the harbour of Arbroath; Mr Watt reporting that every thing was in good order.

Saturday 20th.

In the same manner, and with similar success, the Floating-light and Bell Rock were visited on the 20th of this month.

February.

Sunday, 11th.

Artificers cannot land on the Rock.

The Tender was in a state of readiness for the spring-tides, on the 5th of February, but the winds, though westerly, were so stormy, that she could not go to sea. The weather having moderated on the 11th, though then the period of neap-tides, she went off to change the crew of the Floating-light, and supply that ship with necessaries; and afterwards stood towards the Rock; but as it did not appear above water, a landing could not be effected, though, from the general aspect of things, the Beacon and Building were concluded to be in good order, and the vessel returned to Arbroath on the afternoon of Monday the 12th.

Wednesday, 21st.

Still prevented from landing.

The Tender sailed this morning at 5 o'clock, with a fine breeze at west, having on board the usual complement of artificers, a change of crew, and a supply of provisions for the Floating-light. At 9 she got off to the Rock, but the wind, by this time, blew so fresh, that it was found impracticable to land; every thing, however, about the Building and Beacon appeared to be in good order. At 11, the Tender stood towards the Floating-light, and, after considerable difficulty, the provisions were got on board, and a transfer made of the crews; when the Tender sailed for Arbroath, and got into the harbour at 4 P. M., having been only about eleven hours in making this trip.

1810, March.

Sunday, 11th.

A landing is effected. Large stones drifted upon the Rock.

At 4 o'clock this morning, the Tender sailed for the Rock with the wind at N. by E., when the artificers made a landing at half-past 10, and remained till 1 A. M., having found every thing in good order, excepting some parts of the Railways, which had received damage from the movement of a large drift-stone or traveller, estimated to contain upwards of one ton of rock, which was broken and removed, to prevent its doing more damage. The building, as high as the daily rise of the tide, was now covered with a strong growth of sea-weed. On the course, however, immediately above the Rock, the fuci had been prevented from taking root from the chips of stone which continually washed about the building. Some holes in the Rock, near the Beacon, which, in the year 1807, had been filled with ruble-building, a species of work rather unexpectedly found to withstand the force of the sea, had in the late gales been shaken loose, and laid open.—In the course of the gales of the 25th, 26th, and 27th of March, as is supposed, two large drift-stones or travellers had done considerable injury to the Railways. It also appeared, from certain marks upon the beams of the Beacon, at the height of about five feet above the Rock, that these stones, containing from seven to ten cubic feet each, or upwards of half a ton, had actually been lifted by the sea and driven with force against the Beacon. In the course of these gales, also, the large cask-buoy, used as the moorings of the Tender, had broken adrift. During these gales, the Floating-light rolled very heavily, and had shipped several great seas, but nothing of any consequence happened in the way of damage to the vessel or her appurtenances.

Beacon now rendered very secure.

As the finishing of the Light-house, in the course of next season, depended wholly upon the stability of the Beacon, every possible attention was paid to its safety; and it was most satisfactory to learn, by Mr Watt's report, that every thing about it continued in good order. On almost every visit during the two former winters, some of the bracing-chains were found in a broken state; but since the months of September and October last, when they were removed, and replaced with thirty-six great bars of iron bolted to the principal beams, as shown in Plate VIII., every thing had remained in a state of connected firmness.

Progress of the works at Arbroath.

The hewing or cutting of the several courses, forming the void of the Light-house, was also in great forwardness in the work-yard at Arbroath; and by the latter end of the month of April, the Forty-fourth course, forming part of the store-room, shewn in the section of Plate XVI., was laid on the platform, and ready for shipping to the Rock. The burning and pounding of the Aberthaw lime, and the preparation of other materials, were also going on.

1810, April.

Landing on the Rock precarious in Winter.

The season, though now advanced to the month of April, was still boisterous. The day, however, was getting long, and the influence of the sun began to be felt in checking the frosts, which often stopped both the quarrying operations and the stone-cutters. The lengthening of the day, as well as moderate weather, was a great regulating circumstance in the Bell Rock works; for, during the winter months, only one low-water tide occurred with day-light; and, indeed, in the depth of winter, there may be said to be no very favourable opportunity of landing on the Rock, as low-water at new and full moon happens here about 8 o'clock, which renders the chance of landing extremely uncertain and precarious.

Retrospective view of the works. Mylnefield Quarry.

Previously to entering upon the operations of the season 1810, it may be proper, in this place, to take a retrospective view of the various departments of the work. The granite courses of the Bell Rock Light-house having been completed, for a considerable time, it was only the sandstone quarries that were to be attended to. As formerly noticed, the stone of Mylnefield, like that of most quarries which lie in strata or alternate beds, is liable to split and become useless, from the effects of frost, owing to the natural sap or moisture which they contain. Water, being unlike other bodies which follow the general law of contracting in volume with a reduction of temperature, is found, on the contrary, to encrease in bulk at the moment of congelation, producing the most surprising effects in rending rocks, even with an explosive force. In sandstone quarries, therefore, the work is usually suspended during the months of December, January, February and March, when the frost happens to be intense, as was the case in the winter of 1809–1810, when the thermometer occasionally fell so low as the 17th degree of Fahrenheit. Notwithstanding every precaution in the work-yard at Arbroath, by covering the quarried materials with straw and brushwood, many excellent and valuable stones were lost by the intenseness of the frost. Such, however, was the desire of getting early forward with the work, in order to insure the completion of the building operations in the favourable part of the season, that the writer took the earliest measures for getting an additional supply of stones from Mylnefield; and, by the beginning of the month of April, the Smeaton and Patriot, together with the hired sloop Alexander, were loaded and sent to Arbroath.

Craigleith Quarry.

From this description of the nature of the stone of Mylnefield, it became necessary, for the furtherance of the upper parts of the Light-house during the winter months, that they should be prepared of stone which would admit of being worked without much risk of injury during frosty weather. For the cornice of the building, and the parapet of the light-room, the writer, therefore, made choice of the Liver-rock of the Craigleith Quarry, well known for its durability and beauty, and for its property of not being liable to be affected by frost. By this means also, the iron-work or frame of the Light-room might be fitted to the masonry on the spot where it was to be prepared, which would thereby lessen the actual work upon the Rock. Another advantage attending this arrangement, was the opportunity it afforded of making practical trial of the Balance-crane, with which the masonry of the ensuing season was to be built, as it had been found necessary to make several alterations on its construction.

State of the Works at Edinburgh.

The use of a piece of vacant ground was accordingly got at Greenside, contiguous to the author's house, in Edinburgh, where a number of masons were employed, at the sight of Mr Peter Logan, foreman builder. A very considerable difficulty was, however, experienced in procuring so many principal stones of the liver-rock, of the description and dimensions necessary for the cornice and balcony; the stones of which also formed the Light-room floor in one length, as will be understood by examining Plates XIII. and XVI. But, as these works commenced at Edinburgh in the latter end of October 1809, they were completed early in the month of March 1810, and the whole of this critical and difficult part of the building was then ready for shipping to the Bell Rock. The several compartments of the Light-room were now also in progress. The sheets of silver-plated copper for the reflectors having been ordered from Messrs Boulton and Watt, — the glass from the British Plate-Glass Company, — the cast-iron sash-frames from Mr John Patterson of the Edinburgh Foundery, — while the construction of the reflectors and reflecting-apparatus, together with the framing of the whole Light-room and its appurtenances, were executed under the immediate directions of Mr Thomas Smith, the writer's predecessor, who had now retired from the more active duties of engineer to the Light-house Board.

Practical conclusions about the period of completing the Works, and mode of distinguishing the Light.

Having, in the course of the two last seasons, landed and built upwards of 1400 tons of stone upon the Bell Rock, while the work was low in the water, and before the Beacon was habitable, and finding that it did not now require more than about 700 tons to complete the masonry, the writer concluded, that, barring accidents of a very untoward nature, there was every prospect of the Light-house being finished in the course of the ensuing season. A question, of much importance, however, still remained in some measure undetermined, regarding the characteristic description of the light most suitable for the Bell Rock, so as to render it easily distinguishable from all others upon the coast. There being Stationary-lights already in the Firth of Forth; this mode could not be adopted for the Bell Rock. Revolving-lights had also lately been erected upon the Fearn Islands, the most contiguous Light-house-station to the southward, as will be seen from the General Chart of the coast in Plate III. Considering, therefore, the liability of the mariner to mistake the appearance of lights in stormy weather, or from an error in his course in returning from a distant voyage, it was of the last importance that the Bell Rock Light-house should be easily distinguishable. The most suitable means for accomplishing this seemed to be by the exhibition of different colours from the same Light-room. The only colour which had yet been found to answer, was produced by interposing shades of red glass before the reflectors. But this was the colour used for distinguishing the Light of Flamborough-head, on the Yorkshire coast, and, though about 169 miles to the southward, it would still have been desirable to have avoided the same colour. A train of experiments was therefore made from Inchkeith Light-house, with plates of glass, coloured red, green, orange, yellow, blue, and purple, procured from Birmingham and London. These were fitted to the reflectors at Inchkeith, within view of the writer's windows in Edinburgh. The Tender was likewise appointed to cruise, that more distant observations might be made, for ascertaining the effect of these coloured shades. But after the most full and satisfactory trials, the red colour was found to be the only one applicable to this purpose. In tolerably clear weather, the light of one reflector tinged red, alternating with a light of the natural appearance, with intervals of darkness, was easily distinguishable at the distance of eight or nine miles; while the other colours rendered the light opaque, being hardly distinguishable to the naked eye at more than two or three miles. After various trials and observations made in this manner, both on land and at sea, the writer at length resolved on recommending the use of red, as the only colour suitable for this purpose; and, in order to vary the light as much as possible from that of Flamborough-head, a square Reflector-frame was adopted at the Bell Rock, with two of its faces or sides having red coloured shades, and the other two exhibiting lights of the natural appearance. At Flamborough-head, the Reflector-frame is triangular, and on one side it is furnished with red coloured shades, while the other two sides exhibit lights of the natural appearance. The design at the Bell Rock, on the contrary, was to exhibit a light tinged red, alternating with one of the natural appearance; and, upon this principle, the apparatus was put in a state of preparation.

1810, March.

State of the Works at Arbroath.

In the work-yard at Arbroath things were going forward very prosperously, at the sight of Mr David Logan, clerk of works. The hewing or preparation of the stones for the Light-house was now advanced to within about eight courses of the cornice, which, with the parapet, as already observed, was all set up at Edinburgh, and ready for being shipped when wanted at the Rock. A kiln of the Aberthaw limestone having already been calcined, was partly reduced to the state of powder, and put up into casks, as formerly. The operation of pounding the lime was very tedious and unpleasant, being performed by labourers upon a stone-bench in the lime-house, where it was reduced chiefly by means of friction, between the bench and stones, managed by hand. Due proportions of pozzolano-earth and clean sharp sand were made up in casks, and the oaken trenails and wedges in bundles; but the supply wanted of these materials was, in future, to be comparatively trifling. The building being now considerably above the rise of the tide, the use of mortar was less, while the system of trenailing and wedging was to be discontinued, after the building had reached the top of the stone staircase, or to the height of 13 feet above the solid. The several implements connected with the building operations being also laid to hand, nothing was now required but good weather and favourable tides, to proceed with the works at the Rock.

Gangway or Bridge for the Rock.

1810, April.

Among the preparations at Arbroath for the furtherance of the work at the Bell Rock, was the construction of a gangway or bridge of timber between the Beacon and the Building, instead of the Rope-ladder employed with so much effect last season, as will be understood by examining the second and third years' work, represented in Plate IX. This more stable and commodious way of communicating with the works, was also to be useful as a stage for raising the building materials, instead of the lower crane, the stool or prop of which had become too low, and, as before noticed, had been washed away by the sea in the course of last month. This bridge consisted of two principal beams of Memel timber, measuring 44 feet in length, 6 inches in thickness, and 13 inches in depth. At one end these beams were to abut against the principal beams of the Beacon, and to be strongly bolted to them; at the opposite end, one was to be rested on the sole or instep of the door, while the other was to be let 6 inches into a hole cut into the upper granite course of the Light-house. They were placed 7 feet apart, and formed a roadway of 6 feet in breadth between the rails, which was strongly bound in a lateral direction with cross framing mortised into the principal beams, and otherwise fixed with screw-bolts. The bridge was further to be supported by four diagonal spur-beams, which met in pairs on each side, at the middle of the roadway, and there formed king-posts, to steady and support it. A crab or winch-machine was to be placed upon it, for raising the stones at once from the rock to the level of the top of the solid part of the building.

Wednesday, 18th.

Operations commence for the season. Wooden Bridge is erected.

After making the experiments relative to the distinguishing of the light, the Tender sailed from Leith Roads on the morning of Tuesday, the 3d of April, and got into Arbroath on the 6th, where she lay. Being fitted out for the Rock, with a sufficient stock of water and provisions, and having also on board the beams and apparatus for the wooden bridge, she sailed at 1 o'clock this morning, with eleven masons, three joiners, and two blacksmiths, together with Mr Francis Watt, foreman, in all seventeen artificers, who were to be employed during the ensuing spring-tides, in erecting the bridge between the Beacon and Building. At 3 P. M. she was made fast to the new moorings, which had been laid down for her in lieu of those which had drifted on the 26th of March; but the weather was then so boisterous, that no landing could be made on the Rock till the following morning, at 6 o'clock, when they commenced the operations of the season by laying the deals of the mortar-gallery, or lowest floor of the Beacon. Although the weather continued to be extremely boisterous till the 23d, the Tender's marine barometer oscillating between 29.05 and 29.60, yet the wind being westerly, the artificers were enabled to pursue their operations by landing daily; for, upon this occasion, the Beacon was not taken possession of, and they returned at night to the Tender. On the 24th the weather became very fine; the barometer remaining for several days at about 30.10. The work now proceeded with so much alacrity and dispatch, that by the 28th the fixing of the bridge was completed, and the Tender returned with all hands to Arbroath.

Monday, 23d.

Charles Gray gets one of his fingers severely bruised.

While the Tender waited the operations of the artificers at the Rock, the Smeaton made two trips to it, and laid down six sets of moorings with their float-ing-buoys, so that every thing was now in a state of readiness for the commence-ment of the works. When unloading these moorings, Charles Gray, a seaman, un-fortunately got one of his fingers so bruised between the hatchway of the ship and a mushroom-anchor, that it was found necessary to amputate part of it.

1810, May.

Tuesday, 1st.

The Writer proceeds for the Rock, to begin building for the season.

The Smeaton having come to Leith for the Balance-crane, the writer sailed this afternoon with her for the Bell Rock, to commence the building operations for the season. The weather, for the last eight days, had been extremely stormy, and, though still unfavourable, yet, being moderate, hopes were entertained that she would soon make her way down the Firth of Forth. After beating to windward for a day and a night, however, she was obliged to bear away for Burntisland Roads, where he left the vessel, to pursue his journey by land to Arbroath, accompanied by Mr James Dove, foreman-smith, to whom particularly the change in the mode of travelling was a great relief, as, notwithstanding his having had considerable prac-tice at sea, he was still a great martyr to sickness, and even felt a dislike for every thing connected with a ship, which was strongly marked by the following trifling occurrence. On leaving the Smeaton, Captain Pool, presenting the bread-basket to Mr Dove, observed, that, although he could not eat on board, he might perhaps be thankful of a biscuit when he got on shore; on which Mr Dove gravely replied, that "it would be long to the day before he would be thankful for a sea-biscuit." The object of his journey at this time was to fit up the Balance-crane on the top of the building, and to superintend its operation for a time on the Rock. This useful implement had been constructed in the course of last season, but was not then found to be in a sufficiently serviceable state. It was accordingly new-modelled, and, though an opportunity had been afforded of making trial of it at Edinburgh, in raising the weighty stones of the cornice and balcony of the Light-house, yet the writer wished Mr Dove also to fit it at the Bell Rock. They reached Arbroath on the evening of the 3d.

Saturday, 5th.

The Tender is ready for sea.

The Smeaton arrived at Arbroath to-day with the Balance-crane, which was immediately put on board of the Tender, now ready to proceed for the Rock with the first good weather. The Smeaton then took on board the stone ballast, and platform, laid in her hold for the greater conveniency of stowing and discharging the prepared stones of the building. The wind had now changed to the S.W., and hopes were entertained of a return of good weather. But this being the period of neap-tides, and considering that it might be three or four months before some of the artificers again returned to the shore, as the Beacon was now habitable, it was intimated to them on Saturday, that the Tender would not sail till Monday. They accordingly attended church to-day, with their wonted decency of deportment.

Monday, 7th.

Writer sails with the Artificers for the Rock.

The artificers having been warned to take their quarters on board of the Tender last night, the writer sailed this morning from Arbroath at half-past 2, accompanied by Mr Peter Logan, foreman builder, Mr Francis Watt, foreman mill-wright, and Mr James Dove, foreman smith, together with sixteen artificers, and the regular crew of the vessel, in all counting thirty-two persons; but the Tender having the Hedderwick praam-boat in tow, went slowly off. At 12 noon the Floating-light was hailed, when Captain Wilson, the landing-master, came on board, to take his station for the season, and at 1 P. M. the Tender was made fast to her moorings at the Bell Rock. The praam-boat was immediately hauled alongside, and the apparatus of the Balance-crane laid upon her deck, when she was towed to her moorings, there being too much sea at this time, for attempting to land upon the Rock. As the barometer stood at 30.04, hopes were entertained that the weather would soon improve.

Tuesday, 8th.

Landing impracticable.

The wind was at east to-day, and the sea still broke so heavily upon the Rock, that no landing could be made. At high-water, the spray was observed to fly considerably above the building, perhaps not less than 20 feet, in all about 50 feet above the Rock, while the seas were raging and breaking among the beams of the Beacon with much violence.

Wednesday, 9th.

The Praam-boats ride easily.

The same boisterous state of the weather still continued, and the sea-swell was nothing abated to-day, so that no landing could yet be made upon the Rock. The landing-master, however, went in a boat, and examined the Praam-boat at her moorings, where every thing was found in good order. It is here worthy of remark, that while the Tender and Floating-light rolled much, and occasionally shipped pretty heavy seas, the praam, with a cargo of about three tons on board, was perfectly dry upon deck, and to use the seamen's expression, "rode as easily as an old shoe."

Thursday, 10th.

State of the Building.

The wind had shifted to-day to W.NW., when the writer, with considerable difficulty, was enabled to land upon the Rock, for the first time this season, at 10 A. M. Upon examining the state of the Building, and Apparatus in general, he had the satisfaction to find every thing in good order. The mortar in all the joints was perfectly entire. The building, now 30 feet in height, was thickly coated with fuci to the height of about 15 feet, calculating from the Rock: on the eastern side, indeed, the growth of sea-weed was observable to the full height of 30 feet, and even on the top or upper bed of the last laid course, especially towards the eastern side, it had germinated, so as to render walking upon it somewhat difficult. The smith's forge, which had been removed from the mortar-gallery to the top of the Building, in the month of September last, to give more accommodation to the works of the joiners, was left there for the season,—the bellows excepted, which were kept under cover in the Beacon throughout the winter; and, it is not a little remarkable, that, although the sea had risen to a considerable height, and fallen in great quantities upon the top of the building; yet such was the centrical position of the forge, that it remained quite entire: even the spar of timber, and the small cords which had been stretched for steadying it, and forming an awning of about 8 feet in diameter, for sheltering the smith, were also still in their places. This was a proof that no very heavy seas had broken so high as the top of the solid, otherwise the forge and the apparatus for supporting the awning, must have long since been swept away by the breach of the sea.

State of the Beacon.

The Beacon-house was in a perfectly sound state, and apparently just as it had been left in the month of November. But the tides being neap, the lower parts, particularly where the beams rested on the Rock, could not now be seen. The great iron-bars, however, which measure 3 inches square, and from 7 to 9 feet in length, stretching between the principal beams, in place of the bracing chains, which were found constantly liable to break and unscrew, were in view, and in good order. The whole frame of this fabric was now in a firm and secure state. The floor of the mortar-gallery having been already laid down by Mr Watt and his men on a former visit, was merely soaked with the sprays; but the joisting-beams which supported it had, in the course of the winter, been covered with a fine downy conferva, produced by the range of the sea. They were also a good deal whitened with the mute of the cormorant and other sea-fowls, which had roosted upon the Beacon in winter. Upon ascending to the apartments, it was found that the motion of the sea had thrown open the door of the cook-house: this was only shut with a simple latch, that, in case of shipwreck at the Bell Rock, the mariner might find ready access to the shelter of this forlorn habitation, where a supply of provisions was kept; and being within two miles and a half of the Floating-light, a signal could readily be observed, when a boat might be sent to his relief as soon as the weather permitted. An arrangement for this purpose formed one of the Instructions on board of the Floating-light, but happily no instance occurred for putting it in practice. The hearth or fire-place of the cook-house was built of brick, in as secure a manner as possible, to prevent accident from fire; but some of the plaster work had shaken loose, from its damp state, and the tremulous motion of the Beacon in stormy weather. The writer next ascended to the floor which was occupied by the cabins of himself, and his assistants, which were in tolerably good order, having only a damp and musty smell. The barrack for the artificers over all, was next visited: it had now a very dreary and deserted appearance, when its former thronged state was recollected. In some parts, the water had come through the boarding, and had discoloured the lining of green cloth, but it was, nevertheless, in a good habitable condition. While the seamen were employed in landing a stock of provisions, a few of the artificers set to work, with great eagerness, to sweep and clean the several apartments. The exterior of the Beacon was, in the mean time, examined, and found in perfect order. The painting, though it had a somewhat blanched appearance, adhered firmly both on the sides and roof, and only two or three panes of glass were broken in the cupola, which had either been blown out by the force of the wind, or perhaps broken by sea-fowl.

Thursday, 10th.

State of the Timber Bridge.

Having, on this occasion, continued upon the building and beacon a considerable time, after the tide had begun to flow, the artificers were occupied in removing the forge from the top of the building, to which the gangway or wooden bridge gave great facility; and, although it stretched or had a span of 42 feet, its construction was extremely simple, while the roadway was perfectly firm and steady. In returning from this visit to the Rock, every one was pretty well soused in spray, before reaching the Tender at 2 o'clock P. M., where things awaited the landing party in as comfortable a way as such a situation would admit.

Friday, 11th.

Balance-crane landed. Position of the Entrance-door.

The wind was still easterly, accompanied with rather a heavy swell of sea, for the operations in hand. A landing was, however, made this morning, when the artificers were immediately employed in scraping the sea-weed off the upper course of the building, in order to apply the moulds of the first course of the staircase, that the joggle-holes might be marked off in the upper course of the solid, which, as formerly, had not been done to the finishing course of the season. This was also necessary previously to the writer's fixing the position of the entrance-door, which was regulated chiefly by the appearance of the growth of the sea-weed on the building, indicating the direction of the heaviest seas, on the opposite side of which the door was placed. The landing-master's crew succeeded in towing into the creek on the western side of the Rock, the praam-boat, with the balance-crane, which had now been on board of the praam for five days. The several pieces of this machine having been conveyed along the Railways upon the waggons, to a position immediately under the bridge, were elevated to its level, or thirty feet above the Rock, in the following manner. A chain-tackle was suspended over a pulley from the cross-beam, connecting the tops of the king-posts of the bridge, which was worked by a winch-machine, with wheel, pinion and barrel, round which last the chain was wound. This apparatus was placed on the Beacon-side of the bridge, at the distance of about twelve feet from the cross beam and pulley in the middle of the bridge. Immediately under the cross-beam a hatch was formed in the roadway of the bridge, measuring 7 feet in length and 5 feet in breadth, made to shut with folding boards like a double-door, through which stones and other articles were raised; the folding-doors were then let down, and the stone or load was gently lowered upon a waggon which was wheeled on railway tracks towards the Light-house. In this manner, the several castings of the balance-crane were got up to the top of the solid of the building.

Artificers take possession of the Beacon.

The several apartments of the Beacon-house having been cleaned out and supplied with bedding, a sufficient stock of provisions was put into the store, when Peter Fortune, formerly noticed, lighted his fire in the Beacon, for the first time this season. Sixteen artificers, at the same time, mounted to their barrack-room, and the foremen of the works also took possession of their cabin, all heartily rejoiced at getting rid of the trouble of boating, and the sickly motion of the Tender. The boats had landed on the Rock this morning at 9, and the writer left it again with the landing-master and his crew at 3 P. M., and went on board of the Tender for the night, after having seen some progress made in setting up the balance-crane.

Smeaton arrives with the first cargo.

The Smeaton having been loaded at Arbroath with the first cargo of stones, consisting of thirty-eight blocks of the Twenty-seventh course, got to her moorings at the Bell Rock this morning, and was made fast, though not without considerable difficulty. But, nothing could be done towards delivering her until the balance-crane was got into a working state.

Saturday, 12th.

No communication with the Rock.

The wind was at E.NE., blowing so fresh, and accompanied with so much sea, that no stones could be landed to-day. The people on the Rock, however, were busily employed in screwing together the balance-crane, cutting out the joggle-holes in the upper course, and preparing all things for commencing the building operations.

Sunday, 13th.

Balance-crane ready for use.

The weather still continues boisterous, although the barometer has all the while stood at about 30 inches. Towards evening, the wind blew so fresh at E. by S., that the boats both of the Smeaton and Tender were obliged to be hoisted in, and it was feared that the Smeaton would have to slip her moorings. The people on the Rock were seen busily employed, and had the balance-crane apparently ready for use, but no communication could be had with them to-day.

Theory of the land and sea breeze exemplified.

The wind had now prevailed long from the eastward, and it was remarked on board of the Tender, that, in moderate weather, it generally inclined from the northward in the mornings, and from the eastward and southward, as the sun advanced to the meridian; in this respect, resembling the land and sea breezes, familiar to those acquainted with tropical climates. This phenomenon is accounted for, by considering the state of the inland country, where the Grampian-hills lie about 20 miles northward from the coast, thickly covered with snow. The winds, therefore, in the early part of the day, generally came from these colder regions, towards the milder and somewhat more rare atmosphere of the sea. But in the after part of the day, the heat of the sun, acting more powerfully upon the arable lands and objects in the fore-ground of this mountainous range, rarified the air more highly upon the shores than on the sea, which produced a tendency in the winds to blow towards the land. Extending this view of the subject to the great tracts of snow-covered mountains, in the north-eastern districts of Europe, it is natural to suppose that the current of the winds will be from these colder regions towards the expanse of the Atlantic Ocean. Hence the prevailing winds in the spring of the year are from the eastward, in their passage across Great Britain to the Atlantic.

Monday, 14th.

Smeaton slips her moorings.

The wind continued to blow so fresh, and the Smeaton rode so heavily with her cargo, that at noon a signal was made for her getting under way, when she stood towards Arbroath; and, on board of the Tender, we are still without any communication with the people on the Rock; where the sea was seen breaking over the top of the building in great sprays, and ranging with much agitation among the beams of the Beacon.

Tuesday 15th.

Returns to the Rock.

The Smeaton did not go into Arbroath last night, as the appearance of a northerly or land breeze induced the active spirit of Captain Pool to stand off again for the Bell Rock; but he had no sooner reached his moorings at 5 o'clock this morning, than the wind again shifted to the S.E., and he could not get hold of the ring of the Floating-buoy of his moorings, and was, therefore, obliged to return again towards Arbroath. There was still no communication between the Tender and the Rock, as the sea continued to run very heavily upon it.

Wednesday, 16th.

Is driven to Leith Roads.

The wind had shifted to the N.E. this morning, and hopes were entertained that it might take a more northerly direction, but it continued without change, and for two or three days past the Barometer had been falling, and was now at 29.50. It was, therefore, still impossible to land upon the Rock. The appearance of the weather brought the Smeaton out of the harbour, Captain Pool having become very impatient to get his first cargo landed; but, on his arrival, instead of being able to make fast to his moorings, the writer found it necessary to direct him to proceed for Leith Roads, as the proper place for the vessel in the present state of the weather.

Thursday 17th.

Patriot sent to the quarry for the last cargo of stones.

People at the Rock experience boisterous weather.

The Smeaton had no sooner reached the Firth last night, and anchored in Leith Roads, than the wind came round to the north, and Pool, without delay, once more weighed anchor and sailed for the Bell Rock, which he reached this morning. The Patriot, at the same time, came off from Arbroath with water, fuel, and provisions for the supply of the Floating-light, the Tender, and Beacon-house, and after discharging these, she proceeded for Mylnefield Quarry, for the last cargo of stones wanted for the Bell Rock Light-house. On this trip the writer had great pleasure in dispatching her, as this state of things greatly narrowed the operations. The wind, in the course of the day, had shifted from north to west; the sea being also considerably less, a boat landed on the Rock at 6 P. M., for the first time since the 11th, with the provisions and water brought off by the Patriot. The inhabitants of the Beacon were all well, but tired above measure for want of employment, as the balance-crane and apparatus was all in readiness. Under these circumstances, they felt no less desirous of the return of good weather than those afloat, who were continually tossed with the agitation of the sea. The writer, in particular, felt himself almost as much fatigued and worn out as he had been at any period since the commencement of the work. The very backward state of the weather at so advanced a period of the season, unavoidably created some alarm, lest he should be overtaken with bad weather, at a late period of the season, with the building operations in an unfinished state. These apprehensions were, no doubt, rather increased by the inconveniences of his situation afloat, as the Tender rolled and pitched excessively at times. This being also his first off-set for the season, every bone of his body felt sore, with preserving a sitting posture, while he endeavoured to pass away the time in reading; as for writing it was wholly impracticable. He had several times entertained thoughts of leaving the station for a few days, and going into Arbroath with the Tender till the weather should improve; but, as the artificers had been landed on the Rock, he was averse to this at the commencement of the season, knowing also that he would be equally uneasy in every situation, till the first cargo was landed; and he, therefore, resolved to continue at his post until this should be effected.

State of lower parts of the Beacon. Effects of marine vermes.

At low-water to-day, an opportunity was afforded of examining the lower parts of the Beacon-house. The kneed Bats, or great iron stanchions, employed for fixing the principal beams to the Rock, which will be seen by examining Plate VIII., were found in good order, without the least appearance of movement or decay. The same observation is also applicable to the exterior of the principal beams of the Beacon, wherever the charring of the timber and successive coats of boiling pitch had been applied; but at the foot or sole of the respective beams, where they rested upon a site cut for them upon the rock, where the pitch could not be applied, the òniscus or vermis so destructive to timber exposed to the wash of the sea, had made a considerable impression, and the beams were found to be hollowed out. In several instances, they even stood clear of the Rock, depending only upon the stanchions and bolts for their support. The circumstance of these vermes attacking the sole of the beams, had not been anticipated, otherwise preventive means might have been adopted, by sheathing them with copper, especially where they rested on the Rock.

Friday, 18th.

23 blocks of stone landed and raised with the new tackle.

The company of artificers, lodged on the Beacon, having been increased from sixteen to twenty-two, their time hang very heavily on their hands, till the stones were landed on the Rock. The wind being now N.W., the sea was considerably run down, and this morning at 5 o'clock, the landing-master's crew, thirteen in number, left the Tender; and having now no detention with the landing of artificers, they proceeded to unmoor the Hedderwick Praam-boat, and towed her alongside of the Smeaton; and in the course of the day, twenty-three blocks of stone, three casks of pozzolano, three of sand, three of lime, and one of Roman cement, together with three bundles of trenails, and three of wedges, were all landed on the Rock and raised to the top of the building, by means of the tackle suspended from the cross-beam on the middle of the bridge. The stones were then moved along the bridge on the waggon to the building, within reach of the balance-crane, with which they were laid in their respective places on the building. The masons immediately thereafter proceeded to bore the trenail holes into the course below, and otherwise to complete the one in hand. When the first stone was to be suspended by the balance-crane, the bell on the Beacon was rung, and all the artificers and seamen were collected on the building. Three hearty cheers were given while it was lowered into its place, and the steward served round a glass of rum, when success was drank to the further progress of the building.

One of the stones in danger from the breaking of a bolt.

Having thus had the satisfaction of finding that the bridge and its apparatus answered every purpose for raising the materials; that the balance-crane was no less suitable for building the stones, which, from their dove-tailed form, as before noticed, required that they should be slipped or laid perpendicularly into their sites; and the artificers being now comfortably lodged in the Beacon-house, there hardly remained a doubt that the Bell Rock Light-house would be completed in the course of the current year. It often happens, however, that accidents occur on the first trial of machinery; and, accordingly, in shifting the wheel and pinion work of the winch-machine upon the bridge, from the single to the double-purchase, in order to raise a pretty heavy stone, the bolt of the bush gave way, just as the stone had attained its full height, and was about to be lowered on the bridge-waggon, to be moved within the sphere of the balance-crane. The fall of the stone, though only from a height of 8 or 9 inches, communicated a sudden shock throughout the Beacon-house, and produced an alarm among the workmen for the moment. Had this accident occurred before the waggon was wheeled under the stone, in all probability it would have killed some of those who were at work below upon the Rock; besides breaking the stone and the railway, which must have stopped the work for a considerable time, until another stone could have been prepared and sent from the work-yard at Arbroath.

Saturday, 19th.

15 stones landed.

The Smeaton having been completely discharged last night, sailed at 10 P. M. for Arbroath, to load a second cargo for the Bell Rock. The Patriot had towed off the Dickie Praam-boat to-day, being of a somewhat smaller size, and more handy than the Fernie, which now lay in ordinary, at Arbroath, in case of accident to the Hedderwick or Dickie. The wind, however, being rather unsteady, it was feared that no materials would have been landed; but Captain Wilson, with his usual dexterity and skill, succeeded in transporting fifteen stones, which were raised to the top of the building, by means of the tackle on the bridge, and built by the balance-crane with wonderful facility.

Smeaton makes rapid trips.

This morning at 1 o'clock, the Smeaton got into Arbroath, when Mr Kennedy, engineer's clerk, had the artificers immediately called, who loaded her with the Twenty-eighth course of the building, consisting of thirty-three pieces of stone, besides six casks of pozzolano, six casks of lime, six casks of sand, four bundles of trenails, four bundles of wedges, and eight stone joggles, together with four logs of timber, one Railway-waggon, and a supply of water, beer, fuel and provisions for the Beacon-house. At 2 P. M. she sailed again for the Bell Rock, and reached it at 5, to the surprise of every one, Captain Pool being no less active in his trips than Mr Kennedy was zealous in the dispatch given at the work-yard.

Sunday, 20th.

Prayers first read on the Light-house.

The wind was southerly to-day, but there was much less sea than yesterday, and the landing-master's crew were enabled to discharge and land twenty-three pieces of stone, and other articles for the work. The artificers had completed the laying of the Twenty-seventh or First course of the staircase this morning, and in the evening, they finished the boring, trenailing, wedging, and grouting with it mortar. At 12 o'clock noon, the Beacon-house bell was rung, and all hands were collected on the top of the building, where prayers were read, for the first time, on the Light-house, which forcibly struck every one, and had, upon the whole, a very impressive effect. The artificers then went to their barrack to dinner, and the landing-master's crew went off to the Tender. In the afternoon, the remainder of the Smeaton's cargo was discharged, and she sailed for Arbroath at 11 P. M.

Monday, 21st.

Active exertions of the landing-master's crew.

The Patriot had arrived at Arbroath with the last cargo of stones from Mylnefield Quarry for the Light-house, on the 19th, and was fully discharged to-day, and was now fitting with her ballast and platform for carrying off the worked materials to the Rock. The wind being at south, caused a considerable swell on the Rock, and it was with great difficulty that the landing-master got the remaining ten stones of the Smeaton's last cargo landed from the Hedderwick. His crew were not only completely drenched, but were much exhausted with the fatigue of pulling the loaded praam-boat against the swell of the sea; and on reaching the Rock, it required their utmost exertions to prevent her from driving to leeward upon the rugged ledges which encumbered the eastern creek.

Tuesday, 22d.

Thirty-first course completed.

The dispatch made by the Smeaton in performing her trips between Arbroath and the Bell Rock, was quite surprising, being seldom more than one day absent. On the last trip, for example, she had only left the Rock on Sunday night at 11, and this morning at 8 o'clock, she returned to her moorings with thirty-five pieces of stone. Of these, seventeen were landed to-day, with which the Thirty-first course of the building was completed, and the remainder of the day was occupied in boring the trenail holes in the lower course, fixing the trenails and wedges, and grouting the whole carefully with mortar.

Wednesday, 23d.

The Patriot arrived at the Rock this morning, with her first cargo of building materials for the season, consisting of 42 stones, together with a supply of pozzolano, lime, sand, wedges, trenails, and 8 stone joggles. The Smeaton was completely discharged of her cargo, and sailed again at 2 P. M., when the writer took his passage with her to Arbroath.

Thursday, 24th.

Arrangements for conduct of the work, and safety of the Beacon.

The weather continued moderate at the Rock, with the wind at west, and 18 stones of the Patriot's cargo were landed and built to-day. The Accounts connected with the Light-house service were collected at this period, being paid at the terms of Whitsunday and Martinmas. The writer at the same time arranged some matters more fully in the work-yard, connected with the loading of the materials at Arbroath. In particular, Mr David Logan, clerk of works, was held responsible for providing every thing contained in the Requisition of the foreman-builder; while Mr Kennedy, engineer's clerk, was answerable for the other parts of the respective Requisitions from the Tender and Beacon, and for the dispatch given in the loading and sailing of the vessels. The masters of the stone-vessels were accordingly directed, on their arrival by night or day, to deliver all letters at the office. In the same manner, before leaving the Rock, Regulations for the proper conduct of the works there, were also instituted; where his assistants were also held responsible for the duties of their several departments; Mr Peter Logan, for the execution of the masonry; Mr Francis Watt, for the good condition of the Beacon-house, Railways, and Machinery; Captain Wilson, for the state of the Praams and other boats employed in the landing of materials, and for the safety of the stones and building-materials in transporting them from the ship's hold till they were placed upon the waggons on the Rock. The steward, Mr John Peters, was answerable for making the necessary Requisitions for a sufficient stock of provisions, water and fuel; while Captain Taylor, master of the Tender, was to see a proper stock of these articles landed and kept in store upon the Rock. From the hazardous situation of the Beacon-house with regard to fire, being composed wholly of timber, there was no small risk from accident; and on this account, one of the most steady of the artificers was appointed to see that the fire of the cooking-house, and the lights in general, were carefully extinguished at stated hours.

Friday, 25th.

The weather continued to be extremely fine, with the wind at west, and the barometer standing about 30 inches. The landing operations proceeded briskly, so that the building was to-day ready for the Door-lintel.

Saturday, 26th.

Balance-crane shaft is broken.

The door-lintel being of large dimensions, equal to about a ton and a half in weight, and considerably heavier than any of the other stones of this course, in raising it with the balance-crane, sufficient attention had not been paid to increase the balance-weight proportionally, and an unequal strain being then brought upon the opposite arms of the crane, the upright shaft yielded, and broke at one of the joints; fortunately no person was hurt, though a stop was put to the work for the present. This unlucky accident happened about 4 in the afternoon, when the Patriot, then at her moorings, discharging a cargo of stones, was immediately dispatched to Arbroath with the broken shaft, where she arrived about 2 o'clock on Sunday morning. The writer was at this early hour rather alarmed, by Captain Macdonald knocking at his bed-room door, and calling out in a hollow tone, "that the Balance-crane had given way." An express was immediately sent for Mr James Dove, who, only two days prior to the accident, had left the Bell Rock, and was in the neighbourhood of Arbroath, and when the messenger reached him, he was preparing to go with his friends to the church of his native parish.

The Writer is welcomed in at the door of the Light-house.

The shaft of this crane consisted of four hollow pipes of cast iron, in lengths, the lower one of 8 feet, and the three upper ones of 6 feet, fitted to each other with a flush or square joint, so that the body of the crane might traverse upon them without interruption, as will be understood by examining Plate XVII. There was, unavoidably, a degree of weakness at these joints, which required considerable precaution in shifting or adjusting the balance-weight, according to the strain occasioned by a heavy stone. This accident, though speedily repaired, produced a delay of no less than three days to the building operations, which, together with the time occupied in making provision for a new method of inserting the door-hinges into the building, made this part of the masonry, upon the whole, appear extremely tedious. Having got the door-lintel laid, the writer was not a little gratified on being welcomed, with acclamation, in at the Door of the Bell Rock Light-house. Limited as the height of the building still was, the formation of the door stamped a new character upon it, and the lintel gave it an additional appearance of strength.

Fixtures of the hinges of the door and window-shutters.

The fixtures of the hinges of the door and shutters of the windows are of a peculiar construction, as will be seen in the different diagrams of Plate XIX. They consisted of boxes or cases made of brass, of a dovetailed form, measuring 16 inches in length, and 1 inch in depth in the void; one of these cases was inserted into a cavity cut in the upper bed of one of the rybat-stones on each side of the door or window, and run up with melted lead. Into this case the dovetail-end of the hinge was afterwards introduced, and fixed in its place by driving a middle-piece, after the manner of a Lewis-bat. The advantage of this method is, that, in the event of its being found necessary, at any future period, to renew or repair a hinge, all that becomes necessary is to draw the middle-piece and extract the Lewis from the box, without requiring to cut or mangle the building, as would be found necessary by the usual method of inserting hinges into walls. The hinges and cases were made of fine brass; those for the door weighing 50 lb., and those for the window-shutters being smaller, weighed about half as much.

1810, June.

Friday, 1st.

The weather, during the last week of the month of May, was very favourable for the operations; and the barometer stood to-day at no less than 30 inches and 42 hundred parts. The wind was S.E., and the atmosphere somewhat foggy, but not such as to prevent the landing operations from going forward. The Patriot was now at her moorings discharging; and the landing-master's crew transported one of the praam-boats to the Rock with 14 stones, which enabled the builders to complete the Thirty-third course, being the one immediately above the door-lintel, consisting of 32 stones.

Saturday, 2d.

Shipping makes great dispatch.

The weather still continuing to be extremely fine, the landing-master and his crew left the Tender at 4 A. M., and proceeded to deliver the remainder of the Patriot's cargo, consisting of 14 stones, with a proportion of pozzolano, lime, sand, and Roman cement, together with six bundles of trenails and wedges. She then made sail for Arbroath, and the Smeaton at the same time arrived with the Thirty-fourth course, consisting also of 32 stones. She had previously put a new cable on board of the Floating-light, this being the period at which her winter-tackle was annually shifted. The Smeaton got to her moorings at 11 A. M., when Captain Wilson and his crew immediately proceeded to deliver her, and by 4 in the afternoon she was cleared, and had sailed again for Arbroath to load, having thus been discharged in five hours, being the shortest period in which any cargo had hitherto been delivered at the Bell Rock. This formed a striking contrast with the delivery of the first cargo of the season, which had been on board from the 18th till the 29th of May, or eleven days, in the course of which the Smeaton was put thrice into Arbroath, and once up to Leith Roads, shewing how very dependent these works are upon the state of the weather. To-day there were no fewer than 56 pieces of stones transported to the Rock, being the greatest number hitherto landed in one day.

Sunday, 3d.

Patriot makes a trip in 33 hours.

The dispatch given in the loading department at Arbroath was nothing short of that of the landing at the Rock. The Patriot only got to the Light-house loading-birth last night at 11 P. M., when Mr Kennedy commenced loading her at midnight, with 34 pieces of stone, 9 stone joggles, two casks of pozzolano, two casks of lime, two casks of sand, and three bundles of trenails and wedges: she sailed again at 4 A. M., and got fast to her moorings at 5 in the afternoon, having been absent from the Rock only 33 hours. The landing-master's crew towed the Hedderwick praam-boat alongside, and loaded her with 18 pieces of stone, which were safely landed on the Rock. At 11 P. M. the boats returned to the Tender, having been at work since 4 o'clock this morning. The weather was so inviting at this time, that, contrary to usual practice, a quantity of the stones was laid upon the Rock round the western side of the building, which were afterwards raised by the purchase-tackle on the bridge: the building was thus continued for a longer period than the tide permitted the landing-master's crew to proceed with their operations. Some risk, however, attended this arrangement, as part of the stones were necessarily left on the Rock, exposed to the wash of the sea, from one tide to another. But the workmen being now permanently on the Rock, this could scarcely happen to a great extent, as the sea generally takes a tide or two to get into so rough a state as to be dangerous in cases of this kind. The Thirty-fifth course was laid to-day, consisting of 32 pieces of stone; but it required the work to be continued from 5 in the morning till 8 in the evening, before the trenailing, wedging, and grouting with mortar, were completed; the artificers having of course pay for their extra hours.

Monday, 4th.

Thirty-sixth course laid.

To-day there was a strong breeze of wind from the east, with hazy weather, but, as the mercury still maintained the high state of 30.32, every confidence was felt in the landing operations. The Patriot was accordingly discharged of the remainder of her cargo, and 16 stones, with other building materials, were landed on the Rock, though not without considerable difficulty, from the heavy swell of sea which was running upon it. The artificers also succeeded in building all the stones which were on the Rock, and finished the Thirty-sixth course, consisting of

24 blocks.

The King's birth-day observed.

This being the Birth-day of our much revered Sovereign King George III., now in the Fiftieth year of his reign, the shipping of the Light-house service were this morning decorated with colours according to the taste of their respective captains. Flags were also hoisted upon the Beacon-house and Balance-crane on the top of the Building. At 12 noon, a salute was fired from the Tender, when the King's health was drunk, with all the honours, both on the Rock, and on board of the shipping.

Tuesday, 5th.

Stair-case completed.

Rate of Wages.

The weather still continuing very favourable for the operations, the work proceeded with much regularity and dispatch. Twenty stones were landed to-day from the Smeaton, and the artificers completed the Thirty-eighth or finishing course of the staircase, which brought the building to the height of 45 feet. As the walls were here reduced from 5 feet 9 inches to 3 feet 2 inches in thickness, the scarsement at the level of this course formed a kind of floor or bench 2 feet 7 inches in breadth, at the top of the staircase, intended for keeping the water-cisterns, fuel, and provisions. The laying of this course being attended with a good deal of additional trouble, the artificers were occupied with it from 5 o'clock in the morning till 8 in the evening, when all hands being collected on the building, three hearty cheers were given, and a dram served out, at the completion of the first floor. During this season, nine hours were counted a day's work at the Bell Rock, instead of three hours of tide-work, as in the early stages of the business. The artificers having, therefore, had six extra hours to-day, at the rate of 6d. per hour, each had 3s. per day to receive, in addition to his stated wages of 3s. 4d.; and, as the work was continued on Sundays, they were now making upwards of two guineas per week, free of incumbrance, while the foremen were in the receipt of about double that sum. The inhabitants of the Beacon were consequently in great spirits, both at the satisfactory progress of the work, and at the amount of their extra wages.

Progress of the Works at Edinburgh.

While the work thus proceeded at the Bell Rock, it was making also good progress at Arbroath, as the whole of the courses, excepting three, were now ready for shipping to the Rock. Advice was also received from Edinburgh, that the Light-room Reflecting-apparatus and Revolving-machinery were getting regularly forward, so that every prospect was afforded of the work being brought to a conclusion in the course of the season.

Artificers liable to accident. Small Boat and Life-buoy provided.

As the Light-house advanced in height, the cubical contents of the stones were less, but they had to be raised to a greater height; and the walls being thinner were less commodious for the necessary machinery, and the artificers employed, which considerably retarded the work. Inconvenience was also occasionally experienced from the men dropping their coats, hats, mallets, and other tools, at high-water, which were carried away by the tide; and the danger to the people themselves was now greatly increased. Had any of them fallen from the Beacon or Building at high-water, while the landing-master's crew were generally engaged with the craft at a distance, it must have rendered the accident doubly painful to those on the Rock, who at this time had no boat, and consequently no means of rendering immediate and prompt assistance. In such cases, it would have been too late to have got a boat by signal from the Tender. A small boat, which could be lowered at pleasure, was therefore suspended by a pair of davits projected from the cook-house, the keel being about 30 feet from the Rock, as will be seen from Plate VIII. This boat, with its tackle, was put under the charge of James Glen, of whose exertions on the Beacon mention has already been made, and who having in early life been a seaman, was also very expert in the management of a boat. A life-buoy was likewise suspended from the bridge, to which a coil of line 200 fathoms in length was attached, which could be let out to a person falling into the water, or to the people in the boat, should they not be able to work her with the oars.

Wednesday, 6th.

Trenailing the Stones discontinued.

The landing-master succeeded to-day in transporting 44 stones to the Rock, and the artificers laid the Thirty-eighth course, which consisted of 16 blocks. The trenailing and wedging of the stones being now discontinued, as the building was above the ordinary range of the sea, a great relief was instantly felt, as will be understood from examining the several courses in Plate XIII.; and as the work was thereby much simplified, it was now expected that two courses might be laid per day.

Thursday, 7th.

Number of people on the Beacon. Fitting of window-hinges troublesome.

To-day 12 stones were landed on the Rock, being the remainder of the Patriot's cargo; and the artificers built the Thirty-ninth course, consisting of 14 stones. The Bell Rock works had now a very busy appearance, as the Light-house was daily getting more into form. Besides the artificers and their cook, the writer and his servant were also lodged on the Beacon, counting in all twenty-nine; and at low-water the landing-master's crew, consisting of from twelve to fifteen seamen, were employed in transporting the building materials, working the landing apparatus on the Rock, and dragging the stone-waggons along the railways, of which an idea will be formed by examining Plate XVIII. There were 27 stones discharged to-day from the Smeaton; and the artificers laid the Fortieth course of the building, in which the windows of the water, fuel, and provision store-room occur. The fitting of the hinge-boxes for the window storm-shutters, occupied a considerable portion of time, as has already been described in allusion to the entrance-door.

Friday, 8th.

The comfort of good weather on the Rock.

In the course of this day the weather varied much. In the morning it was calm; in the middle part of the day there were light airs of wind from the south, and in the evening fresh breezes from the east. The barometer in the writer's cabin in the Beacon-house oscillated from 30 inches to 30.42, and the weather was extremely pleasant. This, in any situation, forms one of the chief comforts of life, but, as may easily be conceived, it was doubly so to people stuck as it were upon a pinnacle in the middle of the ocean.

Saturday, 9th.

Balance-crane shifted to-day.

The weather continued to be very agreeable, and ships every where seen upon the sea. At the Bell Rock we had only the Tender and the Floating-light, the Smeaton and Patriot being at Arbroath. The Dickie praam-boat was brought from her moorings this morning, when 9 stones were landed. The artificers were chiefly occupied to-day, in shifting the balance-crane from the top of the solid, to the top of the staircase, across which it was supported on strong beams, while struts were projected under the body of the crane, and butting against the interior of the walls of the building, as will be understood by examining the third year's work of Plate IX. The balance-crane was, however, so constructed, that its foot might have been allowed to rest upon the solid of the building throughout the whole operation, and the shaft lengthened as the building rose, by adding additional pieces, till the whole of the masonry was completed, which would have formed a length of shaft extending to 50 feet. It was, however, found, upon the whole, to be more convenient and economical to lift the crane from floor to floor as the work advanced.

Sunday, 10th.

Crane erected at western Wharf.

Although stones had hitherto been occasionally landed on the western, as well as the eastern side of the Bell Rock, according to the state of the weather; yet, as the railways and apparatus of the eastern creek were much sooner in a working condition than those of the other, and being only 90 feet from the Light-house, while the western Railway extended to 290 feet in length, as will be seen from Plates VI. and XVIII., the eastern creek was generally used in all directions of the wind, when the weather was moderate. To-day, however, the wharf at the western creek had been completed to its full extent, and one of the moveable-beam cranes was erected at it, upon a piece of frame-work constructed of Norway logs, forming also a platform employed in landing the stones.

Two stones upset by the Sea.

In the course of last night, the wind had blown pretty strongly from the S.E., and towards morning it shifted to the S.W., which created a considerable swell of sea. Owing to the time unavoidably occupied in the shifting the balance-crane, and fitting the brass cases for the Lewis-bat hinges of the window-shutters of the provision-store, together with the eagerness, and even impatience of Captain Wilson, the landing-master, on all occasions, to get his part of the business accomplished by the speedy delivery of the stone-vessels, he had landed both the Thirty-first and Thirty-second courses, which were thus piled in rather too great a number at the western side of the building. During the night, though the range of the sea was considered trifling, yet it had upset two of the stones, which, when the tide left the Rock, were found lying at some distance with the Lewis-bats turned downwards. These two courses, being too much at the mercy of the waves, were raised to their places on the building, and, though not laid with mortar for the present, were, nevertheless, out of the reach of heavy seas, and more at the command of the artificers.

A Praam boat is sent from the Rock with her cargo.

Although the praam-boats, from their built, and the construction of their moorings, rode easily with a cargo on deck, as formerly noticed, yet a certain risk also attended this state of things, and the writer rather wished the Smeaton and Patriot to remain at their station, with the stones on board, until an opportunity was afforded of landing and getting them at once laid in their places upon the building. One of the praam-boats had, however, been brought to the Rock with 11 stones, notwithstanding the perplexity which attended the getting of those formerly landed taken up to the building. Mr Peter Logan, the foreman builder, interposed, and prevented this cargo from being delivered, but the landing-master's crew were exceedingly averse to this arrangement, from an idea that "ill luck" would in future attend the Praam, her cargo, and those who navigated her, from thus reversing her voyage. It may be noticed, that this was the first instance of a Praam-boat having been sent from the Bell Rock with any part of her cargo on board, and was considered so uncommon an occurrence, that it became a topic of conversation among the seamen and artificers.

At 1 P. M. the bell rung for prayers, which were read by the writer in the Beacon; after which the artificers went to dinner, and the work again commenced and was continued till 9.

Monday, 11th.

The first operation of the building-artificers this morning, was to lift the two courses laid on the top of the walls last night, and build them with mortar; some of the stones of the upper course, in the mean time, being stowed round the foot of the balance-crane. These two courses consisted each of 16 stones, besides the dovetail joggles for connecting the perpendicular joints, as shewn in diagrams of Plate XIII. The landing-master's crew proceeded this morning to discharge the Patriot, and having loaded the Hedderwick Praam-boat, she was towed to her moorings to remain until the stones could be received at the Rock. In the afternoon the Patriot sailed; and in the evening the Smeaton arrived from Arbroath with another cargo, bringing also letters, papers, provisions, water, and fuel for the Beacon.

Tuesday, 12th.

Stones sent from the Rock are safely landed.

To-day the stones formerly sent from the Rock were safely landed, notwithstanding the augury of the seamen, in consequence of their being sent away two days before. These, together with 14 dove-tail joggles, were immediately taken up to the top of the building, and laid, for the present, without mortar, on the top of the Thirty-fourth course.

Wednesday, 13th.

Floor of the Light-room flat laid.

The artificers were employed with the Forty-sixth course to-day, and in making preparations for laying the Forty-seventh, being the floor for the Light-room stores. In the afternoon and evening, the joiners were employed in fitting up a piece of frame-work, as a centre for supporting the interior ends of the stones composing the Floor course, which projected from the outward face of the building towards the centre of the apartment, as will be understood from Plates XIII. and XVI.

Mr John Reid has got leave ashore, after being three months afloat.

The Floating-light having got her winter cable on board, and being otherwise in good order, Mr John Reid, principal Light-keeper, and acting master, while Captain Wilson was employed at the Bell Rock, having been upwards of three months afloat, it was thought proper that he should now have liberty for a time on shore, that, in his turn, he might relieve Mr Wilson. Mr Taylor, commander of the Tender, accordingly went on board of the Floating-light, leaving the landing-master in charge of the Tender, along with his other duties at the Rock.

Thursday, 14th.

To-day 27 stones and 11 joggle-pieces were landed, part of which consisted of the Forty-seventh course, forming the store-room floor. The builders were at work this morning by 4 o'clock, in the hopes of being able to accomplish the laying of the 18 stones of this course. But at 8 o'clock in the evening they had still two to lay, and as the stones of this course were very unwieldy, being 6 feet in length, they required much precaution and care both in lifting and laying them. It was, however, only on the writer's suggestion to Mr Logan, that the artificers were induced to leave off, as they had intended to complete this floor before going to bed. The two remaining stones were, however, laid in their places without mortar, when the bell on the Beacon was rung, and all hands being collected on the top of the building, three hearty cheers were given on covering the first apartment. The steward then served out a dram to each, when the whole retired to their barrack much fatigued, but with the anticipation of the most perfect repose even in the "hurricane-house," amidst the dashing seas on the Bell Rock.

First letter written from the Light-house.

While the workmen were at breakfast and dinner, it was the writer's usual practice to spend his time on the walls of the building, which, notwithstanding the narrowness of the track, nevertheless formed his principal walk, when the Rock was under water. But this afternoon he had his writing-desk set upon the store-room floor, when he wrote to Mrs Stevenson, certainly the first letter dated from the Bell Rock Light-house, giving a detail of the fortunate progress of the work, with an assurance that the Light-house would soon be completed at the rate at which it now proceeded; and the Patriot having sailed for Arbroath in the evening, he felt no small degree of pleasure in dispatching this communication to his family.

Friday, 15th.

Floors of the Bell Rock and Edystone Light-houses.

The floor-courses of the Bell Rock Light-house lay horizontally upon the walls, as will be seen from the sections in Plates VII. and XVI. They consisted in all of 18 blocks, but only 16 were laid in the first instance, as the centre-stone were necessarily left out, to allow the shaft of the balance-crane to pass through the several apartments of the building. In the same manner also, the stone which formed the interior side of the man-hole, was not laid till after the centre stone was in its place, and the masonry of the walls completed. The number of stones above alluded to are independently of the sixteen joggle pieces with which the principal blocks of the floors were connected, as shewn in the diagrams of Plates VII. and XIII. The floors of the Edystone Light-house, on the contrary, were constructed of an arch-form, and the haunches of the arches bound with chains, to prevent their pressing outward, to the injury of the walls. In this, Mr Smeaton followed the construction of the Dome of St Paul's; and this mode might also be found necessary at the Edystone, from the want of stones in one length, to form the outward wall and floor, in the then state of the granite quarries of Cornwall. At Mylnefield Quarry, however, there was no difficulty in procuring stones of the requisite dimensions; and the writer foresaw many advantages that would arise, from having the stones of the floors to form part of the outward walls without introducing the system of arching: in particular, the pressure of the floors upon the walls would thus be perpendicular; for, as the stones were prepared in the sides, with groove-and-feather, after the manner of the common house-floor, they would, by this means, form so many girths, binding the exterior walls together, as will be understood by examining the diagrams and section of Plate VII., with its letter-press description; agreeably to which he had modelled the floors in his original designs for the Bell Rock, which were laid before the Light-house Board in the year 1800.

31 Persons lodged in the Beacon-house.

Pay and Premiums at the Rock.

The weather still continuing favourable for the operations at the Rock, the work proceeded with much energy, through the exertions both of the seamen and artificers. For the more speedy and effectual working of the several tackles, in raising the materials as the building advanced in height, and there being a great extent of Railway to attend to, which, required constant repairs, two additional mill-wrights were added to the complement on the Rock, which, including the writer, now counted thirty-one in all. So crowded was the men's barrack, that the beds were ranged five tier in height, allowing only about 1 foot 8 inches for each bed, while the greatest extent of floor-room measured only about 8 feet 6 inches across, between the beds on opposite sides, as will be seen in the sections and diagrams of Plate VIII. The artificers commenced this morning at 5 o'clock, and, in the course of the day, they laid the Forty-eighth and Forty-ninth courses, consisting each of 16 blocks. From the favourable state of the weather, and the regular manner in which the work now proceeded, the artificers had generally from four to seven extra hours' work, which, including their stated wages of 3s. 4d., yielded them from 5s. 4d. to about 6s. 10d. per day, besides their board; even the postage of their letters was paid while they were at the Bell Rock. In these advantages, the foremen also shared, having about double the pay and amount of premiums of the artificers. The seamen being less out of their element in the Bell Rock operations than the landsmen, their premiums consisted in a slump sum, payable at the end of the season, which extended from three to ten guineas.

Seamen find one of the lost sets of moorings.

As the laying of the floors was somewhat tedious, the landing-master and his crew had got considerably beforehand with the building artificers in bringing materials faster to the Rock than they could be built. The seamen having, therefore, some spare time, were occasionally employed, during fine weather, in dredging or grappling for the several mushroom-anchors and mooring-chains, which had been lost in the vicinity of the Bell Rock, during the progress of the work, by the breaking loose and drifting of the floating-buoys. To encourage their exertions in this search, Five Guineas were offered as a premium for each set they should find; and after much patient application, they succeeded to-day in hooking one of these lost anchors with its chain.

Experiment of collecting Gas from Fishes.

It was a general remark at the Bell Rock, as before noticed, that fish were never plenty in its neighbourhood, excepting in good weather. Indeed, the seamen used to speculate about the state of the weather from their success in fishing. When the fish disappeared at the Rock, it was considered a sure indication that a gale was not far off, as the fish seemed to seek shelter in deeper water, from the roughness of the sea, during these changes of the weather. At this time, the Rock, at high-water, was completely covered with podlies, or the fry of the coalfish, about six or eight inches in length. The artificers sometimes occupied half an hour after breakfast and dinner in catching these little fishes, but were more frequently supplied from the boats of the Tender. This evening the landing-master's crew brought to the Rock a quantity of newly caught codfish, measuring from 15 to 24 inches in length. The membrane called the sound, which is attached to the backbone of fishes, being understood to contain, at different times, greater portions of azote and of oxygen than common air, the present favourable opportunity was embraced for collecting a quantity of this gas in a drinking-glass, inverted into a pail of salt-water. The fish being held under this glass as a receiver, their bladders were punctured, and a considerable quantity of gas was thus collected. A lighted match was afterwards carefully introduced into the glass, when the gas exhibited in a considerable degree the bright and luminous flame which an excess of oxygen is known to produce.

Saturday, 16th.

Cause of ground swells.

The weather was hazy, and the wind had shifted to-day from west to east, accompanied with a heavy ground-swell in the sea. At the Bell Rock, this was sometimes observed to be the precursor of a gale, while, on other occasions, the swell did not make its appearance till the force of the wind had ceased. Many speculations have been made by naturalists upon the probable cause of ground-swells, so often observed by seamen, and which sometimes appear even without the accompaniment of wind, either before or after. To account for this, it may be noticed, that the waters of the German Ocean or North Sea, from their connection with the Atlantic Ocean, are often affected by gales of westerly winds, which never reach our shores, though they have the effect of forcing an undue portion of the waters of the Atlantic into the British seas, which tend to overfill all the friths and bays, producing the phenomenon of a ground-swell;—a condition of things which may also be supposed to follow from the account given of the gale experienced by the writer off Flamborough-head, on the 19th September 1809, described at page 320.; which might as readily have been checked in its progress, by the contrary wind, before it reached the northern shores, as off the coast of England. This subject is further illustrated by the writer in a paper read before the Wernerian Society, on the bed of the German Ocean, and given in the Appendix, No. V.

Landing-master's dress, and activity of his crew.

The landing-master having this day discharged the Smeaton, and loaded the Hedderwick and Dickie praam-boats with 19 stones, they were towed to their respective moorings; when Captain Wilson, in consequence of the heavy swell of sea, came in his boat to the Beacon-house, to consult with the writer as to the propriety of venturing the loaded praam-boats with their cargoes to the Rock, while so much sea was running. After some dubiety expressed on the subject, in which the ardent mind of the landing-master suggested many arguments in favour of his being able to convey the praams in perfect safety, it was acceded to. In bad weather, and especially on occasions of difficulty like the present, Mr Wilson, who was an extremely active seaman, measuring about 5 feet 3 inches in height, of a robust habit, generally dressed himself in what he called a Monkey Jacket, made of thick duffle-cloth, with a pair of Dutchman's petticoat-trowsers, reaching only to his knees, where they were met with a pair of long water-tight boots; with this dress, his glazed hat, and his small brass speaking-trumpet in his hand, he bade defiance to the weather. When he made his appearance in this most suitable attire for the service, his crew seemed to possess additional life, never failing to use their utmost exertions when the captain put on his "storm-rigging." They had this morning commenced loading the praam-boats at 4 o'clock, and proceeded to tow them into the eastern landing-place, which was accomplished with much dexterity, though not without the risk of being thrown, by the force of the sea, on certain projecting ledges of the rock. In such a case, the loss even of a single stone would have greatly retarded the work. For the greater safety in entering this creek, it was necessary to put out several warps and guy-ropes, to guide the boats into its narrow and intricate entrance; and it frequently happened that the sea made a clean breach over the praams, which not only washed their decks, but completely drenched the crew in water.

Want of the western wharf.

On this, as on many other occasions, the want of the western wharf was particularly felt; for, although it had long been used with great advantage in the ordinary traffic of the Rock, and was now carried to its full extent, it was still not fit for all the purposes of landing weighty materials, otherwise the landing operations would have been accomplished with much more ease and facility to-day. So much, however, had been to do in boring the rock, inserting iron-bats and other operations, accessible only at the lowest tides, that, although Mr Watt and his squad of artificers had embraced every opportunity, by day and night, — for this work to the last was carried on by torch light, — yet the wharf of the western railway was not entirely completed.

Operation of shifting the Balance-crane. Its properties.

The building-artificers were employed to-day in raising the Balance-crane to the light-room-store, where it was supported upon two beams of oaken timber, which were made to rest upon the outward extremity of the floor, or close to the wall of the house. The removal of the crane from one storey to another was attended with considerable trouble. The body of the crane, as will be understood by examining Plates IX. and XVII., was raised upon the shaft at every two or three courses which were added to the height of the building. This mode might have been continued throughout, without once raising the foot of the crane, by simply adding to the length of the shaft. But, all things taken into view, it was considered preferable to lift the whole machine from floor to floor. This was accomplished in the following manner: Two beams of fir-timber were laid across the walls of the house, on which the body of the crane was rested. This new position did not prevent the purchase-tackle of the crane from being worked, and it was therefore applied to lift the foot and the four lengths of the shaft, which were laid aside till successively wanted in the course of building. The foot, with two lengths of the shaft, being placed upon the oaken beams above alluded to; a cutter or spear-bolt was passed through one of the numerous holes in the shaft; when the beams on which the body of the crane rested on the walls being removed, the crane was again in a complete working condition. The Balance-crane had therefore the property of being applicable to raising itself, from stage to stage, as well as of laying the stones, and preserving its equilibrium when loaded. In case, through inattention or accident, an undue proportion of weight had been brought upon one end of the beam of the crane, as was the case when the door-lintel was laid, four spurs or diagonal supports of oak, were attached to the shaft, the lower ends of which rested upon the floor and butted against the wall, while the upper ends fitted into a collar or circular piece of cast-iron, which embraced the shaft immediately under the body of the crane. These preparatory operations occupied a great part of this day, after which there was no further delay occasioned by the Balance-crane, till it was again to be raised to the next floor, except the occasional lifting of the body, and applying additional lengths to the shaft, as the building rose, things which were accomplished without retarding the work.

Sunday, 17th.

Western wharf finished to-day.

It was fortunate, in the present state of the weather, that the Fiftieth course was in a sheltered spot, within the reach of the tackle of the winch-machine upon the bridge; a few stones were stowed upon the bridge itself, and the remainder upon the building, which kept the artificers at work. The stowing of the materials upon the Rock, was the department of Alexander Brebner, mason, who spared no pains in attending to the safety of the stones, and who, in the present state of the work, when the stones were landed faster than could be built, generally worked till the water rose to his middle. At 1 o'clock to-day the bell rung for prayers, and all hands were collected into the upper barrack-room of the Beacon-house, when the usual service was performed.

At low-water this afternoon all hands were employed in completing the western wharf,—a work which had now been in progress for a twelvemonth. One of the moveable-beam cranes was elevated on it, under a salute of three hearty cheers. This wharf was formed of timber, consisting of successive layers of Norway logs, like the Eastern Wharf, as represented in Plate XI., which were raised to the level of the Railways, or about 6 feet in height, and fixed down with bat-bars of iron, measuring 7 feet in length, having been sunk about 12 inches into the Rock.

Remarkable state of the sea at the Bell Rock to-day.

The wind blew very hard in the course of last night from N.E., and to-day the sea ran so high that no boat could approach the Rock. During the dinner-hour, when the writer was going to the top of the building as usual, but just as he had entered the door, and was about to ascend the ladder, a great noise was heard over-head, and in an instant he was soused in water, from a sea which had most unexpectedly come over the walls, though now about 58 feet in height. On making his retreat, he found himself completely whitened by the lime which had mixed with the water, while dashing down through the different floors; and, as nearly as he could guess, a quantity equal to about a hogshead had come over the walls, and now streamed out at the door. After having shifted himself, he again sat down in his cabin, the sea continuing to run so high that the builders did not resume their operations on the walls this afternoon. The incident just noticed, did not create more surprise in the mind of the writer, than the sublime appearance of the waves, as they rolled majestically over the Rock. This scene he greatly enjoyed while sitting at his cabin window: each wave approached the Beacon like a vast scroll unfolding; and, in passing, discharged a quantity of air, which he not only distinctly felt, but was even sufficient to lift the leaves of a book which lay before him. These waves might be 10 or 12 feet in height, and about 250 feet in length. Their smaller end being towards the north, where the water was deep, and they were opened or cut through by the interposition of the Building and Beacon. The gradual manner in which the sea, upon these occasions, is observed to become calm or to subside, is a very remarkable feature of this phenomenon. For example, when a gale is succeeded by a calm, every third or fourth wave forms one of these great seas, which occur in spaces, of from 3 to 5 minutes, as noted by the writer's watch; but, in the course of the next tide, they become less frequent, and take off, so as to occur only in 10 or 15 minutes; and, singular enough, at the third tide after such gales, the writer has remarked, that only one or two of these great waves appear in the course of the whole tide.

Thursday, 21st.

Landing-master's crew have now more leisure.

From Monday 18th till this date, the work went forward in the usual routine, and the building was now in readiness for the floor of the kitchen or third apartment. In the present state of things, the two stone-vessels Smeaton and Patriot, could not be fully employed, as, owing to the greater height of the building, every operation required much more time, in proportion to the tonnage which the vessels brought off to the Rock. Indeed, the original intention of providing two vessels for this department was chiefly to guard against accident, as, in this service, they were much exposed to danger, in the event of which, without a second vessel, the work must have been arrested in its progress. Having now also the full use of the western creek, the process of landing was seldom delayed, excepting from want of demand on the part of the builders; it was still, nevertheless, necessary to keep up the establishment of shipping, for the reason above stated.

Disagreeable state of the weather.

The 19th was a very unpleasant and disagreeable day, both for the seamen and artificers, as it rained throughout with little intermission from 4 A. M. till 11 P. M., accompanied with thunder and lightning, during which period the work nevertheless continued unremittingly; and the builders laid the Fifty-first and Fifty-second courses. This state of weather was no less severe upon the mortar-makers, who required to temper or prepare the mortar of a thicker or thinner consistency, in some measure, according to the state of the weather. From the elevated position of the building, the mortar-gallery on the Beacon was now much lower, and the lime buckets were made to traverse upon a rope distended between it and the building, as will be seen from Plate IX. On occasions like the present, however, there was often a difference of opinion between the builders and the mortar-makers. John Watt, who had the principal charge of the mortar, was a most active worker, but being somewhat of an irascible temper, the builders occasionally amused themselves at his expence. For, while he was eagerly at work with his large iron-shod pestle in the mortar-tub, they often sent down contradictory orders, some crying, "Make it a little stiffer, or thicker, John," while others called out to make it "thinner;" to which he generally returned very speedy and sharp replies; so that these conversations at times were rather amusing. The brass cases of the upper-hinges of the window of this apartment, occurring in the Fifty-second course, occasioned a good deal of detention, on the 20th, in laying it, when the artificers were employed from 4 in the morning till 9 in the evening.

Extra pay.

Responsible situation of the principal workmen.

During wet weather, the situation of the artificers on the top of the building was extremely disagreeable; for, although their work did not require great exertion, yet, as each man had his particular part to perform, either in working the crane, or in laying the stones, it required the closest application and attention, not only on the part of Mr Peter Logan, the foreman, who was constantly on the walls, but also of the chief workmen. Robert Selkirk, the principal builder, for example, had every stone to lay in its place. David Cumming, a mason, had the charge of working the tackle of the balance-weight, and James Scott, also a mason, took charge of the purchase with which the stones were laid; while the pointing the joints of the walls with cement, was entrusted to William Reid and William Kennedy, who stood upon a scaffold suspended over the walls in rather a frightful manner. The least act of carelessness or inattention on the part of any of these men might have been fatal, not only to themselves, but also to the surrounding workmen, especially if any accident had happened to the crane itself, while the material damage or loss of a single stone would have put an entire stop to the operations, until another could have been brought from Arbroath. The artificers having wrought seven and a half hours of extra time to-day, had 3s. 9d. of extra pay, while the foremen had 7s. 6d. over and above their stated pay and board. Although, therefore, the work was both hazardous and fatiguing, yet the encouragement being considerable, they were alwise very cheerful, and perfectly reconciled to the confinement, and other disadvantages of the place.

Carpenter of the Floating-light leaves the service.

During fine weather, and while the nights were short, the duty on board of the Floating-light was literally nothing but a waiting on, and therefore one of her boats, with a crew of five men, daily attended the Rock, but always returned to the vessel at night. The carpenter, however, was one of those who was left on board of the ship, as he also acted in the capacity of assistant light-keeper; being, besides, a person who was apt to feel discontent, and to be averse to changing his quarters, especially to work with the mill-wrights and joiners at the Rock, who often, for hours together, wrought knee-deep, and not unfrequently up to the middle in water. Mr Watt having, about this time, made a requisition for another hand, the carpenter was ordered to attend the Rock in the Floating-light's boat. This he did with great reluctance, and found so much fault, that he soon got into discredit with his messmates. On this occasion, he left the Light-house service, and went as a sailor in a vessel bound for America, — a step which, it is believed, he soon regretted, as, in the course of things, he would, in all probability, have accompanied Mr John Reid, the principal Light-keeper of the Floating-light, to the Bell Rock Light-house, as his principal Assistant. The writer had a wish to be of service to this man, as he was one of those who came off to the Floating-light in the month of September 1807, while she was riding at single anchor, after the severe gale of the 7th, at a time when it was hardly possible to make up this vessel's crew; but the crossness of his manner prevented his reaping the benefit of such intentions.

Patriot makes a trip to Arbroath and back to the Rock, in 24 hours.

The trips of the stone-vessels became more and more remarkable for dispatch. The Patriot having only sailed for Arbroath yesterday morning at 8 o'clock, returned this evening at the same hour with a cargo; when the landing-master immediately got his praam-boats alongside, and came to the Rock with 16 stones, 8 joggles, 8 casks of pozzolano, and the same quantity of lime and sand, with seven logs of timber for the Railways, which were immediately taken up to the Beacon, till they were wanted on the Rock. Such, therefore, was the dispatch given to the loading of the materials at Arbroath, together with the persevering activity of Mr Spink, — who had succeeded Mr Macdonald in the command of the Patriot, — and his mate Mr Peter Soutar, that, although she did not reach Arbroath till the morning of the 21st, at 1 o'clock, yet being instantly loaded, she was made fast to her moorings again at the Rock, after an absence of only 24 hours.

An attempt made to land stones at high-water, with the bridge-apparatus.

The weather was extremely fine to-day, and the artificers laid the Fifty-sixth course, or kitchen-floor, forming, like the other floors of the building, a part also of the outward wall. For supporting the inward extremity of these long stones, until a sufficient weight was built upon the exterior wall, the joiners had erected a piece of frame-work on the floor below on which they rested. This morning at 4 o'clock, the landing-master's crew had commenced their operations, and by 12 noon 34 stones were landed, together with the several articles mentioned above, which discharged the Patriot, and she again sailed for Arbroath. An attempt was made to-day to land materials at high-water with the bridge-apparatus; but, although the water was smooth, yet there was a certain lift in the sea, which occasionally brought a sudden strain on the frame of the bridge, and made the whole shake and jerk in such a manner as to communicate a considerable degree of tremor to the whole fabric of the Beacon-house, shewing that this mode of landing weighty stones could hardly be ventured upon, even in the very finest weather.

Progress of landing the stones. The Seamen become discontented.

The building operations had for some time proceeded more slowly, from the higher parts of the Light-house requiring much longer time than an equal tonnage of the lower courses. The duty of the landing-master's crew had, upon the whole, been easy of late; for, though the work was occasionally irregular, yet the stones being lighter, they were more speedily lifted from the hold of the stone-vessel to the deck of the praam-boat, and again to the waggons on the railway, after which they came properly under the charge of the foreman-builder; the artificers working the several purchase-tackles in raising the stones through the successive stages, from the railways to the bridge, and from thence to the top of the building, as represented in Plates IX. and XVIII. It is, however, a strange, though not an uncommon feature in the human character, that when people have least to complain of, they are most apt to become dissatisfied, as was now the case with the seamen employed in the Bell Rock service, about their rations of beer. Indeed, ever since the carpenter of the Floating-light, formerly noticed, had been brought to the Rock, expressions of discontent had been manifested upon various occasions. This being represented to the writer, he sent for Captain Wilson, the landing-master, and Mr Taylor, commander of the Tender, with whom he talked over the subject. They stated, that they considered the daily allowance of the seamen in every respect ample, and that the work being now much lighter than formerly, they had no just ground for complaint; Mr Taylor adding, that if those who now complained "were even to be fed upon soft bread and turkeys, they would not think themselves right." At 12 noon, as before noticed, the work of the landing-master's crew was completed for the day. But at 4 o'clock, while the Rock was under water, those on the Beacon were surprised by the arrival of a boat from the Tender, without any signal having been made from the Beacon. It, however, brought the following note to the writer from the landing-master's crew.

Sir Joseph Banks, Tender.

"Sir,

"We are informed by our masters, that our allowance is to be as before, and it is not sufficient to serve us, for we have been at work since 4 o'clock this morning, and we have come on board to dinner, and there is no beer for us before to-morrow morning, to which a sufficient answer is required before we go from the Beacon; and we are, Sir, your most obedient servants."

On reading this, the writer returned a verbal message, intimating, that an answer would be sent on board of the Tender, at the same time ordering the boat instantly to quit the Beacon. He then addressed the following note to the landing-master.

Correspondence with the Landing-master.

"Beacon-house, 22d June 1810,
5 o'clock, P. M.

"Sir,

"I have just now received a letter purporting to be from the landing-master's crew and seamen on board of the Sir Joseph Banks, though without either date or signature; in answer to which, I inclose a statement of the daily allowance of provisions for the seamen in this service, which you will post up in the ship's-galley, and at 7 o'clock this evening I will come on board to enquire into this unexpected and most unnecessary demand for an additional allowance of beer. In the inclosed, you will not find any alteration from the original statement, fixed in the galley at the beginning of the season. I have, however, judged this mode of giving your people an answer, preferable to that of conversing with them on the Beacon. I am, Sir, your most obedient servant,

"To Captain Wilson.

Robert Stevenson."

"Beacon-house, 22d June 1810.—Schedule of the daily Allowance of Provisions to be served out on board of the Sir Joseph Banks Tender."—"1½ lb. beef; 1 lb. bread; 8 oz. oatmeal; 2 oz. barley; 2 oz. butter; 3 quarts beer; vegetables and salt no stated allowance. When the seamen are employed in unloading the Smeaton and Patriot, a draught of beer is, as formerly, to be allowed from the stock of these vessels. Further, in wet and stormy weather, or when the work commences very early in the morning, or continues till a late hour at night, a glass of spirits will also be served out to the crew as heretofore, on the requisition of the Landing-master."

"Robert Stevenson."

Writer goes on board of the Tender.

On writing this letter and schedule, a signal was made on the Beacon for the landing-master's boat, which immediately came to the Rock, and the schedule was afterwards stuck up in the Tender's galley. When sufficient time had been allowed to the crew to consider of their conduct, a second signal was made for a boat, and at 7 o'clock the writer left the Bell Rock, after a residence of four successive weeks in the Beacon-house. The first thing which occupied his attention on board of the Tender, was to look round upon the Light-house, which he saw with some degree of emotion and surprise, now vieing in height with the Beacon-house; for, although he had often viewed it from the extremity of the western Railway on the Rock, yet the scene, upon the whole, seemed far more interesting from the Tender's moorings, at the distance of about half a mile.

Two of the Seamen are dismissed the service.

The Smeaton having just arrived at her moorings with a cargo, a signal was made for Captain Pool to come on board of the Tender, that he might be at hand to remove from the service any of those who might persist in their discontented conduct. One of the two principal leaders in this affair, being the master of one of the praam-boats, and who had also steered the boat which brought the letter to the Beacon, was first called upon deck, and asked if he had read the statement fixed up in the galley this afternoon, and whether he was satisfied with it. He replied that he had read the paper, but was not satisfied, as it held out no alteration on the allowance; on which he was immediately ordered into the Smeaton's boat. The next man called had but lately entered the service, and being also interrogated as to his resolution, he declared himself to be of the same mind with the Praam-master, and was also forthwith ordered into the boat. The writer, without calling any more of the seamen, went forward to the gangway, where they were collected, and listening to what was passing upon deck: he addressed them at the hatchway, and stated that two of their companions had just been dismissed the service, and sent on board of the Smeaton, to be conveyed to Arbroath. He therefore wished each man to consider for himself, how far it would be proper, by any unreasonableness of conduct, to place themselves in a similar situation, especially as they were aware that it was optional in him either to dismiss them, or send them on board a Man-of-war. It might appear that much inconveniency would be felt at the Rock by a change of hands at this critical period, by checking for a time the progress of a building so intimately connected with the best interests of navigation; yet this would be but of a temporary nature, while the injury to themselves might be irreparable. It was now, therefore, required of any man who, in this disgraceful manner, chose to leave the service, that he should instantly make his appearance upon deck, while the Smeaton's boat was alongside. But those below having expressed themselves satisfied with their situation, viz. William Brown, George Gibb, Alexander Scott, John Dick, Robert Couper, Alexander Shephard, James Grieve, David Carey, William Pearson, Stuart Eaton, Alexander Lawrence, and John Spink, were accordingly considered as having returned to their duty. This disposition to mutiny, which had so strongly manifested itself, being now happily suppressed, Captain Pool got orders to proceed for Arbroath Bay, and land the two men he had on board, and to deliver the following letter at the office of the work-yard.

"On Board of the Tender off the Bell Rock,
22d June 1810. 8 o'clock P. M.

"Dear Sir,

"A discontented and mutinous spirit having manifested itself of late, among the Landing-master's crew, they struck work to-day, and demanded an additional allowance of beer, and I have found it necessary to dismiss D——d and M——e, who are now sent on shore with the Smeaton. You will, therefore, be so good as to pay them their wages, including this day only. Nothing can be more unreasonable than the conduct of the seamen on this occasion, as the landing-master's crew not only had their own allowance on board of the Tender, but, in the course of this day, they had drawn no fewer than 24 quart pots of beer from the stock of the Patriot, while unloading her.

"I remain, yours truly,
"Robert Stevenson."

"To Mr Lachlan Kennedy, Bell-Rock Office, Arbroath."

On dispatching this letter to Mr Kennedy, the writer returned to the Beacon about 9 o'clock, where this afternoon's business had produced many conjectures, especially when the Smeaton got under way, instead of proceeding to land her cargo. The bell on the Beacon being rung, the artificers were assembled on the bridge, when the affair was explained to them. He, at the same time, congratulated them upon the first appearance of mutiny being happily set at rest by the dismissal of its two principal abettors.

Saturday, 23d.

Progress of the Works at Arbroath.

The Smeaton having landed the disaffected men and delivered the letter, returned to the Bell Rock last evening at 8 o'clock, when the landing-master and his crew immediately proceeded to discharge her, leaving the loaded praams at their moorings for the night. By letters from the work-yard from Mr David Logan, clerk of works, the writer learned, that, when the two courses which the stone-cutters had now in hand were completed, there would only be one more to prepare, and that already several of the masons were about to be paid off.

Sunday, 24th.

The Works are visited by Mr Murdoch of Soho.

At the Rock, the landing of the materials, and the building operations of the light-room-store, went on successfully, and in a way similar to those of the provision-store. To-day it blew fresh breezes; but the seamen nevertheless landed 28 stones, and the artificers built the Fifty-eighth and Fifty-ninth courses. The works were visited by Mr Murdoch junior, from Messrs Boulton and Watt's works of Soho. He landed just as the bell rung for prayers; after which the writer enjoyed much pleasure from his very intelligent conversation: and having been almost the only stranger he had seen for some weeks, he parted with him, after a short interview, with much regret.

Wednesday, 27th.

Sixty-second course laid.

There were 46 pieces of stone landed to-day, 16 of which were built, being the Sixty-second course, in which the upper brass cases for the hinges of the storm-shutters occurred, each of which weighed about 25 lb., or 100 lb. for the four cases with their hinges. The sole or foot of the balance-crane was also shifted, an operation which became necessary at the height of about every 16 feet of the Light-house; and it was now raised from the store-room to the kitchen-floor. The shaft of the crane consisted of one piece of 8 feet, and three of 6 feet, making its whole length 26 feet, of which, about 7 feet were occupied with the body and foot of the crane. The operations of laying the courses in which the hinge-cases of the storm-shutters of the different windows occurred, like those of the entrance-door, being very tedious, the Beacon-bell was rung this morning at the very early hour of 3 o'clock, and as the work continued till half-past 9 at night, the artificers had 8 hours and a half's extra work, which yielded them 4s. 3d. of extra pay.

Thursday, 28th.

Workmen wetted by the sea on the top of the walls.

The Sixty-third and Sixty-fourth courses were laid to-day, consisting of 16 stones each. Last night the wind had shifted to north-east, and blowing fresh, was accompanied with a heavy surf upon the Rock. Towards high water it had a very grand and wonderful appearance. Waves of considerable magnitude rose as high as the solid or level of the entrance-door, which, being open to the south-west, was fortunately to the leeward; but on the windward side, the sprays flew like lightning up the sloping sides of the building; and although the walls were now elevated 64 feet above the Rock, and about 52 feet from high-water mark, yet the artificers were nevertheless wetted, and occasionally interrupted in their operations on the top of the walls. These appearances were in a great measure new at the Bell Rock, there having till of late been no building to conduct the seas, or object to compare them with. Although, from the description of the Edystone Light-house, the mind was prepared for such effects, yet they were not expected to the present extent, in the summer season; the sea being most awful to-day, whether observed from the Beacon or the Building. To windward, the sprays fell from the height above noticed, in the most wonderful cascades, and streamed down the walls of the building in froth as white as snow. To leeward of the Light-house, the collision or meeting of the waves produced a pure white kind of drift, which is attempted to be represented in the Frontispiece to this work: it rose about 30 feet in height, like a fine downy mist, which, in its fall, felt upon the face and hands more like a dry powder than a liquid substance. The effects of these seas, as they ranged among the beams, and dashed upon the higher parts of the Beacon, produced a temporary tremulous motion throughout the whole fabric, which to a stranger must have been frightful.

Saturday, 30th.

Mr John Reid's Report on the Floating-light.

The artificers laid the Sixty-fifth course to-day, forming the fourth or bed-room floor. They had, however, no extra hours' work, a circumstance which had not occurred for several weeks before. Although, from the rapid progress which was now making with the Building, there was every prospect that it would be finished in the course of this year; yet, as the Light-room and its apparatus were very critical parts of the operation, which would necessarily fall to be transported to the Rock at a late period of the season, and were, consequently, liable to many casualties, it was proper to make provision for continuing the Floating-light for another winter, in case the light should not be exhibited from the Light-house. This vessel had now been on her station for three years; and as she lay at anchor in 19 fathoms water, it had, consequently, been impossible thoroughly to examine her bottom. What rendered her state more uncertain, was the condition of the logs of timber employed for supporting the temporary Railways on the Rock for nearly a similar period. These logs were of the common Norway-fir, and when laid down measured about ten inches upon each side; but after lying about three years on the Rock, they were so much wasted by the small insect formerly mentioned, that they would not now square to more than 7 inches, without leaving traces of the ravages of this animal, having thereby lost at the rate of about one-half inch on each side of sound timber per annum. Directions had been given to Mr John Reid, who, during the summer months, had the command of the Floating-light, and who was also professionally a ship-carpenter, to take a convenient opportunity of trimming the vessel, in such a manner as to give her a list first to one side and then to the other, so as to get her bottom as fully examined as possible. This having been done, Mr Reid intimated that he considered her in a sound state. The writer accordingly left the Beacon-house to-day, accompanied by the landing-master, to see some of the side-planks which had been dubbed or dressed with a carpenter's adze, and, on examination, he had the satisfaction to find that they appeared perfectly fresh. This was a matter of some consequence to the work, as it must have been attended with great inconvenience, to have removed such a vessel as the Floating-light, and put another in her place, even for a short period. After this inspection, the writer returned to the Rock, having previously requested of Mr Reid to make a report in writing, which he did in the following terms:

"Pharos Floating-Light, off the Bell Rock,
30th June 1810.

"Sir,

"According to your orders, I have, on several occasions, during this month, careened the Float, and inspected her bottom as much as possible while the vessel is at anchor; but I can see no appearance of the wood-worm in any part of it. There is indeed plenty of sea-weed, mussels, and red-worms (creatures with many feet), but it is not this kind of worm that perforates the planks of shipping; and as this destructive animal generally makes its appearance between wind and water, I am apt to believe that the Pharos' bottom is perfectly sound and healthy. With regard to the beam and knee observed to be working a little, I will send a note of the scantling of the timber that will be necessary for securing it, to Mr Dickie, the carpenter, at Arbroath. I, for one, have no objections to another winter on board, without further repairs; for though she rolls heavily in the trough of the sea, yet she has, upon the whole, been a very kindly ship to me.—I am, Sir, your most obedient servant,

"To Mr Stevenson.

John Reid, Carpenter."

1810, July.

Narrow escape of one of the Masons.

While William Kennedy, one of the masons, was stepping off the bridge into the entrance-door of the Light-house, one of the cast-iron slips of the balance-weight of the crane, weighing about 70 lb., fell from the top of the building and grazed his left shoulder, but, fortunately, in so gentle a manner, that it hardly ruffled the skin; a few inches nearer, it would have carried away his arm or killed him on the spot.

Sunday, 1st.

Writer describes his Cabin.

The artificers laid 12 stones to-day, and the seamen landed no fewer than 34 blocks.—The writer had now been at the Bell Rock since the latter end of May, or about six weeks, during four of which he had been a constant inhabitant of the Beacon, without having been once off the Rock. After witnessing the laying of the Sixty-seventh or second Course of the bed-room apartment, he left the Rock with the Tender, and went ashore, as some arrangements were to make for the future conduct of the works at Arbroath, which were soon to be brought to a close; the landing-master's crew having, in the mean time, shifted on board of the Patriot. In leaving the Rock, the writer kept his eyes fixed upon the Light-house, which had recently got into the form of a house, having several tiers or storeys of windows. Nor was he unmindful of his habitation in the Beacon, now far overtoped by the masonry; where he had spent several weeks in a kind of active retirement, making practical experiment of the fewness of the positive wants of man. His cabin measured not more than 4 feet 3 inches in breadth on the floor; and though, from the oblique direction of the beams of the Beacon, it widened towards the top, yet it did not admit of the full extension of his arms when he stood on the floor; while its length was little more than sufficient for suspending a cot-bed during the night, calculated for being triced up to the roof through the day, which left free room for the admission of occasional visitants. His folding-table was attached with hinges, immediately under the small window of the apartment, and his books, barometer, thermometer, portmanteau, and two or three camp-stools, formed the bulk of his moveables. His diet being plain, the paraphernalia of the table were proportionally simple; though every thing had the appearance of comfort, and even of neatness, the walls being covered with green cloth, formed into pannels with red tape, and his bed festooned with curtains of yellow cotton-stuff. If, in speculating upon the abstract wants of man in such a state of exclusion, one were reduced to a single book, the Sacred Volume, whether considered for the striking diversity of its story,—the morality of its doctrine,—or the important truths of its Gospel, would have proved by far the greatest treasure.

Monday, 2d.

Case of George Dall, an impressed seaman.

In walking over the work-yard at Arbroath this morning, the writer found that the stones of the course immediately under the cornice were all in hand, and that a week's work would now finish the whole; while the intermediate courses lay ready numbered and marked for shipping to the Rock. Among other subjects which had occupied his attention to-day, was a visit from some of the relations of George Dall, a young man who had been impressed near Dundee in the month of February last: A dispute had arisen between the Magistrates of that borough and the Regulating Officer as to his right of impressing Dall, who was bona fide one of the protected seamen in the Bell Rock service. In the mean time, the poor lad was detained, and ultimately committed to the prison of Dundee, to remain until the question should be tried before the Court of Session. His friends were naturally very desirous to have him relieved upon bail. But as this was only to be done by the judgment of the Court, all that could be said was, that his pay and allowances should be continued in the same manner as if he had been upon the sick-list. The circumstances of Dall's case, were briefly these. He had gone to see some of his friends in the neighbourhood of Dundee, in winter, while the works were suspended, having got leave of absence from Mr Taylor, who commanded the Bell Rock Tender, and had in his possession one of the Protection Medals, represented in Plate XII., and alluded to at page 209. Unfortunately, however, for Dall, the Regulating-Officer thought proper to disregard these documents, as, according to the strict and literal interpretation of the Admiralty regulations, a seaman does not stand protected unless he is actually on board of his ship, or in a boat belonging to her, or has the Admiralty-protection in his possession. This order of the Board, however, cannot be rigidly followed in practice; and therefore, when the matter is satisfactorily stated to the Regulating-Officer, the impressed man is generally liberated. But in Dall's case this was peremptorily refused, and he was retained at the instance of the Magistrates. The writer having brought the matter under the consideration of the Commissioners of the Northern Light-houses, they authorised it to be tried on the part of the Light-house Board, as one of extreme hardship. The Court, upon the first hearing, ordered Dall to be liberated from prison; and the proceedings never went further.

Tuesday, 3rd.

Magistrates of Arbroath visit the Bell Rock.

During the three years in which the operations of the Bell Rock Light-house had been in progress, the Magistrates of the Royal Burgh of Arbroath, where the work-yard was established, had shewn the utmost attention in forwarding the works, by every means in their power. In particular, a free or peculiar birth had been given to the vessels of the Light-house service, where a crane was permitted to be erected; and the building materials were allowed to be reshipped for the Light-house, without any additional charge for shore-dues. Indeed, the whole community of this town seemed to view the work, and those concerned with the operations, in a very favourable manner. The writer was therefore happy, at this time, in having an opportunity of giving effect to an arrangement long talked of, with the Magistrates and some of their friends, of taking a sail to the Bell Rock, to see the progress of the works. This having been accordingly intimated to Provost Airth, he gladly embarked in the Tender, along with two of the former Chief-Magistrates, Balfour and Milne, and Bailies Duncan, Fleming, Anson, Wightman, and Kid, together with Mr John Colville, Town-Clerk, Messrs Bruce, Bell, Balfour, Johnston, Christie and Lindsay, &c. in all sixteen. The vessel sailed from Arbroath at an early hour, but the weather became thick and foggy, with the wind at S.E., and it was 2 o'clock P. M., before she reached her moorings at the Rock, which being then covered with water, the party had to wait till about 6 before a landing could be made. During these four hours, the vessel had a very unpleasant rolling motion: the party cast many a weary look towards the Rock for its appearance; and, on landing, much satisfaction was expressed at getting a firm footing upon the railways. The party soon began to clamber up to the Beacon, and, after examining all its parts, crossed the bridge, but only a few ventured to the top of Light-house, from the narrowness of the passages, and difficult position of the ladders. After spending fully three hours upon the Rock, the water began to rise upon the Railways, when the gentlemen again embarked, and were greeted with cheers from the workmen. The wind being fair, and the weather pleasant, the Tender soon reached Arbroath, when the party landed, much delighted with their trip, while the writer was not a little pleased at having thus had an opportunity of gratifying so many of his friends.

Wednesday, 3d.

Number of Artificers on the Rock reduced to 22.

The artificers had yesterday laid the Sixty-eighth course of the building, consisting of 16 stones, of which 10 had also been landed. The Tender having returned from Arbroath this afternoon, the landing-master's crew left the Patriot, and took up their quarters again on board of the Tender. The artificers lodged in the Beacon had of late varied from twenty-six to thirty-one in number; but the Railways being finished, the work now admitted of their being reduced to twenty-two. During the time that the Rock was covered with water, and materials could not be landed, the masons were employed in dressing off and repolishing any inequalities which appeared on the interior walls of the different apartments. The raising of stones from the waggons on the Rock to the top of the building, now about 80 feet in height, had become rather a tedious operation. The lift with the balance-crane in particular being upwards of 45 feet, it required some precaution and trouble in coiling such a length of chain upon the barrel. It therefore became necessary to lessen this operation, by placing a winch-machine on the store-room floor, and projecting a beam from the western window, to form a stage in taking up the stones, as will be understood by examining the third year's work of Plate IX., and the general view of the operations at the Rock represented in Plate XVIII.

Narrow escape of the Smeaton at the Bell Rock. Advantage of Alarm-bells.

Being now within twelve courses of being ready for building the cornice, measures were taken for getting the stones of it and the parapet-wall of the Light-room brought from Edinburgh, where, as before noticed, they had been prepared, and were in readiness for shipping. The honour of conveying the upper part of the Light-house, and of landing the last stone of the building on the Rock, was considered to belong to Captain Pool of the Smeaton, who had been longer in the service than the master of the Patriot. The Smeaton was therefore now partly loaded with old iron, consisting of broken railways and other lumber, which had been lying about the Rock. After landing these at Arbroath, she took on board James Craw, with his horse and cart, which could now be spared at the work-yard, to be employed in carting the stones from Edinburgh to Leith. Alexander Davidson and William Kennedy, two careful masons, were also sent to take charge of the loading of the stones at Greenside, and stowing them on board of the vessel at Leith. The writer also went on board, with a view to call at the Bell Rock, and to take his passage up the Firth of Forth. The wind, however, coming to blow very fresh from the eastward, with thick and foggy weather, it became necessary to reef the mainsail, and set the second-jib. When in the act of making a tack towards the Tender, the sailors who worked the head sheets were all of a sudden alarmed with the sound of the smith's hammer and anvil on the Beacon, and had just time to put the ship about to save her from running ashore on the north western point of the Rock, marked "James Craw's horse," in Plate VI. On looking towards the direction from whence the sound came, the Building and Beacon-house were seen, with consternation, while the ship was hailed by those on the Rock, who were no less confounded at seeing the near approach of the Smeaton, and, just as the vessel cleared the danger, the smith and those in the mortar-galley made signs in token of their happiness at our fortunate escape. From this occurrence the writer had an experimental proof of the utility of the large Bells which were in preparation to be rung by the machinery of the Revolving-light; for, had it not been the sound of the smith's anvil, the Smeaton, in all probability, would have been wrecked upon the Rock. In case the vessel had struck, those on board might have been safe, having now the Beacon-house as a place of refuge; but the vessel, which was going at a great velocity, must have suffered severely, and it was more than probable that the horse would have been drowned, there being no means of getting him out of the vessel. Of this valuable animal and his master, both delineated in Plate X., we shall take an opportunity of saying more in another part of the work.

The Artificers on the Beacon greatly alarmed.

The weather cleared up in the course of the night, but the wind shifted to the N.E., and blew very fresh: and it was with difficulty that a communication could be made with the Tender, after which the Smeaton bore away for Leith about 7 A. M. At 9 she was abreast of Fifeness, and at half-past 1 P. M. got safely into Leith harbour, after a passage of about six hours, which was fully the quickest which the writer had made from the Bell Rock to Leith, a distance of about 88 miles. From the force of the wind, being now the period of spring-tides, a very heavy swell was experienced at the Rock: at 2 o'clock on the following morning, the people on the Beacon were in a state of great alarm about their safety, as the sea had broke up part of the floor of the mortar-gallery, which was thus cleared of the lime-casks, and other buoyant articles; and the alarm-bell being rung, all hands were called to render what assistance was in their power for the safety of themselves and the ma-terials. At this time, some would willingly have left the Beacon and gone into the Building: the sea, however, ran so high, that there was no passage along the bridge of communication; and when the interior of the Light-house came to be examined in the morning, it appeared that great quantities of water had come over the walls, now 80 feet in height, and had run down through the several apartments, and out at the entrance-door. From this state of things the work was stopped for two days, in the course of which the joiners got the mortar-gallery refitted, and the landing-master's crew supplied it with a fresh stock of materials for making mortar. Notwithstanding this state of the sea upon the Rock, the Tender and Patriot still kept at their moorings. Such, indeed, was the practice of the seamen, in this kind of life, that, unless when the wind blew from N.W., or in such a direction as made the vessels ride with their sterns towards the Rock, they never thought of moving from their moorings, unless the vessels were deeply loaded.

Progress of the Light-room works.

On reaching Edinburgh, the writer found the Light-room and Reflecting-apparatus in considerable forwardness at the Greenside Company's works. He had also received advice from Prescot, that the plate-glass for the windows would soon be in a state of readiness; and Messrs Meirs and Son of London intimated, that they would cast the Bells at any time, on receiving a week or ten days notice. The only article connected with the light-room, regarding which there was a doubt, was the coloured glass for distinguishing the light, which had long since been commissioned from Mr Okey of London, who, though a very ingenious artist, was rather an irregular correspondent.

Works at Arbroath completed.

The upper course of the Light-house at the work-yard of Arbroath, was completed on the 6th, and the whole of the stones were therefore now ready for being shipped to the Rock. The operations of the hewers or stone-cutters were thus brought very nearly to a close: only the 23 steps of the stone staircase of the Light-house remained to be dressed; and this piece of work was reserved for some of the principal masons, on their return from the Rock, as the steps could not be conveniently built until the balance-crane and other bulky apparatus were removed from the building. From the present state of the works, it was impossible that the two squads of artificers at Arbroath and the Bell Rock could meet together at this period; and as, in public works of this kind, which had continued for a series of years, it is not customary to allow the men to separate without what is termed a "Finishing-pint," five guineas were for this purpose placed at the disposal of Mr David Logan, clerk of works. With this sum the stone-cutters at Arbroath had a merry-meeting in their barrack, collected their sweethearts and friends, and concluded their labours with a dance. It was remarked, however, that their happiness on this occasion was not without alloy. The consideration of parting, and leaving a steady and regular employment, to go in quest of work, and mix with other society, after having been harmoniously lodged for years together in one large "Guild-hall or Barrack," was rather painful. The completion of this part of the work at Arbroath was felt as an era in the Light-house affairs, by admitting of the discharge of so considerable a number of the artificers. Mr David Logan, by this means also, got off to the Bell Rock, having been hitherto chiefly confined to the operations ashore.

Mr Smeaton's daughter visits the Light-house works at Edinburgh.

While the writer was at Edinburgh, he was fortunate enough to meet with Mrs Dickson, only daughter of the late celebrated Mr Smeaton, whose works at the Edystone Light-house had been of such essential consequence to the operations at the Bell Rock. Even her own elegant accomplishments are identified with her father's work, she having herself made the drawing of the vignette on the title-page of the Narrative of the Edystone Light-house. Every admirer of the works of that singularly eminent man, must also feel an obligation to her for the very comprehensive and distinct account given of his life, which is attached to his Reports, published in three volumes quarto, by the Society of Civil Engineers. Mrs Dickson being, at this time, returning from a tour to the Hebrides and Western Highlands of Scotland, had heard of the Bell Rock works, and from their similarity to those of the Edystone, was strongly impressed with the desire of visiting the spot. But, on inquiring for the writer at Edinburgh, and finding from him that the upper part of the Light-house, consisting of nine courses, might be seen in the immediate vicinity, and also, that one of the vessels which, in compliment to her father's memory, had been named "The Smeaton," might also now be seen in Leith,—she considered herself extremely fortunate; and having first visited the works at Greenside, she afterwards went to Leith to see "The Smeaton," then loading for the Bell Rock. On stepping on board, Mrs Dickson seemed to be quite overcome with so many concurrent circumstances, tending in a peculiar manner to revive and enliven the memory of her departed father; and, on leaving the vessel, she would not be restrained from presenting the crew with a piece of money. "The Smeaton" had been named spontaneously, from a sense of the obligation which a public work of the description of the Bell Rock owed to the labours and the abilities of Mr Smeaton. The writer certainly never could have anticipated the satisfaction which he this day felt, in witnessing the pleasure it afforded to the only representative of this great man's family. Mrs Dickson's stay in Edinburgh was short, as, in seeing so much of the Bell Rock works, she had accomplished the chief object which brought her to this side of the country. On her return to the neighbourhood of Kendal, the place of her residence, she had the kindness to send the writer a portrait of her father, together with the vignette of the Edystone Light-house.

Mr David Logan joins the Works at the Rock.

At the Bell Rock, Mr Peter Logan, foreman builder, was reinforced by the able and active exertions of his son Mr David Logan, who was now relieved from attendance at the work-yard of Arbroath, where the stone-cutters had just completed their operations. In the mean time, the walls of the Light-house were progressively rising, and, on Friday the 6th, the artificers laid the Seventy-first course, consisting of 16 stones, and shifted the foot of the Balance-crane from the kitchen to the bed-room, about 42 feet above the bridge. A considerable time was, therefore, occupied in raising a stone from thence to the top of the building. To remedy this, as formerly alluded to, a beam was projected from the western window of the light-room store, where a winch-machine and apparatus were placed, with which the stones were raised from the bridge to the level of the window-sill. The chain of the balance-crane was then lowered, and hooked into the Lewis-bat of the stone, which was thus hoisted up, and laid in its place on the building, as will be fully understood by examining the progress of the work in Plate IX. This additional tackle from the store-room window gave a wonderful facility to the operation of raising the stones; for, though the time of working upon the walls of the building was now extended to the whole day, yet the period of landing the materials upon the Rock was still unavoidably confined to the few hours during which it was left by the tide at low-water.

Saturday, 7th.

The Patriot is seven days in being cleared of a cargo.

The landing-master's crew commenced at 4 o'clock this morning, and transported 24 blocks of stone and 8 dove-tailed joggles to the Rock in the course of the day, which cleared the Patriot of her cargo, when she sailed for Arbroath, having now been no less than 7 days on the birth. This was, therefore, the most tedious trip since the first cargo of this season, which, as before noticed, had been on board of the Smeaton for 11 days. The stones landed to-day could not be raised to the top of the building, as the joiners had possession of the upper apartment, where they were fixing the framing used for supporting the floor-stones, while building. The stones were, in the mean time, left chiefly on the Rock, though a few were laid upon the bridge.

Saturday, 8th.

Progress of raising the Stones.

To-day the Seventy-second course was laid. The mill-wrights, in the mean time, made preparations for fitting up another winch-apparatus on the bed-room floor, similar to that already described for the store-room, by projecting a beam from its western window, which was to form another stage for lifting the materials. When, therefore, a stone was landed on the Rock, and conveyed along the Railways, within reach of the winch-apparatus upon the bridge, and raised to its level, it was next hooked by the chain of the winch on the store-room floor: having attained that height, it was laid hold of by the chain of the machinery on the bed-room floor; and last of all, it was hooked to the chain of the balance-crane, by which it was raised to the top of the walls and laid in its place. The series of machinery now in motion on the Bell Rock, was very complete, and gave great facility to the landing of the materials. A set of tackle was at work at the landing-cranes on the eastern and western side of the Rock, for lifting the stones from on board of the Praam-boats, and laying them on the waggons: from thence they were wheeled along the Railways to the bridge; from which they were successively lifted, as has been described, by the machinery upon it; then by that in the store-room; next by that in the bed-room, and last of all by the balance-crane,—as will be more particularly seen in the third year's work of Plate IX., and in the General View of the Works, Plate XVIII.

Monday, 9th.

Last cargo of stone shipped at Arbroath.

At Arbroath, the Patriot had now loaded the last cargo of building materials from that port, consisting of 65 pieces of stone, 4 dove-tailed joggles, 18 casks of pozzolano, lime, sand, and cement, with three cart-loads of timber, and the necessary supplies of provisions for the Tender and Beacon-house. From the interest which the inhabitants of Arbroath took in all that concerned the Bell Rock Lighthouse, it soon became generally known that the last cargo from the work-yard was loading. Upon this occasion, the ships in the harbour hoisted their colours, in compliment to the approaching termination of the works; and, at 7 P. M., a great concourse of people collected on the quays, who united in giving three hearty cheers, as the Patriot sailed from the harbour. At the Bell Rock, the building-artificers were at a stand to-day for want of materials, and were employed in dressing off and polishing the interior of the building, while the landing-master's crew were removing lumber from the Rock, which, for the present, was put on board of the Tender. The joiners and mill-wrights were occupied in framing a centre for building the dome-roof of the library.

Tuesday, 10th.

The Patriot reached her moorings this morning, but it was then blowing a fresh gale from W.S.W., and the Tender's boat had much difficulty in getting her hawser reeved through the eye-bolt of the floating-buoy. No materials could be landed on the Rock to-day.

Wednesday, 11th.

The weather being moderate, with the wind at S.E., the landing-master's crew proceeded this morning to discharge the Patriot at the early hour of 3 o'clock; and in the course of the day, 30 blocks and 2 dove-tailed joggles of stone, and 7 casks of pozzolano, lime, and sand, were landed, besides some timber, which occupied them till 8 o'clock P. M., with little intermission. During this time also, the artificers laid the Seventy-third course, consisting of 16 stones.

Thursday, 12th.

Library Floor laid.

The building-artificers laid the Seventy-fourth course to-day, being the floor of the library or strangers' room, which, like the others, consisted altogether of 18 stones; but of the floor courses, as before noticed, only sixteen stones were laid in the first instance, the centre and the stone connected with the man-hole being left for the conveniency of moving the machinery as the building advanced in height. The seamen landed 25 blocks of stone, and the remaining 2 dove-tailed joggles which discharged the Patriot; and at 2 P. M. she sailed for Leith, to load a cargo of the upper courses of the Light-house, which had been worked at Edinburgh. The artificers on the Rock were now reduced to 22, there having been 6 of their number sent ashore at this time. The Smeaton having loaded 48 stones at Leith, with sundry other materials, arrived to-day at the Bell Rock; but the praams were still at their moorings, loaded with part of the former cargo, which the builders could not yet receive.

Friday, 13th.

To-day the building-artificers laid the Seventy-fifth and Seventy-sixth courses, consisting each of 12 stones, and the seamen landed 11 stones, being the remainder of the Patriot's cargo.

Saturday, 14th.

The Seventy-seventh and Seventy-eighth courses were laid to-day: the landing-master's crew discharged 26 blocks of stone, and 20 dove-tailed joggles from the Smeaton, and landed them on the Rock. As it blew very fresh from the S.W., it was a hard day's work for the seamen, who commenced this morning as early as 2 o'clock to load the praam-boats, and it was between 7 and 8 in the evening before the boats returned on board of the Tender for the night.

Sunday, 15th.

The artificers laid the Seventy-ninth and Eightieth courses to-day, consisting of 12 stones each, and had no less than seven and a half hours of extra time, having been at work from 4 o'clock this morning till 9 in the evening, owing to some difficulty which occurred in laying the course, in which the upper storm-hinge cases occurred.

Monday, 16th.

Ring-bar course laid.

Floors described.

The artificers laid the Eighty-first course, consisting of 12 stones from Craigleith Quarry, being one of these worked at Edinburgh, in which a groove, for an iron-ring, was cut, as an additional security for the superincumbent weight of the cornice. In the First course of the Dome of St Paul's of London, a continuous chain had been sunk into a groove, in order to bind the haunches of the arch more firmly together. Mr Smeaton, alluding to this in his Narrative, also inserted a chain into each of his floor-courses at the Edystone Light-house. Being of an arched form, these chains inserted into grooves, cut in the haunch-courses of arches, have a tendency to counteract their pressure outwards. At the Bell Rock, the writer, however, designed the floors in such a manner that each projected from the outward wall of the building towards the centre, and the whole being grooved in a lateral direction, in the joints, like the deals of a common floor, became as one stone, having a perpendicular pressure upon the walls. Even in the dome-roof of the library, though it has a spherical appearance within, yet the stones are all laid upon horizontal beds, the dome being formed by hollowing the under beds, and making them overlap or project inward beyond each other, the pressure being still perpendicular upon the walls, instead of thrusting outwards, as in the case of an arch.

Description of the Ring-bar.

Instead of a continuous chain, as at the Edystone arches, the writer here introduced a flat-bar of the best Swedish iron into the Eighty-first course, having been previously connected in three pieces with scarf-joints and screwed bolts, with nuts. This bar was set on edge in the building: it measured 3 inches in depth, 1 inch in thickness, and was in weight about 400 lb. avoirdupois. This bar was fitted into a groove 3 inches in width, and 4 inches in depth, cut in the upper bed of the course. The bar having been heated as nearly as might be to the temperature of about 150 or 160 degrees of Fahrenheit, it was floated or run up flush with lead, in a very careful and complete manner by Mr John Gibson, plumber of Leith, who entered so much into the spirit of this work, that he attended the operation himself: no pains was, therefore, spared in having this body of melted lead properly connected with the circular bar of iron. By this means the iron was preserved from the accession of moisture, and, being much stronger than copper, it was preferred to that more ductile metal. The stones of this course were soon laid, but the artificers were occupied so long with the application of the ring-bar, that they had been at work from 4 in the morning till 8 in the evening. The Smeaton being discharged, sailed again for Leith, to take on board the last cargo of stones for the Light-house. The artificers could only receive 7 blocks of stone and 7 joggles to-day: the Hedderwick Praam-boat was accordingly left at her moorings with the remainder of the Smeaton's cargo still on board.

Tuesday, 17th.

The Dome course occupies much time in laying.

The seamen landed 2 casks of pozzolano and lime, 4 joggles and 6 blocks of stone, which discharged the praam-boats. The artificers laid 8 stones of the Eighty-second course, forming part of the dome-roof of the library. This course consisted of 16 stones, which were attended with much more difficulty than those of the ordinary courses: from their projecting into the apartment, and being also more easily injured, they required more precaution in laying and in the fitting of the joggles. The artificers were therefore at work to-day from 4 in the morning till half-past 8 in the evening, in laying one-half of this course. From the prevalence of S. W. winds, the Patriot only reached Leith at one P. M. yesterday, and commenced loading this morning, when she took on board 32 pieces of stone. The Smeaton having also arrived at Leith this afternoon, both vessels were now off the station, and it was found necessary to dispatch one of the Floating-light's boats to Arbroath, for a supply of pozzolano, lime, and sand, and also for provisions for the people at the Rock.

Wednesday, 18th.

Landing-master's crew reduced in number.

The building-artificers laid the remaining 8 stones of the Eighty-second course to-day, and had three and a half hours of extra time. The landing-master's crew having no materials to land upon the Rock, were employed to-day in collecting a variety of articles, and clearing the Building and Beacon of implements not now wanted, which were carried on board of the Tender. The Floating-light's boat returned this afternoon from Arbroath, and immediately landed her cargo. The landing-master's crew had for some time past been reduced to nine men, being little more than was necessary for working the Tender when she got under way; but at the Rock they had the daily assistance of a boat and five men from the Floating-light.

Thursday, 19th.

Patriot driven from the Rock.

The Patriot arrived at the Bell Rock this evening at 9 o'clock, with a cargo of the cornice-stones; but, as it blew a fresh gale from the N.E., the Tender's boat could not make fast her hawser to the moorings, and she was obliged to stand in for the Bay of Arbroath. There being, of course, no building materials on the Rock, the artificers were employed in dressing off and polishing some of the joints in the interior of the Light-house. At high-water to-day, it being now the time of spring-tides, there was a great deal of sea upon the Rock: considerable sprays rushed up to the smith's gallery on the Beacon, and the water occasionally rose in jets to the height of 40 feet upon the building.

Friday, 20th.

Ceremony observed at loading the last stone at Leith.

The gale from the N.E. still continued so strong, accompanied with a heavy sea, that the Patriot could not approach her moorings; and, although the Tender still kept her station, no landing was made to-day at the Rock. At high-water, it was remarked, that the spray rose to the height of about 60 feet upon the building. The Smeaton now lay in Leith loaded; but the wind and weather being so unfavourable for her getting down the Firth , she did not sail till this afternoon. It may here be proper to notice, that the loading of the centre of the Light-room floor, or last principal stone of the building, did not fail, when put on board, to excite an interest among those connected with the work. When the stone was laid upon the cart, to be conveyed to Leith, the seamen fixed an ensign-staff and flag into the circular hole in the centre of the stone, and decorated their own hats, and that of James Craw's, the Bell Rock carter, with ribbons; even his faithful and trusty horse Bassey, was ornamented with beaus and streamers of various colours. The masons also provided themselves with new aprons; and, in this manner the cart was attended in its progress to the ship. When the cart came opposite the Trinity-House of Leith, the officer of that Corporation made his appearance, dressed in his uniforms, with his staff of office; and when it reached the harbour, the shipping in the different tiers where the Smeaton lay, hoisted their colours, manifesting, by these trifling ceremonies, the interest with which the progress of this work was regarded by the public, as ultimately tending to afford safety and protection to the mariner. The wind had fortunately shifted to the S.W.; and about 5 o'clock this afternoon the Smeaton reached the Bell Rock. The writer had also the satisfaction soon afterwards to see the Patriot made fast to her moorings; but there was still too much sea to admit of landing upon the Rock.

Monday, 23d.

Many Strangers visit the present interesting state of the Works.

The present interesting state of the Light-house, which had now attained the height of 90 feet, induced a great many strangers to visit the Bell Rock, while the machinery was in operation, and the Light-house and Beacon were connected with the wooden-bridge; and beams were projected from the windows of the store-room and bed-room, for the suspension of the tackle with which the stones were raised. The Stone-lighters and Tender also lay in the offing at this time, while the Praam-boats were occasionally at the landing creeks on the eastern and western sides of the Rock, delivering the stones, which were afterwards wheeled along the railways. The whole, as shewn in Plate XVIII., afforded great pleasure, and excited the surprise of many visitants, who often endured much hardship in open boats, on a passage of from 12 to 20 miles, from the shore. Two parties, under these circumstances, landed to-day, among whom were Messrs Gellatly and Macpherson, accountants, from the Greenside works at Edinburgh. This being the fifth day of the gale, much relief was felt at the Rock on the arrival of the boats.

Tuesday, 24th.

Difficulty of landing and raising the stones of the Cornice.

At 6 o'clock this morning, Captain Wilson and his people left the Tender to load the praam-boats with stones from the Patriot, so as to be ready at tide time for landing them on the Rock. In the course of this day, the whole of the Eighty-third, and 2 stones of the Eighty-fourth courses were landed in safety, which greatly relieved the writer's mind as to the practicability of landing the stones of the Eighty-fifth course, forming the balcony-walk and light-room floor, as shewn in Plates XIII. and XVI. The stones of this course measured 7½ feet in length, and weighed upwards of one ton each. For the safety of these unwieldy and more delicately formed stones, Captain Wilson had made some very judicious arrangements. In particular, he had procured pieces of matting, and the seamen of the Tender and Floating-light had been at work for some time, preparing additional defenders, made of old ropes. By a proper application of these, the stones went safely through the progressive stages of being taken from the hold of the Smeaton, and laid on the decks of the praam-boats, after which they were delivered by the landing-apparatus on the Bell Rock, laid on the stone-waggons, conveyed along the railway to a centrical position under the bridge, and raised by four different sets of tackles to the top of the building, as will be understood by examining Plates IX. and XVIII. These several movements were fortunately accomplished with all the stones, without even a trifling injury being done to any of them. The writer, in the course of this day's work, remarked, that, from the time that one of these large blocks was laid upon the waggon at the landing-apparatus, till it reached the top of the building, then about 95 feet in height, it required, on an average of eight observations, at the rate of 14 minutes for each. Though the number of stones landed to-day was only 18, yet there being still some remains of sea from the former gale, much care and attention became necessary in the management of these unhandy materials. The landing-master's crew, who were frequently working up to the middle in water, were occupied till 10 o'clock at night before they returned to the Tender. The building-artificers were no less constantly employed, though they only laid 8 stones of the Eighty-fourth course to-day, after continuing their operations till 9 o'clock P. M.

Wednesday, 25th.

Eighty-fourth course completed.

The landing-master's crew commenced their operations again this morning at 6, and, in the course of the day, they landed 10 stones of the Eighty-fifth, being the course immediately under that of the balcony; together with 14 dove-tailed joggles for the joints, as will be understood by examining the diagrams of Plate XIII. The building-artificers laid the remaining 8 stones of the Eighty-fourth course. The Patriot having been cleared this evening of her cargo, sailed to Arbroath for a supply of water and provisions for the people on the Rock, as the stock at this time was getting low, from the vessels having of late been much off the station, while employed in bringing the stones from the work-yard at Edinburgh.

Eight stones of the Balcony course laid.

The building-artificers having now 8 blocks of the Eighty-fifth or Balcony course at hand, which, in one length, formed the balcony-path and Light-room-floor, excepting the centre-stone, as will be seen from the diagrams in Plate XIII., above alluded to, they commenced work at 4 o'clock this morning; but such was the difficulty attending the laying and fitting the joggled joints of these long stones, that it was 10 P. M. before they were laid: they had, therefore, no fewer than eight extra hours to-day, which yielded the high rate of 7s. 6d. to the workmen, and 15s. to the foremen, besides their stated wages and provisions. The landing-master's crew transported the remaining 8 blocks of the balcony to the Rock; and, when the last stone was raised in safety through its various stages to the top of the building, three cheers were given by all hands.

Thursday, 26th.

Balcony course completed.

The winds were still moderate, but it rained very heavily at times, and the artificers were very uncomfortably situate on the top of the walls. They, however, persevered in completing the laying of the balcony-course under every disadvantage. The Patriot returned to the Rock this afternoon, with a supply of provisions and necessaries; when she was dispatched to Mylnefield Quarry, for the first cargo of stones for the establishment of houses at Arbroath, about to be erected for the use of the families of the Bell Rock Light-keepers, it being only intended to lodge the keepers themselves at the Rock.

Friday, 27th.

Eighty-sixth course built.

The artificers had finished the laying of the Balcony-course, excepting the centre stone of the light-room floor, which, like the centres of the other floors, could not be laid in its place till after the removal of the foot and shaft of the balance-crane. This stone was accordingly left on board of the Smeaton, to be landed with the last cargo. The Eighty-sixth course, consisting of 8 stones, being the first of the Parapet-wall of the light-room, was landed and built. During the dinner hour, when the men were off work, the writer generally took some exercise by walking round the walls, when the Rock was under water. But to-day his boundary was greatly enlarged, for, instead of the narrow wall as a path, he felt no small degree of pleasure in walking round the balcony, and passing out and in at the space allotted for the light-room door. In the labours of this day, both the artificers and seamen felt their work to be extremely easy, compared with what it had been for some days past.

Sunday, 29th.

The building-artificers laid the Eighty-seventh and Eighty-eighth courses, consisting each of 8 stones; and having made another long day's work, they had eight extra hours pay. The landing-master's crew transported 2 casks of pozzolano, 2 of lime, and 2 of sand, with 23 blocks of stone, to the Rock, which completed the landing of the masonry of the exterior walls of the Light-house. Immediately before dinner the bell was rung, and all hands being assembled, prayers were read as usual in the artificers' barrack-room.

Ceremony observed at landing the last stone.

Captain Wilson and his crew had made preparations for landing the last stone, and, as may well be supposed, this was a day of great interest at the Bell Rock. "That it might lose none of its honours," as he expressed himself, the Hedderwick praam-boat, with which the first stone of the building had been landed, was appointed also to carry the last. At 7 o'clock this evening, the seamen hoisted three flags upon the Hedderwick, when the colours of the Dickie Praam-boat, Tender, Smeaton, Floating-light, Beacon-house, and Light-house, were also displayed, and the weather being remarkably fine, the whole presented a very gay appearance, and, in connection with the associations excited, the effect was very pleasing. The praam which carried the stone was towed by the seamen in gallant style to the Rock, and, on its arrival, cheers were given as a finale to the landing department.

Monday, 30th.

Ceremony at laying the last stone of the walls.

The Ninetieth or last course of the building having been laid to-day, which brought the masonry to the height of 102 feet 6 inches, the Lintel of the light-room door, being the finishing-stone of the exterior walls, was laid with due formality by the writer, who, at the same time, pronounced the following benediction: "May the Great Architect of the Universe, under whose blessing this perilous work has prospered, preserve it as a guide to the Mariner."

Tuesday, 31st.

Machinery partly dismantled.

The artificers were employed to-day in taking down the tackle and machinery from the store-room and kitchen-floors, which were put on board one of the praam-boats, and conveyed to the Tender. The joiners were assisted at low-water by some of the seamen, in preparing the lower parts of the beams of the Beacon-house, for receiving a coat of hot pitch and tar, as usual, before winter, to defend them against the ravages of the insect which, as before noticed, had made a considerable impression on the soles of the beams, where they rested upon the Rock. The Patriot had sailed for Mylnefield Quarry; and the Smeaton, being now discharged, left the Rock for Lord Elgin's works at Charlestown, to load limestone for the light-keepers' houses, to be built at Arbroath. The Tender continued at her moorings, and took on board from time to time such implements and apparatus as were no longer wanted at the Rock. The Floating-light, from the uncertainty attending the period of finishing the light-room and its apparatus, and consequent exhibition of the light from the building, had, perhaps, a long time yet to remain at her station; but one of her boats was to be regularly sent with five seamen, to assist at the operations on the Rock as formerly.

1810, August.

Wednesday, 1st.

Foot and shaft of Balance-crane taken down.

The artificers and seamen were employed to-day, as yesterday, in clearing the building of lumber, and in coating the beams of the Beacon with a mixture of tar and pitch. The body of the Balance-crane was also supported with beams on the walls of the light-room, in such a manner that its machinery could be applied to lowering its foot and shaft down through the apertures left for this purpose in the floors of the several apartments. The machinery of this useful implement thus supported, was yet to be used in laying centre-stones in the floors of the store-room, kitchen, bed-room, library and light-room; and also in taking up the cast-iron sash-frames and other weighty apparatus of the light-room.

Thursday, 2d.

The several apartments of the building being now entirely cleared of the tackle and apparatus connected with raising the materials, the artificers were in readiness for laying the centre-stones of the several floors.

Friday, 3d.

Lord Kellie with a party visits the Bell Rock.

This morning, between 7 and 8 o'clock, the works of the Bell Rock were visited by the Earl of Kellie, the Honourable Mr Methven Erskine, Mr David Monypenny, Sheriff of Fifeshire and one of the Commissioners of the Northern Light-houses (now Lord Pitmilly), and his Lordship's brother, Mr Alexander Monypenny. The party had left Cambo-house, upon the coast of Fife, at an early hour; but the wind being from the south-west, and blowing fresh, had rendered their passage very uncomfortable. When the boat reached the Tender, the party came on board, as it was too early in the tide for landing on the Rock, which was still under water; but when the railways made their appearance, the party proceeded to the western-wharf, and Lord Pitmilly having been the first of the Light-house Commissioners who had landed here, it was named Pitmilly Wharf. After viewing the Rock, which was now partially dry, they ascended to the Beacon-house, and passed along the bridge, with all its difficult steps, to the Light-house, where the servants had contrived to cover a table, made up with detached planks, on which the first breakfast was laid out in the Bell Rock Light-house. After having gone over the whole of the works, they left the Rock about mid-day.

Centre-stone of the Light-room floor laid by the writer.

At 3 P. M., the necessary preparations having been made, the artificers commenced the completing of the floors of the several apartments, and at 7 o'clock the centre-stone of the light-room floor was laid, which may be held as finishing the masonry of this important National Edifice. After going through the usual ceremonies observed by the Brotherhood on occasions of this kind, the writer, addressing himself to the artificers and seamen who were present, briefly alluded to the utility of the undertaking, as a monument of the wealth of British Commerce, erected through the spirited measures of the Commissioners of the Northern Light-houses, by means of the able assistance of those who now surrounded him. He then took an opportunity of stating, that toward those connected with this arduous work, he would ever retain the most heartfelt regard in all their interests.

Saturday, 4th.

Artificers leave the Rock.

When the bell was rung, as usual, on the Beacon this morning, every one seemed as if he were at a loss what to make of himself. There was, however, upon the whole, still much to do to the Light-house, which is only yet to be considered in the state of a house with its outward wall built; but, before being useful or habitable, it must be roofed over, internally finished, and provided with the necessary furniture and utensils. At this period, the artificers at the Rock consisted of 18 masons, 2 joiners, 1 mill-wright, 1 smith, and 1 mortar-maker, besides Messrs Peter Logan and Francis Watt, foremen, counting in all 25; and matters were arranged for proceeding to Arbroath this afternoon with all hands, as it now became necessary to new-model the works there. The Sir Joseph Banks Tender had by this time been afloat, with little intermission, for six months, during the greater part of which the artificers had been almost constantly off at the Rock, and were now much in want of necessaries of almost every description. Not a few had lost different articles of their clothing, which had dropped into the sea from the Beacon and Building; some wanted jackets, others, from want of hats, wore night-caps; each was, in fact, more or less curtailed in his wardrobe, and, it must be confessed, that at best, the party were but in a very tattered condition. This morning was occupied in removing the artificers and their bedding on board of the Tender; and although their personal luggage was easily shifted, the boats had, nevertheless, many articles to remove from the Beacon-house, and were consequently employed in this service till 11 A. M. All hands being collected and just ready to embark, as the water had nearly overflowed the Rock, the writer, in taking leave, after alluding to the harmony which had ever marked the conduct of those employed on the Bell Rock, took occasion to compliment the great zeal, attention and abilities of Mr Peter Logan and Mr Francis Watt, foremen, Captain James Wilson, landing-master, and Captain David Taylor, commander of the Tender, who, in their several departments, had so faithfully discharged the duties assigned to them, often under circumstances the most difficult and trying. The health of these gentlemen was drunk with much warmth of feeling by the artificers and seamen, who severally expressed the satisfaction they had experienced in acting under them; after which, the whole party left the Rock.

The writer meets with his assistants ashore.

In sailing past the Floating-light, mutual compliments were made by a display of flags between that vessel and the Tender; and at 5 P. M. the latter vessel entered the harbour of Arbroath, where the party were heartily welcomed by a numerous company of spectators, who had collected to see the artificers arrive, after so long an absence from the port. In the evening, the writer invited the foremen and captains of the service, together with Mr David Logan, clerk of works at Arbroath, and Mr Lachlan Kennedy, engineer's clerk and book-keeper, and some of their friends, to the principal Inn, where the evening was spent very happily; and after

"His Majesty's health," and "The Commissioners of the Northern Light-houses," had been given, "Stability to the Bell Rock Light-house" was hailed as a standing toast in the Light-house service.

Sunday, 5th.

The author has formerly noticed the uniformly decent and orderly deportment of the artificers who were employed at the Bell Rock Light-house, and to-day, it is believed, they very generally attended church, no doubt, with grateful hearts for the many narrow escapes from personal danger which all of them had more or less experienced during their residence at the Rock.

Monday, 6th.

Plans arranged for building Light-keepers' houses at Arbroath.

Hitherto the account of these works has been given in the form of a Diary; but now that the chief difficulties of the undertaking are over, it is proposed to quote only particular dates in reference to their progress. At the meeting of the Commissioners of the Northern Light-houses, held at Edinburgh in the month of July 1810, it had been resolved to purchase a piece of ground contiguous to the harbour of Arbroath, which presented an unobstructed view of the Bell Rock Light-house, on which a suite of buildings was to be erected, for the accommodation of the families of the light-keepers and seamen of the Tender, and also for the necessary store-houses. Mr Charles Cunningham, Secretary to the Light-house Board, accordingly corresponded with Mr John Nicol, writer in Arbroath, who purchased the ground for the site of these buildings, together with a small court-yard and bleaching-green, as arranged and laid out in Plate XII. In constructing these buildings, and enclosing an extensive piece of garden-ground for the use of this establishment, the artificers, who had just returned from the Rock, were now to be employed.

Duty on stone charged for these buildings.

The Patriot had returned from Mylnefield Quarry to Arbroath with the first cargo of stones, for the use of these operations, which were about to be landed duty-free, when the Custom-house officers interposed, demanding the duty of 33 per cent. on stone carried coast-ways, as the buildings at Arbroath were not considered as coming within the exemption granted for the Bell Rock Light-house. After representing the circumstances of the case to the Board of Customs at Edinburgh, it was found that another petition would have been required to the Lords of the Treasury, before the present exemption could be granted; but the extent of the duty in question being trifling, the Light-house Board declined making any further application, and the duty was therefore regularly paid for the stones of this compartment of the work.

Three years of the lease of the Work-yard given up.

The writer finding that the Bell Rock work-yard at Arbroath, which had been taken upon a lease of seven years, could be dispensed with after the term of Martinmas, thereby leaving three unexpired years of the tack still to run, the lease was cancelled by the landlord, on his being paid one year's rent in name of damages.

This afforded a satisfactory proof of the termination of the works, at least three years sooner than the period calculated upon at its commencement. The great circular platform in the work-yard, shown in Plate XII., which measured 42 feet in diameter, and was sunk 2 feet 6 inches under the level of the surrounding ground, used for laying and marking the courses of the Light-house, before they were shipped for the Rock, contained a great quantity of stones suitable for the interior walls of the light-keepers' houses. The first operation of the builders, therefore, was to remove the stones of this platform to the site of the new buildings.

Friday, 9th.

Base-line measured on the Sands of Barry.

The writer, with a view to making a survey of the coast contiguous to the Bell Rock, or from Fifeness to the Redhead, embraced the present as a convenient time for measuring a base-line. For this purpose, the Sands of Barry, about 9 miles westward from Arbroath, were selected; and he provided himself with the following apparatus: a strong iron-chain of the length of 100 feet, carefully graduated; 5 wooden coffers, each 20 feet in length, 5 inches in width, and 3 inches in depth, on which the chain was to be stretched; 10 oaken stakes, 4 feet in length, and 4 inches square at the top, for marking off distances of 1000 feet; 10 picket-rods of fir timber, measuring 8 feet in length, with cross boards at the top; 2 spars of 20 feet in length, with small red flags for marking the termination at each end of the Line; and one of Messrs Miller and Adie's best Theodolites. With these, he left the harbour of Arbroath at 5 on the morning of the 9th of August, in one of the Bell Rock boats, manned with six seamen, and accompanied by one of his assistants. At 8 o'clock they reached the small village called the Feus; and after walking about two miles and a half along the Sands of Barry, flag-staffs were erected at the extremities of the line intended to be measured, which, in relation to each other, were situate by compass S.W. ½ S., and N.E. ½ N. The next operation was to mark off the first 1000 feet of the line in a general way, with the picket-rods, into spaces of 100 feet. The wooden coffers, or troughs, for levelling and directing the chain, were then laid on the sands, which being naturally very flat, required only that certain places of the track should be partially cleared with the spade. The chain was then stretched by two of the seamen, to a degree of tension which they were directed to give it, by as regular and uniform a strain as possible; and the links being all previously examined, the distances were carefully marked with an iron pricker. In this manner, the whole length of a line, extending to 10,866 feet and 9½ inches was measured. This was altogether a most laborious operation, occupying 14 hours, including the short time the party were at their meals, which were taken on the field. The line having been thus gone over from North-east to South-west, the operation was reversed as a check, from South-west to North-east; the result of which was not a little satisfactory, as the second measurement only varied one inch from the first, though the line extended upwards of two miles. The weather was very favourable; the wind being westerly, and blowing gentle breezes, while the barometer remained steadily at about 29.78.; the temperature was marked three times a day, and averaged 54°. The angles and bearings of the Bell Rock and other objects having been taken from this base-line, were ultimately referred to in constructing the map of the coast delineated on Plate IV.

Trigonometrical Survey of Great Britain.

For a more complete and perfect mode of making such measurements, the reader may consult Colonel Mudge's Account of the Trigonometrical Survey of England and Wales, in two volumes quarto; a work which shows the astonishing accuracy with which that great National Survey is conducted; and also, the correctness to which mathematical instruments have been brought; and strongly illustrates the difficulties which assail man, when he aims at absolute precision, even in the most simple of the arts.

Tuesday, 14th.

Artificers return to the Bell Rock.

The Smeaton having, in the course of the last ten days, lifted such of the moorings as could now be dispensed with, took the Dickie praam-boat in tow, and sailed for Leith, to load the cast-iron sash-frames of the Light-room. On her return to Arbroath, she took on board the stone-steps for the Light-house, 23 in number, to be erected between the passage of the entrance-door and the provision store, as will be seen from the section of Plate XVI. With these she sailed to-day at 1 P. M., having on board 16 artificers, with Mr Peter Logan, together with a supply of provisions and necessaries; who left the harbour, pleased and happy to find themselves once more afloat in the Bell Rock service. At 7 o'clock, the Tender was made fast to her moorings, when the artificers landed on the Rock, and took possession of their old quarters in the Beacon-house, with feelings very different from those of 1807, when the works commenced.

The Smeaton is in danger, and obliged to leave her Station.

The barometer, for some days past, had been falling from 29.90, and to-day it was 29.50, with the wind at N.E., which, in the course of this day, encreased to a strong gale, accompanied with a sea which broke with great violence upon the Rock. At 12 noon, the Tender rode very heavily at her moorings, when her chain broke at about 10 fathoms from the ship's bows. The kedge-anchor was immediately let go, to hold her till the floating-buoy and broken chain should be got on board; but while this was in operation, the hawser of the kedge was chaffed through on the rocky bottom, and parted, when the vessel was again adrift. Most fortunately, however, she cast off with her head from the Rock, and narrowly cleared it; when she sailed up the Firth of Forth, to wait the return of better weather. The artificers were thus left upon the Rock with so heavy a sea running, that it was ascertained to have risen to the height of 80 feet on the building. Under such perilous circumstances, it would be difficult to describe the feelings of those who, at this time, were cooped up in the Beacon, in so forlorn a situation, with the sea not only raging under them, but occasionally falling from a great height upon the roof of their temporary lodging, without even the attending vessel in view, to afford the least gleam of hope in the event of any accident. It is true that they had now the masonry of the Light-house to resort to, which, no doubt, lessened the actual danger of their situation. But the building was still without a roof, and the dead-lights, or storm shutters, not being yet fitted, the windows of the lower storey were stove in and broken, and, at high-water, the sea ran in considerable quantities out at the entrance-door. In the course of this afternoon, the spring-tides being now at the highest, the bridge or gangway was also for a time rendered completely impassable, from the quantity of sea that constantly washed over it. The smith's gallery, at the same time, was also partially broken up, and several bags of coal, a barrel of small beer, and a few casks, containing pozzolano, lime and sand, were all swept off the Beacon. When the sea left the Rock, it was likewise found that two of the cast-iron legs of the sheer-crane were broken, and that some pieces of the Railways had been torn up.

Thursday, 16th.

Mortar-gallery completely broken up.

The gale continues with unabated violence to-day, and the sprays rise to a still greater height, having been carried over the masonry of the building, or about 90 feet above the level of the sea. At 4 o'clock this morning, it was breaking into the cook's birth, when he rung the alarm-bell, and all hands turned out to attend to their personal safety. The floor of the smith's or mortar-gallery was now completely burst up by the force of the sea, when the whole of the deals and the remaining articles upon the floor were swept away, such as the cast-iron mortar-tubs, the iron hearth of the forge, the smith's bellows, and even his anvil, were thrown down upon the Rock. The boarding of the cook-house, or storey above the smith's gallery, was also partly carried away, and the brick and plaster-work of the fire-place shaken and loosened. At low-water, it was found that the chain of the moveable beam-crane, at the western wharf, had been broken, which set the beam at liberty, and greatly endangered the guy-ropes by its motion. It was observed, during this gale, that the Beacon-house had a good deal of tremor; but none of that "twisting motion" occasionally felt and complained of before the additional wooden struts were set up for the security of the principal beams; but this effect had more especially disappeared ever since the attachment of the great horizontal iron-bars in connection with these supports, instead of the chain-braces, shewn in Plate VIII. Before the tide rose to its full height to-day, some of the artificers passed along the bridge into the Light-house, to observe the effects of the sea upon it, and they reported that they had felt a slight tremulous motion in the building, when great seas struck it in a certain direction, about high-water mark. On this occasion, the sprays were again observed to wet the balcony, and even to come over the parapet-wall into the interior of the light-room. In this state of the weather, Captain Wilson and the crew of the Floating-light were much alarmed for the safety of the artificers upon the Rock, especially when they observed, with a telescope, that the floor of the smith's gallery had been carried away, and that the triangular cast-iron sheer-crane was broken down. It was quite impossible, however, to do any thing for their relief, until the gale should take off.

Friday, 17th.

Tender returns to the Rock.

The weather moderated in the course of the last night, and the wind shifted to S.W., when the Tender, which had been for the last two days in the Firth of Forth, stood towards the Rock, and reached it at 7 P. M., but could not come within speech of the inhabitants of the Beacon, though, from signals mutually exchanged, it appeared that all was pretty well. Captain Taylor next spoke the Floating-light, and found no complaint on board. They had, indeed, shipped several heavy seas, yet no damage had been sustained; and during the gale they rode with 60 fathoms of cable veered out. After making these enquiries, he stood towards Arbroath to get the Tender's rigging refitted, and her moorings repaired, which had suffered in the gale. Knowing also that a new floor, and other articles, were wanting at the Beacon, he meant also to supply some of these; but on approaching Arbroath, there was still too much sea upon the bar of the harbour, and he was obliged to stand off again to sea.

Saturday, 18th.

Smith's Anvil, Bellows, &c. washed off the Beacon.

The wind shifted to the westward to-day, and the Tender got into Arbroath. In the mean time, Captain Wilson visited the Bell Rock with a well manned boat from the Floating-light, when he had the happiness to find Mr Peter Logan and his people in perfect health, though, in the course of the gale, they had at times been considerably alarmed, while the sea was making inroads upon their habitation. In searching about the Rock in quest of some of the articles which had been washed from the smith's gallery, it is not a little remarkable, that so ponderous an article as the anvil, weighing 170 lb., should have been found in a hole at the distance of 60 feet from the Beacon, and that the iron pan or hearth of the forge, weighing about 100 lb., was found at the distance of 200 feet from it. Near to this lay one of the cast-iron mortar-tubs; but the smith's bellows, and many other articles amissing, were never found. Captain Wilson foreseeing that there might be a want of fuel on the Rock from the late disaster, had very properly carried two bags of coal from the Floating-light; and, after landing these, he returned to his ship at 2 P. M.

Thursday, 23d.

Light-room sashes landed. Captain Wilson is hurt by one of them.

Both the Tender and the Smeaton having been forced into Arbroath, were detained there with strong gales of westerly wind, till Monday the 20th, when they sailed for the Rock; the Smeaton, with the sash-frames of the Light-room on board, and the Tender, with a supply of provisions and necessaries for the Floating-light and Beacon-house. The wind being at W.S.W. and the weather more moderate, both vessels got to their moorings on the 23d, when all hands were employed in transporting the sash-frames from on board of the Smeaton to the Rock. In the act of setting up one of these frames upon the bridge, it was unguardedly suffered to lose its balance, and, in saving it from damage, Captain Wilson met with a severe bruise in the groin, on the seat of a gunshot wound received in the early part of his life. This accident laid him aside for several days.

Friday, 24th.

The Smeaton being now discharged, sailed again for other articles still wanted from Edinburgh, belonging to the Light-room frame. The masons at the Rock were busily employed in setting up the stair, and in dressing off and polishing the joints of the interior walls of the Light-house: For, although the stones had all been polished to a smooth surface in the work-yard, in order to give the apartments a cleanly and comfortable appearance, as plastering would have been quite unsuitable for such a situation, yet the walls in many parts required to be retouched, when they came to be examined in a more finished state. James Glen, of whom mention has already been frequently made, was assisted by the smith in refitting the gallery, and the other injured parts of the Beacon-house.

Monday, 27th.

Balance-crane removed from the top of the Building.

The sash-frames of the Light-room, 8 in number, and weighing each 254 lb., having been got safely up to the top of the building, were ranged on the balcony, in the order in which they were numbered, for their places on the top of the parapet-wall; and the balance-crane, that useful machine, having now lifted all the heavier articles, was unscrewed and lowered, to use the landing-master's phrase, "in mournful silence."

Wednesday, 29th.

Sir William Rae and Party visit the Rock.

The works were visited at this time by Mr Rae, Sheriff of Edinburgh, now Sir William Rae, Bart., Lord Advocate of Scotland, and Mr Adam Duff, Sheriff of Forfar, now of Edinburgh, ex officio Commissioners of the Northern Light-houses, who, as Members of the Bell Rock Committee, had individually taken much interest in the Light-house affairs. The party further consisted of General Brown, Captain Harry Stuart of the Royal Navy, Mr James Dickson of Leith, and Mr Charles Cuningham, Secretary and Cashier to the Light-house Board. The writer had the pleasure of embarking with these gentlemen at Leith on the 28th, in the Bell Rock Tender, and, after calling at the Light-houses of Inchkeith and Isle of May, the vessel, in the course of the night, got towards the Rock, and next morning the party landed, and minutely examined every thing connected with the operations of the Light-house and Beacon. On this occasion, one of the principal landing-places was named Rae's Wharf, and another Duff's Wharf, as marked on Plate VI. After breakfasting in the Light-house, Sir William proposed, that the foremen, landing-master, artificers and seamen, should be collected on the Beacon, when he expressed the satisfaction which he and his brother Commissioner felt at seeing the present advanced state of the Light-house; and, after alluding to the utility which might result from the publication of the whole proceedings of this work, concluded an address of much tenderness of feeling, by wishing all of us every prosperity and happiness. The party having been highly amused and gratified upon the Rock, again embarked; and at 10 A. M. the Tender sailed for Leith Roads, where she arrived, at 6 o'clock P. M., having made the trip from thence in the short space of about 28 hours.

1810, September.

Sunday, 2d.

Wooden-bridge removed from the Rock.

The writer having accompanied the party to Leith, immediately returned to the Bell Rock, where he was to make arrangements for bringing the operations to a conclusion. The steps of the stair being landed, and all the weightier articles of the Light-room got up to the balcony, the wooden-bridge was now to be removed, as it had a very powerful effect upon the Beacon, when a heavy sea struck it; and could not possibly have withstood the storms of a winter. Every thing having been cleared from the bridge, and nothing left but the two principal beams, with their horizontal braces, James Glen, at high-water, proceeded with a saw to cut through the beams at the end next the Beacon, which likewise disengaged their opposite extremity, inserted a few inches into the building. The frame was then gently lowered into the water, and floated off to the Smeaton, to be towed to Arbroath, to be applied as part of the materials in the erection of the light-keepers' houses. After the removal of the bridge, the aspect of things at the Rock was much altered. The Beacon-house and Building had both a naked look, to those accustomed to their former appearance; a curious optical deception was also remarked, by which the Light-house seemed to incline from the perpendicular towards the Beacon. The horizontal rope-ladder before noticed was again stretched, to preserve the communication; and the artificers were once more obliged to practise the awkward and stradling manner of their passage between them during 1809, as will be understood by examining the second year's work of Plate IX.

Last Stone of the Light-house laid.

At 12 noon, the bell rung for prayers, after which the artificers went to dinner, when the writer passed along the rope-ladder to the Light-house, and went through the several apartments, which were now cleared of lumber. In the afternoon, all hands were summoned to the interior of the house, when he had the satisfaction of laying the upper step of the stair, or last stone of the Building. This ceremony concluded with three cheers, the sound of which had a very loud and strange effect within the walls of the Light-house. At 6 o'clock Mr Peter Logan, and eleven of the artificers, embarked with the writer for Arbroath, leaving Mr James Glen with the special charge of the Beacon and Railways, Mr Robert Selkirk with the Building, with a few artificers to fit the temporary windows, to render the house habitable.

1810, October.

Tuesday, 4th.

Tender sails for Leith, to be sold.

At Arbroath, the building operations for the keepers' houses were left under charge of Mr Peter Logan and Mr Lachlan Kennedy, when the writer proceeded for Greenock, to sail on his annual voyage to the Northern Light-houses. In passing the Floating-light this morning, he went on board, and examined that ship with Captain Wilson, and had the satisfaction to find every thing in the most orderly and cleanly condition. The sailors, with those feelings which usually accompany taking permanent leave of a vessel, hoisted an ensign flag on board of the Floating-light, as the Tender was now on her way to Leith to be dismantled and sold.

The writer must also confess, that, on finally leaving the Sir Joseph Banks Tender, it was not without feelings of regret, as he had spent a considerable portion of the two last summers in this beautifully moulded ship.

A Praam-boat drifts from the Rock.

On the afternoon of the 5th, a signal was observed flying from the main-masthead of the Floating-light, which created considerable alarm at Arbroath, when the Smeaton sailed to inquire into the cause. Upon hailing the Floating-light, Captain Wilson informed Mr Pool that the Hedderwick praam-boat had broke adrift from her moorings, and gave his opinion as to the course to be steered, in order to fall in with her. At 8 o'clock next morning she was observed a few leagues to the eastward, and taken in tow by the Smeaton, to be carried to Leith; but the wind being westerly, after getting above the Isle of May, she was obliged to anchor in Canty Bay, to the eastward of Tantallan Castle; and at noon on the 12th, she got safely into the harbour of Leith, after a very cross passage of six days.

Artificers for the erection of the Light-room landed.

The arrival of the Smeaton had for some days been anxiously watched, as the remaining parts of the Light-room were ready to ship for the Bell Rock. No time was therefore lost in getting her loaded; and, on Thursday the 13th, she again sailed with Mr Dove, and the artificers, who were to fit up the light-room; and on the following day the whole were landed at the Rock. The first operation was to put up a temporary rail round the balcony, with a few iron stanchions, and some ropes, for the safety of the workmen. Captain Wilson and his crew also erected a pair of sheers and a suitable tackle for lifting the cast-iron sash-frames from the balcony to the top of the parapet-wall.

Saturday, 15th.

Dr Barclay and party sail with the writer to the Light-houses.

This being the train in which the Bell Rock matters were left, the writer embarked to-day at Greenock, in the Light-house Yacht, along with his friends, Dr John Barclay, Mr Charles Oliphant, and Mr Patrick Neill, who were to accompany him on a tour to the Northern Light-houses. Notwithstanding the boisterous state of the weather during the early part of the month of September, it now became uncommonly fine; the barometer being found to oscillate within a few parts of 30 inches, and the range of the thermometer, taken daily at 9 A. M., indicated from 43 to 50 degrees. The winds were also chiefly from the west, which being favourable for the ship's course, the trip was not only remarkable for its quickness, but was, upon the whole, the most pleasant which the writer had ever experienced; as will readily be imagined by those who have the happiness to know the excellent qualities of his fellow-travellers, whether considered on account of their manner, intelligence, or scientific acquirements. This opportunity is therefore gladly embraced by the writer of recording their mutual friendships.

Progress of the Light-room works.

On returning from this voyage, the writer landed at the Bell Rock on Sunday the 14th of October, and had the pleasure to find, from the very favourable state of the weather, that the artificers had been enabled to make great progress with the fitting up of the Light-room. From the 14th of September till the 22d, they were occupied in fitting the sole-plate and trimming-path, forming the basement of the window-sash-frames. From the 22d till the 23d, the work executed got two successive coats of oil-paint; and, as it had also been carefully laid over with lin-seed-oil at the foundry, while in a hot state, it was nearly impervious to the effects of the atmosphere, and was likely to be kept free from oxidation. Between the 28th September and 2d October, the sash-frames were raised to their places and screwed together, along with the top-plate or cornice. From the 2d till the 15th, the copper-smiths were employed in erecting the cupola or roof of the Light-room, the several parts of which will be more readily understood by examining Plate XX., with its letter-press description. Besides finding the works in this forward state, the writer had the happiness of seeing the plate-glass for the Light-room safely landed on the Rock. Each of these plates, measuring 32½ inches by 26¼ inches, and one quarter of an inch in thickness, could not have been soon or easily replaced; and their safe arrival was therefore considered a very fortunate circum-stance; which having witnessed, the writer set sail for Leith, where he landed on the following morning.

Friday, 10th.

Loss of Charles Henderson.

The light-room work had proceeded, as usual, to-day, under the direction of Mr Dove, assisted in the plumber-work by Mr John Gibson, and in the bra-zier-work by Mr Joseph Fraser; while Mr James Slight, with the joiners, were fit-ting up the storm-shutters of the windows. In these several departments, the artifi-cers were at work till 7 o'clock P. M., and it being then dark, Mr Dove gave orders to drop work in the light-room; and all hands proceeded from thence to the Bea-con-house, when Charles Henderson, smith, and Henry Dickson brazier, left the work together. Being both young men, who had been for several weeks upon the Rock, they had become familiar, and even playful on the most difficult parts about the Beacon and Building. This evening they were trying to outrun each other, in descending from the light-room, when Henderson led the way; but they were in conversation with each other, till they came to the rope-ladder, distended between the entrance-door of the Light-house and the Beacon. Dickson, on reaching the cook-room, was surprised at not seeing his companion, and inquired hastily for Henderson. Upon which the cook replied, "Was he before you upon the rope-lad-der?" Dickson answered "Yes; and I thought I heard something fall." Upon this the alarm was given, and links were immediately lighted, with which the artificers descended on the legs of the Beacon, as near the surface of the water as possible, it being then about full tide, and the sea breaking to a considerable height upon the building, with the wind at S.S.E. But after watching till low-water, and searching in every direction upon the Rock, it appeared that poor Henderson must have un-fortunately fallen through the rope-ladder, and been washed into the deep water.

The deceased had passed along this rope-ladder many hundred times, both by day and night, and the operations in which he was employed being nearly finished, he was about to leave the Rock when this melancholy catastrophe took place. The unfortunate loss of Henderson cast a deep gloom upon the minds of all who were at the Rock, and it required some management on the part of those who had charge, to induce the people to remain patiently at their work: as the weather now became more boisterous, and the nights long, they found their habitation extremely cheerless, while the winds were howling about their ears, and the waves lashing with fury against the beams of their insulated habitation.

Difficulty attending the procuring of Red-coloured-Glass.

It has already been noticed, that the plate-glass for the sash-frames of the light-room was safely landed on the Rock, and the writer had also the satisfaction of learning to-day that the red-coloured glass for distinguishing the light was in readiness to ship at London. After having corresponded with all parts of the kingdom, in endeavouring to procure red glass of the finest quality, by having it coloured in the furnace, it was mortifying to find that its manufacture was wholly impracticable, excepting in the production of small pieces, containing not more than three or four square inches, similar to those in the compartments of cathedral-windows: which, in the process of shading a reflector, must have induced a number of minute divisions, and necessarily obstructed much of the light. The writer at length resolved on confining his attention to plates of Crown-glass, stained by repeated applications of the litharge of gold, laid on after the manner of gum or paint, which was afterwards subjected to a strong heat in a muffle or furnace, of a peculiar construction, forming altogether a very nice and difficult process. In looking through this stained glass, the eye is not sensible of any effect but that of a fine rich red colour, when the pigment is properly applied; but, on examining a cross section of the glass, the green colour of the Crown-glass is distinctly seen in the centre, while a thin film of red is perceptible on the edges. Although the effect produced in this way cannot be so perfect as if the glass were uniformly coloured in the pot; yet, when applied to the purposes of a distinguishing light, its effects are highly characteristic and beautiful. As the works were now drawing near a completion, and all the essential parts of the light-room apparatus must soon be upon the spot, the writer, after repeated disappointments from Mr James Okey, glass-stainer of London, found it necessary to send Mr John Forrest, superintendant of light-keepers' duty, with instructions to remain there until he got the plates into his possession. He accordingly arrived in London on the 15th of September, and immediately waited upon Okey; but, notwithstanding the numerous letters and pressing calls which had been made upon that artist, explanatory of the necessity of the case; yet, as the plates wanted were to be 25 inches in diameter, and, consequently, about 5 inches more than any he had hitherto been required to make, his furnace was still to rebuild, and his apparatus otherwise to conform to these enlarged dimensions, before he could begin to the Bell Rock plates. In order to insure attention and dispatch, Mr Forrest took lodgings at Clerkenwell, in Mr Okey's immediate neighbourhood, and paid frequent visits to his workshop. Numerous glass-workers in various parts of the country had previously been applied to for this article, but none of them ever produced a single plate.

Monday, 22d.

Mr Robert Hamilton visits the Bell Rock.

The whole apparatus and workmen necessary for completing the exterior of the Light-house being now on the Rock, the writer was desirous of seeing the ball placed upon the top of the cupola, and accordingly embarked at Leith in the Yacht for that purpose. Mr Hamilton, who, as one of the Commissioners, had always taken a most lively interest in the affairs of the Bell Rock, took this opportunity to pay it another visit. The wind was at W.S.W., blowing pretty fresh with the barometer at 29.50; but, in the course of the night, the Yacht got down to the Floating-light, and was kept plying about, within view of it, till morning.

Tuesday, 23d.

The ventilator-ball is set upon the cupola.

The wind had shifted, in the night, to N.W., and blew a fresh gale, while the sea broke with violence upon the Rock. It was found impossible to land, but the writer, from the boat, hailed Mr Dove, and directed the ball to be immediately fixed. The necessary preparations were accordingly made, while the vessel made short tacks on the southern side of the Rock, in comparatively smooth water. At noon, Mr Dove, assisted by Mr James Slight, Mr Robert Selkirk, Mr James Glen, and Mr John Gibson, plumber, with considerable difficulty, from the boisterous state of the weather, got the gilded-ball screwed on, measuring 2 feet in diameter, and forming the principal ventilator at the upper extremity of the cupola of the Light-room, as will be seen from the section in Plate XX. At Mr Hamilton's desire, a salute of 7 guns was fired on this occasion, and all hands being called to the quarter-deck, "Stability to the Bell Rock Light-house" was not forgotten.

Thursday, 25th.

The Light-room is glazed.

The glazing of the sash-frames of the light-room having been completed on Wednesday the 24th, the boats of the Smeaton and Floating-light landed on the morning of the 25th, when the plumbers and glaziers left the Rock; from whom the writer learned the progress which had been made with the work. Among other preparations for the glazing, it was stated, that besides the sheeting provided as a screen, all hands had engaged to give part of their bedding for the better defence of the glass, in case it should come to blow so hard as to endanger the stopping of the work; but although the weather had rather a threatening aspect at the commencement of this critical operation, yet it was got through in a manner much beyond expectation, and in one day and a half the light-room was completely closed; though not without being under the necessity of lighting torches at night, which were, however, screened from the view of shipping.

Saturday, 27th.

The Yacht returns to the Rock, but loses one of her boats.

After the house was glazed, and in a manner externally finished, the writer sailed from Leith for the Rock, on the 27th of October; but, as it came to blow very fresh from W.S.W., a landing could not be effected, and the Yacht was put into Arbroath till the 29th, when the wind became more moderate, and she again stood off. While in the act of putting about, with the sea still running high, one of the two boats astern got entangled and filled with water, when the stem of one of them unfortunately parted, and she immediately sunk. It was indeed with great difficulty that the other was saved, by two of the crew jumping into her, at the risk of their lives; and having baled out the water with buckets, she was got safely on board.

Tuesday, 30th.

Great dexterity of the Landing-master and his crew.

This accident obliged the vessel to be anchored all night in the Bay of Arbroath, and having got another boat she sailed this morning at 5 o'clock. On reaching the Rock, it was found that a very heavy sea still ran upon it; but the writer having been disappointed on the two former occasions, and, as the erection of the house might now be considered complete, there being nothing wanted externally, excepting some of the storm-shutters for the defence of the windows, he was the more anxious at this time to inspect it. Two well manned boats were therefore ordered to be in attendance; and, after some difficulty, the wind being at N.N.E., they got safely into the western creek, though not without encountering plentiful sprays. It would have been impossible to have attempted a landing to-day, under any other circumstances than with boats perfectly adapted to the purpose, and with seamen who knew every ledge of the Rock, and even the length of the sea-weeds at each particular spot, so as to dip their oars into the water accordingly, and thereby prevent them from getting entangled. But what was of no less consequence to the safety of the party, Captain Wilson, who always steered the leading boat, had a perfect knowledge of the set of the different waves, while the crew never shifted their eyes from observing his motions, and the strictest silence was preserved by every individual except himself. Under such regulations, which were observed on all occasions of difficulty, the landings at the Rock proceeded with the greatest regularity, and by this means, safety, and even comfort, were enjoyed, where, under different circumstances, there would have been much peril. The second or attending boat was steered by James Shepherd the experienced coxwain of the Floating-light, whose directions were to keep about two oars' length astern. This boat was generally kept light, and as free of incumbrance as possible, that she might be ready to assist in any case of emergency. The writer is the more particular upon this subject, as he conceives that much of the success of the Bell Rock operations depended on the safety which attended the many thousands of landings made in all sorts of weather.

State of the Railways.

On landing at the Rock this morning, the writer found the Railways much broken up on the eastern-reach and the circular track round the building; while the western-reach, extending to upwards of 290 feet, had also materially suffered. In several places it had got an inclination to one side, by the force of the N.E. seas, which came sweeping round the Rock, and it was evident it could not withstand the gales of winter. The Norway logs, on which these railways were supported, had not only been much reduced in strength, by the ravages of the insect formerly noticed, but, from this cause also, the rails had got a tremulous motion in heavy seas, which had shaken loose several of the bolts. It was, however, so far well that they had already answered the immediate purpose intended by them.

State of the beams of the Beacon.

The Beacon-house was found, upon examination, to be in general in a good state of repair, though the lower parts, where the beams rested upon the Rock, had suffered from the insect. Several of them, as before noticed, had been so much hollowed, where they at first rested on the Rock, that the hand could be introduced into the heart of the log, while the exterior of the timber, for an inch or two in thickness, remained quite entire; the charring of the surface, and the hot-pitch, wherever it could be applied, having completely preserved it. Several of the beams, however, now rested chiefly upon the bolts, which passed through the great iron-stanchions sunk into the Rock, as represented in Plate VIII. But this fabric had nearly served its purpose, and there was a prospect of its being taken down next summer. It has before been noticed that these effects, at the parts where the beams rested, or were in contact with the Rock, had not been anticipated. But, in the event of a similar erection on any part of the British coast, it would be proper to provide against this by sinking the foot of the principal beams 8 inches into the Rock, and shoeing them with sheet lead or copper; though the action of the latter metal with the iron-work might be somewhat objectionable, and might render a coating with tin advisable.

State of the Light-house.

Having examined the Beacon-house, he next passed to the Light-house, by the horizontal rope-ladder represented in Plate IX. The lower part of the building, as high as the perpendicular range of the tide, was coated all over with marine plants; toward the north-east, this appearance had indeed reached about 50 feet in height. On entering the house, he had the pleasure to find it in a somewhat habitable condition, the lower apartments being closed in with temporary windows, and fitted with proper storm-shutters. It may here be remarked as a strong instance of the very fortunate position of the Entrance-door, that although the sea had risen to the height of upwards of 80 feet, on the eastern side of the Light-house, it had not, as yet, been found necessary to have it hung, although Mr Slight was now setting about this operation, by the insertion of the Lewis-bats or tails of the hinges, into their respective brass-boxes, previously built into the walls. There being, as yet, no inner-door for the passage, temporary-hatches were also still wanting for the man-holes of the several floors, to check the sifting air, which, in westerly winds, made the house very cold, and carried along with it particles of dust, which might have become injurious to the reflecting-apparatus.

Condition of the several apartments.

The lowest apartment at the head of the stair-case was occupied with water, fuel, and provisions, put up in a temporary way, until the house could be furnished with proper utensils. The second or light-room store was, at present, much encumbered with various tools and apparatus for the use of the workmen. The kitchen immediately over this had, as yet, been supplied only with a common ship's coboose, and plate-iron funnel, while the necessary cooking utensils had been taken from the Beacon. The bed-room was, for the present, used as the joiners' workshop, and the strangers' room, immediately under the light-room, was occupied by the artificers, the beds being ranged in tiers, as was done in the barrack of the Beacon. The light-room, though unprovided with its machinery, being now covered over with the cupola, glazed and painted, had a very complete and cleanly appearance. The balcony was only as yet fitted with a temporary rail, consisting of a few iron stanchions, connected with ropes; and in this state it was necessary to leave it during the winter.

Light-house put under charge of Mr John Reid.

Having gone over the whole of the low-water works on the Rock, the Beacon and Light-house, and being satisfied that only the most untoward accident in the landing of the machinery could prevent the exhibition of the light, in the course of the winter; Mr John Reid, formerly of the Floating-light, was now put in charge of the light-house as principal keeper; Mr James Slight had charge of the operations of the artificers; while Mr James Dove and the smiths having finished the frame of the light-room, left the Rock for the present. With these arrangements the writer bade adieu to the works for the season. At 11 A. M. the tide was far advanced; and there being now little or no shelter for the boats at the Rock, they had to be pulled through the breach of sea, which came on board in great quantities, and it was with extreme difficulty that they could be kept in the proper direction of the landing-creek.—On this occasion, he may be permitted to look back with gratitude on the many escapes made in the course of this arduous undertaking, now brought so near to a successful conclusion.

November.

Saturday, 3d.

The Boat is washed off the Beacon.

The wind having, on Saturday the 3d of November, shifted to the N. E., with showers of snow, accompanied by a very heavy swell of sea, it was stated, in the monthly return from the Rock, that the water had come in considerable quantities into the threshold of the entrance-door, which, on this occasion, had to be shut. During this gale, it was thought that the Beacon would certainly have been carried away by the force of the tremendous seas which fell upon it, and often washed over it at high-water. The small boat suspended from projected davits at the height of 30 feet above the Rock, as shown in Plate VIII., got full of water by the accidental stopping of the eyelet-hole, while the friction occasioned by the tremulous motion of the Beacon, and beating of the waves, chaffed one of the bow-tackle ropes: she then hung suspended from the stem-tackle, and every sea which came rolling along gave her a new impulse: this soon wore out the remaining tackle, and she was at length swept away, after having kept her position since mid-summer.

Sprays rise 104 feet on the Light-house.

On one occasion, while the inmates of the Light-house were standing on the balcony, looking with attention at the wonderful state of the sea, the sprays conducted by the walls, came full in their faces, and, passing partly over their heads, struck upon the second tier of the glass-panes of the light-room, which is 104 feet from the Rock! During this gale, a thrilling motion was sensibly felt throughout the building, upon leaning against the walls at particular periods, when the seas struck the base of the house. The rise of the spray to the height above mentioned rather surprised the writer, as he had not himself at any time seen it higher than about 70 feet. He had, however, felt the tremulous effect alluded to; and it has already been remarked, that it is not while the gale continues that the sea strikes so hard, or rises to so great a height; but after the abatement of the storm, when the waves begin to break in the manner represented in the frontispiece.

Sprays fly over the Floating-light.

This gale was also much felt on board of the Floating-light. Captain Wilson states, in his account of the weather, that he had to veer out the long-service, or about 90 fathoms of cable, and often to freshen hawse, or to shift that part of the cable which was immediately in the hawsehole of the ship. The seas also which struck the bows of the vessel were generally carried as far aft as the quarter-deck, and were not unfrequently thrown over the stern. This gale was, therefore, considered to have been as severe as that of September 1807, already described. The Light-house Yacht, now acting as Tender at the Rock, having been driven from her station, had taken shelter in Burntisland Roads, ready on the first change of weather to return to the Rock. The Smeaton and Patriot were fortunately in Arbroath, discharging their cargoes of stones from Milnfield, for the establishment on shore.

Mr Reid and Mr Fortune left in the Light-house.

On Monday the 5th, the Yacht again visited the Rock; when Mr Slight and the artificers returned with her to the work-yard, where a number of things were still to prepare connected with the temporary fitting up of the accommodation for the light-keepers. Mr John Reid and Peter Fortune were now the only inmates of the house. This was the smallest number of persons hitherto left in the Light-house. As four light-keepers were to be the complement, it was intended that three should always be at the Rock. Its present inmates, however, could hardly have been better selected for such a situation; Mr Reid being a person possessed of the strictest notions of duty, and habits of regularity, from long service on board of a man-of-war, while Mr Fortune had one of the most happy and contented dispositions imaginable.

Tuesday, 13th.

Experience a heavy gale.

From Saturday the 10th till Tuesday the 13th, the wind had been from N.E., blowing a heavy gale; but to-day, the weather having greatly moderated, Captain Taylor, who now commanded the Smeaton, sailed at 2 o'clock A. M. for the Bell Rock. At 5 the Floating-light was hailed, and found to be all well. Being a fine moon-light morning, the seamen were changed from the one ship to the other. At 8, the Smeaton being off the Rock, the boats were manned, and taking a supply of water, fuel, and other necessaries, landed at the western side, when Mr Reid and Mr Fortune were found in good health and spirits. They reported, that the sea had run very heavily, and rose at times nearly to the balcony of the Light-house, when it fell with great weight and violence on the Beacon-house; that, on Sunday the 11th, the wooden-frame of the western wharf was carried away; and that the railways to the eastward were also much shattered and broken by large detached masses of rock, brought from deep water by the impulse of the sea, some of which left on the Rock were apparently of the cubical contents of several tons. Though none of these stones have yet been traced as belonging to any particular part of the Rock, yet they are all of the same red sandstone. It was intended at this time, that a large stock of coals and water should have been got into the Light-house, before the Smeaton went to Leith, to load the remainder of the apparatus; but this, from the state of the weather, was found impracticable, and she therefore returned to Arbroath, to wait a change of weather.

1810, November.

Saturday, 1st.

Their description of the effects of the Sea upon the Light-House.

It having been intimated at the work-yard, that a log of timber had come ashore at West-Haven, about six miles from Arbroath, James Glen, who knew every piece of timber upon the Bell Rock, was dispatched, to ascertain if it had drifted from thence; and, on his return, reported that the log had belonged to the Western Wharf. Mr Slight having got his apparatus prepared, went again off to the Rock with the workmen, when a large additional supply of water, fuel, and provisions, was also landed. It was now ascertained, that the whole of the western wharf, and part of its connecting railway, had been carried away, and that the circular-track and eastern-reach of the railways were much damaged. Mr Reid farther stated, that, during the late gales, particularly on Friday the 30th, the wind veering from S.E. to N.E., both he and Mr Fortune sensibly felt the house tremble, when particular seas struck, about the time of high-water; the former observing that it was a tremor of that sort which rather tended to convince him that every thing about the building was sound, and reminded him of the effect produced, when a good log of timber is struck sharply with a mallet; but, with every confidence in the stability of the building, he nevertheless confessed, that, in so forlorn a situation, they were not insensible to those emotions which, he emphatically observed, "made a man look back upon his former life."

1810, December.

Thursday, 6th.

The Red-coloured glass arrives at Leith.

The Smeaton was now much wanted at Leith, where Mr Forrest had arrived from London on the 1st, with the plates of red-coloured glass; but the weather continued boisterous, and she was detained in the harbour of Arbroath with a gale at S.W. To-day the writer got notice from Mr Andrew Roger, merchant in St Monance, that some fishermen belonging to that village had picked up a raft of timber, strongly bolted together. This turned out to be part of the timber of the Western Wharf, which had drifted from the Rock on the 11th, and had been ever since floating about the Firth of Forth. It was picked up on the coast of Fife, about nine miles to the westward of the Isle of May.

Saturday, 8th.

The Reflecting apparatus sent from Leith.

The wind having shifted last night, the Smeaton sailed from Arbroath at 10 P. M., for Leith, to take on board the whole of the remaining appurtenances necessary for the exhibition of the Light. She got into Leith harbour on the 9th, about mid-day, when the apparatus was immediately put on board; but the weather was unfavourable for going down the Firth of Forth. To-day, however, the wind being west, with a better appearance, the following persons sailed for the Rock, viz. Mr James Dove, smith, who was to screw together the frame for the Reflecting-apparatus; Mr James Clark, clock-maker, who had constructed, and was now to regulate, the Revolving-machinery for the lights; and Mr John Forrest, who had the general superintendance of the keepers' duty of the Northern Light-houses, and being also foreman for Light-room repairs in the service, was to adjust the reflectors and lamps, and remain at the Bell Rock until every thing was found to proceed in a satisfactory manner.

Friday, 14th.

An attempt is made to land at the Rock.

At day-light this morning, however, the Smeaton was still eight or nine miles from the Light-house, with hardly any wind. In the prospect of effecting a landing, Captain Taylor manned the boat when about two miles distant from the Rock, intending to leave the above persons, and afterwards to take the earliest opportunity of landing the apparatus, the tide being now too far spent for attempting the latter operation. The only articles taken in the boat, besides their personal luggage, were the two boxes of red-glass, which having already cost so much trouble, and requiring so much care, Mr Forrest, with his usual caution, had determined not to lose sight of. The party thus proceeded, but, on reaching the Rock, they had the mortification to find it nearly under water, with such a breach of sea that no boat could approach it. They were, therefore, obliged to return to the ship, perishing with cold, and chagrined with disappointment.

Saturday, 15th.

Reflecting-apparatus safely landed.

The wind still continued from N.W., but, most fortunately for the business of the day, the weather was moderate. Having last night called at the Floating-light, it was arranged with Captain Wilson, that he should attend by day-light at the Rock, with one of his boats, to assist in landing the Smeaton's cargo. The passengers went off first, carrying in their boat the two cases of coloured-glass, and a few other articles, while the Floating-light's boat followed with the machinery; and by noon the whole of the Reflecting-apparatus was got safely into the Light-house. Mr Forrest having thus been enabled to give advice, which reached the writer on the 17th, that all the articles had been safely landed; and foreseeing that every thing would be in readiness in the course of about four weeks, a specification of the appearance of the light was prepared, to the following effect, for public advertisement.

Monday, 17th.

The Light is advertised to the Public.

"Navigation of the North Seas. — A Light-house having been erected upon the Inch Cape, or Bell Rock, situate at the entrance of the Friths of Forth and Tay, in north Lat. 56° 29′, and west Long. 2° 22′, — The Commissioners of the Northern Light-houses hereby give notice, That the Light will be from oil, with reflectors, placed at the height of about 108 feet above the medium level of the sea. The light will be exhibited on the night of Friday, the 1st day of February 1811, and each night thereafter, from the going away of day-light in the evening until the return of day-light in the morning. To distinguish this light from others on the coast, it is made to revolve horizontally, and to exhibit a bright light of the natural appearance, and a red-coloured light, alternately, both respectively attaining their greatest strength or most luminous effect in the space of every four minutes; during that period, the bright light will, to a distant observer, appear like a star of the first magnitude, which, after attaining its full strength, is gradually eclipsed to total darkness; and is succeeded by the red-coloured light, which in like manner increases to full strength, and again diminishes and disappears. The coloured-light, however, being less powerful, may not be seen for a time after the bright light is first observed. During the continuance of foggy weather, and showers of snow, a Bell will be tolled, by machinery, night and day, at intervals of half a minute. Notice is hereby also given, That the Floating-light, moored two and a half miles N.W. ½ N. from the Bell Rock, will, from and after the 1st day of February 1811, be discontinued, and, as soon thereafter as the weather permits, the vessel will be removed from her station."

List of Newspapers.

To give this Notice publicity, it was advertised in the following Newspapers:

SCOTCH.

Edinburgh Weekly Chronicle.
---- Courant.
---- Correspondent.
---- Mercury.
---- Advertiser.
---- Star.
---- Journal.
Leith Telegraph.
Dundee Advertiser.
---- Mercury.
Perth Courier.
Montrose Review.
Aberdeen Journal.
---- Chronicle.
Inverness Journal.
Glasgow Journal.
---- Courier.

---- Western Star.
---- Sentinel.
---- Packet.
---- Herald.
Greenock Advertiser.

ENGLISH.

London Gazette.
---- Globe.
---- Morning Post.
London Courier.
---- Chronicle.
Plymouth Telegraph.
---- Chronicle.
Bristol Gazette.
---- Journal.
---- Mirror.
---- Mercury.
Liverpool Courier.
---- Advertiser.
---- General Advertiser.
---- Saturday Advertiser.
Cumberland Packet.
Newcastle Courant.
---- Chronicle.
---- Advertiser.
---- Tyne Mercury.
Hull and Rockingham Packet.
Hull and Rockingham Advertiser.
York Courant.
---- Herald.
---- Chronicle.
Norwich Mercury.
Hampshire Telegraph.

IRISH.

Dublin Evening Post.
---- Patriot.

Thursday, 27th.

The Light-keepers are left in possession of the House.

The Tender having got a landing made on the 27th December, every thing at the Light-house was found in a prosperous state. Mr Dove and Mr Clark had finished their work about two hours before the Smeaton came in sight; and Mr Slight had also completed all that was proposed to be done to the interior finishing of the apartments this winter; so that Mr Forrest, with Messrs Reid, Bonyman, Leask, and Fortune, the keepers, were now left in possession of the Light-house.

CHAPTER VII.

ACCOUNT OF THE BELL ROCK LIGHT-HOUSE, FROM ITS
COMPLETION IN 1810 TILL THE YEAR 1823, INCLUD-
ING A STATEMENT OF THE EXPENCE OF THE WORK.

1811, January.

When the artificers left the Bell Rock, on the 27th of December 1810, Mr Forrest's first object was to take down the rope-ladder, distended in a horizontal position between the entrance-door of the Light-house and the mortar-gallery of the Beacon, as it prevented the door from being conveniently shut, and thereby occasioned a draught of air through the several apartments, rendering the house uncomfortable, and proving injurious to the lustre of the reflectors. In lieu of this, another rope-ladder, fitted with wooden steps, was suspended from a Lewis-bat, inserted into the sill of the door. This ladder, when hauled up, was stowed in the passage, and thus admitted of the door being shut.

Fresh Provisions fall short at the Light-house.

During the last fortnight of the month of January 1811, the weather had been very unsteady, with gales of wind chiefly from the eastward; which prevented the Light-house Yacht, now acting as Tender, from sailing for the Rock till Thursday the 17th. Mr Forrest and the light-keepers were found in good health, and busily employed in their respective operations, now nearly brought to a close. No communication having been had with the shore for the last three weeks, their stock of fresh meat and vegetables was expended; and, looking forward to the possibility of a continuation of similar weather, they had begun to economise the fuel and water before this day's supply came to hand.

A supply is received.

The next trip which the Yacht made to the Rock was on Tuesday the 29th. A letter from Mr Forrest stated, that he had received a very full supply of every thing, both for the light-room and provision-store, and added, "Let the weather be how it will, we shall not be in want even of the most trifling article, for a month to come."

February.

Friday, 1st.

The Light is exhibited.

The day long wished for, on which the mariner was to see a light exhibited on the Bell Rock, at length arrived. Captain Wilson, as usual, hoisted the Float's lanterns to the topmast on the evening of the 1st of February; but the moment that the light appeared on the Rock, the crew, giving three cheers, lowered them, and finally extinguished the lights. The Yacht had sailed on the 31st of January, for the purpose of taking this ship in tow for Leith, as being no longer necessary here; but in the course of that night, it came to blow so excessively hard from E.SE., that she was obliged to bear away for the Firth of Forth, leaving the Floating-light at her moorings.

Friday, 8th.

A Storm occurs when the House is lighted.

On the 9th, the Yacht returned, and, although a very heavy sea then ran upon the Rock, a landing was effected with a boat-load of coals, water, and fresh provisions. Mr Forrest states in his letter at this time, that every thing on the 1st of February, had been found to answer to his entire satisfaction. He, however, mentions, that the wind blew excessively hard during the three first days after the house was lighted, and that the sprays had risen to the height of 80 feet upon the building. He adds, that, in the course of this gale, all hands had kept watch without intermission for twenty-four hours, with the storm-window-frames at hand, in case of accident, as the plates of glass on the windward side of the light-room had shaken loose, and, by the continued violence of the wind, the putty had been "wrought quite thin, and was softened like mortar." These plates of glass, measuring each 32½ inches by 26¼ inches, were so fitted with brass-guards that they could not possibly be blown out, in an entire state, but were in some danger of being broken, by pressing upon the window-sashes while the putty was thus softened. Mr Taylor, who upon this occasion commanded the Yacht, had considerable difficulty in approaching the Light-house, and observes, "There being now no attending-boat to accompany our landings at the Rock, I find we must not run such risks as formerly, as, in the event of an accident happening to us singly, no assistance can be got. To-day, one of those heavy rolling seas struck the boat, and pitched her upon one of the ledges, but she was got afloat again before the next breach of the sea reached her, and was afterwards carried like a shot out of the creek."

Tuesday, 12th.

Floating-light puts into Anstruther.

The wind having shifted to the west, with moderate weather, the Yacht sailed from Arbroath to-day, to take charge of the Floating-light. Having accordingly received a hawser on board, she cast off the chain-cable moorings, on which a buoy was placed, it being impossible, at this time, to lift the mushroom-anchor. The wind was then at N.NE., and the crew were all extremely happy in the prospect of soon finishing their task, declaring that they had been more tired of the Floating-light during the last twelve days, than all the time they had been on board of her. At 10 P. M., the wind suddenly shifted to W.NW., and when abreast of the Island of May they wore-ship, for the Floating-light was so unmanageable that she could not be stayed or tacked in the usual manner. They then stood to the north shore, and anchored off Crail during the night, in seven fathoms water. On the 14th, the wind being still down the Firth , it occupied the whole period of the flood-tide to get about six miles to windward, and night coming on, Captains

Wilson and Taylor concluded that it would be most prudent for them to put into Anstruther harbour, and there wait for a fair wind. While the Floating-light lay here, the Yacht made a trip to the Bell Rock, and relieved the Light-keepers, when all was found well.

Some of her Crew get married.

At Anstruther a great deal of interest was felt, and people even flocked from a considerable distance, to see a vessel which had been moored, for nearly four years, off the Bell Rock. The singularity and simplicity of her rigging attracted the attention particularly of nautical men, while the thick bed of sea-weed and shell-fish on her bottom, was matter of surprise to every one. The crew had also become so well acquainted in this port, and the neighbouring fishing-towns, that some of them had got married, and if the vessel had remained another week or two in port, the probability is that she would not have had an unmarried man on board.

State of the Floating-light's bottom.

1811, March.

The Floating-light at length arrived at Leith, on the 8th of March, after a passage of no less than three weeks from her station. The account given of the marine productions on the ship's bottom, had excited the curiosity of several of the writer's friends; and, on her arrival, he was accompanied by the Reverend Dr Fleming of Flisk, Dr Leach of the British Museum, and Mr Patrick Neill, Secretary to the Wernerian Society, who examined, with great attention, the numerous crustaceous, testaceous and molluscous animals, and zoophytes, which still adhered in great numbers to her bottom. Mussels of the species called Mytilus pellucidus, were abundant: they were of a large size, the striæ on the shells measuring 3½ inches in length, by 1¼ inch in breadth. Some of the common acorn-shell, Balanus communis, were so large as 1½ inch in diameter. The sea-weeds were chiefly Fucus digitatus and esculentus, and were in general 4 or 5 feet in length. During the time the Floating-light had rode off the Bell Rock, the crew had made a regular practice of picking off considerable quantities of the mussels for fishing-bait for the several vessels in the Light-house service, and also for the artificers at the Rock. It was therefore chiefly in the runs and lower parts of the bottom, where they had never been disturbed, that the animals were in the greatest numbers; and here also the fuci were longest. Next to the keel, the writer measured a compact bed of these mussels and vermes, of the depth of from six to eight inches; and Captain Wilson, upon first seeing her bottom at Anstruther, described it in his letter to be a "complete mussel-scalp." The timber of the ship, however, was quite sound.

Sunday, 24th.

The Light-keepers get their turns of liberty ashore.

The Light-house Yacht had no sooner got her troublesome charge safely into port, to be dismantled and sold, than she returned to the Rock, to supply the Light-house and shift the keepers; but such was the boisterous state of the weather, that no landing could be made till the 22d, when Mr John Reid relieved Mr John Bonyman, who went ashore in his turn. The Yacht then steered for Leith, when the command of that vessel was given to Captain Wilson, while Captain Taylor took charge of the Bell Rock Tender,—situations for which their services had respectively qualified them.

Letter from the Superintendant Light-keeper.

The Yacht, when last at the Rock, brought a letter from Mr Forrest, in answer to a number of queries, on points to which his attention had been directed, during his residence in the Light-house. He replied with so much intelligence and correctness of observation, that it may be proper here to give his letter verbatim.

Bell Rock Light-house, 14th March 1811.

"SIR,

"I received your letter of the 7th of January, desiring me to give you an account of every particular occurrence at the Bell Rock during the winter, including the effects of the sea on the building, the comfortableness of the Light-house as a dwelling, and the ability of the light-keepers for their duty. In answer, I will now endeavour to give you the information wanted, which I shall do in the order of the particulars which you sent me, having, in consequence of your instructions, noticed every thing about the place.

Effects of the sea on the building.

"Nothing extraordinary happened from the time I came here, on the 15th day of December, till the 1st day of February, when the house was lighted to the public. On that night, it appeared as if nature, on the first lighting of the house, were making trial of the sufficiency of the building. During all that night and the following day, there was nothing to be seen but the sea covered with foam as far as the eye could reach. The only damage we sustained, was the loosening of a number of the panes of glass, which I noticed to you in a former letter. During the gale, the sprays did not rise higher than the bed-room windows, or about 70 feet above the level of the sea. I paid particular attention to your directions, as to whether I could feel the house shake; but I was not then very sensible of this effect, the tides being neap, though, at the time of high-water, there was a kind of vibration felt when the sea did not break till it reached the building. The most sensible feeling, however, of this kind which we have, is when there is a very heavy ground-swell after a gale at N.E. On these occasions, the sea rises at intervals on the building, till the sprays are stopped in their course upwards by the cornice; but this only happens when the heavy swell occurs with spring-tides. On the 15th of February, we felt the vibration very sensibly, which had not so much the effect of shaking, as that of the tremor produced by the striking of the alarm bells, on the balcony of the Light-house, in foggy weather, when the storm-shutters, windows, and hatches are shut. During some gales from the S.E., especially when the wind continues two or three days from that quarter, the seas rise to a great height. At high-water, on these occasions, I have observed the Beacon-house, for perhaps a second or two, completely covered with waves and sprays. But every thing about that fabric remains quite entire, without the least damage that I can discover.

State of the Wagon-ways.

"I have done all in my power, with the assistance of the light-keepers, to pre-serve the waggon-ways, and we have frequently forgot ourselves in working at them, till the tide was too far advanced; and, in stormy weather, have been obliged to make a precipitate retreat up the rope-ladder, after a complete wetting. Some of the reaches are notwithstanding much broken up, and it will be a great pity if the remainder do not stand till the summer months, when they can be properly secured; for, at times, in the course of this winter, the Tender's boat has brought us supplies, when, but for the waggon-ways, it would have been just the same as going to destruction, to have attempted a landing.

Remarkable effects of the sea in lifting a piece of lead.

"I often take pleasure in looking at the seas breaking upon the Light-house, and it is awfully grand, at the time of high-water, to observe the sprays rising to such a height on the building, and even to be on the Rock at low-water, when the waves are about to break. Being in a manner only a few yards distant, they approach as if they were about to overwhelm us altogether. But now that we are accustomed to such scenes, we think little of it. You will perhaps form a better idea of the force of the sea, during these gales, when I relate to you, that, on the 15th of February, the large piece of lead that was used as the back weight of the balance-crane, weighing 4 cwt. 3 qrs. 17 lb., or nearly a quarter of a ton, was fairly lifted by the sea, and carried to the distance of six feet from the hole, in which it had lain since the month of August. It was now found turned with the ring-bolt downwards, and it was with great difficulty that four of us could muster strength enough to return it to its former shelf in the Rock.

Direction of the seas which have most effect upon the Light-house.

"All the observations which I have made regarding the effects of the seas and weather on the Light-house, while I have been here, lead me to conclude, that when the wind is from the S., S.W., W., N.W., and even N., the sea has little effect on the building; but, from south to north-easterly, the force of the waves is consid-erable, especially when it comes to blow hard. During the gale of the 22d February, I remarked, that even the heaviest seas, if they broke before they came to the foot of the building, slipped past without giving the least shock to the house; and it is only a very few of the waves that reach the building, in the course of a tide, which cause the vibration alluded to; but we fear those seas only which come from the NE., as they break close upon the house. I may say, in general, that the higher or stronger the wind is, the less power the sea has on the Light-house; the heaviest seas being accompanied with little wind, or occurring after the gale has abated.

Comfortable state of the building.

"With regard to the comfort of this building as a dwelling, I had no other ex-pectation but that, on account of the sea-air, and newness of the walls, the house would have, in the first instance, been damp. It is, however, the very reverse of this, and I may confidently say, that it is as dry round the inside walls, and on the floors, as any house in Edinburgh. This may be chiefly occasioned by the smoke-tube which passes from the kitchen through the upper floors to the cupola of the Light-room, which contributes greatly to the dry state of the building; but we even find the store-rooms and stair-case, which, as yet, have not the benefit of a fire, also comparatively free of dampness. As a proof of this, it may be noticed, that the lower parts of the house dry pretty readily when the floors are washed, excepting, indeed, when a heavy sea runs, and some water comes in at the checks of the windows, and partially wets the lower apartments. It is, however, impossible entirely to keep out wetness at windows, which, for conveniency, must be made to open, especially when so great a body of water occasionally presses upon them. As to the warmth of the house, ever since we got The Jacob's ladder taken down, and the Entrance-door shut, we have been very comfortable. I never heard the least complaint on this head from any of the Light-keepers, and it is a general remark that we are warmer here than ashore.

Qualifications of the Light-keepers.

"With regard to your inquiries about the Light-keepers, I may remark, that Mr John Reid, the principal keeper, appears to like his situation very well, though, at first, when the sea struck hard upon the building, he seemed rather sad, and was perhaps not so confident about it. When he was in that mood, I used to cheer him by telling him it was only a fancy; and as he is a very sensible man, and originally bred a seaman and carpenter, his mind readily complies with a belief in our safety. Mr John Bonyman, the principal assistant, appears to take well with his situation; and having been personally employed as a mason from first to last in the erection, and more fully understanding its nature, he always keeps himself very easy upon this point. Mr Henry Leask, though formerly a shipmaster, yet having for several years been a light-keeper, has been much at home with his family, and his attention is naturally drawn more towards them; however, he appears quite satisfied, though he does not speak very confidently about our habitation, but shrugs up his shoulders, and looks strange when he feels the tremor of the house. As to their qualifications as light-keepers, I have not the least hesitation in stating, that Mr Reid and his assistants are now fully competent for their duty. We proceed agreeably to our written instructions, though there are some parts of them which I shall take the liberty of submitting to you for alteration.

1811, April.

Manner in which they spend their time.

"I will now let you know how we come on with what I may call our domestic life. When the duty of the house is over for the day, we generally take a walk on the waggon-ways, and search about the crevices of the rock for small fishes, when the state of the tides and weather permit; but when that is not the case, we content ourselves without it, and find amusement in reading a small library, consisting of about a dozen of volumes of one kind or other, collected among us; and you know we have the progressive numbers of the Scots Magazine and the Weekly Chronicle, which we receive as regularly as the situation of the place will admit. I may further notice, that it gives the Light-keepers much pleasure to learn that Mr Slight has received orders, in fitting up the strangers' room, to provide it with a book-case, which we understand the Commissioners are to supply with books. On Sunday, we attend to the general rule of the service, doing no more work in the Light-room than is necessary, cleaning only the reflectors, lamp-glasses and windows, operations which are usually over at this season about 12 o'clock, after which we meet for prayers, and read two or three chapters of the Bible.

"I have perhaps tired you with this long letter, but I could not give you the description you wanted in fewer words. I shall only further add, that we all remain in good health, and that every thing connected with the Light-room apparatus is in good order.—I am, &c. &c.

"John Forrest"

"To Mr Robert Stevenson,
"Engineer for Northern Light-houses."

Friday, 2d.

They are left in full possession of the house.

From this very satisfactory communication, it was evident that the Light-house might now be left under the charge of Mr Reid and his assistants. The Tender accordingly sailed this morning, carrying off Mr Bonyman, who had been at Arbroath on leave; when Mr Forrest, who had been upwards of three months at the Rock, came on shore, leaving Mr Reid to instruct his third assistant, Michael Wishart, the mason who had been so severely hurt on the 30th June 1809, by the fall of the moveable beam-crane.

Progress of the ulterior works.

1811, May.

The houses erecting at Arbroath for the families of the Light-keepers, were roofed over in the month of May; at which period, the signal-tower for communicating with the Light-house, represented in Plate XII., had attained to half its height, or about 30 feet. The shipping at this station consisted only of the Smeaton as Bell Rock Tender, the other vessels which had been employed in carrying on the work, having been disposed of by public sale. As soon as the weather permitted, the artificers went off to the Rock to put the Railways in a state of repair after the gales of winter; for this purpose, the Beacon-house was still extremely useful as a smith's shop, while it also served as a store for the implements and bulky articles connected with the fitting up of the interior of the Light-house.

The Lord Justice-Clerk Hope, and a party embark for the Bell Rock.

On the 24th of July, Lord Justice-Clerk Hope, Lord Boyle, Dr Hope, Mr Hamilton, and Mr James Spreull, besides Lady Charlotte Hope and Mrs Hamilton, embarked at Leith in the Light-house Yacht, to visit the Bell Rock. The wind being at SW., and blowing hard, the vessel had to put into Arbroath till the 26th, which prevented the Lord Justice-Clerk and his Lady from visiting the Light-house; but the rest of the party having remained, they had a most convenient landing on the Rock; were highly gratified with their visit, and returned in the Yacht to Leith on the 28th.

1811, September.

State of things at the Rock.

In the course of his annual voyage to the Northern Light-houses, the writer, on the 27th September, touched at Arbroath, and had the satisfaction to find that the Light-keepers' houses were nearly in a habitable state, while the Signal-tower was ready for the plaster-work. Having landed on the following day at the Bell Rock, with Mr James Haldane, who had accompanied him thither on his first visit in the year 1800, they did not fail to express their mutual congratulations on the successful result of those operations which, on the former occasion, had been contemplated at a very distant view. On examining the Light-house, every thing was found to be in good order, and Mr Reid, and his assistants, quite satisfied with their habitation. Mr Dove had completed the copper flag-staff, and also the iron-grating on the outside of the Light-room, for the greater conveniency of cleaning the windows: Mr Slight had made great progress in fitting up the oak partitions, beds, and interior finishing of the house; and had dismantled the upper parts of the Beacon-house, which was now reduced to its state in 1809, as represented in Plate VIII. At low-water, all hands were engaged at the Railways to fortify them also for withstanding the storms of winter; and it was chiefly for this purpose that the principal beams of the Beacon-house were preserved on the Rock. It had been originally intended to erect a stone-slip for the conveniency of landing, till, from experience, it was found that the iron Railways were more suitable to the circumstances of the place than solid masonry; the waves acting with much more force on the solid wall, than on the open railways.

Tender goes adrift.

On the 12th of this month, the Smeaton having been, for several days, at the Rock, landing stores and articles for the artificers, unluckily broke adrift by the failure of the mooring-chain. As it came to blow fresh from W. NW., she narrowly escaped shipwreck; and having been driven eastward as far as Dunnottar Castle, it was not till Tuesday the 15th that she returned. This shewed the uncertainty of making the Tender fast to moorings at the Rock, excepting in fine weather, and pointed out the propriety of keeping her under-way, during her future casual attendance for the supply of the Light-house. This arrangement, however, required that the mate and one seaman should be left on board, while the master and other two were at work in the boat.

Boats suitable for the Bell Rock.

"Bruce's boat."

It may here be noticed, that a boat, in order to be at once safe and convenient for landing at the Bell Rock, should measure not more than from 14 to 16 feet in length of keel. A boat, therefore, of a proper size for parties visiting the Light-house from the shore, will be found too large for landing at the Rock; because, when she has still a depth of water to float her into the several creeks, the tide has not sufficiently ebbed to afford shelter from the breach of the sea, even when there is but a slight swell on the Rock. In like manner, she requires to lie too long in floating off again, and is consequently more apt to be damaged than a smaller boat. A decked vessel, with a float-boat of the dimensions mentioned above, is the safest; or, if a large open boat is used to go from the shore, it should not be less than 20 feet in length of keel, carrying a small boat, upon the plan of "Bruce's Two-half boat." This description of craft may be conveniently stowed into the fore-peak of a large boat, and, when put to use, the two-halves are screwed together with great facility, and used with perfect safety as one boat. For this ingenious contrivance, the public are indebted to the late Mr James Bruce, of the Naval Yard establishment, Leith.

Light-house Stove takes fire.

Owing to inattention on the part of the Light-keepers, the chimney of the temporary stove, which, for the present, was fitted up in the kitchen, had been allowed, on the 20th of this month, to take fire; and though the surrounding apparatus was proof against burning, yet the heat of the tube, which passes through the Light-room, so cracked and damaged six of the squares of plate-glass, that it was judged proper to replace them with others from the stock on hand.

1811, November.

Sprays rise to the height of the Light-room.

The month of November set in with S.E. winds, and the tides and sea upon the shores of the Firth of Forth, rose higher than had been observed for the last thirty years. During this gale, while Mr Leask, one of the keepers, was standing upon the balcony, a considerable quantity of sprays broke over the cornice, so as to wet all his clothes, and to strike against the glass of the Light-room so forcibly, as to alarm those who were within. This was the first instance observed of the sea rising to the height of about 108 feet above the surface of the Rock. The Light-keepers also stated, that when the tide was at the highest, they expected every minute that the Beacon would have been swept away, as it was frequently wholly under water when the sea broke around the Light-house; nor were they altogether at ease as to their own situation. Several large masses of stone were, upon this occasion, thrown upon the Rock; a mass of about two tons, completely blocked up one of the landing-places until it was broken and removed. The Railways also suffered severely, having been dislocated in several places.

Advantage of double windows.

In the course of the month of December, the Light-house had been visited with very severe gales, but the keepers were now gaining more confidence in the stability of their habitation. Captain Taylor, who commanded the Tender, on questioning them when he landed on the Rock, how they had stood out the bad weather, they, to his surprise, replied, "There has been nothing remarkable in the weather." They further stated, "that, when the doors and storm-shutters were made fast, and the double windows shut, all was quiet in the several apartments: it was only when they went to the Balcony that they heard the wind: and that the house had little or no motion by the sea striking it, excepting in storms from the north-east, east, or south-east, but especially from the north-east."

1812.

The Light-house excites much interest.

The light had now been exhibited for twelve months; and it was highly gratifying to the Board to find, from almost every quarter of the coast, by the testimony of those who had seen it at sea, that this important edifice gave universal satisfaction, appearing in all respects to answer the fullest expectations of the mariner. It appeared also from the Album, or book kept at the Light-house, for inserting names, that nearly 500 strangers had landed to see it, in the course of the summer season.

1812, August.

Sir William Rae and Mr Duff visit the Rock with parties.

On the 21st of August, Sir William Rae, Baronet, the Lord Chief-Baron Dundas, General Francis Dundas, Mr Jardine of the Exchequer, and Mr Russell, accountant to the Board, visited the Light-house, when the Chief-Baron expressed his entire approbation of the work and establishment in general. About the same period, Mr Duff landed, accompanied by Mr Foulerton, one of the Elder Brethren of the Trinity-House, Mr Menzies of Pitfoddels, and the late Mr Taylor of Kirktonhill, who were in like manner much pleased. It was, upon this occasion, gratifying to hear Captain Foulerton's remarks of approbation, as his official connection with the English Light-house Board, more especially qualified him for judging of the Bell Rock works.

The Beacon is removed from the Rock.

On Friday the 4th September, at 5 A. M., the writer landed at the Rock with Mr James Slight, clerk of works, who, with eight artificers, was to commence taking down the frame or principal beams of the Beacon-house. This useful fabric might have remained for an indefinite period, but for the ravages of the insect already described, which had now affected the beams so much where they rested upon the Rock, as to render its removal advisable. In this operation the artificers were only employed for about three weeks, although it had occupied nearly the whole of two working seasons to erect it. The Tender made occasional trips ashore with the timber, the great iron stanchions, bracing-bars, and numerous bolts, which were to be employed in the erection of the buildings at Arbroath, and in the works of the Carr Rock Beacon.

Mode of securing timber against the insect.

The only remark which the writer has to make, regarding the erection of such a building as the Beacon-house is, that due precaution should be used in protecting the soles or feet of the beams, where they rest upon the Rock, and are inaccessible to the application of pitch or other preventives. Sheathing with copper might, perhaps, be found the best protection; but, in such situations, the copper should be coated with tin, to prevent any action between it and the iron-work.

Light-house assailed by a gale.

On the 1st of October, Mr Slight, accompanied by several artificers, went again off to the Light-house with the remaining apparatus for finishing the interior of the house, having still the bed-room to fit up, the brass-plates for the safety of the sill and lintel of the entrance-door, and a variety of other small works to complete. The railways were also in want of some additional stays, to fit them for withstanding the storms of winter. These operations, however, were conducted much more slowly since the removal of the Beacon; and it now became necessary to erect the smith's forge upon the balcony of the Light-house, for sharpening tools, and other little operations.

1812, November.

Remarkable shock of the sea.

On Saturday the 14th of November, a very severe storm took place, accompanied with a heavy sea from the S.E. A letter from the Light-house stated, that, "at high-water in the evening, a tremendous sea struck the house, the effect of which was the most alarming that had been experienced perhaps since it was erected. The locks upon the doors were heard to rattle; and what makes this the more singular is, that not another sea of consequence struck the house during the whole tide." Upon further inquiry into this matter, the writer found that the artificers, and two of the light-keepers were then in the kitchen; upon the shock taking place, the whole sprung up to the balcony, imagining for the moment that some vessel must have got upon the Rock, and that the report heard was the discharge of a gun, so sudden and sharp was the sensation which it occasioned. But they soon found that their alarm was occasioned by the sea alone.

Professor Robison's opinion on this subject.

The writer has often thought of this surprising effect of the force of the sea; and he finds it difficult to assign a cause for the motion of the doors in so low a position of the building as the kitchen; otherwise than by supposing a disturbance in the equilibrium of the air, by the sudden displacement of the column of water, which, upon these occasions, rises upon the building. The tremor felt in leaning against the walls in the upper apartments, when it blows fresh, or when the house is struck by a sea, or by a boat coming suddenly against it, may be compared to that which is perceptible in a common house, upon the slamming of particular doors, or when a carriage makes a rattling noise in passing along the streets; but it is attended with no real danger. In confirmation of this, it may be mentioned, that when the late Professor Robison of Edinburgh visited the Edystone Light-house, something having forcibly struck the building, he was sensible of a vibratory motion in one of the rooms in which he was then sitting. But, instead of producing any alarm in the mind of the Professor, he assured his friends, that it was to him the strongest proof of the unity and connection of the fabric in all its parts. This anecdote the writer is desirous of preserving, as it was communicated to him by this eminent person.

View of the Sea, from which the Frontispiece is delineated.

1812, December.

The writer being in Forfarshire at this time, was desirous of seeing the effects of the sea upon the Light-house, after the Beacon had been removed. He accordingly embraced the opportunity of sailing from Arbroath with the Tender, in a pretty hard gale from north-east, at 4 o'clock in the morning of the 9th of December, and, at 7, got close to the Rock. The Light-house now appeared in one of its most interesting aspects, standing proudly among the waves, while the sea around it was in the wildest state of agitation. The Light-keepers did not seem to be in motion; but the scene was by no means still, as the noise and dashing of the waves were unceasing. The seas rose in the most surprising manner to the height of the kitchen windows, or about 70 feet above the Rock; and after expending their force in a perpendicular direction, successively fell in great quantities round the base of the Light-house, while considerable portions of the spray were seen adhering as it were to the building, and guttering down its sides in the state of froth as white as snow. Some of the great waves burst, and were expended upon the Rock before they reached the building; while others struck the base, and, embracing the walls, met on the western side of the house, where they dashed together, and produced a most surprising quantity of foam. Upon this view of the breaking of the seas at the Light-house, the frontispiece for this work has been delineated.

The Sea overruns the Rock at low-water.

Though there was no possibility of effecting a landing to-day, yet the vessel lay off-and-on till low-water, that the writer might also then see the state of the waves upon the Railways. He found that they still continued to make a constant run over them; and that no one could have stood upon any part of the rock, even for the space of one minute, without having been thrown down and carried away by their force. After lying-to till 10 o'clock, the Tender bore away for the Firth of Forth, leaving the inhabitants of the Rock surrounded, and even enveloped by the sea in its utmost fury, yet in a state of comparative comfort, and enjoying feelings of the most perfect security.

Mode in which the Light-house is attended.

The regulations observed in attending the Bell Rock are these. The vessel stationed at Arbroath goes off every fortnight, or in the course of each set of spring-tides, to relieve the Light-keepers, and to supply the house with necessaries; but when the weather does not admit of this, the master's instructions direct him to embrace the first favourable opportunity thereafter. Of the four keepers belonging to this establishment, three are always at the Light-house, while one is ashore on liberty. The regular term ashore is a fortnight, and the duty at the Rock is six weeks. During the rotations, however, in the course of the winter and spring, some of the keepers were detained upwards of three months upon the Rock, while others were four or five weeks ashore. The Tender had made several unsuccessful attempts to effect a landing during this period, and had been twice forced to Leith Roads, and once to the northward as far as Aberdeen. The light-keepers, however, seemed, upon the whole, pleased with their situation; and talked in a feeling manner of the hardships of mariners, whom they often saw tossed about during the storms of winter.

1813.

Establishment for the Light-keepers at Arbroath completed.

In the course of the year 1813, the Light-keepers' houses, at Arbroath, signal-tower, and sea-wall connected with them, were completed; and a garden of upwards of an acre was enclosed, and laid out for the use of the families of the light-keepers, and for supplying the Light-house and Tender with vegetables.

These buildings formed no part of the original design; but the Commissioners were resolved that this establishment should be complete. Had houses been hired in the town of Arbroath, for the light-keepers, much inconvenience would have arisen to the service, especially when the attending vessel was going off to the Rock under night. Besides the principal building occupied by the light-keepers, there are store-houses, and accommodation for the master and crew of the attending vessels, in an adjoining building, where each family has two or three rooms. The top of the signal-tower is formed into a small observatory, furnished with a 5 feet achromatic telescope, a flag-staff, and copper signal-ball measuring 18 inches in diameter.

Signals observed at the Rock.

By means of this, and a corresponding ball at the Light-house, certain signals are daily kept up between Arbroath and the Rock. The chief of which consists in hoisting the ball at the latter place to the top of the flag-staff, where it is kept, when all is well, every morning, between the hours of 9 and 10. But in case the weather should prove so foggy or cloudy at this hour, that the signals cannot be seen, the watch is again set at 1 P. M., and should it then become clear, the ball is again elevated, and allowed to remain till 2 o'clock. This signal is watched by the light-keeper who, in his turn, happens to be ashore on liberty, and who immediately answers it by hoisting the ball at Arbroath. Should the ball at the Rock, however, be allowed to remain down, as is the case when any thing is particularly wanted, or in the event of sickness, the Tender immediately puts to sea.

1814.

Thunder-rod.

The mechanical operations at the Bell Rock, during the year 1814, consisted principally in fitting up a thunder-rod or electrical conductor, on the exterior and western side of the building, as may be observed on the elevation of the Light-house in Plate XVI. This rod is continuous from the top to the foundation of the building, being connected with the sash-frames of the light-room, and the Railways upon the Rock. The best construction and application of rods for conducting the electric fluid, is a problem upon which scientific men are not altogether agreed; some being of opinion, that the conducting-surface should be large; while the slender bell-wires in dwelling-houses are found capable of conveying it in a body sufficient to destroy the premises. The fixing of a plate of any considerable breadth upon the exterior of the Light-house would have been attended with much difficulty; and the writer having consulted Professors Playfair and Leslie, and Dr Brewster, a rod was prepared by Mr Adie, optician, 2¼ inches in breadth, and, where thickest, 1 inch, the external side being slightly rounded, to suit the circle of the wall, and thus presenting the least possible resistance to the sea. The composition of this rod was one ounce and a half of tin to a pound of pure copper; and with its bats, screws, and connecting pieces, it weighed 556 pounds, or about one-quarter of a ton.

Method of fixing it.

In order to fix it to the building, a groove was cut in the exterior wall, as high as the solid part, about half an inch in depth, which was sufficient to receive the edge or thinnest part of the rod. On the higher parts of the building the wall was not cut, the flat side of the rod being simply applied to it; and in its track, brass-bats, previously perforated and screwed, were sunk in the wall to the depth of three inches, and run up with melted lead, at about two feet apart. The rod being cast in lengths of seven feet, the pieces were successively applied to the building, when the precise positions of the holes in the brass-bats were ascertained, marked on the rod, and bored on the spot for screw-nails of ⅝ths of an inch in diameter; the several lengths of the rod being half checked at each end, and the nail-heads counter-sunk, as shewn in Plate XIX. Fig. 10. The cutting of this groove and the bat-holes in the masonry, was done in a very masterly manner by the late Thomas Selkirk, of whom notice is here more particularly taken, as this was the last piece of work which he executed, as well as from his having been acknowledged by his companions to have been one of the best stone-cutters in Scotland.

1814.

A party of the Commissioners and Sir Walter Scott visit the Light-house.

On the 30th of July this year, Mr Hamilton, Mr Erskine, and Mr Duff, Commissioners, along with Mr (now Sir) Walter Scott, and the writer, visited the Light-house; the Commissioners being then on one of their voyages of Inspection, noticed in the Introduction. They breakfasted in the library, when Sir Walter, at the entreaty of the party, upon inscribing his name in the album, added the interesting lines, of which the reader will find a fac-simile on the second title-page.

1815.

Permanent Railways began to be fitted.

Lord President Hope lands at the Rock.

Though the temporary railways originally fitted up for the building operations had been thoroughly repaired, they were often found much in disorder, and required a still stronger mode of construction. In the course of this summer, therefore, part of the western-reach of the new or permanent Railway was fitted up, which was named Hope's Wharf; Lord President Hope having landed upon it in the month of August, from the Latona Frigate.

1816.

Pharos Tender built.

The sloop Smeaton having been originally constructed as a stone-lighter, was not well adapted for sailing, or doing the duty of a Tender. A vessel, of 51 tons register, properly fitted for this service, was therefore built at Leith by Mr Morton, and launched in the summer of 1816, under the appropriate name of The Pharos. Besides her stern-boat, this vessel carries another upon deck, measuring 15 feet in length of keel; she is also sheathed with copper, and laid out with a fore and after cabin.

The Light-house is Painted.

Owing to the sprays of the sea, the colour of the upper part of the Light-house had become much changed, and had acquired a dark olive hue, while, on the western side, the granite courses below were of a whitish-grey; so that the building had now a party-coloured appearance. To remedy this, and especially to prevent the sandstone from imbibing moisture, it was, in the summer of 1816, painted in oil colour, of a greyish tint. The whole of the interior of the house being of polished masonry, was at the same time painted white; while the walls and roof of the library were decorated with pannelled work, in a very tasteful manner. Mr Macdonald of Arbroath the painter, having remained a considerable period in the Light-house, had several opportunities of observing the effects of the sea upon the Rock, and made some striking sketches of its appearance upon the building in storms, which have afforded useful hints to the artist who furnished the draught from which the frontispiece to this work is taken.

1818.

Fuci disappear from the Rock.

On visiting the Light-house in the summer of 1818, the writer was struck with the naked appearance of the Rock, the fuci having in a great measure disappeared. On examination he found that they had been cut off by vast numbers of a species of limpet, curiously striated with blue lines, (the Patella pellucida of naturalists). Among various other changes incidental to the plants and animals on the Rock, the barnacle was found to be fully more prevalent than formerly, and covered all the higher parts, like a greyish coloured scurf. One good effect connected with the disappearance of the sea-weed, was a more complete exposure of several large holes or inequalities in the Rock. Some of those, on the north-eastern side of the Light-house, being of a large size, varying from two to four feet in depth, the writer considered necessary to have filled with ruble-building, which, in an imbedded state, when executed with pozzolano-mortar, had been found to withstand the utmost force of the sea.

1819.

Permanent Railways completed.

In the course of the summer of 1819, Mr James Slight, and his brother Alexander (who had assisted throughout the works in making moulds for the stone-cutters, and in other operations requiring neat and ingenious workmanship), together with Messrs George Dove, Robert Selkirk, James Glen, James Scott, Alexander Brebner, and John Mitchell, completed the remaining parts of the western and southern-reaches of the railways, by the addition of a number of large cast-iron stays or braces, as represented in Figs. 13, 14, and 15, of Plate X. The bats of these new railways were wedged with timber and iron in the usual manner, and the feet of the supports, with their bats and spear-bolts, were plastered over with Roman-cement, with a view to secure them against the effects of oxidation.

Improvement on the entrance to the Light-house by a ladder of brass.

By taking the stores from the railways to the entrance of the Light-house up the sloping exterior wall, the joints of the courses at that part had been somewhat injured. The access also to the door had hitherto been only by a rope-ladder, or, to strangers, by a suspended chair, which was hoisted up by the crane fixed to the building. Both of these were liable to accidents and decay, from the wearing of the ropes by frequent use. In order, therefore, to prevent injury to the building, and to remove these defects, two strong bars of brass, of the same composition as the thunder-rod, were fixed on the building, from the door down to the rock, to answer the purpose of skids; and steps of the same metal, being attached to these bars by screw-bolts, a substantial and convenient ladder, or rather flight of steps, was thus constructed; and, as this apparatus became a fixture, ready entrance to the Light-house was provided for, and could on all occasions of emergency be safely obtained. A connection being also formed between this metallic-stair and the kitchen-chimney, a thunder-rod was thus obtained for the interior as well as the exterior of the house; the whole including the stair, weighing about 3133 pounds, or about 1 ton 8 cwt. of brass.

Sprays rise 105 feet.

In the course of the three last winters, the weather had been so uncommonly mild, that the sea, as appears from the Light-house Returns, had rarely risen upon the building higher than from 30 to 50 feet. But, in October 1819, there were some very severe gales, accompanied with heavy seas, the sprays of which, on the 24th, rose to the height of 105 feet above the Rock. The water had struck the light-room with such force at this time, that one of the assistants, then on watch, started from his seat, imagining that some serious accident had occurred. The writer having landed on the 20th November following, examined into the precise state of matters upon that occasion, when it was stated, that it appeared as if a bucket or two of water had been thrown with violence against the Light-room windows. Mr Reid, principal Light-keeper, and Mr Taylor, commander of the Tender, also confidently observed, that this was the most severe gale which they had experienced since they were connected with the service. It may, perhaps, therefore, be concluded, that the maximum force of the sea at the Bell Rock is to raise the sprays to the height of about 105 feet above the surface of the Rock.

A piece of the highest part of the Rock carried away.

These storms had proved so severe, that the Rock actually lost about 18 inches of its height, a fragment of that thickness having been carried away from the highest part. This spot the workmen had significantly termed "The Last-hope," as marked on Plate VI., in allusion to the imminent hazard which the party on the Rock had incurred in the year 1807. The removal of this highest stratum is the more particularly noticed, as forming a link in the chain of probabilities, leading to the conclusion of the Bell Rock having once been of much greater extent.

1820.

Improvements on the Light-house, Brass-door, &c.

Though the Light-house might be considered as long since finished, various improvements have still at different times been made on it. In the course of the year 1820, an inner entrance-door was hung in the passage, chiefly to prevent the necessity of shutting the outer-door so frequently during the continuance of westerly winds. To save room, and cutting the walls, this door was constructed of brass-pannelled work, and the upper part glazed with plate-glass, to preserve the light. In the original fitting up of the interior of the house, the machinery-weight had been carried through the centre of the several apartments; but this having been found incommodious, the rope was now conducted close to the wall, in a small case; and, by introducing a double-pulley, the weight does not require to be brought higher than the floor of the Light-room-store, from which it descends into the drop-hole formed in the solid part of the building, as shewn in Plate XVI. The store-room for water, fuel, and provisions, was also fitted up this year in a more commodious manner, with cast-iron cisterns, an enlarged magazine for fuel, and a complete set of lockers. The water, which hitherto had been carried from the store to the kitchen in buckets, was now raised by a pump, fitted up after the manner of the beer-pumps in general use in London.

1821.

A new machine for taking up the stores.

The weather during 1821 was comparatively mild, and no storm of any consequence occurred at the Rock. The only work deserving notice that year, was the removal of the small crane from the entrance-door, to the provision-store; where a machine, upon a new principle, was constructed, the barrel or drum of which moves vertically upon its axis, instead of horizontally, while it winds up the chain. By means of this machine, the stores are now taken up to the entrance-door more conveniently; while both the door and passage are entirely relieved of the encumbrance of the crane-apparatus; as will be understood by examining Plate XIV. Fig. 7. and Plate XVI.

Mr Reid retires from the Light-house service.

In the course of this year, Mr John Reid, the principal light-keeper, on account of the state of his health, resigned his situation, and was succeeded by Mr Thomson Milne, reflector-maker. In consideration of Mr Reid's faithful services, the Board put him on the half-pay list, at the rate of 30 guineas per annum.

1822.

Light-house works and model completed. Design for Wolf Rock.

In the year 1822, the several large holes in the Rock, formerly alluded to, were filled up, and that important work completed. The writer may here mention, that he is possessed of a complete model of the Bell Rock Light-house as executed, and of the chief implements mentioned in this work, which he will take measures for preserving to the Public; from a recollection of the interest he should have felt in examining any model of the Edystone Light-house, before he had an opportunity of seeing that work itself. He also, for similar reasons, gives a design, in Plate XXIII., founded on experience, as applicable to the erection of Light-houses on sunken rocks, which more particularly occurred to him after his first visit to the Wolf Rock situate between the Land's End and the Scilly Islands, in the year 1813, under the auspices of the Admiralty, in the Orestes sloop of war, commanded by Captain Smith.

1823.

Severe storm. Carrier-pigeon sent from the Rock.

The year 1823 set in with perhaps as severe a storm as has occurred on this coast since the Light-house was erected. The Pharos, in the course of her attendance on the Rock, was driven first into the Firth of Tay, and thereafter into the Forth, where she was forced to anchor above Queensferry, about 70 miles from her station; and in the course of the winter, it was fully two months before she could effect a landing at the Light-house. The only accident, however, which happened during that period, was the breaking of the ratchet-wheel spring, which keeps the reflector-frame in motion, while the machinery is winding up. Though only of a trivial nature, and unconnected with the stormy effects of the sea, it nevertheless created considerable alarm among the families of the Light-keepers ashore, as the signal-ball was very properly kept down upon this occasion. Their anxiety, however, was relieved in the course of the day, by the arrival of a carrier-pigeon, with a billet from the principal light-keeper, intimating what had happened. A pair of these curious birds had originally been presented to the establishment by Captain Samuel Brown of the Royal Navy. They have now multiplied considerably; and two or more are generally conveyed to the Rock at every trip of the Tender, and let off occasionally for amusement. Their flight between the Light-house and the Signal-tower at Arbroath, upwards of 11 miles, has been ascertained to have been at the rate of about one mile per minute.

Expence and cubic contents of the Work.

In concluding these details, it may be proper to state, from the Abstract Accounts of the expence, quantity of materials, and description of workmanship, given in Appendix, No. VI., that the expence of this important national work amounted to L. 61,331:9:2; and that the cubical contents of the materials used in its erection were about 28,530 feet, and would weigh about 2078 tons.

GENERAL VIEW OF THE BELL ROCK WORKS.

Drawn by G. C. Scott from a Painting by A. Carse.
Engraved by Willm. Miller.

PLATE XVIII.

APPENDIX.

No. I.

CONTAINING A NOTICE OF ADDITIONAL LIGHT-HOUSE STATIONS, LIGHT-KEEPERS' INSTRUCTIONS, FORMS OF MONTHLY AND SHIPWRECK RETURNS.

ADDITIONAL LIGHT-HOUSE STATIONS.

Additional Light-houses.

In noticing the different points alluded to, at page 60., as the most prominent stations for additional Light-houses on the coast of Scotland, we shall follow a course from east to west, including the Orkney and Shetland Islands.

Eastern Coast.

On the eastern coast two light-houses seem particularly to be required, in addition to the present Light on Kinnaird-Head. One of these, at Buchan-Ness, near Peterhead, which becomes a turning-point in the navigation of that coast, as will be seen from Plate III., would be an excellent guide to the southward, for shipping on the long flat shores of Aberdeenshire, and not less useful as a direction for the foul ground or sunken rocks called Rattray Briggs to the northward of Buchan-Ness. Some are also of opinion, that Girdle-Ness, at the entrance of Aberdeen harbour, would be a proper station for a sea or public Light. The next station in the order of position on the eastern coast, is Tarbetness, a centrical point of land extending into the Moray Firth , which leads to Cromarty Roads, a great rendezvous for shipping in stormy weather. A Light upon this projecting point would also be extremely useful as a direction to the numerous small ports of this district, and would prevent the losses which occasionally happen on Culloden Rock, and Halliman's Scars, and by the Firth of Tain being mistaken for a continuation of the Moray Firth . It would also serve as a guide to the narrow passage of Fort George, leading to the eastern entrance of the Caledonian Canal.

Northern Coast.

Several Light-houses are still wanted for the protection of shipping on the Northern Coast. In particular we notice, that although the eastern entrance of the Pentland Firth is already well marked by the Light-house on the Skerries; yet the western approach to this dangerous, but important channel, requires a light upon Dunnet-head in Caithness, which would prevent vessels from mistaking Murkle Bay for the Pentland Firth , and, at the same time, form an excellent guide for the south-western coast of Orkney. Cape Wrath in Sutherland is the north-western point of the Mainland of Scotland, as will be seen from Plate III. A Light-house upon that promontory would be of great importance to the navigation of the dreary coast of Caithness and Sutherland, and as a direction for the sunken rock called the Nun, surveyed by Captain Ramage, in H. M. S. Cherokee in the year 1814; and by him found to lie 15 miles in a north-eastern direction from that shore. A light upon Cape Wrath would likewise serve as an excellent guide to the northern entrance of the Great and Little Minish, or Friths of Lewis and Uist, a central track in the navigation of the Hebrides, now much frequented by shipping since the erection of the Light-house upon Glass, one of the Harris Isles.

Orkney and Shetland Islands.

Perhaps the only additional light still wanted in Orkney, to which it is here necessary to allude, is one upon Nouphead of Westra, to direct shipping on the north-western side of these Islands. In addition to Sumburgh-head Light-house in Shetland, one upon the Out-skerries of Whalsey, on the east, another upon the Scaw of Unst, in the north; and a third on the Skerries of Ve, on the western side, would seem to render these Islands complete in regard to Light-houses.

Western Coast.

The opening of the sheltered passage through the Friths of Lewis and Uist, by the Light-house on Glass, has, in a great measure, superseded the use of the outward course of shipping by St Kilda, which is now seldom taken by coasting vessels, though a Light upon that island would be extremely useful to ships making the land from the Western Ocean. The next Light-house that seems wanting in connection with the navigation of the Minish is one upon the Island of Bara, as a direction to its western entrance by the Firth of Uist. It will only further be necessary, on this coast, to direct our attention to the position of the Rocks of Skerryvore, in order to perceive the importance of a light upon that dangerous reef, which lies about 12 miles south-west from the Island of Tiree. The principal rock here is a circular mass of granite, about 60 feet in diameter, and elevated about 20 feet above the highest tides. The rocks of Skerryvore prove not only a great bar to ships making the coast from foreign voyages, but, it is feared, have been fatal to many vessels sailing along these western shores.

The Rhins, a promontory forming the south-western extremity of the Island of Islay, is another position of importance for pointing out the northern side of the passage from the Atlantic to the Clyde and Irish Sea, between Islay and Bengore Head in Ireland. The Commissioners, at their meeting in the month of January 1823, having ordered a Light-house to be built at this station, it is accordingly in progress. The navigation of the sounds and tracks among the Western Isles would also be greatly facilitated by the erection of four Light-houses, of the smallest class of sea-lights, on stations connected with the inner Sounds of Skye and Mull. One of these lights, erected at the south entrance of the Sound of Mull, would not only be important to that passage, but to the various tracks leading to the Sounds of Islay, and by those of Linnehe and Loing, to the western entrances of the Caledonian and Crinan Canals. The Island Devaar, at the entrance of the much frequented anchorage of Campbeltown Loch, is another station for a small Light, to which the attention of the Board has been directed by the Shipping Interest of the Western Coast.

Southern Coast.

Although the lights upon the Point of Corsewall and Isle of Man, form a good direction for the southern coast of Scotland, yet a light upon the Mull of Galloway would still be of much utility in preventing northern-bound ships from mistaking Glenluce Bay for the Irish Channel; and in leading them along the Scotch side, between the Firth of Clyde and the Irish Sea. Application has also been made for the erection of a small Light upon the Little-Ross Island, at the entrance of Kirkcudbright-anchorage.

INSTRUCTIONS FOR THE BELL ROCK LIGHT-KEEPERS.

Instructions to Light-Keepers.

I.—The Keepers of the Bell Rock Light-house are hereby instructed and directed to keep the lamps of the reflecting-apparatus burning bright and clear, from the going away of day-light in the evening till the return of day-light in the morning. The better to obtain this purpose, the period of night is to be divided into Watches, and each keeper in rotation will mount guard for three hours. The fountains of the lamps being daily supplied with oil, the wicks must be frequently trimmed in the course of the night, but more particularly at the end of each watch.

II.—The motion of the machinery of the reflector-frame must be so regulated, that one of the lights of the natural appearance, and one of those coloured red, shall be exhibited to the mariner in their most brilliant effect, in the course of every four minutes; or the reflector-frame must make one entire revolution in the space of eight minutes.

III.—The keeper on watch will look out for the occurrence of foggy or snowy weather, and during the continuance of either, the bells must be kept tolling both day and night.

IV.—At the end of each watch, the keeper respectively on duty must ring the house or bed-room bell, as the case may be, and thereafter remain at his post until he is relieved by the keeper in person whose turn it is to mount guard.

V.—In the event of any thing getting out of order about the machinery of the reflector-frame, so as to prevent its operation, the Lights, and also the Bell-hammers, if required, must be moved by hand, as nearly to the periodic time as possible, until the repair of the machine can be accomplished.

VI.—Should the stock of Oil in the Light-house by any means be reduced to 150 gallons, between the 1st day of October and the last day of February; or to 50 gallons between the 1st day of March and the 30th day of September, the number of lights on each side of the reflector-frame shall be reduced to three; but in the event of the stock of Oil being respectively lessened to one-half of the above quantities, or that any of the other stores essential to the support of the Light, are getting so low as to endanger its total failure, only one burner shall be lighted on each side of the reflector-frame, or four burners in all.

VII.—Unless, under these circumstances, a supply comes to hand, recourse must ultimately be had to the use of the Wax Candles in store.

VIII.—During any period that the stores or provisions appear to the acting Principal Light-keeper to be in danger of falling short, or in the event of sickness, or under any other circumstances considered of a calamitous and hazardous nature, the signal of distress shall be observed, by ceasing to hoist the Signal-ball at the stated periods, until the arrival of the Attending-vessel.

IX.—In all cases of difficulty, especially such as are referred to by the tenor of the Articles VI. VII. and VIII. of these Instructions, the acting Principal Light-keeper shall use his discretion and judgment in lessening the daily allowance of provisions, water, and fuel, according to his view of the circumstances of the case.

X.—No lights of any kind are to be left in such a situation as to endanger accident by fire. If at any time it should be found necessary to enter the store-room under night, the light must be carried in a lantern.

XI.—The better to ensure regularity and good order in the Light-house-duty, it shall be performed in three distinct departments. The keepers to shift in rotation weekly, from the performance of one department to another. These changes are to take place every Saturday-night.

XII.—The light-keeper performing the duty of the first department, shall, in the course of the day, supply the lamp-fountains with oil, and the burners with cotton; he shall clean the reflecting-apparatus, and all the utensils connected with the trimming of the lights. He shall also take his turn in mounting guard both day and night.

XIII.—The day-work of the second department includes the cleaning of the machinery-case, windows, walls, floors, and apparatus connected with the light-room, not already specified as coming under the first department; he shall likewise clean the balcony and library; the books of which must be dusted or cleaned on the first Saturday of every month. The keeper in this department will also take his turn at day and night watches.

XIV.—The third department includes the cleaning of the bed-room, kitchen, and provision store-room; together with the passages, stairs, and whole utensils connected with these apartments. He shall likewise cook the provisions, and take charge of them from the time of their being served out, until they are set upon the table in a prepared state. The keeper acting in this department shall only be subject to the performance of night-watches.

XV.—The acting Principal Light-keeper will mount guard in his turn by day and night, and do the duty of the first and second departments, but he is hereby exempted from personally performing the duty of the third department; he will, however, serve out the stores, and keep the light-room store in a cleanly and orderly state.

XVI.—The chimney or smoke-tube of the kitchen-range, and the windows of the several apartments, are to be cleaned on the last Saturday of every month, or as soon thereafter as the weather will permit: The performance of which is to be entered into the Monthly Return.

XVII.—The wharfs or cast-iron railways, rope-ladder (now brazen stair), shall, in like manner, be overhauled and examined during the period of spring-tides, on the full and change days of the moon. The condition of these works to be also regularly entered into the Monthly Returns.

XVIII.—The light-keeper on guard is to give immediate notice to the acting Principal-Keeper of the appearance of the Tender, or of any other vessel or boat, which is seemingly approaching the Rock; when the proper signals will be made as to the practicability and safety of landing, and the necessary attendance given; according to the instructions of the Signal-Book.

XIX.—The Keeper on watch between the hours of 9 and 10 in the morning, shall hoist the signal-ball to the flag-staff-head (if the weather will permit), and, in this position, allow it remain during that hour, when all is well; but in the event of foggy or stormy weather, such as shall obstruct the view with the telescope between the Light-house and the Signal-tower at Arbroath, the ball shall be hoisted between the hours of 1 and 2 in the afternoon, should the weather have then improved. These circumstances are to be stated in the Monthly Returns.

XX.—The keepers, in rotation, shall have leave, and be carried ashore in the Attending-vessel, at such periods as may best suit the service. When this occurs in regular succession, each of the four keepers will remain six weeks at the Light-house, and two weeks at Arbroath with their families.

XXI.—The keeper who for the time being is on leave at the establishment at Arbroath, will there attend the duty of the signal-room, from 9 to 10 every morning, and likewise from 1 to 2 in the afternoon, when, from the state of the weather, the signals at the Bell Rock cannot be seen and repeated at the appointed hour in the morning, agreeably to Article XIX.

XXII.—The rotation for leave on shore must be so regulated, that the turns of the Principal and Principal-assistant Light-keepers do not immediately or successively follow each other.

XXIII.—When at the Light-house, the keepers will have Rations of provisions and other allowances, as stated in the annexed Schedule, but while they are on shore they provide for themselves.

XXIV.—In case the Rations served out should not at any time be used, the same must be returned to the store, as no provisions of any kind are permitted to be taken away from the Light-house.

XXV.—The Principal Light-keeper, and, in his absence, the Acting Principal-keeper, is held responsible for the due performance of the duty of the other keepers; for the correctness of the Requisitions made for stores; for the Monthly Returns written by the Assistant or Expectant Light-keepers; for all Entries made in the store and journal books; for the regular and properly serving out of the daily allowance of light-room stores and provisions; for the regular use and cleanly state of the bed and table linen; for the good order of the Light-house furniture, apparatus and appurtenances; that none of the stores be wasted or embezzled, but that the strictest economy and careful management be observed, yet so as to preserve a good and sufficient light.

XXVI.—The light-keepers are hereby prohibited from receiving, bringing, or allowing to be brought to the Light-house, any spiritous liquors, as private stores. The Acting Principal Light-keeper is held responsible for the conduct of his assistants; and the Master of the Tender for the conduct of his men in this respect.

XXVII.—The Bell Rock being the chief station at which Light-keepers are instructed in their duty for the service of the Northern Lights, the Principal, or, in his absence, the Acting-principal Keeper, is directed to superintend this department, and they are respectively held responsible for the certificate they may ultimately give as to the qualifications of Expectant-keepers. Upon production of the certificate to the Engineer, the light-keepers will be found entitled to the premium stated in the annexed Schedule of Allowances.

XXVIII.—Each Expectant-light-keeper is to be resident for at least six weeks at the Bell Rock. In the course of this period he is to practise the whole duty performed in the light-room; to write the Monthly Returns; and carefully to peruse these Instructions. If, at the end of this period, he is found qualified, he will receive a certificate to the following effect: "Bell Rock Light-house," (here insert the date.) "These certify, That" (here insert the name,) "has resided" (here insert the number of) "days at this Light-house; and having been duly instructed in the whole practice of the Keeper's duty in the Light-room, he is considered qualified to act as an Assistant Light-keeper," or is found deficient in certain points, (here state the case as it may be.) "Witness my hand," (Signature of Principal, or, in his absence, of the Principal Assistant Light-keeper.)

XXIX.—The Inventory of the Light-house apparatus, books, furniture, and utensils, is to be compared with the Inventory-book upon the first Friday of the months of May and November half-yearly, or as soon thereafter as the Principal and Principal Assistant Light-keepers are both upon the Rock. Any deficiency in the articles of the Inventory-Book is to be stated in the respective Returns for these months.

XXX.—It being a rule in the Service of the Commissioners of the Northern Light-houses, that access to their establishments shall be free and open to the Public, the keepers are enjoined to pay attention to Strangers, shewing them every civility in their power; and, particularly, to afford their aid and assistance, in cases of Ship-wreck; yet so as not to neglect any thing incumbent upon them, in the proper discharge of their duty as light-keepers.

XXXI.—It is recommended to the light-keepers to be cleanly in their persons and linens, and proper in their apparel in general.

XXXII.—The Light-keepers are enjoined to assemble in the Library, for the purpose of reading the Scriptures, and for Prayers, every Sunday, at 12 o'clock noon, in their Uniform-dress. This service is to be performed by the Acting Principal Light-keeper, or Principal Officer of the Board present. The table is to be covered during this service with a flag; and, when the weather is moderate, the Light-house flag is, at the same time, to be hoisted to the mast-head, and allowed to remain till sunset.

XXXIII.—Should any difference of opinion arise among the Light-keepers about the meaning of these Instructions, the duty shall in such cases be performed agreeably to the explanation and orders of the Acting Principal Light-keeper. In the same manner, in all matters to which these Instructions may not seem fully to apply, the orders of the Acting Principal Light-keeper are hereby declared to be binding upon the respective Light-keepers.

XXXIV.—In case of neglect of duty on the part of any of the Assistant-keepers, the Principal shall, according to the nature of the offence, communicate the circumstances to the Superintendant Light-keeper, on his first visit, or immediately by letter to the Engineer, that the offending party may be reprimanded, put under stoppages, or ultimately dismissed from the service, as the case may require.

XXXV.—These Instructions, with such additional orders as may be issued from time to time, are to be read by the officiating Officer, immediately before reading Prayers, on the first Sunday of the months of May and November.

Edinburgh, 1st August 1823.

ROBERT STEVENSON,
Engineer to the Commissioners of the Northern Light-houses.

SCHEDULE referred to in the XXIII. and XXVII. Articles of the INSTRUCTIONS.

Daily Allowance per Man, 1 lb. Beef; 1 lb. Bread; 2 oz. Oatmeal; 2 oz. Barley; 2 oz. Butter; 3 quarts Beer; Vegetables and Salt no stated allowance; For Tea and other necessaries 4d. per day; For instructing each Expectant-Light-keeper L. 2, distributed as follows, viz. Principal Light-keeper 15s., Principal-Assistant 10s., each of the two Ordinary Assistants 7s. 6d.

MONTHLY RETURN FROM THE BELL ROCK LIGHT-HOUSE, FOR NOVEMBER 1812.

Monthly Return.

Key:
A Spermaceti Oil, in Gallons.
B Wicks in Dozens
C Lamp glasses
D Beef, in Lib.
E Bread, in Lib.
F Oatmeal in Lib.
G Barley, in Lib.
H Butter, in Lib.
I Beer, in Qrts.
J Water, in Gallons
K Coals in Cwts
L Vegetables in Dozens
M Number of People victualled

Light-House Stores received.				Provisions, Water, and Fuel, received.									
Nov. 1812.		A	B	C	D	E	F	G	H	I	J	K	L	M
Stock on hand,		313	593	360	263	243	72	32	2	200	615	60	11	
Sunday,	1.													8
Monday,	2.													8
Tuesday,	3.	200			60	112				160	200	12	6	9
Wednesd.	4.													9
Thursday,	5.													9
Friday,	6.													8
Saturday,	7.													8
Sunday,	8.													8
Monday,	9.													8
Tuesday,	10.													8
Wednesd.	11.													8
Thursday,	12.													8
Friday,	13.													8
Saturday,	14.													8
Sunday,	15.													8
Monday,	16.													8
Tuesday,	17.													8
Wednesd.	18.													8
Thursday,	19.													8
Friday,	20.	100			37					80		4	3	3
Saturday,	21.													3
Sunday,	22.													3

Monday,	23.														3
Tuesday,	24.														3
Wednesd.	25.														3
Thursday,	26.														3
Friday,	27.													·		3
Saturday,	28.														3
Sunday,	29.														3
Monday,	30.														3
Received,		613	593	360	360	355	72	32	25	440	815	76	20	188
Expended,		111¼	12	36	188	188	23½	23½	23½	376	260	19	13½	
Remainder in Store,		501¾	581	324	172	167	48½	8½	1½	64	555	57	6¼	—

Key:
AB Spermaceti Oil. Galls.
AC „ Qs.
AD „ Pts.
BB Wicks in Dozens
CC Lamp Glasses
DD Number of Lamps in Light-Room.
EE Beef in Lib.
FF Bread, in Lib.
GG Oatmeal in Lib.
HH Barley, in Lib.
II Butter, in Lib.
JJ Beer, in Qts.
KK Water, in Gallons
LL Coals in Cwts
MM Vegetables used.

		Light-House Stores served out.						Provisions, Water, and Fuel, served out.								
Nov. 1812.		AB	AC	AD	BB	CC	DD	EE	FF	GG	HH	II	JJ	KK	LL	MM
Stock on hand,																
Sunday,	1.	3	2				24	8	8	10	10	10	16			6

Monday,	2.	3	2				24	8	8	10	10	10	16			6
Tuesday,	3.	13	2			6	24	9	9	12	12	12	18	30		6
Wednesd.	4.	3	2				24	9	9	12	12	12	18		2	6
Thurs- day,	5.	3	2				24	9	9	12	12	12	18		1	6
Friday,	6.	3	2				24	8	8	10	10	10	16			6
Saturday,	7.	3	2		6		24	8	8	10	10	10	16		2	6
Sunday,	8.	3	2			6	24	8	8	10	10	10	16			6
Monday,	9.	3	3				24	8	8	10	10	10	16	40		6
Tuesday,	10.	3	2				24	8	8	10	10	10	16		2	6
Wednesd.	11.	4	0				24	8	8	10	10	10	16			6
Thurs- day,	12.	4	0				24	8	8	10	10	10	16		2	6
Friday,	13.	3	2				24	8	8	10	10	10	16			6
Saturday,	14.	3	2			6	24	8	8	10	10	10	16			6
Sunday,	15.	3	3				24	8	8	10	10	10	16		2	6
Monday,	16.	3	3				24	8	8	10	10	10	16	150		6
Tuesday,	17.	3	3				24	8	8	10	10	10	16			6
Wednesd.	18.	3	3				24	8	8	10	10	10	16		2	6
Thurs- day,	19.	3	3				24	8	8	10	10	10	16			6
Friday,	20.	3	3			6	24	3	3	06	06	06	6			4
Saturday,	21.	3	3				24	3	3	06	06	06	6		2	4
Sunday,	22.	3	2				24	3	3	06	06	06	6			4
Monday,	23.	4	0				24	3	3	06	06	06	6			4
Tuesday,	24.	4	0				24	3	3	06	06	06	6			4

Wednesd.	25.	3	3			6	24	3	3	0 6	0 6	0 6	6		2	4
Thursday,	26.	4	0				24	3	3	0 6	0 6	0 6	6			4
Friday,	27.	3	3				24	3	3	0 6	0 6	0 6	6	40		4
Saturday,	28.	4	0				24	3	3	0 6	0 6	0 6	6			4
Sunday,	29.	3	3				24	3	3	0 6	0 6	0 6	6			4
Monday,	30.	4	0		6	6	24	3	3	0 6	0 6	0 6	6		2	4
		111	1		12	36		188	188	23	23 0½	23 0	376	260	19	13

Carried to return for next month.

Written by M. Wishart, Assist.

Principal or Principal Assistant Light-Keeper's Signature, John Reid, Prinl.

JOURNAL relative to the Duty of the Light-Keepers, and the State of the Weather, &c. at the Bell Rock, for November 1812.

Nov. 1812.		Time of Extinguishing, A.M.	Time of Lighting, P.M.	Night-Watch Set, P.M.	Keeper on First Watch.	Keeper absent on Leave.	Tolling of Bells begun.	Tolling of Bells ceased.
Sunday,	1.	6.50	4.55	5	J. Reid	Wishart		
Monday,	2.	6.20	4.55	-	J. Bonyman			
Tuesday,	3.	6.30	4.55	-	H. Leask			
Wednesday,	4.	6.25	5.	-	Reid	Bonyman		
Thursday,	5.	6.25	4.45	-	Leask			
Friday,	6.	6.40	4.45	-	M. Wishart		8 A.M.	10 A.M.
Saturday,	7.	6.45	4.40	-	Reid			
Sunday,	8.	6.50	4.40	-	Leask			

Monday,	9.	6.40	4.45	-	Wishart			
Tuesday,	10.	6.45	4.35	-	Reid			
Wednesd.	11.	6.30	4.35	-	Leask			
Thurs-day,	12.	7.	4.30	-	Wishart			
Friday,	13.	6.55	4.30	-	Reid			
Saturday,	14.	6.30	4.30	-	Leask			
Sunday,	15.	7.	4.20	-	Wishart			
Monday,	16.	6.55	4.20	-	Reid			
Tuesday,	17.	7.	4.20	-	Leask			
Wednesd.	18.	7.5	4.20	-	Wishart			
Thurs-day,	19.	7.	4.15	-	Reid			
Friday,	20.	7.15	4.10	-	Leask			
Saturday,	21.	7.15	4.10	-	Wishart			
Sunday,	22.	7.	4.10	-	Reid			
Monday,	23.	7.	4.10	-	Leask			
Tuesday,	24.	7.10	4.10	-	Wishart			
Wednesd.	25.	7.10	4.15	-	Reid			
Thurs-day,	26.	7.20	4.10	-	Leask			
Friday,	27.	7.15	4.5	-	Wishart			
Saturday,	28.	7.20	4.15	-	Reid			
Sunday,	29.	7.10	4.10	-	Leask		12 noon	10 P.M.
Monday,	30.	7.10	4.10	-	Wishart			

Nov. 1812.		Foggy, Snowy.	Hazy, H. Rain, R. Clear, C.	Wind Calm, C.	Barom. in Inches at 8 A.M.	Therm. in Degrees at 8 A.M.
			Prevailing State of the Weather.			
Sunday,	1.		R.H.	S.W.	29.40	46
Monday,	2.		C.	W.S.W.	29.50	42
Tuesday,	3.		C.	West.	29.68	42
Wednesday,	4.		C.	N.N.W.	29.69	43
Thursday,	5.		C.	North.	29.70	45
Friday,	6.	Foggy,	C.	North.	29.50	45
Saturday,	7.		C.	N.N.E.	29.60	50
Sunday,	8.		H.	Variable.	29.88	50
Monday,	9.		C.	S.E.	30.10	49
Tuesday,	10.		C.	Variable.	30.12	48
Wednesd.	11.		C.	N.E.	30.30	48
Thursday,	12.		H.R.	N.E.	29.90	45
Friday,	13.		H.R.	S.E.	29.52	42
Saturday,	14.		H.R.	S.S.E.	29.60	43
Sunday,	15.		H.R.	N.E.	29.65	41
Monday,	16.		H.R.	N.E.	29.92	41
Tuesday,	17.		H.	East.	29.41	44
Wednesd.	18.		H.	N.E.	29.70	43
Thursday,	19.		C.	N.N.E.	29.22	45
Friday,	20.		C.	Variable.	29.50	45
Saturday,	21.		H.	N.W.	29.47	50

Sunday,	22.		H.	W.S.W.	29.58	49
Monday,	23.		H.	W.S.W	29.60	46
Tuesday,	24.		H.R.	Variable.	29.50	45
Wednesd.	25.		R.H.	N.E.	29.86	45
Thursday,	26.		R.H.	E.N.	29.66	49
Friday,	27.		C.	S.S.E.	29.97	48
Saturday,	28.		H.	S. by E.	30.23	47
Sunday,	29.	Foggy,	H.	Variable.	30.34	43
Monday,	30.		C.	S.W.	30.15	43
				30)	892.25	1356
				Average,	29.742	45.2

		Supposed rise at High Water on the Building of		Tender's Boat		Sick, and unable for Duty.	Number of Strangers on the Rock.
Nov. 1812.		Tide.	Spray.	Arrives.	Departs.		
Sunday,	1.	8	40				5 Artificers.
Monday,	2.	9	40				
Tuesday,	3.	10	40	8 A.M.	10 A.M.		2 Surveyors.
Wednesday,	4.	11	40	8 A.M.	9.30 A.M.		2 depart.
Thursday,	5.	11	50	10 A.M.	10.15 A.M.		
Friday,	6.	11	70				
Saturday,	7.	10	40				
Sunday,	8.	9	40				
Monday,	9.	9	40				

Tuesday,	10.	8	40				
Wednesd.	11.	8	50				
Thursday,	12.	7	50				
Friday,	13.	7	40				
Saturday,	14.	8	60				
Sunday,	15.	8	96				
Monday,	16.	9	60				
Tuesday,	17.	9	70				
Wednesd.	18.	10	60				
Thursday,	19.	11	50	7 A.M.	10 A.M.		5 depart.
Friday,	20.	11	50				
Saturday,	21.	10	40				
Sunday,	22.	10	50				
Monday,	23.	9	40				
Tuesday,	24.	9	50				
Wednesd.	25.	8	90				
Thursday,	26.	8	40				
Friday,	27.	8	40				
Saturday,	28.	8	40				
Sunday,	29.	9	30				
Monday,	30.	9	30				

Written by M. Wishart, Assist.

Principal or Principal Assistant Light-Keeper's Signature, John Reid, Prinl.

REMARKS regarding any Accident or Particular which occurred connected with the Bell Rock Light-house during the Month of November 1812.

1812.

Nov. 1. The first part of these twenty-four hours strong gales, with much rain, middle and latter parts moderate and changeable.

... 3. Blowing fresh breezes to-day, with fine clear weather. At 8 A. M. the Light-house Yacht's boat landed twenty ankers of spermaceti oil. Mr John Steedman, and Mr William Lorimer, from Mr Stevenson's office, also came to the Rock to do business at the House. Returned by the boat one anker of dregs of oil, with a box of broken lamp-glasses, together with 20 empty casks. One mason went ashore.

... 4. At 8 A. M. the Yacht's boat landed, and made two trips with a variety of articles and materials for the joiners, and provisions for the use of the house. Returned some extra bolts. Mr Steedman and his assistant employed with their instruments measuring the Rock at low-water.

... 5. These twenty-four hours, strong breezes with clear weather. At 10 A. M. the Yacht's boat landed, and took off Mr Steedman and Mr Lorimer.

... 15. A constant gale, with much rain until the 19th, when it fell moderate. The signal-ball was not hoisted to-day, as an intimation ashore that the artificers were ready to leave the Rock.

... 20. Variable weather to-day, with flying showers. At 7 A. M. the Tender's boat landed at three trips, with water, fuel, and provisions, for the use of the House, and ten ankers of oil for the use of the Light-room. At 10 o'clock the boat departed, when Mr Slight, James Glen, Robert Selkirk, and two others, left the Rock to proceed to the shore for the season.

... 23. All these twenty-four hours it blew strong gales, with very hazy weather. Signal-ball not hoisted, owing to the state of the weather.

... 25. Blowing a gale with much rain. Signal-ball not hoisted.

... 26. Do. weather with much sea.

... 29. First and middle parts of these twenty-four hours hazy and variable. Middle parts foggy and calm, with frost. Bells tolling. Signal-balls not hoisted.

... 30. Fine clear weather. Cleaned the chimney to-day.

Written by, M. Wishart, Assist.
Principal or Principal Assistant Light-keeper's Signature. John Reid, Prinl.

To Robert Stevenson, Esq.
Engineer for Northern Light-houses,
Edinburgh.

Note.—Similar Monthly Returns are also sent from the other Light-house Stations, independently of which, the Light-keepers are directed to correspond with the Engineer as often as the circumstances of the Service require.

SHIPWRECK RETURN from Pladda Light-House.

Shipwreck Return.

DESCRIPTION of Vessels or Boats Wrecked within Fifty Miles of any of the Northern Light-House Stations, to be immediately communicated to the Engineer, in so far as the circumstances can be ascertained by the observation or diligent inquiries of the respective Light-Keepers; who are also instructed to render every assistance in their power to Shipwrecked Mariners; without however neglecting the proper duties of their charge.

Date.	Ship, Brig, Schooner, or Sloop, &c.	Belonging to what Port.	Name of the Vessel.	Name of the Commander.
Tuesday, 18th February 1823.	Sloop,	Greenock,	Atlas,	Alexander Duncan.

Where Wrecked.	At what Hour Wrecked, A. M. or P. M.	In what kind of Weather.	No. of the Crew or Passengers Saved.	No. of the Crew or Passengers Lost.	Whence from.	Where Bound.
Island of Pladda, to the S. W. of the Light-house.	At 5 A. M.	Stormy, Hazy Weather. Wind S. S. E.	5	none.	Sydney.	Greenock.

Cargo.	Tonnage.	Supposed Value of the Vessel.	Supposed Value of the Cargo.
British Oak Timber.	75	£ 400 0 0	£ 200 0 0

Principal or Assistant's Signature, William Soutar, Prinl.

Note.—It fortunately happens that no instance of Shipwreck has occurred at the Bell Rock since its erection; and therefore a Return from one of the other Light-house Stations is given.

LETTER accompanying the foregoing Shipwreck Return.

Pladda Light-House, 18th February 1823.

SIR,

I beg leave to inform you, that this vessel was observed by the keeper on watch in the Light-room to be ashore at 5.30 A.M., who gave the alarm to all the inmates of the Light-house; but no assistance could be given to the crew by us till 8.30 A.M., when the tide ebbed so far that they could heave us a rope; then we assisted them in getting their clothes, and themselves, and some other articles, ashore. It is thought by the Captain and crew that the vessel will not be got off. As it happened to be about high-water when she came ashore, she is very far up on the shore, and ebbs almost dry at low-water, although it be neap-tides.

The report given us by the Captain and crew is, that they thought to have weathered this island, as they had the light three points on their weather-bow; but having so little sail set at the time, they observed they were so near the shore they thought the vessel would not stay. Their jib and top-sail was all the sail they could carry to the storm. They say they were in the act of setting a small bit of the peak of their mainsail when the vessel struck, to enable them to keep more to windward of the island.Wednesday, 19th. At low-water, the Captain and crew, with other assistance, stripped the vessel of her sails and materials, which were carefully laid aside, and partly got into the store-house. Nothing more particular about the wreck at this date; but we shall be as serviceable to the unfortunate men as we can.

I remain,
SIR,
Your most obedient humble Servant,
WILLIAM SOUTAR.

To Robert Stevenson, Esq.
Engineer for Northern Light-Houses, Edinburgh.

No. II.

POEM ON SIR RALPH THE ROVER, EXTRACTED FROM
MR SOUTHEY'S WORKS.

INCHCAPE ROCK.

Extracted, by Mr Southey's permission, from his Minor Poems, Vol. III. p. 148.

Inchcape Ballad.

An old writer mentions a curious Tradition, which may be worth quoting. "By east of the Isle of May," says he, "twelve miles from all land in the German Seas, lyes a great hidden rock, called Inchcape, very dangerous for navigators, because it is overflowed every tide. It is reported in old times, upon the saide rocke there was a bell, fixed upon a tree or timber, which rang continually, being moved by the sea, giving notice to the saylers of the danger. This bell or clocke was put there and maintained by the Abbot of Aberbrothok, and being taken down by a sea pirate, a yeare thereafter he perished upon the same rocke, with ship and goodes, in the righteous judgment of God."

Stoddart's Remarks on Scotland.

> No stir in the air, no stir in the sea,
> The Ship was still as she could be;
> Her sails from heaven received no motion,
> Her keel was steady in the ocean.
>
> Without either sign or sound of their shock,
> The waves flow'd over the Inchcape Rock;
> So little they rose, so little they fell,
> They did not move the Inchcape Bell.
>
> The Abbot of Aberbrothok
> Had placed that bell on the Inchcape Rock;
> On a buoy in the storm it floated and swung,
> And over the waves its warning rung.
>
> When the Rock was hid by the surge's swell,
> The Mariners heard the warning Bell;
> And then they knew the perilous Rock,
> And blest the Abbot of Aberbrothok.
>
> The Sun in heaven was shining gay,

All things were joyful on that day;
The sea-birds scream'd as they wheel'd round,
And there was joyaunce in their sound.

The buoy of the Inchcape Bell was seen
A darker speck on the ocean green;
Sir Ralph the Rover walk'd his deck,
And he fix'd his eye on the darker speck.

He felt the cheering power of spring,
It made him whistle, it made him sing;
His heart was mirthful to excess,
But the Rover's mirth was wickedness.

His eye was on the Inchcape Float;
Quoth he, "My men, put out the boat,
And row me to the Inchcape Rock,
And I'll plague the Abbot of Aberbrothok."

The boat is lower'd, the boatmen row,
And to the Inchcape Rock they go;
Sir Ralph bent over from the boat,
And he cut the Bell from the Inchcape Float.

Down sunk the Bell with a gurgling sound.
The bubbles rose and burst around;
Quoth Sir Ralph, "The next who comes to the Rock
Won't bless the Abbot of Aberbrothok."

Sir Ralph the Rover sail'd away,
He scour'd the seas for many a day;
And now grown rich with plunder'd store,
He steers his course for Scotland's shore.

So thick a haze o'erspreads the sky
They cannot see the sun on high;
The wind hath blown a gale all day,
At evening it hath died away.

On the deck the Rover takes his stand,
So dark it is they see no land.
Quoth Sir Ralph, "It will be lighter soon,
For there is the dawn of the rising Moon."

"Canst hear," said one, "the breakers roar?
For methinks we should be near the shore."
"Now, where we are I cannot tell,
But I wish we could hear the Inchcape Bell."

They hear no sound, the swell is strong;
Though the wind hath fallen they drift along,
Till the vessel strikes with a shivering shock,
"Oh Christ! it is the Inchcape Rock!"

Sir Ralph the Rover tore his hair;
He curst himself in his despair;
The waves rush in on every side,
The ship is sinking beneath the tide.

But even in his dying fear
One dreadful sound could the Rover hear,
A sound as if with the Inchcape Bell,
The Devil below was ringing his knell.

1820.

No. III.

ABSTRACT ACCOUNT OF LIGHT-HOUSE DUTIES.

LIGHT-HOUSE DUTIES.

ABSTRACT ACCOUNT of LIGHT-HOUSE DUTIES, furnished to the Committee of the House of Commons, in reference to the Bell Rock Act.

"ABSTRACT STATE of ADDITIONAL DUTIES that will arise from the District to be included in the Collection by the Erection of a Light-House on the Cape or Bell Rock; calculated from the Custom-House Returns, 13th May 1806, at the rate of 1½d. per ton, whether Outwards or Inwards.

' 1804.	Foreign,	Inwards,	93,782		
		Outwards,	67,633		
	Coastways,	Inwards,	239,037		
		Outwards,	170,174	Tons.	
			— — — —	570,626	L. 3566 8 3
' 1805.	Foreign,	Inwards,	81,123		
		Outwards,	73,289		
	Coastways,	Inwards,	259,997		
		Outwards,	203,564		
			— — — —	617,973	3862 6 7½
' 1806.	Foreign,	Inwards,	97,205		
		Outwards,	86,739		
	Coastways,	Inwards,	270,737		
		Outwards,	215,637		

	— — — —	670,318	4,189 9 9
Total of three years,		1,858,917	L. 11,618 4 7½

"The tonnage of the ports of the Firth of Forth, already pay ½d. *per* ton for Inchkeith light, so that the additional duty payable by them, will be only one penny *per* ton, the total tonnage thus paying ½d. is, for the whole three years, 971,482.		
Deduct, therefore, ½d: *per* ton for this amount,	L. 2023 18 5	
Deduct also expences of collection, and the charges of management, say 15 *per cent*.	1742 14 9	
		3766 13 2
"Nett total for three years,		L. 7851 11 5½
"Nett yearly total		L. 2617 3 9½

(Signed) "C. Cuningham,
Secretary to the Commissioners of the Northern Light-houses."

Note.—The District of coast referred to in the above Abstract, lies between Peterhead, in Aberdeenshire, towards the north, and Berwick-upon-Tweed, to the south, both inclusive.

No. IV.

REPORTS RELATIVE TO THE BELL ROCK LIGHT-HOUSE, BY MR RENNIE, AND THE WRITER.

RELATIVE REPORTS.

Containing REPORTS relative to the Bell Rock Light-House, addressed to the Commissioners of the Northern Light-houses, by John Rennie and Robert Stevenson, Civil Engineers.

REPORT by Mr Stevenson.

Edinburgh, 23d December 1800.

During the reign of his present Majesty (George III.), a spirit for discovery and improvement, in maritime affairs, has been pursued with the greatest energy, and crowned with a success, which can only be equalled by the happy effects that have followed to commerce. In proportion, therefore, as the pursuits of the navigator are considered essential to the wealth of the community, every effort to Assist him, in his course through the pathless ocean, must be regarded both as the call of interest and humanity. The most prominent causes of the perfection to which coasting-navigation has been brought, may be ascribed to the accuracy of our charts, and an increase of land-marks, by which the mariner, after braving the dangers of the seas, is enabled to guide his ship with safety into her intended port. It is well known, that before the Maritime Survey of the Orkneys and Hebrides, by Mackenzie; and until an act of Parliament was passed, appointing Commissioners for erecting Light-houses upon the coast of Scotland, mariners were left to grope their way from the Firth of Forth to the Firth of Clyde, without the assistance either of proper charts or land-marks. Under these circumstances, they passed the Pentland Firth , and generally held a course to the northward of the Orkney islands; then steering westward, they sailed on the outward side of the Lewis Isles into the Atlantic Ocean, exposed to many dangers, and unable to avail themselves of the advantages of the sheltered sounds and harbours of the Friths of Lewis and Uist. Hence the difficulty of navigating this district, was long a great bar to the improvement of the Highlands, and to the extension of the British fisheries. It was, likewise, a material drawback to the present flourishing trade, carried on through these sounds to the Baltic and other parts of the northern Continent of Europe.

From the earliest accounts which tradition gives of the navigation of the Firth of Forth, a Light-house upon the Bell Rock appears to have been looked forward to as an essential pre-requisite to the advancement of its commerce: And in proportion to the extent of the one, the call for the other has become more and more urgent, and is now regarded as a matter of the greatest importance.

Since the publication of Adair's Charts, there has been no want of a survey of the Firth of Forth; but this important estuary still remains extremely deficient with regard to land-marks, and the reporter will venture to say, that there is not any where a more dangerous reef in the kingdom, or one that calls more loudly for something to be done, than the Cape or Bell Rock. When, therefore, the extensive benefits derived from those powers, which have enabled the Commissioners of the Northern Light-houses to erect and maintain six Light-houses upon the coast, are considered, it is much to be wished that some measure were adopted for enabling that Board to add to the number of these land-marks, by the erection of one upon this most destructive rock. From the numerous losses by shipwreck, which have happened upon the Bell Rock, it is presumed, that some account of its position and extent, from actual survey,—a few remarks upon the description of building best suited to the situation of the rock,—together with an attempt to point out the extensive use of such a light,—and the ports which appear to be within the limits of any duty to be levied for its support, will not be deemed unnecessary at a time when the public look forward, with anxious expectation, to this Board, in a matter of so much importance, not only to the navigation of the Firth of Forth, but in general, to the eastern coast of Great Britain.

Having finished a design and model of a pillar-formed light-house for the Bell Rock, immediately after the very fatal storm which occurred in the month of December 1799, the next object of the Reporter, was to survey the rock itself, that he might judge more fully of its fitness for the situation. Accordingly, in the month of April following, he set off for the rock, and had reached Fifeness, when, from the state of the weather, he was obliged to return, after an absence of ten days, without accomplishing his purpose. Soon after his return from his annual voyage to the Northern Light-houses, Mr Gray, secretary for the Commissioners, requested of the Board of Customs to grant the use of one of its yachts, to make another attempt. An order having been accordingly obtained for the Osnaburgh cutter, Captain Campbell, then lying at the Elie, the reporter, accompanied by his friend Mr James Haldane, architect, set off for that place. But the Osnaburgh being then under repair, and the period of spring-tides being at hand, it was found advisable to proceed along the coast to West-haven, on the northern side of the Firth of Tay; and upon Sunday the 5th of October 1800, a landing was effected upon the Rock, and an ample opportunity afforded of gaining all necessary information.

The Bell Rock, as appears by the best charts of the coast, is situated at the mouth of the Firth of Forth, in west longitude 2° 22′, and north latitude 56° 29′. It lies nearly fifteen miles from the Island of May, in a north-eastern direction per compass, and twelve miles south-west from the Red-head in Angusshire, which it resembles, being a free-stone of a reddish colour, though of a much harder body, and closer grit. Besides its natural asperities, the surface in general is thickly coated with sea-weed, and, on the higher parts, the barnacle, white buckie or whelk, and limpets, abound, and altogether it presents a very rugged appearance, owing to the sloping of the strata from south, where highest, to north, at an angle of about 30 degrees. The material part of the rock, which lies north-east and south-west, measures, on an average, about 300 feet in length, and 240 feet in breadth. The highest part above the surface of the sea, does not exceed seven feet at low-water of spring-tides; which part, at high-water of same tides, is from nine to ten feet under water. The reporter also found, that the medium height of the foundation of any building erected upon it, will not exceed two or three feet above the surface of the sea at low-water of spring-tides. The above dimensions may be termed the material part of the rock; but, south-west of this, there runs a reef or shoal, of considerable extent, which is only visible in very low tides.

The short time which the Bell Rock is seen above water, and the irregularity of the soundings in its vicinity, are the cause of many wrecks upon it. Indeed, after the water has flowed, in ordinary tides, but a very short time, the most skilful mariner cannot point out its place, without its proper meaths or land-marks in sight, which lie from twelve to twenty miles distant. Under these circumstances, the Bell Rock will be found more dangerous to vessels coming near it, than perhaps any of those reefs upon which Light-houses have as yet been erected.

The Edystone Rock, for example, is about eleven miles from land, situate at the entrance of Plymouth Sound. Before the rock was reduced for the foundation of the Light-house, it was about three feet above high-water of spring-tides. The Longships Rock, situate three miles off the Lands-End, is about forty feet above high-water mark, though barely large enough for the foundation of the Light-house. The Smalls lie fourteen miles off St David's Head; and the rock on which the light-house is built, is about five feet above high-water of spring-tides. The South Rock, lying three miles off the land, between Loch Strangford and Donaghadee, is about four feet under the surface at high-water of spring-tides. The Tour de Corduan, upon the coast of France, is built upon a sunken rock at the entrance of the Garonne, and is said to be about eight feet under the surface of the sea at high-water of spring-tides. And, lastly, the Bell Rock, the subject of this report, lying upwards of eleven miles from land, is from nine to ten feet under water, as before stated.

Ever since the reporter had an opportunity to know the danger and inconvenience that must attend the navigation of the Firth of Forth, while the Bell Rock remains without some signal upon it, to forewarn seamen, he has been much employed in considering what kind of building would be most applicable to its situation; and he has, therefore, endeavoured to obtain as much information as possible about works of this kind. The first light-house erected upon an insulated rock on the coast of Great Britain or Ireland, appears to have been that of the Edystone, which was begun in 1696, and was scarcely finished, when a dreadful storm carried it completely away. This erection was constructed of timber, and was designed and executed by Mr William Winstanly, who, with his artificers and the light-keepers, unfortunately perished in its ruins. The next light-house that was built upon the Edystone Rocks, consisting partly of stone and partly of wood, it was finished in 1709, and was the work of Mr John Rudyard, who, carefully avoiding the errors of his predecessor, lopped off all superfluous ornaments, and produced a plain building; which, after withstanding the fury of the waves for forty-nine years, had the misfortune to be destroyed by fire. The present Edystone

Light-house was begun in 1756, and finished in 1759. It has now stood forty-four years, a memorial of the ingenuity and indefatigable labours of Mr John Smeaton, who, guarding against the defects of the two former buildings, constructed the whole of stone; the blocks of the solid part are curiously dove-tailed into each other; and every thing unnecessarily tending to give resistance to the water is carefully avoided, while the whole is completely fire-proof. The next light-house erected upon a situation of this kind, was the Smalls, which is placed upon eight beams of oak, arranged round a centre one. The latest light-house built on an insulated situation, is that upon the South Rock on the coast of Ireland. The reporter made three successive journeys to this light-house, during its progress: First in 1796, when it was only 12 feet in height; again in 1797, when it was nearly finished; and a third time in the month of August 1800. This light-house is built of granite, quarried in the mountains of Morne. The method of dove-tailing or joggling the stones, and attaching the courses to each other, is different from that of the Edystone; throughout the solid part of the masonry, and eighteen inches within the circumference of the building, six great bars of malleable iron are carried up, each four inches square; and upon the top of every alternate course, a circular plate of iron is let into the stone, and fixed by spear-bolts to the upright bars. The building is of a conical figure, and was built in the course of three years from a design by Mr John Rodgers of Dublin.

Before being properly certified as to the possibility of getting a foundation for a building of any kind upon the Bell Rock, the reporter thought of a Floating-light, like those moored off the Dudgeon-shoal, and other sand-banks on the coast of England. But the foulness of the ground about the Bell Rock, the great depth of water near it, together with the unsteadiness of a light of this description,—and above all, the perplexing uncertainty which must ever attend such a light in a storm, cannot fail to unhinge the confidence of the mariner, and thereby prevent him from making free with his course; and when, from an error in it, or in the distance run, he is disappointed in seeing the light, wrong conclusions are apt to be formed: he supposes that the Floating-light has drifted, and by changing his course, perhaps turns upon the very point of danger. These were considerations from which much relief was felt, upon learning that the rock was large enough to form the foundation of a permanent building; but, till the moment he landed upon it, he was uncertain if a building of stone was applicable; and foreseeing the difficulties which would be avoided, if, instead of carrying up the lower part solid, it could be formed of pillars, after the manner of the Smalls Light-house; reflecting also upon that elegant and useful application lately made of cast-iron, in the construction of bridges, choice was made of this metal, in his first model for the Bell Rock, as being more substantial than timber, and also less liable to corrosion from the action of the atmosphere than malleable-iron. This light-house (see Plate VII.), was to consist of six hollow tubes or pillars, built each to the height of ninety feet, measuring two feet in diameter at the base, and diminishing to six inches at the top, ranged round a common centre so as to form a diameter of thirty-five feet at the base, and eight feet at the top, immediately under the light-room. The pillars were to be cast in lengths or pieces of ten feet each; and at every joint horizontal bars were made to grasp the pillars, and the whole was also connected diagonally with various cross braces. Under the light-room, the building was to be laid out into four heights of apartments for the light-keepers and stores, formed within the range of the pillars, which occupying 45 feet of their height, the part below being of similar height, was left free for the passage of the sea, thus presenting the least possible resistance to the waves. These apartments were to be formed and covered in with strong copper, which, to prevent its acting upon the iron, was to be coated with tin. The lower part, or floor nearest to the sea, was to form an inverted cone, presenting a surface calculated to disperse the seas which might strike against it. In order still more to increase the common base, and strengthen this fabric, Professor Robison advised that a diagonal bar should be attached to the exterior side of each of the pillars.

In this first design, provision was made chiefly against the impulse of the sea, without taking into account the possibility of a vessel or wreck getting near it; but he found, after landing upon the rock, that it was possible for a vessel at high-water to come, without interruption, against the pillars. To guard against misfortune from this quarter, the reporter first thought of defending the pillars in various ways, particularly by throwing a kind of Chevaux de Frise round them, with beams of oak. He, however, found it difficult to suppose any set of pillars of adequate strength to resist the force of a loaded vessel, violently agitated in a winter storm, which must render the pillar-formed construction very uncertain, even after every precaution should be taken to guard against such accidents. Nor ought the danger to which such a mass of metal, constantly exposed to the effects of the marine-acid, to be wholly overlooked, in giving a preference to a circular building of stone, which being a compact figure of solid matter, would resist any force that might be brought against it. The reporter has estimated the Pillar-formed Light-house at L. 15,000; and, although that for the Tower of masonry amounts to L. 42,636, 8s., yet, as it is treading a beaten path, which leads to certainty, it is surely to be preferred in a work of this kind: the foundation-course of stone must be more tedious than that of so many pillars, yet, in this there is nothing impracticable; and when the difficulties of the first courses are surmounted, the superiority of a fabric of stone over one of iron will readily be admitted.

In the model for a building of stone, made since the reporter first landed upon the Bell Rock, he has retained nearly the same elevation as that of the Edystone Light-house, which presents less resistance, and preserves a greater base than perhaps any other figure that could have been thought of. In this design he has also followed Mr Smeaton in the use of oak-trenails to keep the stones in their places, while the work is in progress; but has differed in the mode of diminishing the interior-walls, as the building rises in height. Instead, also, of Mr Smeaton's plan of dove-tailing the stones, and connecting the floors, various other modes are resorted to, for effecting this perpendicularly as well as laterally, with the view of introducing larger materials, and keeping the stones in a more entire state. One of these is by an iron-bat, which is inserted into the joints of the lower courses, while the void or upper courses are to be indented, or let perpendicularly into one another. Upon inspection of the models and drawings of this design, it will perhaps be found to render the construction more simple, to divide the strength of the walls more equally, and, upon the whole, to give that stability which the situation of the Bell Rock seems so peculiarly to require. (See Plate VII.)

Upon comparing the pillar-formed Light-house, with the circular tower of masonry, it is matter of surprise that ever the Smalls Light-house should have been erected upon that plan, unless it were to avoid the additional expence of a stone building. There is, however, one circumstance which materially favours the pillar-formed construction at the Smalls, the want of which becomes a principal objection to its application at the Bell Rock; namely, that the Smalls Rock being five feet above high-water of spring-tides, the pillars are more obviously defended from injury in the event of a vessel or wreck coming against them, and also from the violence of the sea, whereas the Bell Rock, at certain periods of the tide, is from nine to ten feet under water.

When Mr John Rennie, civil engineer, obligingly favoured the reporter by examining his models, he gave a decided preference to the structure of stone, as did Professors Robison and Playfair. And Captain Huddart also, upon seeing the pillar-formed model, mentioned that the Trinity-House did not approve of iron pillars which, in the instance of the Smalls, were considered not so proper as beams of oak. The chief motives which induced the reporter to model a light-house upon the plan of the Smalls, were the uncertainty of procuring a foundation for a stone building; the small resistance which the pillars present to the force of the waves, and the first cost being very considerably less. But although this is true, with regard to the resistance, it must also be remembered, that the pillars come prodigiously short of the weight of a tower of masonry, of the dimensions of the one modelled, containing upwards of 2000 tons; whereas the iron pillars, even in their most improved state, do not exceed 200 tons. When, therefore, the stone light-house is compared with the iron one, all idea of the greater resistance of the former is lost in its solid contents, and in the uniformity of its figure.

In alluding to the great utility of an erection on the Bell Rock, it may, in general, be observed, that it is in the same degree of latitude with the Town of Holstebro in Denmark, and that the Naze of Norway, or entrance to the Baltic, lies north of Holstebro 1° 30′. It therefore follows, that all vessels bound to the Baltic, from, any port south of the River Tweed, must cross the latitude of the Bell Rock, while the degree of east or west longitude, in which such vessels pass, must depend upon the direction of the winds and other circumstances. In order to avoid the enemy in the time of war, it is common for shipping in this track, first to make the land about Buchanness in Aberdeenshire, and from thence take their departure either over seas, or along shore to their respective ports. With regard to ships bound for Archangel and Greenland, they, at all times, make the Islands of Shetland, and from thence take their departure. If, therefore, lines be drawn from Buchanness and Girdleness in Aberdeenshire, to Flamborough Head in Yorkshire, and the mouth of the Tyne in Northumberland, the Bell Rock will only be found to lie from six to ten leagues distant from these courses or lines. So that vessels crossing the mouth of the Firth of Forth, from Buchanness to the Humber and Thames, &c., may not only come in sight of a light upon this rock, but be materially benefited by it, according to the state of the weather, while those upon the course of the nearest line bound for Newcastle and Sunderland, &c. must, in every voyage which carries them north of the Tweed, be essentially served by a light upon the Bell Rock.

It further deserves notice in this place, that the principal estuaries on the eastern coast of Great Britain, are those of the Friths of Moray and Forth, and the Rivers Humber, and Thames. The most material general purpose which would be answered by a Light upon the Bell Rock, is the opening of the Firth of Forth as a place of safety, in storms from south-east, east, and north-east. When mariners at sea are overtaken with a gale under such circumstances, they make for the most contiguous of these four inlets; but are often known to avoid the Forth, on account of this Rock, which, like another Cerberus, guards its entrance. Of this, a melancholy example occurred (which will long be remembered with that regret which never fails to accompany the forlorn case of the widow and fatherless), in that heavy gale at south-east, which happened in the winter of 1799, and drove many vessels from their moorings in Yarmouth Roads, put them past the Humber, and the crews being afraid to make free with the Firth of Forth, even though the wind was fair, were, with others, driven ashore between the Redhead in Forfarshire, and Kinnaird Head in Aberdeenshire, to the number of about thirty sail. Nor were they all saved that weathered Kinnaird Head; several were wrecked in Orkney and Shetland; and the whole loss occasioned by this gale has been stated as high as seventy sail, with many of their crews! amongst which are reckoned two that were known to have been lost upon the Bell Rock. This fatal catastrophe, of which the history of our coast affords few examples, is the more to be lamented, when it is considered that a light upon the Bell Rock, by opening the way to a place of safety, would infallibly have been the means of preventing much calamity, to those who sought safety, with various fortune, in more northern latitudes. In conclusion, it may be observed, that until this improvement of the coast comes from the Commissioners of the Northern Light-houses, it is much to be feared that the cause continuing, the sad effects will not cease.

(Signed) Robert Stevenson.

To the Honourable the Commissioners of the Northern Light-houses.

REPORT by Mr Rennie.

London, 30th December 1805.

Gentlemen,

In consequence of your directions, I set out in a vessel called the Pharos, from Leith, on the 15th of August last, early in the morning, in company with Robert Hamilton, Esq. one of your Commissioners, and Mr Stevenson, your Engineer, to view the Bell or Cape Rock, for the purpose of considering the practicability of building a Light-house thereon. But, owing to the want of wind, we did not get near the Rock till dusk, i. e. about half-past seven, which was near half ebb; but although we were not above a mile distant, we could discover but little of the rock itself. Its situation, however, was sufficiently apparent, by the breakers upon it, which, although the sea was very little agitated where we were, yet the waves were very high on the Rock itself, breaking over it with considerable violence. We approached within less than half a mile of it, and took soundings; but it becoming dark, we judged it advisable to sail further off, and anchored about a mile from the Rock all the night, in expectation we should be able to land on it next morning, which, from the serene appearance of the sky, we doubted not we should be able to effect. We had not dropped the anchor long, when the little wind there was during the day ceased, and it became a dead calm, but, notwithstanding this, there was a heavy swell, and the vessel rolled much. Frequently, during the night, I viewed the place where the Rock lies, and saw the heavy breakers which played about it, till near three quarters flood, when they nearly ceased, and no appearance of such a place was to be observed. They commenced again about quarter ebb, and continued increasing for some time; but, by nine in the morning, the sea became more smooth, and about half-past nine, the rock appearing several feet above water, we left the Pharos in a small boat, and had the satisfaction of landing on it about half-past ten, a little before low water. The spring-tides, however, were rather past their height, being five days after the full moon. We landed on the north-east side of the Rock, in a little bay or inlet, through some breakers, but these were just on the verge of the Rock, for when we got in, the water was quite smooth.

The Rock lies in a direction nearly south-west and north-east, magnetic bearing. That part which was dry, saving some small inlets, I found to be about 280 feet long, and 220 feet wide. Its general surface was about 4 feet above the level of low water, though some places were about 6 feet high. The Rock, however, extends for some distance all round that part which was dry, and dips downward. It extends under the surface for about 400 feet on the south-west side, about 100 feet on the north-east side, and about 50 on the south-east and north-west sides; and on those parts the water is shallow. At about 300 feet south-west, I found about 13 feet water, but, on account of the breakers, could not sound on the low parts of the Rock, or either of the other sides. At the extremities of the main Rock above mentioned, the dip is sudden; the bottom, however, is rocky for a considerable extent round its bed, but the water is deep.

The Rock itself is a hard red freestone, in beds dipping to the south-east, about one in five; these beds are various in their thickness, some being much greater than others; but, generally, well connected together. Such parts as are not immediately exposed to the violent wash of the waves, are coated with a hard crust, and covered with limpets; and, indeed, when it is exposed to the full fury of the sea, there seems to be little appearance of decay, so that I have no doubt, were a Light-house constructed here, no fears need be entertained for the durability of the Rock, as it seems to me well calculated to resist the effects of the waves.

We remained on the Rock for about an hour and a half, when the tide began to flow rather quickly, and having got all the necessary measurements as to height and size, we left it, and returned to our vessel, having been much gratified with the ample view we had of it, and soon after our getting on board the vessel, we weighed anchor at one, and the wind suiting, we arrived at Arbroath about four o'clock.

The Inch Cape, or Bell Rock, lies in West longitude 2° 22'; North latitude 56° 29', as stated by Mr Stevenson. It is about eleven miles distant from the harbour of Arbroath, about ten miles from the Bluff Point of the Sands of Barry, at the northern side of the entrance to the River Tay, and about eleven miles from the Red Head, which lies between Arbroath and Montrose; so that in fact it is about the same distance from the shore as the Edystone Rock, on which Mr Smeaton completed a stone light-house in the year 1759. The soundings on the south-west side, and near to this Rock, as taken at low water, were about 7 fathoms, within half a mile of it; and, in the same direction, about 15 fathoms, bottom rock. About three-fourths of a mile, 19 to 20 fathoms, bottom gravel. At the north-east side, and near to the Rock, the soundings were 6 fathoms. About three-fourths of a mile north-west of the Rock 15 fathoms, and about a mile and a quarter in the same direction 18 fathoms. We did not take the soundings on any other side of the Rock, or at a greater distance; but I was informed they were full as much as those we had taken.

Such being the situation of the Cape or Bell Rock, lying nearly in the direction which vessels generally take in sailing into the Firth of Forth, from northerly directions, or out of it, in sailing to the north or east, it is no wonder that many accidents should arise in hazy weather or dark nights, there being no means of discovering its situation correctly, unless when the land-marks are to be seen, for the deep water lying so close all round the Rock, nothing can be ascertained from soundings, until too near to enable vessels to get out of the way. Breakers, no doubt, frequently point out its situation, but these, in dark nights, and hazy weather, often are not sufficient, and at high-water, even in good nights, are not always discernible; for want of other means, many vessels have been wrecked thereon, and numberless valuable lives and much property lost.

Vessels trading from the Humber, and northwards to the Baltic, to Norway, Greenland, &c. are often, by stress of weather, driven towards the coast, and even those from more southerly ports often share the unfortunate fate of coasting vessels. It is therefore of the utmost importance that something should be done to mark out the situation of this dangerous and frightful Rock.

A Beacon has been proposed, but this would but ill answer the purpose. Nothing, in my opinion, would do it effectually, except a Light-house; and the question is, whether a Light-house could be built on this Rock, and, if so, of what materials it should be composed, and which, in point of strength and durability, are most likely to become a lasting work, without which the mariner can never make free with his course.

Of all the works which could be erected here, perhaps a wooden Light-house would be the cheapest. But were a wooden Light-house to be constructed, I apprehend a solid base of stone must first be constructed, similar to that built on the Edystone by Mr Rudyard; but wood is liable to decay; it would require constant repairs, and would also be liable to be destroyed by fire, as that of Mr Rudyard's was. A Light-house of cast-iron might also be constructed here, and I will allow that it might have a coating of lead, or other metallic substance, so as for a long time at least to resist the effects of the marine acid. But to make a Light-house that would last of such materials, would be nearly, if not wholly, as expensive as one of stone, which I believe, I need scarcely say, no human ingenuity could render as durable; and as the durability of such a work as this is of the utmost consequence, I apprehend a moderate sum of extra expence ought not to be looked on as an object of material consideration, when put in competition with the advantages of durability. But, besides these objections to a work constructed of wood or iron, vessels being apt to be driven against it at high-water, there being at spring-tides from nine to ten feet deep on the top of the Rock, and should the vessel be a large one, and acted on by a heavy sea, it would not be difficult to foretell the consequences.

The durability and efficacy of a stone Light-house has been proved in the most satisfactory manner at the Tour de Corduan, near the mouth of the River Garonne, on the coast of France; at the Edystone, off the mouth of Plymouth Harbour, and in other situations. Why, therefore, with such incontestible proofs before our eyes, should recourse be had to a material new in itself for such purposes, and untried? a material which, if fitted and joined together as it ought to be, would consume nearly as much time in getting the lower part laid, as the laying of three or four courses at the bottom of a stone Light-house, and when the stone-work is got to the height of five or six feet above the Rock, the greatest part of the difficulty may be said to be over; and besides, such a solid mass of materials would resist any violent shock of a vessel which might be brought against it by the sea. I have, therefore, no hesitation in giving a decided opinion in favour of a stone Light-house.

As to the practicability of erecting such a work on the Bell Rock, I think no doubt can be entertained, with such examples before us as the Tour de Corduan and Edystone before mentioned.—In the 4th volume of the Architecture Hydraulique of Belider, an account is given of the Tour de Corduan. It is built on a low rocky island, dry at low water, and whose surface is nearly level; it is covered at high-water, as near as I can ascertain from his draughts and description, about 8 or 9 feet. It is exposed to a very heavy swell of the sea, lying quite open to the Bay of Biscay, from whence it is well known very heavy swells come, and beat against it with great fury; yet this Light-house has resisted the fury of the waves for above 250 years.

The Edystone Light-house is built even in a more exposed situation than that of the Tour de Corduan, and upon a rock whose surface is little larger than the base of the Light-house itself. The top of this rock is shelving, and was seldom covered by ordinary spring-tides before Mr Smeaton began his foundation; the lower part, however, was always covered over at the top of neap-tides. At the lowest place, when he began his work, the rock was dry about six hours each tide, although there the Edystone Rock is less in size than the Cape Rock, yet the advantage of being so long dry, is greatly in favour of building a Light-house; the most difficult and tedious part of the work being the establishment of the four or five lower courses of the foundation.

The higher parts of the Cape Rock, as I have before stated, are little more than six feet above the low water of an ordinary spring-tide. But I apprehend, when a place sufficiently large for the foundation is levelled, its surface will be little more than three and a half feet above the low water of an ordinary spring-tide. I do not think that above three hours' time for work can be expected, which is about half of what was got at the Edystone. The depth of the water all round it, and its exposure to the German Ocean, renders it as difficult a situation to construct a durable work upon as that of the Edystone, if not more so. I doubt, therefore, more time will be required for the work; but this depends so much on the state of the weather, that no certain calculation can be made. It is better, therefore, to reckon on a sufficient time, and this I would beg leave to state at four years; and if it can be done in less time so much the better. The Rock upon which the Edystone Light-house stands is certainly harder than the Cape Rock, and of course required more time to work; but, on the other hand, the Cape Rock lying in a more northerly latitude, and where the weather is more variable, it is likely that greater interruption will be given to the proceedings than in the other; so that, all circumstances considered, the time I have mentioned, I doubt, will be little enough.

Mr Stevenson, to whose merit I am happy to bear ample testimony, has been indefatigable in obtaining information respecting this Rock, and he has made a model of a stone Light-house, nearly resembling that of the Edystone, in which he has proposed various ingenious methods of constructing the work, by way of facilitating the operations. I own, however, after considering these in the fullest manner I have been able, and comparing them with the construction of Mr Smeaton's, I mean in the building, and also that there is undoubted proofs of the stability of the Edystone, I am inclined to give it the preference. No doubt some methods different from the Edystone will require to be put in practice for the foundation; but its general construction, in my opinion, renders it as strong as can well be conceived,—in fact, it may be looked upon as a solid mass of rock. Viewing the matter, therefore, in this light, it will be unnecessary for me to accompany this Report with the design of a Light-house. It will be time enough to make such a design, when the Commissioners shall be in a situation to give orders for the erection, and then I have no doubt Mr Stevenson will furnish much valuable matter towards the perfecting of it.

The total height of the Edystone Light-house, from the lower course of stones on the rock to the top of the platform or balcony-floor, is about 70 feet; from thence to the bottom of the iron-frame of the lantern about 6 feet 9 inches; and the lantern itself is about 8 feet 3 inches; so that the total height to the eve of the cupola is about 84 feet 6 inches. Now, as the Bell Rock lies so much lower than that of the Edystone, I think the height of the shaft or tower of the Light-house should not be less than 80 feet, or, perhaps, a little more, say 85 feet; so that the cupola will, in this case, be about 100 feet above the surface of the rock. With such a height of Light-house as is here proposed, I would advise that the diameter of the base should be greater, and as it is less surrounded by such an extent of rock, it will give facility to the gradual diminution of the effects of the waves breaking upon it; will render the fabric more steady, and, as it will diminish quickly, no great additional surface will be presented to the sea.

The floor of the lower room, i. e. the height of the solid part of the Light-house, I would propose to be about 50 feet, and from thence to the top of the platform 35 feet, making a total height, from the rock to the platform or gallery, of 85 feet. As to the lantern itself, I need say little on that head, as lanterns for light-houses have, of late years, been greatly improved, as well as the lights. The substitution of lamps with reflectors, in place of coal or candle lights, has been found of the greatest advantage to the mariner; and it is not unlikely, from what I have been lately made acquainted with, that the substitution of the hydrogen gas in place of lamps, will not only prove a much cheaper, but a better light than even lamps. I am told that it will not cost above one-eighth of the price of oil. The kind of light to be used is also a matter of consideration, for unless lights are so constructed as to enable the mariner to distinguish between one and another, he may be apt to mistake his situation; but that also can be easily arranged, when this part of the subject comes to require consideration. The new light on the Skerries in Orkney is a revolving one; perhaps a similar one may also be judged advisable here, as, if the Light-house on the Island of May was to be fitted up with reflectors in the usual manner, it would not always be easy to distinguish this from the Cape Rock, unless one of them was to be made a revolving, or the lights to be placed in different situations of the house.

A Light-house has, of late years, been built on the South Rock, near the mouth of Loch Strangford, on the coast of Ireland. This Light-house was begun on the 11th of June 1795, and completed the 25th March 1797. It is 30 feet diameter at the base, and about 15½ feet just below the balcony floor. It is 56 feet high from the rock to the platform or balcony floor, and its shape is the frustum of a cone. It is built of granite from the Mountains of Morne; and the lantern, from the platform to the cupola, is about 12 feet high, and 10 feet wide. The light is a revolving one, and lighted by 10 lamps with reflectors, 3 in the upper course, 3 in the lower course, and 4 in the middle, and makes a revolution in five minutes. This distinguishes it from the Copland lights.

The rock on which this Light-house stands is about 400 yards long, and about 100 wide, and is covered about 18 inches deep at high-water, ordinary spring-tides. The rock is composed of beds of schistus, intermixed with beds of a kind of indurated clay, which are wearing fast away by the washing of the sea; and, unless some speedy and effectual means are taken to secure it, this Light-house will not be of long duration. It has cost about L. 22,000, and it is said that L. 7000 more will be required to secure the rock from washing away. I will not take upon me to say that this sum will be sufficient for the purpose; but it seems to me that it will not be a very difficult matter to secure the rock, if proper means are taken. The channel is here narrow, and the seas cannot be very heavy; indeed Macculloch the Light-house keeper informed me, that they seldom rise above the first landing, which is only about 27 feet from the top of the rock.

In the construction of a Light-house at the Cape Rock, great care will be necessary in choosing stone of the most durable quality, fit to resist the effects of the waves. For this purpose, I examined the rocks lying along the shore nearest adjoining the Inch Cape Rock, but found none of a very durable quality; most of it is a red freestone, softer than the rock itself, which has been much worn away by the wash of the sea, and therefore by no means fit for the exterior work of such a building; and there does not appear to be any fit for that purpose nearer than Kingoodie, about three or four miles from Dundee. This stone is a hard millstone-grit, of an excellent quality; very hard to work, but can be raised in blocks of any size and thickness required. It therefore appears to me to be most fit for the exterior work of a Light-house to be built on the Cape Rock; but as the price the proprietor asks for it is very high, it becomes a question whether the solid part of the building may not be done with the stone from near Arbroath, which, although not fit for exterior work, is yet of a pretty strong quality, and might be used in the solid part of the building, not exposed to the weather or wash of the sea: Or, it may be a question, whether the saving that would arise from using the stone near Arbroath, is a consideration, when put in competition with the superior strength and specific gravity of the Kingoodie stone.

Granite is also a stone that will resist the waves without wearing, and it is therefore a matter of consideration, whether granite stone might not be had from Peterhead or Aberdeen for this purpose. Granite, it is true, cannot conveniently be had in such large blocks as the Kingoodie stone, but it may be had in blocks sufficiently large to answer the purpose, and, if well dove-tailed, and properly cemented together, the whole may be made to act as one solid body of rock.

As to the expence of a Light-house in such a situation, it is not a very easy matter to form any thing like a correct calculation. So much depends on weather, on the untoward circumstances that may probably happen while the work is in hand, that they baffle even the most experienced artist to make the proper allowances. The price and quantity of materials is by no means difficult to ascertain; but the expence of putting them together must be more a matter of guess than of correct and well founded calculation. I have, however, computed the expence that such a work ought to cost, and have made every allowance for contingencies, from my own experience of works in the sea, and from what I have been able to collect from the experience of others, in which, I think, I have made a very full allowance for contingencies, and the cost amounts, by my estimate, to L. 41,844, but I will say L. 42,000, and, I trust, if ever the work is executed, and done with judgment, it will not exceed that sum.

I have gone on the supposition, that the outside is to be made of Kingoodie stone, and the hearting of stone from near Arbroath. I am, Gentlemen, your most humble servant,

(Signed) John Rennie.

To the Honourable the Commissioners of the Northern Light-houses.

REPORT by Mr Stevenson.

Edinburgh, 15th November 1806.

In the year 1800, when the Reporter laid before the Commissioners various models of a Light-house for the Bell Rock, the prospect of the undertaking was so distant, that it then appeared unnecessary to trouble the Board with any scheme for carrying the work into execution; but since the passing of the act of Parliament for this purpose, the case is materially altered. In preparing any method for carrying on a work, the most difficult in its nature, and one to which the common tests of experience can hardly be applied, he is aware, that it is impossible, by any previous arrangement, to determine what will answer in all respects. In so far as the operations on shore are considered, the ordinary rules of practice apply, but, in forming plans for the Rock itself, matters must be adjusted to the situation and circumstances of the case.

Certain measures, of a preliminary nature, are, however, indispensably necessary, while others may be of doubtful application; among the former, it appears to be essentially necessary to provide a vessel to be moored at the distance of from three quarters to one mile north-west of the Rock. She must, of course, be fitted up as a store-ship, with accommodation for the artificers, and ground-tackle for riding in from 17 to 20 fathoms water, on rather a hard bottom. This vessel, besides answering as a store-ship for water and provisions, may occasionally take on board lime, cement, and other materials from the small craft at the Rock, when lying at anchor with them on board may be found inconvenient. There is also another and most important service, which this vessel will fall to perform in terms of the act of Parliament, which is the carrying of a Light upon her mast, for the benefit of shipping, and to enable a duty to be collected, even before the commencement of the work, agreeably to the suggestion of Mr Cuningham.

The Reporter, in order to inform himself more fully regarding the construction of such a vessel, while attending the progress of the Bill in London, visited the Floating-light ship at the Nore, under the command of Mr Bennet, who very politely described every particular connected with the business. He had also frequent communications with Captain Huddart of the Trinity House, who takes a particular charge of the Floating-lights under the management of that Board, since which he has also corresponded with him upon the subject, who has obligingly stated his ideas relative to a vessel and moorings fitted for the Bell Rock. Upon the whole, the Reporter is of opinion, that a dogger, or Dutch-built vessel, is best calculated for this service. Such a vessel would require to be from 80 to 100 tons burden, moored with a mushroom-anchor, weighty iron mooring-irons, having likewise on board a hempen cable of 16 inches in circumference. The mushroom-anchor, which is but a late invention, is now in use at all the Floating-lights on the coast, and even in some of his Majesty's store-ships. Its great property consists in its being hardly possible for a vessel to foul her anchor with it; and the construction is such, that it may be made in part, or wholly, of cast-iron, agreeably to the accompanying model, from which an idea may more easily be formed of its application. (See Plate X.). This vessel must be furnished with such a light as to be readily distinguishable from the Coal-light on the Island of May; and although the Dudgeon Floating-light, off the Norfolk coast, which carries two lanterns, is at a great distance, yet, as it is the nearest Floating-light to the Bell Rock, it may be advisable to distinguish it from that also. As a vessel cannot be dispensed with for the accommodation of the artificers, it will be found to be a great saving to employ her as a store-ship. As this vessel is only meant to answer a temporary purpose, by purchasing one of the Dutch or Prussian prize-ships, now for sale in Leith, she might perhaps be fitted up for about L. 2000.

Although it would be perfectly impossible to do any thing with much effect at the Bell Rock, without a vessel stationed in the offing; yet as she must necessarily be moored at the distance of about a mile from it, to give a sufficient birth for swinging, according to the wind, and also to give sea-room to clear the Rock, in the event of her breaking adrift, the inconveniency and difficulty of the frequent passage between the Floating-light and the Rock must be very considerable. It therefore occurs to the Reporter, that the greatest advantages would arise from the erection of a temporary residence for the artificers upon the Rock during the working-months of summer, and also to answer as a store for some of the materials. The greatest difficulties which Mr Smeaton had to struggle with at the Edystone, arose from the smallness of the rock, which at once precluded any attempt of this kind from being undertaken, and subjected the work to all the disadvantages and trouble so particularly described as experienced in communicating on all occasions with the store-ship. But, from the extent of the Bell Rock, an opportunity may be had for erecting a temporary residence, for facilitating the work. It was under the conviction that such an accommodation might be constructed, that the clause was introduced into the act for allowing the collection of half-duties upon the erection of a Beacon. But, independently of these advantages, the Reporter conceives some erection of this kind necessary, to give confidence to the artificers, in the event of accident to the boats, of which they might lay hold, until assistance could be procured from the store-vessel. This temporary residence is provided for in his estimate for the Light-house, and having modelled it, he proposes that it should consist of beams of timber, not less than 50 feet in length, and of proportional strength; the beams are coupled together at the top, where they form a cabin for the workmen, and, at the same time, answer all the purposes of a Beacon.

The next material object to be considered, is a method which may prolong or extend the working hours at the Rock, especially in the first instance, to low water of neap, as well as spring tides. In this respect we also find, that Mr Smeaton had no alternative, having had barely extent for the foundation of the Light-house; but, in this respect, he had less occasion for such an apparatus, as the top of the Edystone Rock was rather above high-water, although, from its shelving form, the level of the ground-course was not more than nine feet above low water of spring-tides. The ground-course of the Bell Rock, however, will not be more than about two feet above low-water of such tides. It therefore becomes an object of great importance, to construct a water-tight fence round the site of the building, which might be the means of saving a whole season with the work, and securing the proper execution of the lower courses, by enabling the workmen to go on in a more deliberate manner with their operations. The Reporter has had several methods in view for raising a coffer-dam for this purpose to the height of about six feet or thereby, which would allow the work to proceed regularly in moderate weather at low water of neap as well as spring-tides. He has, accordingly, modelled a coffer-dam with this view, which he proposes to be three feet more in diameter than the base of the building, and, from its exposed situation, the greatest attention must be paid to the strength and fitness of the materials. At first he intended this to be of timber, but at length fixed upon cast-iron, strongly connected with iron-bolts, passing through flanges raised upon the joints, which are to be provided with a groove, for the conveniency of tightening them. The whole of this apparatus is estimated to weigh about 40 tons, and is so constructed, that when all the pieces are landed on the rock, and laid in their places, the foundation for them being prepared, they may be set up, and temporarily fixed, in the course of a good spring-tide.

There is no part of this critical work which will be attended with so much difficulty as the landing of heavy materials, nor is there any part of the business that has occupied so much of the Reporter's attention. Mr Smeaton appears to have had a great deal of trouble upon this head; and in conversing with one of those having charge at the South Rock Light-house, on the coast of Downshire in Ireland, while it was building, it was stated, that there was more time lost in getting a regular supply of materials, and more vexation attending this department, than any other part of the operations, although this rock is exposed and dry at every tide, and only 3 miles from the shore, with a beach where vessels were laid to discharge their cargoes; whereas the Bell Rock is about 11 miles from land, forming neither a steep-face, like that of the Edystone, nor a sloping beach, like that of the South Rock, while it is so low in the water, that it can afford little or no shelter to vessels, if brought alongside of it. Under all these adverse circumstances, the landing of the materials becomes a consideration of the most perplexing nature. He has sometimes thought that the depth of water upon the rock might be turned to advantage in landing the stones at high-water; yet this mode has its disadvantages, and could not always be depended upon; others must, therefore, be resorted to, more certain in their application. Vessels of an easy draught of water, and not exceeding 20 tons burden, might in very moderate weather be brought close into some of the small creeks of the rock. Some of these will admit of improvement, where cranes might be fixed for unloading them. This may, perhaps, turn out to be the surest mode upon trial; but it may also be necessary to resort to others, such as having buoys moored in different directions, at a convenient distance from the rock; by making fast a hawser to the buoy best suited to the direction of the wind; the hawser may be veered out till the vessel with the materials gets so close to the Rock as to discharge. Some have even supposed, that the materials may be transported to the Rock under these circumstances by a float of cork or timber, and when the vessel is thus cleared of her cargo, she may be hauled off again, and so make sail. The stones, when landed, if not immediately built, may be stowed into the cast-iron coffer-dam, which, for this purpose, will be found of the greatest use, while the lower courses of the building are in progress; and as the work advances, other plans will present themselves.

In the Report dated 23d December 1800, on the subject of the Bell Rock, the Reporter explained his reasons for laying aside the plan of a cast-iron Light-house, and, after what has since been stated in Mr Rennie's report 30th December 1805, it is unnecessary for him to enter again upon that subject, especially as it has been fixed that the building is to be of stone. The matter which he, therefore, now submits to the consideration of the Board, is, the quarry or quarries from which these materials should be taken. It is to be regretted, that the extensive quarries in the neighbourhood of Arbroath are not of so durable a nature as to render them fit for outside work. On his way from Fraserburgh lately, he passed through Aberdeen, Arbroath, and Dundee, and, in addition to former inquiries, brought with him a note of prices, and specimens of the stone of the quarries of these places. Upon the whole, there seems to be objection to the use of best Arbroath or Red Head stone, for the hearting or inside-work, which may be had for 9s. 4d. per ton. The Mylnefield or Dundee stone at 25s., but for the granite, of the sizes wanted, no price could be quoted. Stone is the principal material that requires consideration. As for lime, we have an extensive choice in this country, and nothing can perhaps answer the purpose better for securing the outside joints than Parker's cement. The Reporter has a specimen of Aberthaw lime, which Mr Smeaton used with so much advantage; it would be no difficult matter to get a cargo of it, which would be sufficient for the whole building.

With regard to the Lantern, and other parts of the building which require to be of metal, without entering into particulars, they will no doubt fall to be made of copper, at least such parts as are more particularly exposed to the action of the air or water. As to the nature of the Light itself, there may be some improvements and alterations upon the present system, before the building is completed; but, after erecting such a fabric as will be necessary at the Bell Rock, no pains will of course be spared upon so essential a part as the quality or description of Light to be exhibited.

Supposing the work to commence in the Spring of the year 1807, it is already time that the store-vessel were in preparation, and the necessary arrangements made for fitting her up as a Floating-light, that the collection of the duties may commence; and, when got to her moorings, the workmen may begin to the temporary residence or beacon, and prepare the rock for the building, which would form the primary operations, and occupy the first Summer. If the beams are found to withstand the storms of winter, the upper part can then be covered in as a residence for the artificers in 1808; and, at all events, be habitable for the Summer of 1809. While these measures are carrying forward, and the site of the building is in progress, the lower course of stones will be in preparation on shore. The place which the Reporter would propose for carrying on these works is Arbroath, as the port most contiguous to the Rock, being situate at the northern side of that range of coast which forms St Andrew's Bay, in which the Bell Rock holds a centrical situation. A passage may be made from Arbroath to the Rock with much more regularity than from the Tay. On the southern side of this great Bay, there is no convenient harbour between the Tay and Fifeness. The stones, being transported from Mylnefield and Aberdeen, would be hewn at Arbroath, and after being laid and marked upon a platform, course by course, would then be shipped for the Rock.

It is unnecessary at this time to enter further into particulars. When the dimensions of the building are finally arranged, it will then be proper to enter into contracts for the materials, and shipping for conveying them, and to provide implements and artificers for the work.

(Signed) Robert Stevenson.

To the Honourable the Commissioners of the Northern Light-houses.

JOINT REPORT by John Rennie and Robert Stevenson.

Edinburgh, 26th December 1806.

Gentlemen,

You having at your meeting on the 10th instant resolved that the Light-house to be erected on the Bell Rock shall be of stone, we, according to your request, went to Aberdeen and Mylnefield, for the purpose of examining into the quality and price at which stone for the erection of the Light-house could be delivered at Arbroath, the place where it is proposed the materials shall be prepared for the work.

At Aberdeen, we found that many additional quarries had lately been opened, some of them of an excellent quality, and capable of producing larger blocks of stone than granite quarries usually do; but still it is doubtful, as has been formerly mentioned, whether any one quarry will be found to produce a sufficiency of large blocks in any reasonable time; but by purchasing from different quarries, a regular supply may be procured for all the purposes wanted, in case you shall determine upon using the granite in preference to stones from Kingoodie. The Aberdeen granite is of so very strong and durable a nature, and has been used in works where the sea has acted upon it for time immemorial, that no doubt can possibly be entertained respecting its adaptation to a work of this kind. There is also every reason to believe, that the Kingoodie stone resists the sea and weather equally well, but we have not been able to collect such positive proofs of this as of the other; for, although a good deal of that stone has been used in the piers of the harbour of Dundee, yet, as this has been mixed with other sorts of the same appearance, and nearly of the same composition of those of Kingoodie, it prevents the possibility of our saying whether some of the stones that have wasted may not be Kingoodie, although we have great reason to believe that they are not. However, where facts cannot be positively ascertained, doubts exist; and we think, that a Light-house upon the Bell Rock is too important a work to suffer even a doubt to exist; and we have no hesitation, therefore, in recommending, that the under part of the building, at least as high as the first apartment, should be of Aberdeen granite; and as this is the great bulk of the work, it may be as well, perhaps, to complete the outer course of granite to the top.

As to the extra price this will incur, we cannot at present correctly say. We have had two offers for granite from the Rubislaw and Dancing-Cairn Quarries. The former by Robert Spalding, is at 10d. per cubic foot, delivered on the quay at Aberdeen, but, as the expence of shipping and shore-dues are not included, this may be fairly reckoned at 2d. per cubic foot more. The other is from Snell, Ranie and Thom, at 1s. 4d. per cubic foot, delivered free on board a vessel at the quay. Now, as the freight from Aberdeen to Arbroath will be about 7d. per cubic foot, and as an agent must be employed to examine and see the stone delivered by the different quarry-men, we suppose that 1d. per foot may be added for commission; so that, exclusive of Government duties, the offer for Aberdeen stones will stand nearly as follows: Spalding's offer, with charges, will amount to 1s. 8d. per cubic foot, and Snell and Company's at 2s. The expence of working the Aberdeen stone will come high, we doubt, for such a work as this. Where dove-tails, and other devices for the security of the building will be necessary, it cannot cost less than 2s. 6d. per cubic foot. Now, taking the price of stone at the average of the above offers, it will amount, with workmanship and freights, to 4s. 4d. per cubic foot, so that the casing or outside course of granite will amount to about L. 7266. Mr Mylne offers to supply blocks of Dundee or Kingoodie stone, put free on ship-board, at 1s. per cubic foot; the freight from thence to Arbroath will be about 4d. per cubic foot, so that the stone will cost at Arbroath 1s. 4d. The working of this stone will cost about 1s. 6d. per foot, making the cost of the Kingoodie stone 2s. 10d.; therefore a casing of Dundee stone would amount to L. 4760, making a difference in favour of Kingoodie stone of L. 2506.

The next question that arises here is, what kind of stone should be used for the hearting of the building, where nothing can affect the stone, of whatever quality it may be; and here the Arbroath or Redhead quarries may come into competition. There are arguments in favour of both; the Kingoodie will be more expensive, but its specific gravity is greater, and it is of a much stronger nature than the Arbroath stone. If Kingoodie stone is used for the hearting, the cost of the stone, with freight and cutting, will be about L. 2124. The Arbroath stone will cost, delivered at the work, about 9s. per ton of 16 cubic feet, and cutting about 1s. per cubic foot, so that the total cost will be about L. 1172, a difference in favour of the Arbroath stone, besides duty, of about L. 952. Now, whether you may agree to pay this extra price we will not venture to anticipate, but we have no hesitation in saying that the Kingoodie stone is the best.

Another object which occupied our attention, was the procuring of a piece of ground at Arbroath, with proper sheds and warehouses, near the harbour, for the purpose of dressing the stones, laying the courses as they are to be in the Light-house, keeping stores, &c. &c. For this purpose we applied to Messrs Duncan and Cargill, who have a ship-builder's yard adjoining the harbour, and who some time since intimated their intention of disposing of it; but we found that the place was not of the dimensions necessary for the work, that the warehouses on the ground did not belong to the ship-yard, and that the people had not finally determined upon disposing of this place. We therefore inquired further, and found a piece of ground much larger than the carpenter's yard, and nearly as well situated, but there are no buildings upon it; and indeed, there is no other spot at all convenient, or near the harbour, that can be had. We therefore saw the proprietor John Taylor, and he has offered to let the whole for seven years, at the rent of Twenty Guineas per annum. The rent is high, but the situation is such as to render it more suitable than any other, and therefore we advise Mr Taylor's proposal to be accepted.

Having now stated the result of the several objects for which our journey northward was undertaken, it may be proper to mention what occurs to us as the best mode of proceeding respecting the measures to be taken for the erection of the Light-house, with the construction that appears best suited to the stability of the work. The first object that naturally presents itself is the establishment of the Floating-Light, now in preparation, respecting which some correspondence has taken place between Mr Stevenson and Captain Huddert of the Trinity Board of London, which is now before you. Their information is very satisfactory, and from the measures taken in advising with the Trinity-House of Leith, it is hoped that every thing relative to the fitting out of the Prussian-dogger, purchased for this service, will be the most complete of the kind, and the sooner she can be got to her moorings the better, that the operations at the Rock may be commenced, and that the duties may be collected for paying the Treasury loan, and otherwise adding to the general fund.

The second object that comes under consideration is the inclosing the piece of ground at Arbroath for a work-yard. This may either be done by a ruble wall or a wooden fence, but the former is preferable, because several buildings must be made for stores, and for floors, to mark out the different courses with the dove-tails as they form the building, so that the ruble wall may form part of these buildings. Sheds must also be erected for the masons to work in.

Thirdly, Two vessels, of about 30 tons each, for conveying stones from Arbroath to the Rock, should, without delay, be contracted for. These vessels must be built strong, and of good materials, and calculated to work well at sea, that no opportunity of going to the Rock may be lost.

Fourthly, A crane for unloading the vessels should be established at Arbroath, and another at the Rock, for landing the materials, as also the necessary tools and triangles, with tackle for setting the stones in the work-yard, and at the Rock likewise, stone-carriages, jacks, &c.

Fifthly, Mooring-chains, anchors, buoys, with ropes, &c., to assist in landing the materials, and for enabling the men to leave the Rock when the tide prevents them from working.

Sixthly, A coffer-dam will be wanted, to the height of 4 or 5 feet, so as to enable the workmen to continue so much longer on the Rock than they could do, were the tide allowed to flow over the foundation when it rises above the level of the Rock.

Seventhly, Although we do not pretend to say that a stage, for the accommodation of the workmen, can with certainty be constructed on the Rock, yet it might be worth while to attempt the establishment of such a work, as, if it did answer, great facility in carrying forward the work would be obtained; and, should the project fail, the timber and iron can be applied to other uses, and the expence of the experiment cannot be great.

Eighthly, A variety of small tools, for cutting the foundation of the Rock, for dove-tailing the stones, and sundry other uses too tedious to mention, will also be wanted.

Ninthly, A quantity of Aberthaw lime should be procured, as well as other lime of the best quality which the country affords, and a small lime-kiln for burning it erected, and no more burned at once than can be used in a short time, that it may be always had as fresh as possible, as the less it is exposed to the air after being burned the better will it cement. Pozzolano or tarras should be got, if possible, to mix with the lime, these making the best cement that has yet been discovered; but, if it cannot be had, manganese, or even burnt ironstone, will form a good substitute. A quantity of Parker and Company's Roman cement will be wanted, to keep the sea from washing out the other cement before it has time to harden in the joints.

Tenthly, Oak trenails will be required for fixing down the stones, while the building is in operation, and the several courses liable to be washed by the waves. Lead for running bolts into the Rock, &c. will also be necessary.

As to the construction of the Light-house itself, we are of opinion, that it is much better to follow what has been found to answer at the Edystone, a situation nearly similar to the present, than, in a work so important, to look for other methods that have not stood the test of trial. It must, however, be observed, that some alteration, suited to the difference of local circumstances, ought to be adopted. The Rock at the Edystone differs both in form and quality from the Bell Rock; it lies in a slanting direction, and the higher part was never covered by the tide. It is of a harder quality, and but small in size; nothing, therefore, was to be found in this case in regard to the wearing or wasting of the Rock; and from its limited size, there was no more space than what merely enabled the engineer to make the erection upon it.

The case at the Bell Rock is very different, the Rock being, on an average, not more than four feet higher than low-water of spring-tides. It is of a softer quality, but the dimensions are large. It therefore becomes necessary that the base should be more extended and flat where it is connected with the Rock, so that when the waves break upon it, they may spend their fury on the base of the Light-house, instead of the Rock itself, and thereby prevent it from wearing away. The tower should also be higher, as the tide rises more upon it than on the Edystone. These, and a few other alterations, will adapt the Edystone plan to the Bell Rock, unless in so far as the light itself is connected; but this need not now be a subject of inquiry. A Plan of the Light-house, nearly similar to what is proposed, is handed herewith, but no plan of the dove-tailing has been made, nor can it well be done at present, as the dove-tails must be suited to the different courses of stone as they come from the quarry; but, as the principle is similar to that of the Edystone, the design may be easily judged of.

It is of much importance, that, in so hazardous a work as the present, recourse should speedily be had to advice when occasion requires; and, as a Quorum at all times cannot be got, it might be advisable to appoint a Sub-Committee of your number, to be called together when necessity may require.

(Signed) John Rennie.
Robert Stevenson.

To the Honourable the Commissioners of the Northern Light-houses.

REPORT by Mr Rennie.

Edinburgh, October 29. 1807.

Gentlemen,

I went to the Bell Rock on the 5th instant, when I found Mr Stevenson with his workmen engaged in preparing the Rock to receive the foundation of the Light-house; also in erecting a Beacon on it, for the double purpose of pointing out to mariners the situation of the Rock more correctly than can be done by the Floating-Light, and as an asylum to the men employed on the Rock, in case they should be overtaken by the tide before the boats had time to take them to the vessel. Mr Stevenson had been constantly engaged in the different operations for about two months, during which time he had never been ashore; and it was fortunate he had taken the resolution of remaining constantly on board, for, without this, there is every reason to believe that the workmen could not have been prevailed on to continue at the work, they having previously shewn a disposition to leave it; but by perseverance, and by allowing them their provisions while on board the vessel and working at the Rock, they have not only been prevailed on to remain at the work, but they now seem to be better satisfied when at the Rock than on shore; and as no accident has happened, although the weather has several times been very stormy, there is great reason to believe that the workmen, being now accustomed to the work, and having gained entire confidence by the success of the past year, will return with redoubled vigour next season, and that the work will proceed with much spirit and regularity.

The work performed in the course of the present season, consists first of preparing the Rock for the foundation of the Light-house to a certain extent; but owing to that part of the Rock where the Light-house is to stand being very uneven in the surface, and some of it within 2½ feet of the level of the sea at low-water of spring-tides, the time at which the men can work is of course very limited; and as there would be great danger of shivering the Rock, if blasting or any other violent measure were resorted to for expediting the work, it has been thought better to proceed in the more secure mode of cutting the stone by picks and chisels, which, as the Rock is hard, and so consumes much time, considerable progress has been made towards this; and I hope, by the end of next June, the whole of the Rock will be completely ready to receive the foundation-course of the Light-house: perhaps it may even be ready sooner; but so much depends on weather, I do not venture to state particularly the time when this most essential object will be completed; but I have great confidence in the zeal Mr Stevenson has shewn in the past season, to prognosticate that he will do all that can be done in the next to expedite the work.

A large beacon, consisting of six main beams of timber, about 13 inches square, and 44 feet long, has been erected on the Rock; it forms a pyramid of about 42 feet high, and a base of the same extent. This is well secured to the Rock with dovetail cramps, and with chains and braces. Near the top are cross-bars to stiffen the upper part of it, which have been found of great use, as the smith's forge for sharping tools was erected there, and for the last fortnight the tools were sharped, and various other works done, which tended greatly to facilitate the operations at the Rock. The workmen continued there during the time the Rock was covered with the tide, which enabled them to begin working the moment the part was uncovered where they were employed, and it likewise enabled them to work till the last moment, when the tide began to cover the work. Had no such asylum been provided, the workmen would not only have lost much time in getting from the vessel to the Rock, but also in getting from it. This beacon is not yet entirely finished: a few good tides would enable the workmen to complete it, and when done, I have great hopes it will be found to resist the storms; indeed it has resisted several even in the unfinished state it is, and therefore is a favourable prognostication that it would be stable when completed.

There is, besides, a provision-chest intended to be placed on its top, and above this a ball and flag-staff, so that I hope it will be a very useful additional mark for mariners to avoid this dangerous Rock, and should be advertised as well as the

Floating-Light.

The advanced state of the year renders it necessary that the operations at the Rock should stand until the spring of the year. This is proposed to be done whenever the beacon is completed; but during the winter every requisite measure should be taken to proceed with the work for the Rock as expeditiously as possible. For this purpose I must beg leave to recommend to the Commissioners that the remainder of the articles mentioned in our Report of the 26th December last, should be provided with as little delay as possible.

The ground taken on lease from John Taylor, at Arbroath, for a wood-yard, has been covered in part with the necessary buildings and workshops, but sheds for the masons to work in during the winter season are not yet done. These may be got of the most temporary kind; if they just keep off the rain it will be enough, and no delay should take place in procuring them.

Several cargoes of Aberdeen and Dundee stones have been laid down and landed at the yard, part of which are worked, and the masons are engaged in working the remainder. I am sorry, however, to say, that neither the supply from Aberdeen nor Kingoodie has been so abundant as could be wished. Unless exertions far greater than has hitherto appeared be made, it will be impossible to proceed with the building on the Rock next season. I accompanied Mr Stevenson both to Aberdeen and Kingoodie. In viewing the former, it appears, that unless stones are purchased from such quarries near Aberdeen, as may turn them out, it is scarcely probable a sufficient quantity of large stones for the lower courses of the Light-House can be had in due time from the Rubieslaw quarries alone. It therefore will be advisable, that Mr Skene empower his agent to purchase from the other quarries whenever blocks of the requisite size can be found. As to the Kingoodie quarry, it only wants a little exertion on the part of Colonel Mylne's agents, as the quantity wanted would be easily got in a few weeks, if exertion such as has been promised be made.

The Floating-Light was completed and moored within the distance of one mile from the Rock on the 9th July, and for some time the people employed at the Rock lodged in her; but the situation in which she was moored has been found not to answer, as, after the gale of the 6th September last, which she rode out with perfect safety, it was found that her cable had been cut by a piece of rock or wreck. She went adrift next day, luckily without receiving any injury, but it has been found that there is no clear ground, (at least that has yet been discovered), less than the distance of about two miles and a half from the Rock, which will render her of no use as a place to accommodate the workmen; another vessel of some sort must therefore be provided. The Yacht has been used since the Float was removed to such a distance, but as neither the manner she was rigged, nor her accommodation, is suitable, nor indeed can she well be spared from attending the other light-houses, she cannot be counted upon in future. In my opinion a proper vessel should be purchased, and fitted up for this purpose, and she will sell at little discount after the work is completed.

One vessel of the description mentioned in the second article of the Report of 26th December 1806, has been built and fitted out. She has been engaged in carrying materials to the Rock; in carrying stones to the yard; and sundry other matters. A second vessel of the like description should be got ready against the spring, to carry the stones and materials to the Rock, &c. Two cranes have been purchased for loading and unloading stones; one has been erected at Aberdeen, and the other at Arbroath; and they both answer the purpose very well. Triangles, and other necessary apparatus are preparing for the work on the Rock, and will be ready against the time they are wanted. Mooring-chains and buoys for the vessels employed about the Rock have also been prepared and laid down.

It was proposed, in the Report of December last, to have a coffer-dam on the Rock, for keeping out the water during a part of the time the tide is flowing; but it rises so quickly here, after having turned, that I do not think a coffer-dam will produce advantages adequate to the expence. It is therefore proposed to do the work without any coffer-dam at all: there has been sufficient trial already made, to satisfy us respecting its practicability without a coffer-dam. The beacon already erected, and which there is reason to believe will stand, renders a stage of the description formerly mentioned unnecessary. It is intended, should this beacon stand over the winter, to erect places for the accommodation of the workmen employed at the Rock on its top. This will greatly facilitate the operations, as before stated.

Most of the small tools mentioned in article 9th of Report of December last, have been procured. Some are still wanting; but these are few. No Aberthaw lime has been procured, nor any pozzolano. Mr Stevenson intends to send the Yacht for a cargo of Aberthaw limestone, as soon as she can be spared from the service of the Light-houses; and, if a vessel is purchased for the accommodation of the workmen at the Rock, she may also be sent for a cargo of Aberthaw lime. I have not been able to procure any pozzolano, although many trials have been made. I have some hopes that a small quantity may still be procured; but I cannot speak with certainty: if not, tarras, or burnt ironstone, must be used. No oak trenails for the stones have yet been got. Mr Stevenson, however, is about to order some from Southampton; and I hope they will be in time for the work. Lead is, at this time, very cheap. I submit it to the wisdom of the Commissioners, whether it might not be advisable to purchase now what may be wanted for the work.

As to the construction of the Light-house, I submitted a plan to your consideration in the month of February last, (see Plate VII.) According to this plan, the works are proceeding; plans of each course of stone have been made; the whole is dove-tailed, but somewhat different from the mode pursued at the Edystone; they are less in length on the outside, but deeper in the direction of the radius of the Light-house, which will render the structure, on the whole, stronger than the Edystone plan. The extension of the base of the building is also much greater; and the base is considerably different. By this means, not only the impulse of the waves on the building will be less, but their action on the part of the rock adjoining the foundation will be much easier. The Rock is softer than that on which the Edystone is built, but it is harder than I imagined when last here. On the whole, I feel confident, that this work will be brought to a successful termination, within a reasonable period. The knowledge which has been acquired by the operations of the last season, impresses me with additional confidence in the practicability of the work, although confident, from the commencement, that, with proper care and attention, such a work might, with certainty, be completed.

The necessity of Mr Stevenson's remaining much at the Rock while the operations are going forward, render it necessary that some person, by way of agent, should be appointed to pay money at Arbroath, and to credit and settle accounts. As to this the Commissioners will order as they think right. I am, honourable gentlemen, your most obedient servant,

(Signed) JOHN RENNIE.

To the Honourable the Commissioners of the Northern Light-houses.

REPORT by Mr RENNIE.

Edinburgh, 12th December 1808.

Gentlemen,

I visited the Bell Rock on the 25th ult. The weather was favourable, but the tide did not ebb so low as to allow me to examine the foundation of the masonry so completely as I could have wished; but as there was little swell, I was enabled to form a tolerable judgment concerning the perfection with which it is executed, and this, I have the pleasure to say, is very favourable.

The Rock was nearly all cut last season, but several parts in the interior was hollow, and others appearing unsound, they could not be cut out without a serious expence in money, as well as a great loss of time. It was therefore judged preferable to make up these places with stone, and, accordingly, 17 stones have been let into different parts of the foundation, which brought the whole on which the Tower stands to a level; on which level, the first course of 12 inches was laid in August, and the outer-edge margin of this course, was nicely fitted all round to the rock, which, in every place except one, as I have been told by Mr Stevenson, projects higher than the upper part of it, by which, the base may be said to be completely indented into the Rock. Above this 12 inch course, two others, of 18 inches, have been laid, and it gives me great satisfaction to inform you, that they are done in a very complete manner, and the mortar, in all the outside joints, has not been at all affected by the sea beating upon it. A very small quantity was out of some of the inside joints, which, I am told, had arisen from the sea catching it (the weather being unfavourable) while the course was laying; this has been directed to be made up, and covered with Roman cement, which will render it as perfect as if no such thing had happened.

It is here proper to remark, that although the pozzolano mortar forms the best of all cements I have seen, yet it does not acquire a sufficient degree of induration to resist the effect of heavy waves for several weeks after it is used. The Roman, or Parker's cement, acquires almost an immediate induration, capable of resisting the heavy waves; but it never acquires so great a degree of induration, nor does it bind the stones so well together as the pozzolano mortar ultimately does. Its use, therefore, is to guard or preserve the pozzolano mortar until it has time to harden, which it does most effectually, and therefore every joint should be plastered over with this cement as soon as laid.

The place where the lower or 12 inch course is above the Rock, should be made up with stone of the same quality as the Rock itself. These stones should be dove-tailed into the rock, and laid with pozzolano mortar, secured by the Roman cement, the same as the other; for if done with harder stone (should the rock waste at all) it would resist the waves better than the soft, and occasion a more speedy waste of the other parts of the Rock than the Tower. All the protuberances of the Rock round the base of the Tower, should likewise be cut off, and smoothed, so as to form a regular curve at the base of the Tower, by this means there will be no place for the waves to catch, and their action will be regular on the whole, and I have no doubt, when so done, there will be little or no wasting in the rock itself.

The operations in the work-yard seem to be proceeding with much regularity, and there is a good stock of materials now there. Two courses are nearly completed on the platform, and as the diameter of the Tower diminishes fast, I have little doubt that there will be several other courses ready by the season that the work can with safety be resumed on the Rock; so that if the next season is at all favourable, I would fain hope the whole solid part of the Tower may be completed; every course of stone will raise it so much above the rock, and, of course, prolong the time of working a tide, until it is above the top of the springs, and then, if materials can be landed at the rock in sufficient quantity, the laying of them on the Tower will proceed with little or no interruption.

To secure a regular supply, another Praam or Stone-lighter should be got ready by the end of April next. Mr Stevenson has already received proposals for the building of one, and the sooner it is set about the better. It will also be necessary to build or hire another vessel, to assist the Smeaton in carrying out the stones from the work-yard; I apprehend it will be best to hire a vessel for that purpose, as the services required of her will be of short duration. About 10 tons more of pozzolano will probably be wanted, and this I have been able to procure through the friendship of the Hull Dock Company; it is already ground, and now lying there to be shipped. A small additional quantity of Aberthaw limestone is likewise to be procured, by the kelp-vessels that trade to Bristol, as a return freight.

It happens, rather unfortunately, that some of the granite quarries about Aberdeen have veins of a soft sort, which I have reason to believe decomposes with the sea and weather. Some of these stones have, unluckily, been sent to the work-yard. My decided opinion is, that all of this kind should be laid aside for the out-side work, and others of a good quality procured in their place. They can be substituted for the Dundee stone, and, therefore, although some loss will by this means be sustained, it will, on the whole, be trivial. I am, Gentlemen, your most humble servant,

(Signed) JOHN RENNIE.

To the Honourable the Commissioners of the Northern Light-houses.

No. V.

REMARKS RELATIVE TO THE GROUND-SWELLS OF THE SEA.

Wasting Effects of the Ocean.

In the Memoirs of the Wernerian Natural History Society, Vol. III. p. 814., and in the Edinburgh Philosophical Journal, Vol. III. p. 42., the subject of the Wasting Effects of the Sea upon the firm ground, is variously treated by the writer; and is here alluded to, in reference to the production of the appearance termed a Ground-swell, so often observed on our shores. In these papers it has been assumed, that the German Ocean, or North Sea, bounded partly by the coasts of Great Britain, Norway, Denmark, Germany, Holland, and France, as will be seen from Plate III., is almost every where wasting and extending its margin, upon the principle of its forming the great receptacle for all the debris of the surrounding countries above mentioned, which have a direct tendency to lessen its capacity for containing the waters which flow into it from the Atlantic, by the apertures between the shores of Scotland and Norway, towards the north, and between Dover and Calais, to the south. These passages may respectively be conceived as admitting a constant quantity, while this great basin is continually receiving the debris of the extensive tracts of country which surround it, through the medium of the innumerable rivers and streams that fall into it.

Wasting Effects of the Ocean.

Upon similar principles, the extensive lakes of interior countries become so many receptacles for the debris of their respective districts; and must in the lapse of time, contain less water, in proportion to the cubical contents of solid matters carried into them. So it is upon the great scale with the basin of the North Sea, from the extensive banks deposited therein, which lessen its capacity, and thereby give a tendency to the water which flows into it to overflow and waste its margin, producing, under various modifications, those heavy swells in the Sea to which we now allude. With this state of things in view, we may now inquire into the effects of the storms which agitate the waters of the Atlantic, and reach our shores only in the form of what has been significantly termed a Ground-swell; which may partly be illustrated from the storm described in page 312. of this work. We accordingly find the waters of the North Sea often in an agitated state, without any apparent cause, though no doubt proceeding from distant storms at sea. Hence, a continued gale from the westward, passing along the Atlantic Ocean, overcharges all the seas and inlets communicating immediately with it. Under these circumstances, although the surface of the North Sea be comparatively smooth, yet having acquired motion to a considerable depth from the distant storm, it continues to produce the effect of a Ground-swell for a considerable period. A swell of this description is almost constantly observable in the Bay of Biscay, owing to its exposure to the Atlantic, and from the configuration of the bounding land between Cape Finesterre in Spain, Ushant in France, and the relative position of the British Isles. Here the Ground-swells, proceeding from the same cause as those of the North Sea, are either the precursors of a gale of wind, or the effects of one which does not reach us.

Similar, though less evident effects, are produced by gales of wind which may be conceived to be confined to the boundary of the North Sea itself. Hence the heavy waves which often break upon the eastern shores of Great Britain, without any apparent cause at the time, are afterwards found to arise from storms at sea. But the heaviest Ground-swells of the North Sea are produced by gales from the north-east, which proceed in a progressive manner along the inclined plane of its bed, until the waves, by impinging upon the bottom and sides of the firm ground, are so disturbed that they ultimately cease, after wasting the whole extent of the shores, and sometimes causing the most destructive effects upon the coast of Holland, forming the southern extremity of this great basin.

<h1 style="text-align:center">No. VI.</h1>

SCHEDULES OF MATERIALS AND WORKMANSHIP.

Materials.

SCHEDULE, CONTAINING AN ENUMERATION OF THE MATERIALS USED IN THE ERECTION OF THE BELL ROCK LIGHT-HOUSE.

Course.	Granite in Pieces.	Sandstone in Pieces.	Granite in cubic feet.	Sandstone in cubic feet.	Tons of Sandstone and Granite.	Sandstone Joggles.	Oak Trenails.	Oak Wedges in pairs.	Pozzolano in Barrels.	Lime in Barrels.	Sand in Barrels.
1	4	14	6	146	10.891				1.5	2.2	1.1
2	52	71	508	876	101.648	13	246	378	13.6	19.9	10.7
3	52	84	808	1269	152.797	13	246	437	16.9	24.8	13.3
4	52	71	696	1009	125.609	13	246	400	14.5	21.2	11.4
5	53	54	593	849	106.258	13	212	336	12.5	18.3	9.8
6	26	71	492	790	94.275	13	194	270	11.8	17.2	9.2
7	26	58	238	767	73.094	13	168	242	8.3	12.3	6.6
8	26	45	196	547	54.148	13	142	268	7.4	11.0	5.8
9	26	45	264	426	50.737	13	142	229	6.3	9.3	5.0
10	26	45	292	606	65.748	13	142	229	7.6	11.0	5.9
11	26	45	339	363	52.006	13	142	229	6.3	9.3	5.0
12	16	37	160	462	45.308	8	108	184	5.7	8.4	4.5
13	16	37	194	347	39.709	8	108	184	5.0	7.4	3.9
14	16	37	168	329	36.423	8	108	184	4.8	7.0	3.7
15	16	37	188	301	35.962	8	108	184	4.6	6.8	3.6

16	16	37	153	321	34.698	8	108	184	4.7	6.9	3.7
17	16	37	182	308	36.000	8	103	184	4.7	6.9	3.7
18	16	37	153	297	32.983	8	108	184	4.4	6.4	3.4
19	16	37	180	304	35.560	8	108	184	4.5	6.6	3.5
20	16	29	196	308	37.077	8	108	152	4.3	6.3	3.4
21	16	29	211	264	35.088	8	92	152	4.2	6.1	3.2
22	16	29	100	311	29.906	8	92	152	3.9	5.7	3.0
23	16	29	177	238	30.615	8	92	152	3.9	5.7	3.0
24	16	29	147	303	32.951	8	92	152	3.9	5.6	3.0
25	16	29	149	235	28.248	8	92	152	3.5	5.2	2.8
26	6	39	142	250	28.780	8	92	152	3.5	5.2	2.8
27		38		315	22.500	8	79	67	3.0	4.4	2.4
28		33		259	18.500	8	66	58	2.8	4.1	2.2
29		26		236	16.857	8	54	61	2.9	4.2	2.2
30		26		249	17.786	8	52	54	2.4	3.4	1.8
31		25		238	17.000	8	50	68	2.2	3.3	1.8
32		26		274	19.571	8	52	69	2.3	3.3	1.8
33		28		302	21.571	8	56	78	2.6	3.8	2.0
34		30		296	21.143	8	60	80	2.7	4.0	2.1
35		32		271	19.357	8	64	80	3.0	4.5	2.4
36		32		266	19.000	8	64	80	2.5	3.7	2.0
37		32		279	19.929	8	64	80	2.3	3.5	1.8
38		24		275	19.643				1.5	2.2	2.0
39		16		138	9.857				1.2	1.8	1.6
40		16		136	9.714				1.2	1.7	1.5
41		14		133	9.500				1.1	1.6	1.4

A	B	C	D	E	F	G	H	I	J	K	L
42		14		142	10.143				1.1	1.6	1.4
Over,	599	1524	6932	16035	1678.590	338	4065	6329	207.1	303.8	165.4

Key:
A Course.
B Granite in Pieces.
C Sandstone in Pieces.
D Granite in cubic feet.
E Sandstone in cubic feet.
F Tons of Sandstone and Granite.
G Sandstone Joggles.
H Oak Trenails.
I Oak Wedges in pairs.
J Pozzolano in Barrels.
K Lime in Barrels.
L Sand in Barrels.

A	B	C	D	E	F	G	H	I	J	K	L
1	4	14	6	146	10.891				1.5	2.2	1.1
2	52	71	508	876	101.648	13	246	378	13.6	19.9	10.7
3	52	84	808	1269	152.797	13	246	437	16.9	24.8	13.3
4	52	71	696	1009	125.609	13	246	400	14.5	21.2	11.4
5	53	54	593	849	106.258	13	212	336	12.5	18.3	9.8
6	26	71	492	790	94.275	13	194	270	11.8	17.2	9.2
7	26	58	238	767	73.094	13	168	242	8.3	12.3	6.6
8	26	45	196	547	54.148	13	142	268	7.4	11.0	5.8
9	26	45	264	426	50.737	13	142	229	6.3	9.3	5.0
10	26	45	292	606	65.748	13	142	229	7.6	11.0	5.9
11	26	45	339	363	52.006	13	142	229	6.3	9.3	5.0
12	16	37	160	462	45.308	8	108	184	5.7	8.4	4.5
13	16	37	194	347	39.709	8	108	184	5.0	7.4	3.9
14	16	37	168	329	36.423	8	108	184	4.8	7.0	3.7

15	16	37	188	301	35.962	8	108	184	4.6	6.8	3.6
16	16	37	153	321	34.698	8	108	184	4.7	6.9	3.7
17	16	37	182	308	36.000	8	103	184	4.7	6.9	3.7
18	16	37	153	297	32.983	8	108	184	4.4	6.4	3.4
19	16	37	180	304	35.560	8	108	184	4.5	6.6	3.5
20	16	29	196	308	37.077	8	108	152	4.3	6.3	3.4
21	16	29	211	264	35.088	8	92	152	4.2	6.1	3.2
22	16	29	100	311	29.906	8	92	152	3.9	5.7	3.0
23	16	29	177	238	30.615	8	92	152	3.9	5.7	3.0
24	16	29	147	303	32.951	8	92	152	3.9	5.6	3.0
25	16	29	149	235	28.248	8	92	152	3.5	5.2	2.8
26	6	39	142	250	28.780	8	92	152	3.5	5.2	2.8
27		38		315	22.500	8	79	67	3.0	4.4	2.4
28		33		259	18.500	8	66	58	2.8	4.1	2.2
29		26		236	16.857	8	54	61	2.9	4.2	2.2
30		26		249	17.786	8	52	54	2.4	3.4	1.8
31		25		238	17.000	8	50	68	2.2	3.3	1.8
32		26		274	19.571	8	52	69	2.3	3.3	1.8
33		28		302	21.571	8	56	78	2.6	3.8	2.0
34		30		296	21.143	8	60	80	2.7	4.0	2.1
35		32		271	19.357	8	64	80	3.0	4.5	2.4
36		32		266	19.000	8	64	80	2.5	3.7	2.0
37		32		279	19.929	8	64	80	2.3	3.5	1.8
38		24		275	19.643				1.5	2.2	2.0
39		16		138	9.857				1.2	1.8	1.6

Course.	Granite in Pieces.	Sandstone in Pieces.	Granite in cubic feet.	Sandstone in cubic feet.	Tons of Sandstone and Granite.	Sandstone Joggles.	Oak Trenails.	Oak Wedges in pairs.	Pozzolano in Barrels.	Lime in Barrels.	Sand in Barrels.
40		16		136	9.714				1.2	1.7	1.5
41		14		133	9.500				1.1	1.6	1.4
42		14		142	10.143				1.1	1.6	1.4
Over,	599	1524	6932	16035	1678.590	338	4065	6329	207.1	303.8	165.4
Over,	599	1524	6932	16035	1678.590	338	4065	6329	207.1	303.8	165.4
43		16		140	10.000				1.1	1.6	1.4
44		16		139	9.929				1.2	1.8	1.6
45		16		135	9.643				1.1	1.7	1.4
46		16		132	9.429				1.1	1.6	1.4
47		18		261	18.643	16		64	2.0	3.0	1.5
48		16		118	8.429				1.0	1.5	0.8
49		16		115	8.214				1.0	1.5	0.8
50		14		114	8.143				1.0	1.5	0.8
51		14		123	8.786				0.9	1.4	0.7
52		16		122	8.714				0.9	1.4	0.7
53		16		115	8.214				1.0	1.5	0.8
54		16		113	8.072				1.0	1.5	0.8
55		16		102	7.286				0.9	1.4	0.7
56		18		258	18.428	16		64	2.0	3.1	1.5
57		16		97	6.929				0.9	1.4	0.7
58		16		104	7.429				0.9	1.4	0.7
59		14		96	6.857				0.9	1.4	0.7

60		14		102	7.286				0.7	1.1	0.5
61		16		100	7.143				0.8	1.2	0.6
62		16		97	6.929				0.8	1.3	0.6
63		16		90	6.429				0.7	1.1	0.5
64		16		86	6.143				2.0	3.1	1.5
65		18		228	16.288	16		64	0.6	0.9	0.4
66		16		83	5.929				0.7	1.0	0.5
67		16		82	5.859				0.6	0.9	0.4
68		16		88	6.286				0.4	0.7	0.3
69		12		76	5.429				0.6	0.9	0.4
70		16		74	5.286				0.6	0.9	0.4
71		16		95	6.786				1.0	1.5	0.8
72		16		77	5.500				2.0	3.1	1.5
73		16		75	5.357				2.5	3.7	2.0
74		18		225	16.071	16		64	2.0	3.1	1.5
75		16		73	5.216				0.6	0.8	0.4
76		16		73	5.216				0.7	1.1	0.5
77		16		82	5.859				0.6	0.7	0.4
78		12		62	4.429				0.5	0.7	0.4
79		12		62	4.429				0.6	0.9	0.4
80		12		75	5.357				0.6	0.9	0.4
81		16		70	5.000				1.0	1.5	0.8
82		16		181	12.929				1.0	1.5	0.8
83		16		190	13.571	16			2.0	3.1	1.5
84		16		257	18.357	16			2.0	3.1	1.5
85		16		298	21.286	16			2.5	3.7	2.0

A	B	C	D	E	F	G	H	I	J	K	L
86		8		62	4.429				0.4	0.7	0.3
87		8		60	4.286				0.4	0.6	0.3
88		8		56	4.000				0.3	0.6	0.2
89		8		52	3.716				0.3	0.5	0.2
90		8		48	3.429				0.2	0.5	0.1
Total 90	599	2236	6932	21598	2075.945	450	4065	6585	255.0	377.9	204.5

Key:
A Course.
B Granite in Pieces.
C Sandstone in Pieces.
D Granite in cubic feet.
E Sandstone in cubic feet.
F Tons of Sandstone and Granite.
G Sandstone Joggles.
H Oak Trenails.
I Oak Wedges in pairs.
J Pozzolano in Barrels.
K Lime in Barrels.
L Sand in Barrels.

A	B	C	D	E	F	G	H	I	J	K	L
Over,	599	1524	6932	16035	1678.590	338	4065	6329	207.1	303.8	165.4
43		16		140	10.000				1.1	1.6	1.4
44		16		139	9.929				1.2	1.8	1.6
45		16		135	9.643				1.1	1.7	1.4
46		16		132	9.429				1.1	1.6	1.4
47		18		261	18.643	16		64	2.0	3.0	1.5
48		16		118	8.429				1.0	1.5	0.8
49		16		115	8.214				1.0	1.5	0.8
50		14		114	8.143				1.0	1.5	0.8
51		14		123	8.786				0.9	1.4	0.7
52		16		122	8.714				0.9	1.4	0.7
53		16		115	8.214				1.0	1.5	0.8
54		16		113	8.072				1.0	1.5	0.8
55		16		102	7.286				0.9	1.4	0.7
56		18		258	18.428	16		64	2.0	3.1	1.5
57		16		97	6.929				0.9	1.4	0.7

58		16		104	7.429				0.9	1.4	0.7
59		14		96	6.857				0.9	1.4	0.7
60		14		102	7.286				0.7	1.1	0.5
61		16		100	7.143				0.8	1.2	0.6
62		16		97	6.929				0.8	1.3	0.6
63		16		90	6.429				0.7	1.1	0.5
64		16		86	6.143				2.0	3.1	1.5
65		18		228	16.288	16		64	0.6	0.9	0.4
66		16		83	5.929				0.7	1.0	0.5
67		16		82	5.859				0.6	0.9	0.4
68		16		88	6.286				0.4	0.7	0.3
69		12		76	5.429				0.6	0.9	0.4
70		16		74	5.286				0.6	0.9	0.4
71		16		95	6.786				1.0	1.5	0.8
72		16		77	5.500				2.0	3.1	1.5
73		16		75	5.357				2.5	3.7	2.0
74		18		225	16.071	16		64	2.0	3.1	1.5
75		16		73	5.216				0.6	0.8	0.4
76		16		73	5.216				0.7	1.1	0.5
77		16		82	5.859				0.6	0.7	0.4
78		12		62	4.429				0.5	0.7	0.4
79		12		62	4.429				0.6	0.9	0.4
80		12		75	5.357				0.6	0.9	0.4
81		16		70	5.000				1.0	1.5	0.8
82		16		181	12.929				1.0	1.5	0.8
83		16		190	13.571	16			2.0	3.1	1.5
84		16		257	18.357	16			2.0	3.1	1.5
85		16		298	21.286	16			2.5	3.7	2.0
86		8		62	4.429				0.4	0.7	0.3
87		8		60	4.286				0.4	0.6	0.3
88		8		56	4.000				0.3	0.6	0.2
89		8		52	3.716				0.3	0.5	0.2
90		8		48	3.429				0.2	0.5	0.1
Total 90	599	2236	6932	21598	2075.945	450	4065	6585	255.0	377.9	204.5

Masonry,	2075.945
Lantern, and its Apparatus,	7.500

Total in Tons,		2083.445

In this Table, 13 cubic feet are allowed to a ton of Granite, and 14 cubic feet to a ton of Sandstone.

Workmanship.

SCHEDULE, shewing the Extent and Description of WORK executed on the Sandstone and Granite employed in the Erection of the Bell Rock Light-house.

Course.	Granite Beds and Joints in superficial feet.	Sandstone Beds and Joints in sup. feet.	Granite facework in superficial feet.	Sandstone facework.	Sandstone polishwork.	Granite boring in lineal feet.	Sandstone boring in lineal feet.	Granite wedge grooves in lin. feet.	Sandstone wedge grooves in lin. feet.	Granite Lewis holes.	Sandstone Lewis holes.
1		500									18
2	1165	3354	132			156	264	208	170	52	71
3	2472	3141	275			208	325	260	421	52	84
4	1832	2980	265			208	325	300	300	52	71
5	1735	2406	220			208	251	300	204	52	54
6	1120	2788	196			104	316	156	349	26	71
7	679	2100	159			69	267	138	185	26	58
8	613	1858	110			78	184	104	164	26	45
9	750	1359	113			82	166	113	125	26	45
10	626	1887	111			87	173	112	145	26	45
11	898	1216	114			91	181	130	156	26	45
12	519	1394	90			51	125	69	120	16	37
13	522	1157	87			51	125	69	120	16	37
14	443	1148	86			51	125	69	120	16	37
15	539	997	84			51	125	69	120	16	37
16	448	1123	82			51	125	69	120	16	37
17	484	1093	80			51	125	69	120	16	37

18	430	1036	79			51	125	69	120	16	37
19	467	1023	84			56	134	74	129	16	37
20	484	952	89			56	110	80	114	16	29
21	513	872	87			56	110	80	114	16	29
22	319	981	82			53	113	76	118	16	29
23	464	829	78			53	113	76	118	16	29
24	361	926	88			59	107	83	111	16	29
25	388	802	77			56	110	80	114	16	29
26	370	818	76			56	110	80	114	6	39
27		1017		70	36		130		78		38
28		943		62	31		99		58		33
29		956		61	31		81		61		26
30		785		61	30		78		54		26
31		754		60	30		75		68		25
32		762		70	35		87		80		26
33		868		73	47		98		97		28
34		908		68	23		100		93		30
35		1022		68	23		106		93		32
36		854		64	21		106		86		32
37		782		71	25		112		100		32
38		502		70	111		24				
39		421		56	37		16				
40		417		56	37		16				
41		391		55	37		14				
42		372		60	44		14				
Over,	18641	50494	2944	1025	598	2093	5306	2933	4859	594	1528

Key:
A Course.
B Granite Beds and Joints in superficial feet.
C Sandstone Beds and Joints in sup. feet.
D Granite face-work in superficial feet.
E Sandstone face-work.
F Sandstone polish-work.
G Granite boring in lineal feet.
H Sandstone boring in lineal feet.
I Granite wedge grooves in lin. feet.
J Sandstone wedge grooves in lin. feet.
K Granite Lewis holes.
L Sandstone Lewis holes.

A	B	C	D	E	F	G	H	I	J	K	L
1		500									18
2	1165	3354	132			156	264	208	170	52	71
3	2472	3141	275			208	325	260	421	52	84
4	1832	2980	265			208	325	300	300	52	71
5	1735	2406	220			208	251	300	204	52	54
6	1120	2788	196			104	316	156	349	26	71
7	679	2100	159			69	267	138	185	26	58
8	613	1858	110			78	184	104	164	26	45
9	750	1359	113			82	166	113	125	26	45
10	626	1887	111			87	173	112	145	26	45
11	898	1216	114			91	181	130	156	26	45
12	519	1394	90			51	125	69	120	16	37
13	522	1157	87			51	125	69	120	16	37
14	443	1148	86			51	125	69	120	16	37
15	539	997	84			51	125	69	120	16	37
16	448	1123	82			51	125	69	120	16	37
17	484	1093	80			51	125	69	120	16	37

18	430	1036	79			51	125	69	120	16	37
19	467	1023	84			56	134	74	129	16	37
20	484	952	89			56	110	80	114	16	29
21	513	872	87			56	110	80	114	16	29
22	319	981	82			53	113	76	118	16	29
23	464	829	78			53	113	76	118	16	29
24	361	926	88			59	107	83	111	16	29
25	388	802	77			56	110	80	114	16	29
26	370	818	76			56	110	80	114	6	39
27		1017		70	36		130		78		38
28		943		62	31		99		58		33
29		956		61	31		81		61		26
30		785		61	30		78		54		26
31		754		60	30		75		68		25
32		762		70	35		87		80		26
33		868		73	47		98		97		28
34		908		68	23		100		93		30
35		1022		68	23		106		93		32
36		854		64	21		106		86		32
37		782		71	25		112		100		32
38		502		70	111		24				
39		421		56	37		16				
40		417		56	37		16				
41		391		55	37		14				
42		372		60	44		14				

Over,	18641	50494	2944	1025	598	2093	5306	2933	4859	594	1528
Course.	Gran-ite Beds and Joints in super-ficial feet.	Sand-stone Beds and Joints in sup. feet.	Gran-ite face-work in super-ficial feet.	Sand-stone face-work.	Sand-stone pol-ish-work.	Gran-ite boring in lineal feet.	Sand-stone bor-ing in lineal feet.	Granite wedge grooves in lin. feet.	Sand-stone wedge grooves in lin. feet.	Gran-ite Lewis holes.	Sand-stone Lewis holes.
Over,	18641	50494	2944	1025	598	2093	5306	2933	4859	594	1528
43		383		60	44						16
44		409		59	40						16
45		395		59	40						16
46		388		58	40						16
47		685		67	231				80		18
48		361		54	38						16
49		352		54	38						16
50		335		54	52						14
51		322		64	44						14
52		315		64	44						16
53		335		58	49						16
54		339		58	41						16
55		318		54	38						16
56		672		65	231				80		18
57		320		51	38						16
58		318		51	38						16
59		301		51	48						14
60		250		60	41						14

61		273		60	41						16
62		298		55	49						16
63		294		51	41						16
64		294		51	41						16
65		645		55	231				80		18
66		277		49	38						16
67		274		49	38						16
68		250		53	57						16
69		192		43	61						12
70		198		43	61						16
71		282		57	44						16
72		259		49	38						16
73		254		49	38						16
74		645		51	247				80		18
75		209		45	45						16
76		247		53	41						16
77		226		57	52						16
78		165		54	61						12
79		221		54	61						12
80		225		52	49						12
81		368			49	38					16
82		679			115						16
83		846			160						16
84		671			148						16
85		165			399						16
86		157			92						8

A	B	C	D	E	F	G	H	I	J	K	L
87		147			91						8
88		138			90						8
89		129			89						8
90		120			88						8
Total 90	18641	66440	2944	3145	4377	2093	5306	2933	5179	594	2240

Key:
A Course.
B Granite Beds and Joints in superficial feet.
C Sandstone Beds and Joints in sup. feet.
D Granite face-work in superficial feet.
E Sandstone face-work.
F Sandstone polish-work.
G Granite boring in lineal feet.
H Sandstone boring in lineal feet.
I Granite wedge grooves in lin. feet.
J Sandstone wedge grooves in lin. feet.
K Granite Lewis holes.
L Sandstone Lewis holes.

A	B	C	D	E	F	G	H	I	J	K	L
Over,	18641	50494	2944	1025	598	2093	5306	2933	4859	594	1528
43		383		60	44						16
44		409		59	40						16
45		395		59	40						16
46		388		58	40						16
47		685		67	231				80		18
48		361		54	38						16
49		352		54	38						16
50		335		54	52						14
51		322		64	44						14
52		315		64	44						16
53		335		58	49						16
54		339		58	41						16
55		318		54	38						16
56		672		65	231				80		18
57		320		51	38						16
58		318		51	38						16

59		301		51	48						14
60		250		60	41						14
61		273		60	41						16
62		298		55	49						16
63		294		51	41						16
64		294		51	41						16
65		645		55	231				80		18
66		277		49	38						16
67		274		49	38						16
68		250		53	57						16
69		192		43	61						12
70		198		43	61						16
71		282		57	44						16
72		259		49	38						16
73		254		49	38						16
74		645		51	247				80		18
75		209		45	45						16
76		247		53	41						16
77		226		57	52						16
78		165		54	61						12
79		221		54	61						12
80		225		52	49						12
81		368			49	38					16
82		679			115						16
83		846			160						16
84		671			148						16
85		165			399						16
86		157			92						8
87		147			91						8
88		138			90						8
89		129			89						8
90		120			88						8
Total 90	18641	66440	2944	3145	4377	2093	5306	2933	5179	594	2240

No. VII.

ABSTRACT-ACCOUNT OF THE EXPENCE OF ERECTING THE BELL-ROCK LIGHT-HOUSE, AND OF EXECUTING THE ULTERIOR WORKS CONNECTED WITH THAT ESTABLISHMENT.

Wages and Premiums.

Wages of artificers while off at the Bell Rock, and in the work-yards at Arbroath and Edinburgh, where the stones were cut and prepared in regular courses,	L. 11,980 15 8	
Premiums to artificers for Sundays' work and extra hours upon the Rock, and in the Work-yard at Arbroath,	998 14 9	
Premiums to seamen, including Sundays' work at the Bell Rock,	473 5 6	
Note.—Masons and smiths were paid at the rate of 3s. 4d.,—mill-wrights 3s. 6d.,—joiners 3s., and labourers at from 2s. 2d. to 2s. 8d. per day; besides lodgings ashore, and victuals while afloat.—The premiums paid to artificers were at the rate of 6d. per hour for extra time; eight hours constituting a day's work at the Rock.—The seamen were paid at the same rate on Sundays as on week days.		
Amount for wages and premiums to artificers, and including premiums to seamen,		L. 13,452 15 11

Building Materials.

35,952 cubic feet of Sandstone from Mylnefield quarry, dressed to the quarry-moulds, and put on ship-board,	L. 3,412 18 5	
Extra dressing in reducing the courses to regular thicknesses at Mylnfield,	667 2 8	

1700 cubic feet of sandstone from Craigleith Quarry for the cornice and parapet wall of the Light-room,	200 0 10	
13,964 cubic feet of granite from Rubieslaw and other quarries at Aberdeen, and from Cairngall near Peterhead,	1,979 1 4	
Extra dressing in reducing the granite stones to the quarry-moulds, and to regular thicknesses, to suit the respective courses, including cartage and charges of shipping,	1,291 7 2½	
40 Tons of Pozzolano-earth in casks,	398 3 4	
60 Tons of Aberthaw-limestone, including freight from South Wales,	78 14 2	
100 Bushels Parker's or Roman cement, including casks and shipping charges,	43 12 0	
6 Tons of Tarras, including casks and shipping charges,	52 19 10	
Casks for carrying lime and sand from the work-yard to the Bell Rock,	38 3 3	
4824 oaken trenails, from 21 to 24 inches and 6195 oaken wedges, from 12 to 18 inches in length,	216 1 6	
Note. — The quarry price of Sandstone varied from 1s. to 2s. 9d., and Granite from 1s. 3d. to 5s. per cubic foot. Pozzolano from L. 6 to L. 14 per ton. Tarras from L. 6, 10s. to L. 11 per ton. Limestone was 1s. per ton. Cement varied from 5s. to 6s. 6d. per bushel; oaken trenails from L. 1 to L. 5 per hundred, and wedges were L. 1: 6: 6 per hundred.		
Amount for Building Materials,		8,378 4 1½

Implements and Machinery for the Works, including Beacon-house, Cast-iron Railways, &c. &c. (See Plates VIII., IX., X., XIV., XVII., and XVIII.)

4662 cubic feet of Memel and Swedish timber, and 480 Petersburgh deals for the use of the Beacon-house, cast-iron Railways and wharfs upon the Bell Rock, and for making moulds for the stone-cutters,	L. 1,436 19 7	
69 tons 9 cwt. of cast-iron for Railways,	812 15 11	
25,893 lb. malleable iron in stanchions, bats, knees, stays, bracing-chains, screw and spear bolts, including other apparatus for the use of the Beacon-house and Railways,	1,244 3 7	

19 Tons 13 cwt. 2 qrs. 3 lb. cast-iron, 14,002 lb. malleable iron, and 505 lb. of brass for cranes, winch-machines, and other apparatus,	1,191 14 7½	
Cordage for cranes, &c.	409 1 0	
Two large Sling or Woolwich-carts, for conveying large blocks of stone, fitted up with wheel and pinion-work for slinging or lifting the stones off the ground,	150 3 6	
15,446 lb. quarry and stone-cutters' tools; 11,934 lb. malleable iron, and 771 lb. steel, used in the work-yard; exclusively of tools, nails, and other furnishings connected with joiners' and smiths' shops; but including stone-jacks and common carts used in work-yard, &c. &c.,	1,567 10 1½	
Note. — The price of fir-timber varied from 3s. to 5s. 6d. per cubic foot; cast-iron from L. 10, 10s. to L. 23:6:8 per ton; chains and axles, &c. 6½d. to 1s. per lb.; quarry and stone-cutters tools from 6d. to 10d. per lb.; Swedish and British bar-iron from L. 21 to L. 29 per ton. Steel was 7d. per lb., and brass 1s. 10d. per lb.		
Amount for Machinery, &c.		6,812 8 4

Shipping.

Price of the hull of a Prussian fishing-dogger,	L. 250 0 2	
Carpenter-work, altering and fitting up the dogger as the Pharos Floating-light,	1,397 12 8	
Two sets of chains, with mushroom anchors, spare shackles and swivels, &c., for mooring her off the Bell Rock, the whole weighing about 13,083 lb. of malleable, and 3200 lb. of cast-iron,	462 9 4	
Outfit in hempen cables, sails and rigging, including 11 tons cast-iron, ballast, ship-hearth, cabin-stoves, alarm-bell, &c.,	1,664 2 3	
Three large copper lanterns, glazed with plate glass, (so constructed, that the ship's masts passed through them), fitted with brass chandeliers for 60 agitable-lamps, each having a small silvered-copper reflector,	397 1 2½	
Freight of a vessel, and expence of laying down the moorings for the Floating-light,	81 5 6	

Wear and tear of the Floating-light riding off the Bell Rock, from July 1807 till February 1811,	1,059 11 5½	
Advertising the mooring and exhibition of the Floating-light, generally, in the Newspapers of the United Kingdom,	227 18 9	
Victualling the crew of the Floating-light, including occasional subsisting money and board-wages while ashore,	1,149 18 7	
Pay of the master, mate, principal and assistant light-keepers, and seven seamen, from 1807 to March 1811,	1,632 12 8	
		8,322 12 5
First Cost and Outfit of the Sir Joseph Banks Tender of 84 tons register, the Sloop Smeaton of 42 tons, the Sloop Patriot of 46 tons, and of four Stone Lighters of about 15 tons each, including wear and tear during the progress of the works,	L. 5,436 9 7½	
Bedding for seamen and artificers during the progress of the works,	349 7 2	
Victualling seamen and artificers afloat, including occasional subsisting money for seamen while ashore,	2,930 12 7½	
Pay of the masters, mates, and seamen of the respective vessels,	2,434 2 2	
Freight of hired vessels bringing stone from Mylnefield, Aberdeen, and Peterhead quarries, and timber and cast-iron from Leith and other ports to Arbroath,	930 17 11	
Port charges and sailing disbursements of the several vessels,	358 8 4½	
Insurance of Shipping, effected only for a limited period,	647 12 6	
14 Mushroom Anchors, weighing 13 tons 7 cwts. 0 qrs. 10 lb. of cast-iron,	235 15 8	
28,456 lb. malleable iron, in mooring-chains, shanks of mushroom-anchors, spare swivels and shackles,	891 11 2	
16 Large mooring buoys of coopers' work, and one of carpenters' work,	456 19 2	

Note.—Pay of the masters of the respective vessels in the service was from L. 5 to L. 6, 6s., mates from L. 4 to L. 5, 5s., principal light-keeper L. 5, 5s., assistant light-keeper L. 3, 15s., seamen from L. 2, 10s. to L. 3, 15s. per month. Officers' occasional subsisting money 2s., and seamens' 1s. 8d. per day.		
The price of the hulls of the vessels were from L. 9, 15s. to L. 10 per ton, and cordage from L. 77 to L. 130 per ton; cordage subject to a discount of 7½ per cent.; other articles generally to 5 per cent.		
Amount for shipping,		14,671 16 4½

Light-room, &c. (See Plates XVI. and XX.)

Lantern or Light-room with tinned copper roof, 8 cast-iron sashes, 8 feet in height, glazed with 48 squares of plate-glass, measuring 13½ by 26¾ inches. Malleable iron stays, copper rings, flag-staff, and signal-ball, &c.	L. 1,135 1 11	
24 Reflectors raised to the parabolic-curve, made from copper plated, in the proportion of 6 oz. of silver to each lb. of copper; arranged upon a malleable iron chandelier, furnished with brass fountains, and argand burners, including a train of Revolving-machinery, and two alarm-bells, set upon tripods on the balcony, &c.	1,287 17 2	
Balcony-railing of cast-iron, with brass supports and top-rail; and a conductor or thunder-rod extending, from the Light-room to the Rock, 216 0 3		
Amount of Light-room, &c.		2,638 19 4

Ulterior Works, &c. (See Plate XII.)

Finishing and Completing the interior of the Light-house, with wainscot partitions,—doors,—trap-ladders,—furniture of oaken-timber for the several apartments,—kitchen range with cast-iron chimney,—tinned-copper oil cisterns—brass and copper bolts and hinges for doors,—window-shutters,—brasslocks,—brass hand-rails for inside stairs,—water-cisterns, and coal magazines, &c.	L. 1,489 16 6	
Erecting permanent Railways upon the Bell Rock, improving the wharfs or landing places, and removing the Beacon-house,	1,338 16 6	

Houses erected for the families of the light-keepers and seamen of the Tender, signal-tower, store-houses, and sea-wall, at Arbroath,	4,500 8 3	
The price of about 1½ acre of ground for a garden, trenching, and enclosing it for the use of the light-keepers, and seamen, and their families,	1,158 18 10	
The price of a pew of 14 sittings in the parish-church of Arbroath, for the use of the Light-keepers and their families,	52 10 0	
Note.—Wainscot 7s. 6d. per foot, brass 1s. 8d. to 2s. per lb.		
Amount for Ulterior Works,		8,540 10 1

Incidents.

Expence of Act of Parliament,	L. 548 8 0	
Travelling charges connected with the work,	312 14 7	
Incidental charges for stamps and postages, including letters for artificers afloat, salary for Engineer's clerk, &c.	882 5 1	
Advertising the exhibition of the Light upon the Bell Rock, and the discontinuance of the Floating-light, on the 1st of February 1811,	219 10 3	
The cost-price of the artificers barracks, platform of aisler-masonry for fitting the courses before shipping them to the Rock,—engineer's office,—smith and joiner's shops,—store-house and stable, estimated at	1,255 5 6	
Rent of the work-yard, and compensation to the landlord for taking it off the hands of the Commissioners before the expiry of the lease,	174 19 6	
Price, hire, and keep of work-horses,	593 5 11½	
481 tons coals, used in the artificers' barracks, smith's-shop, lime-kiln in the work-yard, and at the beacon-house, &c.	347 4 2	
Shore-dues upon materials for the Light-house, and other articles during the progress of the works,	270 9 6	
57½ dozen of flambeaux, for night-work at the Bell Rock,	32 9 6	

Stationery and books for Engineer's office, and shipping,	134 10 8½	
One five feet Achromatic-telescope with brass-stand, steadying-rods, two eye-tubes, a mahogany-stand with night-glass for signal-room,	35 1 0	
Pension, and Sick lists for wages of artificers and seamen when off work, medical attendance, &c.	925 12 2	
Superintendence of engineers, and plans, including L. 300 to Captain Brodie,	4,858 13 5	
Interest upon L. 25,000 of Government loan, up to March 1810,	3,446 11 5	
Treasury fees for Exchequer bonds, &c.	235 10 4	
Note.—Price of coal 13s. 4d. to 19s. per ton. Oats from 20s. to 23s. per boll. Hay from 10½d. to 1s. 3d. per stone of 22 lb.		
Amount for Incidents		14,272 11 1
Amount of gross expenditure in erecting the Light-house, including Ulterior Works,		L. 77,089 17 8

Gross Expenditure.

Deductions.

DEDUCTIONS.

For workmens' barracks, implements, machinery, shipping and old materials, disposed of by public sale, or transferred to the Northern Light-houses for the general service of the Board, at the conclusion of the works.			
By the price of the workmens' barracks, storehouses and offices in the work-yard at Arbroath,	L. 700 0 0		
By old gable-walls, lime-house, and sundries in workyard, and engineer's office,	52 8 2		
By the price of three work horses and carts sold at different times,	86 0 0		
By fulzie of stable and work-yard,	21 17 0		

By stone-shivers sold by public sale at different times, including 232 cart loads for the use of the Roads in the vicinity of Arbroath,	48 4 6		
By artificers' time three weeks at Mylnefield, deducted from Quarry Account,	42 0 0		
By two large Woolwich-carts,	55 0 0		
By sundries, sold in the work-yard, by public sale, at the conclusion of the work,	121 16 5		
By the price of two cast-iron cranes, in use upon the quays at Aberdeen and Arbroath, and a small boring-machine used in the work-yard,	273 3 0		
By broken cast-iron railways,	97 19 0		
By the price of drift timber recovered,	6 10 0		
By a stone-waggon and quarry-tools, sold at Aberdeen,	15 13 0		
By old brass and bell-metal,	12 16 9		
By scrap-iron from the smith's shop,	6 10 8		
By sale of old timber, and the soil taken off the site of the light-keepers houses at Arbroath,	15 3 11		
By the price of the Sir Joseph Banks Tender,	1,510 0 0		
By the price of the Patriot,	400 0 0		
By the price of an old boat and mast belonging to the Patriot,	12 0 0		
By cash, in name of damages, in consequence of sap-wood in the Patriot's hull,	80 0 0		
By the amount of sales of sundry stores,	406 0 0		
By the price of three praam-boats or stone-lighters,	193 0 0		
By the price of the wreck of an old stone-lighter and boat,	10 10 0		

By retaining-money paid during the winter months, to one of the seamen who left the service,	1 11 6		
By interest upon the engineer's deposit-account with the Dundee Banking Company at Arbroath, from the commencement till the conclusion of the works,	26 5 7		
By return-freight of the sloop Smeaton, from Aberdeen to Arbroath,	18 18 0		
By shipping, boats, machinery, implements, stores, and moorings, transferred to the general service of the Northern Light-houses,	3,222 8 7		
By the nett cost and maintenance of the Floating-light deducted, as belonging to the general service of the Northern Light-houses,	L. 7,901 10 7		
By the price of the vessel and her stores when sold,	421 1 10		
		8,322 12 5	
			15,758 8 6
Nett cost of the Bell Rock Light-house, and Ulterior Works connected with that establishment,			L. 61,331 9 2

Nett Cost.

Extracted by
Lachlan Kennedy, Engineer's Clerk.

Average Price of Provisions.

Average Price of Provisions during the Period of the Bell Rock Works.

Beef 6d. per lb. of 17½ oz. avoirdupois.
Ship-biscuit L. 1, 9s. per cwt.
Quartern Loaf 13½d. per loaf, of 4 lb. 5½ oz.
Oat-meal L. 1, 11s. per boll, of 140 lb.
Barley 2½d. per lb. of 17½ oz.
Butter 1s. 8d. per lb. of 24 oz.
Salt 10s. per bushel, of 56 lb.
Whisky 11s. per gallon.
Small Beer 1s. 10d. per Scots gallon, of 8 Scots points.

DESCRIPTION OF PLATES.

DESCRIPTION of the PLATES, as they are mentioned in the Work.

PLATE I.

INCHKEITH LIGHT-HOUSE.

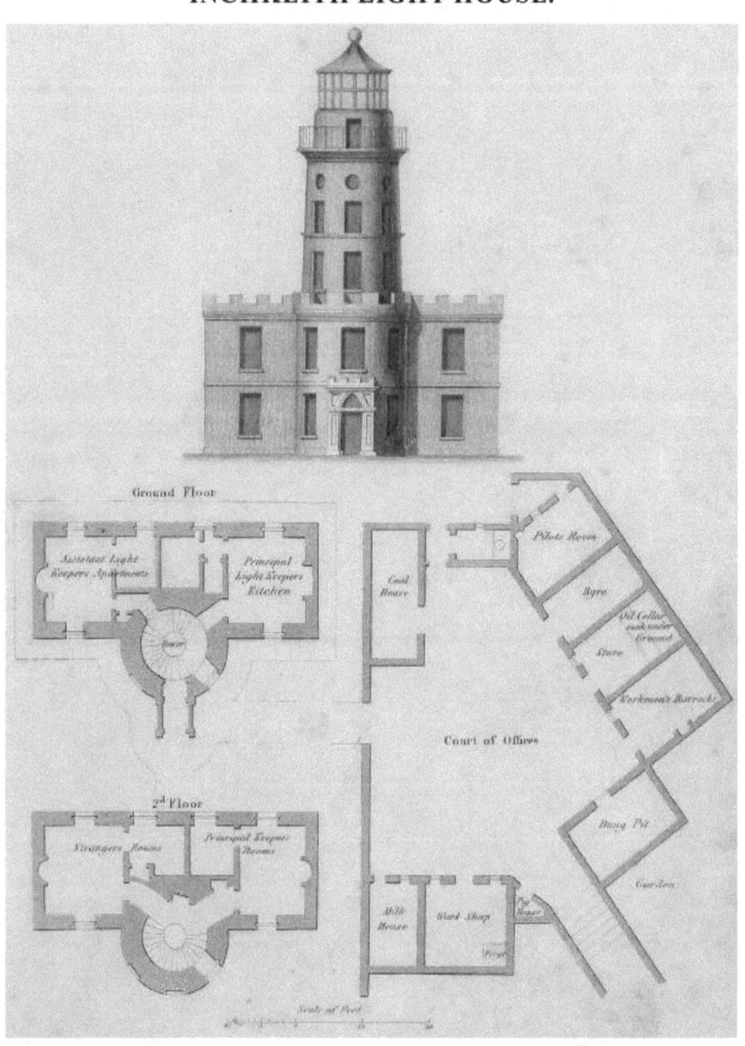

INCH KEITH LIGHT HOUSE.

Drawn by W. Lorimer

PLATE I.

The Light-house of Inchkeith, delineated on Plate I. was erected while Mr Thomas Smith, the writer's predecessor, held the situation of Engineer for the Northern Light-houses. A plan of it is given, as having been the first of these establishments erected upon the new principle; the Reflectors being illuminated with Argand-burners; the Light-room rendered completely fire-proof; and the Dwelling-house fitted for the accommodation of two keepers. But as this establishment is described in the introductory chapter, at page 24, and the names of the several apartments are marked upon the Plate, it seems unnecessary here to enter into detail.

PLATE II.
CARR ROCK BEACON.

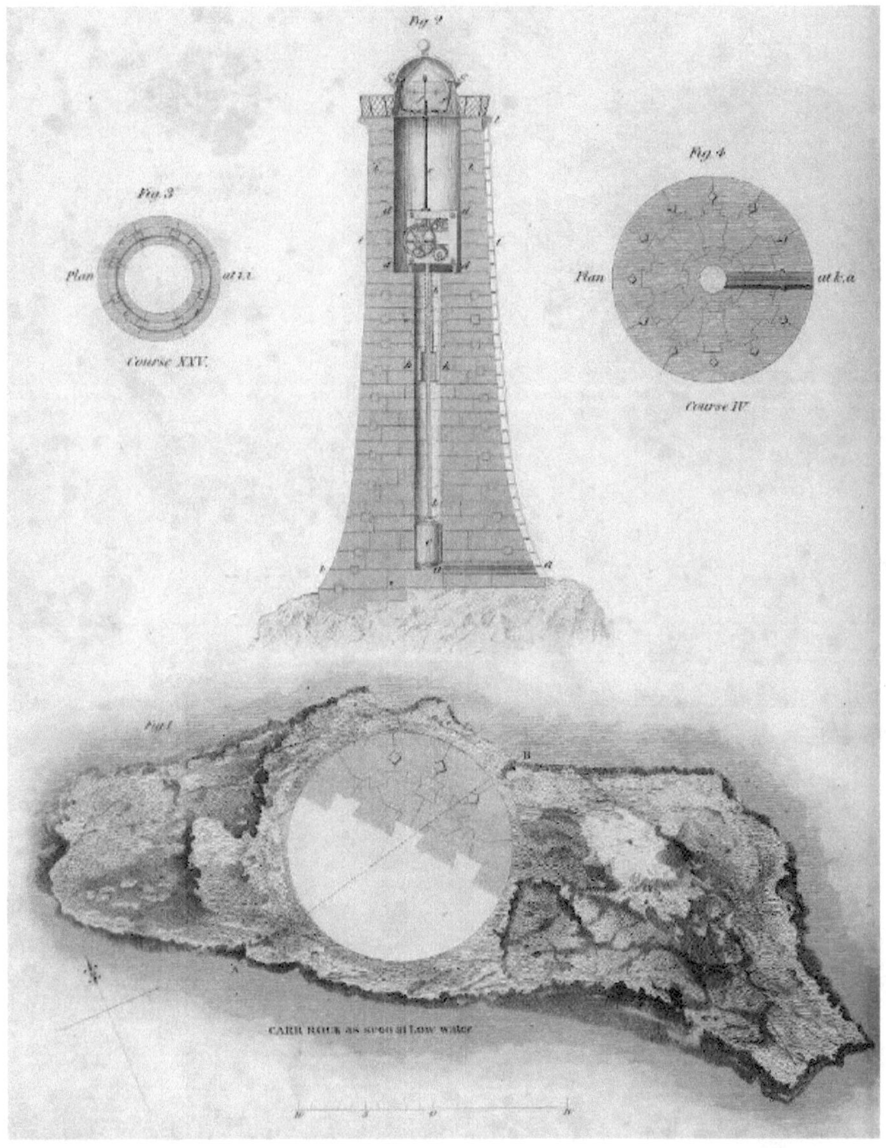

CARR ROCK BEACON AS DESIGNED IN THE YEAR 1810.

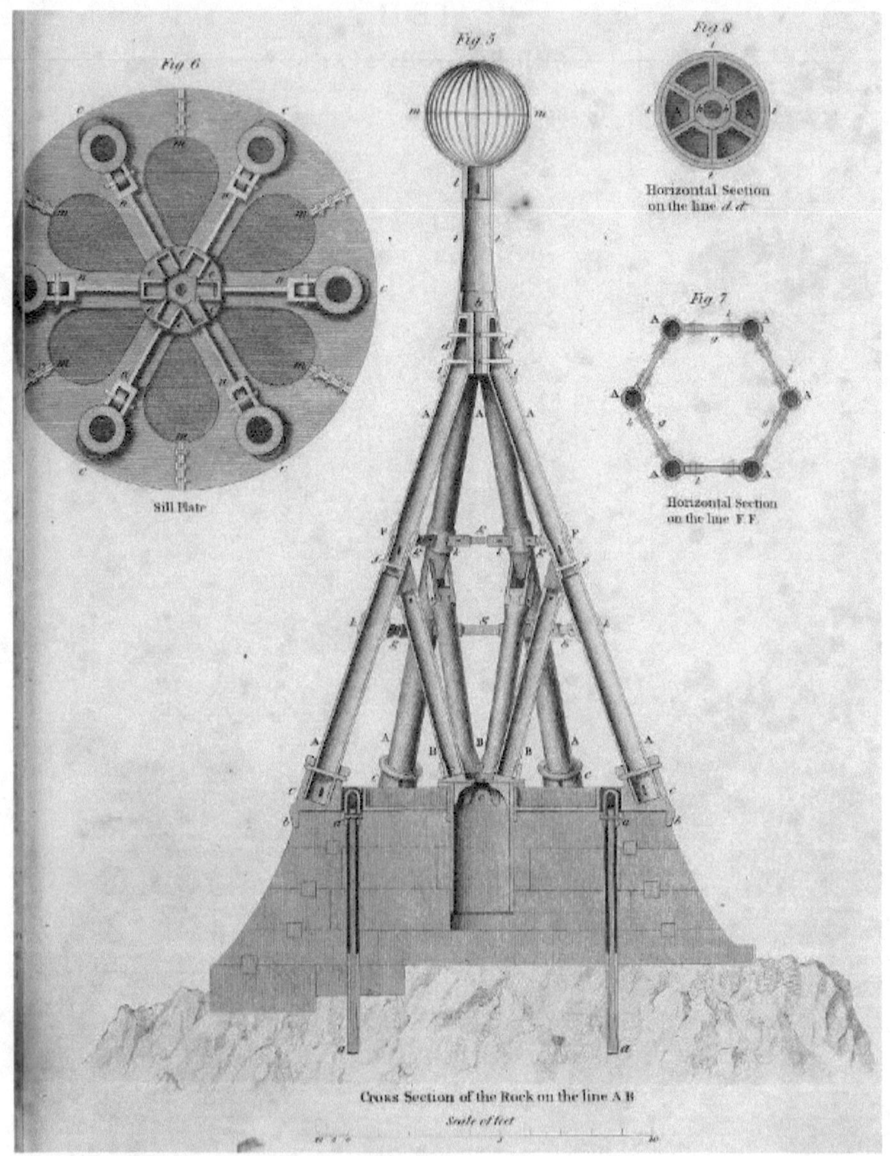

CARR ROCK BEACON AS EXECUTED IN THE YEAR 1821.

Drawn by J. Slight
Engd. by E. Mitchell

PLATE II.

Pl. II.

The Carr Rock Beacon is represented in Plate II. and referred to in the introduction at page 53. The diagram marked Figure 1. is an outline of the rock, shew-

ing the position of the beacon, and plan of the first course of the building, made to a radius of nine feet, cut in a dove-tailed form, after the manner of the courses of the Edystone and Bell Rock Light-houses.

Figure 2. is a section of the rock on the line A, B, Fig. 1. with a perpendicular section also of a tower of masonry and apparatus, for tolling an alarm-bell, which was originally intended for this situation. In Fig. 2. letter a represents an aperture measuring 3 inches in diameter, which was perforated with much labour and care through a block of granite 7 feet in length, previously to its being laid. This canal was intended to admit the tidal-waters into the interior chamber of the building marked b, in which the flood-tide was to act upon an air-tight copper-tank, marked c, and its rod of connection formed into a rack with teeth, by which motion was to be given to a train of machinery, represented at d in the void of the building. The machine was to act on the vertical shaft e, connected with a series of hammers f, placed under the great bell g, which was to have measured 5 feet in diameter, and become the cupola or roof of the building. In this manner the bell was to be tolled to forewarn the mariner of his approach to the dangers of the Carr, and the other extensive ledges of sunken rocks in its neighbourhood. By the rise of the flood-tide, and consequent admission of the waters into the canal a, the tank c, with its connecting rod, not only lifted the bell-hammers f, and, at the same time, also elevated the weight marked h, which, in its descent during ebb-tide, was to have continued the motion of the machinery; and thus, by the alternate operation of the tides, the continual tolling of the Bell was to have been preserved.

It will further be seen from the section of this building, that the masonry of the solid is connected perpendicularly by means of stone-joggles inserted half into the one course and half into the other. But in the void or upper part, instead of the joggles, the bed-joints of the stones were let or sunk about an inch in depth, into each other, as at the Bell Rock, forming so many bands or girths to the work. This will be observed by narrowly examining the section at letter i, with its accompanying diagram Fig. 3., which represents a plan of one of the courses of the void, shewing how the stones were connected horizontally by a system of dove-tailing, as is further represented in Fig. 4., being a plan of a course at the level a, k, in which the perforation is delineated for the admission of the tidal-waters.

The ascent to this building was to have been by means of a ladder of cast-iron or flight of steps, marked a, i, l, fixed on the outward wall by means of screw-bolts fixed into brass-bats, sunk into the masonry, and run up with lead. The entrance-door of this building was formed in the cast-iron frame or pedestal on which the great bell was to have been supported, the access to the interior being by the balcony, round which a cast-iron rail was intended, not only for the safety of the keepers or occasional attendants, but also, in some measure, to defend the bell from the sprays of the sea.

Figure 5. represents the Pillar-formed Beacon, as finished at the Carr Rock in the year 1821. The lower part of this diagram is a perpendicular section of the rock on the line A B, Fig. 1. The masonry is also shewn with two of the six great malleable iron-bats or stancheons marked a in Fig. 5., which passing through the several courses, are sunk about 30 inches into the Rock. The upper part of this diagram represents a frame of cast-iron work, of great strength, fashioned somewhat after the manner of what seamen term a spar or spur beacon, from being made generally of timber, set up in the form of struts or spur-beams. The connection of this frame will be understood from the detached diagram Fig. 6., taken upon the line or level marked b in Fig. 5. From Figs. 5. and 6. it will be observed, that the beacon consists of 6 pipes or hollow tubes, marked letter A, which are inserted into the sockets c, in the sill-plate of Fig. 6, into which these hollow tubes are strongly wedged and keyed with culter or spear bolts, which pass through each of the sockets and base of the hollow tubes at c. Besides the main hollow tubes marked A, other six marked B, are set up as spurs or diagonals, which radiate from sockets cast in the centre of the sill-plate marked e. These diagonals are so situated, and connected by dove-tail or hook-joints, that they butt against the main tubes, and support them at f. The main tubes are further connected by means of horizontal bars of malleable iron, marked g in Fig. 5, laid into grooves formed in the arms of the cast-iron collars F, k, which clasp around the main tubes at these points, immediately above and below their connection with the diagonal tubes. These collars are also keyed with the main tubes by means of spear-bolts. At the point of junction d d, towards the top, the main tubes form segments of a common circle, and rest upon the centre block h, into which they are keyed and wedged. As a further security, a strong cast-iron tubular formed case, marked i i, is made to clasp around the whole upper parts of the main tubes at their point of junction d d, so as to form a girth to them. This tubular case or cap i i, is 8 feet in length, and terminates with a cast-iron ball marked m m, which is 3½ feet in diameter, formed into ribs, connected with the cap i i, by means of a socket, through which a spear-bolt passes, and binds it to the top of the tubular-case at the point l.

Fig. 6. represents the Ballast-plate, which forms the sill or basement of the superstructure. It contains about 8 tons of cast-iron, and is so constructed as to become a cap or girth to the upper course of the masonry which it is calculated to secure, by means of a flange of 6 inches in depth at the outward extremity, marked b b in Fig. 5, where it is let into the stone. This plate is cast in six pieces, connected together at the points m m m m m m, by means of screw-bolts of one and a half inch in diameter (with nuts), passing through flanges raised at the joints of its several compartments. At the points n n n n n n, there were six socket-holes, for the reception of the great stancheons or bolts, marked a a, Fig. 5, which, passing through the masonry, are sunk 30 inches into the Rock, where they are fixed at the lower ends with iron-wedges, driven home by means of a long iron-driver. The ballast-plate is connected with the upper ends of these great stancheons, by means of a shackle and bolt, in such a manner that the more exposed parts may be renewed. The whole is imbedded and run up with pozzolano-mortar, so as to preserve the several parts as much as possible from the effects of oxidation.

Fig. 7. represents a horizontal section of this beacon, on the line F F, shewing the connection of the horizontal malleable iron-bars or braces g g g g, which fit into the grooves of the arms of the collars, embracing the hollow tubes or pillars A A A A, and connecting them by means of spear-bolts at k k k k. The grooves in these arms are so formed as to command the braces, and to contain a quantity of

Parker's or Roman cement, by which the bolts are preserved from the effects of oxidation. These collars and arms, with their connecting malleable iron-bars, form a girth immediately above the diagonal struts or braces B B B, Fig. 5. A similar chain of connection is in like manner formed below the junction of these diagonal struts, with the main tubes, which, like those described above, has the effect of binding the whole fabric horizontally.

Fig. 8. is a horizontal section upon the line d d, delineated upon a scale of double the size of the other parts of the beacon, shewing the connection of the hollow tubes A A A A A A, at the top, where they change their cylindrical form into segments of a circle at the point of contact, so as to embrace the centre-block h h. The top of these tubes thus formed into a compact figure, is cased or covered with the cylindrical cap i i, through which the spear-bolts immediately above and below the points d d, in Fig. 5, are made to pass and bind the whole firmly together.

PLATE III.

GENERAL CHART, SHEWING THE RELATIVE POSITION OF THE BELL ROCK.

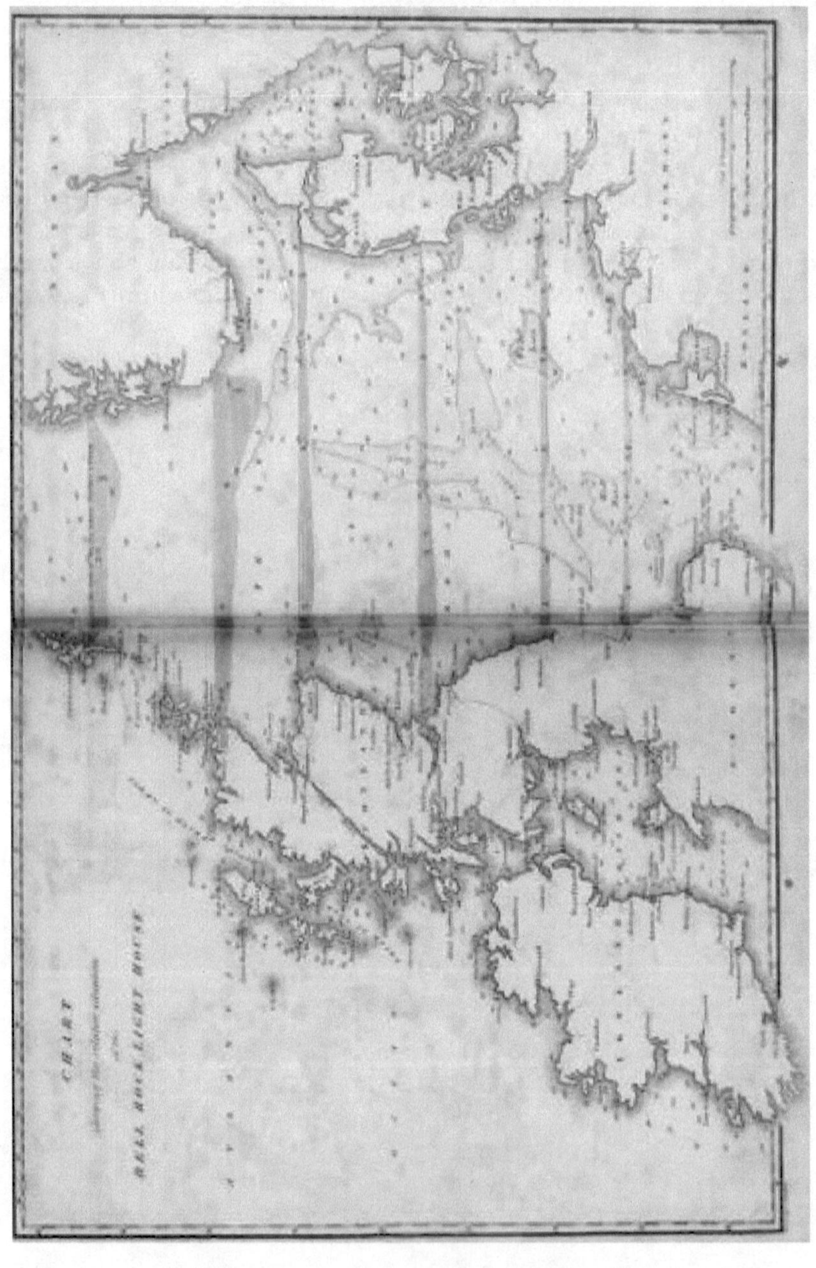

CHART SHEWING THE RELATIVE SITUATION
OF THE BELL ROCK LIGHT HOUSE.

Drawn by J. Steedman
Engd. by W. H. Lizars

Plate III.

Pl. III.

This Plate is reduced from a manuscript-map in the possession of the writer, which is drawn upon a large scale, originally intended for exhibiting the depths of the German Ocean or North Sea, and the situations of the numerous Light-houses on the coasts of the United Kingdom, and opposite Continent, but is here given with the view of shewing the relative position of the Bell Rock.

The chief peculiarity of this map is the sectional lines, exhibiting at one view the relative depths of the ocean, in connection with a theory which the writer has advanced, regarding the wasting of the firm ground by the effects of the sea, as alluded to in Appendix V. These sectional lines, of a deeper shade, are drawn across the German Ocean, from shore to shore. As, for example, between Shetland and Norway, the greatest depth is ascertained to be about 140 fathoms, and so of other examples, extending southward as far as the Straits of Dover. The soundings are all marked in fathoms, and, in so far as regards the east coast of Scotland, have been very generally made from on board of the vessels belonging to the service of the Northern Lights. The forms given to the principal sand-banks, and the soundings in the central and eastern parts of this great basin, have been taken from the best maritime surveys, and nautical authorities. The numerous Light-houses on the respective coasts are coloured; those of Scotland being blue, England red, Ireland green, and the foreign Lights yellow.

PLATE IV.
CHART, SHEWING THE PARTICULAR POSITION OF THE BELL ROCK.

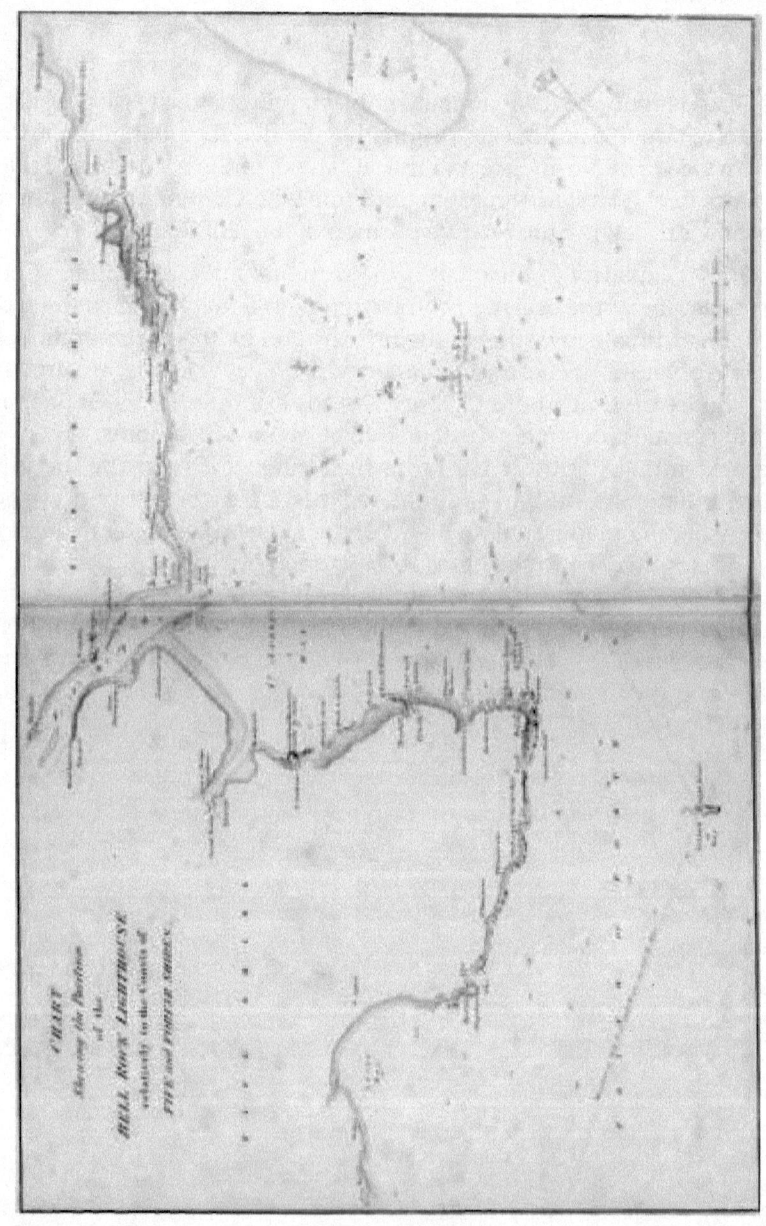

CHART SHEWING THE POSITION OF THE BELL ROCK LIGHT-HOUSE RELATIVELY TO THE COASTS OF FIFE AND FORFAR SHIRES.

Drawn by A. Stevenson

Engd. by W. H. Lizars

PLATE IV.

Pl. IV.

This chart is intended to shew the position of the Rock in reference to the opposite shores of Fife and Forfar, and to the entrances to the Friths of Forth and Tay. The most contiguous point of land, being in the immediate neighbourhood of Aberbrothwick, is distant about 11¾ miles. This chart also exhibits the depths of water, and the nature of the bottom, in the vicinity of the Rock.

PLATE V.

CHART OF THE BELL ROCK, SHEWING ITS POSITION RELATIVELY TO THE SHIPPING EMPLOYED AT THE WORK.

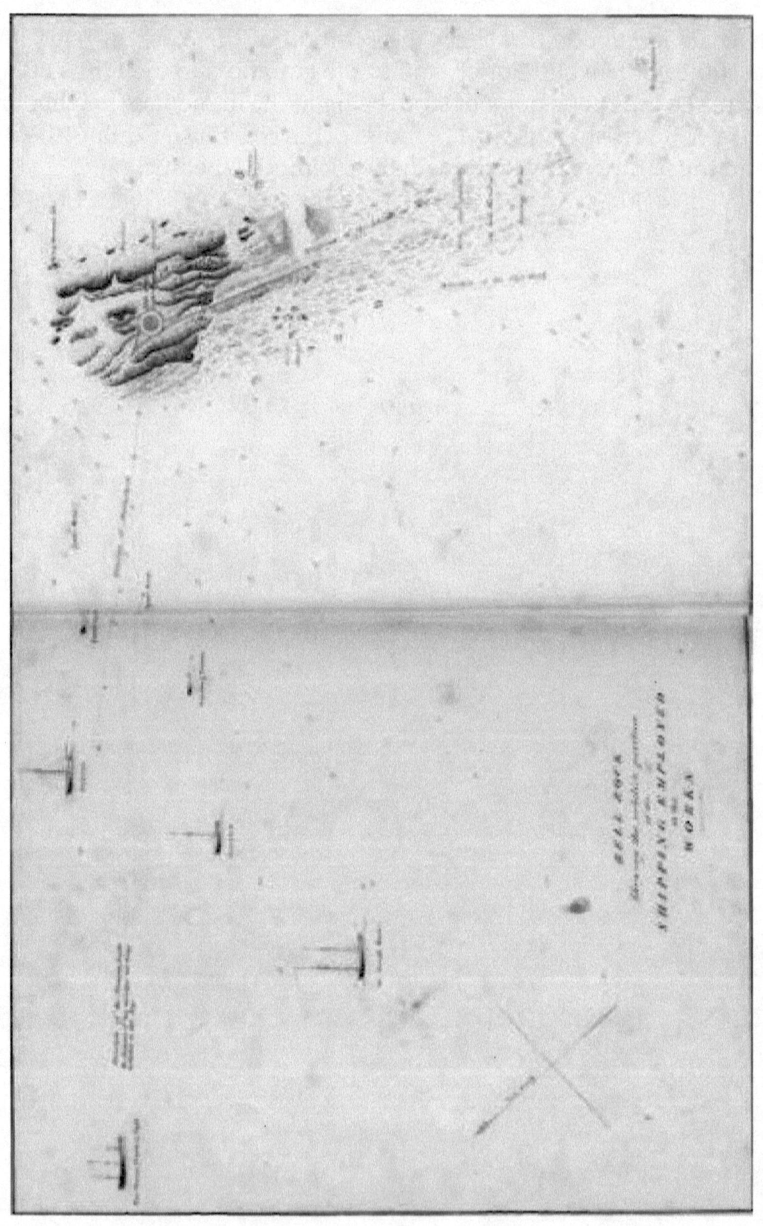

BELL ROCK SHEWING THE RELATIVE POSITION OF THE SHIP-PING EMPLOYED AT THE WORKS

Drawn by J. Steedman

Engd. by W. H. Lizars

PLATE V.

Pl. V.

This Plate represents the Rock at low-water of spring-tides, when that part of it which extends about 1000 feet in a south-western direction from the Light-house, may be traced by the appearance of some detached portions of rock, but chiefly from the sea-weeds which float at the surface of the water. Its greatest extent, in a north-eastern and south-western direction, is about 1400 feet, and in a south-eastern and a north-western direction about 240 feet.

King George III.—This is an insulated rock which lies towards the south-eastern extremity of the Main or House Rock, and has been named in reference to the reign in which the Light-house was erected.

King James V.—is also a detached rock, forming the south-western extremity of the reef, which extends from the House-rock, and is named in reference to that Monarch's memorable voyage round his dominions, about the year 1540, as alluded to in the Introduction, at page 4.

On the north-western side of the Rock, as nearly as may be, the figures of the respective vessels employed at the work are delineated, and the positions of their moorings laid down; with the exception of those of the Pharos Floating-light, whose bearing or direction is only to be understood, as the full distance at which she was ultimately moored would fall beyond the limits of the Plate. The house-part of the Rock is left bare at low-water of ordinary spring-tides, and at high-water of these tides it is from 10 to 12 feet under water; but during the storms of winter, the sea generally breaks over the whole surface of the rock, so as to render walking upon it impracticable, even in the lowest ebbs; while at high water, the sprays fly over the building, or rise to a height of upwards of 100 feet. The reef, which extends in a south-western direction from the House-rock, contains many Travellers or large boulder-stones; affording a proof that the Bell Rock has at one time been of greater dimensions than at present, and these detached stones may be regarded as part of the debris, which have been separated in the lapse of ages from the main Rock.

PLATE VI.

PLAN OF THE NORTH EASTERN PARTS OF THE BELL ROCK, SHEWING THE POSITION OF THE LIGHT-HOUSE, RAILWAYS, AND WHARFS, &C.

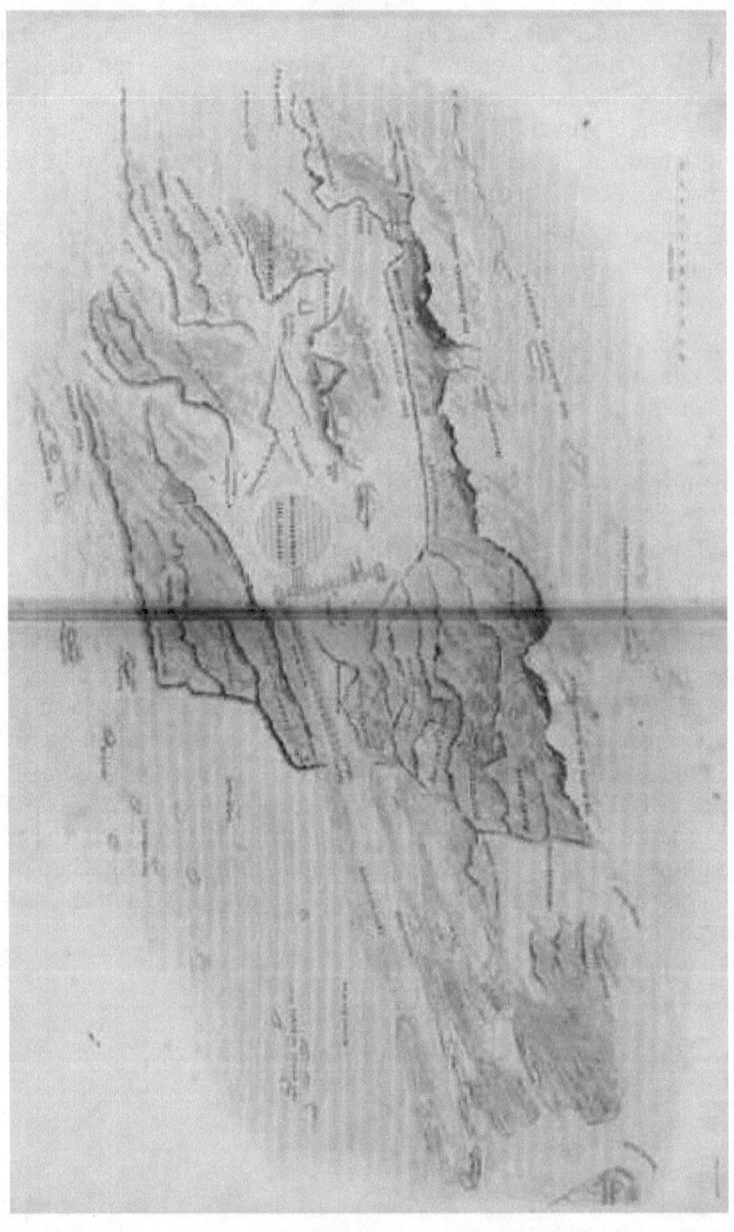

NORTH EASTERN PARTS OF THE BELL ROCK SHEWING THE PO-SITION OF THE LIGHT HOUSE, RAILWAYS, WHARFS, &C.

Drawn by G. C. Scott

Engd. by E. Mitchell

PLATE VI.

Pl. VI.

The description of this Plate, representing the higher parts of the Rock as seen at low-water of spring-tides, affords the writer an opportunity of mentioning many distinguished names connected either officially, or in a friendly manner, with the erection of the Light-house. In corresponding about the state of the Rock, he has often found the advantage of this particular nomenclature of its different parts, as affording a reference to all its localities.

Site of the Light-House, and Railway-Tracks.—The site of the Light-house, which will be seen from the Plate, was fixed by the writer in a central position of what may be termed the House-Rock. From this, as a centre, the Railways ramify in various directions. Upon these the materials for the erection of the house were conveyed, and they are still partly preserved, as convenient foot-paths and wharfs, in landing stores for the Light-house. The portions of the Railway-tracks marked with light dotted lines, were only used during the continuation of the works; while those of a deeper shade represent the permanent railways.

Site of Captain Brodie's Beacon.—The late Captain Joseph Brodie, of the Royal Navy, was perhaps not less known to the public as the fortunate bearer of Lord Duncan's dispatches announcing the victory obtained by the British fleet off Camperdown, than for his unwearied exertions in keeping up the interest of the public, relative to the important results to navigation which would attend the erection of a Light-house upon the Bell Rock, of which notice is taken at page 88.

Site of Mr Stevenson's Beacon.—The position of the Beacon or temporary erection delineated in Plate VIII., was fixed upon the southern side of the site of the Light-house, with the ultimate view of obtaining shelter from the breach of the north-east seas. It was farther important, for the conveniency it afforded of a communication during the progress of the works, by means of a wooden bridge, which will be understood by examining Plate XVIII.

Haldane's Ledge—is situate on the south-eastern side of the Rock, where the writer made his first landing with his friend Mr James Haldane, architect, as noticed at page 91.

Gray's Rock.—Toward the eastern side of the Rock, there is a small outlier, or reef, important as a low-water-mark, which is named Gray's Rock, in compliment to the late Mr John Gray, Writer to the Signet, and the first Secretary to the Light-house Board, as noticed in the Introduction, page 5.

Smith's Rock,—situate on the eastern side of the Light-house, derives its name from the late Mr Thomas Smith, who introduced Reflecting-Lights upon the coast of Scotland; and was the first Engineer to the Board, as noticed at page 7.

Cuningham's Ledge.—This ledge of rock has its name from Mr Charles Cuningham, Writer to the Signet, and successor to Mr Gray, as Secretary and Cashier to the Light-house Board.

Port Hamilton.—This creek is situate at the south-eastern extremity of the House-rock, and derives its name from Mr Robert Hamilton, Sheriff of Lanarkshire, and ex officio one of the Commissioners of the Northern Light-houses; who first landed here in the year 1805, accompanied by Mr Rennie and the writer, with a view further to ascertain the practicability of erecting the proposed Light-house, as noticed at page 95. Mr Hamilton has been a zealous member of the Bell Rock Committee since the period of its institution in the year 1807, and, from his literary habits, he has taken much interest in the pages of this work.

Port Rennie—is situate in the north-eastern part of the House-rock, and derives its name from the late Mr John Rennie, the celebrity and extent of whose works as a Civil Engineer are well known to the public. Mr Rennie was consulted by the Light-house Board relative to this work. His reports will be found in Appendix, No. IV.; and his plan in Plate VII.

Port Stevenson—enters from the north-eastern side of the Rock, and forms the principal landing-place in that direction; it was named for the writer by Mr Hamilton, at the landing above alluded to, in the year 1805.

The Abbot's Ledge—forms the north-western extremity of the House-rock, and derives its name from a tradition (for we can find no authentic record) of one of the Abbots of Aberbrothwick having erected an Alarm-bell, to forewarn mariners of their danger in approaching the Bell Rock.

Sir Ralph the Rover's Ledge—forms the south-western extremity of the House-rock, and takes the name of Sir Ralph the Rover from a noted pirate who is said to have landed upon it, and carried away the Alarm-bell. This traditionary story is beautifully alluded to in a ballad by Mr Southey in his Minor Poems, which, with his permission, is included in Appendix, No. II. page 438.

Dunnichen Ledge,—on the north-western side of the Rock, is named in compliment to Mr Dempster of Dunnichen, who is mentioned in the Introduction, page 5.

Dunskey Ledge,—which is contiguous to the former, is named in compliment to Sir James Hunter Blair of Dunskey, first Preses of the Commissioners of the Northern Light-houses, as mentioned at page 6.

Arniston Ledge.—Named in compliment to the late Lord Chief-Baron Dundas of Arniston, who, while Solicitor-General and Lord Advocate of Scotland, took an active part in Light-house affairs; and visited the Bell Rock in the year 1812, as noticed at page 413.

Rattray Ledge.—In compliment to Mr Baron Clerk Rattray, who, while Sheriff of the Shire of Edinburgh, as noticed at page 98, was ex officio one of the Commissioners of the Northern Light-houses, and, as one of the Bell Rock Committee, took much interest in the work.

Hope's Wharf—forms the termination of the permanent railway toward the west. It was named for the Right Honourable Charles Hope, Lord President of the Court of Session, who landed here in the year 1815. While Lord Advocate of Scotland, he took a warm interest in the affairs of the Northern Light-houses, and in 1803 brought the first bill into Parliament for the erection of the Bell Rock Light-house, as noticed at page 93.

Pulteney Ledge.—So named in compliment to Sir William Pulteney, who, as a Member of Parliament, took a lively interest in the bill brought forward for the Bell Rock Light-house in the year 1803, as alluded to at page 92.

Banks Ledge.—Named in compliment to Sir Joseph Banks, who was Vice-President of the Board of Trade in the year 1806, when the Bill for the Light-house was in Parliament, and who took much interest in it, as noticed at page 101.

Cochrane's Ledge—is named in compliment to Admiral Sir Alexander Cochrane, who first called the attention of the Light-house Board to an erection upon the Bell Rock, as mentioned at page 85.

Port Erskine—forms the principal landing-place on the western side of the Rock, and derives its name from the Honourable Henry Erskine, who, when Lord Advocate of Scotland, and ex officio one of the Commissioners of the Northern Light-houses, brought the second Bill for the Bell Rock Light-house into Parliament, which passed in the year 1806, as stated at page 100.

Ulbster Ledge.—Named in compliment to the Right Honourable Sir John Sinclair, Baronet, of Ulbster, Chairman of the Committee of the House of Commons, and who brought up its report relative to the Bell Rock bill, as stated at page 103.

Kellie Ledge.—Named in compliment to the Earl of Kellie, who visited the works at the Bell Rock in the year 1810, as noticed at page 378.

Pitmilly Wharf—formed the western extremity of the landing-wharf in use during the Light-house operations, and was named in compliment to Mr Monypenny, now Lord Pitmilly, who, while in the commission both as Sheriff of Fife and Solicitor-General of Scotland, was a member of the Bell Rock Committee, and visited the works in the year 1810, as stated at page 378.

Kinedder Ledge—is named in compliment to the late Mr William Erskine, Sheriff of Orkney and Shetland, and a member of the Bell Rock Committee. From Mr Erskine's literary pursuits, he took a lively interest in this work, before he left the Light-house Board, and also after he was raised to the Bench, where he took his seat as Lord Kinedder.

The Abbotsford.—This spot, where the waters of the two principal and opposite landing-places meet, is named in compliment to Sir Walter Scott, Baronet, of Abbotsford, who landed here in the year 1814, as noticed at page 419, when he wrote the beautiful and expressive lines inserted in a fac-simile of his handwriting in the 2d Title-page.

Rae's Wharf—forms the extremity of the southern reach of the permanent railway, and derives its name from Sir William Rae, Baronet, who, in the several capacities of Sheriff-Depute and Lord Advocate of Scotland, has long been a member of the Light-house Board and Bell Rock Committee. His Lordship visited the Rock in 1810, as noticed at page 387.

Duff's Wharf—derives its name from Mr Adam Duff, Sheriff of the shire of

Edinburgh, and a member of the Bell Rock Committee, who repeatedly visited the works at the Bell Rock while in progress, particularly in the year 1810, as noticed at page 387.

Port Boyle—takes its name from the Right Honourable David Boyle, Lord Justice-Clerk, who, while Solicitor-General of Scotland, was a member of the Bell Rock Committee, and visited the Light-house in the year 1811, as noticed at page 411.

The Crown Lawyers.—This name is given to two detached rocks, which lie on the south-eastern side of the House-rock, in allusion to the Lord Advocate and Solicitor-General of Scotland, who are ex officio Commissioners of the Northern Light-houses, as noticed at page 6.

The Maritime Sheriffs.—This name comprehends a range of rocks, also on the south-eastern side of the main Rock, in reference to the Sheriffs of maritime counties, who are ex officio Commissioners of the Northern Light-houses, as noticed at page 6.

The Royal Burghs,—A group of rocks lying on the south-western side of the House-rock, so named from certain of the Chief Magistrates of the Royal Burghs of Scotland who are ex officio Commissioners of the Northern Light-houses, as noticed at page 6.

Telford's Ledge—is named in compliment to Mr Thomas Telford, Civil Engineer, who was requested by Sir William Pulteney to visit the Bell Rock professionally in the year 1803, as noticed at page 92.

Downie's Ledge—derives its name from the late Mr Murdoch Downie, a Marine Surveyor of considerable eminence, who suggested a plan for erecting a Light-house on the Bell Rock, as noticed at page 93.

Neill's Pool—derives its name from Mr Patrick Neill, a particular friend of the writer's, who first visited the Bell Rock in 1808, as noticed at page 235. The surface of this pool measures about three fathoms across, and a fathom and a half in depth, when the tide leaves the Rock. The bottom is generally covered with boulder-stones, which are whirled about with much force when the sea is in a state of agitation.

Stuart's Track—is on the south-western side of the Rock, derives its name from the late Captain Harry Stuart of the Royal Navy, who visited the Bell Rock in the year 1810, as alluded to at page 387. Captain Stuart took an early interest in the plans for the Light-house, both by Captain Brodie and the writer.

Bruce's Ledge—was named in compliment to the memory of the late Mr James Bruce of the Naval Yard, Leith, who frequently visited the Bell Rock, and to whose ingenuity the Light-house service is indebted for the improved construction of a boat, delineated in Plate XI. and noticed at page 412.

Russell's Ledge—is named in compliment to Mr Claud Russell, Accountant to the Light-house Board, who visited the Rock in the year 1812, as mentioned in page 414.

Scoresby's Point,—the most northern part of the Rock, named in compliment to the writer's friend Captain Scoresby junior, who has so much extended our information regarding the Polar Regions.

Trinity Rock.—This rock is named in compliment to a Committee of the Trinity House of Leith, consisting of Messrs Thomas Grindlay, John Hay, and Thomas Ritchie, who gave their advice and assistance in the fitting out and mooring the Floating-light in the year 1807, as alluded to at page 110.

Balfour's Ledge—is named in compliment to the late Provost Balfour of Arbroath, who felt the most lively interest in the Light-house affairs. In his hospitable mansion the writer occasionally resided while the works were in progress.

Leitch's Ledge—is named in compliment to the writer's friend Mr Quintin Leitch, who visited the Rock in the year 1818. Mr Leitch is further noticed at page 43.

Pillans's Ledge—is named in compliment to the writer's friend Mr James Pillans of Leith, who took an early interest in the erection of the Light-house, and who signs the Report of the Merchants of Leith regarding it, as noticed at page 96.

The Last Hope.—This name was given by the writer to the highest part of the rock, in allusion to the narrow escape which he and the artificers made in the year 1807, by the timeous arrival of James Spink, the Bell Rock pilot at Arbroath, as noticed at page 149. Spink is a remarkably strong man, whose tout ensemble is highly characteristic of a North-country fisherman. He usually dresses in a pé-jacket, cut after a particular fashion, and wears a large flat blue bonnet. A striking likeness of Spink, in his pilot-dress, with the badge or insignia on his left arm, which is characteristic of the boatmen in the service of the Northern Lights has been taken by Howe, and is in the writer's possession.

Forrest's Passage.—This gully or opening on the eastern side of the Rock, is sometimes taken as a track by boats in certain states of the sea and tide. It derives its name from the late Mr John Forrest, Superintendant of Lightkeepers' duty in the service of the Northern Lights, who is particularly noticed at page 406.

Logans' Reach.—This reach or compartment of the Railway, on the eastern side of the Light-house, is named in compliment to the late Mr Peter Logan, foreman-builder at the Bell Rock, and his son Mr David Logan, clerk-of-works, whose active and faithful services, in their respective departments, have been too often noticed in this work to admit of reference to particular pages.

Watt's Reach—has its name in compliment to Mr Francis Watt, foreman-millwright, whose services have also already been often particularised in the course of this work, and whose exertions in erecting the beacon and temporary-railways did much credit to his zeal and intrepidity. The writer also often profited by his ingenuity, in reference to the various pieces of machinery employed at the works.

Kennedy's Reach—derives its name from Mr Lachlan Kennedy, who, as Accountant and Cashier in the Engineer's Office, discharged the various duties of his situation in a manner equally creditable to himself and satisfactory to his employers. An Abstract-Account of the expence of the work, as drawn up by him, appears in the Appendix, No. VII. page 475.

Slights' Reach,—named in compliment to Mr James Slight, and his brother Alexander, who were chiefly employed in drawing the courses of the building at large, and in making the various and nicely formed moulds for fashioning the stones. They also fitted up the interior of the house, and the permanent railways on the rock; and made a complete model of the Light-house.

The Smiths' Forge and Ledge—named in compliment to Mr James Dove, foreman-smith, and his assistants, who have been frequently alluded to in these pages. It was here that the forge was erected at the commencement of the works on the Rock; and on the connecting ledge the first or experimental cargo of stones was landed.

Reid's Ledge—is named in compliment to Mr John Reid, the first principal Lightkeeper at the Bell Rock, who retired from the service in the year 1821, as noticed at page 422.

Selkirks' Ledge,—named for Mr Robert Selkirk, principal builder, and his brother Thomas, who was the principal stone-cutter at the work.

Wishart's Ledge—is named for Mr Michael Wishart, some time principal builder at the Rock, as noticed at page 291.

Glen's Ledge.—This ledge has its name from Mr James Glen, millwright and joiner, particularly noticed at page 279.

John Watt.—A detached rock on the western side of the main rock, named for John Watt, principal mortar-maker at the Bell Rock.

Peter Fortune.—A detached reef on the western side of the Rock, named for a well known character in the Light-house service, as noticed at page 299.

Gloag's Track—leads into Port Hamilton, and is named for Mr Robert Gloag, who commanded the Light-house Yacht in the year 1807, and who has otherwise had a good deal of connection with the Light-house service.

Macurich's Track—on the western side of the Rock, is named in compliment to Mr Thomas Macurich, mate of the sloop Smeaton, and afterwards commander of the Bell Rock Tender, who had a very narrow escape in a boat off the Rock, as noticed at page 253.

Webb's Rock—is named in compliment to Mr Joseph Webb, one of the King's pilots at Yarmouth, who superintended the fitting out and mooring of the Floating-light, as noticed at page 108.

Sinclair's Track—is named in compliment to Mr George Sinclair, who, in 1807, commanded the Floating-light, and acted as landing-master.

Wilson's Track—named for Mr James Wilson, landing-master, whose active and enterprising conduct is often noticed in the course of this work. In the year 1815, Mr Wilson left the Light-house service, when he was appointed one of the Harbour-masters of Leith. The speaking-trumpet which he used at the Bell Rock was presented to him, with the sanction of the Light-house Board, when a suitable inscription was engraved on a plate of silver attached to it.

Taylor's Track—leads into Port Erskine, and derives its name from Mr David Taylor, who commanded the Sir Joseph Banks Tender during the progress of the works, and afterwards became Light-house Storekeeper at Leith.

Calder's Track—situate on the north-western side of the Rock, derives its name from Mr Thomas Calder, who commanded the Light-house Yacht, and other craft, connected with the works, as noticed at page 260.

Soutar's Track—derives its name from Mr Peter Soutar, who was one of the Praam-masters while the works were in progress. In 1815 he succeeded Mr James Wilson in the command of the Light-house Yacht.

Pool's Track—is named for Mr Robert Pool, commander of the Smeaton stone-lighter, a very active and persevering seaman.

The Engineers' Ledge,—situate on the eastern side of the Rock, is named in compliment to certain of the Engineer's assistants, who, though belonging more especially to his general or private business, have nevertheless been occasionally employed in the department of the Bell Rock, particularly Mr John Steedman, Mr John Thin, Mr William Lorimer, Mr G. C. Scott, and Mr Robert Shortreed, some of whose names are attached to several of the Plates.

The Artificers.—A name given to a parcel of detached rocks, lying on the north-western side of the main Rock, in allusion to the numerous artificers employed at the works, many of whom are now moving in spheres of more extended usefulness, and, did our limits admit, would be deserving of particular notice, as may be learned from page 379.

The Mariners.—This is also a group of detached rocks on the north-eastern side of the Rock, which in like manner is named in compliment to the exertions of the Seamen, who, as men-of-all-works, gave a helping hand to every operation; and many of whom deserve the warmest acknowledgments of the writer.

Strachan's Ledge,—situate on the north-eastern side of the Rock, was named for Mr Robert Strachan of Leith, who fitted out the Floating-light, and narrowly escaped being lost upon the Rock, when approaching it in a boat which was upset in the year 1808, as noticed at page 244.

Craw's Horse.—Another detached rock, deriving its name from a narrow escape which the sloop Smeaton made in foggy weather, as noticed at page 364, while James Craw, who had charge of the stable, and was principal carter at the work-yard of Arbroath, was on board, with his favourite horse, on his way to Leith, to convey the upper part of the Light-house, from Edinburgh, to be shipped for the Bell Rock. The horse alluded to was a remarkably strong and powerful animal, measuring about 16 hands in height, and having, in the language of jockies, a great deal of bone. It is not a little remarkable, that while the work was in progress, this animal must actually have drawn the materials of the Light-house, extending to upwards of 2000 tons in its finished state, perhaps three or four times, in removing the blocks of stone from the ship to the work-yard, again to the platform, and from the work-yard, when they were to be shipped for the Rock, besides occasional movements to and from the hands of the stone-cutters. A sketch of this animal, and of his master James Craw, will be found at Fig. 21. Plate X. The horse having failed from age, towards the close of the work he was removed to the Island of Inchkeith, to go at large, where he died in the year 1813. The fame of this animal's labours, together with his strength and excellent proportion as a draught-horse, having attracted the notice of Dr John Barclay, that eminent anatomist procured the bones, and set them up in his Museum. This valuable collection, it is understood, is to be bequeathed to the College of Surgeons of Edinburgh; so that the bones of the Bell Rock-horse, to use the Doctor's own language, "will be seen and admired as a useful skeleton, and a source of instruction, when those of his employers lie mingled with the dust."

PLATE VII.

ORIGINAL DESIGNS FOR THE BELL ROCK LIGHT-HOUSE.

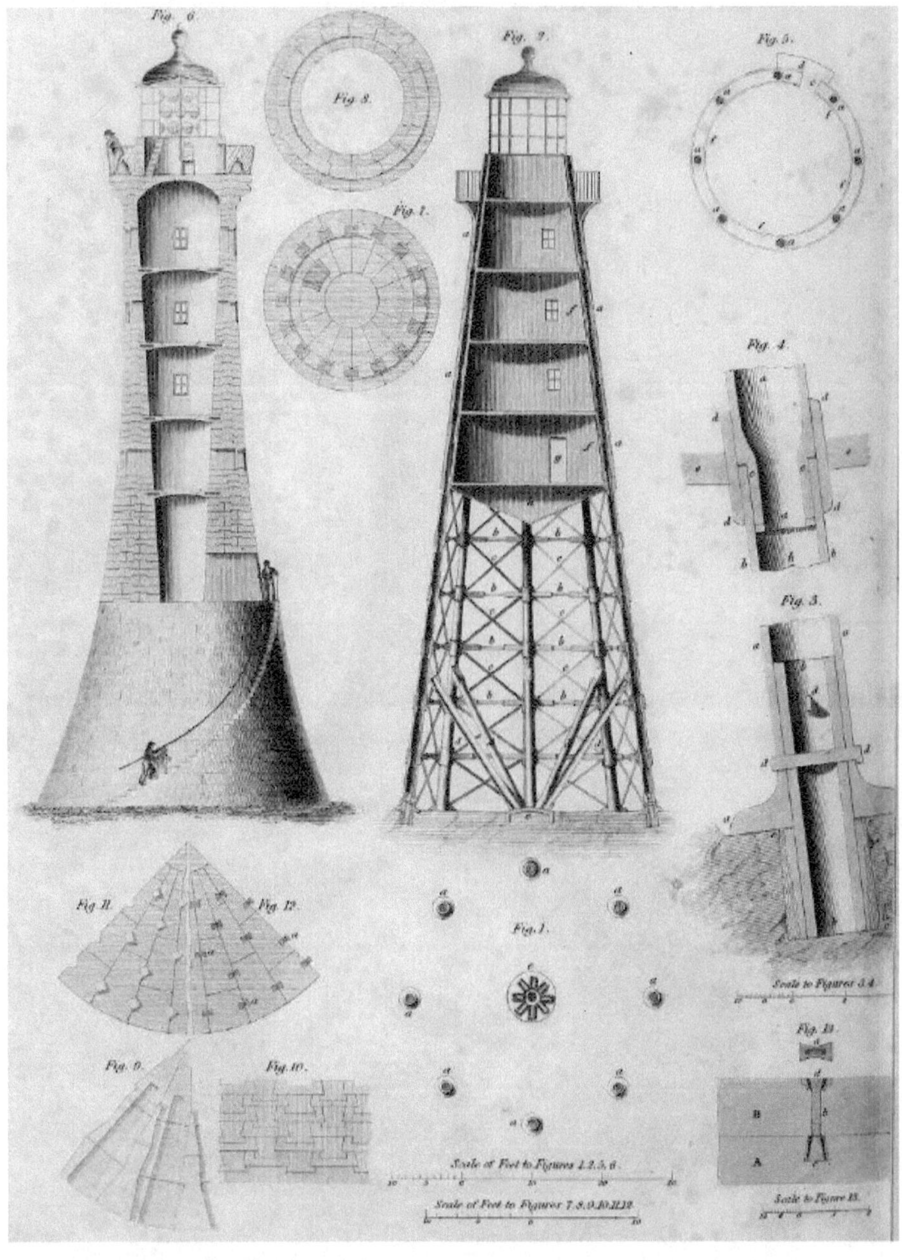

DESIGNS FOR THE BELL ROCK LIGHT HOUSE BY MR. STEVEN-SON.

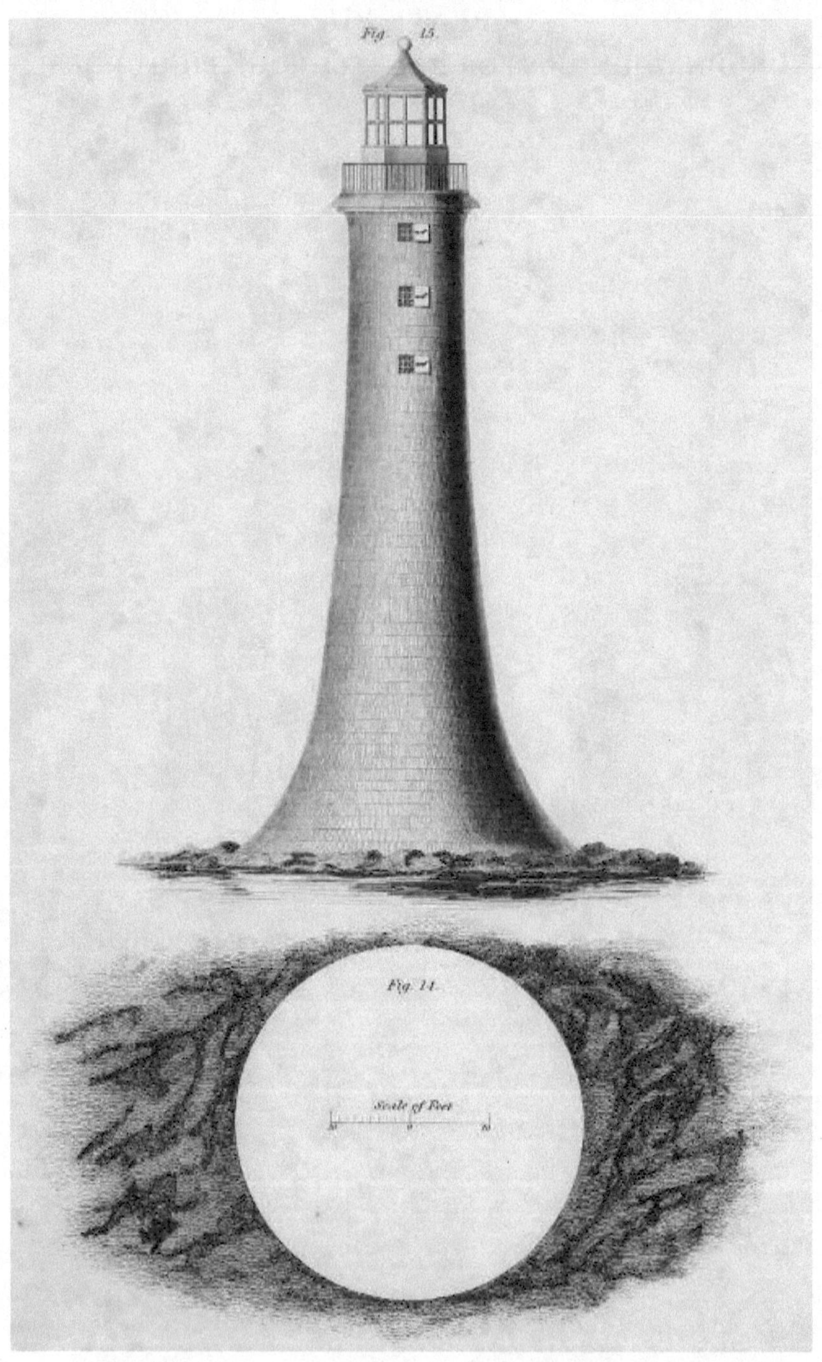

DESIGN FOR THE BELL ROCK LIGHT HOUSE BY MR. RENNIE.

Drawn by J. Slight

Engraved by R. Scott

PLATE VII.

Pl. VII.

Fig. 1. shews the sites of the principal and diagonal supports of cast-iron of the Pillar-formed Light-house, modelled by the writer prior to his landing on the Rock in the year 1800, as alluded to in his report, included in the Appendix, No. IV. at page 440. This Figure is a Plan in which letters a a a a a a a a point out the feet of the eight principal columns; e the central shoe or socket, intended to receive the feet of the diagonal supports or braces, which correspond in number with those of the main columns. This fabric, at the base, was to form a common diameter of about 35 feet, diminishing to 12 feet at the top, or immediately under the Light-room.

Fig. 2. The great columns in this design, which are sunk into the Rock, and the diagonal braces d d d d, which butt against, or step into the shoe c, are also strongly connected by the braces b b b b b b b b, and cross ties marked c c c c c c. The habitable part of this building is formed by two concentric rings of copper, marked a f, a f, the one upon the outside, and the other upon the inside, of the main columns. The space between these rings was to be filled with plaster-of-Paris, or some light substance, to render the apartments air-tight. Letter g is the position of the entrance-door, and the space below the first floor, marked h, is a coal magazine. The better to throw off the sprays of the sea, the lower part, as will be seen from the diagram, is of a conical form inverted.

Fig. 3. Shews the mode of fixing the principal columns, to the Rock, and of building or connecting them together, being an enlarged section of the foot of one of the main columns. The hollow cylindrical tube marked b b, is sunk 24 inches, and acts as a steady pin or joggle to the column which is wedged into the Rock, as shewn at c c c c, by driving oaken and iron wedges alternately, instead of running them up with melted lead. The next length of the column, marked a a a a, is slipped over this tube, and has a seat cut in the rock at right angles to the oblique direction of the column, to which it is connected by the cutter or spear-bolts marked d d d, whose directions respectively cross each other, as shewn in the section.

Fig. 4. represents one of the joints of the main columns, which occur at every 7 feet of their length, from the rock to the habitable part of the Light-house. This description of joint is what is technically termed spigot and faucet; a a is the upper half, b b b the lower, c c the joint, d d d d the collar-piece clasping the joint, and connecting it with the horizontal arms or braces e e, which, in Fig. 2, are marked b, and in connection with the cross ties c, and diagonal-supports d, bind the whole firmly together.

Fig. 5. represents the lower floor of the five apartments, in which a a a a a a a a, as in the foregoing Figs. 1, 2, and 3. shew the main columns passing between the outer covering and inner lining of copper. Letter c marks the entrance door, shewn at g, in Fig. 2., in which d is the plat at the top of the ladder, formed on one of the columns, which may also be conceived as passing up through the habitable part of the building; the floors of which are formed with plates of cast-iron.

Fig. 6. represents a Light-house of masonry, modelled by the writer immediately after his first landing upon the Rock. The better to illustrate this design, the solid or lower part is given in elevation, and the upper or habitable part in section. Compared with the Edystone Light-house, upon the principles of which it was designed, the chief differences consist in the exterior spiral-formed stair, intended to afford permanent access to the Light-house, and also to serve as a landing quay or wharf at high-water. The steps of this stair were to be 3 feet in length, forming a kind of scarsement upon the outer-wall, there being nothing to obstruct the force of the sea under the stair; as it formed part of the main-wall, it may be conceived calculated to have become a kind of spiral buttress to the building. In the upper or habitable part, the interior walls diminish gradually, instead of forming abrupt scarsements, and the floors were laid horizontally, instead of being arched.

Fig. 7. Shews one of the floors, each stone of which forms part of the outward walls, extending inwards to a centre stone, independently of which they were to be connected, by means of copper-batts, with a view to preserve their square form at the extremity, instead of dove-tailing. These stones were also modelled with joggles sidewise, upon the principles of the common-floor, termed Feathering in carpentry; and also with dove-tailed joggles across the joints, where they formed part of the outward wall, as shewn in this figure.

Fig. 8. is a plan of one of the courses of the void or habitable part of this design, shewing both the joggles of the end joint and the girth, raised upon the upper beds of the courses, and sunk into the groove cut in the lower beds of the respective covering courses.

Figs. 9. and 10. exhibit different modes of connecting the stones and courses of the solid of the building, both perpendicularly and horizontally, by means of dove-tailing. But as a certain degree of weakness is unavoidably incident to every system of dove-tailing, and, as the method of forming the bed-joints of the void above alluded to is equally effective, in its application to the solid or lower part of the building, as represented in Plate XXIII., this is considered preferable to the dove-tailing system.

Fig. 11. is part of a course, shewing a simple mode of connecting the stones in water-buildings, so as to avoid dove-tailing, and preserve, as much as possible, the entire figure of the stones. This is effected by inserting square joggles into the joints, and allowing these joggles to project 6 inches into the course immediately above, thereby forming a connection horizontally between the stones of a course, and vertically with the several courses.

Fig. 12. is also a course of masonry, in which the square or entire form of the materials is preserved, while the stones are bound both horizontally and vertically, by means of metallic-batts and plates, as represented in the enlarged diagram described in the following Figure.

Fig. 13., a is the dove-tailed cross-head or plate; b is a section both of the batt and plate, in their places, shewing their connection with two courses of the building marked A B; c shews the mode in which the batt is fixed into the lower course, by means of wedges; d the upper end of the batt and plate, which is also wedged, and appears, when in its place, as in Fig. 11., marked also a a a. But these several modes of connecting the materials of masonry are considered more or less objectionable, when compared with the girths delineated in the design represented in Plate XXIII.

Figs. 14. and 15. are a reduced plan and elevation of the Bell Rock Light-house by Mr Rennie, in the year 1807. They will be found so obvious upon inspection, as not to require explanation, and are here preserved as the only plans or drawings furnished for this work by that eminent engineer.

PLATE VIII.

BEACON-HOUSE.

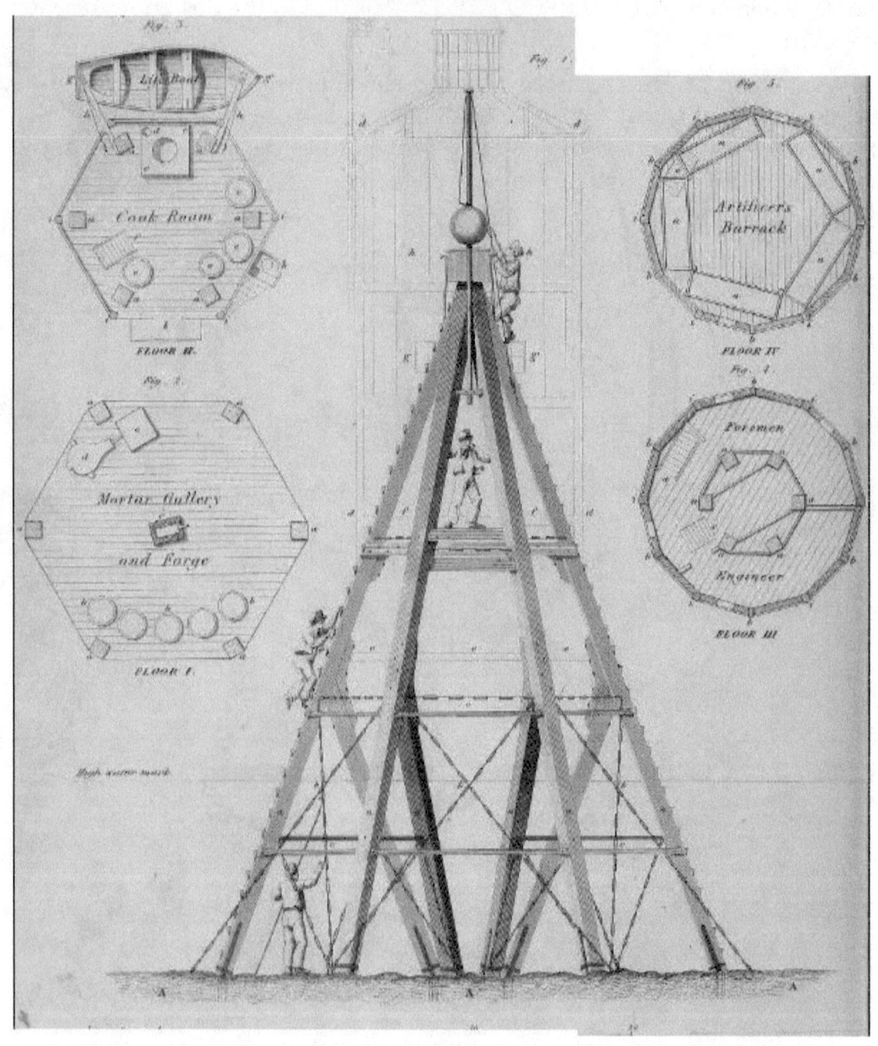

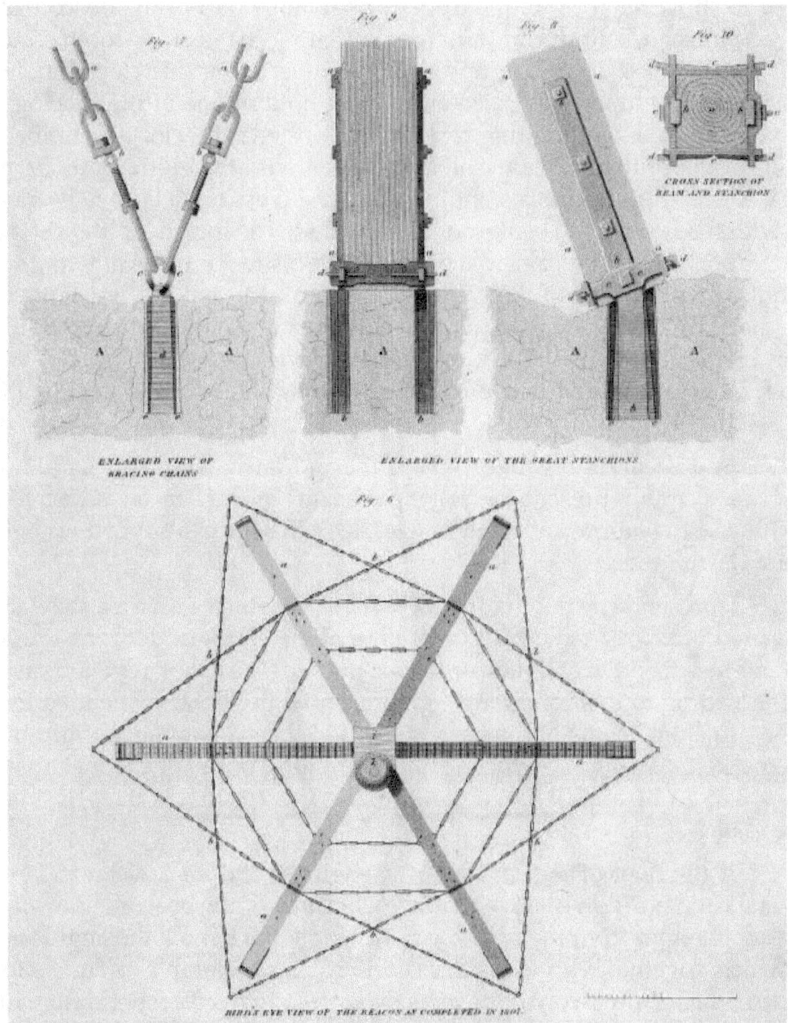

BELL ROCK BEACON

Drawn by W. Lorimer
Engd. by W. H. Lizars

PLATE VIII.

Pl. VIII.

Fig. 1. represents the Beacon-house, which was used as a barrack for the artificers during the working seasons of 1809 and 1810. Letter A A A is the surface of the Rock. The principal legs or beams, with their diagonal supports, radiating from the centre of the plan, are marked a a a a a a, and the bracing chains b b b, as completed in the year 1807. In 1808 the bracing-chains were removed, and the malleable iron-bars marked c c c were substituted. The dotted lines d d d d d, are intended to show the form of the upper or habitable part of the Beacon as it was ultimately finished, with its lantern, for ventilating the barrack-room. One of the figures characterised as sailors, and used for illustrating this elevation, is represented as standing upon the Rock, and laying hold of one of the bracing-chains. The next figure is ascending the trap-ladder, formed with cleats of timber nailed upon one of the principal beams; he is on a level with the mortar-gallery, marked letter e e e. The third figure is standing upon the cross or collar-beams, nearly on a level with the floor of the cook-room, marked f f. The fourth, or highest figure, is standing upon one of the principal beams, with his feet on a level with the top of the windows in the floor of the cabins of the engineer and his assistants marked g g; the head of this figure being within the artificers' barrack, marked h h. With one hand he is supposed to be touching the provision-chest, marked i, and with the other he is laying hold of the rope for hoisting the copper signal-ball k upon the flag-staff.

Fig. 2. represents the gallery where the mortar-makers and smiths latterly worked. a a a a a a represent the principal beams of the Beacon cut across; b b b the position of the mortar tubs and lime-casks; c the smith's anvil; d his bellows; e the hearth or fire-place.

Fig. 3. represents the floor of the cook-room, in which a a a a a a shew the principal beams cut across; b the platt or landing at the entrance-door; c c the coboose or cooking-hearth; d the chimney or smoke funnel; e e e e the provision casks; f the trap stair leading to the floor above; g g the small life-boat, suspended by davits from the principal beams of the beacon; i i i i i i i the six angular upright posts cut across, marked d in Fig. 1., which form the framing of the hexagonal apartments or floors marked III. and IV. Letter k represents the position of the privy, and stair leading to it.

Fig. 4. is the floor of the cabins of the engineer and his assistants. Letters a a a a a a mark the position of the six principal beams of the beacon, now approaching closely together from their diagonal direction: b b b b b b the angular upright posts, which, together with those marked i i i i i i, as referable to Fig. 3., form the upper apartments into twelve sides; c is the trap-ladder, corresponding with letter f in Fig. 3., which communicates with the cook-room floor below; d is another ladder, leading to the artificers' barrack above.

Fig. 5. represents the upper floor, or that of the artificers' barrack-room, on a level with the top of the principal beams, marked a in Figs. 1, 2, and 3. In this diagram a a a a a represent the ground-tier of beds, which were ranged in five heights, excepting at the space over the man-hole, leading up to this apartment, where there was only three heights of beds; c represents the trap ladder answerable to letter d of Fig. 4.

Fig. 6. represents what may be termed a bird's-eye view of the Beacon, as completed in 1807, and before it was converted into a barrack. In reference to Fig. 1., letter a represents the six principal beams, forming a common base measuring about 35 feet across, including the bracing-chains, which are marked b b b b b b. These beams meet in a point at the top, where they rest upon a block of beechwood, to which the upper ends of the beams were fitted, the whole being girded with strong malleable iron rings or hoops, keyed with spear-bolts. Here the provision-chest i, and signal-ball k, are represented as resting upon the top of the principal beams.

Fig. 7. is an enlarged view of two of the bracing-chains, marked a a, with their tightening shakle marked b b, meeting in the ring c c. Letter d represents one of the batts, which were sunk into the rock A A about 20 inches, and wedged with timber and iron, as shewn at e e.

Fig. 8. represents a side view of one of the beams of the beacon, marked a a a a, cut across immediately above the great stancheons b b b b, with its bolts, which were fitted upon each side of the beam; c c represent the clasp-plates, which embraced each foot of the beacon, with its two stancheons. These clasp-plates were fixed with spear-bolts, as shewn at d d. Letters e e represent the wedging with timber and iron, referred to in Fig. 7.

Fig. 9. represents a front view of a like portion of one of the principal beams, as in Fig. 8.; a a a a shew the stancheons on each side of the beam, and b b the lower extremity of the stancheons sunk into the Rock A; c c one of the clasp-plates; d d d d the spear-bolts.

Fig. 10. is one of the principal beams, a cut across at the clasp-plate c c c c. Letters b b are the great iron-stancheons; and d d d shew the spear-bolts.

PLATE IX.

SHEWING THE PROGRESS OF THE WORKS DURING THE SECOND, THIRD, AND FOURTH YEARS' OPERATIONS.

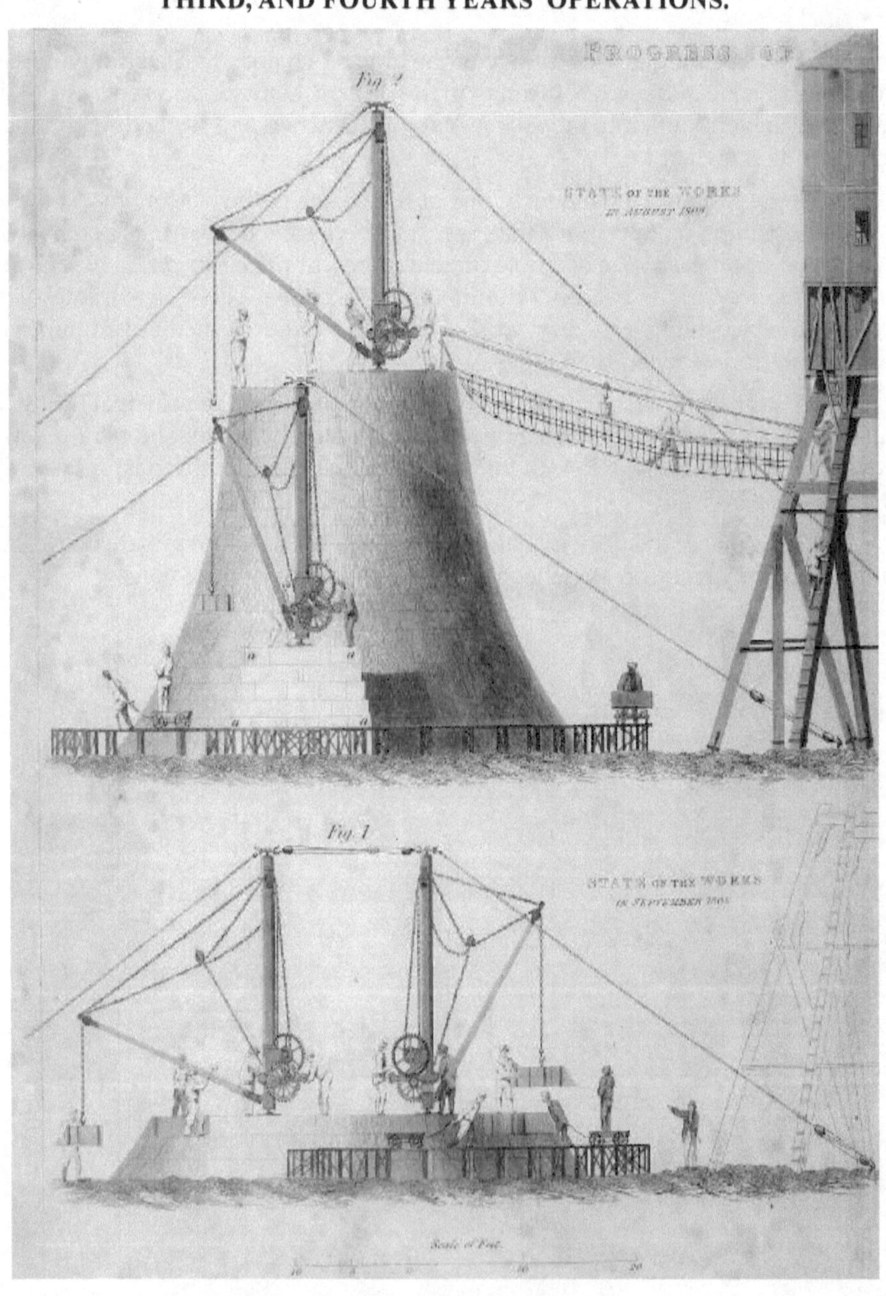

PROGRESS OF THE BELL ROCK WORKS.

Drawn by J. Slight.
Engd. by W. Miller.

PLATE IX.

Pl. IX.

Fig. 1. shews the state of the works about the close of the second season, or year 1808, with two of the moveable beam-cranes, with their guy tackles and working gear, which will be more particularly described under Plate XIV. These are placed upon the top or fourth course of the building. In the fore-ground, part of the unfinished railways are seen, with waggons and artificers at work; and on the right the beacon is partly traced in faint lines.

Fig. 2. represents the state of the works in the month of August 1809, at the close of the third season's work, when only one of the cranes was set upon the building; the other, as the work increased in height, and became less in diameter, was placed upon a temporary stool or prop of masonry, marked a a a a. This prop was found extremely useful, as, by elevating one of the cranes upon the top of it, the lift of the materials was divided, and brought more conveniently within reach of the higher crane, which at this period was about 30 feet above the Rock. In the fore-ground of this diagram, part of the circular track of railway round the building is seen. On the right, a part of the Beacon-house appears with the rope-ladder of communication, extending from the top of the solid of the Light-house to the mortar-gallery. On the rope-ladder a figure is represented walking from the Beacon to the Light-house, and a tackle, with its travelling pulley, is also stretched, for conveying the mortar-bucket, to the builders.

Fig. 3. represents a section of the void or habitable part of the Light-house as it appeared in the month of August 1810, when the masonry was nearly completed. On the right is an elevation of part of the Beacon-house, but instead of the rope-ladder of communication, a bridge of timber is constructed. Letters a a represent the top of the solid, or level of the entrance-door of the building, from which the stair-case ascends to the several apartments. Resting on the sill of the door at b, is seen one of the beams for supporting the road-way of the bridge, and below this, at the point c, is the step of one of the diagonal braces of the bridge, where it is inserted about 6 inches into one of the courses of the solid masonry. Regarding the frame-work of the bridge, it may only further be noticed, that the road-way was chiefly suspended from the king-posts d d.

Letter e represents a block of stone, in the act of being raised from the rail-way on the Rock, to the level of the bridge, by means of the crab or winch-machine marked f, with wheel and pinion apparatus; the pully of the working chain is suspended from the cross beam g, which rests or is supported upon the top of the king-posts. One of the figures on the bridge at h, is in the act of pushing forward a truck cart or waggon i, to receive the stone e; when raised through the aperture in the road-way, it is then lowered upon this waggon, and removed towards the building within the sphere of the several purchases or machines, by which it is transported to the hands of the builders.

Letter k refers to a life-buoy, and a coil of rope, kept in readiness upon the bridge, in case of accident by the fall of any of the people from the building or beacon while the Rock was covered by the tide. l l represent two of the fire-buckets, which were hung round the beacon, under the projection immediately above the cook-room. The stone marked e, in the second stage of its progress towards the top of the building, is now seen immediately above the lintel of the entrance-door, the purchase chain, by which it is suspended, passes over a pulley at m, attached to the beam n n, which is projected from one of the windows of the Light-room store, where it is supported upon a block of timber, so as to admit of the chain passing under it. The further end of this beam, being within the Light-house, was bolted to an upright post marked o o, and the whole apparatus was worked by means of the crab or winch-machine at p, similar to that upon the bridge marked f f. The stone e is next supposed to have gained the height of the floor of the bed-room, where another apparatus, similar to those at f and p, is placed. Here a figure is represented at q, with a rod in his hand, in the act of hooking the chain of the balance-crane into the Lewis-batt, fixed in the stone e, still in its progress to the top of the building. r r r represent the strong oaken beams placed on the floor of the library, on which the foot of the cast-iron balance-crane is supported. s s two of the four diagonal braces of oak timber, bolted into a collar-piece of cast-iron, clasping the upright shaft of the crane at t t, and butting against the upright stretchers at u u; intended as a security to the walls, in case the balance-crane should at any time get out of equilibrium. The two figures marked v v, are represented as working the balance-crane, and are supposed to be standing upon a moveable platform x x, suspended from the body of the crane by rods of iron y y. This platform or stage, with the artificers upon it, being moveable with the body of the crane, gave great facility and conveniency to those who wrought it. z is the balance-weight, move-able by the machinery along the balance-beam of the crane, to keep the whole in a state of equilibrium, according to the varied load suspended from the working or opposite beam; accented á represents the moveable block or cross-head of mal-leable iron, with two eyes, into which the chains of the crane were hooked, when the body (comprehending the machinery and beams) was to be elevated upon the shaft in the progress of building. But the cross-head, together with the other appa-ratus of this machine, will be better understood by examining Plate XVII., with its letter-press description. b′ b′ b′ represent the form and position of the Light-room in dotted lines; c′ the mortar-bucket made to traverse upon the guide-rope d′ d′, stretched between the building and the mortar-gallery of the Beacon; the end of the rope attached to the building being fixed to the stanchion é, inserted into one of the Lewis batt-holes, on the balcony of the Light-room.

PLATE X.

VARIOUS IMPLEMENTS AND APPARATUS CONNECTED WITH THE WORKS.

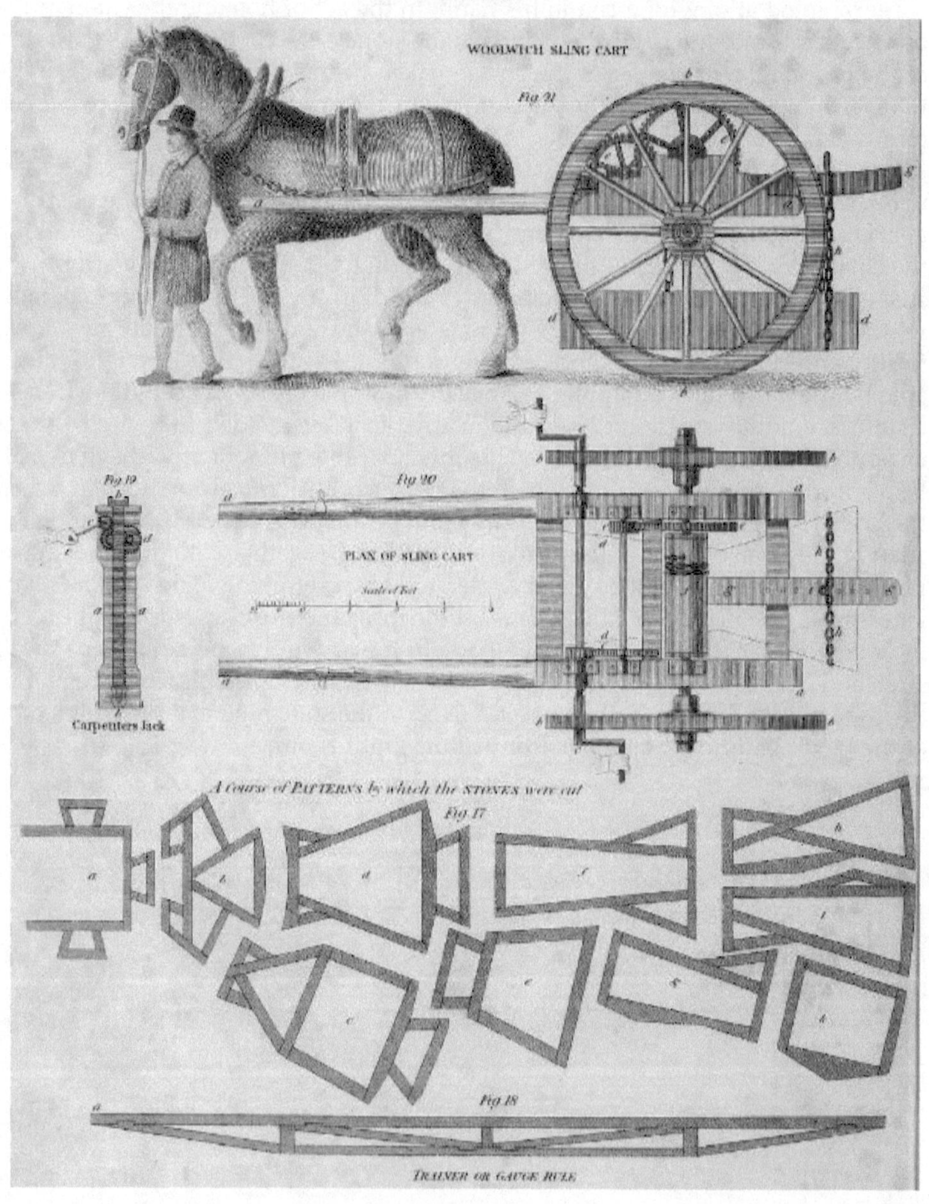

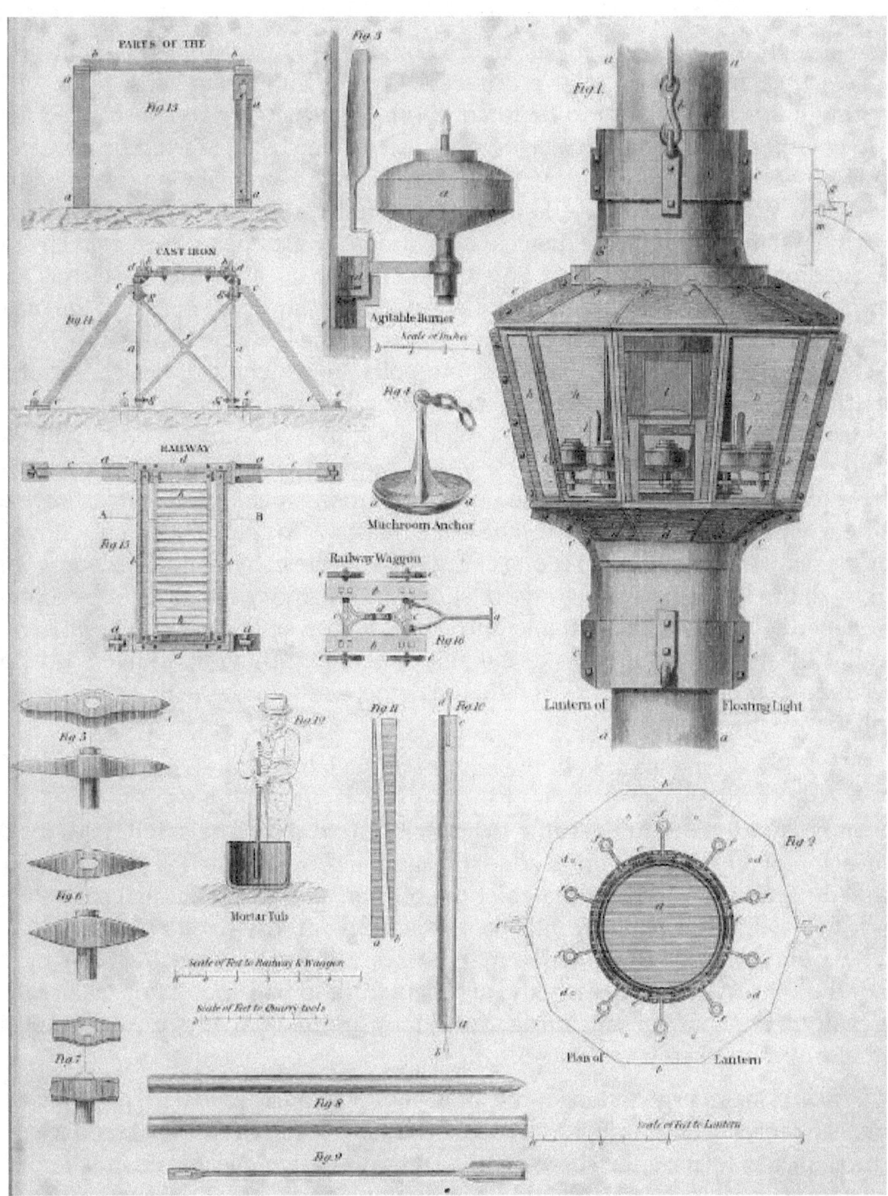

CERTAIN IMPLEMENTS CONNECTED WITH THE BELL ROCK WORKS

Drawn by G. C. Scott
Engd. by E. Mitchell

PLATE X.

Pl. X.

Fig. 1.—is an elevation of one of the three large copper Lanterns carried by the Pharos Floating-Light, which was moored off the Bell Rock while the Light-house was erecting. In order to relieve this vessel of the cumbrous yards with which Floating-lights were in use to be fitted, these lanterns were so constructed as to clasp round the masts, and traverse upon them. This was effected by constructing them with a tube of copper in the centre, capable of receiving the mast, and through which it passed. The lanterns were first completely formed, and fitted with brass flanges; they were then cut longitudinally asunder, which conveniently admitted of their being screwed together on the masts, after the vessel was fully equipped and moored in her station. Letters a a a a shew part of one of the masts, b one of the tackle-hooks for raising and lowering the lanterns at pleasure, c c c c c c c c c c the brass flanges, with their screw-bolts, by which the body or case of the lantern was ultimately put together; d d d shew the position of certain holes in the bottom for the admission of air, f f f f the holes at the top, connected with the ventilation, to which the collar-pieces e e and g g form guards against the immediate effects of the weather. The detached diagram, upon an enlarged scale, shows the air-hole, which is marked m. The letters h h h h shew the part of the lantern which was glazed with plate-glass; i is one of the glass shutters, by which the lamps were trimmed; the lower half being raised, slides into a groove made for its reception; k k shew the range of ten agitable burners or lamps, out of which the oil cannot be spilt by the rolling motion of the ship. Each lamp having a silvered-copper speculum or reflector l l placed behind the flame, was found greatly to increase the brilliancy of the light.

Fig. 2.—is a cross section of the bottom of the lantern, shewing the mast a cut across, b b is the sole or bottom of the lantern, c c the flanges at the junction of the body, in reference to the same letter in Fig. 1.; d d d d the small holes for the admission of air, e e e the brass zone or chandelier, with its ten arms and sockets marked f f, &c. in which the stalks of the burners are inserted. The chandelier is made to traverse horizontally into a corresponding groove fixed upon the interior cylinder or case, through which the mast passes, and upon which the whole moves up and down. When, therefore, the lamps require to be trimmed or taken out of the lantern, the chandelier is turned until they are respectively brought opposite to the shutter marked i.

Fig. 3. is an enlarged view of one of the agitable burners a, with its reflector b, which last measures four inches over the lips, and is raised to the parabolic curve of three inches focus; c the socket, d the section of the moveable chandelier in its groove, answerable to letters k and l, Fig. 1., and f and e Fig. 2. In reference to Fig. 3., e e is a section of part of the central cylinder of the lantern and mast of the ship.

Fig. 4. represents one of the Mushroom-Anchors, constructed wholly of cast-iron, used for mooring the Floating-Light and other craft off the Bell Rock, to which part of the mooring-chain is attached. This diagram seems so obvious as to require no particular description. Towards the head a a the shank is strengthened by means of four feathers or brackets raised upon it, somewhat resembling the connecting gills of the vegetable mushroom. These anchors weighed from 14 to 21 cwt.

Figs. 5. to 9.—Quarry Tools.—Fig. 5. is a common stone-pick, weighing from 8 to 10 lb., shown with and without the handle, which measured about 2 feet in length, but is here shortened. Fig. 6. is the Aberdeen or granite pick, weighing from 6 to 16 lb. Fig. 7. is a quarry hammer, weighing from 6 to 8 lb. used for jumping or boring batt-holes in the Rock, and the trenail-holes in the courses of the building. Fig. 8. represents the boring-irons for the trenail-holes, measuring 1¾ inches in breadth at the cutting end, and varying in length according to the depth of the respective holes. Fig. 9. is the scraper used for cleaning the holes; the perforated end being applied with a piece of rag for drying up the moisture.

Fig. 10. represents one of the oaken trenails used for keeping the stones in their places while the building was within the ordinary range of the sea. The positions of these trenails may be traced in the small circular holes of the courses, in Plate XIII. Their lower ends were cut with a saw-draught as at letter a, into which a small wedge marked b was inserted, and the trenail having been driven home, the small wedge had the effect of tightening or fixing it. The upper end c was then cut off flush with the upper bed of the stone, when it was split, and another small wedge, marked d, driven into the chisel-mark, which completed the operation of fixing the trenails into their places.

Fig. 11. represents a pair of the oaken wedges inserted into corresponding grooves cut into the perpendicular joints of the stones in each course of the solid or lower part of the Light-house, as may be traced in the small oblong holes, marked in the joints of the courses in Plate XIII. These wedges were chiefly intended for bringing the dove-tailed parts of the stones to a general bearing. The thick end of the wedge marked a being dropped into its groove, the smaller end of the corresponding wedge b was then inserted, and driven home till some degree of tension or firmness was obtained. This operation of trenailing and wedging was followed from Mr Smeaton's practice at the Edystone Light-house.

Fig. 12. is a section of one of the cast-iron mortar-tubs, with its pestle, shod or loaded with a piece of malleable iron.

Figs. 13. to 15.—Cast-Iron Plate-railway.—Fig. 13. is a longitudinal view of one length of the cast-iron railways erected upon the Rock; a a a a represent the stools or upright supports, b b are the tracks of the roadway, c c one of the side stays or braces. Fig. 14. is a cross section on the line A B of Fig. 15, in which a a is the support with its cross-brace f, bolted at g g g g; b b are the railway tracks, c c c c the stays, with their connecting bolts on each side, d d the sleeper or horizontal brace connecting the top of the stools, and forming a chair or seat for the rails and grated roadway; e e e e represent the batts and spear-bolts, with which the whole was connected to the Rock, by the process of wedging with timber and iron. Fig. 15. is a plan of the finished railway; a a a a are the feet of the stools, b b the side rails or waggon-tracks, c c the stays or side braces, d d the sleepers, and h h the grated footpath. The weight of a yard in length of the railways complete, of the height of four feet, as represented in these diagrams, may be estimated about 5 cwt.

Fig. 16. represents a plan of one of the railway waggons; a is the iron handle made to hook upon either end of the waggon, so as to prevent the necessity of turning it; b b is the body of the waggon, consisting of two pieces of oak timber, bolted upon the upper part of the double frame intended for accommodating the wheels to the circular track of the railway round the building. The upper and under frames are connected with the bolt c c, so as to admit of the movement above alluded to. For the same reason, a joint was formed in the perch or middle of the frame at d. The trucks or wheels e e e e were of cast-iron, measuring 15 inches in diameter. These waggons were always left upon the Rock, being simply turned upside down, or off their wheels, in a particular part, and were seldom moved by the sea, as they weighed about 2 cwt. each.

Fig. 17. The ten diagrams, marked a, b, c, d, e, f, g, h, i, and k, are a set of moulds for one course of the solid part of the building, by which the stones were cut and prepared in the work-yard previous to their being shipped for the Rock. The application and connection of these diagrams will be better understood by examining the courses of the building in Plate XIII.

Fig. 18. a Trainer or Rule, framed of timber, applied by the builders, for ascertaining the exact position of the stones of the respective courses. a is the eye or socket on which it was fitted to a steady-pin placed exactly in the centre. This rule was used chiefly for ascertaining the radiating direction of the stones, from the centre towards the circumference, being laid agreeably to corresponding notches and lines marked upon their upper-beds, so as to preserve band throughout the work, and prevent difficulty with the closing or finishing stones.

Fig. 19. is a perpendicular section of the carpenter's jack, used with much advantage for shifting and turning the stones in the work-yard. The case of this machine was made of elm, and strongly bound at the ends with iron. It measured 4 feet in height, its greatest breadth 12 inches, and its thickness 6 inches. a a is the stock or case, b b the rack, fashioned at the lower end somewhat like the claws of a carpenter's hammer. The upper end is of a forked form, both ends being conveniently applicable to the varied positions of the stones; c and d are the wheel and pinion work; e the handle by which the machinery is worked, affording a purchase or mechanical advantage in the ratio of about 64 to 1.

Fig. 20. is a plan of the useful machine called The Woolwich Sling-Cart, applicable to transporting large blocks of stone suspended between the wheels by means of a Lewis-batt. When a stone was of considerable length, it became necessary to employ a chain to steady it at the farther end, the application of which will be seen in this and the following figure. a a a a represent the shafts and body of the cart, b b b b the wheels, c c the handles passing between the spokes of the wheels, by which the machinery is worked for lifting the stone. The dotted line d d d d represents a plan of a stone in its state of suspension, e e e the wheel and pinion work, f the barrel or cylinder on which the chain turns as the stone is raised; g g is the tail-beam with its chain h h, and steady-pin i.

Fig. 21. represents the sling-cart in its working state, with letters corresponding to Fig. 20. Here the Bell Rock carter, and his horse, are shown, already noticed in the description of Plate VI., page 498.

PLATE XI.

THE SHEER-CRANE, LEWIS-BATT, PRAAM-BOAT WITH CARGO, SLOOP SMEATON DISCHARGING, AND BRUCE'S TWO-HALF ATTENDING-BOAT.

APPARATUS CONNECTED WITH THE BELL ROCK WORKS.

Drawn by G. C. Scott
Engd. by W. Miller.

PLATE XI.

Pl. XI.

Fig. 1.—The Sheer-Crane at Duff's Wharf. a a a are the working-sheers, to the upper extremity of which the purchase-chain a, e, g, is attached; from the hook marked i, the stone k is suspended by the sling-chain i, k, which was lengthened or shortened according to the state of the tide. b b are the upright-sheers; c c the diagonal or supporting sheers. Those last, though acting as braces, had also a motion upon the connecting block d at the top, from which the pulley e is suspended, and over which the purchase-chain passes. This motion had the effect of giving the stone a kant inwards, when the working-sheers came to the perpendicular, so as to lay it upon the waggon f, to be wheeled along the railways, as will be understood by examining Plate XVIII. The crab or winch machine g g, fixed upon the Rock at one side of the railway, with batts and spear-bolts, was worked with a less or greater purchase, according to the weight of the stone to be lifted. The large wheel measuring 3 feet 3 inches in diameter, formed the single purchase, and the smaller wheel of 2 feet 6 inches, with its pinion of 6 inches, when connected with the former by an intermediate pinion, formed the greater purchase, exerting a power in the one case in the ratio of about 20 to 1, and in the other of 98 to 1.

Fig. 2. is a front view of the machine described above, with corresponding letters. At letters h h, will be seen more distinctly the cast-iron bed, with the snugs or flanges for the reception of the lower ends of the sheers a a a and b b b b, with their journal-bolts. This apparatus, along with the other parts of the works, have been modelled for preservation.

Fig. 3. represents one of the malleable iron Lewis-batts, with which the stones were lifted from stage to stage, after leaving the hands of the stone-cutter. This useful implement consists of six members, viz. the palm, which is in three pieces, marked a, b, c; the palm-bolt d d; the shackle e. The spear-bolt f, for preventing the palm-bolt from drawing, was seldom used in practice.

Fig. 4. is a section of one of the praam-boats, shewing her cargo on deck, and more particularly the form and application of the mushroom-anchor and chain-moorings of the Bell Rock craft. a a is the cargo upon deck; b b is the hold or compartment under deck, calculated to contain a sufficient number of empty casks, for floating her, in the event of receiving injury at the rock. c c mark the fore and after peaks, for containing warps, kedge-anchors, grapplings, defenders, and other tackle; d marks the position of the bits and cross-tree to which a hook at e was fixed, for attaching the end of the mooring-chain; f is the slit in the stem, answerable to a hawse-hole, through which the mooring-chain passed almost on a level with the deep water-line, and was ultimately fixed by the ring g, to the lower swivel of the floating buoy h, and also with the mushroom-anchor i at the bottom, connected with a length of chain extending to about twice the depth of the water.

The detached diagram towards the stern of the praam-boat, consisting of a mushroom-anchor, a larger and smaller floating buoy, with their respective chains, represent the state of the moorings while the praam-boats were employed at the Rock. The small buoy k, with its chain l, was connected at the ring accented l′ to the hawser-chain of the praam. When she was unmoored, this small buoy prevented the end of the chain from sinking. In this manner the praams were conveniently disengaged, or attached to the large buoy h. When at their moorings, the small buoy k was unhooked and stowed below, the strong mooring-chain being now drawn through the hawse, or slit at f, and the ring at l′ being simply laid into the hook at e.

Fig. 5. is a perspective view of the sloop Smeaton at her moorings, delivering a cargo of stones, with one of the praam-boats along-side. In the back ground, the Light-house is seen partly built, together with the Beacon-house. Two of the three figures shewn on the deck, near the mast, are working the winch-machine of the ship in raising a stone from the hold, while the figure, in a lying posture, is holding-on the end of the tackle-fall, as described at page 144. A stone is seen in the main hatch of the ship, suspended from the end of a short boom nearly at right angles to the mast. The figure near the companion or cabin-stair is working one of the guy-tackles. On the praam's deck, part of a cargo may be seen, and the figure towards her stern is laying hold of the stone, suspended in the tackle, to guide it to its birth, while the other contiguous figure is working an opposite guy-tackle. To avoid confusion, only five figures are here introduced. The praam-boat is understood to be lashed head and stern to the ship, having three or four large wooden defenders slung between them, to prevent the vessels from injuring each other with the undulating motion of the sea. The Smeaton's sails are handed, and the main and gaff-booms braced to one side, to give room upon deck, in bringing the stones out of the hold. The only peculiarities about the fitting of the Smeaton, were her large main hatch, for the conveniency of loading and discharging; her winch-machine was pretty powerful, exerting a force in the ratio of about 20 to 1, independently of the purchase-tackle; her cargo was also carried upon a temporary platform laid in the hold.

Fig. 6. is a perspective view of the smith's forge, which was partly fixed with batts upon the Rock; and also of the Foundation-pit, with a number of figures pumping water from the excavated site of the Light-house. The pumps for this purpose were laid in an inclined direction, made of a square form, and very simple in their construction; the pump-spear with its leathern valve, being worked by the artificers, who laid hold of a rope attached to the end of it. In the back ground of this diagram, the Floating-light is seen as if through the haze of the atmosphere.

Fig. 7. represents an Attending-boat, occasionally used during the summer months for visiting the Rock, and relieving the light-keepers. a a is a section of the principal boat, measuring 22 feet in length of keel, and equipped in her rigging after the manner technically termed Lateen-sails, which were originally introduced into use on the Firth of Forth by Mr Thomas Bruce of Grangemuir. These sails are considered more safe than the common lug-sail, from their greatest breadth being carried very low on the mast. But the chief peculiarity of this boat is the launch or "two-half boat" of Mr James Bruce, which she carries, for more conveniently communicating with the Rock, as alluded to at page 412, and further described in Thomson's Annals of Philosophy, vol. viii. p. 58. In this diagram b is the two-half boat, stowed the one-half within the other, between the main and fore masts, c c the two halves about to be joined and used as one boat, d d the stern view of these boats in a separated state, e e the chatter and catch-bolt for connecting the boats together, after the manner of a ship's rudder, f f f f the bolt holes, by which the upper parts of the boats are connected and held together.

PLATE XII.

WORK-YARD, LIGHT-KEEPER'S HOUSES, SEA-WALL AT ARBROATH, AND SEAMEN'S PROTECTION-MEDAL.

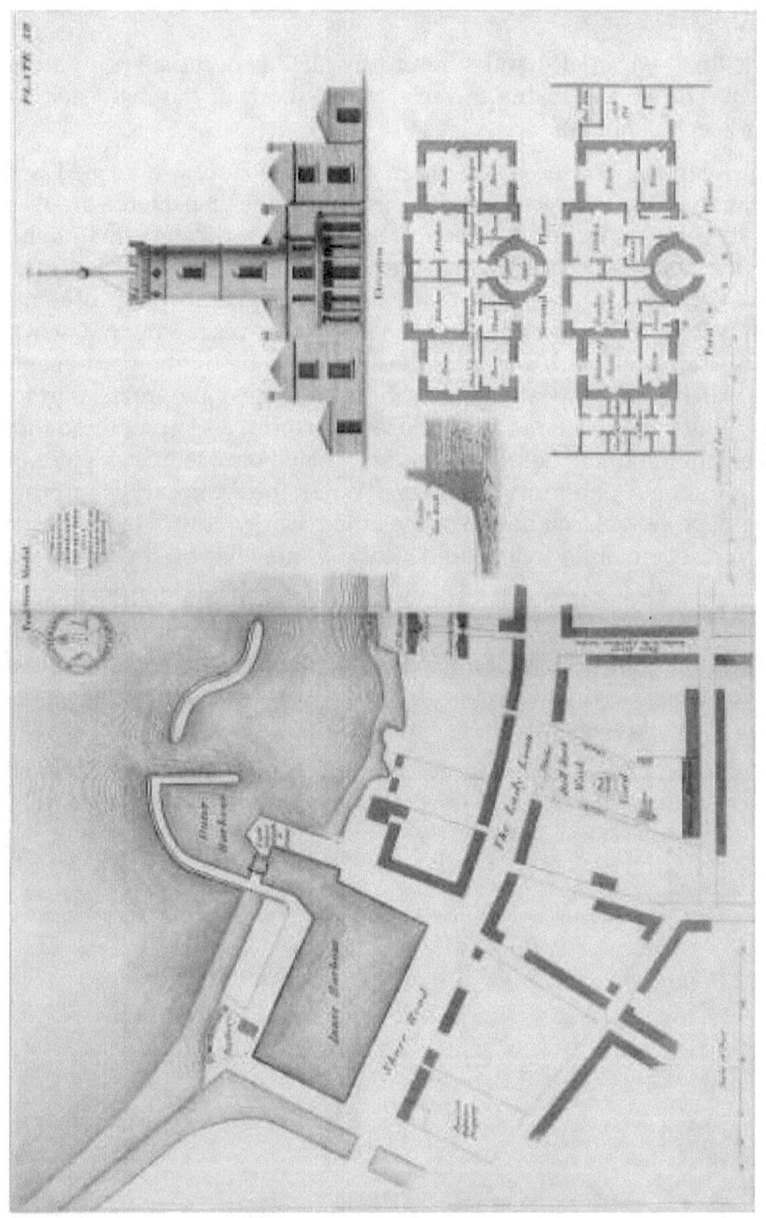

PLAN OF THE HARBOUR AND PART OF THE TOWN OF ABER-BROTHOCK

PLANS & ELEVATION of the LIGHT KEEPERS HOUSES & SIGNAL TOWER

Drawn by D. Logan
Engd. by W. H. Lizars

PLATE XII.

Pl. XII.

Work-Yard.—The left-hand side of this Plate is occupied with a plan of the harbour of Arbroath, shewing the relative positions of the Bell Rock work-yard and light-keepers' houses.

Light-Keepers' Houses.—The other side of the Plate is occupied with a plan and elevation of the light-keepers' houses; but as the apartments are respectively marked, it seems unnecessary to enter farther into particulars, than to notice that each family has three rooms, with other conveniencies. Connected with this establishment, there is also a signal-room at the top of the tower, represented in the elevation, where a five-feet achromatic telescope is placed upon a stand. On the roof a flag-staff is erected, and here the signals made by the light-keepers at the Rock are watched and repeated. On the opposite side of the small court formed by these buildings, there is a range of houses for stores, and accommodation for the seamen belonging to the Bell Rock Tender. The whole occupies a piece of ground extending to about one-third of an acre. While the works were in progress, the large telescope was placed at one of the attic-room windows of Provost Balfour's house, which commands a view of the Rock, as may be observed from the Plate.

Sea-Wall.—The diagram laid down on the left of the light-keeper's houses, represents a section of the wall erected for the protection of the property against the encroachment of the sea. It extends to about 100 feet, and consists of a face-wall of stone from Mylnefield quarry, backed with Arbroath stone, and a granite pavement along its seaward base.

Protection Medal.—The diagram in the central part of this Plate represents the obverse and reverse of the seamen's protection medal, described at page 209.

PLATE XIII.

PLANS OF THE SEVERAL COURSES OF THE MASONRY OF THE LIGHT-HOUSE.

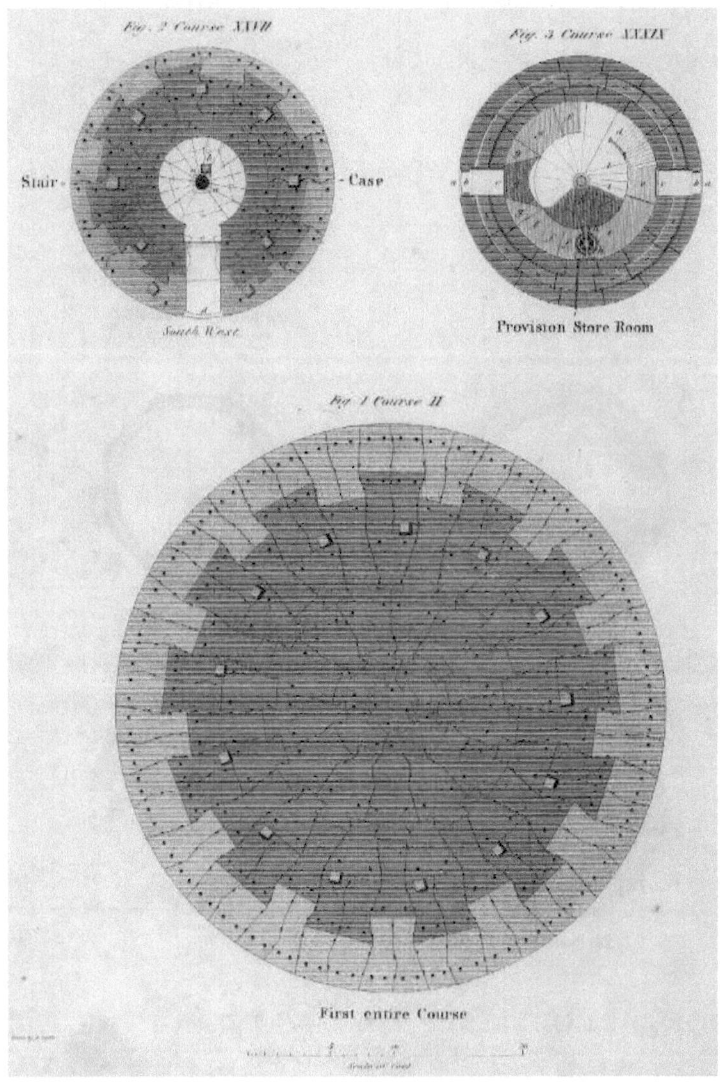

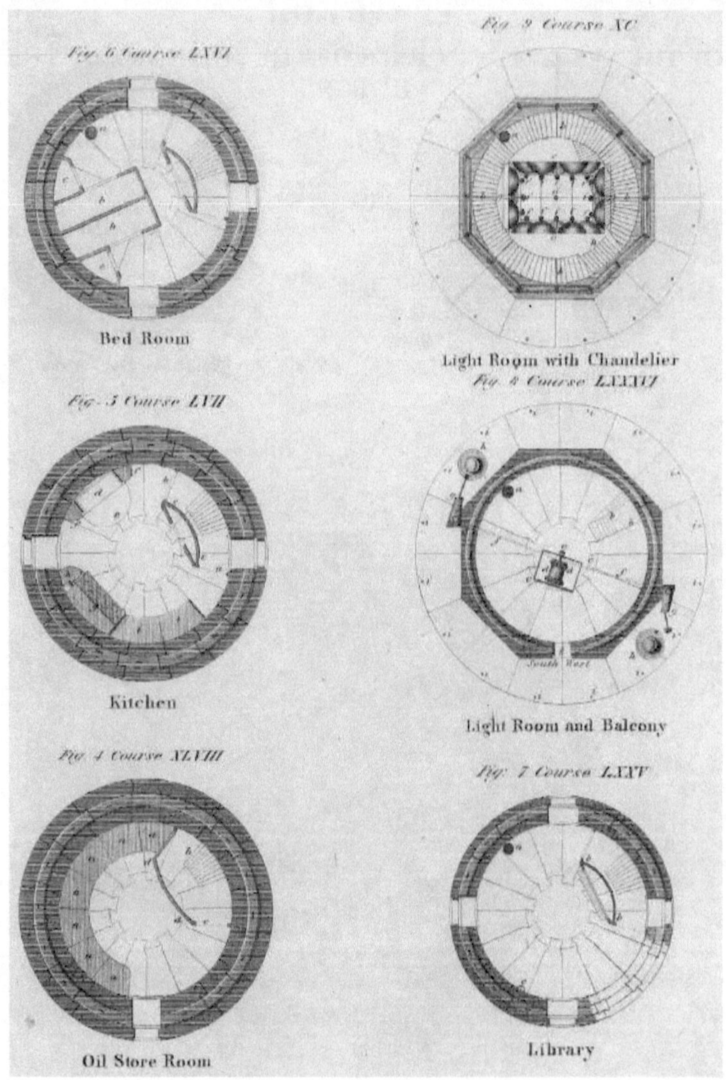

PLANS OF THE COURSES OF THE MASONRY OF THE BELL ROCK
LIGHT HOUSE

Drawn by D. Logan.
Engd. by W. H. Lizars

PLATE XIII.

Pl. XIII.

As the ground or imperfect course of the building could not be ascertained till towards the second year's work, when the site of the Light-house was excavated, this course is represented in Plate XV.

Fig. 1. Plate XIII., is the first entire course, which measures 42 feet in diameter. The dove-tailed method of connecting the solid part of the Light-house here delineated, extends to the height of the entrance-door, as will be further understood by examining the section in Plate XVI. The outward stones of this course are of a lighter shade, being intended to represent the granite blocks, while the central part of a darker shade, represents the sandstone. The thirteen small square or cubical stones in the Plan of this course, shew the upper sides of the joggles, sunk half into the one course, and penetrating half into the superincumbent one, acting as so many steady-pins, calculated to guard against any force tending to affect the fabric horizontally. By tracing the bounding-lines of the stones, from the centre to the circumference, it will be observed, that the whole are connected by means of a system of attachments technically termed Dove-tailing, by which the stones may be said to hook laterally into one another, forming a vertical bond of connection; but it is on the gravity of the materials that the chief dependence is placed for the stability of the fabric. The small circular dots, of which there are four in the centre-stone, and two in each of the others, shew the position of the oaken trenails, measuring 1¾ inch in diameter, and varying in length from 16 to 26 inches, so as to pass through the upper or last laid course, and penetrate 6 inches into the course immediately below. Besides these circular holes, others of an oblong form were cut in the joints, as will also be observed from the Figure. These last were for the reception of wooden wedges, driven in pairs perpendicularly into the joints of the stones, with a view to bring the dove-tailed parts to a uniform bearing, before the joints were grouted with mortar; the bond throughout the building being carefully preserved, by placing the perpendicular joints over the middle of the stones immediately below, being what is technically termed "Breaking-band,"—a system universally attended to in good masonry.

Fig. 2. represents the upper side of the 27th course, or first of the Stair-case, which measures 6 feet 4 inches in diameter within walls, and 19 feet 8 inches over walls. This course is elevated 32 feet 8 inches above the Rock at the foundation of the first stone, as will be seen in the section of Plate XVI. Here the granite casing is discontinued, and sandstone only is in future used. It will be observed, that the same system of dove-tailing is attended to in the stair-case as in the solid: this unavoidably occasioned the working of the stones into very awkward forms, and required the utmost precaution in landing them on the Rock with safety.

The parts of this course which are not shaded, shew the plan of the entrance-door, passage, and circular void of the stair, crossed by the radiating lines of the steps, as also the form of some of the stones of the top of the solid. a a represent the base of a column of cast-iron, which renders the drop-hole for the machinery continuous from the floor of the oil-store down to the level of the passage, and so through the centre of the solid, as shewn in the section Plate XVI.; b is a small stove placed in the stair-case; c is the position of the Inner door, of brass, as shewn in Fig. 2. Plate XIX., the upper part of which is glazed with plate-glass, to preserve the light of the stair-case; d is the position of the entrance-door, which is fashioned agreeably to the circular form of the building, and is strongly bound with the brass-hinges, as also shewn in Figs. 1. and 2. of Plate XIX.

Fig. 3. is the 39th course of the building, and first of the provision-store, and is 45 feet 11 inches above the foundation. This apartment measures 11 feet 9 inches in diameter within walls, and 18 feet over walls. From the floor to the roof the height is 8 feet 7 inches. Here the dove-tailed system, excepting at the end joints, and in the centre stones of the floors, was laid aside. At this level another system of connecting the courses was adopted, by means of a zone or belt, which was raised or worked upon the upper bed of the stones, and fitted to a corresponding groove in the course laid immediately above, as may be seen by tracing the diagrams representing the habitable parts of the house. This zone or belt, together with the horizontal plan of the floors, form the chief distinctive differences between the Designs of the Edystone and Bell Rock.

Fig. 3. The parts in this Figure which are not shaded represent the two windows of this apartment with the landing at the top of the stone stair-case. a a represent the storm-shutters, which will be more fully seen in Plate XIX. b b are the outer glazed windows; c c the inner glazed windows; d the open trap-ladder, with its brass hand-rail, leading to the light-room-store; e e the cast-iron coal magazine; f f f f the water-cisterns, of cast-iron, lined with a mixture of pitch and sand, and containing each 150 gallons; g g g g the four cast-iron magazines, for containing the provision casks, and various implements; h h the machinery, placed on a level with the top of the water-cisterns, for raising the stores from the entrance-door of the building to the Light-house; i i is the hole perforated through the wall for the passage of the chain for lifting the stores, the operation of which will be better understood by examining Plate XVI.; k the cast-iron stage upon which the light-keepers stand when they work the machinery for taking up the stores; l l the cast-iron steps leading to the stage k.

Fig. 4. is a plan of the floor of the light-room store, being the 48th course, which is 55 feet 10 inches above the foundation. This apartment, within walls, measures 11 feet 10 inches, over walls 16 feet 10 inches, and its height is 8 feet 7 inches. The shaded part of the floor marked a a a a a a a, represents the copper oil-cisterns, coated with tin, calculated to contain one whole year's stock of oil, or about 1100 gallons. This apartment being chiefly occupied with these cisterns, there is only one window in it; b is the trap-ladder, and shews also the manhole, measuring 3 feet in its greatest length and 2 feet in breadth; c the store-room door; d d the position of the oaken pannelled partitions, which separate and inclose the store-room from the stair.

Fig. 5. being the kitchen floor, forms the 57th course, which is elevated 65 feet 8 inches above the foundation. This apartment measures 11 feet 11 inches in diameter, over all 16 feet, and its walls are 8 feet 9 inches in height. This room, in the position of its windows, manhole, and trap-ladder, is similar to what has already been described in reference to Figs. 3. and 4. In Fig. 5, a is the door leading to the apartment below; b the door leading to the trap-ladder of the apartment above; c c the oaken partitions, formed into lockers, which shut off the stair from the apartment; d is the cast-iron kitchen range or fire-place, which stands free and unconnected with the walls, forming a connected piece of pannelled work, extending from the floor to the ceiling; e is a strong cast-iron fender, and also a receptacle for the ashes; f f copper coal-boxes, formed into seats, on each side of the fire-place; g the cook's table and locker; h the handle of the pump, by which water is raised from the provision-store or the second floor below; i i other lockers, also formed into seats.

Fig. 6. is the bed-room floor, or 66th course of the building, and is elevated 75 feet 8 inches above the foundation; it measures 11 feet 11½ inches in diameter, and over all 15 feet 6 inches; the walls are 9 feet in height. The windows, manhole, trap-ladder, doors, and oaken partition are similar to what have already been described in the floors below; a shews the position of the aperture for the cast-iron funnel leading from the kitchen-chimney through the several apartments to the cupola of the Light-house; b b the bed-frames, forming two bed-places in breadth, which are three tiers in height, reaching from the floor to the roof, and capable of accommodating six persons; c c lockers on each side of the beds, for the use of the four light-keepers.

Fig. 7. the next in order is the floor of the Strangers'-room or Library, being the 75th course of the building, which is 85 feet 11 inches above the foundation. The diameter of this floor is 12 feet, it measures 15 feet over walls, and the height of the roof, at the centre, is 11 feet 1 inch. The walls, windows, and other particulars of this apartment are nearly similar to those formerly described; a is the cast-iron funnel leading from the kitchen-chimney; b b the oaken framed book-case; c the tube through which the machinery-rope is conducted by the side of the walls of the several apartments, to the ceiling of the Provision-store.

Fig. 8. is the Light-room floor, or 86th course of the building, which is elevated 97 feet 9 inches above the foundation; within walls the floor measures 11 feet in diameter, over walls 13 feet 6 inches. The stones of the floor of this apartment, as will be observed, extend from the centre stone to the circumference of the balcony, varying from 7 feet to 7 feet 6 inches in length. The parapet-wall of the light-room, as will be seen from the Plate, has its outward face of an octagon form, but is worked circular within. In the several courses of the parapet, the principle of the zone or belt in the beds of the stones is still continued, and also the dove-tail of the end joints. The Light-room measures from the floor to the top of the stone work, or sole of the glazed sash-frames, 6 feet. a is the circular aperture for the cast-iron smoke-tube leading from the kitchen-chimney; b b is the manhole of this floor, having its landing towards the centre of the apartment, instead of being close to the wall, as in the several floors below. To have formed the length-way of the man-hole of this floor along the wall, would have occasioned the cutting of the stones in the dome-roof of the Library, in a manner hurtful to the strength of the building, which was conveniently avoided by introducing a platt in the ladder, instead of ascending more directly as by the trap-ladders of the floors below; c c is the case of the revolving-machinery, which gives motion to the Lights; d d is the drum or barrel, with its connecting wheels, on which the rope is coiled, from which the weight is suspended; e the position of the upright shaft for supporting the chandelier on which the reflectors are ranged, which is put in motion by its connecting train of machinery. The dotted lines marked f f shew the direction of the grooves cut in the floor for the horizontal shafts, which derive their motion from the machinery, and work the hammers of the two alarm-bells placed on the balcony; g g the bell-hammers with their cases; h h the bells, weighing each 5 cwt., which are tolled during the continuance of foggy or snowy weather; i i, &c. are the screwed batts of brass, forming the fixtures of the balcony-rail; k the Light-room door communicating with the balcony, which measures in the clear 5 feet in height, and 1 foot 10 inches in breadth.

Fig. 9. is a plan of the Lantern, showing the position of the trimming-path, and reflector-frame. The height from the foundation to the sill of the sash-frame is 102 feet 6 inches, and from thence to the lining of the cupola 13 feet four inches. a is the smoke-tube leading from the kitchen to the cupola; b b b b the cast-iron grated trimming-path, on which the light-keepers stand when they trim the lamps; c c the reflector-frame or chandelier, on which three tiers of reflectors are ranged; d the upright shaft; f f, &c. the position of the fountains for the reflector-burners, g g the position of the shades of red-coloured glass, by which the light is distinguished; h the iron trap-ladder communicating with the trimming-path.

PLATE XIV
MOVEABLE BEAM CRANE.

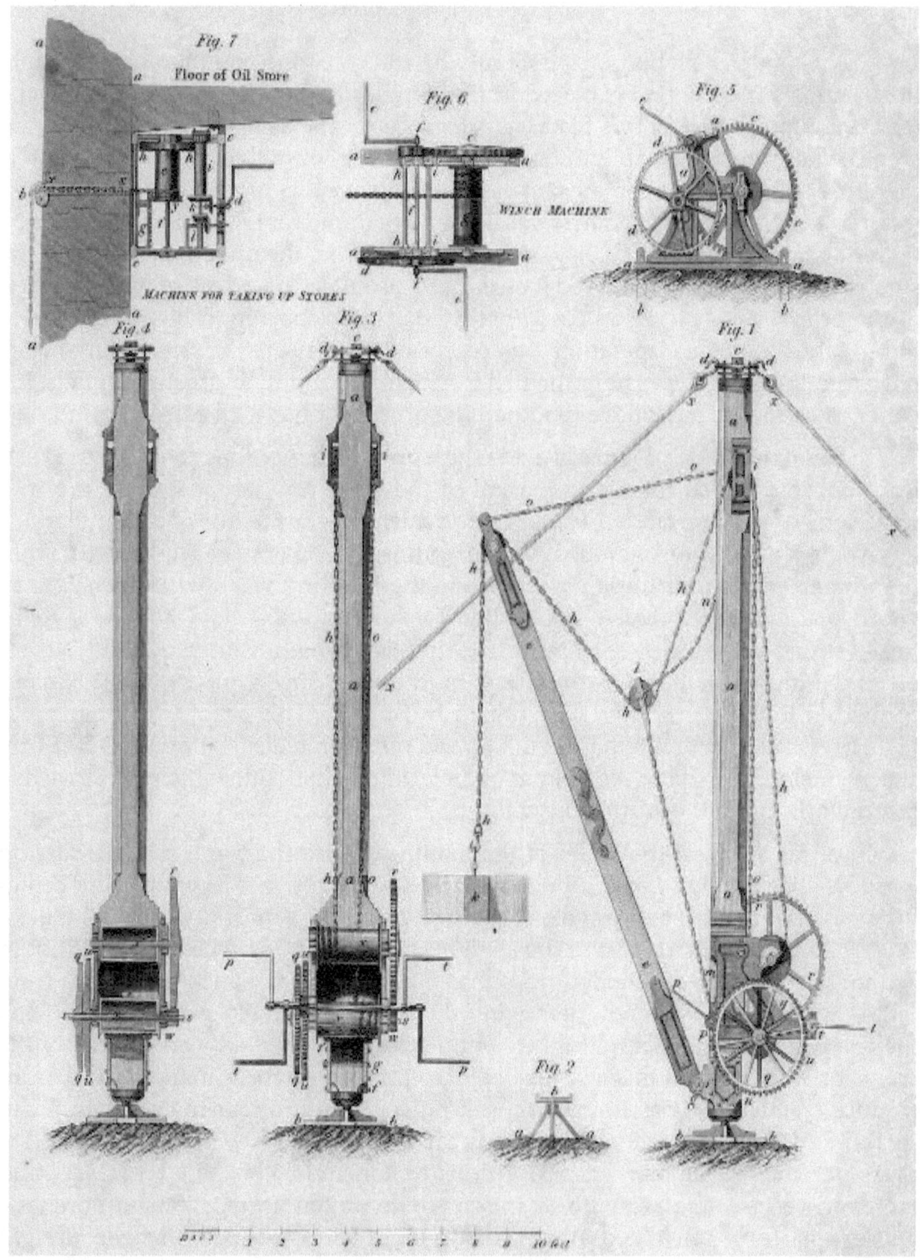

MOVEABLE BEAM CRANE &C.

Drawn by A. Slight

Engd. by A. Wilson

PLATE XIV.

Pl. XIV.

Fig. 1. is an Elevation of the Crane. In cranes of the common construction, the beam is a fixture, and is placed at right angles to the upright-shaft; but in the machine represented in this Plate, its attachment is at the lower extremity of the crane, where it is moveable up and down upon a journal or bolt. This crane is therefore termed a Moveable-beam-crane. The moveable property of the beam, in so far as the writer knows, is new, and possesses the advantage of laying any stone within its range perpendicularly on its site. This, from the dove-tailed form of the stones at the Bell Rock, rendered it essentially useful to this work, to which a crane of the ordinary construction could hardly be said to be applicable. At the Edystone Light-house this operation was performed by means of Triangular-sheers; but, from the greater extent of the Bell Rock works, and their greater depth in the water, such means must have rendered the process of building extremely tedious.

In reference to this Figure, a a a is the upright shaft of the crane; b b the cast-iron foot into which the lower journal of the shaft was stepped; c the cap into which the upper journal works, and into which two of the hooks d d of the four guy-ropes x x x x were entered, for commanding the top of the upright-shaft. From the immersed state of these cranes, while the building was low in the water, a guard-plate was introduced, and bolted to the cap, which laid hold of a collar raised round the journal, to prevent the cap from being unshipped by the waves; e e is the moveable beam, formed and built of two strong pieces of oak timber, connected in the centre by a serpentine row of bolts. This beam was mounted at the upper and lower extremities with strong cast-iron plates; f marks the cast-iron sheers or cheeks, fixed to the bottom of the upright shaft, into which the moveable beam works upon the journal or bolt g.

In order to direct the strain of the main purchase-chain h h h h h h passing over the cheek pulley i fixed upon the shaft, and to prevent its effect from bringing home the moveable beam e e to the upright shaft, a martingale or tail-block l is introduced and made fast to the shaft at m. When the purchase-chain is not in action, the block l is suspended from the small chain at n, which prevents it from falling too low, and thereby deranging the position of the purchase-chain. That the beam may be made applicable to laying the stone marked k, at the foot of the crane, or at the utmost reach of the beam, a chain or purchase marked o o o, is introduced, which also passes over a cheek-pulley i on the opposite side of the shaft. By this additional apparatus the beam is capable of being elevated or depressed at pleasure. The handle marked p p, with its pinion and connecting wheel q q, and larger wheel r r, together with its intermediate pinion, form the main purchase, and exert a force calculated at the rate of about 98 to 1. When a smaller weight was to be lifted, and greater speed wanted, the handle was transferred to the axle s, whose pinion being always in gear with the wheel r r, produced an accelerated motion, with a power in the ratio of 20 to 1; at the same time, the handle t t, with its pinion in action with the wheel u u, worked the beam e e, so as to lay a stone perpendicularly with the greatest facility within any part of its range.

Fig. 2. is the cast-iron tripod, used as a prop to the moveable beam, when applied as a lever, for lifting the crane; a a a mark the foot, b the cross head, having a stud which works into a circular hole perforated in the top of the tripod. By this simple apparatus, the crane could be moved and shifted either perpendicularly or horizontally, with a facility which added greatly to the conveniency of the operations. When the tripod was applied to use, it was placed under the heel-plate of the moveable beam marked v, and when rested upon it, the beam became a lever of great power.

Fig. 3. is an Elevation of the Working-gear of the Moveable Beam-Crane. a a a is the upright-shaft, as in Fig. 2.; b b the cast-iron foot; c the cap with its guard-plate; d d guy-hooks for commanding the top of the shaft; f f the edges of the sheers or cheeks, for the heel of the moveable beam; g the bolt or journal on which the beam is moveable; h h the purchase-chain; i i the cheek pulleys; o o the moveable beam-chain; p p the two main purchase-handles; q q the smaller wheel of the main purchase; r the greater wheel, with the intermediate pinion w, connected with the axle s of the wheel q q. The handles and pinion t t are connected with the wheel u u, for working the moveable beam-purchase; x is the drum or barrel for the main purchase-chain; y the barrel of the purchase-chain of the moveable beam.

Fig. 4. is a Section, shewing the connection of the purchases for working the beam, and lifting the weight: the axle s, of the lesser wheel q, with its intermediate pinion x of the main-purchase, work through the eye or centre of the wheel u u, and barrel y of the beam-purchase. x and r refer to the corresponding letters in Fig. 3.

Fig. 5. is an Elevation of the Winch-machine. The machines, used for the various purposes of landing the materials and raising them to the top of the building, were framed or made of cast and malleable iron. a a a a are the cheek plates or frames in which the axles of the machinery work. Those employed upon the Rock were fixed down by means of spear-bolts, to four bats, as shewn at b b; but in other situations they were fixed by straps of iron to beams of timber. The cheeks a a a a were connected by means of three strong bolts passing through hollow tubes, which butted against the inner sides of the cheeks and kept them in their places. The large wheel marked c c measures 3 feet 3 inches in diameter, and the smaller wheel d d is 2 feet 6 inches: these, with their respective pinions, of 6 inches in diameter, exerted powers respectively of 20 to 1, and 98 to 1, being of a size similar to the cranes; as one set of wheel and pinion patterns were made to answer the several machines employed at the work. Letter e is one of the handles connected with its axle and pinions, which, at pleasure, is made to work with a double or single purchase, by simply slipping the axle out and into gear with the larger and smaller wheels.

Fig. 6. is a Plan of the Winch-machine. a a a a is the sole of the frame, shewing the bat-holes for fixing it down; c is the large, and d the small wheel, with its axle; e e the handles, with their axle and pinions f f f; letter g is the barrel attached to the axle of the large wheel, with part of the purchase-chain; h h is the axle of the small wheel and intermediate pinion; and i i one of the hollow pipes through which the bolts pass for connecting the two cheeks or frame of the machine together.

Fig. 7. refers to a machine fixed to the walls of the Provision-store, for raising the stores from the railways to the entrance-door, as pointed out in Plate XVI. a a a a a section of part of the walls of the Provision-store, in which a hole x x is perforated, and lined with a copper tube, for the passage of the purchase-chain; b is the pulley, with its case, over which it works; c c c is the frame of the machine; and d the handle, with its bevelled pinion. The distinctive feature of this apparatus is the vertical motion of the barrel, by which it receives and discharges the chain always at the same point; the direction also of the chain may thus be altered almost close to the barrel, which in this case was the chief desideratum. To effect this purpose, the barrel is made to move vertically upon the axle f, by means of a screw y, upon its lower end, which works into a corresponding screw-rack g; in its operation, the wheel h h is worked by the cylindrical upright-pinion of brass, marked i. The two pairs of bevelled wheels, supported upon the small intermediate frame l, are introduced, for applying a double or single purchase, according to the load to be raised.

PLATE XV.

FOUNDATION-PIT, OR EXCAVATED SITE OF THE LIGHT-HOUSE.

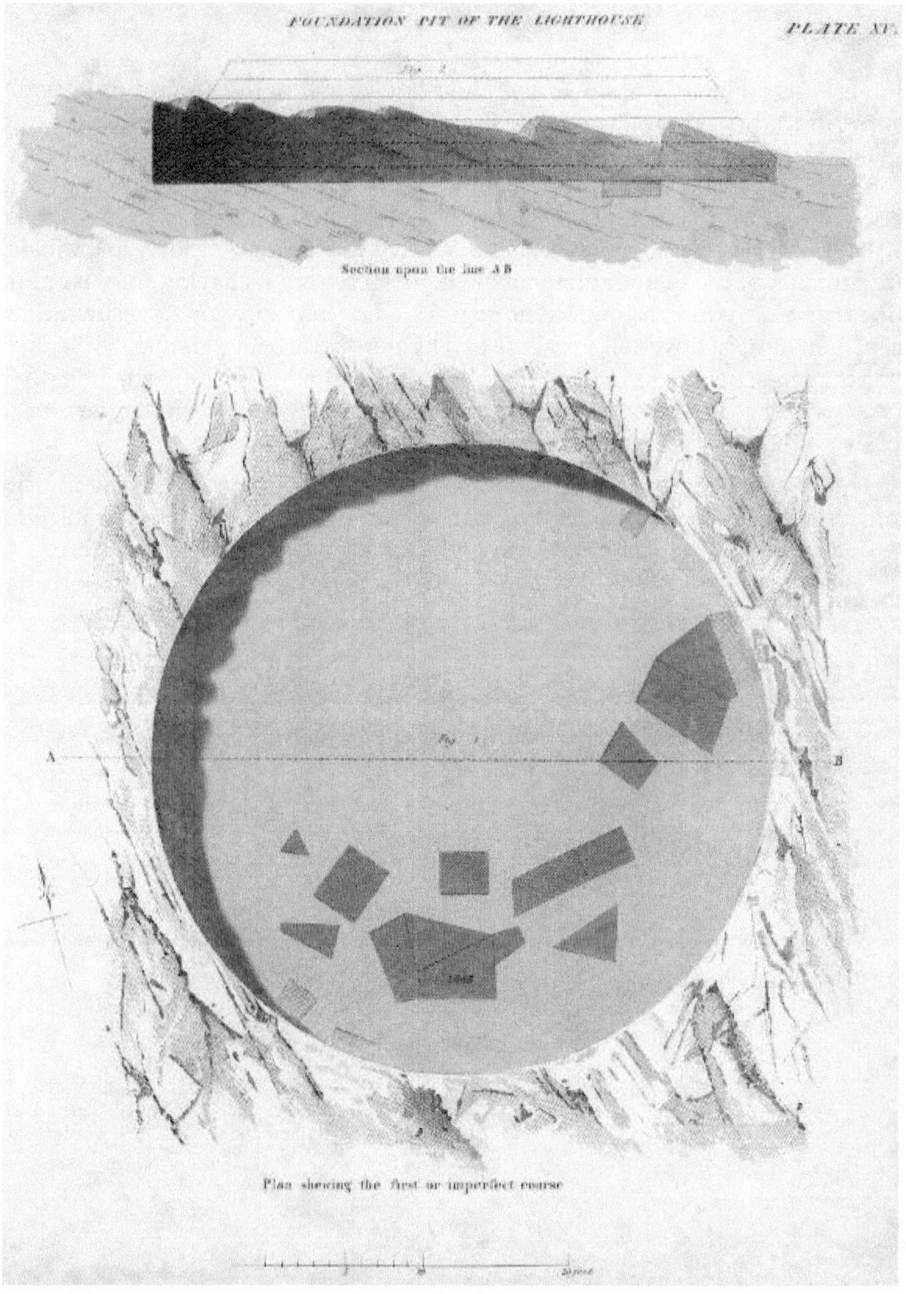

FOUNDATION PIT OF THE LIGHTHOUSE.

Drawn by J. Slight.
Engd. by W. H. Lizars

PLATE XV.

Pl. XV.

Fig. 1. is a Plan of the site of the Light-house, and of the ground or imperfect course, in readiness for receiving the first entire course of the building, represented in Plate XIII. Fig. 1. The dark shaded figures delineated upon the Plan in Plate XV. represent the stones of the ground-course, consisting of 18 detached pieces, which vary in their forms according to certain irregular holes in the Rock. From the same cause, the stones of this imperfect course vary in thickness from 6 to 18 inches. The situation of the Foundation-stone will be seen from its having the year of our Lord 1808 cut upon it, as noticed at page 237. The four exterior stones, which are cut somewhat of a dove-tail form, are of a lighter shade being granite, while the 14 interior pieces, being of sandstone, are of a darker shade. The dark shading on the northern side of the Plan represents merely the shadow of the higher parts of the Rock round the excavated site of the Light-house.

Fig. 2. is a Section of the Foundation-pit, upon the line A B, varying in depth from 18 inches to 5 feet, representing also the dip or inclination of the strata; while the dotted lines above show the form of the lower part of the Light-house.

PLATE XVI.

ELEVATION AND SECTION OF THE LIGHT-HOUSE.

ELEVATION AND SECTION OF THE BELL ROCK LIGHT HOUSE.

Drawn by D. Logan
Engd. by W. H. Lizars

PLATE XVI.

Plate XVI.

Fig. 1. is an Elevation of the Light-house, with the brazen-ladder leading up to the entrance-door. Part of the Rock and railways are seen, on which several figures are at work, landing stones from a boat, as at low-water of spring-tides. The small aperture bored through the outward wall between the door and the window of the

Light-room-store, is for the passage of the chain for raising the stores, as described in Fig. 7. Plate XIV. The two leaves of the entrance-door are shewn folded back upon the walls. The first window above the door seen in this view of the building, is that of the Light-room store; the second is one of the bed-room windows; and the third is in the Library; immediately over this are the cornice and balcony-rail, through which last is seen the Light-room door, with the alarm bells on each side. Through the glazed sashes, the reflectors are seen arranged upon the chandelier, connected with the revolving apparatus. On a level with the lower part of the cupola is the signal-ball. On the ensign-staff a flag is hoisted, with a light-house in the field, used as a complimentary signal in the service of the Northern Light-houses.

Fig. 2. is a Section of the Light-house, shewing parts of the Rock and ground-course. a a show part of the railways; b the brazen ladder leading to the entrance-door, which is marked c. In the central part of the solid of the building is shewn the cylindrical drop-hole d d, which passes through the centre-stones of each course, and forms part of the range of the machinery-weight. On each side of the drop-hole, throughout the solid, and walls of the stair-case, are seen the stone-joggles e e, &c. as they occur in the several courses, and were noticed in the description of Plate XIII. Figs. 1. and 2. At the entrance-door a figure is represented receiving stores into the house. Immediately behind him, one of the leaves of the inner door, of brass, appears folded back into its recess in the wall, the upper part being glazed with plate-glass, for the admission of light to the stair-case. In continuation of the range of the machinery-weight above alluded to, and extending between the solid and the ceiling of the provision-store, a column of cast-iron, marked x x, passes up through the well-hole of the stair. The provision store, with which the stone stair communicates, is formed by a scarsement of the walls at the level of letter f, on which the water-cisterns, lockers for provisions, and coal magazine, are ranged. Over these a stage or platform of cast iron is erected, on which a figure is seen at work at the machinery for raising the stores from the railways to the entrance-door of the house. The purchase-chain of this machine passes over the pully at g, as described in Plate XIV. Fig. 7.

The next apartment in ascending the oaken trap-ladders leading through the several apartment, is the Light-room-store, marked h, occupied chiefly with 7 copper oil-cisterns, which are strengthened with polished brass bars forming the front into pannels. This, and the several apartments above are partitioned off from the stair with a pannelled framing of oak. The kitchen i, over the store-room, is chiefly occupied with the fire-place, (though not seen in this section), which, with its cast-iron pipe or chimney ascending through the different rooms to the cupola, stand free, or are not embedded in the walls of the house. On the right-hand side of the kitchen a figure is seen at the cook's table and lockers; and on the left are seen the oaken trap-ladder set close to the wall, and the lockers, by which it is partitioned off from the apartments. A similar arrangement takes place in the bed-room marked h, occupied chiefly with the oaken bed frames, described in Fig. 6. Plate XIII. The apartment marked l is the Strangers'-room or Library, which contains a small collection of books. The furniture is of oak timber, executed in Mr Trotter of Edinburgh's best style. The walls were painted by Mr Macdonald of Arbroath, in handsomely decorated pannel-work; and from the dome an antique bronze lamp is suspended. The upper apartment m forms the Light-room and Lantern, rendered fire-proof, as every thing is of stone or metal, excepting a small oaken table and chair for the use of the light-keeper on watch; accented m′ is the copper-ball, shown as hoisted for the signal "All is Well." The reflecting apparatus and revolving machinery with which the Light-room is occupied, will fall to be described under Plate XX.

PLATE XVII.

BALANCE-CRANE.

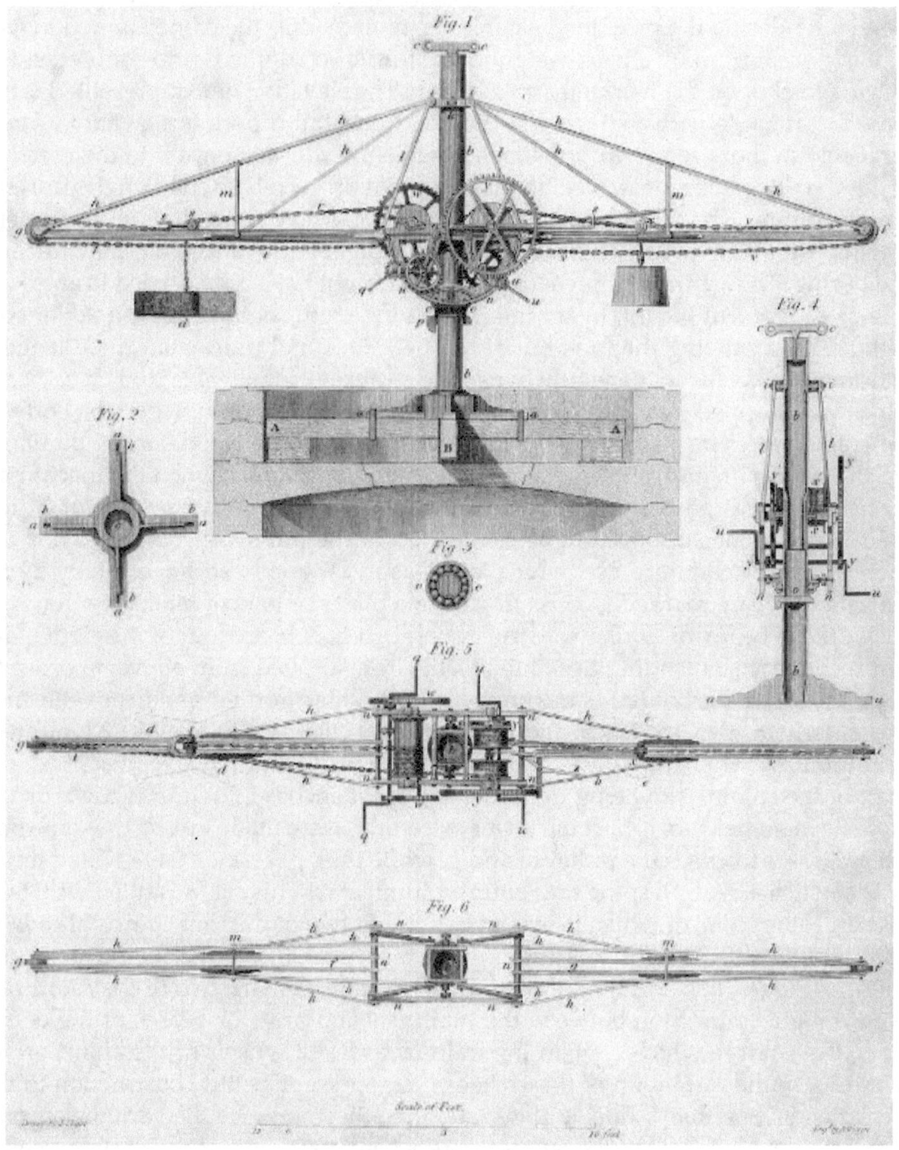

BALANCE-CRANE.

Drawn by J. Slight
Engd. by A. Wilson

PLATE XVII.

Pl. XVII.

Fig. 1. is an elevation of the Balance-Crane, constructed for building the upper part of the Bell Rock Light-house, when the guy-ropes of the Moveable Beam-crane, became "too taunt," as sailors express it, or were too near the perpendicular, thereby rendering the machine unstable. To remedy this, the crane alluded to was kept in equilibrium by a back-weight of cast-iron, so adapted as to counteract the varying load upon the working arm or beam. The elevation here represented is the same in principle with that used at the Bell Rock, but differs somewhat in form, agreeably to more recent improvements made in order to adapt it to the erection of the Carr Rock Beacon. a a is the cast-iron foot or socket, into which the upright central column b b is stepped, being a tube of cast-iron put together in convenient lengths, with flush joints, after the manner of spiggot and faucet, fitted by turning and boring. The centre column of this machine might have been carried to any suitable or convenient height, by adding length to length, as the building advanced, without once moving the foot; but at the Bell Rock, not more than three lengths of from 6 to 9 feet were generally in use. c c represent a malleable iron cross-head, which was stepped into the void of the central shaft or column, when the body of the crane was to be elevated. This operation was accomplished simply by hooking the main-purchase and traveller-chains into the eyes c c, when the machinery of the crane was employed with great facility as a locomotive power for lifting itself; d is a stone supposed to be suspended in the purchase-chain; and e is the back-weight or counterpoise, which, at pleasure, was moved horizontally along the balance-beam marked f, consisting of two plates or bars of malleable iron; g is the working-beam, of similar construction; h-h, h-h, h, h, are four of the eight main and secondary suspending ties of malleable iron, applied from above, in order to leave the lower part of the crane unobstructed. This afforded great conveniencey particularly at the Carr Rock, and also at the erection of the Melville Monument of Edinburgh, where the space for the workmen was extremely circumscribed, the shaft of the column not being more than 10 feet 6 inches in diameter towards the top. The main ties h-h, h-h, at the lower extremity, were made fast by the same bolt which passes through the pulleys f and g, while the upper ends were bolted into a collar, which is seen clasping the central column at i i. This collar is fitted with four friction-rollers, one of which is seen at k. l l shew two of the four principal rods or bars of malleable iron for connecting the Crane, and answering the purpose of a king-post to the ties h-h, h-h, of the frame-work; m m mark two of the four braces forming a connection between the main ties and arms or beams of the crane. The cheeks n n n, which contain the train or series of wheels of the crane, are of cast-iron. In the formation of these cheeks they present as little obstruction to the workmen as possible, while, at the same time, they embrace the various journals or axles of the machinery. The upper part is connected by a square framed collar of malleable iron, seen at Fig. 5. fitted with friction rollers, and, like the collar above alluded to, works round the central column. This lower collar is connected with the cheeks of the crane by studs passing through them, and fixed by means of screw-nuts. The lower part of the frame is in like manner connected with the upright shaft, by a collar, which is moveable upon friction-balls of cast-iron, contained in a circular race or chamber o o, a plan of which, shewing the balls, is given at Fig. 3. The whole machine thus fitted, is supported upon the central shaft by means of the cutter or spear-bolt p. The winch handle marked q, is that with which the main-purchase chain r, passing over the pulley s, is worked, from which the stone d is suspended. Connected with the main-purchase, a wheel, marked w, of 30 inches diameter, is worked by a pinion of 5 inches, mounted upon the axle of the handle q, producing a power or force in the ratio of 18 to 1; this power may at pleasure be increased by throwing another pinion on the same axle into gear with the wheel marked n′, of 16 inches diameter.

The handle u u is connected with the main-traveller s, balance-chain v v v, and their traveller x, to which the back-weight e is appended. The main-traveller wheel y measuring 36 inches in diameter, with its pinion of 5 inches marked u, exerting a power in the ratio of 21 to 1, serves to work the main-traveller. On the same axle with the pinion u, is another pinion, working two wheels, as seen in Fig. 4, which gives motion to the balance-traveller. These two combinations of wheels are so arranged, that, by working the small levers m and z, they can with facility be thrown in and out of gear, so as to work the traveller either together or separately. The whole weight of the Balance-crane, here represented as resting upon the oaken beams A A B, on one of the floors, weighed about three tons; but the balance and working beams having latterly been made of malleable iron, and the other parts of the machine considerably lightened, it did not exceed more than two tons in weight when used at the Carr Rock.

Fig. 2. The cast-iron foot of the Crane is necessarily very ponderous, and weighs about half a ton. The toes a a a a extend about 5 feet; b b b b are the batholes for fixing it down, in case of its at any time getting off the balance, but, in practice, these bats were seldom applied. When the crane was supported over the void or central holes left in the floors during the progress of the work, the toes were clasped to the oaken beams A A B, formerly noticed, represented as resting on one of the upper floors of the building, B, in Fig. 1., being a cross section of the lower beam, with its levelling-block; c, the socket for the central column, or upright shaft, is 10 inches in diameter at the upper side, and diminishes to 9 inches, that the column may become fixed into it by the pressure of the machine.

Fig. 3. o o, in reference to Fig. 1., represents the collar-chamber, filled with cast iron friction-balls, upon which the body of the machine rested, and traversed horizontally with the greatest facility.

Fig. 4. is a perpendicular section taken across the cheeks and wheels with a view to shew the train of the machine more fully. a a is the foot; b b two lengths of the central column, or hollow cylinder, with their spiggot and faucet joint in the middle, shewing also that the metal is about an inch and a quarter in thickness; c c the cross-head, referred to in Fig. 1.; i i the upper collar, shewing its connection l l with the king-posts or main rods; n n the cast-iron cheeks, with the lower collar, and the chamber for the friction-balls; o the cutter or spear-bolt, which supports the whole machine; u u the traveller handles, the main-purchase handles not being embraced in this section; y y the wheels and pinion of the main traveller; accented y′ y′ the wheel and pinion of the balance-traveller x x. In the central part of this figure, the barrel or drum x of the traveller-chains is seen, and also the middle collar x, with its friction rollers.

Fig. 5. is a plan of the body of the Crane, in reference to Fig. 1. b is a cross section of the central column, seen in connection with the upper collar d d; with a stone suspended from the end of the main-beam; e e the back weight suspended from the balance-beam: f and g the extremities of these two beams; h′ h′ h′ h′ four horizontal braces, extending from the cast-iron cheeks to the middle of the beam. Letters n n n n the cast-iron cheeks of the body; q q the main purchase-handles; r the main-purchase chain; s its traveller; t t the traveller-chain; u u the traveller handles; v the balance traveller-chain; x its traveller; w w the main-purchase wheels; y y the traveller wheels; z the lever, for stopping the main traveller-wheel.

Fig. 6. is a plan of the frame work of this machine: b is the upright column, with the upper malleable iron-collar, shewing its connection with the king-posts l l of Fig. 1.; f and g are the extremities of the main-purchase and balance-beams; m′ m′ the horizontal rods connecting with the main-ties; h h, &c. the main ties; h′ h′, &c. the horizontal braces; n n n n the cheeks or frame of the wheels and machinery, with the two great bolts marked n′ n′, by which the frame was principally connected; these bolts being passed also through the interior ends of the balance and working beams.

PLATE XVIII.
GENERAL VIEW OF THE WORKS.

Drawn by G. C. Scott from a Painting by A. Carse.
Engraved by Willm. Miller.

PLATE XVIII.

Pl. XVIII.

This Plate gives a Perspective view of the Works at the Bell Rock, taken by Carse, at low-water of spring-tide, from on board the Light-house Yacht, in the month of July 1810, at the distance of about half a mile in a southern direction from the Rock, and is here reduced from a picture in the possession of the writer. In the fore-ground a boat is introduced, approaching the Rock with a party of strangers, and another is leaving it, supposed to be receiving orders from a figure on the Rock, who is pointing towards her. In the back-ground, the shipping belonging to the work is introduced, viz. the Tender, a Schooner, and the stone-vessels Smeaton and Patriot, with the Floating-light. In the distance, the hills of Fife and Forfar are seen, but the entrance to the Firth of Tay is intercepted by the beams of the Beacon-house. Between the Light-house and Beacon, or in the direction of the chain and stone suspended from the Wooden-bridge, the ruins of the Abbey of Aberbrothwick are seen. The operation of landing the stones with the sheer-crane at Duff's Wharf, toward the right, is seen; and also one of the moveable beam-cranes, in a working position, at Pitmilly Wharf, on the left.

The principal lines of the railways, with waggons, and a variety of operations which are in progress, form a very busy scene upon the Rock. On the praam-boat's deck, toward the left of the picture, Captain Wilson, the landing-master, is represented with a speaking-trumpet in his hand; and at the foot of the Beacon-house, Mr Francis Watt, foreman mill-wright, is supposed to be giving directions about some operations. On a level with the entrance-door of the Light-house, the bridge of communication is situate, and four blocks of stone are seen, in progress of being raised from the railways to the top of the building, viz. one is suspended from the winch-machine upon the bridge, another from the beam projecting out of the window of the Light-room store, a third from the bed-room, and a fourth from the Balance-crane, which last is about to be laid upon the parapet-wall of the Light-room. Here the operations are going forward under the direction of Mr Peter Logan, foreman builder. In the open gallery of the Beacon-house, Mr Dove, the foreman smith, is seen at work, with the smoke of the respective fires of the forge and cook-room. The tackle, distended in a diagonal direction, from the balcony of the Light-house, to the mortar-gallery of the Beacon, shews the mode of raising the mortar-buckets. The figure on the small scaffold suspended from the balcony, shews the method of pointing the walls with Roman cement.

PLATE XIX

ENTRANCE-DOOR, WINDOWS, HINGES, AND THUNDER-ROD.

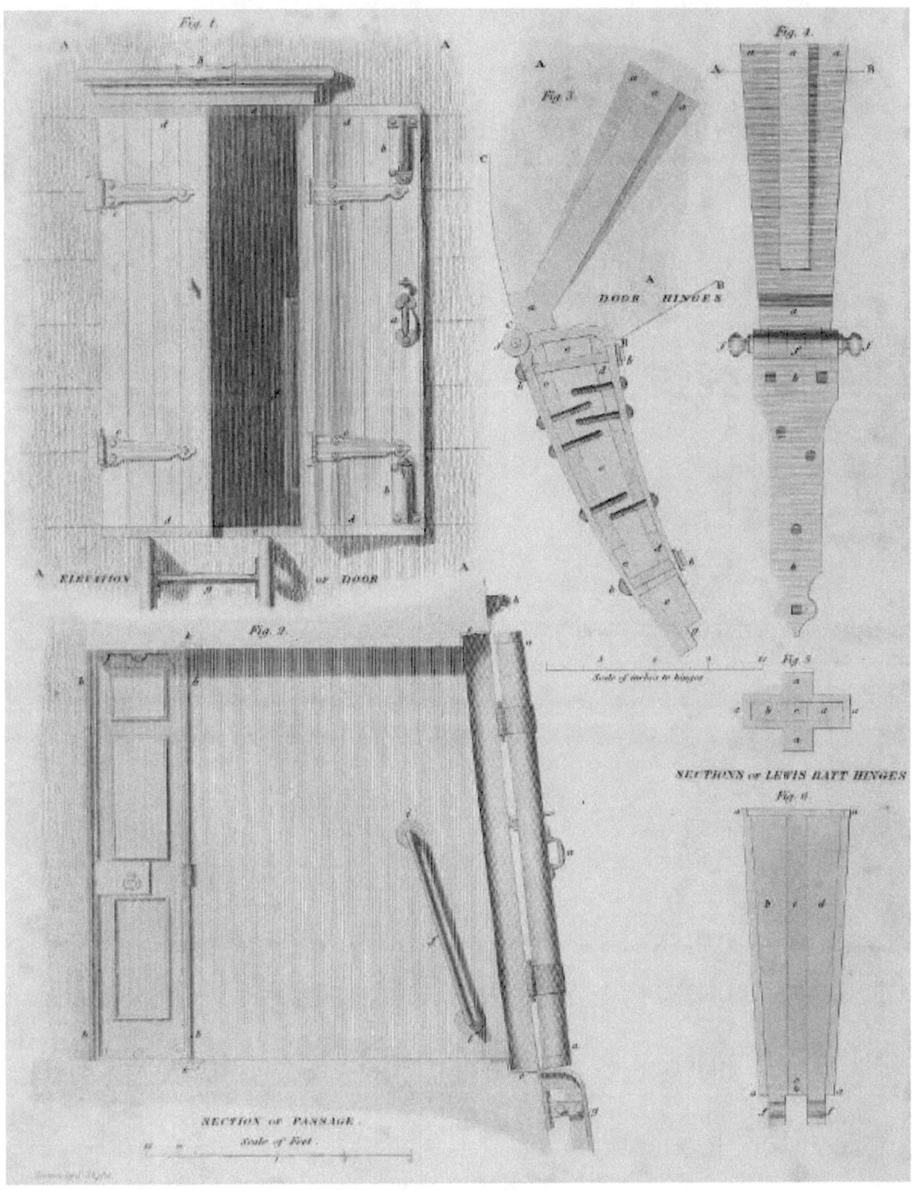

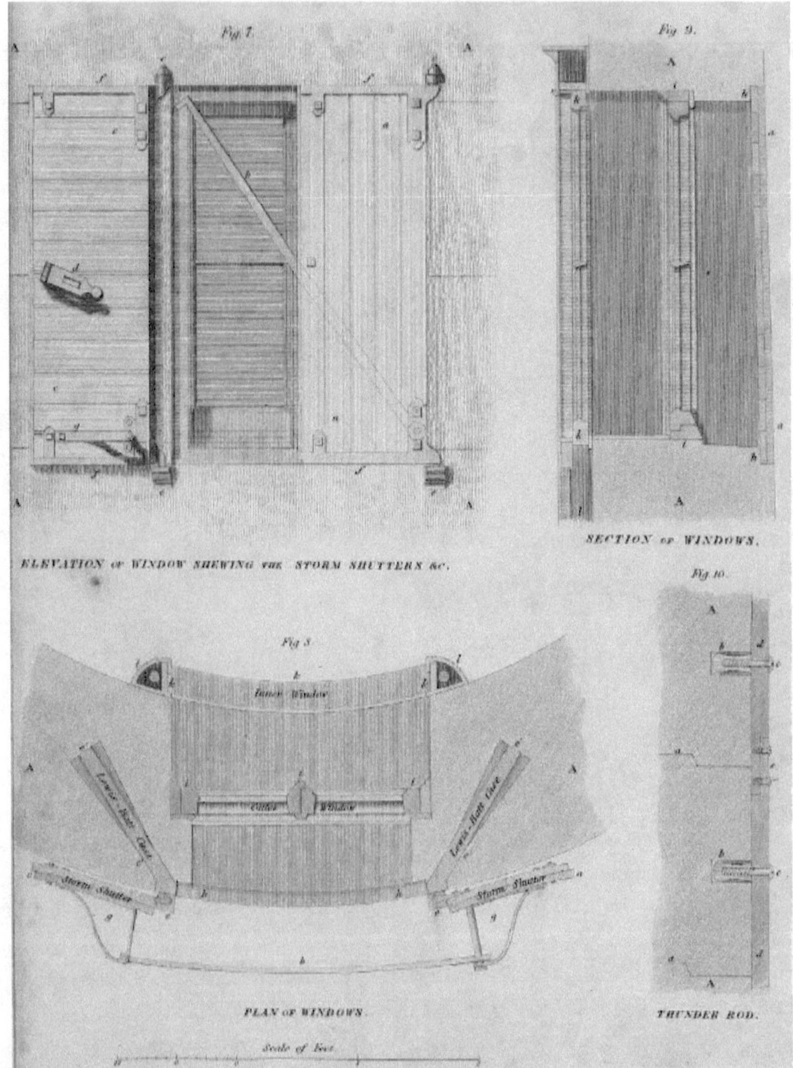

ENTRANCE DOOR, WINDOWS, HINGES AND THUNDER ROD.

Drawn by J. Slight
Engraved by R. Scott

PLATE XIX.

Pl. XIX.

Fig. 1. represents part of the outward wall A A A A, and entrance-door, one leaf or half of which is open, and the other shut; a, one of the handles for opening and shutting it, connected with a thumb-latch; b b the bolts for securing the door when shut; c c c c the hinges; d d d d the brass guard-plates at top and bottom of the door, for defending the timber. The door is framed of fir-wood, and measures 6 feet 4 inches in height in the clear, besides the brass-checks upon which it shuts at top and bottom, which are of 2 inches in depth, as shewn at e in Fig. 1., and also by an end view in Fig. 2. The two leaves form a common breadth of 2 feet 10 inches in the clear. A cornice of brass is formed on the lintel of the door answerable to an eaves-drop, in which a friction roller h is placed, for the chain of the crane, with which the stores are raised. The door, when shut, finishes flush with the building, and is therefore of a circular form, framed and double lined, the whole being put together with white-lead paint: each leaf measures 5 inches in thickness at the hinge side, and diminishes to 2½ inches at the meeting edges, as will be understood by examining the section in Fig 3. When the leaves of the door are thrown open, they are kept in their places by catch-hooks of brass, to prevent gusts of wind from shutting them suddenly; f shews a moveable handle or piece of brass rail, within the passage, for laying hold of in stepping off the brazen ladder to enter the house; g shews the upper extremity or highest step of the ladder, which terminates at the sill of the door.

Fig. 2. shews the relative position of the outer and inner entrance-doors, in which a a a is an end view of the former; b b b b a front view of one of the leaves of the inner brass door; e e the outer door check, faced with plates of brass; f the moveable handle or rail, for the greater conveniency of entering the threshold; g the termination and upper step of the brazen-ladder, attached to the building, for communicating with the Rock. h, section of the cornice and friction-roller. The passage being only 2 feet 10 inches in breadth, the rails or moveable handles f, on each side, are made to slide into brass sockets i i, sunk into the walls, and, like the inner door, are flush with the wall when not at use. k k the sockets for the centre-pin hinge of the inner-door.

Fig. 3. is a cross section of one of the leaves of the entrance-door, shewing the position of the brass-case of the hinge-bat, as it lies in the building. A A part of the walls, B B part of the side-walls of passage, C C part of the surface of the outward wall. a a a a is the brass-case, containing the Lewis-bat-tails or palm of the hinge, (described in Plate XI. Fig. 3.); b b b b the working-tails; c c the outside lining; d d the inside lining; e e e the frame-work of the door, with the bolts and nails connecting the hinges; f the joint of the hinge, shewing the journal pin-hole; g the half-check joint of the door.

Fig. 4. represents a front view of the door-hinges, lettered in reference to Fig. 3. a a a a is the brass box or case, which is built into the wall for containing the palm-end of the Lewis-hinge; b b is the exterior or working tail, with its screw bolt and nail holes; f f f the double-joint and slip-pin.

Fig. 5. is a cross section of the Lewis-box on the line A B of Fig. 4. with its dove-tail feathers; a a a a shew the parts of the Lewis-bat b c d, as it lies in the box, which is built into the wall.

Fig. 6. represents a longitudinal section of the box and palm of the hinge, shewing its position, in reference to the cross section in Fig. 5. a a a a a is the brass box; b and d are the dove-tailed compartments of the palm; c is the tongue or locking-piece; e the pin hole, perforated in the locking-piece, for drawing the parts of the palm in the event of the joint wearing and requiring to be renewed; f f is the slip pin-hole in the other two parts of the palm of the Lewis. The weight of one of the entire hinges of the door, with its Lewis-tail and brass-box was 56 lb., and consequently the four sets for the door weighed about 2 cwt.

Fig. 7. shews the elevation of one of the windows of the Light-house, with part of the exterior wall marked A A A A; one-half of one of the storm-shutters, marked a a, is closed, and the other marked c c, is open; b is a bar of brass, which folds across the window when the shutters are closed, and is used as a stretcher, for preserving them in their places when opened. It will be observed by comparing the close shutter a a with the open one c c, that they are double or cross boarded; they are also fastened with hammered copper nails; d is the clasp used as a handle, which also locks the shutter; e e e e the ends of the dove-tailed hinges as they appear projecting through the walls; f f f f the working-tails of the hinge, forming at the same time the guard-plate of the shutters, as described in Fig. 1. Letter g, upon the open shutter, shews one of the brackets connected with the stretching-bar b, for keeping them open, as will be better understood by examining the following Figure.

Fig. 8. is a plan of one of the window-sills, and a section of one of the storm-shutters, with part of the walls A A, shewing the position of the Lewis-bat cases; a and c, the storm-shutters in an open state; b the stretching-bar in its place, when the shutters are open; e e the exterior ends of the Lewis-bats, with their cases é é é é, which are built into the wall, and, together with the other parts of the hinge, weigh about 28 lb., or 1 cwt. for each set, being one-half of the weight of the door-hinges; g g the brackets connected with the stretching-bar; h h the check in the wall for receiving the shutters; i i the stiles or framing of the outer-window, which opens in two leaves; k k k the framing and case of the inner window, which slides up and down in one sash; l l the balance-weight of the inner-window.

Fig. 9. is a perpendicular section of one of the windows, shewing the triple mode of shutting them during stormy weather. A A a section of a part of the walls. a a, the storm-shutter; h h the check in the building for its reception; i i the frame of the outer-window; k k the inner-window; l the case into which the inner-window drops when not in use.

Fig. 10. A A is a section of part of the thunder-rod and outward wall. a a shew part of the zones or bond-belts, noticed in Plate VII. Fig. 7., and Plate XVI. Fig. 2.; b b the brass-bats let into the wall, for attaching the thunder-rod with the screws c c, which vary from 2 to 3½ feet apart; d d the thunder-rod, made of the best gun-metal, and weighing at the rate of 7 lb. per lineal foot in the range of the sea, or from the Rock to the entrance-door, and from thence to the Light-room, at the rate of about 4 lb. per lineal foot; e is the joint technically termed Half-checking, by which the pieces, of about 7 feet in length, are connected by two screws at each joint, as shewn in the section. This rod, which extends from the Light-room to the Railways, forms an exterior Conductor, while another, which is not seen here, is connected with the chimney, brazen ladder and railways, and completes the interior conducting process.

PLATE XX.
BALCONY AND LIGHT-ROOM.

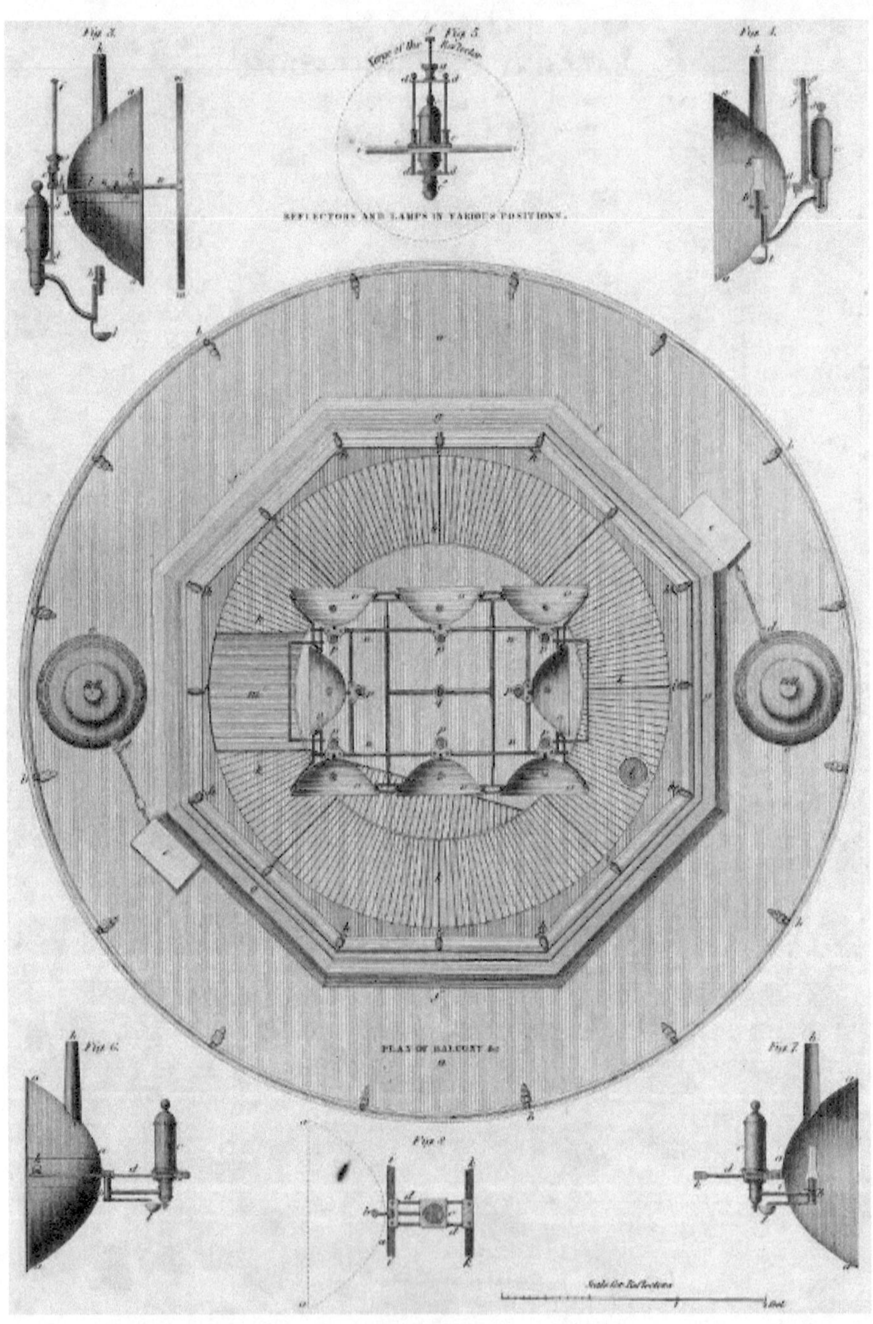

LIGHT-ROOM AND BALCONY.

Drawn by W. Lorimer
Engd. by J. Moffat Edinr.

PLATE XX.

Pl. XX.

Fig. 1. a a represent the Balcony or walk round the exterior of the Light-room; b b, &c. the brass bats, made in the form of the paw of an animal, are used for supporting the balcony-rail; c c the two Alarm-Bells; d d the hammers by which they are tolled, during the continuance of foggy or stormy weather; e e the case for defending the levers which work the hammers; f f f the stone parapet-wall of the Light-room, of an octagon form on the outside, and circular within; g g g the cast-iron sill of the lantern; h h, &c. the angular cast-iron pillars or mullions, formed by the junction of the contiguous parts of two of the sash-frames; i i, &c. the smaller upright bars, forming the astragals or principal divisions of the sash-frames; k k, &c. the grated cast-iron trimming-path; l the smoke-tube, leading from the kitchen through the cupola or roof; m the trap-ladder leading from the light-room-floor to the trimming-path; n n the reflector frame or chandelier, on which are seen 8 of the reflectors marked o o, &c. with their oil-fountains p p, &c. the whole being framed or built upon the moveable upright-shaft q.

Fig. 2. is a section of the dome-roof of the library, the parapet-walls of the light-room, the lantern and its cupola. a a is the balcony, shewing the position of the Alarm-Bells, and cast-iron rail; which last is made in the form of meshes, with a massive coping of brass; f f the parapet-wall of the light-room; g g the cast-iron sill of the lantern; h h, &c. the angular pillars or mullions; i i, &c. the astragals; k k the grated trimming-path; l l the smoke-tube passing through the cupola; n n, &c. the reflector frame, on which 20 reflectors, marked o o, &c. with their fountains p p, &c. are ranged; q q the upright shaft upon which the reflector-frame is built, and which is connected with the revolving-machinery; r r, &c. the copper smoke-tubes from the respective reflectors; s s the cross-bars supporting the upright shaft at t t; and u u a copper receiver for any accidental drop from the upper or central ventilator marked v′ v′ v′, while the letters v v v v mark the exterior line of the cupola; w w the external cornice of the lantern, used as a gutter or eaves-drop, from which the rain-water is conducted off the roof in small pipes to the para-pet-wall of the Light-room; x x the handles which the light-keepers lay hold of; and y y the exterior grated path on which they stand when cleaning the outside of the windows; z z z the steps fixed to the parapet of the Light-room and lantern, by which they ascend to the cupola; á á the copper-tube, used as a flag-staff; b′ the signal-ball, hoisted daily at the Light-house, between the hours of 9 and 10 o'clock in the morning, when "All is Well:" The ropes for raising this ball pass over two pulleys fixed in the top of the flag-staff, and are let down through the interior of it: c′ c′ part of the cornice of the building, shewing the mode of connecting the horizontal and perpendicular joints of the Library-roof; d′ d′, &c. shew the zone or bond-belt worked in the beds of the courses, as mentioned in the description of Plate VII. Fig. 7., Plate XVI. Fig. 2., and Plate XIX. Fig. 10.; e′ e′, &c. from the en-largement of the scale, shews more distinctly than any of the other diagrams, the mode in which the horizontal joggling of the joints of the Light-room and other floors of the building is accomplished; f′ the door leading from the Light-room to the balcony; g′ g′ g′ the case and machinery for causing the Reflecting-apparatus to revolve, so as to distinguish this Light from others upon the coast; h′ h′, &c. the connection-rods, with their various wheels of communication, for changing the direction, and giving motion to the Bell-hammers; i′ i′, &c. the brass tubes for supplying fresh air to the Light-room; k′ the Time-piece, set upon brackets fixed in the wall, for regulating the Revolving-machinery, and for the direction of the light-keepers in changing the day and night watches; l′ a bracket of cast-iron attached to the machinery-case, for supporting the foot on which the upright shaft works; m′ the bevelled wheels connected with the interior machinery and upright shaft, which can be thrown out and into gear at pleasure.

In describing the Reflecting-apparatus delineated in Fig. 3., we may notice, that, agreeably to the laws of optics, almost inconceivable effects are produced by the use of these specula, by which portions of a sphere are illuminated, whose radii seem to be proportionate to the elevation of the radiant point, and the particular state of the atmosphere. Taking these conditions into view, the Revolving-light at the Bell Rock has been seen, from an elevated position on the land, at the distance of about 35 miles. According also to observations which have been made upon Sumburgh-Head Light, in Shetland, which is elevated about 300 feet above the medium level of the sea, it has been seen from a ship's deck at the distance of about 27 miles. Similar effects are also expected to be produced with light refracted through glass-lenses. These, it is believed, are about to be made trial of in the Tour de Corduan, at the entrance of the Garonne, with what are termed Polygonal Lenses, being one large lens, built or composed of a number of small lenses, as suggested by Dr Brewster, in the Edinburgh Encyclopædia, in the year 1811, under the article "Burning Glass."

Fig. 3. a a a represents one of the reflectors, measuring 25 inches over the lips, in a finished state, as now in use at the Bell Rock and Northern Light-houses in general. They consist of a circular sheet of copper, measuring, when flat, 26¼ inches in diameter; weighing 11½ lb. on an average; and plated with silver in the proportion of 6 oz. to each pound avoirdupois of copper. These plates are formed into the Parabolic curve by a very nice process of hammering, and afterwards set into a bezil or ring of brass; b is the lamp, being an Argand-burner, with a circular wick, of about three-fourths of an inch in diameter. If the parabolic figure of the reflector could be constructed and its form preserved with perfect accuracy, the magnitude of the flame of the lamp employed for its illumination would be of less importance. From certain experiments now in progress, the writer is in expectation that considerable improvements may be introduced, in the construction of reflectors, and that additional modes of distinguishing the Light-houses on the coast will be obtained. c is a cylindrical fountain of brass, which contains 24 oz. of oil, suitable for the consumpt of the lamp for about 18 hours, or equal to its expenditure during the longest night in Shetland. A great improvement upon the Burner-apparatus has lately been introduced into the Northern Lights, by affording the light-keeper an opportunity of cleaning the reflector without the obstruction of the burner: the oil-pipe and fountain of the burner is connected with the rectangular frame d, and moveable in a perpendicular direction upon the guide-rods e and f, by which it can be let down and taken out of the reflector, by simply turning the handle g, as will be more fully understood by examining Fig. 5. In this way, the necessity of lifting the reflector, or deranging its focus, is avoided. Although a properly trimmed lamp, especially upon the Argand principle, does not emit smoke, yet the heat and effluvia arising from it, are sufficient to oxydise or sully the upper part of the reflector: an aperture of an elliptical form, measuring about 2 inches by 3 inches, is therefore cut in the upper part of the reflector, to which the copper-tube h is attached. Letter i, immediately behind the reflector, refers to a cross section of the main-bar of the chandelier or frame on which the reflectors are ranged, each being made to rest upon three knobs of brass, one of which, as seen at k k, is soldered upon the brass band l, that clasps the exterior of the reflector.

To distinguish the Bell Rock Light from others on the coast, as noticed at page 401, it is made to revolve, and to exhibit periodically a bright light of the natural appearance, alternating with a red coloured light. This last effect is produced by means of shades of red glass, one of which, represented at m m, is also set in a brass bezil, and made to slide horizontally upon two rods marked n n, into corresponding sockets, fixed upon the reflector-frame at o, so as to enable the light-keeper to trim the lamp without entirely removing the red coloured shade. In the present aspect of the shade, the rods are drawn out to their full extent; but when set for use, the shade is pushed in till its bezil and that of the reflector are within half an inch of each other.

Fig. 4. is a section of the reflector a a, shewing the position of the burner b, with the glass chimney accented b′ b′, and oil cup b, or receiver for any drop that may fall from the lamp. The letters c, d, f, and g, in reference to the corresponding letters in Fig. 3., shew the oil-fountain in its place when the burner is in use.

Fig. 5. has reference to the apparatus for moving the burner up and down, so as to admit freely of the reflector being cleaned. In the present position, c, the fountain, is moved partly down; d d, &c. shows the rectangular frame on which the burner is mounted; e e the elongated socket-guides; f the rectangular guide-rod, connected with the sockets on which the perforated check-handle g slides; accented c′ is a cross section of the oil-pipe, where it joins the valve of the fountain.

Figs. 6, 7, and 8. These three diagrams represent a different mode of withdrawing the burner from the reflector, for the conveniency of cleaning it. In Figs. 3, 4, and 5., this is supposed to be done by a perpendicular motion of the burner; but in Figs. 6, 7, and 8. it slides horizontally. Fig. 8. is a horizontal section of the reflector a a a, and its apparatus, the letters in which correspond with those of Figs. 3, 4, and 5. The advantages attending this mode, are the rendering of the apparatus more steady, by its having two points of support upon the bars i i and k k; while its motion is more direct. The part of the reflector cut out for the admission of the burner in this case, being that which is partly intercepted by it, little of the reflecting surface is thus lost; and this mode may therefore be considered an improvement upon the perpendicular manner of lifting and lowering the burner.

PLATE XXI.
FRONTISPIECE
BELL ROCK LIGHT HOUSE

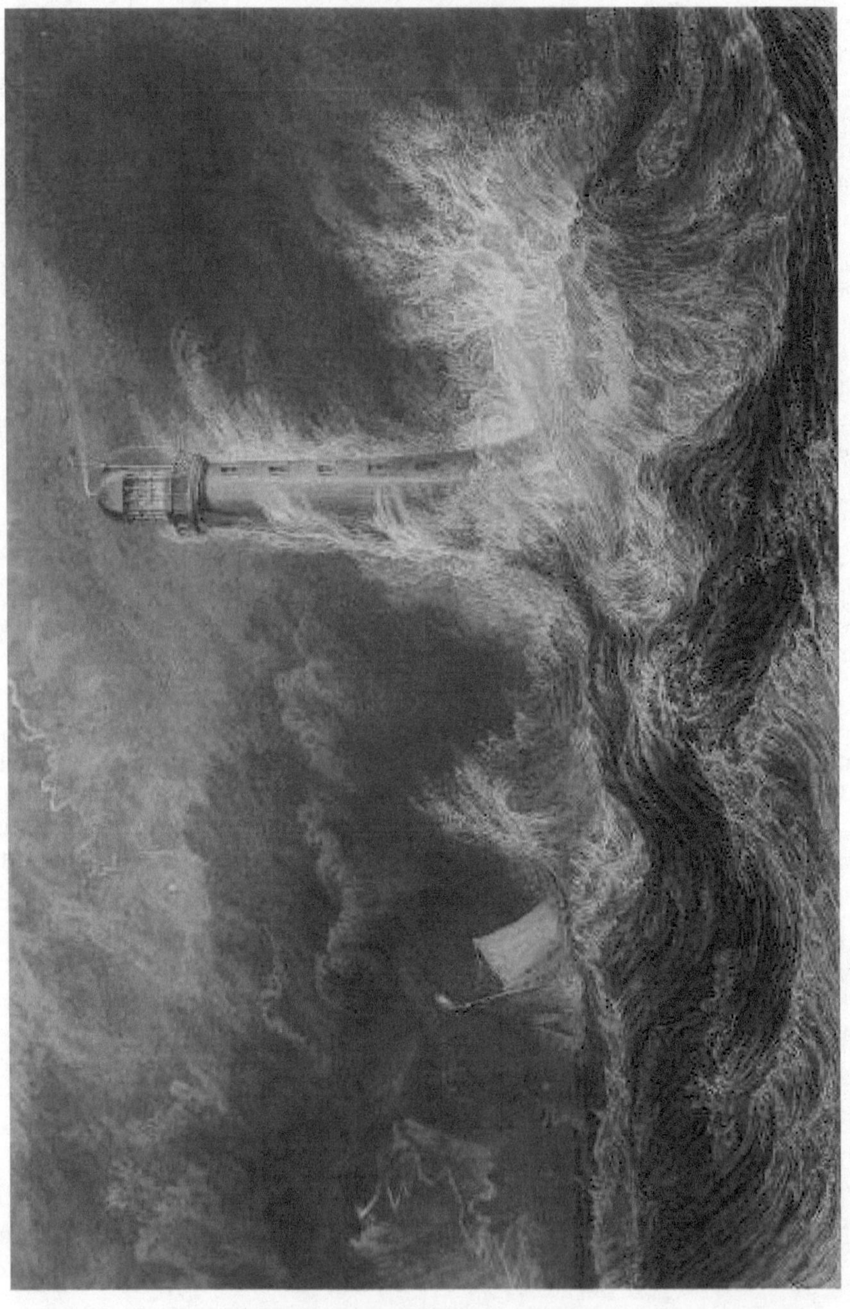

BELL ROCK LIGHT HOUSE

DURING A STORM FROM THE NORTH EAST.

Drawn by J. M. W. Turner R. A.
Engraved by J. Horsburgh.

PLATE XXI.

Pl. XXI.

This scene, which is intended to represent the Bell Rock after a storm at northeast, will hardly admit of any adequate description, from the evanescence of the form of the waves upon these occasions. It is, however, founded upon observations made at the Light-house, between the years 1810 and 1822, or during twelve successive winters. The great rise of the sea during a gale, as delineated in the Vignette to the Narrative of the Edystone Light-house, being so surprising, the writer was at much pains to ascertain the effect also at the Bell Rock; and the maximum height of the sprays hitherto observed has been about 105 feet, or as high as the central part of the Light-room windows.

Mr Andrew Masson, an artist who in early life had been at sea, having expressed a desire to reside in the Light-house for some time during winter, that he might observe the waves in a storm, was readily furnished with an opportunity. He went there in the month of December 1816, and remained for six weeks and four days, when he produced various sketches of the appearances which he witnessed; and Mr Macdonald, noticed at page 519, made several outlines from actual observation, in the winter of 1820. All of these were put into the hands of Mr Turner, Royal Academician; who gave the very spirited drawing from which Mr Horsburgh, an artist of much promise, has succeeded in producing the striking representation in the Frontispiece. The writer has also the pleasure of acknowledging the obligations he owes to Mr Williams, author of Views in Greece, for his friendly advice and assistance.

It may here be remarked, as not a little surprising, that while the sea is running nearly to the height represented in the Frontispiece, the entrance-door of the Light-house, or at least one of its leaves, may nevertheless be left open; and the portion of water which on these occasions makes its way into the passage, is found to be very trifling. This is owing to the fortunate position of the door; for, while the sprays on the eastern side fly with the quickness of lightning to the top of the house, the waves separate below, and are sent round the building with such force, that their collision upon the lee-side produces the wonderful appearance in the picture; where a downy spray, white as snow, rises at some distance from the house, to the height of 20 or 30 feet above the medium surface of the sea, and comes in minute particles upon those within the entrance-door, producing a sensation as if dust were falling upon them.

PLATE XXII.

VIGNETTE OF SECOND TITLE-PAGE.

BELL ROCK LIGHT-HOUSE

VIGNETTE OF SECOND TITLE-PAGE.

Drawn by Miss Stevenson.
Engraved by J. Horsburgh.

PLATE XXII.

Pl. XXII.

The night scene of the Bell Rock Light-house, in the Vignette of the Second
Title-page, was drawn by Miss Stevenson, from a sketch by the masterly hand

of Mr Skene of Rubislaw. To Miss Stevenson, also, as an amanuensis, the writer takes this opportunity, with parental affection, of acknowledging his obligation for almost the entire manuscript written to his diction. The reader will be gratified to find, in connection with this Vignette, inserted at page 64., a fac-simile of the handwriting of Sir Walter Scott, Bart. in the expressive and beautiful lines which he wrote in the Album kept at the Light-house, as noticed at page 419.

PLATE XXIII.

DESIGN FOR A LIGHT-HOUSE, SUGGESTED UPON VISITING THE WOLF ROCK SITUATE EIGHT MILES S. S. W. FROM THE LAND'S-END.

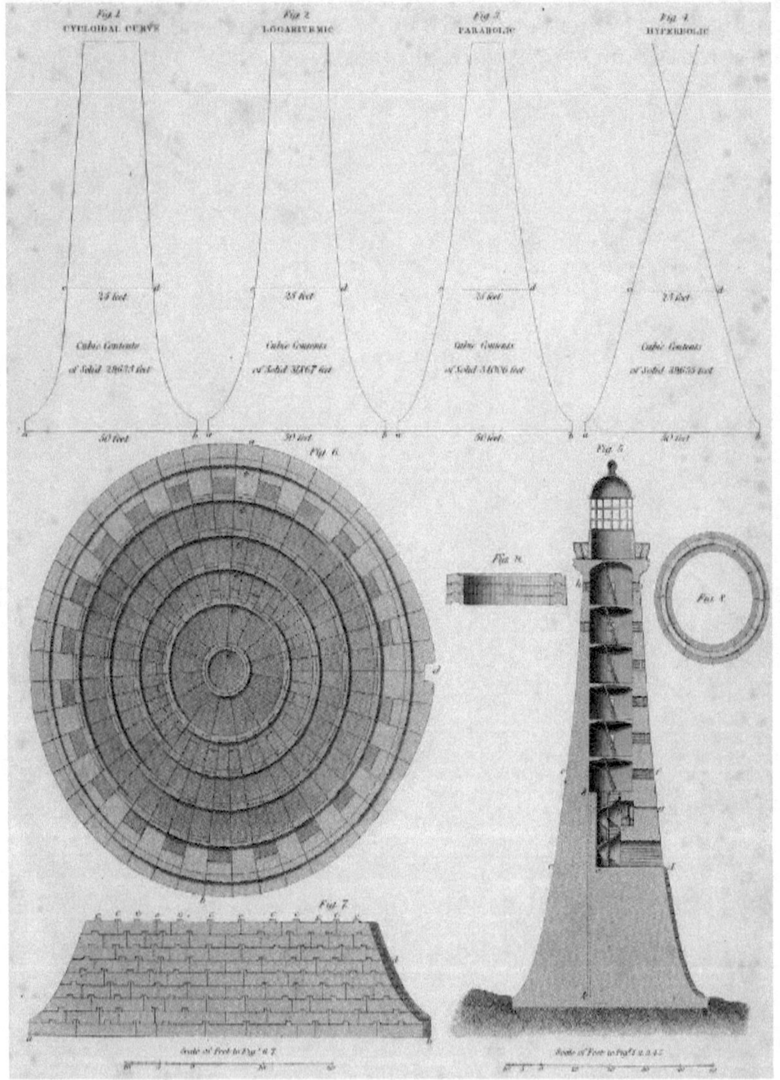

SKETCHES OF A NEW DESIGN FOR A LIGHT HOUSE.

Drawn by G. C. Scott
Engd. by J. Moffat Edinr.

PLATE XXIII.

Pl. XXIII.

In the range of aquatic buildings applicable to the purposes of a Light-house, which the writer has examined, he was forcibly struck with the magnitude of the Tour de Corduan, on the French coast. This magnificent edifice measures about 145 feet in diameter at the base, and 150 feet in height. Its cubical contents may perhaps be stated at the immense quantity of 339,432 feet; of which the basement alone forms about 200,000 feet. This building has undergone considerable alterations since its completion in the year 1609, as appears from Belidor's Architecture Hydraulique, tom. ii. At the time of its alteration from a coal fire to an oil light with reflectors, the upper parts in particular seem to have been greatly simplified, by the removal of several of its exterior ornamental appendages.

The Edystone Light-house, owing to the smallness of the rock, as appears from Mr Smeaton's Narrative of this celebrated building, measures only 26 feet in diameter, at the level of the first entire course; but if there had been space on the Rock for extending it equally on all sides, the ground-course, according to the curve of the outward walls, and the position of the foundation-stone, would have measured 32 feet in diameter. The height of the cupola of the Edystone Light-house is 90 feet, and the cubical contents of the masonry is about 13,147 feet. The Bell Rock Light-house, measures 42 feet in diameter at the base; its height, from the foundation to the cupola, is 118 feet; and the cubical contents of the masonry, as appears from the Table in Appendix, No. VI. is 28,530 feet.

Though the design represented in Plate XXIII., is more or less applicable to several situations upon the coast, yet the writer, in making this Sketch, had special reference to the Wolf Rock, which, as noticed at page 423, he visited in the Orestes sloop of war, commanded by Captain Smith. The extreme dimensions of the upper surface of this rock are about 115 feet, by 90 feet. It is not liable to be covered by the ordinary rise of the tide, though little of it appears above water in spring-tides. The Rock consists of grey porphyry, and is extremely hard. Its outline is somewhat uniform, and the depth of water in its vicinity is from 20 to 40 fathoms. The dangerous position of this reef, in reference to the navigation of the British Channel, led to the proposition of having a Light-house upon it many years since. The erection, however, was ultimately made upon the Long-Ships Rocks, lying about one mile off the Land's-End.

With the construction and dimensions, therefore, of the Light-houses above alluded to in view, the design delineated in this Plate is given, as the result of the writer's knowledge and experience on subjects of this kind. Without, however, entering into particulars as to the mode in which such an operation should be conducted, he merely notices, in reference to the various curves delineated in Figs. 1, 2, 3, and 4. as applicable to Light-houses upon sunken rocks, that he prefers the curve of the diagram represented in Fig. 3., as the outline of a building for a situation like the Wolf Rock.

Fig. 1. is formed by the supposed revolution of the cycloidal curve round the axis of a building, whose base is 50 feet, and which, at the entrance-door or top of the solid, measures 25 feet in diameter; the lines produced beyond these dimensions, which would form the habitable part of the Light-house, being tangents to the curves below. Between the base a b, and its parallel c d, this Figure contains 29,635 cubic feet.

Fig. 2. is in like manner formed by the revolution of the logarithmic curve round the axis of a building of similar dimensions at the base and top of the solid with Fig. 1., and contains 31,867 cubic feet.

Fig. 3. is obtained by the revolution of a parabola round the axis of the supposed building. The contents of the solid part, ascertained as in the two former Figures, is 34,006 cubic feet, being 4,371 cubic feet more than that of the cycloidal curve, and 2,139 cubic feet more than in the logarithmic curve.

Fig. 4. is formed by the revolution of the hyperbola between the two parallels a b, and c d, and contains 39,655 cubic feet, or 5,649 cubic feet more than the parabola. But, from the divergent nature of this curve, it is not applicable to the purposes of a Light-house tower, in its pure or simple form.

Fig. 5. is the section of a design formed by the revolution of the parabola round the axis of a building, as its asymptote, whose base a b, measures 56 feet in diameter, and parallel c d, at the top of the solid, is 36 feet; and height to the entrance-door, 35 feet. The contents of this Figure between these parallels is calculated at 45,000 cubic feet; but the whole of the masonry of the design is estimated at 70,624 cubit feet. Its general features may be stated as similar to those of the Edystone and Bell Rock Light-houses, the parts being only enlarged and the parabolic instead of the logarithmic curve, adopted for its outline. In this design, the parabolic curve is continued from the basement to the cope-stone of the Light-room, exclusively of the projection for the cornice and balcony. The masonry is intended to be 120 feet in height, estimating from the medium level of the sea, of which the solid, or from the foundation to the entrance-door, forms 35 feet, the stair-case 25 feet; and the remaining 60 feet of its height is occupied with six apartments, and the walls of the Light-room. In the stair-case a recess is formed for containing the machinery, for raising the stores to the height of the entrance-door; here a small hole, marked g g, is perforated through the building, for the admission of the purchase-chain. The thickness of the walls immediately above the solid, marked c c, is 12 feet; at the top of the stone staircase or level e f, they are 8 feet, and where the walls are thinnest, as at h i, immediately under the cornice, they measure 2 feet. k k represents a drop-hole formed in the courses of the stair-case and solid, for the range of the weight of the machinery of a revolving Light. The ascent to this building, as at the Bell Rock, is intended to be by an exterior stair or ladder of brass, and the interior communication between the several apartments by means of flights of circular oaken-steps.

Fig. 6. represents the first entire course of this design, drawn to a scale double the size of the former Figure, and shows the manner in which the courses are proposed to be built or connected with each other. In every building of this kind, it is proper that two or more of the lower courses, according to the situation and circumstances of the rock, should be sunk or imbedded in it. Since the erection of the present Light-house on the Edystone, the practice of dove-tailing and trenailing stones in water-buildings has been occasionally followed; and there can be no doubt that in some instances it is attended with advantage. But it is also true, that, independently of the extra quantity of rock and workmanship required, the stones are thereby greatly weakened, and rendered much more difficult to be landed in safety in such situations, and that there is often more apparent than real utility in cutting them agreeably to this system of building, as the great bond of the fabric still resolves itself into the gravity of the materials. It may likewise be noticed, that, unless in very peculiar circumstances, the process of trenailing stones newly laid in mortar ought to be avoided, as it becomes necessary to bore holes into the course immediately below, which is apt to break the bond of the mortar by the tremulous motion of the jumper or chisel and hammer.

To avoid these disadvantages, and more effectually to preserve the square or simplest form of the stones, it is proposed, in this new design, to adopt the same mode throughout, that was followed with the courses of the void or habitable part of the building at the Bell Rock, viz. to have zones or joggle-belts worked on the upper beds, and corresponding grooves cut into the under beds, of all the stones. In the plan represented in this Figure these zones are intended to be 1 foot in breadth, and 1½ inch in depth or thickness, forming the concentric rings, marked c c c c c c, which become so many girths to the course, superseding the necessity both of the dove-tailing system, and of the cubic joggles described in Plate XVI.

In tracing the general aspect of Fig. 6., it may be observed that the outer circle of stones is more lightly shaded, being intended for granite, while the hearting or interior part is of a darker shade, as descriptive of sandstone. The whole course of the building here represented, is uniformly simple, and when laid in its place, no mode of attachment can be conceived more effectually to add to the strength and connection of the fabric than these circular belts. Letter d refers to the recess worked in the outward wall of the solid, measuring 2 feet in breadth and 1 foot in depth, for the reception of a flight of brazen-steps for ascending to the entrance-door, instead of the greater projection of the spiral-formed stair delineated in Plate VII., Fig. 6., or the uncertain means of communication by a rope-ladder. The recess alluded to on the outward wall is worked with a small projection, which gradually falls into the circle of the building, without presenting any abrupt face to the waves. A stair of this description, upon a sloping wall, is ascended with great ease.

Fig. 7. is a section of part of the solid of the building, of which a b is the foundation course, and, in reference to Fig 6., letters c c, &c. correspond with the zones or joggle-belts; d d, shew a section of part of the brazen-ladder, answerable to the purposes of a stair, and a pair of skids, for preventing the joints of the building from being injured in taking up stores to the Light-house. This ladder may also be applied as a part of the thunder-rod, as is the case at the Bell Rock.

Fig. 8. is a plan of an entire course of the void or habitable part of the Light-house, showing one of the joggle-belts of the bed-joints. The form of joggle for the end-joints here shewn is also simple, and suited for preserving the strength of the materials more entire than the method of dove-tailing.

Fig. 9. is a section of three courses of the void of the building, showing the connection of the bed-joints.

FINIS.

Lector House believes that a society develops through a two-fold approach of continuous learning and adaptation, which is derived from the study of classic literary works spread across the historic timeline of literature records. Therefore, we aim at reviving, repairing and redeveloping all those inaccessible or damaged but historically as well as culturally important literature across subjects so that the future generations may have an opportunity to study and learn from past works to embark upon a journey of creating a better future.

This book is a result of an effort made by Lector House towards making a contribution to the preservation and repair of original ancient works which might hold historical significance to the approach of continuous learning across subjects.

HAPPY READING & LEARNING!

LECTOR HOUSE

LECTOR HOUSE LLP

E-MAIL: lectorpublishing@gmail.com

9 789353 422714